Czechoslovakia
Since
World War II

Also by Tad Szulc

Twilight of the Tyrants

The Cuban Invasion (with Karl E. Meyer)

The Winds of Revolution

Dominican Diary

Latin America

The Bombs of Palomares

Portrait of Spain

Czechoslovakia Since World War II

TAD SZULC

THE VIKING PRESS

NEW YORK

This book is for Seweryn

Contents

Book Five: THE NIGHT AGAIN

Czechoslovakia
Since
World War II

The Dusk

In Which a Glance Backward at

Certain Events and People

Provides Insight into Things to Come

I

The Liberation
of Czechoslovakia:
The Red Army Arrives

The contemporary drama of Czechoslovakia—the Soviet-led invasion of August 1968 and its tortured aftermath—opened nearly a quarter of a century earlier in a whirlwind of historical ironies. Those ironies punctuated the whole period when the 1968 Prague Spring was in gestation and when, tragically, it was being mutilated and destroyed.

The Czechoslovak story, then, begins in 1945. The scene is Prague on May 9, a city covered with battle scars and filled with smashed barricades, welcoming the Soviet troops and tanks that liberated it from more than six years of Nazi occupation. Four days before, on May 5, Czech patriots had launched their uprising against the dwindling German garrison as the Soviet forces approached the beautiful old capital from the east and the American armies came from the west. Acrid smoke was still rising from the burning buildings and curling among Prague's eight hundred spires and towers, lingering over the stone statues of the saints on Charles Bridge and clinging to the castle and Saint Vitus Cathedral on Hradčany Hill that looks down on the millennial city. The warm spring sun filtered through the smoke, giving Prague her legendary golden hue, but the joy of the liberation was marred by knowledge that two thousand citizens had been killed and forty thousand injured and wounded in the rebellion.

At dawn on May 7, halfway through the brief Czech rising, the German High Command had signed the act of total and unconditional surrender to the Allies at Reims, in France, and all hostilities were to cease at midnight May 8. But the rear guard of the fleeing Nazi units still sought to hold on to Prague and a near-by SS division was called in to crush the uprising and cover the evacuation. The Germans' hope was to extricate themselves and to surrender to the Americans as far west as possible instead of being caught in the path of the Soviet advance.

Shells from artillery guns emplaced atop the heights of the left bank of the Vltava rained across the river, down Pařižska Street and into the Old Town Square, the *Staré Město*. Direct hits were scored on the fifteenth-century Town Hall, and the damage can still be seen, deliberately left unrepaired by the Czechs, in the rear of the lovely edifice. The shattered back wall overlooks a tiny memorial park where the once independent Bohemian leaders—the spiritual and nationalist heirs of Jan Hus's Protestant Reform warriors—were executed by victorious Roman Catholic Habsburg Austrians after the 1620 battle of the White Mountain during the Thirty Years' War, one of the most depressing moments in the Czechs' frequently depressing history.

That war with Austria was the second time that Czech heresy had challenged a ruling church and its related political system. The first time was Hus's original rebellion in the fifteenth century, which ended in the reformer's being burned at the stake. The third important time, of course, was in 1968—against Moscow's ideological church and *its* power system. Time, to be sure, will tell whether this attempt, too, has failed. My own notion, after watching the dramatic events of 1968 and 1969 at close range, is that, the Soviet Union's invasion of Czechoslovakia notwithstanding, these events were not the end of another brief and brave episode in the tortured history of the Czechs and Slovaks but, instead, marked the beginning of a fundamental metamorphosis of Communism as we have known it in this century, if not of its ultimate collapse.

Czechoslovakia's experience of 1968 and 1969 must, then, be appreciated in the context of profound changes and nascent movements not only in Communist Eastern Europe—including the independent policies pursued by Yugoslavia and Romania—but in the Soviet Union as well. The stirrings of dissent in the Soviet lands—the reawakening of protest among the national minorities and the increasingly frequent trials of dissenting intellectuals in Moscow—help to establish this point. The Prague Spring of 1968 and its aftermath cannot and should not be explained as a historical accident produced in a vacuum or with clichés about the Czech's Hussite inspiration and their Schweikian reflexes. History may move in tortuous and tragic ways, but there was an inevitable logic in its course from 1945 to 1969, and there is no reason to think this logic will fail to apply in the future.

In the meantime, the Czechs retain their penchant for preserving the symbols of their national tragedies. In the Old Town Square there stands the Nazi-battered Town Hall, next to the grassy plot where the Habsburgs killed the twenty-seven Bohemian notables on June 21, 1621. Across the cobblestone square is a monument to Johann Amos Comenius, the seventeenth-century bishop, philosopher, and educator, its cenacle adorned with Hus's promise that one day the Czech people will be masters of their own affairs. (The whole baroque beauty of Prague, its castles and its towers, dates back to the bloody days of the Counter Reformation.) In the light of what happened in Czechoslovakia in August 1968, it appears ironically in character that shortly after the war the Czechs mounted on a stone pedestal in front of the Štefánik Infantry Barracks in Prague's Smíchov district the first Soviet tank to enter their capital in May 1945. For in Wenceslas Square, when the police are not looking, flowers and candles are placed at the foot of the equestrian statue of Saint Wenceslas (the tenth-century Bohemian duke murdered at a church door for his moral reforms) to honor the memory of Prague's youths killed by Soviet tank fire in 1968. Soviet tanks, indeed, seem to have framed Czechoslovakia's history from 1945 on.

Actually, Soviet tanks need not have captured Prague at all in 1945— and therein lies the first of the many ironies of the Czechoslovak drama. It could have been, instead, the American tanks of General George S. Patton's Third Army, and then the postwar history of Europe might have been written altogether differently.

As Winston Churchill recalled in *Triumph and Tragedy*, he, Marshal Stalin, and President Roosevelt had agreed at the Yalta Conference three months earlier that "Berlin, Prague, Vienna could be taken by whoever got there first." By mid-April 1945 it looked as if the Americans would get to Prague first, if they wanted to.

This was the military situation in those crucial and chaotic days: the Third Army had swept through Bayreuth and on April 19 its left flank elements had penetrated Czechoslovakia. The Patton army's right fist swung to the south along the Danube, smashing into Austria and capturing Linz on the way to Vienna, considerably southeast of Prague. (As subsequent developments demonstrated, the American presence in Austria in the first week of May forced the Soviets to agree to a quadripartite occupation of this country and not to insist on the unilateral rule they had attempted to impose. This, in turn, led to the creation of a neutral and democratic Austria after the 1955 state treaty. The analogy does not apply directly to Czechoslovakia, which as an Allied nation would not have been subject to a Big Four occupation. Yet it is arguable that Prague's liberation by the Americans could have exercised a psychological influence in strengthening Czechoslovakia's postwar democratic institutions and rendering them less vulnerable to the ensuing Communist power bid.)

At this point, as United States forces were entering Austria and Czechoslovakia, Churchill became convinced that the Allies' deteriorating relations with the Soviet Union—two months after Yalta the Allies were already at loggerheads with Stalin over Austria and over the composition of Poland's provisional government—would greatly benefit from the American occupation of Prague, at least as a bargaining factor. To keep Czechoslovakia outside the Soviet orbit was, naturally, another preoccupation of the British Prime Minister. Accordingly, he instructed Foreign Secretary Anthony Eden, then in Washington, to obtain the agreement of the United States. And on April 21 Eden concurred in a telegram to Churchill: "It might do the Russians much good if the Americans were to occupy the Czech capital, when no doubt they would be willing to invite the Soviet Ambassador to join the United States and ourselves, in contrast to the behaviour the Russians have shown to us."

Their point was that a Western presence in Prague *ahead* of the Russians would provide a political balance that was already alarmingly lacking elsewhere. In the case of Bulgaria, Romania, and Hungary— three former Nazi allies liberated by the Red Army—the Soviets kept out American and British civilian and military members of Allied Control Commissions for months while local Communist apparatuses were built up. In Poland, like Czechoslovakia, an Allied country, the Western Allies' political influence had been effectively eliminated. The British view was that if Americans were to enter Prague first a Western commitment for the welfare of Czechoslovakia would be created. A significant element in this reasoning was that, since April 5, a Provisional Government of National Unity had been in temporary residence at the east Slovak city of Košice, waiting to move on to Prague. This government, organized in Moscow a few days earlier, was headed by President Eduard Beneš—the respected statesman who exiled himself from Czechoslovakia after the 1938 Munich Pact—but the key positions were held by Communists. It seemed reasonable under the circumstances to anticipate that Dr. Beneš

Vestern moral or physical support in the days and months to
at an American presence in Prague might provide it.

hurchill showed considerable prescience in this whole matter,
1948 were to prove. And it is useful to note that Czechoslo-
he *only* Eastern or Central European nation, aside from
be liberated by both American and Soviet troops. Elsewhere,
s had done the job alone.

30 Churchill took up the issue directly with President Truman,
an three weeks earlier had succeeded Roosevelt at the White
his message:

be little doubt that the liberation of Prague and as much as possible
tory of western Czechoslovakia by your forces might make the whole
to the postwar situation in Czechoslovakia, and might well influence
r-by countries. On the other hand, if the Western Allies play no signifi-
in Czechoslovakian liberation that country will go the way of Yugo-

se, such a move by Eisenhower must not interfere with his main opera-
ast the Germans, but I think the highly important political consideration
1 above should be brought to his attention.

esident Truman and the State Department at first reacted favor-
hurchill's proposal. In his *Memoirs* Truman reports that Acting
of State Joseph C. Grew had urged him to ask the Joint Chiefs
o consider the idea seriously," on the theory that if the Amer-
.es could push to the Vltava, which runs through Prague, "it
would give us something to bargain with in our dealings with the
Russians."

After consulting with the Joint Chiefs, President Truman cabled
Churchill on May 1 that General Eisenhower's attitude toward operations
in Czechoslovakia—approved by the President—was the following:

The Soviet General Staff now contemplates operations into the Vltava Valley.
My intention, as soon as current operations permit, is to proceed and destroy any
remaining organized German forces.
   If a move into Czechoslovakia is then desirable, and if conditions here permit,
our logical move would be on Pilsen and Karlsbad. I shall not attempt any move
which I deem militarily unwise.

Eisenhower did, indeed, move on Plzeň (Pilsen) and Karlový Vary
(Karlsbad) and, in the south, on České Budějovice on the Vltava's upper
reaches. The Second Division, lent to Patton by the First Army for the
April offensive, raced two hundred miles south to reach Czechoslovakia's

borders on April 19 and to join with the Third Army's Sixteenth Division in the assault on Plzeň on the night of May 4. Plzeň fell on the morning of May 5 to the advance armored units of the Sixteenth and Second Divisions, two hours after the German General von Majewski had surrendered to Czech patriots. Almost simultaneously, the Czechs were rising in their capital.

As the chronicler of *The Story of the Second Division* was to write, the Plzeň people greeted the American tanks with even greater enthusiasm than the Parisians had shown their liberators. Plzeň's mayor welcomed Major General Robertson, the Second Division commander, with the traditional bread and salt. Czech children happily climbed on top of the tanks, and there was dancing in the streets all night.

But, immediately, the Czechs began pressing the United States commanders to move on Prague. Josef Mattas, a Communist leader of the Plzeň uprising, reminisced about it in a 1968 interview with a Prague weekly:

> The Americans were here, but Prague was still calling for help. Lieutenant Colonel Sytek, the liaison officer between the American Army and our units abroad, came to see me and we went together to ask General Wilkie [divisional assistant commander] for it. . . . General Wilkie could not decide anything alone, but he promised us to wire General Eisenhower in Nuremberg. A message came that we were to wait until four a.m. . . . At four a.m., a wire came that Eisenhower could not authorize action there, that in the matter of Prague another decision had been taken. . . .

It was at this stage that political considerations in Washington and military hesitations in the field lost the Prague prize for the Allies. Churchill, who remarked in his memoirs that "there was no agreement to debar him [Eisenhower] from occupying Prague if it were militarily feasible," recalled that while the Russians agreed to the American advance to the Karlový Vary–Plzeň–České Budějovice line, they had on May 4 "reacted strongly" against the idea of the Third Army's pushing all the way to the Vltava and Prague.

Eisenhower had broached the idea. Brigadier General John R. Deane, head of the United States Military Mission in Moscow, reported in his book on America's alliance with Russia that General Alexei Antonov, the Soviet Army's Chief of Staff, reacted to this proposal with a "violent protest." "The fine hand of the Soviet Foreign Office could be seen in Antonov's attitude—Czechoslovakia was to be in the orbit of the Soviet

Union and Czech gratitude to America for the liberation of her capital was not part of the program."

This Soviet opposition found an echo in Washington. As President Truman wrote, "To be sure, I agreed with Churchill that it would be desirable to hold the great cities of Berlin, Prague, and Vienna, but the fact was that, like the countries of Eastern Europe, these cities were under Russian control or about to fall under her control." And, he went on, "The Russians were in a strong position, and they knew it. On the other hand, if they were firm in their way, we could be firm in ours. And our way was to stick to our agreements and keep insisting that they do the same. . . ."

This was why, at dawn on May 6, Eisenhower instructed Patton to reject, in effect, the Czechs' pressure on his commanders and to halt his thrust into Czechoslovakia along the semicircular front running from Karlový Vary through Plzeň to České Budějovice. At this point, Patton's tanks were within only two hours of Prague from either Karlový Vary or Plzeň. With the German resistance in western Czechoslovakia in a state of total collapse and the Russians still some distance east of the Vltava Valley, the Third Army had the Czech capital at its mercy, but the top-level American decision was not to exercise this tempting option.

Churchill desperately tried once more to change the situation. As late as May 7, with the Vltava Valley a virtual military vacuum except for the German SS division seeking to quell the uprising, he wired Eisenhower: "I am hoping that your plan does not inhibit you to advance to Prague if you have the troops and do not meet the Russians earlier. I thought you did not mean to tie yourself down if you had the troops and the country was empty."

It was on that very day that history chose to play its first irony on Czechoslovakia.

Presumably acting alone and under the insistent demands of the liberated Czechs in Plzeň and elsewhere, Patton secretly, and characteristically, sent emissaries to Prague on May 7 to propose to the newly organized Czech National Committee, directing the uprising, that American armor enter the capital at dawn on May 8. However, Patton's envoys explained, given the highly delicate political situation, this would be undertaken *only* at the request of the Czech National Committee.

The man who received the Americans happened to be Josef Smrkovský, the Communist underground leader who ostensibly acted as the Committee's Vice-President but was, in fact, its real head. (For tactical reasons, the Communists preferred to have a non-Communist as President of the Committee—he was General Lev Prchala—even though the Prague uprising was largely engineered by them. The postwar political pattern of Czechoslovakia—and the Communist *modus operandi*—was already beginning to emerge.) At thirty-four, Smrkovský was among the most outstanding Communist leaders in Czechoslovakia, having remained in the country and fighting in the underground while most of the Party's top figures were sitting out the war in Moscow—as, for example, were Klement Gottwald and Rudolf Slánský—or hiding in occupied France or serving in Nazi concentration camps. Once a baker and trade-union activist, he had risen to the high post of a Party Secretary in 1937 when he was twenty-six, and, under the Nazi occupation, to the chairmanship of the clandestine Fourth Central Committee.

Now, speaking for the National Committee, but not necessarily with its knowledge and certainly without the approval of the new coalition government in Košice, Smrkovský told General Patton's emissaries that the Czechs in Prague would rather be liberated by the Russians than by the Americans, although Soviet forces were still a good day's march away from Prague's city limits. Many years later—in 1967, when it was no longer ideologically forbidden to acknowledge the American role in Czechoslovakia's liberation—Smrkovský was to explain in a public speech that he had turned down Patton's offer out of concern that the American occupation might adversely affect future Communist plans for Czechoslovakia, a worry that the lower-ranking Plzeň Communists evidently had not shared. Churchill, as it developed, was not just conjuring up ghosts in his frantic dispatches to Truman and Eisenhower.

But Patton had to accept Smrkovský's decision and, consequently, Soviet forces under Marshal Ivan S. Konev entered Prague on the morning of May 9. As Eisenhower later matter-of-factly reported to the Combined Anglo-American Chiefs of Staff, United States troops had halted along the line they held since May 5, "while the Red Army cleared the east and west banks of the Moldau [Vltava] River and occupied Prague."

The Czechs' hope that it might be different was well expressed in a postcard that an elderly employee of a Prague hotel furtively handed my wife in December 1968, as we were being expelled from Czechoslovakia under, of all things, Polish pressure (Poland, where I was born, had participated in the August invasion) on the grounds that as a correspondent for *The New York Times* I had exceeded my professional functions. The card, obviously a treasured memento, shows on its face crossed United States and Czechoslovak flags over the silhouettes of marching American soldiers and an applauding population against the background of Prague's towers. Over the crossed flags, the lettering announces: "YANK SOLDIER'S SONG—Music by Old. Blechai—Words by Bill Powell." It carries a red German 1.20-mark stamp with Hitler's profile and a cancellation mark proclaiming: "ČSR–USA—Liberation of Plzeň—5.5.1945."

On the other side, the forgotten lyricist is identified as "Sgt. Bill Powell." The printed words say, in English and Czech:

> In Czechoslovakia The Day of Victory. The Pilsen Folk Did
> Welcome Us With "Nazdar! A Hurah!" It Was A Day With Tears
>   And Cheers, The Greatest Day In
> Many Years. The Yanks Will Long Remember The Folk We Love
>   So Dear. It Dear.

In the space for the address a faded typewritten line in English tells of "Our thanks to American army," and in Czech, "*Děkujeme americké armádě!*"

It is a voice from the past. It reminds one that, indeed, Czechoslovakia's current drama did begin almost a quarter of a century ago.

One curious thing about the events of May 1945 is that Smrkovský, the man who made it possible for the Soviets to occupy Prague and subsequently helped to bring about the Communist takeover of Czechoslovakia, found himself imprisoned for four years during the Soviet-directed purges of the 1950s and, then, became the principal target of Moscow's hatred as one of the chief progressive Communist figures in the Prague Spring of 1968. There is a fascinating counterpoint in Czechoslovakia's history of the last quarter of the century in the incredibly tortuous political lines forced upon some of the country's leading Communist figures. In no Communist country, not even Hungary and Poland, have so many key personages moved between power and prison and power again, between disgrace and rehabilitation and disgrace anew. Their startling readiness to accept the sublime heights and the abominable depths and their capacity to rationalize each of their successive fates offer an extraordinary insight into the psychology and the sense of blindly unquestioning devotion of so many Communists to their church-like Party.

Smrkovský was only one of these human links between 1945 and 1968. Thus, while he made his fateful May decision in Prague, a fifty-year-old

Communist general named Ludvík Svoboda, earlier in command of the Czechoslovak Army Corps attached to Marshal Konev's forces, became the "non-party" Defense Minister in the Provisional Government of National Unity that had moved from Moscow to Košice. Though both Smrkovský and Svoboda were veteran Communists, there is no reason to suppose they knew each other in these vital days. Likewise, neither of them could possibly suspect that in reward for their days of glory and their subsequent roles in the 1948 takeover—Svoboda could have prevented it—they would be sentenced to prison by their fellow Communists barely six years later. Most certainly it could have never crossed their minds that in another turn in fortune's wheel, they would join forces as members of a famous quadrumvirate that would defy the Soviet Union past the brink of an armed intervention—General Svoboda as the loved and grandfatherly President of the Republic and Smrkovský as the immensely popular Chairman of the Czechoslovak National Assembly.

Another significant link between 1945 and 1968 is provided by Gustav Husák, a Slovak lawyer with an intellectual bent and a Communist career paralleling in Slovakia that of Smrkovský in the Czech lands. Only thirty-one when the Slovaks rose in 1944 against the Germans, he was Commissioner of Interior of the Slovak National Council, Deputy Chairman of the then illegal Slovak Communist Party, and a member of its Central Committee. In August 1944 Husák flew with a Slovak National Council delegation from a secret airfield in Slovakia to Moscow. In March 1945 he joined the Communist team negotiating the political future of Czechoslovakia with the London-based government-in-exile of President Beneš. His colleagues later remembered that he was one of the few Communists to argue at that stage for a federal republic granting Slovakia autonomous rights. He rose quickly in Communist and government affairs in Prague after 1945, but in 1951 he, too, found himself in prison on charges of Slovak "bourgeois nationalism." After nearly nine years in prison and a subsequent rehabilitation, Husák logically emerged as one of the reformist leaders of 1968. Yet, a year later, preaching "realistic" policies toward the Soviet Union, he forsook liberalism to succeed Dubček as the Moscow-blessed First Secretary of the Czechoslovak Communist Party.

While Smrkovský, Svoboda, and Husák in 1945 helped to shape the nation's future, the other men who were destined to soar to exalted fame or opprobrium in 1968 were still lost in obscurity. Of the two members of the 1968 quadrumvirate, besides Svoboda and Smrkovský, Alexander Dubček in 1945 was an unknown twenty-three-year-old Slovak Communist who had been twice wounded in the Slovak uprising and whose brother, Julius, had been killed. Oldřich Černik, Premier of Czechoslovakia during the spring days of 1968 and still Premier after the political defeat of the liberals in 1969, was a young locksmith in Ostrava. A hardworking Communist apparatus man who earned his engineer's degree studying at night, Černik reached the limelight only in 1960 when Antonín Novotný, the Stalinist President of Czechoslovakia, made him Minister of Technology in his cabinet. Unlike Husák, he had not suffered imprisonment—except for his brief capture by the Russians after the invasion—but like him, he was to make a remarkably smooth transition from Communist orthodoxy to liberal heresy and back to orthodoxy again.

Another relevant example of an ideological acrobat among Czechoslovak Communists is Lubomir Strougal. A twenty-one-year-old Prague law student when Marshal Konev's tanks rolled into Prague, Strougal was Novotný's Minister of Interior, controlling the Stalinist-oriented secret police, in the 1960s. In 1968 he found it possible to serve as Deputy Premier in the reformist regime. Seven months later, easily coming to terms with the Soviet invasion, Strougal joined Husák and Černik in a "realistic" power triumvirate, even more outspokenly pro-Soviet than his two colleagues.

But the only fully predictable link between 1945 and 1968 was Novotný himself. In a Nazi concentration camp when Prague was freed, he quickly rose in the Stalinist hierarchy, earned Soviet admiration for his role in the trials of the 1950s, and irritatingly presided over Czechoslovakia until his unlamented ouster in 1968. Neither then nor after their invasion did the Russians lift a finger to bring him back to power. Of those whose careers bridged the full span from 1945 to 1968, Novotný is the only truly forgotten man of Communist politics.

The Prague Checkerboard

In 1945 it was not too difficult for the Czechs, unlike the Poles or even the Romanians and Hungarians, to be reasonably warm in greeting the Soviet liberators. Czechoslovakia had no tradition of anti-Russian sentiment, the Communist Party there had been legal between the wars (in contrast with the rest of Eastern and Central Europe), and it was perfectly respectable to be a Communist. Some of Czechoslovakia's best writers, for example, often contributed before the war to *Rudé Právo*, the Party's official organ. After the Munich Pact, the Soviet Union was the only major world power to oppose the sacrifice of Czechoslovakia to Hitler made by Neville Chamberlain and Edouard Daladier.

The 1939 Soviet-German Nonaggression Pact, the Soviet Union's recognition of a Nazi puppet Slovak state, and its diplomatic break with Beneš's exiled government were obviously blows to the Czechoslovaks, but they were quickly overtaken by the outbreak of the war. Later, President Beneš voluntarily, and even willingly, worked out arrangements for the postwar period with Czechoslovak Communist leaders in the Soviet Union and, in March 1945, his government moved its headquarters to Moscow.

Still, Czechoslovakia was basically a Western-oriented nation and, given a choice, it would probably have opted for liberation by the Americans. As we have seen, there were men both in Czechoslovakia and abroad who feared dire consequences if the country were to be entirely left to the Soviets and their Czechoslovak Communist friends. Already on May 6 a worried Churchill was cabling President Truman that matters in Eastern Europe had come to a point where a conference with Stalin was essential. "Meanwhile," he told the President, "we should hold firmly to the existing position obtained or being obtained by our armies in Yugoslavia, in Austria, in Czechoslovakia, on the main central United States front, and on the British front." This was the prelude to Potsdam.

His plea for Czechoslovakia was, in effect, that the American forces at least remain where they were in Karlový Vary, Plzeň, and České Budějovice. But this, too, was in vain. For politically optimistic reasons, the United States decided in December to pull its troops out of Czechoslovakia and back to the pre-established occupation zones in Germany and Austria.

Churchill's fears notwithstanding, no overt Communist regime was installed in power in Prague in the wake of the Soviet tanks. For nearly three years after 1945 Czechoslovakia enjoyed a honeymoon of freedom, or at least an illusion and a reprieve. A coalition government of democrats of Western persuasion and Communists quietly assumed office under the presidency of Beneš, who at the age of sixty-one returned to the Hradčany Castle he had left for exile in 1938.

In contrast, in Bulgaria, Romania, and Hungary—which until the closing years of the war had fought alongside the Nazis and switched sides only with the approach of the Soviet armies—Moscow quickly and forcibly imposed its own men and, one by one, replaced the shaky coalitions with firmly rooted Communist regimes. In Poland, which lies across the vital communication lines from Russia to East Germany, Stalin first dispatched a purely Communist provisional government from Moscow to Lublin and agreed to include Stanisław Mikołajczyk's group from the London government-in-exile as junior partners in the new Warsaw regime only after a battle of heroic proportions with the British and the Americans. In the Soviet occupation zone of Germany the establishment of a Communist regime, the embryo of the future "German Democratic Republic," was no contest, what with the prompt departure of Anglo-American forces and the massive presence of Soviet troops. Finally, in Yugoslavia, Marshal Tito had no need of the Russians to proclaim a Communist state of his own and Albania at once slid into his sphere.

Czechoslovakia was a different story. Ever since Tomáš Garrigue Masaryk constructed the Czechoslovak Republic in 1918 from the ruins of the shattered Austro-Hungarian Empire and until the Nazi occupation in 1938–1939, it had been the only functioning democracy in Eastern Europe. The rest of that part of the world had been made up of semifascist kingdoms, and Poland was a fascistoid republic. Both Masaryk and Beneš, who became President in 1935 on the retirement of his mentor and friend, had been linked with the left-of-center National Socialist Party (which was founded in 1898 and has absolutely nothing in common with German National Socialism). The Czechoslovak Communist Party, organized in 1921 in the industrial town of Kladno, near Prague, had had a traditional following among workers and the intelligentsia. Its prewar membership had stood only at about eighty thousand, but its influence in Czechoslovak political life was considerably greater than that figure indicates and, as one of the country's four main parties, it had usually controlled some ten per cent of the vote. (In 1925 it had scored its greatest victory, electing forty-one deputies to the three-hundred-seat parliament and trailing only five seats behind the front-running Agrarian Party.)

[handwritten marginal note: Why such gt strength under Repub? and before depression?]

Under Nazi occupation, Communists in both the Czech regions and Slovakia consolidated their positions, taking advantage of the political vacuum. And it was they who were largely responsible for the Slovak uprising in August 1944; they were also active in the Czech underground. Domestic resistance by other groups was sporadic, ill-organized, and not very effective. In the wake of the Soviet advance into Czechoslovakia in 1944, Communist organizers emerged into the open and the Party structure, with no other viable political force ready to oppose it, rapidly developed. When President Beneš reached Moscow in March 1945 for the final negotiations leading to the establishment of a peacetime government, Communist power in Czechoslovakia was already a fact to be reckoned with. Faced with this situation and with the obviously major role the Soviet Union was playing in Europe, Beneš evidently saw no choice but to enter into a coalition.

Favoring this choice were the realities of postwar Europe, but also the absence of any historic anti-Russian sentiment in Czechoslovakia. (This was in marked contrast with neighboring Poland, which until 1918 had lived for nearly a hundred and fifty years under a Russian-Austrian-Prussian partition and was invaded by the Soviets in September 1939.) While Stalin had assured Beneš in 1943 that Ruthenia, the mountainous region adjoining the Ukraine, would be restored to Czechoslovakia after the expulsion of the Nazis, and had later changed his mind and annexed the province to the Soviet Union even before the Czechoslovak leader returned for the political negotiations, Beneš and most Czechoslovaks seemed prepared to swallow this. As for the future, Beneš had faith in Czechoslovakia's democratic tradition and in the Kremlin's honorable intentions.

Contacts between Beneš's government in London and the Russians and the Czechoslovak Communists had been fairly constant. In December

1943 Beneš's visit to Moscow brought a Soviet-Czechoslovak Friendship and Alliance Treaty. In 1944 it was the Czechoslovak Ambassador from the London government-in-exile who approached the Soviets to obtain arms for the Slovak uprising, then in preparation, in which the Communists figured prominently. A Czechoslovak-Soviet agreement of May 1944 provided for Czechoslovak administration of liberated areas.

Thus, there was a background of liberal-Communist cooperation when Beneš and his Foreign Minister, Jan Masaryk, the son of Tomáš Masaryk, flew to the Soviet capital to open the political talks. Unlike the Poles, they were not inhibited by bitter feuds between two underground armies—one loyal to the London government and the other to Moscow—and they did not have to face, as did the Polish exile government, the tragedy of executions and deportations by the Russians of thousands of their citizens.

Moreover, from Soviet and Czechoslovak Communist standpoints, Beneš was eminently acceptable. He and his associates could not be tarred with the "reactionary" brush that was being so generously, and not altogether undeservedly, applied to other London governments-in-exile. It is also quite likely that from the outset the Communists regarded Beneš as essentially naïve and that they opted for patience, instead of engaging in an unnecessary and premature tug-of-war that might reflect adversely on the Soviet image, certain that in the end they would carry the day.

While Beneš and Jan Masaryk led the London group, the Communist team was made up of the Czechoslovak Party's disciplined top veterans. As its head was Klement Gottwald, the forty-nine-year-old Secretary-General of the the Party. Although he was a lifetime follower of the Moscow line, he talked to Beneš in 1945 of Czechoslovakia's "own path to socialism." His second-in-command was Rudolf Slánský, forty-four, a Jew, who after four wartime years in Russia, including a stint on the Kiev Partisan General Staff, had gone to Czechoslovakia in 1944 as the Party's chief secret representative. Another key negotiator was Václav Kopecký, forty-eight, a Communist journalist and propaganda expert, who had spent the entire war in the Soviet Union and earlier was the Czechoslovak delegate to the Comintern. Finally, there was Gustav Husák, the only man on the team to be back in the limelight in 1968–1969, who, as Internal Affairs Commissioner of the Slovak Council, acted as a spokesman for Slovak interests.

The Moscow talks took about a week—with Beneš under steady pressure from the Communists, who immediately presented their own cabinet list—and on April 4, 1945, President Beneš and the Communist Party agreed on their National Unity government. At first sight, it appeared that Beneš had done extremely well under the circumstances. He was personally confirmed as the President of the Republic. Of twenty cabinet seats, only seven went to Communists. Edward Taborsky, a Czech diplomat and historian who accompanied Beneš to Moscow, recalls in his *Communism in Czechoslovakia* that the aging President was rather pleased with Gottwald. "Gottwald's emphasis on the special Czechoslovak way toward socialism and his evident desire not to sever economic links with the West made a good impression on President Beneš. . . . Dr. Beneš felt that Gottwald's dislike of orthodoxism and his relatively high level of practical common sense would cause him to avoid extreme solutions as much as possible." Dr. Taborsky even offers the intriguing thought that had Yugoslavia's Marshal Tito broken with Soviet discipline then, Gottwald "might have considered such a course safer" than throwing himself on Stalin's mercy. Thus, the first intellectual seeds of Czechoslovak Communist heresy may have already been planted twenty-three years before the Prague Spring.

Pleased as President Beneš might have been with the results of his negotiations, a closer look suggests that, instead, he had built himself a menacing Trojan horse. The Premier was Zdeněk Fierlinger, fifty-four, an old-line Czech Marxist Social Democrat and Beneš's prewar and wartime Ambassador to Moscow. As Beneš was to discover to his dismay before too long, Fierlinger, ostensibly a Social Democrat, was a dedicated ball-carrier for the Communists—and the Soviet Union. Of the four deputy premiers, two were Communists. Gottwald was a deputy premier on behalf of *Czech* Communists and Viliam Široký on behalf of *Slovak* Communists. There were no truly separate Czech and Slovak Communist organizations in 1945 (in fact, a Czech Communist Party has never been created to match the Slovak Party), but this was the only way to force Beneš to accept two Communist deputy premiers. Široký, a forty-three-year-old Party veteran who spent most of the war in Moscow and helped lead the Slovak uprising, emerged later as a particularly sinister personage.

The cabinet proper was composed of sixteen ministries, of which, to the delight of Western observers, only five technically went to the Communists. But these five ministries—Interior, Information and Culture, Education, Agriculture, and Social Welfare—were strategic seats of power, and they presently gave the Communists the means of controlling Czechoslovakia.

The Interior Ministry, and with it the police and the secret service, went to Václav Nosek, fifty-three, a prominent labor-unionist and Party leader who was a vice-president of the London State Council, the exile government that Beneš headed. Information and Culture was placed in the hands of Václav Kopecký along with the control of the official press, broadcasting, theater, film, and other artistic activities supported by the state. The Education Ministry was handed to Dr. Zdeněk Nejedlý, a highly respected music critic and professor at Prague and Moscow universities. Nejedlý, then sixty-seven years old, was regarded by the Party as its principal intellectual, but was popularly known as the "Red Grandpa." Agriculture was entrusted to Július Ďuriš, forty-one, a prewar Slovak Communist Member of Parliament and a highly disciplined Party veteran. He had spent four war years in German prisons. Taborsky makes the point that, in naming Nosek to the Interior Ministry and Ďuriš to Agriculture, the Communists secured the organs "which were to play a key part in their early agricultural policies based primarily on the distribution of land confiscated from the expelled Germans and the native 'traitors.' " According to Taborsky, these two ministries were converted "into agencies of the Central Committee of the Czechoslovak Communist Party, carrying out to the letter the Party's directives."

As for the Defense Ministry, the Moscow conferees had unanimously agreed that it should go to a "nonpartisan" figure. But, it was Ludvík Svoboda, the Communist general and later a Hero of the Soviet Union, who was named to it.

To counterbalance this formidable Communist team, President Beneš could lean chiefly on Jan Masaryk, well known in the West and popular at home, who remained Foreign Minister and his closest associate. Among the other non-Communist ministers, only Foreign Trade Minister Hubert Ripka, who had been Information Minister in London, Industry Minister Bohumil Laušman, and Food Minister Václav Majer were destined to play important, albeit brief roles. The others were quickly forgotten by history.

As soon as this rather peculiarly constructed cabinet was agreed upon, President Beneš went from Moscow to Košice, recently liberated by the Soviet armies, to establish his government officially on Czechoslovak soil. Five weeks later, when the Russians instead of the Americans took Prague, the new regime was solemnly installed in the ancient Bohemian capital.

Once in Košice, the Beneš government issued, on April 5, its "Program of the First Government of Czechs and Slovaks on Native Soil." The Communists had a central role in drafting it—in fact, they handed it to Beneš when he was still in Moscow—but the Košice Program carefully refrained from sounding like a Communist document and, indeed, seemed like something the British Labour Party could have easily produced, although it demanded the expulsion of ethnic Germans and Hungarians from Czechoslovakia. Thus, "state direction" was proposed for banking, main industries, insurance, and energy sources, but not a word was breathed about nationalizing private property. In agriculture, not even "state direction" was recommended, and the accent was on the redistribution of confiscated land to small and medium farmers. (This, of course, was to be the Communists' hidden weapon.) The Communist strategy in 1945 was to emphasize moderation and cooperation, liberal "agrarian reform," and all the other policies likely to win support at home and applause abroad. For the time had not yet come to rock the boat.

The over-all package presented to the Czechoslovaks may, indeed, have appeared attractive. But the questions inevitably arise what Beneš thought he could accomplish in the long run with a Communist-riddled government at a time when Soviet power and Communism were spreading throughout Eastern Europe and, conversely, what his partners were likely to do to him and to Czechoslovak democracy. Both Beneš and Masaryk were too intelligent and too experienced not to realize the potential dangers of handing over the ministries of Defense, Interior, and Information to the Communists in a country filled with Soviet troops, bordering on the Soviet Union, and so clearly fitting into the emerging Soviet postwar geopolitical system.

If they needed examples, they only had to look to Romania, where, a few weeks before the negotiations in Moscow, the Russians had mounted a brutal and successful coup that deposed the coalition government headed by General Nicolae Radescu, who had joined with a group of "home Communists" on August 23, 1944, to oust the fascist regime of Ion Antonescu and switch Romania from the Nazi to the Allied camp in the still raging war. The Radescu coalition, under the aegis of young King Michael, had seemed to threaten Soviet interests because it included not only non-Communists but also nationalist-minded domestic Communists who were at odds with the long-exiled Moscow group. (It may be noted that these "home Communists" were Eastern Europe's first Communist nationalists, predating the Tito rebellion in Yugoslavia by four years, the Polish and Hungarian nationalists by almost twelve years, and the

Prague Spring by nearly twenty-four years. It is even more interesting to note that these men and their successors have been back in power since 1965, defying the Soviets with their Romanian national Communism even after the Russian invasion of Czechoslovakia.) Inasmuch as the prewar and illegal Romanian Communist Party never exceeded one thousand members and its growth after August 1944 was somewhat less than remarkable, the Kremlin had to apply its own direct power to swing the situation. The man chosen for the job was Deputy Foreign Minister Andrei A. Vyshinsky, the white-haired Bolshevik who earned world fame as the chief prosecutor in the Moscow trials of 1937.

Vyshinsky arrived in Bucharest late in February 1945 and immediately requested that King Michael dismiss the Radescu cabinet for failure to "maintain order" and appoint as the new Premier a pro-Soviet politician named Petru Groza, who headed the so-called Plowmen's Front. Reminding the King that one million Soviet troops were stationed in Romania, Vyshinsky gave him exactly 125 minutes to replace Radescu with Groza and until noon of the next day to name a full new cabinet. Otherwise, he warned Michael, "Romania might cease to exist as a sovereign state." Groza's National Democratic Front, which was to last only two and a half years before the Russians put in a pure Communist regime, was installed on March 6—less than a month before Beneš formed *his* government with the Communists.

But as they prepared to fly from London to Moscow, President Beneš and Jan Masaryk seemed to feel that they had to trust the Communists—the Romanian example and the parallel Polish controversy notwithstanding. As Beneš was to acknowledge later, when it was already too late, "I still believed in the sincerity of the Soviet leaders." This, of course, could be ascribed to naïveté on the part of a well-meaning and honorable man. Just as obviously, Beneš's ostensible naïveté was a major element in the Communists' own early strategic planning. But nothing is quite that simple, and this was not the whole story.

The truth is that both historically and in terms of the new situation in Europe, Beneš's and Czechoslovakia's options were extremely limited in 1945. They were, in fact, just as limited in relation to the Soviet Union and Communism as they had been in 1938 in relation to Germany and Nazism. Abandonment by the West, despite its Western orientation and proclivities, is the destiny that has haunted Czechoslovakia ever since Tomáš Masaryk founded the republic in 1918 (ironically with the support of President Woodrow Wilson). The recurring theme of this whole story is that Czechoslovakia always is the "Lone Man of Europe."

Having helped to create Czechoslovakia, the West proceeded to wash its hands of it when Hitler demanded and received the Sudetenland (his "last territorial ambition in Europe") in 1938 and again in 1939 when the Nazis marched into Prague. Beneš, the embattled President, learned his first bitter lesson of the West's loyalty to its stepchild. Apprised on September 30, 1938, that Britain and France had capitulated to Hitler and Mussolini and agreed to Czechoslovakia's dismemberment by Germany, Poland, and Hungary—"they decided about us, without us"—Beneš slowly and heavily told his cabinet that "there is no precedent in history for treating an independent nation and state in such a way. . . . I found out that the big states and nations do not at this time consider small states and nations as equals."

This clearly marked the beginning of Beneš's bitterness toward and lack of faith in the West—toward Britain and France for signing the Munich agreement and, less pronouncedly, toward the United States (whose President Roosevelt told the French, as they sought support during the Czechoslovak crisis, that from America there would be "not one man, not one cent"). In exile in London, Beneš once more discovered that the West had little interest in Czechoslovakia. Though Czechs and Slovaks had fought in the French and the British armies since the outbreak of the war, it was only in 1941 that Beneš won official recognition for his exiled government by Britain and the United States. His meeting with President Roosevelt in Washington in 1943 apparently did little to fill him with optimism for the years to come.

As Beneš and Masaryk faced the Communists during the negotiations in March and April 1945, then, it is not really incredible that they were prepared to accept such a far-reaching compromise in forming the postwar government. The alternative would have been to go back to London without even the slightest hope of influencing politically the future course of events in Czechoslovakia, letting the Soviet Union either first set up a local "coalition" regime on her own terms—as she had already done in Romania and was now doing in Poland—or immediately impose purely Communist rule. (It is interesting to note in this context that among the charges leveled against Rudolf Slánský in his 1952 "treason" trial was the accusation that he had criticized Gottwald for not having captured total power for the Communists already in 1945 and for having waited until 1948.)

What Beneš, already a sick and tired man, seems to have decided, then, was to roll with the punch and hope for the best, knowing full well that the West would no more lift a finger to aid Czechoslovakia in 1945 than it had in 1938 and 1939. Despite Churchill's first warnings in April, Western policy, and especially the trend of American policy, was to disengage as rapidly as possible in Europe and concentrate on the war in the Pacific. The Yalta Conference and subsequent Anglo-American exchanges with Stalin had given him virtually free rein politically in Bulgaria, Romania, and Hungary. Though the British and the Americans were to fight a rear-guard political battle over Poland throughout the spring, there was no reason to believe that they would take on the Czechoslovak case.

It was the supreme tragedy of Beneš's life that at every turn he had to make awesome decisions. It may have been in his or in the Czech character that when faced with overwhelming odds he invariably chose the compromise and the conciliation. In 1938 he decided not to resist the Germans, though his nation was willing to fight; as he explained in a speech to the cabinet after Munich, "it was difficult to decide whether to accept the conditions and save the nation or to fight and let ourselves be murdered. . . . History will judge what was correct." Beneš's choice in 1938 was, in a sense, the genesis of his choice in 1945 when he accepted the postwar government and in 1948 when he accepted the Communist sweep into power. And, thinking of subsequent Czechoslovak history, the decision not to resist the Soviet invasion of 1968 had, in the same sense, its roots in the same attitude.

III

Beneš on the Eve

It was in loneliness and growing isolation that President Beneš sought to lead his divided and confused nation from wartime chaos to a semblance of peacetime order. But he was swimming against the tide of history in Czechoslovakia and in all of Europe. His office at Hradčany Castle, majestically rising over the city of Prague and the swift-flowing Vltava River, was no longer the real center of authority in the Republic. In truth, this elderly and almost pathetic yet proud man had carried back from exile the mantle of executive power, but not the power itself.

Now, as the spring turned into summer—the first summer of freedom from oppression in Czechoslovakia in seven years—the seat of effective power shifted to a gray building in downtown Prague that housed the Central Committee of the Communist Party. There, a group of determined men planned and plotted a return to oppression for Czechoslovakia, this time in the name of the Marxist-Leninist faith. They had the powerful support of the Soviet Union, whose troops still held most of the country and whose "technical advisers" were quietly but deliberately helping to force Czechoslovak parliamentary democracy to commit suicide.

And, as usual, the West—currently concerned with the Pacific war, the fate of Poland, and the expansionism of Tito's Yugoslavia—did not seem to care about the clouds again gathering over Czechoslovakia. Washington and London seemed satisfied that a democratic coalition ruled under President Beneš, a respected democrat, and there was no desire to inquire what might be the disturbing reality behind this pleasant illusion.

The reality, of course, was that the Communists were tirelessly working to transform the Party into the leading political force in the country and to infiltrate and capture every possible existing organization from the

27

trade-unions to farmers' cooperatives, women's, youth, and student groups, athletic clubs, and neighborhood-improvement associations. One of their foremost instruments in this enterprise were the local National Committees, ostensibly tied to the National Front government but, increasingly, Communist Party operational units—parallel structures to the Party's own overt regional, district, municipal, and plant committees. (They were to be maintained throughout the subsequent period of Communist rule as useful ancillary organizations.)

As to the Communist Party itself, a powerful membership drive was launched at once. Václav Kopecký's control of newsprint allocation to the newspapers and his deft handling of the radio placed the state's entire propaganda machine at the Party's service, and the press media emphasized that the Communists were democratic-minded social reformers and urged all Czechoslovaks to join the Party.* Citizens were not only encouraged, invited, and cajoled to join the Party, but Communist agents made it clear everywhere that a membership card opened the doors to better jobs, advancement, official favor, and the like. This was especially true in industrial plants, offices, and among the basically conservative farmers whom the Communists sought to attract and convert with the land redistribution program operated by Václav Nosek's Interior Ministry and Július Ďuriš's Agriculture Ministry. Under this system, Nosek confiscated the lands of the ethnic Germans and Hungarians and others who were classified as "traitors" or "collaborators" during the Nazi era and Ďuriš parceled it out to the farmers against a payment equivalent to a year's crop yield.

Many distinguished foreign observers, journalists and diplomats alike, accepted these Communist professions of democratic faith and procedure fairly easily. Articles in the American press and elsewhere reported in pleased wonderment that it was a Communist Minister of Agriculture who was distributing land to the new farmer-owners and that Czechoslovakia was an unusual case where capitalism and socialism were peacefully permitted to compete side by side. This was precisely the impression that the Soviets and the KSČ hoped to create abroad while the efforts went on to construct a politically unbeatable Communist Party at home.

The great membership drive may have violated the Leninist concept that the Communist Party should be an elite "vanguard of the proletariat" and not a gigantic political organization. But, at this stage, the strategy

*In Czech, incidentally, the word "party" is *strana*, which means "side"—the Party's Czech initials are KSČ—and the nation was thus invited to take the Communists' "side."

was to capture ultimate power the parliamentary way—Italian Communists were simultaneously attempting the same thing—and for this goal the Party had to be as big as possible. Consequently, KSČ membership, which totaled 80,000 before the war, had risen to 1,159,164 by May 1946 —a year after the Beneš government took office—and the strength of the National Socialists and the Catholic People's Party decreased accordingly.

This Communist Party operation was directed at a nation-wide level by Party General Secretary Slánský, assisted by the sixty-one-year-old Antonín Zápotocký, Chairman of the Revolutionary Trade-Union Movement (ROH) and future President of Czechoslovakia; Jaromír Dolanský, fifty, an intellectual economist and the Party's Deputy General Secretary; and Josef Smrkovský, just elevated to the Politburo, having kept the Americans out of Prague. In Slovakia, Party activity was headed by Karol Smidke, forty-eight, Deputy Chairman of the Slovak Communist Party and of the Slovak National Council; Karol Bacílek, a remarkably ruthless man who was to acquire a most sinister reputation in the years to come; the ubiquitous Husák, now Deputy Chairman of both the Slovak Party and the Slovak Council and Slovak Commissioner for Transportation and Public Works; and Laco Novomeský, an intellectual, who along with Husák was to suffer later for his Slovak inclinations. The key Prague organization was in the hands of forty-one-year-old Antonín Novotný, a one-time mechanic who was freed from the Nazi concentration camp of Mauthausen in 1945 and immediately plunged into Party work. He replaced Smrkovský at the head of the Prague operation when the latter rose to the Politburo; this was the first time their fates became intertwined. They were to remain so in the 1950s and again in 1968.

In the National Front government, Deputy Premiers Gottwald and Široký and the five Communist cabinet ministers (aided by Premier Fierlinger and Defense Minister Svoboda, and, more often than not, with easily obtained cooperation from several National Socialist members of the cabinet) closely coordinated their activities with Slánský's Party leadership downtown. In the Party hierarchical sense, it was debatable whether it was Gottwald or Slánský who really ran things. But, in practical fact, this mattered little because they were in constant contact.

At the lovely Czernin Palace, below Hradčany Castle, Foreign Minister Jan Masaryk planned and executed Beneš's hopeful foreign policy of maintaining ties with the West as well as with the Soviet Union. But his top deputy was Vladimir Clementis, an urbane forty-three-year-old

Slovak Communist, loyal to the Party both in wartime London and then in Prague.

A well-oiled Communist apparatus, then, functioned at all levels throughout Czechoslovakia from the moment the Beneš government established itself in May 1945. The elderly man at Hradčany Castle was virtually powerless to control a situation that was quickly slipping out of his hands, and this was particularly true in the case of persecutions and atrocities against the Sudeten Germans, which the Communists—and many others—actively encouraged.

While Beneš had supported and signed the laws expelling the Germans and the Hungarians from Czechoslovakia and confiscating their property, he rapidly became appalled at the beatings, imprisonments, and murders of thousands of members of these minorities. Much as the Czechs and the Slovaks had suffered under the Nazis, the retributions against German families, many of which had lived in Czechoslovakia for centuries, constituted one of the least attractive pages in the nation's history. Nazi methods were used against them by the frequently Communist-controlled local political bodies, occasionally acting as courts, and the crowds they so easily assembled. When Beneš or his representatives attempted to intervene against the brutalities, they were largely ignored. Communists controlled the Interior Ministry and the police, and virtually nothing could be done to halt the revenge.

In these and other matters of maintaining some sort of political balance in Czechoslovakia, Beneš could expect no Western support. The government he had formed had been recognized in the West, and both Churchill and Truman seemed convinced that, basically, all was well in Prague. At the Potsdam Conference in July 1945 the chief East European topic was Poland, and the concerns of the Anglo-American allies were the holding of free elections in that country, participation of non-Communists in the government, guarantees for Polish soldiers who had fought in the West and now contemplated returning home, etc. The Allies were anxious to prevent the establishment of an oppressive Communist government in Poland, in whose defense the war had been started in 1939, but, clearly, it had not occurred to them that the same danger lurked in Czechoslovakia. Beneš, in his first address after the liberation, on May 12, had in effect made his peace, telling the Czechoslovaks that while in 1938 "the Western world did us a great wrong . . . let it be stated that the war has made good that injustice." Czechoslovakia, then, was again being left to her own devices by the Western allies, and Beneš made no known effort to change their minds.

In October 1945 United States forces bade farewell to Plzeň, and in December they completed their withdrawal from Czechoslovakia. The last external source of support for Czechoslovak democracy, if not for Beneš himself, had thus been removed. Churchill was no longer Britain's Prime Minister and his successor, Clement Attlee, seemed to feel no concern for Czechoslovakia. The United States had dropped atomic bombs on Hiroshima and Nagasaki, and the war with Japan was victoriously concluded. Now the American cry was to "bring the boys home" and to seek no new entanglements in Europe.

But for Beneš the problems were mounting. Czechoslovakia had not suffered major destruction in the war, Prague was virtually intact, and the highly developed national industry was in a reasonably good state, but the over-all economy was deteriorating. The 1945–1946 winter brought shortages and unemployment, and the ensuing chaos and discontent helped the Communists in their drive for strength.

Consequently, when the first postwar parliamentary elections were held on May 26, 1946, coinciding with the Party's first postwar Congress —the Communists polled 38 per cent of the popular vote (42 per cent in the Czech regions and 30 per cent in Slovakia) and captured 114 out of the 300 parliamentary seats—almost three times the number of seats it had won in 1925, its best prewar year. The immediate reaction of its opponents was jubilation that the Party had failed to win an absolute majority despite its huge membership. Beneš's National Socialists received 18.2 per cent of the vote, the Catholic People's Party 15.8 per cent, and Premier Fierlinger's Social Democrats 12.8 per cent. The Communists now were the largest party in the country and could, on that basis, form a new government, but the 114 Communist deputies alone were a minority in Parliament, and it was hoped that the other parties would resist joining them to form a majority.

This hope, however, was promptly dashed by Fierlinger who, as a fellow Marxist, declared himself in alliance with the Communists and added the Social Democrats' 39 seats to the Communist Party's 114—making a total of 153 seats, exactly an absolute majority of 51 per cent. This move earned Fierlinger both a reputation as "gravedigger" of Czechoslovak democracy and subsequent rewards in the highest Communist councils. (The Soviet invasion of Czechoslovakia twenty-two years later was to find

Fierlinger still an active and devoted advocate of the Soviet and the Communist orthodox line.)

On the strength of the Communists' popular vote majority and their parliamentary alliance with the Social Democrats, President Beneš had no choice but to appoint Gottwald the new Premier of Czechoslovakia. On July 3 Gottwald named a new twenty-six-member cabinet, including nine Communist ministers. Three other ministers were Social Democrats who would presumably cooperate with the Communists; with his own vote, Gottwald thought he could command thirteen votes, or half the total, in the cabinet. The Communist Party appeared to be well on its way to establishing the Soviet brand of socialism in Czechoslovakia through parliamentary rule—a development that nobody could dispute.

Two and a half months before the Czechoslovak elections, Winston Churchill had warned of the new dangers. On March 5 at Westminster College in Fulton, Missouri, he proclaimed that "from Stettin in the Baltic to Trieste in the Adriatic, an iron curtain has descended across the Continent." He was speaking of the denial of free government in Poland, the Soviet stranglehold over East Germany, Bulgaria, and Romania, Communist rule in Yugoslavia and Albania, the approaching liquidation of the Hungarian coalition, and, presumably, the situation in Czechoslovakia. Klement Gottwald's anointment as the Communist Premier in Prague in the summer seemed to confirm Churchill's assessment of affairs in Eastern Europe.

Yet Czechoslovaks, as history continuously demonstrates, are an unpredictable people and, by 1947, both the Kremlin and Czechoslovakia's Communists developed reasons for concern over the country. Despite the Communists' ostensible parliamentary control, no real progress seemed to have been made toward the ultimate objective of assuming total power and eliminating the vestiges of non-Communist democracy and non-Communist policies. On the contrary, this objective had become quite elusive.

Problems developed in the field of foreign policy. For the first time since the pullback of troops in 1945, the West was reacting to the Soviet Union's inroads in Europe. In Washington on May 22, 1947, President Truman signed what was to become known as the Truman Doctrine of intensive military and economic aid to Greece and Turkey. Fearing that the Communist rebellion in Greece, assisted by Yugoslavia, Bulgaria, and Albania, might lead to a complete takeover of the country, the United

States decided not only to shore up Greek political institutions but also, if needed, to intervene directly. In his *Memoirs*, Truman recalls inquiring from the Navy whether squadrons of American warships could easily enter Greek ports. Turkey was aided so as better to withstand direct Soviet pressures and to be able to resist should Greece fall under Communist domination.

Two weeks later, on June 5, 1947, in a speech at Harvard University Secretary of State George C. Marshall unveiled a vast plan of United States economic cooperation with Europe—the Marshall Plan. A conference to set the Plan in motion was to be held in Paris during the summer, and Secretary Marshall pointedly invited the East European countries to join it.

It is likely that in Czechoslovakia the Truman Doctrine and the Marshall Plan made a strong impression not only on advocates of maintaining ties with the West, like Beneš and Masaryk, but also on key Communist leaders, notably Premier Gottwald. For Czechoslovakia desperately needed foreign economic aid. The Communist-oriented experiments with the economy had not been wholly successful, and the inability of the nation to overcome the wartime disruptions made the idea of membership in the Marshall Plan highly attractive. Masaryk succeeded in convincing Gottwald and his Communist colleagues that Czechoslovakia should participate in the American program. Hurried consultation with Warsaw showed that the Poles were thinking along the same lines. On July 4— without any discussions with the Soviet Union—the Czechoslovak cabinet *unanimously* voted to join the Marshall Plan.

News of this decision was received with profound shock in Moscow. Only a few days earlier the Soviets had engineered a political coup in Budapest, a repetition of the Romanian coup of 1945, bringing down the coalition government and installing a Communist regime in Hungary. The notion that Czechoslovakia would simultaneously place a foot in the enemy camp must have struck the Kremlin as not only dangerous but downright absurd. Premier Gottwald was, therefore, invited to Moscow to explain his action, and he flew there on July 7 with Foreign Minister Masaryk and Justice Minister Prokop Drtina, a Socialist.

Their meeting with a raging Stalin at the Kremlin gave the Czechoslovaks the first taste of what it meant to defy Soviet wishes. In retrospect, there is a familiar ring to the urgent summons being sent to the heretic Communist leader and the riot act being read to him by Soviet chiefs. Taborsky reports in his book that Gottwald told Masaryk and Drtina after his Kremlin session, "I have never seen Stalin so furious. . . . He reproached me bitterly for having accepted the invitation to participate in the Paris Conference. He does not understand how we could have done it. He says that we acted as if we were ready to turn our back on the Soviet Union."

Immediately, Gottwald and Masaryk telephoned Prague to report and an emergency cabinet meeting was called later that day. The ministers voted to reject the invitation to join the Marshall Plan with the same unanimity with which they had voted three days earlier to accept it. Beneš, who could have intervened, albeit at the risk of a showdown, was felled in a stroke. On July 10 the Czechoslovak government issued a statement that "Czechoslovakia's participation would have been explained as a deed aimed against friendship with the Soviet Union and the Slav allies." Moscow offered Czechoslovakia two hundred thousand tons of wheat as a consolation prize.

Early in 1968 I asked a leading Czechoslovak Communist economist in Prague why the country's economy had remained so deficient for so many years after the war. "I can tell you simply that this is the result of Stalin's prohibition to Czechoslovakia to join the Marshall Plan, followed by twenty years of building Socialism the Soviet way," he told me. "Our efforts at economic reform are an attempt at compensating for these errors of the past."

This, then, was another root in what was to be the flowering of the Prague Spring of 1968.

If Klement Gottwald had run into a storm in Moscow because of his experiment with a Communist foreign policy independent of the Soviet Union, new storms awaited him in the field of domestic politics.

The first signs came in the summer. Czechoslovaks, the citizenry as well as the politicians, were drawing away from the Communist Party and its policies. The other parties in the National Front began to think that the KSČ's popularity had peaked out with the elections, and they proceeded to act accordingly. Though the Communist Party's membership was, in fact, still ascending, the growth was only of 20,000 members between May 1946 and August 1947. By contrast, Beneš's National Socialist Party, which lacked the formidable propaganda and patronage resources of the Communists, picked up around 100,000 new members during the same period for a total of 650,000, more than one-half of the KSČ enrollment. Politicians were calculating that in the elections scheduled for May 1948 the Communists could not repeat their performance of corralling thirty-eight per cent of the popular vote. The combined votes of the National Socialists, the People's Party, the anti-Fierlinger Social Democrats, and the small Slovak parties promised to cut deeply into the KSČ's strength.

This erosion of Communist prestige was the sum of many factors. The discontent over the economic situation that in 1946 had favored the KSČ started to turn against the Communists now that Gottwald was Premier. Many in the middle classes were disturbed by the rapid rhythm of industrial nationalization which had reached sixty per cent of the country's plants and factories in June 1947, although the Košice Program had not called for it. The excesses of the police and the Interior Ministry were backfiring, as the nation's feeling of vengeance against "traitors," and against the ethnic Germans and Hungarians, ebbed. Justice Minister Drtina, one of the few outspoken anti-Communists in the cabinet, felt secure enough to busy himself blocking the activities of his colleague Nosek. Monsignor Jozef Tiso, President of the Nazi-puppet Slovak Republic during the war, had been hanged in April after a dubious trial, but now the Justice Ministry rode herd over political trials. A reaction was thus setting in against the Communists, and the hurried reversal of Czechoslovakia's plans to participate in the Marshall Plan may also have played a part in it.

But Gottwald's most serious problems were on the national level with the Social Democrats and in Slovakia with the majority Democratic Party. In Prague, the leadership of the Social Democratic Party disowned Fierlinger's 1946 pact with Gottwald to operate jointly "along the Socialist line." At a party congress in Brno in November 1947 Fierlinger was ousted from the chairmanship by a 283-to-182 vote and replaced by Industry Minister Bohumil Laušman, a more moderate Social Democrat. In Slovakia the Democratic Party was increasingly challenging Communist control of the Slovak government headed by Husák.

The net effect of these developments was that the Communists lost the prospects of a peaceful and parliamentary conquest of power, the cherished goal of Gottwald's careful policies. Gottwald had hoped that the electoral victory of 1946—and the working alliance with the Social Democrats—would lead to a landslide at the polls in 1948 and the final liquidation of Beneš and his allies. Now that this no longer was in the cards, the Communist Party abruptly switched tactics and prepared for a classical program of direct action. Having miraculously survived Stalin's fury over the Marshall Plan incident, Gottwald could not risk a political defeat at home. He made one last attempt to mend his political fences by inviting the National Front parties to form a new pro-Communist bloc. But the Social Democrats, the Socialists, and the Catholics of the People's Party simply boycotted his conference. Already under mounting criticism by Communist leaders everywhere, Gottwald at once issued battle orders for a final confrontation with the "bourgeois" enemy. The new objective was the conquest of power at any cost.

Gottwald's chosen instrument in attempting to control the Slovak situation was Gustav Husák, who immediately displayed his talents for ruthless political maneuver that were to stand him in such good stead in 1968 and 1969. On October 6 the Husák government announced the discovery of a conspiracy of "high treason" in Slovakia and proceeded to arrest 380 persons, chiefly members of the Democratic Party. On October 30 the Communists staged a violent manifestation by the Slovak trade-unions to demand the resignation of the Democrats from the Slovak government. In a preview of what was to happen in Prague less than four months later, Husák, without consulting his Democratic ministers, blandly announced that the whole government had resigned. Though a new Slovak government was presently formed, with the Communists still in the minority, Husák had achieved the atmosphere of crisis that was required for his future moves.

Meanwhile, Gottwald too set the tone for further actions. Speaking to the Party's Central Committee in Prague on November 27, he acknowledged that "impatience and even doubts" existed within the ranks over the policy of coexistence with non-Communist parties. "Some comrades" felt that the "bourgeoisie" should have been dealt a mortal bow in 1945, instead of being joined in a coalition, he said—presumably referring to Party General Secretary Slánský. Reverting to the line employed by Communist leaders in other East European countries, he reported that the international situation was also deteriorating. "Foreign reactionaries," he said, were threatening Czechoslovakia, while "domestic reactionaries" were infiltrating the National Front. The National Socialists and the Catholics had cooperated with the "fascist plot" that Husák's police had uncovered in Slovakia. And so on.

The honeymoon of 1945 was now clearly over. Ahead lay open warfare. Late in November Masaryk flew to Washington to explain the Czechoslovak situation to President Truman. It is doubtful that he received anything beyond expressions of sympathy.

The new year—1948—opened with the kind of bad news for the Communists that only served to harden their determination to go for the democrats' jugular. The Public Opinion Research Institute in Václav Kopecký's Ministry of Information informed the Party that a recent poll had shown that in the May 1948 elections for the Chamber of Deputies the Communists would win only twenty-eight per cent of the popular vote, as compared to the thirty-eight per cent obtained two years earlier. And in student-association elections held in Czechoslovak universities in December, Communist candidates had polled only twenty per cent of the vote. The Party was thus even losing the youth.

So the time had come for action. Throughout Czechoslovakia, the Party began organizing *Akcni Výbory*, revolutionary Action Committees in industrial plants, on farms, and in towns and villages. Slánský set up a special task force at the Central Committee to coordinate preparations for what evidently would be a *putsch* at the first opportunity. The Interior Ministry established close surveillance of leading non-Communist politicians. An espionage plot, said to involve United States military attachés in Prague, was unearthed by the security police. Unexplained arrests of democratic figures began occurring in the Czech lands and in Slovakia. A tense and nervous atmosphere pervaded Prague.

The crisis finally erupted on Friday, February 13, when parliament met to hear Justice Minister Drtina report on the investigations of the alleged plot "against the Republic." Drtina, who throughout the three years of the coalition regime had been the single most courageous opponent of the Communists in the cabinet, charged the Interior Ministry with undue interference in the investigations. He then apprised the deputies of the extent of Communist control of the police: Of the nine heads of departments in the security division, five were Communists; all three commanding posts in the main office of the political police were held by Communists.

In the middle of his exposition, a report reached the Chamber of Deputies that Interior Minister Nosek had the day before fired eight non-Communist commanders in the Prague police force and replaced them with men loyal to the Party. The aroused democratic deputies now demanded the reinstatement of the dismissed commanders and voted to censure Nosek. This was the turning point. After both Gottwald and Nosek ignored this vote, twelve non-Communist ministers resigned on February 18, bringing the fall of the government and forcing Beneš to name a new cabinet. The resignations were not immediately accepted by Beneš, however, and feverish negotiations went on for several more days. The KSČ Politburo sat in permanent session at Gottwald's Prague villa (which was said to be connected by direct telephone lines with the Interior Ministry's security division and with the Soviet Embassy).

On February 19 a new and threatening ingredient was added to the crisis cauldron. This was the sudden arrival in Prague of Soviet Deputy Foreign Minister Valerian A. Zorin, until recently Ambassador to Czechoslovakia. Zorin insisted that he had come to supervise negotiation on Soviet grain deliveries to Czechoslovakia, but few Czechoslovaks took this explanation seriously. As was to become evident in the next few hours and days, Zorin's mission in Prague was strikingly reminiscent of the visit to Bucharest three years earlier by Andrei Vyshinsky, another Soviet Deputy Foreign Minister, to force a change in government.

That he had come to influence events in Czechoslovakia—the second Soviet intervention in eight months—became amply clear the moment he left Ruzyň airport in the company of Vladimir Clementis, the Communist Deputy Foreign Minister of Czechoslovakia. Calling at once on Masaryk, in bed with a fever at his Czernin Palace apartment, Zorin told him that the Soviet Union was alarmed by the activities of "reactionary" elements in the Czechoslovak republic. The deteriorating world situation required a greater loyalty by Czechoslovakia to the Soviet Union and its "Slav" allies. A soft-spoken man—not a table-pounder like Vyshinsky—he advised Masaryk that Moscow simply wished to see Gottwald's political efforts crowned with success. It was a highly elegant way of telling Masaryk that the Soviet Union desired a *coup d'état* in Czechoslovakia.

Zorin was blunter with Laušman, Chairman of the Social Democrats. If his party maintained contacts with oppositionist ministers—who, he suggested, were tied to "foreign reactionary governments"—"the Soviet Union might be forced to safeguard Czechoslovakia's independence," he warned. Food Minister Ivan Pietor was advised that "the Soviet Union never deserts her friends."

Though no Soviet troops were stationed in Czechoslovakia at the time, Zorin seemed to be indicating that, if needed, a military intervention would take place. He never made it absolutely clear, but from the instant he landed in Prague, Beneš and his associates had to live with the threat of a Soviet invasion or, at least, a civil war. As Beneš was to say later, it was Munich all over again. And, to be sure, those words about safeguarding Czechoslovakia's independence and about the Soviet Union never deserting her friends were to be heard again in Prague two decades later. Patterns of Soviet behavior do not much change.

Besides the possibility of a Soviet intervention, however, Beneš had to contend with powerful and menacing internal pressures. As part of the preparations for a *putsch*, the Czechoslovak Communist Party had reactivated the armed People's Militias, the successors of the 1945 revolutionary militias which had been dissolved by the government in 1946.

The national commander of the militias was General Josef Pavel, a one-time worker who had studied at the Lenin School in Moscow and subsequently became the most distinguished Czech volunteer officer in the International Brigades in the Spanish Civil War. He had commanded the famous Dimitrov Battalion and early in 1939, as the Spanish Republic stook at the brink of final defeat, he organized the last detachment for the Brigades. Pavel had returned from France after internment during the Second World War and immediately joined the security apparatus of the Communist Party. General Pavel's deputy was Josef Smrkovský.

The evening of February 20 Smrkovský issued orders that "a state of battle" was being declared for all the militiamen in Prague as of six a.m. the next day and that all seven thousand of them would receive two hundred cartridges each for their rifles. From Brno, workers at the local defense plant dispatched trucks with the ammunition. Simultaneously, the Politburo issued a directive to all regional and district committees to "make preparations for purging the National Front of reactionaries, to begin in the factories with the organization of workers' defense corps." A state of war, indeed, had been declared.

An additional pressure on Beneš, who had finally accepted the twelve ministers' resignations, was the arrival in Prague of nearly seven thousand Communist delegates to the Congress of the Revolutionary Trade-Unions that the Communist Party had presciently scheduled for February 22. The stage was, then, set for the confrontation.

The only force capable of withstanding this mounting Communist pressure was the Army. But Defense Minister Svoboda, the Communist general who had joined the government in Košice as a "non-party man," was predictably on the side of the revolution. As the crisis developed, Svoboda said publicly that Czechoslovakia could maintain her freedom only under Soviet protection and in "the camp of progress and democracy." On February 23, addressing a meeting of the Renewed National Front, organized by the Communists, at the Old Town Hall, he pledged that "the Army goes with the nation. . . . Who disturbs the unity of the nation is a menace and must be removed." That same day Beneš had summoned Svoboda to Hradčany Castle to ask whether the armed forces would stand by the government if the police and People's Militias attempted to capture power, and Svoboda had answered that the Army would be loyal if he had a written order from the President to send it into action. Forthwith, Svoboda put into practice his promise to remove those "disturbing the unity of the nation" by confining to quarters all top-level anti-Communist officers.

It was this effective alliance of the three men controlling most of the armed power of the Republic—Ludvík Svoboda, Josef Smrkovský, and Josef Pavel—that in the end forced Beneš to accept the new government which Gottwald, supported by Zorin, had been trying to impose for days. In Slovakia it was Gustav Husák who drove the final nail into the coffin of Czechoslovak democracy. As Chairman of the Slovak government, he informed the opposition ministers, who constituted a majority, that they were dismissed because their ideological colleagues in the Prague government had resigned, and, in their places, he named Communists and their followers. It was a move quite in character with his actions twenty-one years later.

In the gray afternoon of Wednesday, February 25, Eduard Beneš received from Klement Gottwald at Hradčany Castle the new cabinet list approved by Valerian Zorin. He hesitated before placing his signature on it, but Gottwald produced the names of hundreds of "reactionaries" who might suffer if the President demurred. Remembering the day of Munich when "they decided about us, without us," he signed Gottwald's paper.

BOOK TWO

The Night

In Which the Long Night

Descends on the Land of

Czechs and Slovaks

I V

The People's Democracy

As of February 25, 1948, Czechoslovakia was a People's Democracy—with all that this name implied in terms of the evanescence of civil freedoms and total subordination to the interests and wishes of the Soviet Union.

With the takeover in Prague, Eastern Europe was now completely within the Soviet sphere.

In Poland, where all pretense of a coalition government had vanished, Bolesław Bierut was chief of state and Władysław Gomułka the First Secretary of the Communist Party (called the Polish Workers' Party). Both were old-guard Communists, although not necessarily of the worst kind. (Gomułka, in fact, in the years to come played a series of vital but seemingly contradictory roles, if one views the basic changes in a Communist leader's political line as contradictions at all.)

In Romania, the illusion of nonpartisan rule under Premier Groza and King Michael had crumbled on December 31, 1947, when the young monarch had to flee; a few months later Gheorghe Gheorghiu-Dej became the Party's First Secretary, fronting for the powerful "Moscow Communists" of the once-exiled Romanian Bureau of the Comintern.

In Hungary, the Communists—acting with the support of the Soviet Union through Marshal Klimenti E. Voroshilov, Chairman of the Allied Control Commission for Hungary, and Ambassador Georgy M. Pushkin—first did away with the Smallholders Party and then prepared to swallow the Social Democrats to install the bullet-headed Mátyás Rákosi as the boss of the ruling Communist Party, János Kádár as his deputy, and László Rajk as a key Politburo member and as Interior and later Foreign Minister. As Jozsef Révai, editor of the Communist Party's newspaper,

43

was to remark later, "our force was multiplied by the fact that the Soviet Union and the Soviet Army were always there to support us with their assistance." The operational pattern of the Soviet viceroys was thus identical: Vyshinsky in Bucharest in 1945, Voroshilov and Pushkin in Budapest in 1947 and 1948, and Zorin in Prague in 1948.

Events in one country of Eastern Europe inevitably have a quick echo in the others, so the Yugoslav rebellion of 1948 and the subsequent fates of men like Hungary's Rajk, Poland's Gomułka, Romania's Pătrăşcanu, and Bulgaria's Traicho Kostov were to have important effects on Czechoslovakia's destiny. They are, therefore, a part of the Prague story.

Because the Communists for their own tactical reasons were in no hurry to destroy at once the entire image of the Czechoslovak democracy, Beneš was induced to stay on as President, at least in name. Likewise, Masaryk was retained as Foreign Minister. General Svoboda continued as "nonpartisan" Defense Minister. Of the twenty-two other cabinet posts, the Communists took twelve and the balance went to four Fierlinger-controlled Social Democrats and a group of political nonentities allegedly representing the non-Communist spectrum.

Where it mattered, however, the Communists had their own men— Svoboda in charge of the Armed Forces and Nosek at the Interior Ministry. The courageous Prokop Drtina (who failed in a suicide attempt after the *putsch*) was replaced in the Justice Ministry by Alexei Čepička, Gottwald's son-in-law and a tough Communist of the postwar generation. Whereas the older Communists who had lived during the democratic period of the Masaryk Republic retained certain sentimental links with their defeated victims, Čepička represented the new breed of hard-eyed modern Communists, businesslike technocrats of ideology and power. He immediately restored the People's Courts abolished right after the 1945 liberation, launched his Juridical Two-Year Plan designed to revamp the Czechoslovak judiciary, and busied himself drafting a Forced Labor Camps law.

Why Beneš had agreed to lend his name, in effect, to the Communist coup by remaining President is a question that may never be satisfactorily answered. Some of his close friends and associates believed that he feared that a spectacular protest resignation on his part might lead to civil war and to a Soviet intervention. Others think that Beneš felt he could exercise a restraining influence on the Communists as long as he was President, even if only nominally. Having chosen not to fight the Germans in 1938, when his nation and his army stood ready to do so, he showed a certain consistency in his refusal to embark on a confrontation in 1948. And, after all, he was an exhausted and sick man who had suffered two major strokes and no longer had the will to struggle. But, in a real sense, he did leave executive power, or what remained of it, when he departed on February 27 from Hradčany Castle for his country home in Sezimovo Ústí, south of Prague, never again to set foot in the Presidential quarters. (It may be pertinent to note that when General Svoboda, at the age of seventy-two, became Czechoslovakia's President in the spring of 1968 he angrily refused to sign a proposed list of "collaborationist" cabinet ministers presented to him the day of the Soviet invasion by pro-Moscow Communists, including the indestructible Fierlinger, and the Soviet Ambassador. But to compare Beneš with Svoboda twenty years later and in a completely changed context may be an altogether unwarranted exercise in historical judgment. Moreover, the defiant Svoboda of 1968 had by 1969 become the pliant Svoboda.)

A related question is why Masaryk was willing to serve as Foreign Minister of Gottwald's People's Democracy. With Beneš's departure from Prague, Masaryk was the last significant official link between Communist Czechoslovakia and the West, but his effectiveness was limited by the number of Communist officials surrounding him at his Ministry. Presumably, Masaryk served as useful window dressing for the Communists, blunting, as it were, the sharp edge of the events. Masaryk, on the other hand, in the opinion of his friends, hoped to be able to fight the good fight a while longer—like Beneš, evidently hoping to influence the situation for the better by his very presence.

Be that as it may, Masaryk's dilemma lasted only two weeks. On the morning of March 10 his broken body was found in the courtyard of Czernin Palace, four stories below the bathroom window of his ministerial apartment. The circumstances in which Masaryk died remain a mystery twenty-two years later. Theories, documented to a greater or lesser extent, and circumstantial evidence available at the time point to either a suicide or a murder. Those who accept the suicide explanation speak of Masaryk's despondency and fits of depression in the days preceding and following the *putsch*. They also contend there was no known reason why the Soviet secret police would wish him murdered. (Here they may err in applying Western logic to Soviet thinking.) Those who are convinced he was murdered—and who think the deed was done by the MGB, the Soviet Ministry of State Security—claim there were signs of struggle in the apartment, and they point out that Masaryk would never have killed himself—he was the strongly influenced son of a moralist father who had once written a book condemning suicide. Finally, he may have been assassinated by totally unknown third parties.

Jan Masaryk was laid to rest next to Tomáš Masaryk at the tiny cemetery at Laný, the small town twenty-five miles from Prague where the old President had his summer estate. But the story did not end there: the whole question of Jan Masaryk's death was reopened during the Prague Spring of 1968, as the new Czechoslovak regime ordered an inquiry into it. The inquiry, during which Czechoslovak newspapers freely raised the theory of an MGB murder plot, came to a quiet and inconclusive end after the Soviet invasion, but it had served the purpose of reviving the Masaryk legend—one of the most significant elements in reawakening Czech nationalism after twenty years of night. Conversely, the Masaryk issue became an outstanding irritant to the Soviet Union in her dealings with the Dubček regime. Thus, Jan Masaryk in death may have done more for Czechoslovak liberalism than he had been permitted to do in life. However, in December 1969 the Husák regime, winding up the earlier investigation, announced that Masaryk's death had been the result of an "unfortunate accident." This was a strange compromise, discarding both the official verdict of suicide and the unofficial but widely held view of murder.

Now Premier Gottwald was ready to push ahead with the plan fully to communize Czechoslovakia. Deputy Foreign Minister Vladimir Clementis was promoted to replace Masaryk, and on March 11—only twenty-four hours after Masaryk's death—Gottwald presented his government to Parliament and obtained a vote of confidence by 230 voices in favor and no nays. Seventy deputies chose to stay away.

At the same time, the Party embarked on a membership drive—the week of March 7 to 15 was named "Gottwald's week of membership enrollment"—without parallel in Communist history anywhere in the world. While the KSČ's membership stood at 1,159,164 in May 1946 (roughly 9 per cent of the total population) it had soared by November 1948 to 2.5 million (18 per cent). The overwhelming majority of the new members signed up after February 25, including many pro-regime Social Democrats. This meant that one in every three Czechoslovak adults was now a Party member, something that Lenin never visualized when he defined the Communist Party as the vanguard of the proletariat. The Gottwald enrollment drive had almost overnight turned the KSČ into the world's second largest Communist Party. (After the Soviet Union's, where Party membership then stood at 8 million, or 4 per cent of the population. Proportionally, then, there were four and a half times more Communists in Czechoslovakia than in the Soviet Union.) About one-third of the members were women and, among them, one-half were housewives, emphasizing how deeply ideological proselytizing had reached into the fabric of family life.

Professionals, too, rushed to embrace the Party. According to figures collated by Edward Taborsky in *Communism in Czechoslovakia*, before February 1948 there were only 143 lawyers in the Czech lands who belonged to the Party—and only five of them were in Prague—but the total skyrocketed to 1,049 out of 1,940 members of the bar after the *putsch*. Though the enrollment binge slowed down in 1949—membership dropped to 1,788,381 members and 522,683 candidate-members—the Party's ancillary strength was expanded by one million members of the Communist Youth Movement, the ČSM, which organized young people between the ages of fourteen and twenty-six into twenty thousand units throughout the country.

Study of these figures inevitably raises the perplexing question of the political opportunism of the Czechs, unpleasant as this subject may be. This apparent national proclivity of the Czechs has recurrently manifested itself—between 1938 and 1945, then in 1948, and again in 1968 and 1969. There is the citizenry's haste to join the Party after the February coup, the nation's quiescence during the dark period of 1948–1968, the quick swing to the reformers of mid-1968, and, finally, the extraordinary rationalizations behind the acceptance of the "realistic" pro-Moscow leadership by even some of the most outstanding liberals after April 1969.

To be sure, awesome pressures were at work on the Czechs during each of these periods. Even before the 1948 *putsch*, subtle and sometimes quite unsubtle pressures were applied to individual citizens to join the Party in order to win personal or professional advancement. After the coup, savage purges by Action Committees eliminated "opponents of the revolution" from vital sectors of national life and scared others into accepting the new *status quo*. Subsequently, unabating police terror kept the population in line.

But there is a difference between passive acceptance of the inevitable and active support for a system that, at least in private, a majority abhorred. A case in point, oddly enough, was Slovakia, which contributed only 236,000 members to the Party—only ten per cent of *its* population. Whether this relative standoff was due to Slovakia's essentially rural character—aside from the industrial centers of Bratislava, Košice, and a few other towns, the country is primarily agricultural—or to its intense nationalism, the fact remained that the Slovaks took less enthusiastically to Communism. This was so even though Soviet troops had single-handedly liberated Slovakia and the top echelons of the national Party structure included such prominent Slovaks as Karol Bacílek, Viliam Široký, and, increasingly, the controversial and complex Dr. Husák.

One possible explanation for this phenomenon is that after the coup the national leadership of the KSČ in Prague lost interest in the cause of Slovak autonomy. Dr. Husák, on the other hand, in a curious political move shortly after the takeover which he had so forcefully assisted, brought into the Slovak Party's high ideological echelons the liberal-minded Slovak Communist poet Laco Novomeský—this at a time when Communist intellectual orthodoxy, or sterility, was riding high in Prague. At the same time, another Slovak whose nationalism was years later to play a crucial role in Czechoslovak history, arrived at his first post in the Communist hierarchy. He was Alexander Dubček, a worker in a yeast factory in Trečín, in central Slovakia, and he was made Organizing Secretary of the local Party's district committee.

The offensive to turn Czechoslovakia into a full-fledged People's Republic was directed by the "big three" of Czechoslovak Communism, Gottwald, Slánský, and Zápotocký. Second-level commands were in the hands of Information Minister Václav Kopecký, who was busily imposing the Stalinist cultural line on the nation's artists, intellectuals, and journalists, and Jaromír Dolanský, the man concerned with fitting Czechoslovakia's economic structure into the Soviet concept of development. Josef Smrkovský had lapsed into one of his periods of political obscurity, though he remained on the Central Committee. General Pavel held a high post in the national security apparatus. But Oldřich Černik, one of the great figures of 1968, was still an unknown locksmith in Moravia at the Vítkovice iron works, studying engineering at night and learning the ropes in the Party's district committees of Opava and Ostrava.

The process of rebuilding Czechoslovakia ranged from purges and arrests to lawmaking. The headquarters of non-Communist political parties were raided and their publications stopped. Non-Communist officials were ousted from ministries and other official organizations by the Action Committees or on orders "from above." "Bourgeois" enemies of the regime were jailed or sent to work in the mines, industrial plants, or farms. In October Justice Minister Čepička established a special State Court for Crimes Against the Republic, which could be anything the regime wanted them to be. Those who succeeded in evading arrest tried to flee the country, an act which had become a crime in itself. Among those who made it abroad was Hubert Ripka, a minister in Beneš's precoup cabinet and one of his closest advisers.

Among the first victims of the new regime was General Heliodor Pika, wartime chief of the Czechoslovak Army mission in Moscow representing the Beneš government, a delegate to the Paris Peace Conference, and a Deputy Chief of Staff of the Army after 1945. Pika, who during the war had access to secret intelligence communications between London and Moscow and the resistance groups at home, was in a position to document the degree of wartime cooperation between the Beneš government and the Czechoslovak Communists in Moscow, and also seemed familiar with the wartime activities in the Soviet Union of Ambassador Fierlinger and General Svoboda (then commanding the Czechoslovak corps attached to the Soviet Army). He was arrested and executed in 1949 on charges of "treason." When the Czechoslovak Military Court posthumously rehabilitated him late in 1968—after the Soviet invasion but, interestingly. with President Svoboda's blessings—it was made clear that his main crime had been knowing too much and that his arrest and trial had been arranged partly in order to minimize the role of the Western powers in the liberation of Czechoslovakia; and official propaganda subsequently portrayed the United States as deliberately refusing to take Prague in 1945, so that Czech patriots could be slaughtered by the Nazis.

On May 9—a national holiday marking the third anniversary of Prague's liberation by the Soviet troops—the Parliament, acting as a Constituent Assembly, approved a new constitution for Czechoslovakia, replacing the 1920 charter. Meeting under its new chairman, Fierlinger, the Assembly passed the Constitution, which formed a curious hybrid between a West European parliamentary system and the Soviet example. But what mattered was not the relatively liberal language of the new document—it offered, for instance, guarantees against arbitrary arrest and provided that "as a rule" the press could not be censored—but how Gottwald and his associates were going to implement it. There were enough loopholes for ministers like Nosek and Čepička to use the Constitution as arbitrarily as they wished, and their way of conducting the affairs of state left little hope that the implementation would be lenient.

On May 30 the new government held the scheduled elections for the National Assembly—elections that the Communist Party's own poll in January predicted would be lost—and the result was the choice of 239 Communists and 61 others (mostly fellow travelers). Gottwald now had his working majority in parliament, but it was only a theoretical situation inasmuch as the National Assembly had become a mere rubber stamp for the regime. Among those elected were Slánský, Clementis, and Husák.

Now, the regime could use parliament to legalize retroactively the nationalizations of industrial and other private property. While the May 9 Constitution served this purpose in terms of doctrine, nine separate nationalization acts were voted subsequently during 1948. The private sector in industry and commerce was cut down to 5.1 per cent, and this percentage comprised businesses employing fewer than fifty employees. All domestic wholesale and all foreign trade were instantly placed in the hands of the state.

Concerned as Gottwald still was with outward legality for his government's acts, he pressed President Beneš to sign the new Constitution. He repeatedly visited the ailing old man at his retreat, but Beneš refused. On June 7 he signed, instead, the document of his resignation from the Presidency after thirteen years in office. In the accompanying letter to Gottwald, he expressed the pathetic hope that "the Republic be spared from all calamities, that all citizens live and work in mutual tolerance, love, and forgiveness, that they wish for others the freedom which they themselves should conscientiously enjoy." As Beneš watched the presidential flag being lowered from his Sezimovo Ústí villa, Klement Gottwald was in Prague addressing an emergency session of his cabinet. In what appeared to be a sincere tribute to a man who had become his personal friend, though an ideological enemy, the Communist Premier spoke of Beneš as "a distinguished successor to the President Liberator, the leader of the struggle for liberation and also the co-creator of the new order."

On September 3 Beneš died. Two years later, he and the elder Masaryk —the "President Liberator"—became targets of a vicious propaganda campaign directed by Moscow and the Czechoslovak Communist apparatus. It was to last until 1968, when the Prague Spring brought their political rehabilitation and an explosion of love and respect for Czechoslovakia's only two democratic presidents.

Under a government reorganization on June 14, Klement Gottwald became, at the age of fifty-two, the President of Czechoslovakia, and the "first worker to reside at Hradčany Castle," as one of his sycophantic admirers was to say. No longer believing that Czechoslovakia should follow her "own path" to socialism, he was unquestionably the most powerful man in the country, as both President and Party Chairman, both posts carrying full executive powers. He had survived Stalin's anger over the Marshall Plan affair—he was punished during 1947 by not being named Czechoslovak delegate to the founding meeting of the Cominform in Moscow (his emerging rival Slánský went instead)—and could look back with satisfaction at his nineteen years at the helm of the Party.

Antonín Zápotocký was appointed Premier to succeed Gottwald, and Slánský stayed on as the KSČ General Secretary (not suspecting that his own days in power were numbered). The only visibly disappointed men were Zdeněk Fierlinger and Education Minister Zdeněk Nejedlý, the "Red Grandpa," both of whom had hoped to be anointed as chief of state, even if in their case the job would have been a purely ceremonial one. Gottwald traveled to the Crimea for his summer holidays—and to see Stalin—and returned to Hradčany Castle ready to implement fully the new order.

V

The Weaving of the
Iron Curtain, 1948–1951

Czechoslovakia was now firmly in the Soviet orbit. In Hungary, the last vestiges of non-Communist resistance vanished when the Social Democrats merged with the Communist Party on June 14, 1948, to form the new Hungarian Workers' Party under Rákosi. To judge from these accomplishments, the first half of 1948 was highly successful for the Soviet policies in Eastern Europe. But, simultaneously, the Communist world was shaken to its very foundations by Yugoslavia's break with the Soviet Union over the issue of national independence and, concomitantly, over the basic question whether socialism (or Communism) may follow its "own path" of development in each country or must follow Moscow's guidance. This decision of 1948 to go it alone—made by Josip Broz Tito, Yugoslavia's wartime Partisan chief, Communist Party Chairman, and later, Marshal and President of the Republic—was a seismic shock of such magnitude that the world Communist movement never recovered from it entirely, and the Soviet Union's leading role in international Communism was never the same again.

Yugoslavia's rebellion against Moscow was the first overt challenge to the sanctity of the Kremlin Communist church—the first meaningful and menacing Communist heresy since 1917—and for the first time it actively introduced the dimension of "National Communism" into Communist affairs. It firmly established the distinction between the Communists who fought the war in their own countries, the "home Communists," and those who for the most part sat it out in the Soviet Union, the

"Moscow Communists," and set in motion an ideological and political struggle that lasted for the next twenty years.

From a respectable historical perspective of more than twenty years, it is now beyond question that it was Tito's Yugoslavia that unleashed the forces of nationalism in the Soviet Union's Communist realm. Yugoslav influence and inspiration can be detected in the Polish and Hungarian rebellions of 1956 (though Yugoslavia chose to refrain from condemning the Soviet tanks' intervention in Budapest), in Albania's defection from the Soviets in 1961 (ironically, for her own anti-Yugoslav reasons), in Romania's quietly mounting and still continuing defiance of Moscow throughout the 1960s, and, finally, in Czechoslovakia's Spring of 1968. To be sure, no conscious or articulated "Titoism" is to be found in any of these situations, but a common strain of Communist nationalism runs through all of them, and it goes back to the spring of 1948 in Belgrade. And, ironically, Tito was throwing down his nationalistic gauntlet in Stalin's direction just as Stalin was completing the imposition of his will on Czechoslovakia and virtually destroying its national identity.

It has been long and fervently believed that the power of ideologies may shape the fate of men and nations. Karl Marx evidently believed it and so did Lenin and Trotsky and the ensuing generations of Communist followers who lived and died for the principles and slogans of world "proletarian unity" and "socialist justice." And it was an accepted corollary that the Soviet Union, the birthplace of the Communist revolution, was to be forever the fountainhead of this ideology. The magnetism exercised by Moscow and the blind loyalties it aroused in some otherwise brilliant men everywhere made it possible for Communism—and, with it, Soviet sway—to spread across Eastern and Central Europe and the Balkans in the wake of World War Two. These loyalties to the idea of Communism and to the hallowed concept of the Party could not be broken by persecutions, betrayals, or the destruction of the reputations and lives of some of the greatest among the faithful. And, yet, this extraordinary spell was broken in Yugoslavia in 1948, not because Tito saw himself as a better interpreter of Marx and Lenin, but simply because nationalism asserted itself as a power incomparably greater than the Communist ideology. The issue in Yugoslavia was not the search for a better or more humane Marxism—as was to be the case twenty years later in Czechoslovakia, where a brief but logical synthesis of nationalism and "Socialism with a Human Face" emerged—but a naked contest between two sets of national interests. Only many years later, when Yugoslavia was reasonably secure in her national independence, did Tito allow the development of the natural evolution toward civil freedoms and a fairly advanced form of Marxist humanism.

As Milovan Djilas, one of the chief architects of Yugoslavia's rebellion against Moscow (and later a victim of Tito's own domestic ideological inflexibility), was to remark, what had happened in Yugoslavia and was still happening in the Communist world was "the twilight of ideologies." Writing of events in his own country, Djilas commented in his book *The Unperfect Society* that "the Balkan nations have survived for centuries, stretched out between East and West, by establishing their distinctive character precisely as a synthesis between their own and outside, between native and alien, social patterns and aspirations. . . . Nothing could be more portentous for these nations than to make a bridge with other nations regardless of their systems and ideologies, while keeping their own identity. . . . Nothing can be loftier and nobler for their striving and creative sons than to remain open to all the winds—to find their own answers." In 1952 the late Louis Adamic, who in *The Eagle and the Roots* wrote one of the most perceptive early books on Tito's Yugoslavia, explained even more clearly the rationale of Yugoslavia's deliberate but regretful defiance of the Kremlin:

> The Yugoslav background takes in the Greek and Latin classics, Christianity, the Renaissance, Enlightenment, and other facets of "Western" culture. Tito, [Edward] Kardelj, [Mosha] Pijade, *et al.*, grew up in a "Western" environment. They're Marxians, and Marxism is a "Western" criticism of Western civilization and Christianity. They all have read stacks of Russian literature, and some of it is distilled in their makeup. But they're steeped, too, in South Slavic lore and letters, and they're just naturally more of the "West" than the "East"—or of neither, turning critical eyes at one and then at the other, seeing good and bad in both. Their essence may be something between the two with a core and a drive of its own.

What Djilas and Adamic say in this context about Yugoslavia obviously applies to Czechoslovakia, likewise "stretched out between East and West." What is true in the Yugoslav background is even more so in the country of Jan Hus, Comenius, Kafka, Karel Čapek, and Masaryk. The historical and cultural logic of the Yugoslav rebellion against the Soviet Union in 1948, inevitably had to assert itself in the actions of the Czechoslovak Communists of the 1968 breed, who, like their Yugoslav cousins, also grew up in a "Western" environment blended with Slavic influences.

The conflict between Tito and Stalin—and it is relevant to note that it concerned two powerful personalities as much as their countries—had its roots in early wartime disagreements. These, in turn, stemmed from the fact that Tito, commanding a Partisan army that grew to eight hundred thousand men in 1945 and immobilized thirty German divisions for a good part of the war, was not prepared to welcome Stalin's guidance when he felt that the policies laid down suited not Yugoslavia's but the Soviet Union's long-range interests. Determined to lead Yugoslavia to Communism after the war, but under his and not Stalin's control, Tito thus chose to destroy his anti-Nazi but right-wing rival, General Draža Mihajlović, despite anguished radio appeals from Moscow for more "flexibility" to avoid offending Britain and the United States. Though a devoted lifetime Communist, Tito must have remembered how close the Comintern had come before the war to abolishing the illegal Yugoslav Communist Party because, in Moscow's judgment, it was producing no results. Presumably, he wanted no new pressures from the Kremlin after the war and saw no reason why he should put himself in the position of having to accept postwar coalitions, with non-Communists that could only weaken his own power. Watching the preliberation dealings between Beneš and Gottwald, he must have guessed what was likely to be the pattern of Soviet policy in Eastern Europe—the classical coalition in which "Moscow Communists" would eventually conquer power at the expense not only of non-Communists but of "home Communists" as well —and he was not interested in playing the game.

But Tito also intended to be master in his own house and to formulate his own foreign policies regardless of Soviet wishes. (For example, during the five months when Soviet troops were present in Belgrade and sections of northeast Yugoslavia in 1944, these allied soldiers were responsible for 1340 rapes of Yugoslav women and 1204 violent robberies, according to Vladimir Dedijer, Tito's biographer. The Marshal's reaction was to complain energetically to the Soviet command, something that no other Communist leader in Europe would have dreamed of doing. A tighter rein was forthwith placed on Soviet troops.) In the spring of 1945 Tito ignored Stalin's words of caution when his territorial interests in the Trieste area and southern Austria clashed with the resistance of the United States and Britain. As Stalin, who was not yet ready for a showdown with the West, kept relaying Churchill's and Truman's complaints to him, Tito replied that "we don't want to be used as a bribe in international bargaining." In October 1946 the Yugoslavs shot down two United States Air Force transport aircraft over their territory. Many respected East European specialists hold, in fact, that in the immediate postwar days Tito was much more of a Communist revolutionary and even adventurer in foreign policy than Stalin, who followed a more careful line to avoid premature Western reactions.

When the Cominform was created in September 1947 as a successor to the old Comintern disbanded during the war to allay Western suspicions, the two Yugoslav delegates—Djilas and Edward Kardelj, another close Tito associate—were among its most enthusiastic supporters. Next to them, Rudolf Slánský was a pale presence, still chiefly concerned with establishing firm Communist rule in Czechoslovakia, and it is yet another irony that Slánský was soon to become a baffled victim of his Yugoslav colleagues' drastic shift in policy toward the Cominform. But already, state-to-state relations between the Soviet Union and Yugoslavia were deteriorating. Tito was rapidly becoming convinced that the Yugoslavs were the losers in the system of joint stock companies organized in Yugoslavia by the two countries in 1946 and 1947. These companies, established in a number of Russia's satellites, were the forerunners of an even more complex commercial and economic structure of bilateral agreements under which manufactured products, raw materials, and foodstuffs were exported to the Soviet Union at prices set in Trade-Rubles of fluctuating value, in return for which the satellites received whatever the Soviet Union could spare, accumulating enormous trade balances that looked splendid on paper but were of little other use. Trade-Rubles are a Soviet commercial currency arbitrarily and artificially pegged to individual commodities. Tito also took exception to the Soviets' foot dragging on re-equipping his army with modern weapons. Living in a predatory world, he reasoned, Yugoslavia in 1948 needed something better than obsolete early World War Two arms.

To compound his growing disenchantment, Tito was resentful of Stalin's interference with his plans to reorganize the Balkans. The Yugoslav Marshal's idea was federation with Bulgaria, to be followed by a broader Balkan union incorporating Romania in the northeast and Albania in the southwest. It is not unreasonable, given Yugoslavia's geographical position, size, and relative military and economic strength, to think that Tito visualized such a Communist Balkan alliance, or union, as an instrument to be directed from Belgrade. Stalin, who believed that a Yugoslav-Bulgarian federation would be good for Moscow (the Bulgarians were almost completely under Soviet political domination and the old unresolved dispute between them and the Yugoslavs over Macedonia would inevitably weaken Belgrade), agreed to Tito's plan, but he vetoed, for the time being, the rest of Tito's design. This, in turn, led Tito to change *his* mind—on the correct grounds that to federate with Bulgaria alone would move a "Trojan horse" into Yugoslavia.

Tito's next step was to decide to incorporate Albania into Yugoslavia without waiting for other developments—thus applying to Albania the same treatment Stalin had been dispensing to Yugoslavia. Early in 1948, acting on a supposed request from Tirana, Tito dispatched a fighter aircraft wing to Albania and prepared to move in two Yugoslav divisions. The Soviet Union, which had her own strategic interests on the Albanian Adriatic coast, encouraged the pro-Moscow faction of the Albanian Communist Party, headed by First Secretary Enver Hoxha, to appeal for Soviet help. At this point, Stalin, who in any case felt he should have been consulted on the dispatch of the aircraft, told Tito to desist: the Yugoslav leader was overstepping the decent bounds of unilateral Communist action.

A series of urgent consultations between the two governments followed this exchange. In a final attempt to solve the dispute, in March Tito, not willing to go himself, dispatched Djilas and Kardelj to Moscow, where Stalin informed them that "it is not your mistakes, but your policy" that he found objectionable. Djilas recounted this interview in his 1961 book, *Conversations with Stalin*. What concerned Stalin was that a Balkan union would be an entity over which Moscow would have little or no control. Tito, on the other hand, realized that if he gave in on this Balkan dispute, nothing would remain of his cherished independence. His reaction was that Yugoslavia had no choice but to go it alone.

While it could be argued that Tito had recklessly contrived an artificial crisis with his contradictory Balkan politics, the underlying issue was whether Yugoslavia was free to pursue *any* kind of future politics without Stalin's approval, and both men knew it. The complicated Balkan game, which Tito presently dropped in favor of building up his defenses against the Soviet Union, was a test case. The battle lines, then, were drawn.

On April 12, 1948, Tito called into session the Central Committee of the Yugoslav Communist Party to prepare his followers for the worst. He told the Committee that the problem with the Soviet Union was "not a matter of any theoretical discussion" but, fundamentally, of "relations between one state and another." When Moscow soon thereafter made its classic charge that Yugoslavia was turning its back on the Soviet Union, the Yugoslav Party shot back that "no matter how much each of us loves the land of socialism, the Soviet Union, he can, in no case, love his own country less."

Between April and June, Stalin sought to resolve the Yugoslav problem through the traditional procedure of liquidating the man who had defied him. Immense pressures were applied to bring about Tito's fall, and the Soviet Union employed all the political resources at its command. Playing on Serb nationalism within the Yugoslav federation, it attempted to subvert the Serb Communist Party against Tito. It tried to infiltrate the Yugoslav secret police and to win over Yugoslav army chiefs. But Tito's personal following was too great to be eroded so easily. His secret police remained loyal, and it devoted its efforts to detaining several thousand Soviet sympathizers. The harder the Russians pressed, in fact, the stronger Yugoslav nationalism became.

By late June, Stalin faced the first of the great dilemmas that were to plague him and his successors thereafter. Even if the immediate crisis could be patched up, to let Tito get away with his challenge would be to invite Communist governments and parties elsewhere to try their luck. Ruling a multinational state and himself a Georgian, Stalin was obviously aware of the tremendous power of unleashed nationalism, but he was not prepared to preside over the liquidation of the empire he had barely completed acquiring. However, having failed to dethrone Tito through political means, Stalin could still resort to armed intervention. Russia and Yugoslavia had no common border, and an invasion would have to be coordinated with Bulgaria, Hungary, and Romania, Yugoslavia's three immediate neighbors. This could plunge the Balkans into a major war and, besides, Stalin was not sure of the loyalties of the three satellites. Tito, of course, was aware of all these realities.

The only remaining line for Moscow was exorcism and demonology. This task was entrusted to the Cominform, which, on June 28, 1948, issued from Bucharest a ringing declaration reading Yugoslavia, in effect, out of the international Communist movement. Tito and his followers were charged with the full catalogue of sins against Communism, ranging from "Nationalism, Trotskyism, and Menshevism" to failure to collectivize Yugoslavia's agriculture. Among others, the signature of Rudolf Slánský was affixed to the Cominform writ.

But, this being the tradition among Communist countries, the Soviet Union made no attempt to break diplomatic relations with Yugoslavia. There was a certain subtlety in this strategy: it turned the dispute with

Yugoslavia into an ideological conflict, whereas the Yugoslavs regarded it as a purely state-to-state problem. This approach, subsequently described as "defense of socialism," was to be used by Moscow in all cases involving rebel client states. It simply did not behoove the Soviet Union to allow itself to be dragged into an international dispute with another Communist country; an ideological battle, on the other hand, had the advantage of playing on the sympathies and perplexities of Communists everywhere—and on their often unshakable faith in Moscow. Additionally, it avoided exacerbating nationalistic sentiments. Perhaps not surprisingly, therefore, the Yugoslavs reacted to their excommunication by the Cominform with sorrow and genuine astonishment. Their first response was that the Yugoslav Communist Party was, indeed, as faithful to Marxism-Leninism as the Soviet Party, and, to disprove the Cominform charges, they set out on a massive program of agricultural collectivization and other orthodox Communist policies. But, in time, an ideological response was apparent, too, one of economic liberalization and more "human" Marxism, and it merged with nationalistic sentiment not only in Yugoslavia but throughout the Communist bloc. Moscow was to find out that playing with ideologies is a dangerous game, when ideologies themselves begin to ebb and slip into the twilight.

In July Tito presided over the Party's Fifth Congress, which represented the country's 470,000 registered Communists. In anticipation of a new round of Soviet pressures, it served to close the ranks even closer around him. Andrei Vyshinsky, Soviet Deputy Foreign Minister, visiting in Belgrade to participate in a Danube River conference, used his presence there to probe for weak points in the Yugoslav armor, but found none. Tito was in full command of the situation. At the age of fifty-six, he was in superb physical and mental condition (though his Partisan associates called him affectionately *Stari*, the Old Man).

The next Soviet move was an economic blockade—Soviet trade with Yugoslavia dropped in 1949 to one-eighth of the 1948 volume—and the deliberately fabricated impression that Tito might still face military action, a threat that Tito took with some seriousness. As he was to report later, there were 1397 incidents along Yugoslavia's borders with the Cominform countries between July 1948 and December 1949.

Louis Adamic, who had a long discussion with Tito in January 1949 on the possibility of a Soviet invasion, quoted him as saying:

"An attack upon us is . . . not excluded. . . . If an attack is tried, it probably won't come before next summer [1949] and the Soviet Army won't participate. We'll repel it easily even if our neighbors use Soviet arms. The chances are their soldiers won't want to fight us; their hearts won't be in it. Those who may be thinking of such an adventure know this as we do, and so it may not materialize. . . . Of course, if the Soviet Army itself attacks us, say, with a lot of Asian divisions, it won't be easy. But that's hardly conceivable. . . . There are several reasons why the Soviet Army wouldn't be thrown against us: I'll give you two. First, it would deepen the disillusionment the progressives everywhere feel toward the Soviet Union because of the Cominform resolution; and, second, it would create an even greater disturbance in the world than, say, the coup in Czechoslovakia did early in 1948."

History has proved that Tito's calculations were correct. It may have also proved that an attack on Yugoslavia was staved off by Stalin's realization that the Yugoslavs would fight back and that an invasion could lead to unpredictable situations that Moscow would be unable to control.

In the end, then, the Soviet Union failed to eradicate the Yugoslav cancer, albeit knowing full well that it threatened to infect the rest of the Communist body politic. Incapable of burning out the malignancy, Moscow proceeded to isolate it the best it could. But this effort, too, was doomed to failure. The contagion stubbornly kept reappearing elsewhere, posing successive dilemmas for one set of Kremlin leaders after another.

To isolate the menace of national Communism in Eastern Europe, the Soviet Union embarked, with diabolical and inquisitional fervor, on a course that was to bring on the worst Communist mass terror since the purges of 1936–1938. No country in the Communist bloc was spared the Soviets' preventive vengeance. Strangely, it was Czechoslovakia, one of the most docile satellites, that was dealt the worst blows. In Moscow's extraordinary demonological formula, the principal ingredients were Titoism, Trotskyism, and a Spanish past. To these cardinal ideological sins, invoked separately or in the same breath, were attached earthly crimes such as treason, espionage, Zionism, wartime betrayal of comrades to the Gestapo, and secret links with the British Intelligence Service, the Central Intelligence Agency, and assorted security organs of lesser "reactionary" countries. These accusations were aimed almost without exception at Communists in leading positions, including those who may have been feted and acclaimed at the Kremlin only weeks or days before their sudden and unexplained arrests.

At first sight, this wild mixture of ideological and criminal accusations seemed so absurd as to make many people in Eastern Europe seriously wonder whether the aging Stalin had not become irrational and whether his associates had not lost touch with reality. How, indeed, could the public have seriously been expected to believe that so many of the official leaders, with admirable records of prewar and wartime imprisonment in the struggle for Communism and of underground resistance to the Nazis, had suddenly turned out to be sinister Trotskyites and Titoists, secret enemies of the Soviet Union and traitors to their own countries? Accustomed as so many Communists were to switches in the Kremlin's policies in the postwar years, the charges hurled at their erstwhile idols tended to tax the imagination of the faithful. Moscow may have been even risking a credibility gap in issuing its denunciations, but there was considerable method in this apparent madness.

The principal Soviet objective in staging the ruthless and violent counteroffensive against "Titoism" was to liquidate the concept of "national Communism" where it had emerged and nip it in the bud where it might later develop. In this sense, there has always been consistency in Soviet policy: having recognized during the Yugoslav crisis of 1948 and 1949 the danger to itself inherent in independent brands of Communism, the Kremlin moved to smash them in Poland and Hungary in 1956 and in Czechoslovakia in 1968. Moscow sought to solve two intimately related problems: nationalism in the satellite countries threatening the monolithic unity of Communism under Soviet guidance, and nationalist contagion being transplanted to the Soviet Union itself.

As to the first, as Marshal Tito's declaration of independence was painfully demonstrating, "national Communism" by definition rejected the so-called leading role of the Soviet Union in Communist affairs. But this, in turn, implied a fundamental threat to the Soviet Union as a national power in Europe and to its world-wide influence. Inasmuch as the Soviet Union had deliberately set out after the war to surround itself with a new type of *cordon sanitaire* of East European satellites, it stood to reason that it would not gladly tolerate the erosion of this bloc. That Communists rather than discredited reactionaries stood behind this threat to Russia rendered it only the more dangerous. If Titoism could not be at once curbed in Yugoslavia, it certainly could not be permitted to raise its head in other Communist capitals.

As to the second, a flowering of nationalism in Eastern Europe, especially in the Communist context, could deal a mortal blow to the very integrity of the Soviet Union. The memories of nationalism in the Ukraine and among the Crimean Tatars, the Armenians, the Georgians, the Latvians, the Mongols, and other Soviet minority groups were too fresh to permit the risk of their reawakening. Soviet leaders had not forgotten how many Ukrainians and Tatars had sided with the Nazi invaders in the 1940s against "Mother Russia," and they were constantly aware of the explosive potential of the nationalities problem at home.

Under these circumstances, nationalism in general and Communist nationalism in particular had to be taboo. It may have suited Moscow tactically to allow a certain measure of highly controlled nationalism, or even autonomy, in a region like, for example, Slovakia to strengthen local Communists during a takeover period. But it is a matter of record that the Soviets in 1945 had strenuously opposed a federative state of Czechs and Slovaks and were to lash out furiously at Slovak nationalism in the 1950s. When a Czecho-Slovak federated state finally came into being after the 1968 invasion, the Russians imposed safeguards against any true regional nationalism.

In dealing with the national minorities issue, historically bedeviling Eastern and Central Europe, Moscow always took care to subordinate the minorities to its own and Communism's strategic interests. Romania, for example, benefited from the transfer of sections of Transylvania with large Hungarian minorities because it suited the Soviets to balance the relative regional power of Bucharest and Budapest. (The Kremlin lived to regret this readjustment.) Macedonian nationalists were encouraged in Bulgaria's favor against Yugoslavia, as were Albanian nationalists. And so on. But in the broader sense, nationalism, to say nothing of national Communism, was a threat to be eradicated mercilessly. And the way to deal with it was to portray it as a revisionist movement contrary to the tenets of Communism and "proletarian nationalism." Tito thus became a "bourgeois nationalist"—a label enriched, for good measure, with the adjective "fascist." The charge of "nationalist" was now the mark of profound ideological betrayal.

The epithet "Trotskyite" was added gratuitously, not because Tito evinced any Trotsky-like inclinations or deviations, but because it offered the orthodox faithful an easy mental association with the man depicted for decades as the outstanding revisionist heretic of Marxism-Leninism.

The third and most fascinating ingredient of the anti-Tito exorcism formula was the Spanish Civil War background. Singling out the East Europeans who had fought in Spain was not a capricious exercise, either, and in a way the Soviet leaders demonstrated in it greater prescience than they may have realized at the time. There was a double motivation for the Kremlin's regarding with suspicion the former volunteers in the Spanish Republican Army. One was that the Communists who had fought in

Spain—many of them had remained in France after the Republican defeat as prisoners of the Germans or fighting in the French underground—had had considerable exposure to Western experience and what the Soviets called "cosmopolitanism." The second was that these East European "volunteers for liberty," as they called themselves, were largely idealistic Communists, and one could not be certain that this idealism would not reassert itself in less convenient circumstances for the Soviet Union. This was a correct, if cynical, assessment; Moscow had been destroying East European and even Russian fighters in the Spanish Civil War (to say nothing of refugee Spaniards) long before the Second World War and the emergence of Titoism. Yet today the Communist scene in Europe is crowded with these "volunteers for liberty," and many of those who survived the war and the purges rose half a generation later as progressive leaders in Eastern and Western Europe.

Indeed, the story of the East European members of the International Brigades forms a special chapter in Communist history, one that provides considerable light. For the Spanish experiences of these men created in time something of an instinctive fraternity among them. And the roster is truly impressive.

Czechoslovakia's Josef Pavel fought in Spain as commander of the Dimitrov Battalion. Among other Czechoslovak veterans, František Kriegel, a physician, was the immensely courageous member of the Party's Presidium under Alexander Dubček before the Soviet invasion. Artur London became Deputy Foreign Minister in February 1949. Osvald Zavodský was at that time Chief of State Security. Leopold Hoffmann headed President Gottwald's personal security service after 1948 but became chairman of the National Assembly's Armed Forces and Security Commission in 1968. Laco Holdoš was in 1950 Vice-President of the Slovak National Council. Otakar Hromadko was the Party representative at the Military Academy in 1950. Otto Šling, secretary of the Party's committee in the Czechoslovak unit of the Brigades, became secretary of its regional committee in Brno. Antonín Svoboda was the chief of the Armed Forces Section of the Party's Central Committee after 1948. Karel Dufek, a career diplomat, served as director of the Foreign Ministry's foreign-press section in 1968. Most of these men were Communist progressives, and many of them were caught in the web of the Titoist trials of the 1950s.

Among the Yugoslavs, Tito himself operated in Paris in 1936 as the head of an "underground railway" channeling East European volunteers into Spain. He was assisted by Edward Kardelj and Boris Kidrič, the future head of Yugoslavia's State Planning Commission. Djilas, who had not then met Tito, was an active recruiter in Belgrade for the secret Aid-for-Spain organization. Of the nearly two thousand Yugoslav volunteers in Spain, twenty-four were to become Partisan and subsequently regular Army generals, including Chief of Staff General Ivan Gošnjak. Koča Popović, a poet, Partisan general, and at one point Yugoslavia's Vice-President, fought in Spain, and so did Aleks Bebler, later Deputy Foreign Minister; Vladimir Popović, who was to become Ambassador to the United States; and Branko Ćopić, a leading Yugoslav Communist who commanded the Fifteenth International Brigade.

Poland contributed Karol Świerczewski, who under the name of "General Walter" rose to the command of the International Brigades after leading the Fourteenth Brigade and the crack 36th Division. Świerczewski, who had once been a professor at the Moscow Military Academy, in 1945 became Poland's first postwar Defense Minister. He was mysteriously assassinated in March 1947. General Marian Spychalski, who succeeded him as Defense Minister, had commanded the Dambrowski Brigade in Spain.

Among the Bulgarians, General Ivan Kinov, a Brigade commander in Spain, was Chief of the General Staff in 1949. Raiko Danianov, a veteran of the Dambrowski Brigade, was Vice-President in the early 1960s.

Luigi Longo, now General Secretary of the Italian Communist Party and a leading spokesman for the autonomy of national Communist parties, served as Inspector General of the International Brigades. His predecessor, the late Palmiro Togliatti, was director of tactics for the Spanish Communist Party.

But a handful of Communist hard-liners also knew service in Spain. László Rajk, Hungary's Interior and later Foreign Minister, was the political commissar of the Rákosi Battalion in the Thirteenth International Brigade and was severely wounded in action. Ernö Gerö, a highly sinister personage in the Hungarian Party's highest echelons, was a Comintern political agent in the Spanish war. Albania's onetime Chief of Staff and present Premier, Mehmet Shehu, was a deputy battalian chief. Klement Gottwald was political adviser at the International Brigades' Albacete base in 1936. Walter Ulbricht, the indestructible General Secretary of the East German Party, spent some time in Spain with a German NKVD unit looking, not surprisingly, for Trotskyites.

From the Soviet military contingent, Ivan Konev, Rodion Malinovsky, Kirill Meretskov, Konstantin Rokossovsky, and I. Nedelin survived the purges of the Spanish veterans and rose to fame as wartime marshals. But such top Soviet representatives as General Ian A. Berzin, Arthur Stashevsky, Vladimir A. Antonov-Ovseenko, and Michael Koltsov were executed in 1937 and 1938 on their return to the Soviet Union.

That the Spanish veterans were quickly spotted as potential Titoists was clearly spelled out by President Bierut in Poland. Addressing the plenary session of the Central Committee of the Polish Party in November 1949, Bierut charged that many former volunteers in the Dambrowski Brigade in Spain, commanded by General Spychalski, were "fascist police spies" who had infiltrated themselves after the war in the top echelons of the Polish government. Ironically, this speech came four days after the Polish-born Soviet Marshal Rokossovsky, a Spanish veteran, replaced Spychalski as Defense Minister.

In Czechoslovakia, Premier Gottwald told the Central Committee on February 22, 1951:

> After the fall of Republican Spain, a large number of the Brigades' volunteers found themselves in camps in France. They lived there in very bad conditions and they were targets of pressure and blackmail first by the French espionage services, then American and later German and others. These espionage services, taking advantage of the poor physical and moral condition of the volunteers, have thus succeeded in enrolling many among them as their agents. Those who were enrolled by the Americans and the French directly served the western imperialists and those who were enrolled by the German Gestapo were transferred, after the defeat of Hitler's Germany, to the American espionage services, as were all the Gestapo agents.

The Soviet leaders had, therefore, succeeded with amazing ideological legerdemain in creating a package of charges in which Titoism, "bourgeois nationalism," Trotskyism, and Spanish Civil War experience were neatly tied together with fascism, treason, espionage, and employment by the Gestapo and every imaginable Western intelligence agency. Moscow also produced an extra ingredient, Zionism, to play on the always latent anti-Semitism of Eastern Europe.

All this was to be used as Moscow's formidable weapon against the spread of Titoism in Eastern Europe. But it also was to serve the parallel —and equally vital purpose—of separating "Moscow Communists" from "home Communists." Whether Titoist or not, there were many Communist leaders springing up who had been formed politically either in wartime resistance movements at home or under alien influences in the West. In the Soviet judgment, the time had come to reassert the sway of the

"Moscow Communists," men who had spent the war in the Soviet Union, possessed unquestionable loyalties to it, and returned to their countries to look after Moscow's interests.

Feuds between "home Communists" and "Moscow Communists" had been brewing throughout Eastern Europe long before the final Tito split with the Soviets, and purges might have been in the offing even if the proud Yugoslav Marshal had not chosen to defy the Kremlin.

The issue in Romania, for example, centered on the fact that a group of men in the small, illegal Romanian Party—and long at loggerheads with the Romanian Bureau of the Comintern—had swiftly moved into power positions prior to the arrival in 1944 of a Moscow contingent in the liberated country. In what may well have been the very first symptom of nascent national Communism, these domestic leaders proceeded to compound their offense by refusing to move over. Headed by Ana Pauker, the Kremlin's chief Romanian agent, a forbidding-looking woman, the Moscow Communists assumed the offensive against the "locals" after winning some support in the Bucharest apparatus. They scored in 1946 with the execution of former Party General Secretary Stefan Foris and again in April 1948 with the arrest of Justice Minister Lucretiu Pătrăşcanu. In Poland, Bulgaria, and Hungary preparations were also under way for showdowns. The Yugoslav schism triggered instant action along all the fronts.

But, with the inevitable irony accompanying all East European trends, an unnoticed event occurred in Bucharest just as Pătrăşcanu was being imprisoned. A quiet apparatus man named Nicolae Ceauşescu was elected to the Central Committee of the Party, initiating a career that was to make him in time one of the leading apostles of national Communism in the Soviet realm.

The lightning of the great Titoist purges first struck in Poland, and its chosen target was forty-three-year-old Władysław Gomułka, First Secretary of the Polish Workers' Party and the country's Deputy Premier.

As seen from the standpoint of Soviet strategy in 1948, it was perfectly logical that Gomułka was immediately singled out for political liquidation. Preventive liquidation was a classical weapon, as Soviet history of the 1930s had amply demonstrated. In fact, there is reason to believe that the decision to remove him had been taken even before the final break between Tito and the Soviet Union. The problem with Gomułka was not that he was a Titoist, that he was preparing to lead Poland along a course similar to Yugoslavia's, or that he was engaged in secret conspiracies with Tito, even though these charges naturally were made. The point was that, in the opinion of the hypersensitive Russians, Gomułka might develop Titoist—or nationalist Communist—tendencies if allowed to remain in power. That he was regarded as "unreliable" stemmed essentially from the fact that he was a "home Communist" who had risen to prominence in the illegal Party and in the anti-Nazi Communist underground long before the contingent of "Moscow Communists" arrived in the wake of the advancing Soviet troops, although since 1945, when he was named First Secretary, Gomułka had worked smoothly with his "Moscow" Party colleagues.

Gomułka's dubiety was further compounded by his noticeable nationalist sentiments, evidently accentuated by his wartime resistance experience; and in Poland nationalism is historically related to anti-Russian sentiment. Gomułka was born when much of Poland, including Warsaw, had belonged to Czarist Russia and, like so many men of his generation, he had been brought up in an anti-Russian environment. And, like many "home Communists," he saw no contradiction between Polish nationalism and Communist ideology. For the Soviet Union, which regarded excessive patriotism as a contradiction of the theory of "proletarian internationalism," this was dangerous indeed. Already during the war he had shown his independent streak, often defying Moscow's radioed orders to his resistance units, and, according to one version of the events, he had personally blocked the practice of certain Communist leaders of betraying to the Gestapo members of the London-led underground army. Men who were close to Gomułka during the war claim that his disagreements with Moscow were many and not infrequently bitter.

With the advent of peace, this tough, unsmiling, and uncompromising man maintained his own views on what should happen in Poland. In 1944, for example, he talked to associates of a "Polish way to socialism." Presently, he became involved in an argument with Moscow over the removal to the Soviet Union of industrial installations from the German zone that had been annexed by Poland. His reasoning was that Poland, economically smashed by the war, could hardly be expected to recover if she were deprived from the very outset of vital industrial plants in her new western provinces.

Gomułka clearly could not be trusted by Moscow at a time when Titoist rebellion was beginning to rock the Communist boat. In mid-June 1948 he found himself under sudden and unanimous attack at a meeting of the

Central Committee for having stressed the historical importance of Poland's independence in his main speech. Under normal circumstances, his speech would probably have gone unnoticed, but this obviously was the chance his enemies were waiting for. Rank-and-file revolts do not erupt spontaneously, as a rule, in Central Committees. Presently, his colleagues began pressing him to resign quietly "in the interest of the Party."

Gomułka compromised by agreeing to take a vacation. This spared him attendance at the June 28 Cominform session in Bucharest at which Tito was formally excommunicated from the Communist movement. But in July he abruptly resumed his role as the Party's First Secretary. This was total insubordination, and the Party reacted by declaring him a "nationalist" guilty of "rightist deviations." The crisis continued until the end of August, when, at a dramatic Central Committee meeting on August 31, Gomułka recognized the "veracity" of charges against him and agreed to resign. Among those who denounced him most virulently were Zenon Kliszko, the Party's secretary in charge of cadres and one of his closest associates, and General Spychalski, who had served as chief of intelligence in Gomułka's underground army and was shortly to come under suspicion himself. The next day the Central Committee announced its decision to remove Gomułka from the post of First Secretary and the "unanimous approval" of this move by the national congress of the Party. Gomułka was also fired as Deputy Premier and Minister of the Regained Territories. Bolesław Bierut, who all along called himself a Socialist, was chosen to replace him as First Secretary of the *United* Polish Workers' Party, the new party formed from the merger of the Communists with the fellow-traveling Socialists. The first phase of the Polish purge was complete.

A year later the purge was resumed and Gomułka's accusers of 1948 became the victims. First, however, Gomułka was brought back from oblivion to publish in the September 7 issue of *Trybuna Ludu*, the Party's official organ, an attack on the "Tito clique." But this was not sufficient to assure Moscow that the danger in Poland had passed. On November 7, 1949, the Russians forced Bierut to accept Marshal Rokossovsky as Poland's Defense Minister in place of Spychalski, the only instance when a Soviet officer was openly named to command the armed forces of a satellite state. (Born in Poland, he had been a Soviet citizen all his adult life, but now Bierut promptly took care of the technicality of granting him Polish citizenship.)

A Central Committee meeting between November 11 and 13 became a forum for a new wave of assaults on Gomułka. Though he defended himself stubbornly and methodically, he was accused of collaboration with the Nazis and of "lack of confidence" in the Soviet Union, an expression that was to become painfully familiar. He was forthwith expelled from the Party. At the same time, the Central Committee denounced General Spychalski and Kliszko as "fascist police spies" and protectors of "Trotskyite" Spanish War veterans and likewise ejected them from all their posts. The Polish military establishment was purged and nineteen officers were executed. Among those imprisoned were Spychalski and Army counterintelligence chief General Wacław Komar. A savage wave of arrests swept the country, with Jews as the favorite victims.

In August 1951 agents of Urząd Bezpieczeństwa, the secret police known by its initials, U.B., arrested Gomułka at a mountain resort where he lived in quiet retirement. The apparent reason was that Moscow was insisting on a Titoist show trial in Poland following the "confessions" and executions of top Communist leaders in Bulgaria and Hungary and coinciding with the massive trial then in preparation in Czechoslovakia. In all three cases, the "evidence" was successfully assembled, as the accused were broken down by the Soviet-directed interrogators. But Gomułka went on resisting, to the dismay of his tormentors, and almost miraculously outlasted the purges. This was the end of the first chapter in Gomułka's fantastic political trajectory.

The only major Communist leader of 1944 to be in power again a quarter of a century later, Władysław Gomułka strangely personified the whole process of synthesis in those extraordinary years that bridged the postwar liberation in Eastern Europe and the tragedy of Czechoslovakia in the late 1960s. But there was to be a striking parallel between his destiny and that of Gustav Husák, both of them brutally tortured prisoners in the 1950s and, later, close ideological allies in the cause of preserving orthodox Communism. Both men are enigmas and both are deserving subjects for an in-depth study on the psychology of Communist leaders.

With the Polish situation reasonably in hand in the spring of 1949, the attention of the Kremlin crusaders then turned to Bulgaria and Hungary.

In Albania, however, the pro-Moscow faction in the Communist Party —which at that stage was paradoxically the *nationalist*-minded group— took care of the situation alone, with brutal and astounding speed. Prior to the Tito-Stalin break, the dominant wing of the Albanian Party was controlled by Deputy Premier and Interior Minister Koçi Xoxe, a onetime provincial tinsmith, although Enver Hoxha, the Western-educated intellectual, held the post of the Party's First Secretary. This was so simply because Xoxe was a virtual puppet of the Belgrade regime, which ran Albania and its Communist Party very much the way Moscow would have hoped to run all *its* satellites. It was the Xoxe faction that favored union with Yugoslavia. Hoxha and his people, on the other hand, were Albanian Communist nationalists who wished maximum independence for their tiny and utterly underdeveloped nation. Albania's economic situation required it to be the client state of a larger Communist power, but Hoxha's intriguingly successful geopolitical theory was that the farther away the protector was located, the better for his country. So he opted for the relatively removed Soviet Union over neighboring Yugoslavia (and, in 1961, for the utterly remote China over the Soviet Union). A bizarre but extremely valid case of "national Communism," Albania was to act according to her own political logic when she violently denounced the Czechoslovak invasion in 1968 and quit the Warsaw Pact on the theory, naturally shared by China, that it was a case of one revisionist striking at another revisionist. It was a splendid example of Balkan deviousness blended with tortuous Communist ideology.

In any event, Hoxha and Chief of Staff Mehmet Shehu, the Spanish War veteran, acted within hours of the Yugoslav-Soviet break to assert their power. On June 29, 1948, the day after the Cominform excommunicated Yugoslavia, the Albanian Party's Central Committee, now completely in their hands, denounced the Yugoslavs as "traitors and Trotskyites." Xoxe, once a Tito protégé, immediately realized which way the wind was blowing and he, too, joined in the attacks on Tito. But this was no longer good enough. In August Xoxe was fired from his Party and government posts. In November he was arrested. In June 1949 he was secretly tried and executed. A month earlier his closest associates—Politburo member and chairman of the State Control Commission Pandi Kristo, Politburo member and chairman of the State Planning Commission Nosti Kerentyi, Deputy Interior Minister Vaske Koletzki, State Security Police chief Vargo Mitrojorji, and Central Committee propaganda head Huri Nota—were sentenced to long prison terms. The following year Hoxha and Shehu carried out a second "consolidating" purge aimed at Politburo member Abedin Shehu (no kin to the Chief of Staff) and others. Titoism, then, was liquidated in Albania in favor of a nationalistic trend that the Russians warmly applauded until it turned against them more than a decade later.

In Bulgaria, the problem was more complicated. Here, charges, "evidence," and trials had to be prepared, and it was not until March 1949 that the Soviet security advisers and their Bulgarian colleagues were ready to move.

Selected for the gallows in Bulgaria was Traicho Kostov, Acting Premier and Political Secretary of the Party's Central Committee, which made him the country's top Communist. Kostov, who joined the Party in 1919 at the age of twenty-two, was so devoted to the cause that in 1924 he jumped out of the fourth-floor window of the Sofia police headquarters hoping to die rather than break down under torture and give away his comrades. He survived his suicide attempt with two broken legs and a smashed back, but for the rest of his life was a crippled hunchback. His stamina was so great, however, that Kostov emerged as Bulgaria's principal "home Communist" during the war and, in 1948, as the logical heir to the aging Georgi Dimitrov, once head of the Comintern and later Premier of Bulgaria.

Kostov was a complicated person, and this cost him his life. On the one hand, he was a totally dedicated Communist and an admirer of the Soviet Union. As Bulgaria's leading Communist, he lent his name to the postwar purges of "bourgeois elements" that resulted in 2138 executions after sentencing by "People's Courts." No other Communist country in Eastern Europe had engaged in terror on this scale. Then, after the signing of the peace treaty with the Allies in 1946, another outburst of vengeance brought death to Nicola Petkov, the leader of the leftist opposition Agrarians, and many others; both Dimitrov and Kostov were unquestionably associated with these killings, as they were with everything else in Bulgaria. On Kostov's fiftieth birthday, December 27, 1947, the Party newspaper told him in a congratulatory editorial: "Great are your achievements, Comrade Kostov, as the builder of the Party, as the teacher and instructor of the Party members."

But Kostov also had an independent mind, at least when it came to dealings with the Soviet Union and the national interests of Bulgaria. Certainly not a "Titoist" in the Moscow sense, he nevertheless tangled with the Kremlin over such issues as the joint Soviet-Bulgarian stock companies and the deliveries of Bulgarian products to the Soviet Union. At one point, in fact, he invoked the State Secrets Law to keep vital economic data away from the Soviets, a most unusual gesture of defiance. But Moscow's greed was creating the same problems in Bulgaria as it had created in Yugoslavia, Poland, and Romania, and Kostov went as far as to complain personally to Stalin. He also took a negative stand on Tito's original proposal for a Yugoslav-Bulgarian federation, though at first both Stalin and Dimitrov had approved of the idea. All in all, then, Kostov was not a man to be trusted when the time bomb of Titoism exploded and the Russians felt they had to clean up Eastern Europe fast.

Vulko Chervenkov, the man the Kremlin *did* trust (he was Dimitrov's brother-in-law, among other things), was assigned the task of liquidating Kostov. On April 5, 1949, Kostov was consequently fired from all his Party and government jobs and accused of having pursued "an insincere and unfriendly policy toward the U.S.S.R. during the trade negotiations and on the question of furnishing economic information to Soviet representatives." It was also charged that he tolerated "nationalistic tendencies within the state apparatus and, in fact, has encouraged them."

A series of show trials followed almost immediately, involving thirty-three Bulgarian officials, including ten cabinet ministers, in addition to Kostov. The charges against them ran from "Titoism" to being "fascist spies" and agents of American, British, and Yugoslav intelligence services. Kostov himself was said to have conspired with the United States Minister to Bulgaria. The purge reached so deep into the apparatus that the list of "traitors" included the Army Chief of General Staff, General Ivan Kinov (the onetime Spanish War volunteer); the Chief of Army Intelligence, Peter Vranchev; the Chief of the Army Political Department, General Boyan Balgaranov; the directors of the State Security Police, Stefan Bogdanov, Georgi Ganev, and Nikolai Zadgorsky; the Governor of the Bulgarian National Bank, Tsanyu Tsonchev; Finance Minister M. Sakelarov; Transport Minister S. Tonchev; Vice-Premier Dobri Terpeshev (who had commanded Bulgarian Partisans during the war); Minister of Foreign Trade Yordan Bozhilov; and Minister of Electrification Ljubomir Kairakov.

The system used by the Bulgarian security specialists and their Soviet advisers was to obtain signed "confessions" from all the accused before bringing them to the courtroom for the actual trial. These "confessions" were obtained through a combination of torture, brutality, and patient and ever-mounting psychological pressure reaching the point where the accused was in the end virtually convinced of his own guilt. Under a technique copied from the Moscow trials of the 1930s, all the "confessions" were cross-indexed in the sense that one inculpated all the others.

Kostov, too, signed a "confession." But the moment he was brought to the courtroom in Sofia and asked to confirm it verbally, this tough old

Communist rebelled. Ridiculed earlier during the trial as a hunchback, he may have remembered that day twenty-five years ago when he jumped out of the window rather than betray his principles. Now he proceeded to tell the court that the confession he had signed in prison was false and taken from him under duress. The flushed court officials immediately cut his microphone dead and Kostov was forced to halt his angry peroration. His fellow prisoners and the state witnesses were made to repeat the accusations against him. What happened to Kostov during the night is not known, but the next day in court he begged forgiveness for his outburst. He also wrote a letter to the Party that he repented for his "lies" in the courtroom and pleading that his life be spared so that one day he might atone for sins. (The only known previous instance in Communist history of a courtroom denial of a signed confession concerned Nicolas Nicolaievich Krestinski, in the prewar Moscow trials. Krestinski had been charged with Trotskyism, "rightist deviation," and espionage, and in court he said that he knew from his own experience that only during the trial would he have a chance to tell the truth. Naïvely, he said, "I had thought that unless I told what I am telling today—that all was false—my statements would have never reached the chiefs of the Party and the government." Krestinski fought all day to establish his innocence, but the next day he recanted and admitted he had acted out of a "an acute sentiment of false shame." He was convicted and executed.)

But Kostov was the only one to be executed in the 1949 Bulgarian purge; all the others accused were imprisoned. Additional trials of lesser Communist officials followed, with prison sentences again being meted out. Between 1949 and 1950 the Bulgarian Communist Party expelled nearly 93,000 members, almost one-fifth of the total membership. In June 1950 a leading Communist official remarked that the Party still suffered from "nationalism, cosmopolitanism, Kostovism, and Titoism." In death, Traicho Kostov thus became a Communist political adjective of derision.

As the Kostov trial was being prepared in Bulgaria, László Rajk was arrested in Hungary on June 14, 1949. To let even one country escape the show trials, the Soviets presumably reasoned, would be to show weakness and to invite another Tito type of disaster.

At the age of forty, Rajk was certainly a "home Communist." Having fought in Spain at the head of the Rákosi Battalion and having spent two years interned in France, he returned to Hungary in 1941 and was promptly arrested by the Germans, but he managed to run the activities of the illegal Communist Party from prison. In 1944 he was taken to a

Nazi concentration camp in Germany. Back in Hungary again after the war, Rajk rapidly rose to prominence in the Budapest Communist Party organization.

When the Social Democrats merged with the Communists in June 1948 to form the Hungarian Workers' Party, Rajk became a member of the fourteen-man Political Committee (Politburo), a member of the strategic eight-man Party Secretariat, and Minister of Interior. In the latter capacity, he was responsible for the imprisonment of Hungary's Jozsef Cardinal Mindszenty. But no sooner was Rajk installed in the Party's top hierarchy than warfare erupted between the "home Communists," including himself, and the "Moscow Communists," headed by Mátyás Rákosi, the Party's General Secretary.

The attack, classically, came from the Moscow faction and it was led by Ernö Gerö, who was Rajk's colleague on the Political Committee. It is pertinent to note that Gerö had known Rajk in Spain, not as a fellow "volunteer for liberty" but as a Comintern agent primarily concerned with the politics of the Spanish Communist Party. In any event, at an all-night session of the Politburo early in July 1948 Gerö accused Rajk of preparing an armed coup to take over the Workers' Party. He said that Rajk was organizing a special police unit at the Budapest Radeczky barracks, equipping it with modern weapons, and placing it under the direct orders of his Interior Ministry. Rajk rejected the charge that he was mounting a *putsch* and insisted the Soviet military command was aware of his plans to reorganize the Radeczky force. Although Yugoslavia's split with Moscow had already occurred, Gerö did not yet charge Rajk with Titoism. In what became a temporary standoff, Rajk was switched from the Interior Ministry to the Foreign Ministry while retaining his Party posts.

For nearly a year Rajk enjoyed comparative tranquillity. In fact, on May Day 1949 he was the most acclaimed Party leader after Rákosi himself. On May 15 he was elected to Parliament. But on June 16 Rákosi and Gerö struck again. Rajk was suddenly arrested, dismissed from all his posts, and expelled from the Party. He was accused of being a "fascist spy," a "Titoist," and a Trotskyite. The Moscow wing of the Party had completed its preparations and now the stage was set for a show trial.

Though the court proceedings, lasting from September 16 to September 24, closely resembled other "Titoist" trials elsewhere in Eastern Europe, the Rajk case was conducted with special artfulness. Rajk and his trial companions were accused not only of links with Tito, but also of conspiratorial connections with Noel and Herman Field, two Americans representing the Unitarian Service Committee, and through them, it was said, Allen Dulles and the Central Intelligence Agency. Noel Field had been secretly arrested in Hungary and his brother Herman was being held in Poland, though the Warsaw government denied knowledge of this.

Another special dimension in the Rajk trial was the establishment of the first major link between the "Titoist" purges and the former Spanish Civil War volunteers. (This was to be reflected with extraordinary vigor in the Czechoslovak trials three years later.) To a much greater extent than in the Warsaw proceedings centered on the Gomułka case, the Kremlin had decided to prove that Communist Spanish War veterans were actual or potential traitors and that they formed a special and highly dangerous group.

On September 24, 1949, the Budapest People's Court sentenced Rajk, member of the Communist Party's Organizational Committee Tibor Szonyi, and Central Committee member András Szalay to death by hanging. Rajk had "confessed" that while in Spain he had been an agent of Admiral Horthy's secret police, and all of the accused agreed in their confessions that Tito was "the vilest of traitors, the number-one puppet of American imperialism." From the transcript of the Rajk trial, it appears as if Tito, and not Rajk, had been the real defendant, and of course this was in a large sense true. Pál Justus, a former Social Democrat and Vice-President of the Hungarian Radio Corporation, was sentenced to life imprisonment, and scores of other persons received lesser punishment. Two high-ranking Army officers with experience in Spain—Lieutenant General György Pálffy, Chief of Staff and head of the Army's Political Division, and Colonel Bela Korondi—were tried separately in a military court and executed.

But this was not all. In the summer of 1950 a new purge brought the imprisonment of Arpád Szakasitz, a Social Democrat who had been chairman of the Hungarian Workers' Party and head of state; the Party's Deputy General Secretary, György Marosan; Justice Minister and Party Central Committee member Istvan Ries; Army Chief of Staff General László Solyom; Army Chief Inspector General László Kuthy; and the Director of the Kossuth Military Academy, General Kalman Revai. The civilians were punished for their Social Democratic past and the military officers—again many of them Spanish War veterans—for alleged involvement with Rajk and "Titoism."

In the spring of 1951 the third phase of the purges resulted in prison sentences for such outstanding "home Communists" as János Kadár, a Party deputy general secretary since 1948 who had replaced Rajk as Interior Minister. Czechoslovakia alone had thus far escaped the waves of terror rolling across the Communist bloc, but she was living only a reprieve, and the noose was already tightening. Terror was, inevitably, begetting more terror, and the question could be fairly asked whether the Soviet Union was not, historically, losing the day rather than saving it. In a speech on September 12, 1949, Tito offered his own prophetic analysis: "Every working class is capable of fighting and winning the new social order. Bayonets have never correctly spread a progressive idea and brought social transformation, but only enslavement."

VI

The Great Purge

In 1949 Czechoslovakia gave the outward appearance of a well-adjusted Soviet satellite state. Except in Slovakia, always a special case, the "Moscow Communists" led by Gottwald, Slánský, and Zápotocký were firmly in command. Those who could be regarded as "home Communists" held subordinate posts: Josef Pavel as Deputy Interior Minister; Josef Smrkovský, Director of State Farms and Forests and Deputy Agriculture Minister; Antonín Novotný, head of the Prague Party organization and member of the Central Committee whose loyalty to Moscow could not be questioned.

Gottwald, who had had his difficulties with Moscow, was now Stalin's junior partner in the sweeping personality cult that had developed in Czechoslovakia since the takeover. He was constantly described as "Stalin's best disciple," and his portraits appeared everywhere in Czechoslovakia next to Stalin's. All the Party and government institutions were geared to imitate the Soviet example, and the monotonous ideological principles of Soviet Communism pervaded the press and Czechoslovakia's cultural and intellectual life. The flavor of the new policies—or lack of it—could be found in an avalanche of official pronouncements.

For instance, the Minister of Information and Culture, Václav Kopecký, a tireless speechmaker, told the Party's Central Committee in May 1949: "Taking over the cultural heritage of the past, we are reappraising the fruits of Czech and Slovak literature and carrying out the revision of the literary works created in the bourgeois epoch. We see to it that only such works of our national literature are propagated among the people as can . . . contribute to the spiritual rebirth of the nation and help us in our socialist efforts."

Kopecký brought to the job of being Czechoslovakia's cultural czar a background as a journalistic propagandist. He did not hesitate to tell the Central Committee that "the new literary and artistic production is an important agent of the ideological and cultural rebirth in our country and is destined to play a great role in the socialist education of the broad masses." The regime was the "guardian of ideological purity," he said, which would purge the country of "bad literature" in order to do away with the "leftovers of bourgeois and petty-bourgeois ideology" and "ideologically confused intellectualism."

To put his notions into practice, Kopecký took over all the libraries and bookstores in Czechoslovakia and dispatched his agents to purify private collections. Edward Taborsky has estimated that seven million books from private libraries "were consigned to scrap paper," three million were moved to public libraries, and four million were locked away pending ideological decisions. Most of the works of pre-Communist Czech and Slovak writers were banned—and this included poetry and drama as well as the writings of the now officially hated Tomáš Masaryk and of Karel Čapek, generally considered Czechoslovakia's leading contemporary writer. Čapek was blacklisted because, presumably, he had written in 1924 a little book entitled *Why I Am Not a Communist,* in which he said that "in spite of the lies in the Party program, no proletarian culture exists. . . . If Communism pushes forward and dismisses the so-called bourgeois culture as unnecessary junk, then good-by." To take the place of the "bourgeois culture," Kopecký flooded the country with the outpourings of younger writers willing to compose in the "socialist realist" style—and in tune with the ideas of his Soviet counterpart Andrei Zhdanov, as well as with the works of Marx, Lenin, and Stalin, the Russian novels of Maxim Gorky and other approved writers, and such fascinating volumes as Gottwald's *Report to the Central Committee* and Slánský's *Report on the Unified Agricultural Cooperatives* (which sold 928,250 copies).

Zdeněk Nejedlý, the doddering Education Minister, announced shortly after the takeover that "we shall change human nature in accordance with our needs. . . . We shall not be satisfied with the innate gifts of man." This concept was put to work in Czechoslovakia's schools and universities, first with a purge of teachers and then with a purely Marxist-Leninist curriculum. Russian became a required subject, even though many students made it a point not to learn it after eight years of classes.

The film industry, long a pride of Czechoslovakia, was reduced, in

Kopecký's words, to the mission of providing people "with worthy motion pictures which would convince by their truthfulness and would be an incentive for our construction effort and a source of enthusiasm for joyful socialist work." The man put in charge of this program was Jiří Hendrych, who was to rise to the Party Presidium and, incredibly, open inadvertently the doors to the liberalization of 1968.

In the economy, collectivization and prompt industrial deliveries to the Soviet Union became the outstanding features of the system. No Czechoslovak leader ever thought of complaining to Stalin that the Soviet Union was unilaterally reaping the fruits of the labor of Czech and Slovak workers. Instead, friendship with the Soviet Union was the national slogan and the Czechoslovak-Soviet Friendship Society approached a membership of 2.2 million. Whether the motive was genuine friendship or genuine opportunism, the Society's rolls showed that every seventh citizen of the republic belonged to it.

Under the circumstances, it would seem absurd to suspect that Czechoslovakia was threatened with "Titoism" or anything like it. But as early as 1949, Moscow launched its first efforts to prove that, indeed, the Tito threat was lurking in the shadows.

It may have been a case of self-fulfilling prophecies, but evidence now available shows that as soon as the Rajk trial was over in Hungary, Soviet security services and a select group of Czechoslovak secret police, a "parallel police," went to work building up a Titoist affair in Czechoslovakia.

The history of the great Czechoslovak Communist purge arrests and trials between 1949 and 1954 (though arrests went on, less spectacularly, right up to 1967) is vital for the understanding of the events of 1968 and 1969.

In the first instance, it explains the Prague Spring of 1968 as the explosion of pent-up emotions and frustrations after the bloody Stalinist repression. With the exception of the Soviet trials of the 1930s and certain events in China in the 1950s and 1960s, nothing on a comparable scale had ever swept a Communist country in terms of Party power struggles and the wanton political destruction of an entire generation. Even today it is impossible to estimate precisely how many Czechs and Slovaks were imprisoned or deprived of means of decent livelihood after 1949. Tentative statistics assembled by the Rehabilitation Commissions in 1968 suggest tens of thousands of arrests and hundreds of thousands of dismissals from jobs. It was not accidental, then, that the leaders in the 1968 liberalizing experiment like President Svoboda, Josef Smrkovský, Gustav Husák, and Josef Pavel had been victims in the earlier persecutions.

In the second instance, the purges of 1949–1954 offer extraordinary insight into the Communist parties' operative and psychological techniques, as evidenced in the political liquidation of the Prague Spring men and the return in 1969 to sordid Communist orthodoxy. They also tell a great deal about the human and political make-up of the men who played significant roles in the 1950s and were to hold the center of the stage in 1968 and 1969. The story of how President Gottwald and his allies purged the KSČ in the early 1950s is an ominous prelude to the history of the 1969 purges conducted by Husák—after he had once more shifted his allegiances.

In 1969, in a changed world and with the Communist monolith already severely cracked, the process had to be infinitely more careful and sophisticated, but the angry rhetoric, with its dark hints of "antisocialist" conspiracies concocted in the West and in "Zionist" centers abroad to soften Czechoslovakia for the final "imperialist" blow, is strangely reminiscent of the words uttered in the 1950s to justify the savage purges.

At first, the arrests, imprisonments, and executions during 1949 seemed to bear little visible relationship to the Yugoslav affair already preoccupying the Kremlin. Instead, they appeared to be individual and often capricious cases of the settlement of old Communist accounts so typical of the postwar years, although occasionally they were related to premonitions of the Prague leadership. The execution of General Heliodor Pika, arrested in 1948, was the outcome principally of disputes concerning wartime intelligence dealings with the Russians, as was to be demonstrated in his posthumous rehabilitation *after* the 1968 Soviet invasion. There is likewise no satisfactory explanation for the July 1949 hanging of Dr. Milada Moraková, a middle-level government official, the first woman to be executed for "high treason" in Czechoslovakia. Sentenced each to twenty years in prison in the same trial were Dr. Vojtech Jandecka, chief of the First Department of the Government Presidium and chairman of an association of ex-Nazi-concentration-camp prisoners, and Dr. František Boublik, who served in the Government Presidium until the 1948 takeover. Curiously, both men were formally rehabilitated in May 1969 (they were actually released when an amnesty was declared in 1960) following court testimony by a physician that they had been severely tortured to force them to sign "confessions." Just as curiously, if not ominously, they and several other rehabilitated former prisoners complained publicly that their applications for rehabilitation were being examined by the same State Security officials who had extracted their confessions nineteen years earlier. The agents, removed during the Prague Spring, had quietly resumed their posts under the regime of Gustav Husák, an ex-prisoner.

The year 1949 also brought mass arrests by the Communist regime of Roman and Greek Catholic priests. Running as usual a year behind Hungary, where Cardinal Mindszenty had been imprisoned in 1948, Czechoslovakia arrested and convicted Josef Beran, the Roman Catholic Archbishop, and sentenced him to a fourteen-year term. (Poland's Stefan Cardinal Wyszynski, however, was not arrested until 1954, as the Polish Catholics stubbornly fought for their church.) Archbishop Beran, who was infinitely more popular and democratic-minded than Mindszenty, had spent three wartime years in Nazi concentration camps. In this first of three church purges, Bishop Stepan Trochta of Litoměřice was condemned to twenty-five years' imprisonment, while Brno's Bishop Karel Skoupy, then sixty-three years old, received twenty years along with Bishop Josef Hlouč of České Budějovice. Thousands of priests, monks, and nuns were jailed; others were forced to work in factories and on farms. While the bishops were tried on charges of "treason," "espionage," and contact with the Vatican, the removal of the priests, monks, and nuns was more openly designed to destroy the church as a functioning entity. The operation went hand in hand with the systematic destruction of the "bourgeoisie" as a social class. Summing up these efforts, the Justice Ministry was to announce proudly in 1958 that "former exploiters, members of the bourgeoisie and petty bourgeoisie [merchants, storekeepers, doctors, lawyers, office workers, nuns, and priests] comprise seventy per cent of all sentenced persons."

There were countless such arrests and trials during 1949, but the first detention to be subsequently linked with the Titoist purges was that of Dr. Evžen Löbl, then a Deputy Minister of Foreign Trade. His arrest on November 24 came two months after the Rajk trial in Hungary. And it was significant, as it developed later, that Dr. Löbl happened to be a Jew and a Slovak.

In reconstructing the immensely complex story of the Czechoslovak purges, three separate phases are distinguishable in the preparation of the trials.

The first phase covered roughly the first part of 1950, when the Soviet and Czechoslovak security authorities were groping for a pattern and seeking to fit the "evidence" obtained in the Budapest trials as well as possible into the Czechoslovak situation. This particular effort was entrusted to the Soviet MGB—the Ministry of State Security—at the same time that Moscow began to press the regime in Prague to produce a Titoist show trial. But the fact that it was to take four years for the full process to run its course suggests strongly that at the outset there was considerable uncertainty about which direction to go in—and how far—in purging the KSČ leadership.

It is clear, however, that the first targets, agreed on in Moscow, the Prague Interior Ministry, and among top Party leaders, were to be the "bourgeois nationalists" (specifically Slovaks), Spanish Civil War veterans, persons with wartime connections in the West, and the Jews. The aging Stalin was rapidly developing those anti-Semitic sentiments—he had called the Jews "those rootless cosmopolitans"—which were to find culminating expression in the Moscow "Doctors' Plot" and the parallel purges of Soviet Jews. The combination of Slovak nationalists, Spanish veterans, "Westerners," and Jews was not altogether illogical if the object of the exercise was to prove a Titoist conspiracy. The classical demonological ingredients were all there and, presently, the security machine was set in motion.

The sinister element was, of course, that the highest chiefs successively used one group of men to liquidate another and to be disposed of, in turn, by the next group. This pattern makes it fairly evident that the over-all planning was being done in Moscow rather than Prague, on the simple theory that the Czechoslovak Party and security bosses were not likely to be engaged in digging their own graves.

As the first phase opened, the hard core of the ruling apparatus in Prague was composed of President Gottwald, also the Party Chairman; General Secretary Rudolf Slánský; Premier Zápotocký; Deputy Premier Široký; and Karol Bacílek, a Slovak member of the Party's Politburo. On the security side, power was ostensibly vested in Interior Minister Nosek; Deputy Interior Ministers Josef Pavel and Oskar Valeš; and the Interior Ministry's State Security Chief Osvald Zavodský. The last three were all Spanish Civil War veterans.

As events were soon to demonstrate, actual police power was in the hands of Justice Minister Čepička and Ladislav Kopřiva, chief of the Cadres Section in the Party's Central Committee. The key man in operations was Kopřiva, who not only controlled the Party apparatus, but was also busily creating a "parallel" secret police in cooperation with the Soviet MGB "advisers." A rough, violent man given to loud outbursts of fury, Kopřiva was to be the gray eminence in the approaching months, along with General N. T. Likhachev and two men named Makarov and Galkin who were the chief Soviet MGB "advisers" in Czechoslovakia. Likhachev and Makarov were high-ranking MGB officers who came to Prague almost immediately after the end of the Rajk trial, where they had served in an "advisory" capacity.

The appearance in Prague of the MGB group coincided with a communication from Mátyás Rákosi to Gottwald that the Rajk trial had produced "evidence" incriminating certain persons in Czechoslovakia in "Titoist" conspiracies. Similar information came to Deputy Interior Minister Valeš who was in charge of contacts with security services in other East European countries.

The first overt sign that the Czechoslovak Party was turning on its own officials in connection with the "Titoist" situation came with the disclosure in *The New York Times* on October 24, 1949, that Foreign Minister Clementis was reportedly under suspicion for being too "independent-minded" and having dangerously strong Slovak nationalist proclivities. Dr. Clementis, who had spent most of the war in London, had worked closely with the Soviet diplomat Valerian Zorin during the final preparations for the 1948 *putsch*, and became Foreign Minister after the death of Jan Masaryk, whose deputy he had been for three years. Now he was in New York, heading the Czechoslovak delegation to the United Nations General Assembly, and he was very clearly disturbed by the news. *The Times*' story happened to appear exactly a month after the sentencing of Rajk and his associates in Budapest, and the long catalogue of charges of "bourgeois nationalism" hurled at the Hungarian Communists must have suggested to Clementis that there might be considerable truth in the reports he was reading.

As a reporter for the United Press covering the United Nations, I was among the scores of newsmen who daily hounded Clementis for comment on his allegedly impending liquidation. In perspective, it was a bizarre situation; a man being publicly asked whether the government he represented as Foreign Minister was indeed on the verge of throwing him in prison if and when he returned home. But this is how modern journalism is practiced, and Clementis had the grace to understand it and refrain from unkind response. As I recall those days—my first exposure to the Czechoslovak problem—Clementis merely smiled and puffed on his pipe as we followed him in and out of General Assembly meetings at Lake

Success. But on at least one occasion, he said that "of course" he would return to Czechoslovakia when the United Nations session ended at Christmas.

What went on in his mind—and between him and Prague—is obviously unknown. But word of Clementis's evident concern must have reached Prague, because late in November his wife Ludmila arrived in New York with what were purported to be personal assurances from President Gottwald that all the stories were "imperialist" inventions and that the government retained the fullest confidence in him. Looking back at the evidence now available, one cannot exclude that at that point Gottwald himself may have been honestly convinced that Clementis was in no danger. The coincidence of the arrest of Dr. Löbl that same week somehow did not strike home. But the purge plans were not being hatched by Gottwald, as far as anyone knows, but by the tiny inner circle in Prague built around Kopřiva, Bacílek, and Čepička (Gottwald's son-in-law) and directly linked to Moscow. While Clementis unquestionably had been marked as a purge target immediately after the Rajk trial—*The New York Times* story was accurate here—sixteen months were to elapse before the prosecutors were ready to launch the proceedings. The scope of the trials in preparation required long and tedious months of spadework.

Clementis returned to Prague on January 2, 1950. Four days later his private secretary, Théo Florin, was arrested in the street by state security agents. When Clementis began making irritated inquiries, Nosek told him he knew nothing about it. He then appealed to Gottwald and Slánský. Three days later Gottwald telephoned Clementis to say that Florin's arrest was not political and that the case would be rapidly solved. It never was.

Between January and May the state security apparatus produced a number of seemingly, or actually, unrelated arrests. Some of them were made by the Interior Ministry's regular secret police and others by Kopřiva's "parallel" force. Again, there were indications that the various segments of the Czechoslovak security machine were working at cross-purposes or, at least, without much coordination. But there were also ominous signs that Kopřiva and his twenty-six MGB advisers were quietly engineering the destruction of the regular political police. (This phenomenon was to recur late in 1968.)

The first arrests were principally aimed at more or less known Spanish veterans, but it should have been an alarming tipoff to the many highly placed "Spaniards," especially those in the security services. Apparently acting on orders from above, state security agents detained five Spanish veterans and a sixth person closely associated with them: Dora Kleinová, who had served as a physician with the International Brigades; Alice Kohnová, a volunteer; a Communist named Pavlik and his wife, who had both fought in Spain; Vlasta Veselá, who was in the Brigades' health services; and her husband Feigl, a wealthy businessman secretly dedicated to Communist causes whom she had met in France after the fall of the Spanish Republic. It appeared that they had been mentioned at the Budapest trials by Tibor Szönyi, the executed Organization Secretary of the Hungarian Party, as members of the Czechoslovak branch of the "Titoist" and "espionage" center supposedly set up by Noel Field, the mysterious American around whom much of the Rajk show trial had revolved.

These six seemingly minor arrests were to become immensely significant because, as far as the Kopřiva operatives were concerned, they provided the needed direct link with the Budapest conspiracy. In the second place, they established a connection between these alleged "Titoist" agents and a large number of important Party, government, and security officials with Spanish War backgrounds. The common denominator was that Mrs. Kleinová, Mrs. Kohnová, the Pavliks, and the Feigls had remained friendly with the fellow Spanish War veterans who now held eminent positions in Czechoslovakia. This was the method through which Kopřiva and his Soviet colleagues were preparing to do away with the established security apparatus and the non-Moscow Communists in high posts.

Meanwhile, a quick secret trial was arranged for the six "Spaniards." Vlasta Veselá Feigl committed suicide in her cell at the Ruzyň prison in suburban Prague during the investigations. The others were turned over to the Hungarian authorities.

Looking back at these techniques employed in 1950, one is struck by the similarity in the methods used then and in late 1968 and 1969 to clean out the liberals and moderates in the Czechoslovak state security services. In both cases, the system was guilt by association and guilt derived from personal backgrounds. In both cases, the men in the security services cooperated in their own political destruction. And, incredibly, some of these men lived twice through the same experience.

If a relatively identifiable pattern was beginning to emerge with the first arrests of the Spanish War veterans and their linkage with the Budapest trials, perplexing dimension came with sudden blows aimed at Communists of impeccably orthodox backgrounds and firm Moscow connections, and, at a wide spectrum of the non-Communist middle class.

Thus, the Central Committee, meeting on February 24–26, 1950, surprisingly expelled from its membership and from the Party itself Vilém Nový, the pliant editor of *Rudé Právo*, the official KSČ newspaper. Nový was accused of being an "agent of imperialism" and he was arrested. (This ever-loyal Moscow Communist was to lose his standing in the Party again with the advent of the 1968 liberalization. After the Soviet invasion he became one of the chief ideologists of the return to the orthodox line.) Another high official charged at the same time with being an "imperialist spy" and a contact with Noel Field was Milan Reiman, a department chief in Premier Zápotocký's office. According to Kopřiva's announcement to the Central Committee, Reiman had "committed suicide" during the investigations, another victim in the long line of alleged, induced, or real political suicides in Czechoslovakia.

Just as inexplicably, Defense Minister General Svoboda was removed on April 25 from the post he had held since the 1945 liberation, and General Jan Drgač was fired ten days later from his post as Army Chief of Staff. This was the beginning of a purge in the armed forces that was to assume considerable proportions. For the time being, General Svoboda was kicked upstairs to become, at the age of fifty-four, Deputy Premier in charge of the State Office of Physical Training and Sports, clearly a meaningless job. But the technique in 1950, as in 1968–1969, was often to move a man from a key position to an empty sinecure before doing away with him altogether. The new Defense Minister was Čepička.

Simultaneously, the Kopřiva squad opened a frontal assault on the immensely juicy target that was the Czechoslovak Foreign Ministry. Here, the operation seemed to make more political sense because Czernin Palace had all along remained outside the grasp of the Moscow Communists. Not only was Clementis, as Minister, a Slovak with a wartime London past, but among the high officials there were Spanish veterans, men who had spent the war either in the West or in Nazi concentration camps, and a number of Jews.

The thirty-five-year-old Deputy Foreign Minister Artur London, for example, had all the possible strikes against him: he had fought in Spain; he later worked in the French resistance against the Germans and was imprisoned in a Nazi concentration camp; he had a French Communist wife and had lived for a few years in France after the war; and he was a Jew. He also had the misfortune of having known Noel Field and of having received a small loan from Field's Unitarian Service Committee while staying at a Swiss sanatorium. Deputy Foreign Minister Vavro Hajdu, then thirty-six years old, was in London during the war, had broadcast for the BBC, and was a Jew. Karel Dufek (who, as chief of the ministry's foreign-press section in 1968, had the task of informing me of my expulsion from Czechoslovakia as a *New York Times* correspondent) was a veteran of Spain, served as a diplomat in Turkey and Britain, and was the chief of the ministry's Communist Party unit. Eduard Goldstücker, a Jew, was counselor in London in 1949 and later Minister to Israel. One of the few men in the Czechoslovak cast of characters who remained politically consistent for twenty years, Goldstücker was to emerge after his imprisonment in the 1950s as one of the chief architects of the Prague Spring. Finally, the entire diplomatic service still employed a considerable number of Jews as well as non-Communists, and increasingly it was suffering from embarrassing defections to the West.

With the detention of Dr. Löbl—later singled out in the trials as the "first member of the conspiracy to be arrested"—the Kopřiva witch-hunters now concentrated on the Foreign Ministry and the Ministry of Foreign Trade as principal areas for proving the existence of a "Titoist plot." As officials in both ministries inevitably had to maintain professional contacts abroad, "evidence" against them could be easily procured. Because some of the Foreign Ministry men also had close personal connections with state security officials, largely through their past Spanish associations, the Kopřiva operatives were eventually able to follow this trail to neutralize the secret police and, later, to take on the top Party leadership. Little by little, then, the framework of the purges was acquiring shape.

The Soviet advisers, however, had clearly started out without a blueprint and their task was comparable to the assembling of a blank jigsaw puzzle, not quite knowing what would emerge in the end. The same process was to be repeated in 1969, when Moscow and the new Czechoslovak leadership undertook to prove that the Prague Spring had been a "rightist counterrevolution" painstakingly plotted from abroad. Artur London's book on the purges of the 1950s, *L'Aveu dans l'engrenage du procès de Prague*, quotes a former Spanish volunteer, Alois Samec, who initially worked with the Soviet advisers:

> It was in the autumn of 1949, after the Rajk trial, that they arrived in Czechoslovakia. They were saying that surely we must also have among us a conspiracy against the state . . . that the enemies who wanted to overthrow the socialist regime

were infiltrated in all the wheels of the Party and the government apparatus. . . .

According to the instructions they gave us, we carried out arrests of persons who "could have" had activities against the state through their functions or relationships. It was only afterward that one looked for proof. . . . I had received the order of one of the Soviet advisers, Borisov, to hand him personally a copy of every part of the testimony obtained from an accused person. I called his attention to the fact that the General Secretary of the Party was already receiving a copy of the summaries. He put me brusquely back in my place and ordered me not to discuss his instructions.

I also had contact with other Soviet advisers, notably Likhachev and Smirnov. They collected compromising information about everybody, especially about people holding high functions, including Slánský and Gottwald. . . .

From their arrival, they began to infiltrate all the wheels of [state] security through the offices of "men of confidence" who were devoted to them body and soul. In this way they rapidly succeeded in creating within [state] security—where they were supposed to be working officially—a parallel police obeying them only.

Samec also told of all the interrogations' summaries being immediately translated into Russian.

The "parallel police" quickly and efficiently established surveillance over Clementis and his principal associates during early 1950. Artur London writes that already in 1949 he was periodically called in for lengthy questioning by security officials at their Dejvice headquarters or at the Interior Ministry on the subject of his acquaintance with Noel Field and his other foreign ties. That he was a Deputy Foreign Minister was no deterrent to the security agents. Clementis himself had been complaining to London and Hajdu that he was being shadowed by men who were not his regular bodyguards.

Finally and inevitably the ax fell on Clementis. On March 13, 1950, President Gottwald summoned him to Hradčany Castle to ask for his resignation on the grounds that he had carried out a "deficient" personnel policy in his ministry. The next day Clementis's resignation was announced in Prague.

According to Czechoslovak officials familiar with the events of 1950, there are valid reasons to believe that the Soviets had demanded the immediate arrest of Clementis, but that Gottwald resisted out of a personal sense of loyalty and because he thought the "evidence" thus far amassed against the dismissed minister was not quite convincing. Presumably, Gottwald deserves credit for at least having tried to maintain a modicum of decency toward his comrades. Clementis thus won a reprieve of nearly a year.

The second phase in the preparations of the trials was inaugurated on May 23, 1950, when Ladislav Kopřiva emerged from the murky shadows of the Central Committee's Cadres Section to become head of the newly created Ministry of State Security. (He was replaced in the Cadres job by Bruno Köhler, one of his most trusted associates.) The state security services under Osvald Zavodský were simultaneously detached from the Interior Ministry and placed in Kopřiva's new ministry. The Interior Ministry itself lost all its power. Again, there are reasons to believe that Gottwald used his influence to prevent the arrest of Václav Nosek and Deputy Minister Pavel. Although Nosek had long been a faithful servant of the Moscow cause, he was vulnerable because he had spent much of the war in London and had close ties with Clementis. Pavel, of course, had the Spanish background against him.

At the end of May, then, the Moscow Communists had captured all the key positions in Czechoslovakia. Kopřiva was the police czar. Čepička held the armed forces. Široký became the new Foreign Minister while retaining the post of Deputy Premier. And no time was wasted in launching an open attack on the "enemies" of the Republic. Speaking at the Ninth Congress of the Slovak Communist Party on May 24, the day after Kopřiva took over the security apparatus, Široký had this to say of his fellow Slovak, Clementis:

> Comrade Clementis emigrated after the occupation of the republic in 1939. After the conclusion of the Soviet-German pact, which had great importance for progressive humanity because it crossed the low and treacherous plans of the Anglo-American imperialists, he stood up against the Soviet Union and adopted the attitude of a class enemy.
>
> He maintained this attitude of a class enemy during the Soviet-Finnish conflict and during the liberation of the Western Ukraine and Western White Russia by the Soviet armies. In London, Comrade Clementis was associated with the bourgeois emigrants surrounding President Beneš, and his activities and his broadcasts were all on the bourgeois line. He also maintained this attitude as Undersecretary and as Minister of Foreign Affairs. This deviationist did not consider future developments after the war in terms of class warfare.

Široký's speech officially opened the hunting season on "Titoists" and "bourgeois nationalists." Slovakia, which was nationalist, was the obvious place to start the hunt.

Though Clementis was the first target of attack, Široký used the Congress to smash Slovakia's entire autonomous structure. Husák, who had been removed nineteen days earlier as chairman of the Slovak Board of

Commissioners, was denounced by Široký as a "nationalist" and a follower of Clementis. Laco Novomeský, the famous Slovak poet, a friend of Husák's and a member of the Board of Commissioners, received the same treatment. So did Dr. Karol Smidke, head of the Slovak National Assembly and the Slovak Association of Partisans.

Controlling all the strategic positions in the Party and the government and having dismantled the Slovak edifice, the Moscow group now appeared ready to stage the planned trials. But there must have been a desire for perfection in the scenario, or some hidden sources of potential opposition may still have had to be liquidated. The witch-hunters stayed their hand for another six months, consolidating their positions.

Much of this time was used to construct "evidence" for the forthcoming arrests. Artur London recalls, for example, that Kopřiva interrogated him about Zavodský, still ostensibly the head of state security services, to establish whether he had been guilty of "treason" during the war and had collaborated with the Gestapo in France. Massive files were assembled on virtually every Party official of any importance. It was as if Moscow and its Prague associates were still uncertain just how to proceed, as if a director had gathered an immense cast but could not set the production in motion because the script somehow did not hang together. In the sinister make-believe world of contrived trial preparations, the analogy is perhaps not amiss.

Presently, the order to move was given and, in December 1950, Kopřiva's agents began to fan out across the country on their ominous assignments.

The most notable Communist leaders caught in the dragnet before the end of the year were Otto Šling, secretary of the Party's regional committee in Brno (the second most important after Prague and one which tended to be relatively liberal, as events in 1969 continued to show), and Mrs. Marie Švermová, a member of the Party Presidium, Deputy General Secretary, and head of the Central Committee's Organizational Department. In Šling's case, the presumed reason for his detention was his role as the secretary of the Czechoslovak Communist Party unit in the International Brigades in Spain and his Jewish origin. But Mrs. Švermová's arrest was bewildering even to those close to the "inner circle." She was the famous widow of Jan Šverma, a Moscow Communist and wartime resistance hero, and the sister of Karel Švab, Deputy Minister of State Security who no longer was able to protect her. Šverma had visited the Czech volunteers in Spain in the summer of 1937 with a Party delegation, and this conceivably may have been held against his widow. But the line of reasoning was not to become clear until Gottwald issued the official version months later. In the meantime, these arrests were kept secret from the public, as the Kopřiva ministry was preparing to strike again.

In anticipation of new arrests, the government busied itself demoting potential victims from top jobs. Whenever feasible, the policy was to retain people who had already been deprived of high posts. There must have been a motive for the prompt arrest of Šling and Mrs. Švermová, but men like Clementis and Husák remained untouched though already long out of public life. General Svoboda lived in oblivion in the sports post. In October 1950 General Pavel was removed from his job as Deputy Interior Minister and named commander of the border guards; in December he was sent to the Party's Central Committee school as a student, which was patently ridiculous. "But," he told Artur London, "this is nothing compared to what threatens us. . . . We must expect soon to have our Rajk affair here." Antonín Svoboda, a Spanish veteran, was fired from the directorship of the Armed Forces Section of the Central Committee. Otakar Hromadko, also a fighter in Spain, ceased to run the Party committee at the Military Academy.

On December 2, in the second attack on the church, nine Roman Catholic dignitaries were sentenced to heavy prison terms by a Prague court for "treason and espionage." Jan Opasek, Abbot of the Benedictine monastery at Brevnov, was condemned to life imprisonment. The titular bishop of Olomouc in Moravia received twenty-five years.

Then, starting in January 1951, the Great Purge exploded with a wave of arrests unparalleled in Czechoslovak history.

According to no less an authority than Karol Bacílek, former Minister of State Security, who told his story in 1968, Anastas Mikoyan, one of Stalin's closest collaborators, visited Prague early that year to advise President Gottwald that the Soviet Union considered a "Titoist" show trial an absolute necessity. Gottwald demurred, but a telephone call from Stalin ended his resistance. Kopřiva received his instructions directly from Lavrenti Beria.

In this second phase of the trial preparations, as many as twenty-five thousand persons are believed to have been arrested—in the Party, the government, the armed forces, the security services, and virtually every sector of Czechoslovak life. It hit Czechs and Slovaks and Christians and Jews alike, engulfed Spanish veterans, wartime resistance leaders, former prisoners of the Nazis, loyal Moscow Communists, and just about everybody whom Beria, Likhachev, and Kopřiva chose to suspect. Refugee Spanish Communists were exiled to Ústí-nad-Labem in northern Bohemia.

Official blessings for the purge were given by the no longer reluctant President Gottwald in a speech before the Party's Central Committee on February 22, 1951, when he named Otto Šling and Mrs. Švermová as the leaders in the conspiracy of "traitors and plotters" who planned to grab power and turn Czechoslovakia into "another Titoist Yugoslavia." As the nation recoiled in horror and disbelief, the greats of Communism one after another fell from grace and into prison. Artur London was one of the first to be arrested, on January 28; Laco Holdoš, Slovak Secretary of State for Culture, on February 2; Karel Švab, Deputy Minister of State Security, on February 16—he was said to have refused to cooperate any further with the MGB; Clementis, finally, on February 27. By fall, among other Slovaks Gustav Husák, the poet Novomeský, Karol Smidke (who had been the chairman of the Slovak National Assembly and was to die in prison in 1952), and Leopold Hoffmann, who was then Gottwald's own personal security chief, were imprisoned.

In another of these ironical twists, the thirty-year-old chief secretary of the Trečín District Committee, Alexander Dubček, was elected to the Central Committee of the Slovak Party about the time Husák was being imprisoned for Slovak "nationalism" and "Titoism." Curiously, then, Dubček's rise in the Communist apparatus coincided with the disgrace of Husák, the man who on Moscow's behest was to oust *him* for "revisionist errors" eighteen years later. There is no reason to think that at that earlier juncture the two men had more than a nodding acquaintance.

Pavel and Smrkovský were also arrested during 1951—Smrkovský in April, a month after he lost his job as the head of State Farms and Forests. In the security services, Zavodský followed his boss Švab into prison by a few days. Then it was Deputy Interior Minister Valeš. Antonín Svoboda and Otakar Hromadko were captured in February. General Bedrich Reicin, Deputy Minister of Defense (and a Jew), and General Jan Kopold of the General Staff were arrested in March.

From the Party leadership, six out of the nineteen regional secretaries, including Otto Šling, were imprisoned in the first wave. So were Bedrich Geminder, head of the International Relations Section of the Central Committee (and a Jew); Josef Frank, Deputy General Secretary of the Party (and a Jew); and an ex-editor of *Rudé Právo*, André Simone (also a Jew).

In the government, the arrests included Deputy Foreign Minister Vavro Hajdu, a Jew, detained on April 2; Deputy Minister of Foreign Trade Rudolf Margolius, a Jew; Deputy Minister of Finance Otto Fischl, a Jew; and the head of the economic section of the Presidency, Ludvík Frejka, a Jew. Arrested men in the Foreign Ministry, in addition to Clementis, London, and Hajdu, included Eduard Goldstücker, Karel Dufek, Information Department chief Bedrich Klinger, Jiří Hájek (who lived to be Foreign Minister of the Prague Spring), Pavel Kavan, who was press attaché at the London embassy, and numerous others. Also caught in the roundup was the American William N. Oatis, the Associated Press correspondent in Prague, who was later sentenced to twenty years in prison for "espionage."

The great prisons of the Prague area—Pankrac, Ruzyň, and Koloděje Castle (once Gottwald's summer residence)—Leopoldov in Bratislava, and every other jail in the country were bursting with the prisoners disgorged daily by the security vans.

General Svoboda was arrested late in 1951, after Gottwald removed him from the Deputy Premiership for Sports on the peculiar grounds that there were already too many ministers around. Actually, Svoboda's arrest resulted from a deception-within-a-deception: a falsified telegram had been sent from Moscow to Kopřiva by unknown persons saying that "Stalin doesn't trust Svoboda." This, of course, was enough to lead the white-haired Hero of the Soviet Union straight to prison, but just as oddly nobody in Moscow undertook to correct the error. Five days before Svoboda became Czechoslovakia's President in 1968, he recounted for a Prague newsman the charges against him: that he was a "member of the British Intelligence Service," that in 1945 he had driven a Czechoslovak officer to Plzeň to meet United States troops there and thus provided the Americans with "important material," and that, finally, he had been preparing a "coup." The charges were patently absurd because in April 1945, when American forces entered Plzeň, General Svoboda was sitting in Košice as Defense Minister in the new Moscow-blessed government. Yet, in the frenzied and almost demented atmosphere of Prague in 1951, nobody even thought of questioning these accusations.

When the Central Committee met in Prague on September 6, it was generally assumed, even among the purgers themselves, that the roundup operation preceding the show trial was completed. In addition to the thousands of arrests, nearly a hundred and fifty thousand persons had been expelled from the Party. Virtually every Czechoslovak who could have conceivably been suspected of *anything* subversive was safely in prison, and scores of key personalities—from Pavel to Clementis and from Smrkovský to Husák—were being tortured and interrogated day and night by Kopřiva's special security "referents" working on trial "evidence" in liaison with their Soviet MGB "teachers." But, as usual, Moscow had another surprise in store for Czechoslovakia. And, as usual, the West seemed to know little and care less about the country's fate.

The Soviet surprise for the Czechoslovaks was the third phase in the trial preparations. In the strict sense, it overlapped the second phase because the wave of arrests initiated in January 1951 was not to run out its wild course until the end of the year. But for historical purposes, the opening of this third phase can be set at the September 6 session of the Central Committee.

It was then that in a bewildering act the Central Committee fired Rudolf Slánský from the General Secretaryship of the Party. Again, as in Poland with Gomułka in August 1948, a spontaneous "democratic" rebellion could not have occurred against the Party's top figure without overwhelming external pressure. As far as the Czechoslovak Communist Party was concerned, Slánský was an admired and powerful leader who shared with President Gottwald the stewardship of the nation's political fortunes. The question, then, is who wanted Slánský's removal and why.

Slánský's Communist credentials were perfect even from Moscow's suspicious viewpoint. He had joined the Party at its foundation when he was in his early twenties. Along with Gottwald, four years his senior, he formed the backbone of the leftist "Karlin Faction" which had won Stalin's support in the struggles of the 1920s. He was a humorless, doctrinaire Stalinist who never deviated from the Kremlin line. His war years were spent in Moscow until 1944, when he was secretly sent home as the Party's chief emissary in Czechoslovakia to prepare the postliberation Communist operations. In 1947 Slánský succeeded even in overtaking Gottwald as Moscow's chief favorite when the President had nearly ended his own career by agreeing to let Czechoslovakia join the Marshall Plan. Stalin's wrath against Gottwald was demonstrated when Slánský was chosen instead of him to represent Czechoslovakia at the foundation of the Cominform. Slánský remained the KSČ's permanent delegate to the Cominform and, in June 1948, was among the signers of the document that excommunicated Tito's Yugoslavia. On December 20, 1949, when the Titoist purge was beginning to take shape in Czechoslovakia, Slánský was still riding so high that he was chosen to deliver the official eulogy of Stalin on the occasion of his seventieth birthday at a special session of the Central Committee. In April 1951, when the Kopřiva and MGB machine was already in high gear, the Cominform's journal *For Lasting Peace, for a People's Democracy* published a lengthy article by Slánský praising the "genius" of Stalin, and *Rudé Právo* dutifully reprinted it in Prague.

The mystery, not fully clarified to this day, was what happened between April and late July 1951 to turn the Kremlin against Slánský and order his liquidation. It is clear, however, that the decision against Slánský was taken in Moscow without even consulting Gottwald and his most intimate collaborators. Thus, when Slánský celebrated his fiftieth birthday on July 31, the Czechoslovak Party awarded him the Order of Socialism and the Central Committee, over Gottwald's and Premier Zápotocký's signatures, sent him a warm telegram of congratulations. Václav Kopecký, Minister of Information and the Party's chief propagandist, wrote an editorial in *Rudé Právo* describing him as "an outstanding example of a Communist revolutionary," a "devoted and fiery fighter under the banner of Lenin and Stalin," and a "close and faithful collaborator of Klement Gottwald." As Communist parties traditionally put great stock in birthdays, Slánský also received congratulatory telegrams from all over Eastern Europe and the world.

It might have struck him as odd that no telegrams came from Moscow and that the Soviet press totally ignored his birthday. Such omissions do not occur by accident in the Soviet Union, which emits protocolary signals with the subtlety of the Delphic Oracle, and Slánský was surely sufficiently experienced in Kremlin ritual to realize that something was ominously amiss. But Prague had not yet been formally advised of the impending Slánský disgrace and, on August 18, *Rudé Právo* insouciantly reported that workers in the Letov aircraft plant had the day before renamed it the Rudolf Slánský Aircraft Works to show their "gratitude and love" to this "closest collaborator of Comrade Gottwald."

Exactly three weeks later *Rudé Právo* informed the population that the Central Committee had relieved this "devoted and fiery fighter under the banner of Lenin and Stalin" of his job as General Secretary for his errors in "selecting Party cadres" and improperly interfering with the agencies of the government. Gottwald assumed his post. In the newspaper's September 8 issue, Information Minister Kopecký rushed to explain to what must have been highly perplexed readers that Slánský had sought to turn the Central Secretariat he headed into the "leading Party organ" and that this organ had been operating "over the heads and without the knowledge of responsible comrades."

What went on behind the closed doors of the Central Committee's session is not known, but evidently Moscow and its Prague agents were not yet ready to do away with Slánský altogether. He was allowed to recant and to remain on the Politburo, as the fourth man after Gottwald, Zápotocký, and Široký. Inexplicably, he was also named a Deputy Premier. At the same time, however, Party apparatus chiefs throughout the country were put on guard against him in a highly confidential circular reporting that, at the Central Committee plenum,

> Comrade Slánský admitted with Bolshevik frankness his errors and explained the danger which they represented for the Party. . . . By entrusting Slánský with a responsible position in the state administration, it gives him the possibility of remedying the consequences of his mistakes and shortcomings by his work, and of proving the sincerity of his self-criticism in the new sphere of his activities. . . . The frank admission of the errors and the self-critical pronouncement of Comrade Slánský is the basic precondition for his adequately fulfilling the tasks in his new sphere of action to the benefit of the working class, the Party, and the building of socialism.

This, unquestionably, was putting Slánský on probation, but it was generally assumed that his demotion was an internal Party matter not related to the raging purge of "Titoist traitors and plotters" denounced by Gottwald in February. It had been no secret in top Communist circles that Gottwald and Slánský were often in conflict, if not in direct power rivalry, and the presumption was that Gottwald was settling his private accounts with his colleague. Nothing had been said of treason or "Titoism" in the Central Committee circular, yet Slánský may have realized the awesome dangers facing him when Gottwald remarked pointedly to the Committee that *not only* Šling and Mrs. Švermová were responsible for placing "conspirators" in key positions.

Just what lay behind this new scene remained unclear. It is possible that Gottwald himself was still resisting Soviet pressures for Slánský's final liquidation as he had earlier resisted the whole idea of show trials. Early in November, for example, Slánský's collected works were published in Prague under the title *For the Victory of Socialism*, and *Rudé Právo*, always a step behind the times, praised it as "further important help for the study of the history of our Party and for the improvement of the ideological level of its members."

But, in attempting to reconstruct the events, it now appears certain that the Kremlin had concluded that a star victim was required for the forthcoming trials to make them plausible. People like Šling, Mrs. Švermová, Husák, Clementis, Smrkovský, Pavel, London, or Löbl added up to a rather improbable and incongruous collection of "conspirators," and the trial planners must have felt that someone of the caliber of Traicho Kostov or Rajk was needed to lead the cast and crown the proceedings. Why Slánský and not, for instance, Gottwald or Zápotocký, was chosen is still a matter of conjecture. As Artur London recounts in his book, his prison interrogators kept telling him throughout 1951 that the Party "needs a trial" and making it clear that no decision had been reached how to construct it. London's impressive account shows that until November security "referents" were seeking testimony from their myriad prisoners in a variety of directions as if trying to find the right track in the darkness. It is also useful to recall London's report on his conversation with Samec, the Czech security agent working with the MGB in 1948, in which he told of the Soviet "advisers'" orders to submit to them all interrogation summaries, even though copies were already being sent to the General Secretary of the Party, who was then Slánský. And, significantly, Samec had also told London that the MGB specialists "collected compromising information about everybody . . . including Slánský and Gottwald."

That, in the end, Slánský was picked for the star of the trial may well have resulted from the fact that he was Jewish. The earlier arrests at high levels of the government had strongly focused on Jews, and Stalin was himself increasingly obsessed with the Jewish question. This, then, may have been the decisive factor.

Be that as it may, Rudolf Slánský was arrested on the night of November 24, 1951. An official communiqué four days later informed the nation that "hitherto unknown circumstances have recently been established which prove that Rudolf Slánský has been guilty of active antistate activities" and, therefore, was being detained "for purposes of investigation."

Gottwald never explained what these "unknown circumstances" may have been and how they had suddenly emerged. Scores, if not hundreds, of important prisoners had been interrogated for nearly a year and it does not seem likely that "evidence" against Slánský had unexpectedly materialized between the middle and the end of November. Addressing the Central Committee on December 6, 1951, Gottwald announced that "new revelations" had proved Slánský's "leading part in the conspiracy against the Party and the state." Overnight Slánský had thus turned into a "Titoist" and a "traitor."

To unveil Slánský's "leading" role in the "conspiracy," the Party assembled in the lovely chandeliered Spanish Hall of Hradčany Castle the largest crowd of outside guests ever invited to a Central Committee session. After announcing that Slánský had been stripped of all his official posts and expelled from the Party, Gottwald proceeded to read the indictment, according to which the ousted General Secretary "had knowingly supported all diversionist activities of hostile and criminal groups" and had "tried to create a special Party center behind the back of the Prime Minister." Linking Slánský to the earlier purge victims, Gottwald said that "during the course of the investigation of the various apprehended underground groups it became obvious that Slánský actively participated in these plottings, or better, he was the leading participant in the anti-Party and antistate plot." To cap these accusations, Gottwald added that "we have seized plans and unshakable evidence that the espionage service of the Western imperialists planned to organize and execute the escape of Slánský to the West."

The stage was now set for Czechoslovakia's great show trial.

Although it took the Kremlin three years to establish the existence of a "conspiracy" in Czechoslovakia, yet another year was needed to bring the trial to fruition. With thousands of persons in the prisons and the need to build a coherent court case out of such diverse elements as "Titoism," "Trotskyism," "bourgeois nationalism," "Zionism," and "Western imperialist espionage," the Prague prosecutors and the interrogation "referents" had their work cut out for them. Not even in the Moscow trials of the 1930s did the Soviet prosecutors have a task so complex. To take all these charges at their face value would have inevitably led to the conclusion that only a miracle had saved Communist Czechoslovakia from foundering long ago in a quagmire of treason and delivering her, defenseless, into the hands of the malevolent West—and of Tito.

But the Prague leadership had an explanation why Czechoslovakia had succeeded in remaining a Communist state despite all this deep-seated subversion in its midst. The explanation is vitally important in understanding not only the history of 1951, but also 1968 and 1969. It is found in the speech delivered by Defense Minister Čepička to the National Congress of the KSČ on December 18, 1952, three weeks after the completion of the Slánský trial:

Basing themselves on the last world war, from which the Soviet Army emerged not only as a victor but stronger than ever before, the imperialists came to the conclusion that an attack on the Soviet Union, just as the Hitlerite attack, could end in nothing but catastrophe for them. Therefore, they began their preparations for an attack on the Soviet Union in a number of directions and with a number of alternatives, so as to be insured for any event.

On the basis of one of these alternatives, Czechoslovakia, an immediate neighbor of the Soviet Union, was looked upon as one of the most important military bases for an attack on the Soviet Union. After 1945, the Western imperialists convinced themselves with their own eyes that the Czechoslovak people, a people under the leadership of the Czechoslovak Communist Party and Comrade Gottwald, would never voluntarily become an obedient executor of these incendiary intentions and plans. Consequently, they wanted to master Czechoslovakia with the aid of a base, treacherous Fifth Column. The American imperialists assumed that it would be more advantageous for them if, until the last moment before the attack, *Czechoslovakia should continue to be a country outwardly and officially belonging to the camp of peace and a formal ally of the Soviet Union.*

At a moment beneficial to the imperialists, the Fifth Column in Czechoslovakia was to have opened a front for the benefit of the imperialist aggressors. So, during the battle a dagger was to have been plunged into the back of the Soviet Union. For that the Czechoslovak Army was to have been misused. Therefore, its supreme commander, Comrade Klement Gottwald, was to have been removed by violence. It is clear that the Fifth Column could not carry out its plan *if it were prematurely exposed, as were Tito and his band in Yugoslavia.*

Therefore, particularly great attention was devoted to camouflaging the undermining activities of the hostile Fifth Column in the Army, and exposure was avoided by all means. Only in the extreme event of premature exposure of the traitors and wreckers the Army and the remaining armed forces in our country were to have been conducive to interference and to the adoption of steps which, as in Tito Yugoslavia, would have enabled the traitors and wreckers to take over by force the Communist Party and the state apparatus.

The imperialists, who have learned a lesson from the defeats suffered by their Trotskyite wreckers' agents in the struggle with the Soviet Union, selected the most complicated and insidious forms of wrecking activities in the Army. On the basis of these directives, all members of the antistate plot carefully concealed even the slightest disagreement of the Party. Many times did the American agents Slánský, Reicin, and company declare outwardly their faithfulness to the cause, urging that the example of the Soviet Army be followed. In reality, however, they acted differently.

This wrecking activity of the band of plotters was guarded by all means from exposure. All threads of the Party and state machine were in the hands of Slánský and thus, on the instructions of American imperialists, Slánský could bar all attempts to expose them. Until the middle of 1948, Beneš, whose post of Supreme Commander-in-Chief made it possible to frustrate any attempts to expose and mend affairs, kept his powerful protective hand over the intrigues in the Army.

It is not surprising that the traitors and plotters felt themselves to be completely safe, assuming that the way to their final goal was open to them. But at that very time the worker's fist of Comrade Gottwald struck the traitors like lightning. . . .

In the autumn of 1950 Comrade Gottwald, as Supreme Commander of the Czechoslovak armed forces, decided to carry out changes in the higher ranks of the Army, a decision that changed the situation existing up till then. A crushing blow was inflicted on the treacherous plans of the enemy.

Shortly after the imprisonment of Šling in the autumn of 1950, Comrade Gottwald, on the basis of specific facts, came to the conclusion that the hostile activity, to the extent to which it was then exposed, bore all the hallmarks of the betrayal of Tito, and despite the fact that at that time it was still unknown that Slánský was the chief representative of this danger, Comrade Gottwald took a number of steps directed toward the timely averting of danger. Hoping for the support of the American imperialists and their myrmidons, traitor Slánský, even after the imprisonment of Šling, did not consider his criminal cause to be doomed. It is known by what a mendacious method he tried to draw suspicion away from himself and to place the chief guilt on Švermová, Šling, and others. Finally, in the face of evidence, he was forced to admit his betrayal, including the intrigues organized by him in the Army. He paid the price of his betrayal. . . .

It would have been impossible to eliminate the damage and for the defensive capacity of our country to have grown so rapidly during the short period of two years, *if we had not received help from the closest and best friend of the Czechoslovak people—Comrade Stalin!* [italics added].

When one reads this speech now, it has the eerie reminiscent sound of the speeches and articles emanating from the ruins of the Prague Spring. Čepička's painstakingly constructed argument that Slánský and his associates had, until the bitter end, attempted to keep alive the impression that Czechoslovakia was a "socialist state" allied with the Soviet Union better to run their Fifth Column, was repeated in strikingly similar terms in 1968 and 1969 by pro-Moscow leaders alluding to Dubček, Smrkovský, and their associates.

In these echoes of the past reverberating almost two decades later, not only the tone but the very words seemed identical. Jan Pelnař, the man who replaced Pavel as Interior Minister following the Russian invasion in 1968,* in an interview published in *Rudé Právo* on June 19, 1969, said:

In the course of 1968, internal forces activated with the assistance of foreign enemies of socialism . . . opened a concentrated attack on the state bodies, the Army, and the police. . . . The aim of these attacks was to disintegrate the police

---

* History was savagely repeating itself for Josef Pavel. In 1951, as we have seen, he was removed from the Interior Ministry and arrested on charges of subverting the security forces to soften Czechoslovakia for the "final" blow by the "imperialists." In 1969, already ousted from his job as Interior Minister, he faced the same charges again.

ability to act. . . . The center of their attention was the situation in the Army and Security. They reckoned that the way would be free for them since the Army, Security, and the organization of the state administration would collapse. . . .

The Ministry of Interior succeeded in obtaining some material documenting the the plans of Western intelligence to disintegrate the unity of the Socialist camp and the Socialist system in Czechoslovakia. . . . If we compare these plans with the concrete activity of anti-Socialist forces in Czechoslovakia in the past period, we find they are almost identical.

In 1952, of course, the purge was immensely aided by the investigators' ability to obtain corroborating "confessions" from their victims.* The year spent by the MGB-directed "referents" between Slánský's arrest and his trial in obtaining and matching the "confessions" of hundreds of persons is an extraordinary example not only of modern methods of psychological pressure but, above all, of the ultimate willingness of many a loyal Communist to sacrifice himself, his human self-respect, and his intellectual sense of objective truth to the cause of the Party.

As the numerous accounts of the survivors indicate, it was not only torture and duress but also the infinite patience and cunning of the interrogators that finally brought forth the desired "confessions." Artur London makes the point in his book that he reached the stage during his imprisonment when he would have testified that his year-old son was a Trotskyite, had this been asked of him, and that in numerous instances the sentenced men became so convinced of their own "guilt" that they were sincerely shocked when they were declared innocent in subsequent rehabilitation proceedings. London also chillingly reports that his wife, a devoted Communist and the daughter of Communist parents, wrote to him in prison that she could not go on being married to him if the charges that he betrayed the Party were proved in court. Only after she became finally convinced that the trial was a frame-up did Mrs. London find it possible to rebuild her emotional ties with her husband.

The stars among the "referents" were a Major Doubek, the Commander of Ruzyň, and a Captain Kohoutek, who before the war was on an anti-Communist police squad in Ostrava. They worked closely with Kopřiva and the MGB agents.

In the final preparations of the trial, the "referents" went beyond individual "confessions" of guilt to weave an immensely artful web of "evi-

---

*It may be valid, in thinking ahead to the events of 1968, to ask whether similar "confessions" might not have been extracted from Dubček and his colleagues had they been kept prisoners and tried after being abducted in Prague and taken to Moscow on August 21.

dence" in which each person in the case neatly accused the others of complicity. Slánský, for example, testified that he had placed "Titoists" and "traitors" in highly sensitive positions in the Party, the Army, and the government. Clementis, London, Hajdu, and the others were made to corroborate this in the case of the Foreign Ministry, and Pavel, Zavodský, and Švab in state security. Under the system of mutual incriminations, one former Spanish volunteer would admit that he worked together with others in acting as Gestapo informers in the French camps after the defeat of the Spanish Republic. London and Pavel "admitted" they headed a secret organization of Spanish veterans which, in turn, was linked with "Titoists" and American intelligence through Noel Field. The most innocent personal relationships were thus turned into conspiratorial acts. When several ex-"Spaniards" including Pavel, London, and Zavodský dined in Prague with Luigi Longo, the Italian Communist leader who had served as the Inspector General of the International Brigades, trial "evidence" made it appear as a "Titoist" plot action. Jewish defendants willingly connected the "antistate conspiracy" with "Zionism," implicating themselves and each other. The advantage of this system of cross-accusations was that nobody could deny in open court a signed "confession" without being immediately faced with the testimony of his codefendants. In the end, the whole thing became nightmarishly plausible in this weird world of beautifully meshing "confessions."

On November 27, 1952, the seventh and last day of the great show trial at Pankrac prison, Chief Prosecutor Josef Úrvalek was thus able to proclaim triumphantly in his summation that "Czechoslovakia will not be a new Yugoslavia" after fourteen defendants and thirty-three witnesses—all of them perfectly coached and rehearsed by the security "referents"—had "confessed" all the crimes of which they had been accused. (For reasons known only to the prosecutors, the hundreds of principal prisoners were divided in various groups for separate trials, though it was not quite clear what criteria were being applied. But the chief trial was that of Rudolf Slánský and his thirteen codefendants—twelve of the fourteen were Jews.) As London, one of the fourteen, was to write later, there had not been a single "false note," so superbly had the actors and *mise en scène* been prepared. Perhaps the most Kafkaesque feature of these proceedings was that the condemned men sought out their "referents" in court to find approval for their behavior, as anxious children will do with exacting parents or teachers.

That same day the sentences were handed down, after all had been duly found guilty. Eleven of the accused were condemned to death and three to life imprisonment. Sentenced to die were Slánský; Clementis; Bedrich Geminder, former chief of the Central Committee's International Relations Section; Ludvík Frejka, former head of the economic section of the Presidency; Josef Frank, former Deputy General Secretary of the Party; General Bedrich Reicin, former Deputy Minister of Defense; Karel Švab, former Deputy Minister of State Security; Rudolf Margolius, former Deputy Minister of Foreign Trade; Otto Fischl, former Deputy Minister of Finance; Otto Šling; and André Simone, ex-editor of *Rudé Právo*.

Sentenced to life in prison were London; Vavro Hajdu, former Deputy Foreign Minister; and former Deputy Minister of Foreign Trade Evžen Löbl, who had been arrested two years earlier.

The trial, as Prosecutor Úrvalek said, meant the destruction in Czechoslovakia of the same "band of traitors" as that of "László Rajk in Hungary . . . Traicho Kostov in Bulgaria . . . Koçi Xoxe in Albania . . . Pătrăşcanu in Romania . . . Gomułka in Poland." Put in those terms, their crimes ruled out any clemency; consequently President Gottwald turned down the appeals. All those sentenced to death except Slánský wrote to Gottwald before being hanged on December 3, to declare their innocence and to tell him that they had "confessed" only "in the interest of the Party and socialism."

The epilogue to the Slánský trial seemed awesomely to benefit the treatment the defendants had received from "socialist justice." It was narrated in the liberal Prague weekly *Reportér* in 1968:

> When the eleven condemned had been executed, Referent D. found himself, by chance, at the Ruzyň with the [Soviet] adviser Galkin. Present at the meeting were the driver and the two referents who had been charged with the disposal of the ashes. They announced that they had placed them inside a potato sack and that they left for the vicinity of Prague with the intention of spreading the ashes in the fields. Noticing the ice-covered pavement, they then had the idea of spreading the ashes over it. The driver laughed as he told that it had never before happened to him to be transporting fourteen persons at the same time in his Tatra, the three living and the eleven contained in the sack.

The liquidation of the Slánský group in December 1952 left at least sixty persons to be tried in connection with the Center of Conspiracy Against the State, and uncounted thousands arrested on more or less vague grounds. Many of them had been in prison for as long as three years awaiting trial or release, and now the regime faced the problem of disposing of all these cases. The responsibility was handed to Karol Bacílek, the Slovak Communist of the "inner circle" who served briefly as Minister of State Control, a newly created post, and, in June 1952, replaced Kopřiva as Minister of State Security. In February 1953 he also became Deputy Premier. It was during his tenure as Czechoslovakia's chief policeman that thirty-five of his fellow Slovaks—a group of the 1944 Communist partisans headed by Commander Viliam Zingor—were sentenced by a Bratislava court in 1951 to a total of 230 years in prison for "treason" and "antistate activities."

Now an event took place in Moscow that was destined to reshape the history of Communism, set in motion new rivalries and power struggles, and, at the same time, release a powerful stream of hope in both the Soviet Union and Eastern Europe that despotism might finally dissolve and something resembling freedom might begin to flower. This was the death, at the age of seventy-three, of Josef V. Stalin on the night of March 5, 1953. He died less than two months after suffering a "hemorrhage of the brain" and losing consciousness and the power of speech.

But in Czechoslovakia, Bacílek went to work on the pending cases though Stalin had already died, and Gottwald followed him to the grave three weeks later, after returning from the Moscow funeral of his mentor. Indeed, despite the execution of Beria following Stalin's death and the sudden "thaw" in the Soviet Union that brought thousands of prisoners streaming back from Siberian prisons, the night of terror went on in Czechoslovakia. The reshuffled Prague leadership was as Stalinist as ever, with power now resting in the hands of Antonín Zápotocký, Gottwald's successor as President; Široký, still Premier; Antonín Novotný, who had replaced Slánský as the General Secretary; Defense Minister Čepička; Deputy Premier and security boss Bacílek; Deputy Premier Dolanský; and the propaganda chief Kopecký. It was a close-knit clique forming the Party's Politburo, and it was not about to halt the purges simply because Stalin had died. The country remained hermetically sealed off from Western cultural influences, playing jazz was a criminal offense, and an American diplomat who was a first-rate clarinetist bootlegged jazz to young Czechs at risky secret jam sessions.

Presently, Bacílek devised the idea of dividing the top prisoners into seven groups for the purpose of separate trials: economists, Trotskyites, Slovak "bourgeois nationalists," security officials, Army officers, diplomats, and a catchall contingent including Smrkovský and Vilém Nový.

The Politburo approved Bacílek's plan, and the trial machinery was reactivated.

First to be tried were the diplomats, whose cases came up in May 1953. Those sentenced included Goldstücker (to life imprisonment) and Dufek. In all, 350 members of the Foreign Service were fired or imprisoned. Later, in the security group, Josef Pavel was condemned to twenty-five years in prison for being a "Western agent." He is believed to have been the most atrociously tortured man in the history of the Czechoslovak purges. His colleague Valeš got twenty-two years.

Among the uniformed officers, Smrkovský received eight years. General Drgač, fired from the General Staff when Svoboda was dismissed as Defense Minister in 1950, was sentenced in the late spring. Svoboda himself had been in prison since 1951 after the falsified "Stalin telegram," but was never actually tried. Hromadko and Antonín Svoboda, the liaison men between the Army and the Party, received twelve and fifteen years respectively.

Partly because of the fears and tensions generated by the purges and partly in protest against the currency reform that forced the Czechoslovaks to exchange their money at the rate of fifty old crowns for one new crown, a workers' rebellion suddenly exploded in Plzeň on June 1, 1953. An industrial town in western Bohemia, Plzeň is the site of the big Skoda automotive works and the home of the ancient breweries that have made Pilsen beer world famous. But Plzeň had also been liberated by American troops in May 1945 and its people were more Western-oriented than most Czechoslovaks.

In what was the first open defiance of a Communist regime in Eastern Europe since the end of the war, hundreds of Skoda workers broke out of the plant on that Monday morning, ramming the gate with a heavy truck, and presently became engaged in a running battle with the plant's People's Militia units. An eyewitness reported that a militiaman shot a woman worker, and the enraged crowd trampled him to death. From the plant, some five thousand workers marched on the City Hall to protest the currency reform, chanting, "We won't take this robbery!"

At the City Hall, Plzeň's mayor, Josef Mainzer, came to a window to pacify the crowd, but the mood was now growing ugly. "Comrade Workers," he told them, "you have a workingman for President. . . . You have a government in favor of labor and the workers. Everything we do is in the interest of the workers." But the crowd was growing impatient.

Shouts of *"Fuj! Hanba!"* (Phooey! Shame!) erupted. Then they took up the chant of, "We want a new government. . . . We want free elections!" Presently, rocks and stones began flying against the building and the workers sang the Czechoslovak anthem. Windows were smashed, and workers began climbing through them into the hall. One worker grabbed the microphone through which Mainzer had spoken. "We want free elections!" he shouted. "Finally we've rid ourselves of this villainous band of Communists!" The crowd below, responding, chanted again, "We want free elections!" Meanwhile, the workers inside the building started tossing busts of Stalin, Malenkov, Gottwald, and Zápotocký out of the windows. They threw out a Soviet flag and documents of various sorts. The crowd set them on fire. The fever of success overtook the crowd. "We have overthrown the government!" the men said. "Freedom is back!" In that odd way in which rumors are believed and accepted as facts, the workers told each other that similar demonstrations had broken out in Prague and in Slovakia. Then, a man took the microphone to say that Plzeň needed help.

It did, indeed, because Plzeň was an isolated situation. Two trucks arrived in the square carrying Army troops with bayonets on their rifles. Carloads of secret police followed them. But the security forces were not prepared to face the crowd and they remained passive. The crowd decided to march on the Plzeň prison to liberate the prisoners. They ransacked the courthouse, again hurling Stalin and Gottwald busts out of the windows and burning records. A police car was captured and a large American flag was flown from it. Applause broke out. A column of workers marched to where there had been a memorial monument to American dead in Plzeň's liberation. Another group made its way to the site of the now long-removed statue of Tomáš Masaryk. A sign there proclaiming LONG LIVE THE SOVIET UNION was burned. At the City Hall square, someone produced a large portrait of Beneš and it was placed in one of the City Hall's windows.

At noontime the crowd began to disperse. Many demonstrators went home to eat. In their absence, units of the border guard took over the square, and soldiers sealed it off, standing shoulder to shoulder in two rows. But in the afternoon, the crowd reassembled. When the workers from the Skoda afternoon shift joined the ranks of the demonstrators, there was jostling and fighting with the troops. A worker hit a policeman with a briefcase filled with rocks. A fire truck came on the scene, connected its hoses to the hydrants on the square, and proceeded to hose the crowd. A worker produced a sharp knife and sliced the hoses. There was a brief standoff between the demonstrators and the border guards and police. Then Army troops from Prague began converging on the square—infantry trucks, motorcycles, tanks, and artillery. A tank wheeled around and lowered its cannon to face the crowd. The mass of demonstrators began to ebb away because, as an eyewitness remarked, "You cannot fight a tank with bare hands." Plainclothesmen started arresting people. By early evening the square was empty except for the troops, who settled down for an occupation that was to last a week.

The next day agents of the state security police fanned out over Plzeň to check the plants and shops for the names of the workers who had not reported to work on Monday and were, presumably, among the rioters. Those who could not explain their absence were summarily fired. For a week troops and militia units patrolled the city. In the countryside surrounding Plzeň additional military contingents were kept in readiness to move into town if necessary. Then arrests began. The STB rounded up enough of the June 1 demonstrators to fill all the Plzeň prisons and jails.

It was the end of the June rebellion, but the ripples that Stalin's death had produced in the heretofore still waters of the Communist empire went on widening. A week after, another uprising occurred in the Soviet bloc.

On June 13 the youth of East Berlin rose against the Russians and for one glorious day fought Soviet tanks with rocks and Molotov cocktails. It was the second sign of stirring in the Soviet monolith, but in Czechoslovakia, where Plzeň had been the first sign, it inevitably produced a further hardening and more terror.

In September Bacílek resigned as Minister of State Security—the ministry itself was abolished—and went to Slovakia to take over the leadership of the Slovak Party from Široký, who preferred to concentrate on the Premiership. Police duties were taken over by the new Interior Minister, Rudolf Barák, a fast-rising young Communist. At this point the purge machinery was still running on its own momentum, and as late as March 1954 Osvald Zavodský was executed after President Zápotocký refused to commute his sentence.

Bacílek's arrival in Slovakia sped up the trials of the "bourgeois nationalists," and the star of these proceedings was Gustav Husák who had already spent nearly three years in prison. His long-awaited day in court in April 1954, however, brought him a life sentence. Laco Holdoš, once the State Secretary of Culture, received thirteen years, and the poet

Novomeský ten years. The Slovak Party's Central Committee, on which Alexander Dubček had now served for three years, presumably approved of these sentences. There is no exact count of Slovaks imprisoned or sentenced, but between February 1968 and February 1969 Slovak courts received 2013 applications for rehabilitation of purge victims.

The thousands of condemned men and women were presently parceled out among the high-security prisons—Pankrac and Ruzyň in Prague and Leopoldov in Bratislava—and scores of mines and state farms where they were kept at hard labor. Hundreds upon hundreds found themselves working in the Jachimov and Příbram uranium mines, which were the nearest thing in terms of harsh punishment to what the Soviets had to offer in Siberia. Curiously, the Czechoslovaks went to these mines and camps with total hopelessness, just when Soviet prisoners, excited by the winds of hope that Stalin's death had brought to their country, began rioting in the concentration camps of Vorkuta. In Czechoslovakia, another year was to elapse before her citizens could feel the first breezes heralding the approach of the dawn.

VII

Winter Stays On
in Czechoslovakia

The de-Stalinization movement began to roll across the Communist world almost immediately after the old dictator's death, gaining greater and greater momentum in 1954 and 1955. Already on April 3, 1953, Beria announced that the Jewish "Doctors' Plot" had been a frame-up. Stalin had removed Beria from the Ministry of State Security in November 1951 and replaced him with S. D. Ignatiev, but now Beria was a deputy premier, again in charge of security, and he proceeded to carry out his private vengeances. On April 7 he ordered the arrest of Mikhail Ryumin, who had served as Ignatiev's right-hand man, and had him executed for "fabricating" the doctors' affair. This particular execution was quite pertinent to Czechoslovakia, because Ryumin, as Deputy State Security Minister, was also directly in charge of the preparations for the Slánský trial and of all other police work in Czechoslovakia.

The next stage in the de-Stalinization process—and in the simultaneous Moscow power struggle—was Beria's own arrest on June 26, 1953, under pressure from Nikita S. Khrushchev, the Ukrainian leader who was emerging as the new boss of Soviet politics. Beria was shot during a Soviet Party Presidium meeting—probably on December 1, 1953, according to the version Khrushchev gave to the French Socialist Senator Pierre Commin. In the ensuing months, numerous members of what became known as "Beria's gang" were likewise executed, including Beria's onetime deputy Viktor S. Abakoumov and the two men who had planned and conducted the Rajk trial and the purges in Czechoslovakia, General Likhachev and his aide Makarov.

Quite clearly, the Kremlin—and Khrushchev, who formally became the Soviet Party's First Secretary in September 1953—was striving to free itself as best it could of Stalin's heritage and, among other things, getting ready to reverse itself on the question of the "Titoist conspiracy" and its bloody consequences. With this changing policy in Moscow and the liquidation of the MGB men responsible for the anti-"Titoist" operation, the Hungarian government late in 1954 cleared Noel Field of all the charges upon which the Rajk trial had been based and set him free after five years in prison. (Field had been arrested by Czechoslovak security agents under MGB guidance and turned over to the Hungarians.) The Polish authorities, who for years denied any knowledge of the whereabouts of Herman Field, Noel's brother, suddenly released him from a Warsaw prison. The "Titoist" fantasy was thus coming apart.

But the Czechoslovakian regime—always out of step with broader Communist trends, good and bad alike—plodded ahead along its Stalinist course, oblivious of reality and ignorant of history. Novotný, Zápotocký, and their colleagues were conspicuously insensitive to the winds of change. A posthumous personality cult still surrounded Gottwald, though *Rudé Právo* no longer monotonously praised Stalin along with him. Lip service to the new Soviet concept of "collective leadership" was as far as the Prague bosses would go. On April 24, 1953, the Prague government approved a new Education Act drafted, it said proudly, with the "direct help of Soviet experts" and designed for the "education of a new generation of proud and courageous builders of socialist society." Throughout the year, the Czechoslovak apparatus went on with its purges and trials, continuing them well into 1954, with the execution of former security chief Zavodský and the sentencing of Gustav Husák to life imprisonment.

In November 1954 President Zápotocký and Party chief Novotný proudly unveiled the huge bronze statue of Stalin atop Letná Hill, looking down at Prague and the Vltava River. This was twenty months after Stalin died, and Zápotocký and Novotný obviously were not too closely attuned to Khrushchev's thinking if this gesture was designed to win them favor with the new Soviet leaders. The only thing Novotný had done to fit into the new state of affairs was to confer upon himself the title of the Party's First Secretary in September 1953, after Khrushchev had gained the same title in the Soviet Party. But, then, Novotný was to pay one day with his political life for his stubborn inability to comprehend history.

Having destroyed most of the old Party apparatus through executions and imprisonments, Zápotocký and Novotný busied themselves bringing up a new generation of loyal followers, men who someday were to fill their shoes. With Husák, Smrkovský, Pavel, and so many other once famous Communist chieftains safely put away in the prisons, the way to advancement was speedier than ever before. All that was required was an unquestioning dedication to the Party line and the instinct of a good *apparatchik*. And among the promising new men thus making their way up the Party ladder were the young Slovak Alexander Dubček, and the Czech Oldřich Černik, one month his senior. In 1953 Dubček, already on the Slovak Party's Central Committee, was named Leading Secretary of the Party Regional Committee of Banská Bystrica, one of the principal towns of Slovakia. A year earlier Černik, was chosen Regional Secretary of Ostrava, the big steel and coal mining city of northern Moravia. This was an exalted post for a man so young, and an official biography remarked that "his political reliability, even at this early stage, can be regarded as solid in view of the fact that he participated in the purging of non-Party elements as a member of the Action Committee of the National Front organization" in 1948. This was generous praise, considering that in 1948 Černik was only twenty-six years old and a Party member for less than three years.

About the time Dubček was scaling another rung on the Party ladder, General Svoboda was secretly released from prison: the only known instance of Stalin's ordering redress of an injustice and the Prague leadership's dragging its feet in carrying it out. The details of Svoboda's imprisonment, even its precise duration, remain unclear to this day, as the elderly President is still loathe to discuss it and no record is available. But in an interview with a Prague newspaper in March 1968 Svoboda gave this amazing version of his release from what was roughly a little more than a year in prison, following the falsified telegram from Moscow that "Stalin doesn't trust Svoboda":

While they had me locked up and I sat in Ruzyň, on November 23, 1952, I believe it was, at our embassy in Moscow a reception took place in honor of Comrade Gottwald. My son-in-law was a secretary in the embassy, and my daughter studied in Moscow at that time. And, as happens at receptions and celebrations, toasts were drunk to all sorts of things and a high officer of the Soviet army, General Kozlovski, suddenly lifted his glass and said, "I drink to the health of General Svoboda." Our people at the embassy knew the truth concerning me, that I had been in jail for quite some time already, and therefore there was silence after the toast. Then, when someone rose in this silence and explained my situation as it really was, Kozlovski told my daughter to call home to Prague and tell my wife that the Soviets trust me and that Svoboda is innocent. And a real telegram by Stalin was sent to Prague: "Please set General Svoboda free." I found out about this discussion in Moscow while I was in prison. And you can imagine how I felt, even as a prisoner, when my wife told me that my Soviet comrades trusted me.

But if you think my getting out of prison was easy, then you're wrong. Karol Bacílek came to visit me in prison and passed on to me greetings from Gottwald, telling me that my imprisonment was more or less of a mistake. So I asked Bacílek, "Why am I sitting here?" "We are afraid that you will escape or that you will commit suicide," was his response.

Understandably, I didn't like these excuses, so I spoke quite directly and said that if I were in any way guilty then Bacílek, Zápotocký, and also Gottwald would be sitting here with me too.

Bacílek then asked me about six questions, wanting to know how and with whom I had worked, and then he went away. About a week later they let me out of Ruzyň. So actually, Stalin, who as you know wasn't in any way softhearted, indirectly saved my life. I must say that their behavior toward me in prison was quite decent.

Despite his release, Svoboda's full rehabilitation "still took a long time." The journalist who interviewed him commented, "After the General was released from prison, he still remained a person from whom it was politically safe to keep at a distance. . . . He looked for a job and started working in a collective farm."

Svoboda's job was that of a bookkeeper at an agricultural cooperative at Trebic. He might have spent the rest of his life there if Khrushchev, visiting Prague for the Tenth Congress of the KSČ in June 1954, had not inquired about him. They had known each other on the Ukrainian front during the war, and now Khrushchev wanted to see the General. The embarrassed Czechoslovak leaders immediately brought him back from Trebic, where he had been for over a year, and, as the Prague journalist remarked, this "helped to make the General a human again, so that he got his rights."

Still, the Prague leaders were uneasy about producing Svoboda publicly. Shortly after the Party Congress, Novotný told him, "You will talk at the Dukla memorial, but we're not going to publicize the fact that you have been rehabilitated." Novotný, who evidently resented the Soviet pressure on Svoboda's behalf, angrily refused to give him a post in the government, saying, "He will only make complications." The Party seemed to abhor the idea of releasing, rehabilitating, and restoring to power its victims—even though this process was now occurring in much of Eastern Europe—and, as a compromise, it finally agreed to let Svoboda be "elected" to the National Assembly in October 1954. Two months later, however, the General was raised to the Assembly's Presidium.

Entering the Assembly, he found that its chairman for over a year was Zdeněk Fierlinger, who had thus finally been rewarded for his 1945–1948 services to the Party. (In 1954 Fierlinger was given the additional and vastly more important position of a Politburo member.) This was the second time that Svoboda's and Fierlinger's paths crossed—the first was when the General served as Defense Minister in Fierlinger's 1945 coalition government—and there still was to be a third time, in 1968, in circumstances of nightmarish drama.

Svoboda's release in 1953 was a fluke and an exception, but with the passage of time even the most obdurate Party opposition to a fresh look at the trials had to crack. Soviet MGB advisers had left Czechoslovakia by May 1954, and, in a sense, the KSČ was on its own.

In October, for example, Artur London was visited at the Leopoldov prison by an anonymous military prosecutor who asked him questions about Josef Pavel's case. This was the first recorded instance of doubts arising in any segment of the Prague establishment. London told the prosecutor not only that the accusations against Pavel had been fabricated, but that this applied to all the trials including his own. The officer, London recalls in his book, turned "pale" and promised to report the conversation to his superiors. Yet a long silence followed. The road back was to be long and slow.

Early in 1955, however, an important step was taken in the direction of relaxing police terror in Czechoslovakia and finding some way out of the increasingly embarrassing situation in which tens of thousands of citizens were kept in the Republic's prisons and jails. This was the creation of a special Commission on Socialist Legality in the Central Committee. The commission was headed by Květoslav Ineman, forty-five, a controversial veteran Party member who had spent the war in Nazi concentration camps and later served as a department head in the Central Committee of the Party's Prague organization and whose political career was to take bizarre turns in later years.

Ineman apparently ran his four-man commission under the direct control of Interior Minister Barák. There are reasons to believe that Barák —elevated at the June 1954 Party Congress to full membership in the Politburo ahead of older and better established leaders—was the moving spirit behind the investigation, which marked the start of the first serious effort to review the purge trials of 1951–1954, and that Zápotocký and Novotný accepted it with the greatest reluctance. Whether Barák was a budding progressive or just a realist is a matter of conjecture. With a few notable and honorable exceptions, the political allegiances and viewpoints of Czechoslovak Communists have fluctuated so wildly over the years that fair and precise historical judgments are virtually impossible. Seeming evolution has so often been followed by regression (and vice versa) that even if one resists the temptation to apply the epithet of opportunism it is rarely possible to think of most of these careers in terms of a logical or linear maturation process.

In the specific case of Barák, which later was to acquire considerable importance, it may appear surprising that at this particular juncture of events the Party's hard-line leadership had vested such power in a man of his presumed inclinations. On the one hand, it may be argued that the perplexed leadership needed a front man of Barák's type. But, on the other hand, subsequent events demonstrated that Novotný was not the world's best judge of human nature and something less than a master at the game of politics. Yet, the speed with which the situation was changing in the Communist world left the Prague leadership with fewer and fewer options. With the Hungarian regime fully rehabilitating Rajk in the spring of 1955 and Khrushchev traveling to Belgrade to make peace with Tito, Czechoslovakia's insistence on keeping thousands of men in prison on "Titoist" charges was becoming untenable, if not downright absurd.

The role of Květoslav Ineman is even more controversial than Barák's. London was visited by Ineman and his commission at the prison in May 1955 to be questioned on the background of the Pavel and Oskar Valeš cases—it was the first follow-up on the military prosecutor's inquiries about Pavel seven months earlier—and his impression was definitely favorable. Ineman told him that his own case could not yet be touched because he had been tried with the Slánský group, but on this and subsequent visits he appeared to be genuinely concerned with uncovering whatever evidence might point to the illegality of the trials. He frequently warned London and others to beware of the State Security Service on the grounds that it would fight to the bitter end to prevent the exposure of the "evidence" it had fabricated. Other versions, however, portray Ineman as a secret informer of Novotný and a man bent on obstructing the rehabilitation of the purge victims. Between 1960 and 1968 Ineman was the director of a state publishing house, a job he lost with the coming of the Prague Spring. After the Soviet invasion, he turned into a rabid pro-Soviet conservative and became associated with the most extreme reactionary hard core of the Party. In 1969, with Dubček already ousted, he bitterly denounced in *Rudé Právo* the Communist progressive journalists. It may be that as a cog in the great Party machine hardly noticed by history, he rejected the injustices of the 1950s but could not divorce himself from the Communist orthodoxy that had filled most of his adult life.

Be that as it may, the pressures building up in 1955 around the top leaders and, presumably, the influence of Barák, Ineman, and others were increasingly felt. In mid-1955 Major Doubek and Captain Kohoutek, the two key "referents" of Ruzyň prison and the architects of much of the "evidence" used in the purge trials, were arrested and sent to prison. Some months earlier their former MGB bosses had been executed.

In the prisons, the treatment of the inmates improved almost miraculously. Jindra Kotal, a Deputy Minister of Interior in charge of prisons and himself a former prisoner in a Nazi concentration camp, made a point of visiting Leopoldov in the summer of 1955 to check on the conditions. Among those he found there were Pavel, Valeš, Löbl, London, Hajdu, Goldstücker, Holdoš, Hromadko, and Antonín Svoboda. He inquired about their needs, offered them better cells, and, as London tells it, volunteered to send books to read.

Already in late 1954 London had been allowed on several occasions to be visited by his wife, who no longer thought him guilty of "betraying" the Party, and he had smuggled out through her his account of the 1952 events, written on small sheets of paper. Mrs. London used this information to badger the more and more friendly high Party officials to review her husband's trial. In October 1955 London, who suffered from a lung ailment, was transferred to a sanatorium at Pleš. The Party insisted that it be kept secret, but, clearly, his rehabilitation was being actively prepared.

A month later, Smrkovský, Pavel, Valeš, and several others were released after Party investigators had found that they had been framed. They had been in prison for four years. On February 2, 1956, London was officially cleared—the first defendant in the Slánský trial to be so rehabilitated—and given back his freedom. He had been in prison almost exactly five years. Only a year earlier, Captain Kohoutek had told him that no matter what happened, he must always remain faithful to his trial "confession" because "you must not forget that you have been condemned for the crime of high treason and you must enter the skin of your new personality." Now he was free and Kohoutek was in prison in one of those amazing reversals of Communist justice. But other men—Husák and Löbl among them—still faced long periods of imprisonment, for the Party's wheels turned slowly when it came to the redress of injustice. And, as Tito remarked in a speech in July 1955—after his armistice with Khrushchev—the Czechoslovak Communist Party was finding it difficult to admit its mistakes publicly because "the dead cannot be resuscitated."

Late in 1955 Alexander Dubček, the loyal and promising *apparatchik*, received a leave of absence from the Slovak Party's Central Committee and his Banská Bystrica secretaryship to go to Moscow to attend the CPSU's Superior Political School—a special mark of distinction. A protégé of the Kremlin, he was to remain there for three years while crucial events were rocking Czechoslovakia and the rest of the Communist world.

VIII

Risings to the North and South

The scientific theory of history favored by Marxist-Leninists excludes by definition the precise diagnosis of how and when a revolt fed by emotions may spring from the hearts and minds of men. Such a revolt is not calculable in coefficients of determinism, cyclical projections of economic trends, or dialectical analyses. It is, therefore, impossible and, indeed, unnecessary to say with any degree of precision just how and when the great revolt of 1956 burst forth in Eastern Europe.

What is certain, however, is that this revolt was born from the youth and inspired by the poets, the writers, the journalists, the artists, and the philosophers—just the kind of people whom the Communist orthodoxy could neither understand, regiment, nor accept. During Stalin's lifetime, the emotions and the ideas existed but were stifled and repressed by the prevailing terror and the sense of hopelessness that went with it. Zhdanov in the Soviet Union, Kopecký and Ladislav Stoll in Czechoslovakia, and Jakub Berman in Poland controlled and perverted all the channels of cultural expression, dictating and imposing their grotesquely mediocre standards of "socialist" taste. Stalin's death thus became a milestone and a symbol of the hope that free thought and creativity might begin to return. This hope was a thing of instinct rather than of knowledge, and it spread slowly but irreversibly over Eastern Europe, turning finally into a fearsome revolutionary force.

On June 1, 1953, as we have seen, Czech workers held their first anti-government manifestation in Plzeň. On June 13 the youth of East Berlin lived a day of glory fighting the Soviet tanks. Their act of defiance was

promptly quelled, and it took more than two years, while political controls were being gradually relaxed, before thinkers and writers and artists
could take stock of their positions and relate the weapons of their creative
talent to political action. But they were not acting in a vacuum or without
tradition. In Eastern Europe the poets, who can be both artists and philosophers, have always been revolutionaries. The Revolution of 1848,
the romantic "Spring of the Peoples," could not have exploded without
them against the rule of the Triple Alliance. Adam Mickiewicz in Poland,
Jan Neruda in Bohemia, and Bolintineanu in Romania were bards of
freedom against oppression, just as Pushkin was in Russia. And so in
1956 Poland had the middle-aged Adam Ważyk, a Communist, and the
aging Antoni Słonimski, not a Communist, to start the wheels going
round; in Czechoslovakia there were Jaroslav Seifert and František
Hrubín, both Communists. In the Soviet Union itself they had their kinship with Yevgeny Yevtushenko and Andrei Voznesensky.

If a date is needed to record the moment the East European intellectual
revolt began in earnest, then August 21, 1955, is probably it—the day the
Warsaw literary weekly *Nowa Kultura* published the lengthy and bitter
epic "Poem for Adults" by Ważyk. Ważyk had devoted most of his adult
life to becoming the nearest thing to Poland's Stalinist poet laureate. Suddenly, this was what he had to say of his country under Communism:

> The great migration builds a new industry,
> Unknown to Poland but known to history.
> It is fed on empty words,
> Living wildly from day to day despite the word of preachers,
> In poisonous coal gas, in slow torture
> A working class is smelted from the migrants.
> Much is wasted. And thus far, there is only dross. . . .
>
> When the vulture of abstraction picks out our brains,
> When students are locked up in textbooks without windows,
> When language is reduced to thirty incantations,
> When the lamp of imagination is extinguished,
> When the good people from the moon deny us the right to our taste,
> Then truly oblivion is dangerously near.
> Have I lost the gift of seeing, or the gift of convenient blindness?
> I am left with but a short note, with these verses of new sorrow. . . .
>
> They ran to us shouting:
> A Communist never dies.
> It never happened that a man did not die.
> Only the memory abides.

The worthier the man, the greater the pain.
They ran to us shouting:
Under Socialism a cut finger does not hurt.
They cut their finger.
They felt pain.
They lost their faith. . . .

We ask for this on earth:
For people who work hard,
For keys to open doors,
For rooms with windows,
For walls without parasitic rot,
For a hatred of little documents,
For holy human time,
For safe homecoming,
For a simple distinction between words and deeds.
We ask for this, for the earth we know
And did not win in a dice game, for which a million perished in battle:
For a clear truth,
For the bread of freedom,
For ardent reason.
We demand this every day.
We demand through the Party.

This declaration of war against the system and the establishment was not lost on Jakub Berman, the man who incongruously combined the functions of czar of Polish culture and head of the Polish secret police. Berman instantly fired Paweł Hoffman, editor of *Nowa Kultura*, and summoned a special session of the Polish Writers' Association to expel Ważyk so that in the future he could be kept out of public print.

But for the first time since Gomułka refused to be expelled from his post of First Secretary of the Party in 1948, the Polish Communist establishment had an open fight on its hands. The Association declined to fire Ważyk from membership. Hoffman, an old-line Communist warhorse, took the floor to say, "Comrade Berman is usurping the right to judge what is good and what is bad in literature, what serves the Party and what is anti-Party. But there are many writers and critics here who know more about literature than he does, and there are also many comrades who have worked longer and with no worse results for the Party than he."

What Ważyk had written in his "Poem for Adults" and what Hoffman had said in its defense represented a basic challenge posed by Communists who had suddenly developed a sense of intellectual independence. It was a challenge against the monopoly of ideas and policies always held by the Party apparatus and a defiance of Party discipline. And it was the kind of challenge that was to haunt East European Communist establishments in the years to come. As a potent explosive charge planted within the system, the Polish intellectual thrust was infinitely more dangerous to Moscow than Tito's "national Communism." In a real sense, then, Ważyk's plea for "a clear truth . . . the bread of freedom . . . ardent reason" was inevitably answered by Soviet tanks in Budapest's Csepel Island and the rest of the city in 1956 and on Prague's Václavské Náměstí on August 21, 1968. The devastating point was clear: that Communist orthodoxy must pit machine gunners against poets and tanks against ideas. It might have given Ważyk a feeling of historical achievement had he known that one of the first objectives of the Soviet tanks when they occupied Prague would be to surround the building housing the Czechoslovak Writers' Union. He was truly the spiritual godfather of the Prague Spring.

In Warsaw Ważyk and his allies succeeded in winning the first round in their battle with the Party during the summer and fall of 1955. The regime, beset by economic troubles and perplexed by the de-Stalinization process in the Soviet Union and elsewhere, chose not to press for a new showdown with the intellectuals. Instead, it tried to roll with the punch and for a while allowed Polish journalists a measure of press freedom they had never experienced. University students were permitted to develop the weekly *Po Prostu* into a crusading liberal publication, and it overnight soared to fame and excited prominence. Newspapers and periodicals followed suit, not to be left behind, and, suddenly, a delicious sense that Poland had an almost free press spread throughout the country. And the revolt, once under way, did not halt there. Long-silent playwrights, novelists, and film makers gave forth with their creations. But, as was to happen in Czechoslovakia, time was needed for the rest of the population to emerge from the long, lethargic night and, above all, to believe that there were "good" Communists alongside the "bad" ones it knew so well. The process never reached fruition in Poland because other events occurred elsewhere and no coherent political leadership emerged from the Party's progressive ranks to capitalize on the rebellion. Yet, the road that led to Prague began in Warsaw.

Quite unexpectedly, the next blow for Communist liberalization or at least the appearance of such a blow was struck in Moscow.

Its author was Nikita Khrushchev, and his instrument for demolishing the memory and the cult of Stalin—and much that the Soviet Communist apparatus had represented under him for more than a quarter of a century—was a famous secret speech on the night of February 24-25, 1956, before 1436 delegates attending the Twentieth Congress of the Soviet Communist Party.

For reasons that may have ranged from a desire to consolidate his own position once and for all in the savage environment of Soviet politics to a realization that to survive in a complex and changing world Soviet Communism must cleanse and rejuvenate itself, the sixty-two-year-old Khrushchev delivered so complete an indictment of Stalin and his practices that the Communist movement could never be the same again, denouncing him for his "mass repressions," his "persecution mania," his "despotism," the murders of his closest associates, fabricated purges and trials that cost hundreds of thousands of lives, an obsession with his own "personality cult," the creation of the legend of his wartime "military genius" when in reality he was a coward who nearly lost the war for the Soviet Union, his disastrous break with Tito, and a catalogue of other crimes, malpractices, and errors so long that it took Khrushchev from midnight to dawn to recite them.

In offering his conclusions, Khrushchev set a tone which even his own expulsion from leadership and a gradual return to Stalinism under his successor could not eradicate: "We must abolish the cult of the individual decisively, once and for all . . . condemn and eradicate the cult of the individual as alien to Marxism-Leninism and not consonant with the principles of Party leadership and the norms of Party life, and fight inexorably all attempts at bringing back this practice in one form or another."

The Communist Party, he said, "must restore completely the Leninist principles of Soviet socialist democracy . . . fight the arbitrariness of individuals abusing their power. The evil caused by acts violating revolutionary socialist legality which have accumulated during a long time as a result of the negative influence of the cult of the individual has to be completely corrected."

The thirty-thousand-word secret speech, supported by thirty pieces of documentary evidence culled from secret Party archives, was the most dramatic and important event in postwar Communist history. It rocked the Soviet Communists and, within days, began sending shock waves through every Communist party in the world. After Khrushchev's denunciation of Stalin's crimes and the "evils" perpetrated against "socialist legality," and his proclamation of "different roads to socialism," there could be no return to the old Communist methods, even if the very effect of the secret speech was to create situations throughout Eastern Europe that later induced Stalinist relapses. The impact of Khrushchev's speech was to survive both his own power interventions in Poland and Hungary and the 1968 invasion of Czechoslovakia. It was striking to hear the liberals of the Prague Spring use words almost identical to Khrushchev's to justify *their* rebellion against violations of "socialist legality," and the Soviet invasion could be regarded as rejection of the Khrushchev doctrine. Yet Brezhnev's ultimate acceptance of the compromise of "unity within diversity" in June 1969 at the world conference of Communist parties was a recognition of the character of Communism as Khrushchev had defined and predicted it during that dramatic February night in 1956.

It is improbable, entreaties to the delegates to the Twentieth Congress notwithstanding, that Khrushchev really expected his secret speech to remain secret for long. A secret cannot be kept by 1436 persons and, significantly, Khrushchev himself ordered a version of his text prepared "for the use of foreign Communists." In short order, most of the foreign Communist parties received the speech to be communicated to their members at closed meetings. Under the circumstances, it was inevitable that the document would fall into non-Communist hands in the West and, indeed, the Central Intelligence Agency obtained it from sources within an East European Communist Party. On June 4, 1956, the United States Department of State published it in English for the whole world to see.

The secret speech was precisely the inspiration that Communists and non-Communists in Eastern Europe needed to press their demands for a measure of justice, freedom, "different roads to socialism," and decent management of national affairs. In Czechoslovakia, as elsewhere, it was an invitation to action. In Prague as in Warsaw and Budapest, the newspapers did not publish it for obvious reasons, but Western radio stations, leaks from Party organizations where it was being discussed, and word-of-mouth description made it widely known to all those who cared.

Needless to say, men like Novotný and his colleagues hardly welcomed it. Not only had Khrushchev denounced Stalin and, through the exorcism of his ghost, attempts to perpetuate Stalinism in Czechoslovakia, but he had openly undermined the anti-Titoist campaign which since 1951 had been the political foundation of the present leadership. Novotný himself had risen to the top Party post partly because of what was officially described as his "crucial" role in "unmasking" the Slánský "conspiracy."

And now Khrushchev had spelled out at the Twentieth Congress the fallacy of the whole anti-Titoist policy:

The willfulness of Stalin showed itself not only in decisions concerning the internal life of the country but also in the international relations of the Soviet Union.

The July Plenum of the Central Committee studied in detail the reasons for the development of conflict with Yugoslavia. It was a shameful role which Stalin played here. The "Yugoslavia affair" contained no problems which could not have been solved through Party discussions among comrades. There was no significant basis for the development of the "affair"; it was completely possible to have prevented the rupture of relations with that country. This does not mean, however, that the Yugoslav leaders did not make mistakes or did not have shortcomings. But these mistakes and shortcomings were magnified in a monstrous manner by Stalin, which resulted in a break of relations with a friendly country.

I recall the first days when the conflict between the Soviet Union and Yugoslavia began artificially to be blown up. Once, when I came from Kiev to Moscow, I was invited to visit Stalin, who, pointing to the copy of a letter lately sent to Tito, asked me, "Have you read this?"

Not waiting for my reply, he answered, "I will shake my little finger—and there will be no more Tito. He will fall."

We have paid dearly for this "shaking of the little finger." This statement reflected Stalin's delusions of grandeur, but he acted just that way. . . .

No matter how much or how little Stalin shook not only his little finger but everything else that he could shake, Tito did not fall. Why? The reason was that, in this case of disagreement with the Yugoslav comrades, Tito had behind him a state and a people who had gone through a severe school of fighting for liberty and independence, a people which gave support to its leaders.

You see where Stalin's delusions of grandeur led. He had completely lost consciousness of reality; he demonstrated his suspicion and haughtiness not only in relation to individuals in the U.S.S.R., but in relation to whole parties and nations.

We have carefully examined the case of Yugoslavia and have found a proper solution which is approved by the peoples of the Soviet Union and of Yugoslavia as well as by the working masses of all the people's democracies and by all progressive humanity. The liquidation of the abnormal relationship with Yugoslavia was done in the interest of the whole camp of Socialism, in the interest of strengthening peace in the whole world.

But even before the secret speech, the pressures on the hard-line Communist regimes of Eastern Europe were mounting from day to day. The ruling parties—and their foes—hardly could have guessed that Khrushchev was preparing to denounce Stalin. (There had been, to be sure, certain hints that Stalin was being undeified. Anastas Mikoyan, the old dictator's jack-of-all-trades, had strangely failed to mention Stalin's name even once when he addressed the Polish Party's Central Committee early in February. A close study of *Pravda* would have revealed that Stalin's legend was quickly fading.) But in Prague, Warsaw, and Budapest the increasingly worried top leaders were already beginning to respond, albeit slightly, to the rising ferment within their parties, and it was dawning on even the most close-minded of them that some form of accommodation or compromise was necessary. The tension brought on by Stalin's death and its effects in the Soviet Union would have to be defused sooner or later.

In Hungary something of a thaw had begun as early as July 1954, when Rákosi and his more liberal Premier, Imre Nagy, agreed to release János Kadár, who had been imprisoned in April 1951 on charges of "espionage," "treason," and "Titoism." During his three years in Vac prison, he had been subjected to torture of extraordinary cruelty and refinement. But now Rajk was about to be cleared and Rákosi and Nagy thought it wise to set Kadár free, although he was to remain a "nonperson" for two more years. (It should be noted that Kadár was being liberated in Hungary just as Gustav Husák and scores of others were being sentenced to lengthy prison terms in Czechoslovakia. The political awakening in Prague was, indeed, a slow process.)

Then, shortly after Ważyk set astir the intellectual community in Poland, Hungarian writers, too, began stirring. The kinship between Poles and Hungarians is considerable, as was to be proved again less than a year later, and empathy between Warsaw and Budapest was inevitable. Writers like Gyula Háy and the well-known experimental novelist Tibor Déry started speaking out publicly against the Soviet doctrine of Communist allegiance in literature—here their target was the shopworn "socialist realism" still pushed by Moscow years after Zhdanov's death—and against continuing interference in literature and the arts by Party bureaucrats. In a widely circulated memorandum, Déry complained of "antidemocratic methods which paralyzed the cultural life of the country." Soon, several members resigned from the executive committee of the Hungarian Writers' Union to show their agreement with Déry's views. As in Poland, the Writers' Union in Hungary reached out for leadership in the incipient revolt against the *status quo*.

In April 1956 Czechoslovak writers in turn fell into step with their Polish and Hungarian counterparts. They were riding the crest of a wave of palpably increasing dissatisfaction within the KSČ and the country at large, a dissatisfaction so pronounced that even as orthodox a man as President Zápotocký had to take it into account.

In his New Year's address to the nation, Zápotocký had begun to dismantle the anti-Titoist demonology in Czechoslovakia, remarking defensively that it had all resulted from "misleading information and the diversionary activities of the enemy." He suggested that Czechoslovak-Yugoslav relations should be improved and acknowledged that the "propaganda campaign which developed after the breach went at times too far."

But even after Khrushchev's speech, the Prague leadership was not rushing headlong into wholesale rehabilitations. When the KSČ's Central Committee met in March 1956, Novotný performed an acrobatic rhetorical feat in exonerating Gottwald from any suspicion that he had created his own personality cult and, instead, blamed the Party as a whole for surrounding the dead President with a "false" aura of untouchability. Novotný also discovered that Stalinist influences led "some" justice and security officials erroneously to think they were "the main power in the class struggle" and could proceed with "excesses" and "arbitrariness." Barák outdid even Novotný when he told the Central Committee that, actually, it was Slánský's fault in "illegally" permitting Tito's name to be linked to his. Blithely ignoring that his "confession" had literally been beaten out of him, Barák announced that Slánský had "welcomed the atmosphere created by the wrong accusations against the leading Yugoslav comrades." This astounding charge was nothing less than accusing Slánský of having deliberately committed suicide and, furthermore, holding it against him as a selfish and "antisocialist" act.

Only in a situation of major disarray could leading figures have stooped to declarations of such absurdity, insulting the intelligence of even the lowest hack on the Central Committee. And that the Party was in total disarray was proved during the April 1956 Plenum of the Central Committee. There, desperately in need of a scapegoat, Novotný and his "collective leadership" partners arranged to fire Alexei Čepička from his posts of Deputy Premier and Defense Minister, simultaneously, depriving him of membership in the Politburo and in the Central Committee. No official explanation was given for this decision to throw to the wolves the man who for nearly eight years had been among the leading executors of purges and repressions. (That Čepička, who only a short time before had expressed Czechoslovakia's "gratitude" to Stalin for saving her from the fangs of "imperialism," was the late Gottwald's son-in-law no longer mattered.) But sacrificing Čepička, presumably as a man who had considered himself "the main power in the class struggle," was evidently meant to still the rising criticism in the country and the simmering revolt within the KSČ itself. But it was in vain.

Feelings were running high, and it was at this point that the writers got into the act to defy the regime. The forum for this defiance was the Second Congress of the Union of Czechoslovak Writers, held late in April 1956. Until then, the Union, organized in 1949 by Kopecký as part of his vast propaganda machine, had been a docile tool of the establishment. Its membership was limited, the authors wrote in accordance with whatever the Party line happened to be at the time, and their reward was publication of their works by Kopecký's publishing houses. For a nation with as powerful a literary tradition as Czechoslovakia, the years after 1949 were ones of sterile mediocrity; those who refused to toe the line confined themselves to translating foreign books or writing poetry sufficiently obscure to escape the censor.

When the congress met in the National Assembly building on April 23, the Party leadership was confident that it would be just another rubber-stamp affair. In fact, it was prepared to make the writers feel good, and President Zápotocký appeared in person to deliver a lengthy speech in which he informed them that "the Party has never prescribed and never will prescribe to the writers regarding their literary work." This might have been passed in silence in 1949, but it was 1956 and the writers were not in the mood to listen uncritically to such patent falsehoods. Besides, they had a great deal on their minds, and they proceeded to express it in a torrent of accusatory speeches. During the floor revolt, Jaroslav Seifert, at the age of fifty-five Czechoslovakia's most outstanding lyric poet, rose to demand the release from prison of his fellow writers and other citizens unjustly condemned during the Great Purge. A onetime Communist expelled from the Party as far back as 1929, Seifert spoke passionately of his isolated and imprisoned colleagues. (One of them was Laco Novomeský, the Slovak poet who had been sentenced to a ten-year term after having been expelled from the Writers' Union for "knowingly propagating unpatriotic, cosmopolitan tendencies.")

František Hrubín, Miroslav Florian, and Miroslav Holub and several other poets and writers followed Seifert to denounce the pressures and humiliations of the Stalin-Gottwald period and to describe in detail the Party practices in forcing them to write according to the official line. They told of Paul Reiman, a Sudeten German whom Kopecký had named to decide what books would be published even though he lacked both literary knowledge and adequate command of the language. The both accurate and prophetic slogan the rebellious writers proclaimed at the congress was "The Writers—Conscience of the Nation."

Once it had recovered from its shocked surprise, the regime struck back. Many of its leaders were sufficiently aware of the situation in Poland and Hungary to realize the dangers now being posed in Czechoslovakia. During the session of April 28, Zápotocký accused Seifert and Hrubín of being "demagogues," and the Party machine succeeded in extracting from the congress a declaration recognizing the KSČ as the "inspirator and organizer of a great revolutionary change" and thanking it for its "correct and wise suggestions." In the strange world of the Communist mentality, a formal resolution no matter how phony carries more weight than reality. The Party, therefore, was reasonably satisfied that it had beaten down the rebellion although both Seifert and Hrubín were elected to the Union's Central Committee.

But the Writers' Congress was not all there was to the nascent Czechoslovak rebellion. In May Holub, Florian, and several other writers began editing a magazine called *Květen* (*May*) and built around it a somewhat clandestine *Květen* group for discussion and stimulation of their literary work. Other young intellectuals followed the *Květen* example, organizing study and reading circles that met at the homes of the members. Forbidden literature was read and circulated. Gradually the spark was returning to the Czechoslovak cultural life. The Czechoslovak cinema industry succeeded in freeing itself to a degree of the official ideological influence, allowing young producers and directors to exercise their imagination. Alois Polednak, named in 1956 to head the film industry (he emerged in 1968 as a man of singular courage and conviction), announced that "the Party accepted the principle of confidence in and responsibility of the film makers."

Next, it was the turn of the students. Also in May a series of resolutions sent to the government demanded the abolition of the 1953 Education Act, which Soviet experts had helped to draft, and charged that the Party-controlled system of higher education was totally inadequate. (An example of this state of affairs was the official admission in 1955 that forty per cent of the university students dropped out before their junior year.) Secondary education was likewise criticized on the grounds that it failed to prepare the students for the universities.

Concerned as the regime may have been over the divisions and uncertainties in the KSČ, it could not stomach all this besides. The writers' revolt had struck at the core of the Party's ideological and propaganda position, while the students' criticisms and demands, often supported by their professors, threatened to subvert an entire generation. To sacrifice Čepička was one thing, and it was done gladly, but to stand still for a basic questioning of the Party's wisdom was something else again. The pretense of a more liberal attitude was at once dropped and a counter-offensive was set in motion.

First Kopecký took pen in hand to charge in *Rudé Právo* that the student critics sought "to push our school system back not only to the era prior to 1953, prior to February 1948, but even back to its state during the First Republic." At a national congress of the KSČ on June 11, Novotný took the floor to denounce "reformist illusions about harmony and reconciliation of class interests . . . voices demanding freedom for bourgeois and antisocialist propaganda . . . views reflecting the petty-bourgeois criticism of Party policy," and attempts to "smuggle" into the Party opinions which under the pretext of "freedom" sought to set the clock back to the pre-1948 days. Thriving on self-criticism, as Communists so often do, he disclosed that when the Party's Central Committee had met in March to discuss Khrushchev's secret speech of a month before, some of its officials in charge of ideology had shown basic doubts about the "very foundations of Marxism-Leninism." The implication seemed to be that a great many people had misinterpreted Khrushchev's speech and that it was up to the Prague ideologues to set them straight.

While the Prague leaders were thus attempting to silence the burgeoning opposition, the situation in Poland and Hungary was rapidly acquiring characteristics they could only regard as alarming. Not only were the intellectuals' rebellions in full swing, but they were spilling over into practical politics, and, worst of all, the regimes appeared to be caving in under the pressure.

In Poland, Bolesław Bierut still ran the country as President and the Party's First Secretary. But liberalizing pressures had forced the Party quietly to release Gomułka late in 1954, roughly the time that Kadár in Hungary had his freedom restored. The difference, at least at that point, was that Gomułka had never been tried and sentenced and this made his discreet liberation easier. On March 12 Bierut died during a visit to Moscow, and overnight Gomułka became the most important personage in the country, even though he remained silently at his home and a Party functionary named Edward Ochab was named First Secretary. From a distance. Gomułka nevertheless exercised the kind of influence that Charles de Gaulle had during his self-enforced retirement from politics. In other words, everybody knew that it was only a question of time before the taciturn Gomułka would return to power. Meanwhile, the Party and government proceeded to purge themselves through the dismissal of Jakub Berman on May 6, following the ouster from the Politburo of Stanisław Radkiewicz, secret police chief at the time of the 1948–1949 trials. Thirty thousand persons were freed from prisons. General Spychalski and Zenon Kliszko were released and returned to Party positions.

In Hungary pressures were mounting from the intellectuals for the rehabilitation of Imre Nagy, a relatively progressive man who had served as Premier from 1953 to 1955 but was then relegated to obscurity. The Party was not quite prepared to bring Nagy back to power, but on March 27 Rákosi took another step of vast significance. In a speech to the Central Committee, he announced that recent investigations allowed the Supreme Court to establish that the Rajk trial as well as others connected with it had been based upon "fabricated charges" made by Lieutenant General Gábor Péter and his associates in the Hungarian secret police (the AVH). According to Rákosi, the AVH had abused its power. The next step was for the Supreme Court to review a series of old cases and to order the liberation of some three hundred "baselessly convicted" persons. Three weeks later, Rákosi publicly admitted "mistakes" committed under his regime. He had gone so far to undermine the political position of his rule—and his personal standing—that Hungarians freely speculated about his forthcoming fall.

Events tend to escalate in such situations, and the Hungarian intellectuals were encouraged to demand further advantages. Their principal weapons were the Hungarian Writers' Union and its publication, the *Irodalmy Ujság* (*Literary Gazette*). Writers no longer confined themselves to demands for literary freedom but criticized the regime on all fronts. At the April General Assembly of the Writers' Union, the membership rejected by one hundred votes to three the candidate proposed by the Party for Secretary-General and elected instead a non-Communist poet. Their new Presidium included such antiregime writers as Pál Ignotus and Lajos Kassák.

The Writers' Union had established itself as the center of antiregime criticism and grievances, but it soon acquired sister organizations. Later in the spring young intellectuals, writers, journalists, and composers belonging to the League of Working Youth (DISZ) of the Communist

Youth Federation established the Petöfi Club—named after Sandor Petöfi, a famous Hungarian lyric poet who was killed in 1849 on the barricades. His nineteenth-century credo fitted perfectly the 1956 situation: "When the people shall rule in poetry, they shall be close to ruling in politics as well." The Petöfi Club undertook to sponsor frequent discussions on a whole range of political, economic, and social topics. Even Army cadets attended the meetings. It was hard to believe, but the Party newspaper *Szabad Nép* in an editorial on June 24 called the Petöfi Club a valuable forum, recommending to Hungary's leaders to participate in its debates. A week earlier, the club had debated the Rajk rehabilitation and greeted his widow with "stormy applause." On June 27 more than five thousand persons stood in the streets to listen over loudspeakers to a club debate during which the Nagy case was mentioned publicly for the first time. The meeting lasted all night and turned into a near riot against the Rákosi regime. Presently, the unrest spread from Budapest to the countryside, and, according to one Hungarian Communist writer, peasants came in carts to village booksellers to pay 100 forints for a copy of *Irodalmy Ujság* that normally sold for 1 forint.

All this activity seemed unbelievable in a Communist state. To the hard-line leaders in Prague, the Hungarian Party was endangering not only itself but also all the "people's democracies" in the region.

Then, on June 28, a warm Thursday, the action switched back to Poland. Not unlike the 1953 Czechoslovak workers' rebellion in Plzeň, the rising at Poznań was essentially economically motivated. But an important difference was that Poland was in a rebellious mood. The workers at the Zispo metal plant were demanding pay rises, but nobody in Poznań, a western Polish city, or Warsaw cared to hear them out. A thirty-man delegation had gone to the capital and warned the Minister of Machine Industry that a strike would be called for June 28 if the workers' demands were not met. Strikes are not tolerated in Communist countries, and the delegation was warned that if the workers went into the streets, they would be met by tanks.

Word of this threat was sent back to Poznań, and, on the morning of June 28, some sixteen thousand Zispo workers set out from the plant to march three miles to Freedom Square in the downtown area. Like so many Pied Pipers, they were joined along their route by additional thousands of men and women from other factories. Marching, they sang ancient patriotic songs and religious hymns. They carried banners demanding

BREAD AND FREEDOM. Eyewitnessses said later that a hundred thousand persons participated in the initial demonstration. At the Town Hall, there were no officials willing or ready to meet the workers, and presently the rumor spread that the delegation which had gone to Warsaw was under arrest. So the huge crowd moved toward the U.B. headquarters to confront the secret police. As in Berlin and Plzeň in 1953, this Polish crowd began to shout, "Out with the Russians!"

Firing broke out. Policemen fired on the crowd and the workers and young people broke into the stores of arms of the People's Militia to equip themselves for combat. Streetcars and trucks were overturned to serve as barricades. Now it was a real revolution. Another crowd went to the prison and instantly captured it. Prisoners were released and secret files burned. The authorities summoned Army troops, but the soldiers refused to shoot at the people. According to one account, a tank was turned over to the rebels by its crew.

Late in the day, units of special security troops from Warsaw reached Poznań. These forces were completely loyal to the government and, unlike the regular city garrison, felt no local loyalties. They brought tanks and artillery and trained them on the rioting crowds. For two days fighting raged throughout Poznań. At the end of the rebellion, fifty-four people had been killed and over two hundred injured. By July 1 it was all over.

Poznań shook Poland as no event had done since the end of the war. But the Polish leadership, caught in mounting turbulence, saw it as part of a larger process. So did the outspoken Polish press: articles began appearing telling the nation that the Poznań uprising had resulted from the workers' just demands.

But this was where even Khrushchev, the man who indirectly had helped the Poznań bomb to explode, drew the line. On July 2 an official Moscow statement attributed the riots to "provocateurs and diversionists paid by foreign sources." The East German press spoke of "imperialist agents." No matter what encouragement he seemed to be offering the progressives, the Soviet Union was reverting to form; its vital interests were at stake and this took precedence over ideological musings. It was an ominous sign that the Hungarians should not have ignored. (Incredibly, Tito joined in the chorus of condemnations, saying that Poznań was the work of "foreign agents." Strong Communist regimes do not take kindly to such challenges of authority, and Tito was no exception.)

In Prague, Novotný's regime seemed to derive perverse joy from Poznań and its aftermath, for the event served to vindicate the Czechoslovak Party's warnings that relaxation of controls only invited "counterrevolutionary" and "imperialist" activities. As the liberal wave in Poland continued to surge, despite Soviet admonitions, Prague reacted as if Poland were an enemy and not a sister "socialist" state. The border with Poland was sealed off to prevent "subversive" contagion from infiltrating into Czechoslovakia; Polish radio stations were jammed—as if they were the BBC, the Voice of America, or Radio Free Europe; and the Czechoslovak press denounced Polish intellectuals as enemies of socialism. It spoke of "revisionism" and openly criticized Adam Ważyk, the progressive Marxist philosophers Leszek Kołakowski and Jan Kott, and the newspaperman Wiktor Woroszylski, who had written that the Poznań workers had a just cause.

But in Hungary, as in Poland, the liberalization process gained momentum every day, and Poznań was a stimulant rather than a deterrent. On July 18 Mátyás Rákosi, as had been predicted, was removed from his position as the Party's First Secretary at a Central Committee session attended by Soviet Deputy Premier Anastas Mikoyan. Mikoyan, who on Stalin's behalf had ordered Gottwald in 1951 to launch the Great Purge, was one of the few top-level survivors of the post-Stalin power struggle in Moscow and was now Khrushchev's East European trouble shooter. It is widely believed that Rákosi's fall was Mikoyan's handiwork, but it would be wrong to conclude that the Soviets were pushing liberalization with one hand in Hungary while discouraging it in Poland with the other. Moscow rarely has sympathy for failures, and Rákosi had simply become a liability. He was guilty of the two contradictory sins of being identified with the Rajk purges, which the Kremlin now wished to forget, and of having allowed too much freedom in Hungary.

The man chosen to replace him was the rather sinister Ernö Gerö, an unconditional representative of the Moscow faction. But, curiously, the same Central Committee session named Kadár to the Party's Secretariat and to the Politburo. Conceivably, Moscow was still hedging its bets in Hungary. But for Kadár it was a formidable leap back to the power center.

In Warsaw, meanwhile, a crucial power struggle was under way. There were the conservatives, known as the Natolin group, after the village near the capital where Soviet Ambassador Panteleimon Ponomarenko held meetings with his Polish friends at his weekend house, and there were the progressives. The first group, encouraged by Ponomarenko, pushed for a return to Stalinist practices; the progressives, including the intellectuals, obviously wanted a Communist democratization. On July 22, the twelfth anniversary of Poland's liberation by Soviet forces, Premier Bulganin spelled out in a public speech the official line of the former:

> We cannot close our eyes to the attempts that are being made to weaken international links among Socialist countries under the slogan of so-called national characteristics. . . . These are attempts to undermine the power of people's democracy under the pretense of widening democracy.
>
> Poznań . . . is proof that international reaction has not abandoned its attempts to restore capitalism in the Socialist countries. . . .
>
> Facts are known when elements hostile to our cause utilized the press organs in the Socialist countries in order to sow their poisonous seeds. Certain managers of these press organs have yielded to hostile influence, forgetting that the Party press should be above all a faithful and consistent herald of the Marxist-Leninist idea and a militant propagator in the struggle for building socialism.

As tensions rose intolerably, the shaky Party leadership turned to Gomułka, who was patiently awaiting the inevitable call at a health resort, where he was recovering from a lung lesion. But, again like General de Gaulle, he would accept the call only on his own terms. These terms included readmission to the Party before he made the slightest commitment, and the elimination from the government of men he considered to be identified with policies that had to be changed. Ochab and Party leaders of all persuasions called on him continuously, but Gomułka would not budge from his conditions. Finally, on August 4, an official announcement informed the nation that the Party card had been restored to "Comrade Gomułka." It was becoming increasingly clear that only Gomułka could restore unity to the Party and bring down the fever in the country. But the men who had once put him in prison still wanted to delay the inevitable denouement. Suggestions were made that he rejoin the leadership in a less exalted position than the First Secretaryship. Gomułka hit back with silence. And this silence also excluded any answer to the question which faction in the struggle he considered himself most attracted to. But in September, after the regime had embarrassed itself further through an attempt to conduct a series of trials in Poznań, Gomułka cast his lot with the liberals—a faction with growing national support; Ochab and Jozef Cyrankiewicz had already joined it. (Curiously, Chairman Mao Tse-tung told Ochab in Peking early in the autumn that the Chinese Party supported the Polish liberals against the neo-Stalinists.)

Gomułka's new attitude included a deep interest in economic reforms and here, too, his advisers were drawn from the progressives' camp.

By now, the Poles were thoroughly aware of where Gomułka stood and that he was a contender for power—the country's liberal editors had taken care of that. His standing had become so great that even Moscow was eager to have him back in the leadership, albeit in a position where he would be surrounded by pro-Soviet conservatives. He was quietly offered a seat on the Politburo and his former post as Deputy Premier. But this did not interest or satisfy Gomułka. He was determined to come back at the head of his own group and to eliminate men he considered pernicious to Poland's welfare. (One of the latter was Defense Minister Rokossovsky, so in addition to all the other tensions, Gomułka was now openly defying the Russians.) A major crisis was approaching the point of explosion.

On October 14 the Politburo met in Warsaw to decide on the date for the next Central Committee meeting that was to solve the crisis. In an unprecedented step, Gomułka, who was a simple Party member, was invited to attend. The Central Committee meeting was set for October 19, and Gomułka's supporters throughout Poland urged industrial plants and other "work centers" to drown Warsaw in a sea of resolutions demanding his election as First Secretary. The pro-Soviet group fought back, marshaling support among *its* clientele. Then, word came from Moscow that the Soviet Union might intervene militarily if the situation deteriorated too much. The liberals prepared to fight, and, through a ruse, Ochab and Cyrankiewicz named General Wacław Komar to head the special security troops. Komar, who had spent years in prison because of his service in the Spanish Civil War, could be counted upon to bring his elite units over to the liberal—or Polish—side in a clash with the Russians.

Presently, Khrushchev sent a message that he would like to attend the Central Committee meeting as a guest. Ochab replied that the time was inopportune. Khrushchev insisted and wired that he was coming regardless of the Poles' wishes. His obvious aim was to force Poland to keep Marshal Rokossovsky as Defense Minister, but the Polish Party reacted by naming Gomułka as its First Secretary at a secret Politburo meeting on October 18 without waiting for the required Central Committee session and approval.

On October 19 the showdown began. Early in the morning, Khrushchev landed at the military airport in Warsaw with an impressive contingent of top Soviet politicians and Army chiefs—Mikoyan, Molotov, and Kaganovich, Marshal Konev, Supreme Commander of the Warsaw Pact forces (the Communist military alliance had been organized in May 1955), Army Chief of Staff General Alexei Antonov, and ten full generals. As the events of 1968 were to demonstrate again, the Soviet Union believes in collective intimidation on the highest level.

The first clash came even before Khrushchev could leave the airport. He tangled with Gomułka only to discover that the former prisoner had been named the Party's First Secretary the day before. According to published accounts, Khrushchev then shouted, "There has been an act of betrayal. We had to come. It is not only a question of Polish-Soviet relations. You are endangering our position in Germany. You're menacing the whole Socialist camp."

"Betrayal" is a concept that has an obsessive value for Soviet leaders. It was hurled at Tito, at Gomułka, at the Hungarians, and finally at the Czechoslovaks over a twenty-year period. It tells more about the Soviet attitude toward other Communist parties, Eastern Europe, and, indeed, the world than any other set of words or insights.

At the Belvedere Palace, at the end of the long Ujazdowskie Alley, Khrushchev furiously battled Gomułka, Ochab, and other Poles for his right to attend the Central Committee meeting. Then Gomułka was informed that Soviet troops were advancing on Warsaw from bases in Poland, the Soviet Union, and East Germany. Gomułka and Ochab asked Khrushchev whether this was true. The Soviet leader conferred briefly with his generals and returned to the room to say that, indeed, Warsaw was on the point of being surrounded.

As the story of that tense morning has been reconstructed, Gomułka is said to have told Khrushchev that unless Soviet troops were withdrawn immediately, he would not continue negotiations. He further told him that he would address the nation over the radio to apprise it of the situation. This was the critical moment of the whole crisis and this was the difference between Warsaw and the situations that were to arise a few weeks later in Hungary and twelve years later in Czechoslovakia. Poland had in Gomułka and his followers a firm leadership prepared to fight, if needed.

After a moment of silence, Khrushchev said, "We shall order all troop movements to be halted." But the Soviet units kept advancing. At Central Committee headquarters, as the Russians waited at the Belvedere, Gomułka was confirmed as First Secretary and Marshal Rokossovsky was dropped from the Politburo. At noon Gomułka resumed negotiating with Khrushchev while his followers went to Warsaw factories to obtain resolutions supporting him in the crisis. University students lined up behind the leadership. Sixty miles from Warsaw, General Komar's tanks blocked a Soviet armored column. Gomułka once more said he would not negotiate "under Soviet guns." General Konev contributed what many years later became a historic phrase: his troops, he said, were merely engaged in "routine maneuvers." At two a.m. of October 20 Khrushchev and Gomułka finally agreed on a brief joint communiqué stating that the Soviet leaders had visited Warsaw. No mention was made of Polish-Soviet "friendship," as Khrushchev had demanded. The Russians agreed to pull their troops back to their bases in exchange for Gomułka's promise of subsequent negotiations and a pledge that Poland would remain in the Warsaw Pact and would allow the Soviets to go on stationing troops in the country. Khrushchev dropped all his efforts to influence the composition of the new Politburo. In the early morning the Soviet team flew home, and, it appeared, the Poles had won the confrontation by not blinking.

On October 22 Gomułka went on the radio to explain his program:

What is constant in socialism boils down to the abolition of the exploitation of man by man. The roads of achieving this goal can be and are different. The model of socialism can also vary.

Within the framework of relations among Communist and workers' parties and among Socialist states, each country should have full independence, and the rights of each nation to a sovereign government in an independent country should be fully and mutually respected. This is how it should be, and I would say this is how it is beginning to be.

The road of democratization is the only road leading to the construction of the best model of socialism in our conditions. . . . We shall not allow anyone to use this process of democratization to undermine socialism. Our Party is taking its place at the head of the process of democratization and only . . . the Party can guide this process.

The Polish crisis ended on October 22, and on October 23 the Hungarian crisis began. But, in a sense, they formed parts of a truly indivisible whole. Since early in the year, Poland and Hungary had marched together along what Gomułka had called the "road of democratization" in socialism. Now the Poles' apparent triumph in their showdown with Khrushchev propelled the Hungarians into their defiance of Moscow. But the bloody tragedy of Hungary brought, in turn, another dimension of tragedy to Poland.

Hungary's virtually completely free press had reported the Polish struggle in detail. It told the Hungarians of Khrushchev's attempt at intimidation, of the final confrontation, and of Gomułka's speech pledging a socialist democracy. This was all that was needed. Hungary's campaign for greater freedoms had been progressing in a rising crescendo all year. On October 6 Rajk had been ceremoniously reburied, along with the other victims of the 1949 trials, in a gesture designed to wipe off the shame of the purges. Demands for Nagy's return to power grew daily, becoming the country's overwhelming political issue. Then came news of Gomułka's triumph and, on October 22, Budapest began moving again. More than five thousand persons attended a rally at the Building Industry's Technological University which lasted for eleven hours; expressions of solidarity with Poland were given and a ten-point list of demands by Hungarian youth presented. This last included the withdrawal of Soviet troops stationed in Hungary.

The next day thousands of students led by a group of rebel writers marched on the Polish Embassy and the monument to Józef Bem, the Polish general who came to Hungary in 1848–1849 to help her fight for her freedom against Austria and Russia. Soon the citizens of Budapest joined the youths, and before the day was over three hundred thousand persons filled the city's sunlit streets in a wild and continuing demonstration of joy over Poland's success and of hope that it would be repeated in Hungary.

Before twilight the crowds began moving from the Bem monument to Parliament Square, across the Danube. As darkness fell, shouts arose for the huge red-lit star on the Parliament building to be switched off, and this was done to a roar of cheers. Then the crowd started demanding the presence of Nagy and his inclusion in the government. Hours later a delegation of writers persuaded Nagy to come from his apartment, and an official led him to a balcony of the Parliament building to address the multitude. He spoke briefly, asking the crowd to disperse, but he could barely be heard. Meanwhile, Gerö, just back from a visit to Belgrade with Premier András Hegedüs, spoke over the radio in tones later described as "truculent." This deeply irritated the Hungarians, and cries of "Down with Gerö!" and "Death to Gerö!" echoed across the capital. In another section of Budapest, a crowd brought a huge statue of Stalin crashing down, and there were shouts of "Russians go home!" The head of the Stalin statue was spat on and smashed to bits.

Shortly after Gerö's speech, a crowd of young people went to the Radio

Budapest building to demand that the students' list of demands, now consisting of sixteen points, be broadcast. While a delegation negotiated inside, AVH security troops with rifles and drawn bayonets moved into the crowd. After nine p.m., tear-gas bombs were dropped from the upper floors; then, suddenly, AVH men rushed from the entrance and started firing in all directions. United Nations investigators reported later that at least three persons were killed. The firing from the windows of the Radio Budapest building went on for twenty minutes, and there were more casualties. Presently, the crowd began to retreat, but a group of youths carried high the bloodied clothes of one of the killed. News of the shooting reached the people still massed in front of Parliament, and the crowd reassembled in the narrow streets around the radio station. Truckloads of regular Army troops and three tanks arrived on the scene, but the officers and soldiers refused to fire on the demonstrators. Continuing fire from the radio building hit the tanks, killing two Army officers and more youths. Thereupon, workers from the industrial suburbs commandeered trucks and rushed to Radio Budapest with weapons given them by soldiers. At the Army barracks, the arms stores were thrown open to the workers. At a factory, a group of workers captured one thousand rifles and ammunition. AVH troop carriers were overturned and burned while demonstrators shot at the radio station with light weapons.

At the offices of the Party newspaper, *Szabad Nép*, where another crowd demanded the publication of the students' sixteen points, AVH troops fired on the people, killing a number of them. But the rioters, now armed, succeeded in occupying the building before dawn, and others burned bookshops selling Russian books. District police stations and Party headquarters were occupied without resistance on the morning of October 24. More arms were thus obtained.

Soviet tanks and troops entered Budapest early on October 24, and violent fighting developed between them and rampaging crowds supported by the police and Hungarian Army units. In a series of seemingly contradictory radio announcements, the Budapest population learned that the sixty-year-old Nagy had been named Premier—this was one of the student demands—and that the "government had applied for help to Soviet formations stationed in Hungary." It was not made clear how or when the request for the Soviet intervention was made and, looking back at the events, it appears highly improbable that Nagy would have made it. This, then, was a precedent for anonymous requests for Soviet military interventions—repeated in Prague in 1968.

In Budapest and throughout the country "Revolutionary and Workers' Councils" took over the functions of government from the Communist Party. The uprisings had now turned into a full-blown revolution with many Hungarian Army units fighting alongside the armed civilians against Soviet tanks. Only the AVH security troops supported the Russians.

On October 25 Soviet tanks guarding the Parliament building, where Premier Nagy's office was located, suddenly began firing in support of the AVH on an unarmed crowd of some twenty-five thousand persons, including women and children, massed in front of the building waiting to see Nagy. Estimates of the number killed in this massacre range from three hundred to eight hundred. But Nagy was under detention by the hard-liners at Communist Party headquarters a block away, where Soviet Politburo members Mikhail Suslov and Mikoyan were negotiating Gerö's removal as First Secretary and his replacement with Kadár. When the crowd moved toward Party headquarters, panic broke out within, as the pro-Soviet Communist leaders and the AVH officers feared for their lives.

It appears possible that the Russians' desire for Gerö's removal may have been motivated by a wish to bring the revolution to an end and halt the fighting. Gerö fled to Soviet-held areas, and Nagy was allowed to come to the Parliament building to form a new government, which he did on October 27, inviting both Communist and non-Communist ministers to join. The Party proceeded to announce that the new government would immediately start negotiating with the Soviet Union for the withdrawal of her forces. In what was a victory of sorts for the insurgents, a ceasefire was ordered by the government on October 28; the urban guerrilla tactics of the "Freedom Fighters" had allowed them to neutralize the Soviet tanks to a considerable extent, and the invading army was making remarkably little progress in smashing the revolution. At Kilián Army barracks, Hungarian troops under Colonel Pál Maléter successfully withstood Soviet assaults.

On October 29 Nagy abolished the AVH and thereby freed himself of the pressures of its leaders. On October 30 he formally did away with the one-party system. Kadár, speaking as First Secretary of the Communist Party, agreed with this liquidation of the dominant role of Communism in Hungary, "to avoid further bloodshed." Free elections were promised by one cabinet minister. Representatives of the moribund Independent Smallholders Party and the National Peasant Party entered the cabinet and, between them, held as many ministries as the Communists. Nagy publicly denied that he had called for the Soviet intervention.

When the new government took office on October 30, the ceasefire had come fully into effect, and for the first time in a week there was no sound of firing in the battered streets of Budapest. The same day Soviet troops began to leave the city. Normal work was to be resumed on Monday, November 5, and, meanwhile, an intense new political life was rising in Hungary. Political parties and Revolutionary Councils were being formed everywhere. It seemed as if the revolution had really succeeded. Hope arose that a bright future was around the corner. Thousands of AVH prisoners, many of them brutally tortured, were released. And, on November 2, Cardinal Mindszenty was set free.

But on November 3 events took a turn that later proved to be ominous. Nagy dropped several Communist ministers from the coalition government with the result that this caretaker cabinet (pending elections) had the same distribution among parties as that approved by the Allied Control Commission in 1945. The clock, it seemed, had been set back eleven years. And as the Nagy regime proceeded with its organization, Colonel Maléter, now Lieutenant General, was named Defense Minister.

As for Kadár, he formed a new party—the Hungarian Socialist Workers' Party—and in a radio speech said that Hungarian writers, journalists, students, workers, and peasants "fought in the front lines against the Rákosi despotism and political hooliganism." The new party, he said, would defend socialism and democracy, "not by slavishly imitating foreign examples, but by taking a road suitable to the economic and historic characteristics of our country." He appealed to the other parties to "overcome the danger" of a foreign intervention by consolidating the government. It appeared that the Communists had resigned themselves to their defeat and that Kadár had turned himself into a nationalist leader. But his tactics were considerably more complex.

They matched, in fact, the reports Nagy had been receiving that since November 1 new Soviet units were entering Hungary. Kadár, apparently, was carrying out his political deceit to give his Soviet friends time to regroup their forces. Nagy called Soviet Ambassador I. V. Andropov and told him the return of the Soviet troops was a violation of the Warsaw Pact agreement and that Hungary would denounce the treaty if the reinforcements were not withdrawn. Simultaneously, he requested Moscow to enter into negotiations for the final evacuation of troops. Andropov advised Nagy that the Soviet Union was prepared to negotiate and that the new troops were arriving to relieve the units that had been fighting in Hungary. This, Nagy replied, was not a satisfactory explanation and Hungary would turn to the United Nations.

When new information reached him of additional Soviet military penetrations into Hungary, Nagy informed Andropov that his government was immediately withdrawing from the Warsaw Pact. Later, the cabinet approved this move and proclaimed Hungary's neutrality. Before the microphones of Radio Budapest, Nagy said, "We appeal to our neighbors, countries near and far, to respect the unalterable decision of our people. It is indeed true that our people are united in this decision as perhaps never before in their history. Working millions of Hungary! Protect and strengthen with revolutionary determination, sacrificial work, and the consolidation of order, our country—the free, independent, democratic, and neutral Hungary."

By evening of November 3 negotiations with the Soviet Union for the withdrawal of troops had advanced considerably. It was even agreed that the last contingents would leave with bands playing military music. A few details remained unsolved, however. At ten p.m. the Hungarian negotiators, led by Defense Minister Maléter, arrived at the Soviet Military Command at Tököl, near Budapest, for a banquet in their honor and the final session. Discussion proceeded until midnight on a series of minor points. Throughout the evening Maléter kept Nagy, in Budapest, informed by telephone of the progress of the talks.

Shortly before midnight, however, Nagy discovered that communications with his delegation at Tököl had been interrupted. Reconnaissance parties sent out from Budapest toward Tököl failed to return. A report of the United Nations Special Committee on the Problem of Hungary said that

discussions between the Soviet military delegation and the Hungarian military delegation at Tököl were in fact interrupted by the entry of a personage "who bore no insignia of rank"—General [Ivan] Serov, Chief of the Soviet Security Police. Accompanied by Soviet officers, he announced that he was arresting the Hungarian delegation. The head of the Soviet delegation, General Malinin, astonished by the interruption, made a gesture of indignation. General Serov thereupon whispered to him; as a result, General Malinin shrugged his shoulders and ordered the Soviet delegation to leave the room. The Hungarian delegation was then arrested. In vain, therefore, did Mr. Nagy, at 5:56 a.m. [November 4], broadcast an appeal to Generals Maléter and István Kovács and other members of the mission to return to their posts at once to take charge of their offices.

At five-twenty a.m., thirty-six minutes before he sent out his orders to his generals, Nagy appeared at Free Radio Kossuth in Budapest to broadcast to his people: "This is Imre Nagy speaking, the President of the Council of Ministers of the Hungarian People's Republic. Today at daybreak Soviet troops attacked our capital with the obvious intention of overthrowing the legal Hungarian democratic government. Our troops are in combat. The government is at its post. I notify the people of our country and the entire world of this fact."

As cannon fire was heard over Budapest, Nagy dictated this statement:

> This fight is the fight for freedom by the Hungarian people against the Russian intervention, and it is possible that I shall be able to stay at my post only for one or two hours. The whole world will see how the Russian armed forces, contrary to all treaties and conventions, are crushing the resistance of the Hungarian people.
>
> They will also see how they are kidnaping the premier of a country which is a member of the United Nations, taking him from the capital, and therefore it cannot be doubted at all that this is the most brutal form of intervention. I should like in these last moments to ask the leaders of the revolution, if they can, to leave the country. I ask that all I have said in my broadcast, and what we have agreed on with the revolutionary leaders during meetings in Parliament, should be put in a memorandum, and the leaders should turn to all the peoples of the world for help and explain that today it is Hungary and tomorrow, or the day after tomorrow, it will be the turn of other countries, because the imperialism of Moscow does not know borders and is only trying to play for time.

At seven-fourteen a.m., Free Radio Kossuth broadcast this announcement in both Hungarian and Russian: "The Hungarian government requests officers and soldiers of the Soviet Army not to shoot. Avoid bloodshed! The Russians are our friends and will remain our friends also in the future."

At eight-seven a.m., Free Radio Kossuth went off the air.

Nagy appears to have left his office after dictating his last statement and gone to the Yugoslav Embassy to seek asylum. About that time, at six a.m., a pretaped announcement from Kadár was broadcast from a radio station at Szolnok, a hundred miles southeast of Budapest, that he was forming the Hungarian Revolutionary Worker-Peasant Government. Kadár asked the people to disarm the "counterrevolutionary gangs" and to assist the new government in fulfilling its program.

As Nagy's protector, the Yugoslav government proposed that Kadár provide a written guarantee that Nagy and his party would be allowed to return freely to their homes, or, if this were not possible, to go to Yugoslavia. Nagy rejected Kadár's countersuggestion that he should go to Romania. He also refused to meet Kadár's demand that he resign from his position in the government, offer a "self-criticism" of his activities, and declare himself in sympathy with the Kadár regime. The Yugoslavs told Kadár they would agree to Nagy's departure only if Kadár guaranteed in writing that he would be granted safe conduct to return freely to his home. Kadár wrote back that the Hungarian government had no desire to apply sanctions to Nagy and members of his group for their past activities.

As the United Nations report tells the story of Nagy's final hours of freedom, on November 22, eighteen days after he had taken asylum, "a bus arrived at the Yugoslav Embassy to take the party to their homes. Soviet military personnel arrived and insisted on entering the bus, whereupon the Yugoslav Ambassador asked that two embassy officials accompany the bus to make certain that Mr. Nagy and his party reached their homes as agreed. The bus was driven to the Headquarters of the Soviet Military Command, where a Russian lieutenant colonel ordered the two Yugoslav officials to leave. The bus then drove away to an unknown destination escorted by Soviet armored cars."

Subsequently, Kadár announced publicly that Nagy and his companions had gone to Romania in accordance with their request. But on June 17, 1958, a year and a half later, first Moscow and then Budapest admitted that a secret trial had been held and that Nagy and General Maléter had been executed.

There is no way of tracing precisely Nagy's and Maléter's whereabouts between the time of their arrest and their execution. Some reports say that Nagy was actually taken to Romania after he left the Yugoslav Embassy, and was brought back to Budapest in June 1957. The trial is said to have lasted over a month and, according to these reports, much of the evidence against Nagy and Maléter was prepared in Moscow. We do not even know the date of their deaths.

The day that Nagy went to the Yugoslav Embassy, Cardinal Mindszenty made his way to the American Legation to ask for protection. He had been free for eight days. As of this writing, he is still there as a "guest" of the United States government.

The Soviet intervention in Hungary proved, of course, that there was no such thing, as far as Moscow is concerned, as "different paths to socialism," no matter what Khrushchev might have said in his secret speech

and Gomułka repeated hopefully after what he thought was his triumphant confrontation with the Russians in Warsaw. It was Khrushchev,
having aroused the hopes of the Communist world with his denunciation
of Stalin and his methods, who had ordered the smashing of the Hungarian revolt, and he was Kadár's partner in the liquidation of Nagy. He
might have liquidated Gomułka too if the situation in Poland had gotten
out of hand during the Hungarian revolt.

The end of the Hungarian revolution at a cost of thousands of lives
wrote *finis* to that country's hopes for an evolution toward its own form
of socialism or any modicum of democratization. And the example of
Hungary slowly withered away the Poles' hopes. Gomułka gradually allowed the Polish reforms to erode away. By the time the Prague Spring
bloomed in Czechoslovakia twelve years later. Hungary and Poland had
become pliant followers of Moscow—to the extent of participating with
their armies in the invasion of Czechoslovakia.

But in late 1956 and 1957 it was the loyal Czechoslovak Communist
leadership that emerged triumphant from the Polish and Hungarian
dramas. Novotný and Zápotocký were proved right in their view of the
Communist world—even though Khrushchev urgently summoned Zápotocký to Moscow in January 1957 to reassure himself that all was well in
Czechoslovakia—and they no longer had to go through the pretense of
relaxing political and intellectual controls at home. Stalin's massive statue
still stood on Letná Hill, overlooking Prague; Husák and many others
remained in the oblivion of Czechoslovak prisons, and it was again fashionable for the regime to bear down with severity on the intellectuals who
dared to question the wisdom of the Party. The thaw of 1956 was frozen
again by the cold winds of 1957. There seemed to be nothing bright in
prospect for Czechoslovakia.

BOOK THREE

The Dawn

In Which the First Light Pierces the Darkness and the Sun Begins to Rise

IX

False Dawn or First Light?

After the Polish and Hungarian uprisings, the years in Eastern Europe were essentially downhill in terms of liberalization, of "humanizing Marxism," until at least late 1960. But it would be inaccurate to think of the late 1950s as a simple return to the period preceding Stalin's death. It was a time of controlled regression studded with startling contradictions and rich in new stirrings. It was also a formative period for the emerging generation of Communist leaders, a time of rethinking and reformulating positions and preparing for a comeback. This is not to imply, of course, that the liberal leaders of 1956 were consciously retrenching, let alone deliberately conspiring, to produce fresh rebellions when the right moment came again. The history of Eastern Europe in those years was much more complex, more spontaneous and instinctive.

For one thing, the international situation was markedly different from the immediate postwar period when for all practical purposes Stalin had succeeded in keeping his satellite empire sealed from outside influences. Now there was increasing travel, the beginnings of tourism, rising trade with the West, a quickening circulation of ideas, and, all in all, a growing sense of participation in world affairs. Eastern Europe's isolation had ended and even the bloodbath inflicted by the Soviet tanks in Budapest could not change this state of affairs. For another thing, the historical truism was being demonstrated that there may be gains—and sometimes quiet victories—even in defeat. There was a new sense, felt instinctively if not proven empirically, that the Soviet monolith had been cracked and that the fissures which had first appeared with Stalin's death and spread with Khrushchev's secret speech and the Polish and Hungarian challenges would deepen and widen with the passage of time. In ordering the

Hungarian intervention, the Kremlin had temporarily arrested this trend, but it had no magic wand to make the waves recede forever. And the waves were building up again, at first far out of sight, then closer and closer to the Soviet breakwater. There was a brief writers' revolt in Bulgaria, the most reliable of Soviet satellites, in 1957; ferment in tightly controlled Romania in 1956 was followed by dangerous storm warnings in 1957, *after* the Hungarian uprising; and in Czechoslovakia the intellectuals were feverishly, if discreetly, experimenting with new ideas, increasingly finding sympathies among the younger men in the Party apparatus.

For Khrushchev and the Soviet Union, then, the period offered a moratorium of sorts. But the possible advantages of this moratorium, in terms of constructing a viable relationship with Eastern Europe, were lost in the confusions and contradictions of Moscow's foreign and domestic problems and never understood. Oscillating wildly between coexistence and renewed political warfare with Tito's Yugoslavia, bogging down in pointless intrigues in the East European capitals, first thawing and then freezing his relations with the United States, hungrily involving himself in the affairs of Fidel Castro's revolutionary Cuba, and, in general, conducting a foreign policy of breathlessly contradictory fits and starts, Khrushchev succeeded in opening a schism with China, losing Albania altogether, and simultaneously encouraging new trends of defiance elsewhere in the Communist world.

I have expressed my belief that the invasion of Czechoslovakia in August 1968 and the formal liquidation of the Prague Spring were only an episode in the long struggle for humanizing, liberalizing, democratizing, and nationalizing socialism in Eastern Europe—certainly *not* the end of the whole process. Hungary 1956 was a lost battle, but it was not a war won by the Soviet Union, as the developments of the next decade were to show; and, by the same token, Czechoslovakia was another lost battle but just as certainly *not* a lost war. The August invasion and Alexander Dubček's fall from power in April 1969 evoked in the West the feeling that this was "the end of a dream." But it is already possible to acquire a broader sense of perspective. The "dream" perhaps after all has not ended.

This perspective, I believe, may be made more meaningful through an understanding of the over-all East European process following the quelling of the Hungarian revolution. It is therefore important to turn our attention to the quiet happenings in Romania that, already in 1957, were acquiring a special significance in East European history.

This Romanian phenomenon could be called "Romanian parallelism." From the very outset, it was a nationalistic position, concerned more with the assertion of Romania's national rights and identity within Communism than with liberalization or democratization within Communism. A slowly developing interest in these latter aspects appeared only in the late 1960s, but by then, paradoxically, Romania had gone much further than Czechoslovakia in effectively challenging the Soviet Union and insisting on her independence. Bucharest was able to make this challenge, which included a violent public condemnation of the Czechoslovak invasion, with impunity because of the extraordinary subtlety and artfulness of its policies.

The Romanians' behavior was, in fact, infinitely more nationalistic even than the Yugoslavs'. Whereas virtually no anti-Russian tradition in Yugoslavia had existed before 1948, fear and hatred of Russia, as of the Turks, was a major factor in Romanian history. When Czarist Russia helped Romania to end centuries-long Turkish domination, the price she exacted was a swatch of Romanian territory. In the 1830s, following this sobering experience, the Romanians spent a fortune building a line of fortifications against the Russians that made Bucharest the world's best defended capital after Paris. In World War Two, the Soviet price for liberating Romania, whose troops had first fought on the Nazi side and succeeded in occupying Odessa, was the annexation of Bessarabia. There are even sound reasons to believe that the Russians and the handful of Romanian "Moscow Communists" took a dim view of the August 23, 1944, *coup d'état* executed by King Michael and his generals together with Romanian "home Communists" that switched Romania from the Axis to the Allied camp. Moscow would have preferred to see Bucharest liberated by Soviet troops, even though the coup dealt a blow to the German armies. This incident continues to rankle, and to feed the resentment against Moscow on the part of Romanian "home Communists."

Another factor in explaining Romania's nationalism is that she is a non-Slav nation in a Slav sea. The Romanians are descended from the ancient Dacians, an Illyrian tribe famous for toughness and combativeness which was finally tamed by the Romans. Romanian culture and language are essentially Roman and Latin in origin, and all along Romanian intellectuals and politicians, monarchists and Communists alike, have felt a cultural superiority over their Slav neighbors. When the Romanian Communist regime became actively engaged in emphasizing the country's nationalism, stress was placed on this Dacian-Roman heritage; Slavic and Russian influences tended to be dismissed as secondary. (This Romanian sense of special identity is considerably more pronounced than that of the Hungarians, who likewise are not Slavs but whose rather obscure origins are traced more in the direction of Mongol Asia than to a great world civilization.)

All this said, however, the Bucharest leaders made a point of being good and loyal Communists—up to a point. In 1948 the Cominform act of excommunicating Yugoslavia was drawn up in Bucharest, and the Romanian Party signed the document. But no "Titoist" purges and trials took place in Romania, despite Moscow's and the MGB's pressures. The Romanian Party's General Secretary, Gheorghe Gheorghiu-Dej, might have been fronting for the Moscow-directed group within the Party headed by "Red" Ana Pauker, but he had the sense to realize that his own head would roll if he allowed a "Titoist" purge. Instead, Gheorghiu-Dej accomplished in May 1952, six months *before* the execution of the Slánský group in Prague, the rather extraordinary feat of purging the *Moscow* Communists in the Romanian Party. Eliminated from the leadership were Ana Pauker, Vasile Luca, and Teohari Georgescu, the three secretaries of the Central Committee in charge, respectively, of foreign affairs, planning, and secret police.

Whether or not this purge was an overt act of defiance of Moscow remains a matter of debate, even though since 1962 the Bucharest leaders have insisted this was so, presenting it as *the* turning point toward Romania's independent policies. Paul Lendvai, a highly perceptive commentator on the East European scene, in his book *Eagles in Cobwebs* recommends caution in accepting this claim at face value, pointing out that in Stalin's life such a "purge" would hardly have been possible without Moscow's agreement. Soviet troops were still stationed in Romania, and the Kremlin would not gladly suffer such impertinence. Lendvai suggests that Moscow may have simply found it expedient to sacrifice the Pauker trinity for the sake of peace in the Romanian Party and to offset the country's dissatisfaction during an acute economic crisis. But the fact remains that Gheorghiu-Dej was able to eliminate his rivals largely because General Emil Bodnaras, forty-eight, until then Moscow's chief delegate in Romania in charge of the armed forces, had switched sides to join the "nationalists." It may have been more than a coincidence that

Bodnaras is a Bessarabian, a native of the region annexed by the Soviet Union. In any event, the shake-up marked the end of the Moscow group's influence in Romanian politics and, as events have shown, the subsequent policies increasingly and, with a consistency lacking elsewhere in the Communist world, emphasized Romania's national identity.

On the other hand, Gheorghiu-Dej permitted no experiments in political relaxation, even after Stalin's death in 1953. In April 1954 former Justice Minister Pătrăşcanu was executed after six years in prison; evidence now available indicates this was an internal settling of old accounts on the part of Gheorghiu-Dej and his security chief, Alexandru Draghici. It was the only known political execution in Romania since 1946.

On the day after Pătrăşcanu's death, a thirty-seven-year-old member of the Party's Central Committee named Nicolae Ceauşescu was elevated to the Secretariat and the Politburo. A onetime Communist Youth leader, a Central Committee member since 1948, and a perfect *apparatchik*, Ceauşescu was a protégé of Gheorghiu-Dej's. It was his good fortune that the Politburo decision to execute Pătrăşcanu was taken hours *before* he joined this body. Ceauşescu was thus able to emerge in later years as a leader with "clean hands," free to rehabilitate Pătrăşcanu posthumously, condemn Gheorghiu-Dej, and stand before the world as a chief of state with an untarnished reputation and the right to protest against violations of "socialist legality." It is also relevant that when, in 1968, Ceauşescu rose against the Soviet invasion of Czechoslovakia and turned Romanian independence into a major factor in East European affairs, one of his closest associates was the Bessarabian Bodnaras.

There is an interesting parallel between the careers of Ceauşescu and Alexander Dubček. One tends to think of both of them as East European Communists of the second generation, certainly as compared to the Brezhnevs, Gomułkas, Kadárs, and Husáks. But to what extent are the Stalinist excesses of the earlier generation reflected on them? Ceauşescu was on the Central Committee when Pătrăşcanu was killed, and as a member of the Politburo, he joined with the Party leaders in 1956 to prevent a post-Stalin liberal explosion in Romania. Dubček, as we have seen, was on the Central Committee of the Slovak Party in 1954 when Husák and the other Slovak nationalists were condemned to long prison sentences. He is not known to have protested this action, any more than he is known to have protested Soviet actions in Hungary two years later. However, if, in the end, the Romanians and the Czechoslovaks do not hold their pasts against Ceauşescu and Dubček, it may be specious, if not downright arrogant, for others to do so. It is in any case clear that as "home Communists," relatively free of the psychotic tensions of Stalinism and of the guilt complexes about the purges of the 1950s, they could develop a sense of identity with their peoples that none of their predecessors achieved. Both were products of the orthodox Communist apparatus and there was nothing in their early careers to indicate that they had special qualities of leadership. This in itself says a great deal not only about the two men but also about present-day Communism and Eastern Europe. In contrast to some earlier great figures in the Communist world, neither is flamboyant or even particularly articulate. They represent a new breed of plain-speaking, acharismatic leader, which may have been exactly what East Europeans needed and wanted after the brain-dulling rhetorical haranguers of the Moscow school.

For different reasons, as we shall see later, Ceauşescu and Dubček became the only European Communist leaders who enjoyed and commanded widespread popular support and sympathy among Communists and non-Communists alike, who were accepted as *national* leaders. (Tito was, of course, a special but important case: the wartime chief of a national resistance movement and the leader of a national defiance of the Soviet Union. In a moment of insight, Khrushchev captured this reality when he said in his secret speech that Stalin had failed to overthrow Tito because the Yugoslav had "behind him a state and a people who had gone through a severe school of fighting for liberty and independence, a people which gave support to its leaders.")

In any event, Gheorghiu-Dej and his associates, including Ceauşescu, were by 1958 busy drafting their blueprint for national independence. At that point, however, Khrushchev decided to withdraw the Soviet troops that had been stationed in Romania since the end of the war. This was apparently a part of his short-lived "peace strategy" in 1958, but it is totally unclear whether he did it on his own initiative (and, if so, why) or to meet Romanian demands. Either way, it was a move that Brezhnev was acutely to regret ten years later.

In Czechoslovakia, the period after the Hungarian rising showed, at first, a hardening of the political line. The tone was set by President Zápotocký when he visited Moscow in January 1957 in response to Khrushchev's urgent summons. Total approval for everything the Soviet Union represented was given; it was, emotionally, a return to Stalinism. On his arrival in Moscow, Zápotocký announced that "for the people of

Czechoslovakia friendship with the Soviet Union is most fundamental." This was precisely what the Kremlin wished to hear, and, pleased with the Czechoslovak attitude, Soviet President Klimenti Voroshilov told Zápotocký in a banquet toast, "The Czechoslovak Communist Party members are the best, the closest, and the dearest friends of . . . the Communist Party of the Soviet Union."

During his Moscow visit, Zápotocký made a point of making a pilgrimage to Stalin's tomb in the Kremlin and to lay a wreath with the words "To the Great Leader of Socialism—J. V. Stalin." The Prague leaders, easily given to wishful thinking, had evidently concluded that Khrushchev's secret speech eleven months earlier had been an indiscretion to be elegantly forgotten. Accordingly, *Rudé Právo* wrote in an editorial on January 29 that "the ambiguous word 'de-Stalinization' stands only for the idea of weakening and giving way to the forces of reaction. . . . It serves as a hiding place for two other very evident ideas— the loosening of friendship and the betrayal of the alliance with the Soviet Union. . . . Those who beat the drum of de-Stalinization and so-called national Communism follow the official tune composed and conducted by the American State Department."

That Novotný and Zápotocký would feel more at home in a well-arranged Stalinist—or post-de-Stalinization—world than among the uncertainties of liberalization had been made clear in a rather remarkable statement of Zápotocký's back in 1945: "After long years of personal experience, I can assure you that often I gain more by submitting to a decision, even though I may consider it unjust, than by obstinately protesting against it."

No sooner had the dangers of liberalization been pushed back with Russia's intervention in Hungary than Zápotocký and his friends began to silence those who had been so "obstinately protesting." Their immediate target, naturally, were the writers. Already in December the youth newspaper *Mladá Fronta* denounced them for a lack of "true Marxist-Leninist spirit," and in January it chastised them for "escapist" tendencies. When the Slovak Communist Party convened in April, speeches of praise for the Soviet Union were blended with attacks on the critics of the system.

All this activity served to set the stage for the Third Congress of the Czechoslovak Writers' Union late in June 1957, when the regime was able to apply punishment for the writers' rebellion of the preceding year. At the June 28 session of the Writers' Congress, the poet František Hrubín was forced to apologize publicly for his speech the year before that had set in motion the intellectuals' uprising. Again, the Party demonstrated its proclivity for self-delusion and for confusing appearance with reality as it delightedly accepted Hrubín's recantation as an assurance that all was well again in the Czechoslovak literary world. For Hrubín's personal capitulation had not the remotest link with the real world of the writers, who simply went underground and never abandoned their struggle for intellectual and political freedom. The Party inflicted other minor punishments on writers and editors, but it could not break their spirit. Jaroslav Seifert did not recant and remained on the Union's Presidium. The Květen group stayed together and both *Květen* and *Nový Život* managed to go on publishing. From all this continuing, if less ostensible ferment, a generation of writers emerged who ten years later helped to deliver the *coup de grâce* to the Moscow Communists in Czechoslovakia. In addition to Seifert and Eduard Goldstücker, who had been released from prison in 1956, there were the poet Jan Procházka, who was twenty-eight years old in 1957; the playwrights Ivan Klima, twenty-six, and Václav Havel, twenty-one; and the Slovak novelist Ladislav Mňačko, thirty-eight, among others.

It took the slow-reacting and self-deluding regime two years to discover that it had failed to lead Czechoslovakia's intellectuals back to "socialist realism." When it did, the Party ordered a special meeting of the Writers' Union in March 1959 to expel Seifert and four other liberals from the Presidium and to install in their place the Stalinist ideologues Ladislav Stoll and Jiří Taufer and a half-dozen obedient hacks. A few months later, the Party thought it had struck another mortal blow by closing down both *Květen* and *Nový Život*. But the writers were busy writing for the "drawer"—an exercise that proved to be more explosively revolutionary than the conspiracies to which the Party was so accustomed from its own experience.

In the political field, re-Stalinization in Czechoslovakia was so successful that when Khrushchev visited Prague in July 1957—a month after a Central Committee session fired a new salvo of plaudits to the Soviet Union—he happily told the workers at the giant ČKD metallurgical plant, "We are leaving you with the conviction that the cause of Leninism in Czechoslovakia is in good hands." Unlike the Czechoslovak leaders, however, Khrushchev had the good taste not to mention in the same breath the cause of "Stalinism."

Prague also slowed down the process of reviewing the sentences of the victims of the Great Purge. Too many prisoners had already been released and rehabilitated, as far as the regime was concerned. Consequently, Interior Minister Barák—who had a hand in many of these releases—rose at the June 1957 meeting of the Party's Central Committee to declare that there had been "erroneous interpretations of our laws" resulting in what he called "false conclusions that the observance of socialist legality implies a certain liberalistic attitude toward perpetrators of criminal acts." Eating crow, along with many of his colleagues, he criticized the Supreme Court and other courts for too much leniency in punishing crimes against the "construction of socialist society." *Rudé Právo* quoted Prosecutor General Bartuška's complaints about "serious liberalistic tendencies in the judicial practice" and his indignant charge that there were important Party members and government officials who "wished to see the main front of the struggle for the strengthening of socialist legality in revisions of trials and arrangements for clemency," who had forgotten that "class enemies and their allies wanted to exploit the Party's criticism of matters of socialist legality for their own benefit."

Then in September Barák's investigating commission submitted its report to the Central Committee confirming most of the sentences handed down during the purges. The Barák report, which it had been believed, before re-Stalinization set in, was taking another direction (and there is evidence to suggest that Barák signed the report reluctantly), also concluded that the "unmasking" of Slánský had "greatly helped the Party" and that his death sentence was "just and equitable." The only consolation was that men who had already been released partly through Barák's earlier efforts—Smrkovský, Pavel, Goldstücker, London, and many others—were not rearrested.

The final touch was that the two men who *were* rehabilitated in 1958 were Major Doubek and Captain Kohoutek, the two chief "referents" at Ruzyň prison and the principal authors of the "evidence" in the Slánský trials. They had been convicted in 1955 for fabricating evidence, and their arrest had followed the Moscow executions of their MGB bosses. Kohoutek now went into quiet retirement, but Doubek was named to an important post in the Czechoslovak travel agency, Čedok, and was further rewarded with an appointment to the management of the Czechoslovak pavilion at the Brussels International Fair in 1958, while many of his victims still lingered in prison. As it was to be after the 1968 invasion, the power of the secret police was being reasserted and could once more look after its own. Also in 1958, in a classic demonstration of how "socialist legality" worked in the 1950s, a regional court in Jihlava, in southern Moravia, sentenced six monks of the Premonstratensian Order to prison terms ranging from one to four and a half years for "subversion against Czechoslovakia." Seven nuns were likewise sentenced in Brno. This was the third instance of proceedings taken against the church since 1948, though admittedly a limited one, and the charges against the monks showed the spirit still pervading Czechoslovakia's judicial apparatus. It appears that the monks had publicly expressed "dissatisfaction" with the proceedings of the government against the churches and religious orders during the earlier purges: this was defined as "general hatred of the people's democratic system" and, therefore, as "subversion." The Jihlava court was thus able to classify the monks' attitude as a criminal offense.

In November 1957 President Zápotocký, the pliant, colorless, and not intensely disliked man who took pleasure in folk music, died in Prague at the age of seventy-three. He was replaced in the Presidency by Novotný, who combined the post with his First Secretaryship of the Party. As the third "worker-President" to move into Hradčany Castle, Novotný, the onetime metal worker, was now undisputed leader of Czechoslovakia. But his ascent to the Presidency made no difference whatsoever in the political picture. Around him in the Presidium were all the tired old faces of Czechoslovak Stalinism and a smattering of younger but equally obedient men, such as Barák. The cast of Presidium characters was still made up of Široký, the tough Slovak who had been Premier since 1953; Bacílek, the former State Security Minister and now head of the Slovak Party; the propaganda chief, Kopecký; the economist, Dolanský; and the aging Fierlinger. In June 1958 the Party congress added to the Presidium Jiří Hendrych, a budding ideologist and onetime film-industry head who was destined to replace Kopecký in the propaganda czardom; Pavel David, an obscure Slovak *apparatchik* still obsessed with "bourgeois nationalism"; and Otakar Šimůnek, an engineer who rose to be Minister of Chemical Industry and then chairman of the State Planning Commission, the first "technocrat" to reach the top ranks of the KSČ.

To consolidate his hold over Eastern Europe after the explosive chain reaction of 1956, Khrushchev had to end his shaky honeymoon with Yugoslavia. The dilemma was whether it was worse for him and the Soviet Union to tolerate Yugoslavia's steadily developing independence in the political, economic, ideological, and military fields or to eat his words of the secret speech in which he had berated Stalin for his "shameful role" in breaking with Tito. But the consolidation process required a demonology, just as one had been needed in 1948. With Hungary prostrated and Poland pushed against the wall, Moscow had no other available ideological enemy within the Communist world except Yugoslavia, and thus the only dialectical decision Khrushchev could rationally make was to produce Tito again as the official villain of Marxism-Leninism.

To an outsider, such a drastic about-face might have seemed dizzying, not to say inconsistent and embarrassing, if Khrushchev wanted to be taken seriously after the tremendous watershed in Communist history caused by his 1956 secret speech. But to a Communist schooled in the turntable flexibility offered through the instrumentality of Marxist dialectics, Khrushchev's assault on Tito made perfect sense. An ideological enemy was necessary, and if one did not exist it would have to be invented. Khrushchev had a special gift for this sort of foreign-policy acrobatics—as he demonstrated during that same year in his dealings with the United States, when he went full circle from the "Spirit of Camp David" to a new Cold War freeze and back again to *détente*.

At the same time, it was a demonstrable fact that Yugoslavia was a highly disturbing presence in Communist Eastern Europe. Politically, she was moving toward virtual neutrality in the East-West conflict through Tito's policies of nonalignment. She had committed the cardinal sin of accepting United States aid—after Stalin had forbidden the Communist-bloc countries to join the Marshall Plan—and between 1949 and 1955 this assistance totaled 600 million dollars in economic aid and 588 million dollars in the military sphere. Above all, Yugoslavia was turning into a model of relative prosperity under Tito's heretical guidance, while the rest of the Communist world wallowed in economic crises, low living standards, inadequacy, and Party-line managerial confusion. The contrast between Yugoslavia and Czechoslovakia was a case in point. Though numerical comparisons are dangerous and misleading because of Czechoslovakia's Moscow-inspired system of statistical measurements in terms of index and percentage figures, it was obvious by 1958 that Yugoslavia had forged ahead in increasing per-capita incomes. In industry, the annual growth rate in Yugoslavia was 12 per cent as compared to 10.9 per cent in Czechoslovakia, according to the official figures. The Yugoslav achievement was particularly impressive because the country had no prewar industrial base worth mentioning, while Czechoslovakia was highly industrialized. Furthermore, Yugoslav productivity was the result of a steadily decentralized system—ushered in by the 1950 decision to launch a collective-management experiment—and Czechoslovakia's was based on the murderously harsh method of enforcing centrally established production norms.

But the chief difference was in living standards. Czechoslovakia followed the Stalinist inspiration of concentrating on heavy industry at the expense of consumer goods, while Yugoslavia sought to develop both. In 1958 Yugoslavia had the world's second highest rate of growth in Gross National Product, but Czechoslovakia was lagging far behind even some semideveloped nations. In agriculture, Czechoslovakia imposed nearly total collectivization practices. The Yugoslavs, faced with the historical problem of the Balkan agricultural deficiency, had in 1953 decided pragmatically to abandon the inefficient forced collectivization and to encourage individual farming. The result was higher and more diversified land production. In 1958 a visit to Prague stores selling foodstuffs or consumer goods revealed striking shortages. But in Belgrade, Zagreb, and other Yugoslav cities, the customer usually had adequate supplies and a varied choice.

On another level, the Czechoslovak economy was plagued with worker absenteeism, which stood at about 9 per cent in 1958, as the workers looked for excuses to stay home because "why bother?" Job-hopping—constant changes in employment—affected about half of the total labor force in 1953 and more than a quarter in 1958, when so-called antifluctuation measures were applied. In Yugoslavia, where decentralization had ironically produced a degree of unemployment, absenteeism was negligible and job-hopping no more frequent than elsewhere in the Western world. The collective-management system of workers' councils offered incentives that the ideologically straitjacketed economies in Eastern Europe could not risk. Only in the mid-1960s did Czechoslovakia, Hungary, or Romania dare to experiment with pay incentives, profit sharing, and collective management. Even Soviet economic planners, rediscovering Evsei Liberman's ideas, began playing with cash incentives for the workers.

For all these negative and positive reasons, therefore, Khrushchev felt justified in launching a second ideological offensive against Tito. Unlike Stalin, however, he was sensible enough never to consider overthrowing Tito by "shaking his little finger" or anything of the sort. He was too realistic, pragmatic, cynical. The attack was purely ideological—or just for show—and it had limited objectives, as the Yugoslavs realized with wry amusement.

No regime was more pleased with this second anti-Titoist campaign than Novotný's group in Prague. Czechoslovak prisons were still full of victims of the Titoist purges, and a revival of anti-Tito demonology gave the KSČ leadership the sense of security it had lost in 1956.

The offensive was first launched from Bulgaria in 1958, when the Soviet Union encouraged the reopening of the Macedonian question, a subject always dear to Bulgarian hearts. The break with Tito in 1948 had started over Tito's policies on Bulgaria and Albania, so it was logical that the second round should also be initiated on Bulgarian territory. Accordingly, Khrushchev arrived in Sofia in June 1958 to attend the Seventh Congress of the Bulgarian Communist Party and used the occasion to announce that the Cominform's excommunication of Yugoslavia ten years earlier had been "basically correct." This diagnosis was offered by the same man who two years earlier had proclaimed that "the 'Yugoslav affair' contained no problems which could not have been solved through Party discussions among comrades" and that "it was completely possible to have prevented the rupture of relations with that country."

Having explained in Moscow in 1956 that "the liquidation of the abnormal relationship with Yugoslavia was [being] done in the interest of the whole camp of Socialism," Khrushchev argued in Sofia that Tito was a "revisionist" who had helped in the Hungarian uprising (presumably a reference to the asylum offered Imre Nagy at the Yugoslav Embassy in Budapest after the Soviet tanks overthrew his regime), and who was a "Trojan horse" in the Communist movement. Tito, who was not nearly so worried in 1958 as he had been in 1948 by the Soviet denunciations, confined himself to the observation that "there was so much mention of Yugoslavia at the Bulgarian Party Congress that it reminded me of a congress of Yugoslav factions."

The Czechoslovak Communists enthusiastically followed suit in denouncing Tito. When the KSČ held its congress in June, immediately after Khrushchev's visit to Sofia, Novotný in almost identical words said that the 1948 Cominform resolution against Yugoslavia had been "correct in principle." While he deplored the 1949 resolution urging an uprising against Tito, he charged the Yugoslavs with distorting and falsifying Marxism-Leninism "from opportunistic, nationalistic, and subjectivistic positions." On June 23 the KSČ Congress dutifully approved a special resolution criticizing the "un-Marxist revisionist attitude proclaimed by the Yugoslav Communist League." In fact, the Czechoslovaks had anticipated Khrushchev's attack by earlier thrusts of their own. A publication of the Czechoslovak Central Administration for Land Survey and Cartography in 1957 referred to Yugoslavia as a "revolution which has only partly succeeded," mentioned derisively the "so-called Workers' Councils," patronizingly described the Yugoslav economy as "stagnating" and developing "haphazardly," and noted a trend toward the "restoration of the bourgeois system." When the CPSU boycotted the Yugoslav Party Congress in April 1958, the KSČ did likewise (in a gesture that was to be repeated under direct Soviet orders in 1969). The Czechoslovak ambassador in Belgrade attended the congress as an observer but left the hall right behind the Soviet ambassador when a high Yugoslav official chided Moscow for its attitude toward Tito's Party.

There was one thing, however, of which Tito could not yet be accused by his detractors: liberalism in Yugoslavia's internal politics. Political liberalization was not to accompany Tito's economic experimentation and flexibility in foreign policy until 1966. The secret police, the UDBA, still rode herd on political dissidents, Communist or not. In 1958 the most celebrated prisoner in Yugoslavia was forty-seven-year-old Milovan Djilas, a former Partisan general and once the nation's Vice-President. Djilas's crime had been to argue publicly that political freedom and dissent must accompany economic reform, to criticize the excesses of the new Communist bureaucracy in his 1953 book *The New Class*, and to reveal, in *Conversations with Stalin*, his many dealings with the late Soviet dictator. To pay for these offenses, Djilas had been expelled from the Party's Central Committee in 1954 and, subsequently, imprisoned. He was to spend nine years in prison and to emerge, in time, as one of the few original modern Marxist philosophers in Eastern Europe before the Prague Spring.

That Khrushchev's anti-Titoist campaign of 1958–1959 did nothing to further the interest of Communist unity is a matter of record. Instead, these years brought the Soviet Union two new formidable problems which, more than a decade later, still remained insoluble, threatening in the most fundamental way what was left of the Soviet-led Communist ideological system. One was China, and the other was Cuba.

The schism between Moscow and Peking began to take shape in 1958 over the issues of national interest. Stalin had decisively helped Mao Tse-tung to victory on the Chinese mainland in the years between the end of World War Two and 1949, but the historical enmity and rivalry between these two Asiatic powers soon overshadowed their ideological links. The question, quite simply, was whether the Russians or the Chinese would determine Peking's political and military policies. The precise origins of the dispute remain unclear, but the roots of this conflict may well be found in the Korean War, when the Chinese crossed the Yalu River to engage American and South Korean forces in open warfare and the Soviets confined themselves mainly to verbal broadsides against Washington, a cautious attitude which the Chinese clearly resented. Then, in 1958, Moscow refused to continue to assist the Chinese in developing nuclear weapons on the not unreasonable grounds that, things being what they were, the Soviet Union might one day become the primary target of Peking's bombs. As the ill feelings escalated, the Soviet Union withdrew its thousands of technical advisers from China, reduced its economic aid to Mao's regime, and, finally, faced the Chinese with the choice of "swimming with us or sinking alone."

But it is possible that the Sino-Soviet dispute has even deeper roots. W. Averell Harriman, who was the American ambassador in Moscow at the end of World War Two, remembers Stalin telling him in private conversations that Mao was a "margarine Communist," not worthy of trust. As Harriman told me in a recent conversation, Stalin had hoped that a different and pro-Soviet Communist Party would emerge in China without Mao and this is why he agreed at the Yalta Conference to recognize Chiang Kai-shek's Nationalists. He switched to Mao, Harriman said, when Chiang began collapsing.

China, as reluctant to capitulate as Yugoslavia had been ten years earlier, responded with ideological attacks on the Soviet leadership. In the way of Communist politics, Mao hurled the same epithet—"revisionist"—at Khrushchev that the Soviets had hurled at Tito. To complicate matters, Peking, proclaiming its allegiance to Stalin's memory, also denounced Tito as a "revisionist," but for reasons diametrically opposed to Khrushchev's. To Tito, on the other hand, both China and the Soviet Union were Stalinist. All these exchanges marked the beginning of the wildly confusing semantic battle in Communist international politics, in which one Communist's "rightist deviationist" is another's "leftist deviationist," in which progressivism, conservatism, dogmatism, sectarianism, and revisionism hold different meanings for different Communists. The events in Czechoslovakia in 1968–1969 gave this distracting game of words a still more bewildering dimension as China and Albania denounced Soviet "revisionists" for invading the Czechoslovak "revisionists'" land and then rallied around to the propagandist defense of Prague.

But the semantic contest had deep implications. The Soviet-Chinese dispute opened up an Asian "second front," and it cannot be excluded that one ingredient in the Kremlin's decision to invade Czechoslovakia was the belief that the Soviet Union must be firmly secured in Eastern Europe in order to have maximum freedom and resources to cope with the Chinese threat. In this sense, then, China is part of the Czechoslovak story.

In any event, the Soviet Union sought in classical Stalinist fashion to settle this problem through self-deluding but loudly ringing declarations. In November 1960 Khrushchev summoned eighty foreign Communist parties to Moscow to join the CPSU in issuing formal condemnations of China and Yugoslavia. Some of them, like the obedient Czechoslovak Party, enthusiastically signed the document. Others, like the Romanians and the Italians, did so against their better judgment. But Khrushchev lost the North Vietnamese and North Korean parties. This was the beginning of the erosion of Moscow's role as *the* leading Communist capital in the world. Despite their obedience at the time, the Czechoslovaks could not have failed to hear the siren song of national Communisms at the 1960 Moscow conference.

Prior to the open break with China, Khrushchev succeeded in involving the Soviet Union in Cuba—with disastrous consequences for the Soviet cause. This was a case of political and ideological greed, awesome miscalculations, and ultimately a clash with a man as resilient and independent as Tito and Mao.

On January 1, 1959, in Cuba, a bearded thirty-three-old guerrilla leader named Fidel Castro Ruz brought down the dictatorship of President Fulgencio Batista, climaxing a rebellion that had started two years earlier, in the easternmost Sierra Maestra mountains. Castro, an instinctive, brilliant politician of Marxist persuasion, was the head of the liberal and non-Communist 26th of July Movement, which both Moscow and the Cuban Communist Party witlessly chose to ignore until almost the last moment. For twenty-one months, the Communists regarded Castro and his Movement as "bourgeois" *putsch*-makers and therefore ideologically repugnant. In September 1958, when Castro was in sight of victory, the Cuban Party (which had once contributed ministers to Batista's regime) sent an emissary to the Sierra Maestra to negotiate with him. This was five months after the Communists had brought about the failure of a general strike called by the 26th of July Movement by their refusal to cooperate. There are also reasons to believe that in 1957 a Communist Youth agent, acting on Party instructions, had betrayed and delivered four pro-Castro students to the Batista police and their deaths.

Once in power, as Premier of the revolutionary government, Castro made his decision to defy the United States. His aim was a radical social revolution throughout Latin America, and he realized that this could be accomplished only through a clean break with "Yankee imperialism." Seizing American property in Cuba and rejecting economic assistance proffered by the still hopeful Eisenhower administration, Castro turned to the Soviet Union for help in carrying out his ambitious plans. Castro was a pragmatic man who was ready to take what Moscow would grant him, but who had a long memory and was not planning to substitute sub-servience to the Soviet Union for subservience to the United States. This, however, Khrushchev did not understand, and within a month of Castro's victory, he dispatched Anastas Mikoyan to Cuba, which he patronizingly regarded as a candidate for satellitehood. At that moment, the Soviet Union trapped itself in Cuba, and it has been unable to extricate itself to this day.

Khrushchev's vision of a strategic foothold ninety miles from American shores and his hungry readiness to finance and equip the Cuban revolution was eventually to cost Moscow around a million dollars a day. But, true to the Soviet Union's tradition of involving its satellite states in its own operations, Khrushchev also decreed that economic assistance, trade, and technical expertise must flow to Cuba from all of Eastern Europe. Inevitably, the heaviest burden fell on Czechoslovakia. In addition to her continuing required sales and deliveries of raw materials and industrial products to the Soviet Union, Czechoslovakia now had to send experts, weapons, food, and industrial equipment to Cuba. (Later, Czechoslovak equipment was to go to Vietnam as well.) As Karel Dufek, the Foreign Ministry's press chief, remarked to me in Prague in 1968, "There is no revolution in the world in which Czechoslovak weapons are not being employed." Then, when United States–Cuban diplomatic relations were broken early in 1961, Cuba named Czechoslovakia to represent her interests in Washington.

There also was a fascinating human link between Czechoslovakia and the Cuban revolution. This link was in the person of Dr. František

Kriegel, a liberal Communist physician of Jewish origin. Dr. Kriegel, a Polish-born militant Communist since 1924, when he was sixteen, had been graduated in medicine from Prague's Charles University in 1934. Two years later, he had gone to Spain, where he served until 1939 as a doctor with the International Brigades. He spent a year interned in France, and, with the outbreak of World War Two, he joined the medical services of Czechoslovak units fighting with the Western Allies. In 1945 Dr. Kriegel returned to Czechoslovakia and was chosen a member of the Presidium of the Prague District Communist Party. There he worked with Smrkovský, Novotný, and Lubomir Strougal—men with whom he was destined to cross paths again during the Prague Spring, when he played a key and dramatic role. In 1949, after the Communist takeover, he became Deputy Minister of Health. It was both a mystery and a near miracle that he was not arrested and purged in the early 1950s—what with his Jewish origin, official prominence, and Spanish Civil War and Western Front past—although he was fired from his ministerial job in 1952 and spent the next eight years working in Prague clinics as a heart specialist. In 1960 the KSČ dispatched Dr. Kriegel, by now a jolly, balding fifty-two-year-old man, to act as adviser to the Cuban revolution's health services. He remained in Cuba until 1963, savoring the Caribbean sun and refreshing his memories of the Spanish Civil War, and then returned to Prague, plunging immediately into progressive Communist politics.

X

1960: New Hope in
a New Decade

In Czechoslovakia, the advent of 1960 and the opening of a new decade seemed to have a special psychological impact. Put in the plainest terms, the people now could say that at last the "Terrible Fifties" were over. Something new was in the air, something that whispered to the people that a change would come in their lifetime, that perhaps it was not too far away.

And, indeed, 1960 began to bring hopeful changes, even though structurally Czechoslovakia was fitted still more firmly into the Soviet political system. A new constitution, approved by the National Assembly on July 11, elevated Czechoslovakia's status from a People's Democracy to a Socialist Republic. Until then, only the Soviet Union had held this exalted rank in the orthodox Communist world—to indicate her advancement on the road to full-fledged Communism as defined by Marx, Engels, and Lenin. (Romania became a Socialist Republic in 1965.) This constitution, which replaced the May 9 Constitution of 1945, did away with the last vestiges of Western parliamentarism which, at least on paper, had existed during the life of the Czechoslovak People's Republic. Now, the new constitution said in its preamble, a "virtual completion of socialist construction" had been achieved in Czechoslovakia and "socialism has won in our country. . . . We have entered upon a new stage of our history and [are] determined to proceed to new and higher goals . . . in completing socialist society and gathering forces for the transition to Communism."

But, in practice, this transition brought about the strengthening of harsh Soviet-type legal provisions, such as the formal creation of "local people's courts," the omission in the new charter of any reference to the right to small private landholdings or businesses, and the pledge made by Novotný in addressing the Central Committee on April 15, 1960, to eradicate "all remnants of the liberalistic, pseudodemocratic principle of the separation of powers." This last point, copied from the Soviets, meant the unification of all government and Party functions under the control of the KSČ and the abolition of even the theoretical independence of the legislature and judiciary. In practice, obviously, the separation of powers in Czechoslovakia had ceased to exist long before, since the Party representatives in the armed forces, the security services, and all the ministries participated in all decision-making and most of the ministers were members of the Central Committee. And the National Assembly and the court system did what they were told by the Party.

But human behavior cannot be legislated in a constitutional law. While the triumph of structural socialism in Czechoslovakia was being proclaimed, life was moving away from it, and sweeping Novotný and his cohorts along. Thus, either in jubilation or in order to make the nation better swallow the new constitution, an amnesty was proclaimed, bringing freedom to Gustav Husák, imprisoned for nine years, to most of those condemned in the Slovak "bourgeois nationalist" trials, and to those caught in the other proceedings dating back to the Great Purge, such as the economist Evžen Löbl.

As soon as he was liberated, Husák went to work for the Pozemni Stavby construction firm in Bratislava. Other former high officials released from prison in 1955 and 1956 were making a comeback to a decent life. Josef Smrkovský, freed in 1955, had spent a year as an employee in the State Farms and Forests Administration and had been appointed head of the farm cooperative in Pavlovice, in Moravia. Later, he was transferred to manage the Jestřebí cooperative, in northern Bohemia. General Pavel was still working at the Czechoslovak Union of Physical Training. General Svoboda, freed in 1953, and since 1954 a member of the National Assembly, was a high official in the Institute of Military History in Prague. Still loyal to the Soviet Union, he was active in the Czechoslovak-Soviet Friendship Society and in the Union of Antifascist Fighters.

On the same day that the National Assembly approved the new Soviet-style constitution, Alexander Dubček was elected to the Central Committee of the KSČ and named to membership in the Party's Secretariat—another of those ironic coincidences haunting Czechoslovak Communist history. Still another was, of course, that Dubček was entering the inner sanctum just as Husák was being freed from prison. The fates of these two Slovaks seemed always to cross.

Dubček's ascension to the Central Committee and the Secretariat was a rather extraordinary accolade. It is apparently not known what or who prompted the leadership to select him for the key Secretariat job, placing him ahead of many well-known, experienced, and probably deserving apparatus figures. At the age of thirty-nine, he was completely unknown on the national scene, despite his tenure on the Slovak Party's Central Committee and his three years in Moscow. And his liberal and progressive leanings, even if he held them in 1960, would not have endeared him to Novotný, still busy exorcising the devils of "revisionism" and associated sins. The best guess is that the Party felt that new blood was needed in the Secretariat, and that Dubček seemed to qualify, being a model *apparatchik*, an easy man to get along with, and a noncontroversial Slovak (the Party tried at all times to assure Slovak representation in its highest bodies). In a sense, Dubček became the Slovak counterpart to Oldřich Černík, a Moravian, also thirty-nine, and likewise a fast-rising apparatus man who had joined the Secretariat in 1956.

In the structure of the KSČ, the Secretariat is the strategic political organ. The secretaries distribute among themselves responsibilities for the Party cadres, armed forces, security organs, economy, foreign policy, and so on. The Secretariat also coordinates the work of the special departments of the Central Committee—such as those concerned with the armed forces, security, international relations, propaganda, etc. While the Politburo (soon renamed the Presidium) fills the principal guiding political and ideological role, the Secretariat carries out day-to-day policy, personnel, and administrative functions—which obviously gives it immense power. If it is aggressively handled, it can even overshadow the Presidium. (Probably the only justified charge made against Rudolf Slánský in 1951 was that, as the General Secretary, he had attempted to turn the Secretariat into the "leading organ," ignoring the Politburo.)

When Dubček joined the Secretariat in 1960, he was one of nine members. At the head was Novotný, the First Secretary; the only other Presidium member in the Secretariat at the time was Jiří Hendrych, the ideologue. The other members, in addition to Dubček and Černík, were Bruno Köhler, the man who replaced Kopřiva as chief of the Central Committee's Cadres Department during the purges; Vladimir Koucký, virtually the Soviet Union's representative in the Czechoslovak Party;

Vratislav Krutina; Antonín Krček; and František Zupka, a prewar Communist member of Parliament. The last three were complete non-entities.

In the Presidium, controlled by the old guard, the only relatively refreshing presence was Interior Minister Barák, who had also acquired the post of Deputy Premier. The other newcomers—Hendrych, Pavel David, and Šimůnek—did nothing to change the conservative and Stalinist character of the group. Barák, on the other hand, had been attempting to do so in his circuitous and contradictory ways ever since his surprise election to the Politburo in 1954. In 1959, when re-Stalinization was still in full swing, Barák undertook to tangle with Novotný on a whole range of issues and principles. And it is pertinent to note that he became the first high-level Communist official to challenge the regime and its philosophy, while men like Dubček and Černík, the future architects of the Prague Spring, took everything in stride.

Barák began this challenge when he returned to public life after a serious illness in 1957–1959. The interlude may have given Barák the time and opportunity to rethink his own position and that of the KSČ in the changing world. In any event, Barák challenged the extent of Novotný's personal power—strongly intimating that Novotný was beginning to behave like a little Stalin—and questioned the concept advanced in the new constitution, then in its final drafts, that there must be no separation of powers among the Party, the executive government, the legislature, and the judiciary.

Failing to win support for his position in the Presidium, and finding no encouragement for a new review of the old trials, Barák did a second extraordinary thing: he spelled out his criticism in a confidential letter to Khrushchev. By now, the Constitution had been approved, eliminating the "pseudodemocratic" concept of a separation of powers, and his letter thus constituted a major breach of Communist discipline. Adding insult to injury, he wrote that, in his opinion, Czechoslovakia's economic difficulties were linked with the "slow and indecisive" liquidation of the "cult of personality." Finally, he informed the Soviet Premier, certain members of the Presidium had participated in the preparation and organization of the political trials of the 1950s. This clearly put the finger on Novotný himself, as well as on Bacílek, who had served as State Security Minister, on Bruno Köhler, and, to a lesser extent, on Kopecký. This bordered on subversion, and, not surprisingly, Khrushchev sent Barák's letter to Novotný.

What followed was a sordid episode, with all the classical Stalinist overtones, leading to Barák's destruction. First, he was removed in June 1961 from his post as Interior Minister (in which he controlled the secret police). Then, the Party began to build up a political and criminal case against him. Major V. Jenyš, Barák's private secretary, was pressed to accuse his chief of a conspiracy to oust Novotný from power and to replace him as President and First Secretary, but Major Jenyš refused, and the plan was changed. He and Barák together were accused of embezzling a thousand dollars from government funds. This extraordinary charge apparently resulted from an incident in 1960, when Novotný, heading the Czechoslovak delegation to the United Nations General Assembly—it was the year that Khrushchev, Castro, and other heads of government attended the session—drew the thousand dollars from the delegation's funds to buy a special camera for himself. When the perplexed delegation insisted that the money be refunded (so that its books would balance and none of its members would be accused of embezzlement), Barák ordered Major Jenyš to deliver it from Interior Ministry funds to the delegation office in New York, against a receipt.

The scenario for this amazing affair had been prepared by Lubomir Strougal, a thirty-seven-year-old pro-Moscow Communist who succeeded Barák as Interior Minister after an undistinguished stint as Agriculture Minister, and Miroslav Mamula, chief of the Central Committee's Eighth Department (Security and Armed Forces) and one of the most sinister personages in Czechoslovakia. How improbable was the Strougal-Mamula plan was demonstrated on the night of January 24, 1962, when President Novotný himself dramatically burst into Barák's office to arrest Major Jenyš for embezzling the thousand dollars. To complete the picture, Novotný brought along Premier Široký, Interior Minister Strougal, Mamula, and Mamula's assistant, L. Procházka. Barák was also invited to witness the arrest. That the President of the Republic would personally undertake to arrest a minor official in the middle of the night for a possible irregularity involving a negligible amount of funds is certainly bizarre. It is perhaps even more bizarre that Strougal and Mamula were both to regain key power positions after the Soviet invasion in 1968. As recounted later by Dr. L. Schwarz, the attorney for Barák and Jenyš, Novotný's expedition turned into low comedy:

> After placing Mr. Jenyš under arrest, Mr. Novotný turned to Mr. Strougal and asked whether he was entitled to do so. . . . Mr. Strougal answered that he wasn't certain but that, after all, Mr. Novotný was Head of State, Commander-in-Chief,

and First Secretary. . . . Mr. Jenyš said, "Comrade President, this cannot be true!" But Mr. Novotný shouted him down, objecting to being addressed as "Comrade" and saying that he was expelling Mr. Jenyš from the Party. Mr. Procházka then took Mr. Jenyš to the Ruzyň jail without any warrant for his arrest.

Shortly afterward, Barák, too, was arrested on the embezzlement charge. The Příbram Superior Military Court sentenced him to fifteen years in prison and Jenyš to ten years as an "accomplice." But there was a political giveaway in this "criminal" case: an internal Party document blamed Barák's 1957 report for being "misleading and useless." Barák vanished from public life.

Barák's internment in 1962 put an end to the first progressive rebellion in the top ranks of the Czechoslovak Communist Party. His behavior may have been quixotic and naïve, especially in complaining to Khrushchev over Novotný's head, but nobody in the Party leadership—including specifically Dubček and Černík—made the slightest overt gesture in Barák's defense.

So powerful were the new contradictions within the KSČ that six months after Barák's sentencing a fresh commission was named to look into the question of the purge trials. Heading this commission was Drahomír Kolder, a young *apparatchik* from Ostrava who had been appointed to the Party's Presidium in 1961. Chiefly interested in economics, Kolder favored liberalizing economic reform in Czechoslovakia, and it was thanks to him that Ota Šik, the liberal Communist economist, was brought in to engineer the needed changes. (Later, Kolder and Šik were to clash when the former devoutly espoused the Soviet line in doing away with the Czechoslovak democratization.)

One reason why the Novotný regime was forced to reopen the eight-year-old affair of the Slánský trial was that Khrushchev embarked on his second de-Stalinization campaign at the Twenty-second Congress of the CPSU in October 1961 and, as usual, Novotný followed Moscow's example or at least acted as if he did.

This second de-Stalinization campaign appeared to result from pressures within the Soviet Union, where Khrushchev had just defeated a Molotov "anti-Party" conspiracy, from the growing disarray in the Communist world, and from the over-all international situation. It seemed convenient to mend fences everywhere and thaw out the Cold War. In 1961 Khrushchev had already called off the second anti-Tito operation and begun once more to court Yugoslavia. Problems with the Chinese were becoming increasingly serious for the Soviet Union, and Khrushchev evidently reasoned that some unity in Eastern Europe would be helpful. But instead of curing his East European headaches, Khrushchev acquired two new ones: one in Albania and the other in Romania.

Both the Albanian and the Romanian headaches were directly related to the issues of nationalism in the Communist movement and, indirectly, to China, and Soviet difficulties with these two countries must be regarded in the context of the Moscow-Peking feud. Albania remains China's chief political spokesman in Eastern Europe, and Romania's independence in the Communist world is largely guaranteed by her policy of equidistant neutrality between China and the Soviet Union. (And it should be noted that the Soviet-Chinese quarrel came out in the open at the 1960 congress of the Romanian Communist Party.)

The additional dimension in the Soviet Union's conflict with Albania in 1961 was Yugoslavia. In 1948 the Albanians had been saved from virtual annexation by Yugoslavia only by Stalin's break with Tito. Therefore, Khrushchev's reconciliation with Tito in 1955 had posed a mortal danger to Enver Hoxha and his associates. They were aware that among other demands made by Tito as the price for political peace with Moscow was their removal, and they knew that a Soviet-Yugoslav alliance could easily lead to the sacrifice of Albania to the Yugoslav appetite. Hoxha survived this crisis by swiftly eliminating all potential pro-Soviet and pro-Yugoslav figures in his government and by dint of sheer endurance. When Khrushchev launched the second anti-Yugoslav campaign in 1958, the Albanians, albeit still suspicious, were more at ease.

But the suspicions grew again when Khrushchev visited Tirana in May 1959. Presumably, he went to prepare the Albanians for the fact that, once more, he was going to make up with the Yugoslavs. But by all accounts the trip was unsuccessful. The Albanians had no faith in Khrushchev's reassurances, and they took a dim view of his advice that their economy should be based on agriculture at the expense of industrial development, so dear to the hearts of the Tirana leaders. Khrushchev, of course, was hoping to diminish Soviet investments in the Albanian economy. The striking thing, however, was that he made the same mistake the same year with Romania and with the same deplorable consequences.

Whereas Albania's salvation in 1948 was the Soviet-Yugoslav split, her survival in 1960 resulted from the Soviet-Chinese split. Deciding to play the Chinese card, the Albanian delegates to the Romanian Party Congress supported Peking's position in speeches at a secret session. Khrushchev sought vengeance by supporting a *coup d'état* by pro-Soviet elements in Tirana the next month (it failed), and through an attempt to starve out the Albanians by sharply reducing food aid shipments in the midst of a bad drought. At the conference of Communist parties in Moscow in November, Khrushchev and Hoxha nearly came to blows. The conference document denouncing Yugoslavia no longer pacified the Albanians; they distrusted the Soviets and had resolved to play Peking against Moscow. A Soviet attempt at reconciliation during the Albanian Party's congress in February 1961 failed completely. Hoxha gave all his attention to the Chinese delegates and none to the Soviet.

Thereafter, Khrushchev returned to tough tactics. He withdrew Soviet, Czechoslovak, and other allied technicians out of Albania, pulled the Soviet submarines out of the Vlora base on the Adriatic, and, finally, announced that all Soviet aid would be canceled. Instantly, China stepped into the breach, offering Albania the same 125 million dollars in credits that the Soviet bloc had just denied her. Now the rift was official and complete and in November diplomatic relations were broken. This was something that never before or after happened between Communist countries. Khrushchev's only recourse was to make virtue out of necessity and proclaim that Albania was guilty of Stalinist deviations.

In a way, Albania became to the Soviet Union what Cuba was to the United States. She was a tiny country on the periphery of the Soviet empire, but her reckless nationalism and defiance could not be smashed despite the immense, nuclear-backed Soviet power. Lacking common borders with the Soviet Union and with Russia's pliant satellites surrounding her, Albania need not fear a conventional land invasion. Where Cuba had turned to the Soviet Union for help, Albania had turned to China. Now both world empires—the American and the Soviet—were faced with the inadequacy of their overwhelming power to deal with the challenge of defiant nationalistic small states and their consequent lack of political leverage.

The Romanian crisis, coinciding with the Albanian one, was more subtle and quiet, subdued in tone but nonetheless effective in fact. It did not even produce a showdown. In the sophisticated and cautious ways of Romanian Communist diplomacy, however, it was in the long run even more dangerous to the Soviet Union. Essentially, it amounted to a declaration of Romania's political, ideological, and economic independence in the Communist world. But it had other overtones: the Bucharest leadership, not unlike the Albanian, had detected practical benefits for Romania from the widening Soviet-Chinese controversy.

The Romanian challenge took the dual form of an economic dispute with Moscow and of a political stand of emancipation. The first revolved around the Soviet Union's concept of an "international division of socialist labor" in Eastern Europe, and it was symbolized by a clash over the steel mills at Galați near the Danube delta.

The Soviet idea was that the East European economies should become fully integrated under the umbrella of the Council for Mutual Economic Assistance (Comecon), which had been organized in 1949 as a counterpart to the Marshall Plan. In practice, this would have meant that Soviet-guided Comecon planners would determine which country should concentrate on industry, and on what type of industry, and which country should dedicate its main efforts to agriculture and incidental industry. Once this process was set in motion, the blueprint indicated, the industrialized countries would exchange products with agricultural countries. The Soviet Union would be assigned both an industrial and an agricultural role because of her size and economic diversity. East Germany, Czechoslovakia, and Hungary, which already had industrial structures, would be the industrial powers of Comecon. Poland would fall between two stools, since her industry had been considerably developed since the war but she was still an agricultural country. Romania and Bulgaria, on the other hand, would dedicate themselves to farming. This was a streamlined version of the earlier arrangement under which the Soviet Union had taken from the satellites what she needed through the system of forced deliveries and dumped on them what she did not need. (One commodity that the Soviets were already beginning to dump on Eastern Europe— and on other underdeveloped countries in Asia and Africa—was the expensive Cuban sugar received from the Castro government in exchange for Soviet oil, industrial equipment, and foodstuffs.)

To this whole concept Romania took deep and powerful exception. President Gheorghiu-Dej and his chief economic planner, Alexandru Birladeanu, made it instantly clear to Moscow that Romania did not propose to turn herself into a "vegetable garden" for the benefit of the Soviet Union or Comecon and that she intended to proceed with developing industry, alone if need be. The Soviet notion of integration, they argued, would adversely affect the Romanian national interest. Much as Romania wished to cooperate with Comecon, she would not do so at the expense of her own welfare. Almost simultaneously, the Romanians informed Moscow that they were interested in credits and equipment to expand the production capacity of the Galaţi steel mills.

The Soviet Union countered with the angry charge that Romania was violating the norms of the "socialist division of labor" and with the statement that inasmuch as there was no need to increase the scope of Galaţi, the Romanians should not count on Soviet help. Gheorghiu-Dej flew to Moscow for a tense meeting with Khrushchev, at which he informed him that Romania would seek Western cooperation in building up Galaţi. As soon as he returned to Bucharest, he ordered bids to be opened to all Western firms. (In time, contracts were granted to British, West German, French, Italian, and American companies.) Faced with the prospect of being completely left out, the Soviet Union expressed interest in bidding as well and was awarded the contract for a cold-rolling mill on even-term competition with the Westerners, according to a policy that Romania was to follow in all her economic projects in the ensuing years.

In the political field, Romanian independence was expressed forcefully at a lengthy session of the Party's Central Committee in late November and early December 1961. Gheorghiu-Dej and his top associates—notably Premier Ion Gheorghe Maurer and Presidium member Nicolae Ceauşescu —used the Central Committee Plenum to attack the Soviet interference in the affairs of the Romanian Communist Party.

They also presented the argument that Romania had begun to "de-Stalinize" even before Stalin's death in 1953. In a sense, this was a continuation of the old struggle between the "home Communists" and the "Moscow Communists." Speakers described the wartime and postwar history of the Romanian Party as one long battle between the "home Communists" and "alien elements" and "immigrant groups." They spoke of comrades' risking arrest and execution at the hands of the pro-Moscow leaders after the liberation for having fought "with the International Brigades against Franco in Spain or in France against the German occupation." They berated the "Moscow Communists" for importing the Stalin personality cult into Romania, working with the Molotov "anti-Party" clique in minimizing the importance of the anti-Nazi uprising in August 1944 and then in preventing and hindering the promotion in the Party of those members who "were connected with the working class and the people."

As Paul Lendvai remarks in *Eagles in Cobwebs*, this Central Committee meeting "with its strongly nationalistic and implicitly anti-Soviet overtones was a covert manifesto of independence. . . . The Plenum, whose significance was overlooked at the time, was the first major step toward the Party's full identification with the Romanian people." Among other steps taken at the time to reawaken Romanian nationalism—which, by definition, had to be anti-Soviet—the Bucharest leadership "rehabilitated" the memory of the late historian Nicolae Iorga, an outstanding spokesman for Dacian-Romanian nationalism.

The beauty of the Romanians' tactics was that Moscow could not openly quarrel with them. Ostensibly, they were denouncing Stalinism and the Molotov "anti-Party" group from whose conspiracies Khrushchev had barely managed to save himself a few months earlier. The real meaning of the Romanian pronouncements, albeit shrouded in Byzantine subtleties, was clear, but Bucharest was not spoiling for a break, and, knowing how to stop at the water's edge, was not forcing the Soviet Union into a drastic reaction. The Soviets, with their hands full in China and Albania, did not want a showdown either. Thus, the Romanians could chalk up gain after gain and get away with it. And there was always the shadow of China and the Romanians were flirting with it, too.

Thus Soviet policy in Eastern Europe had become dangerously caught in the web of Khrushchev's efforts to fend off the "anti-Party" plotters at home and to justify the dispute with China and Albania. The new de-Stalinization led to tolerance of Romania's maneuvers, to the second reconciliation with Tito, to a Moscow-conducted purge in Bulgaria in 1962 to make Premier the relatively moderate Party First Secretary, Todor Zhivkov, and inevitably to greater permissiveness elsewhere in Eastern Europe. Even Khrushchev's confrontation with President Kennedy in October 1962 over the clandestine placing of Soviet nuclear missiles in Cuba could not distract him from these policies in Eastern Europe. (In fact, Cuba's shift toward China as a result of Castro's bitterness over the subsequent withdrawal of the missiles made it even more imperative for Khrushchev to persist on the de-Stalinization course.) And the immediate beneficiary was Czechoslovakia.

XI

Ferment

For once, events in Czechoslovakia began to move with a certain speed. In October 1962 Novotný finally convinced himself that the huge statue of Stalin on Letná Hill—the biggest statue of Stalin in the world, which he and Zápotocký had so proudly unveiled eight years earlier—was an anachronism. Workers were called to remove the monument with as little ostentation as was possible in dismantling an enormous bronze figure surrounded by a plethora of smaller figures in "socialist realist" stances. To the people of Prague, this was the symbol that times were changing. The removal of the statue—exactly one year after Khrushchev had re-dedicated himself to de-Stalinization at the Twenty-second Congress of the Soviet Party—did not mean, of course, that Novotný and his partners were about to throw in the sponge and *really* de-Stalinize Czechoslovakia. It was, instead, a tactical move made to cope with rising unrest in the Party and throughout the nation.

On the political front, there were new demands from the intellectuals and young Communists to bring Czechoslovakia out of the ideological ice age. The smashing of the Hungarian rebellion had receded into the historical past and new forces were gathering to challenge the entrenched rulers. On the economic front, crisis following crisis added fuel to this political discontent. The long years of mismanagement and of ideological, rather than professional, guidance of the economy were producing bitter fruit. Confusion at the top, worker absenteeism, and job-hopping brought the annual increase in industrial labor productivity down from 7.7 per cent in 1959 to 5.7 per cent in 1961 and 3.1 per cent in 1962. For a highly industrialized country like Czechoslovakia, hampered by unrealistically ambitious development plans and burdened with Soviet-ordered exports to Cuba and other "Third World" countries of products that were desperately needed at home, this shrinkage in labor productivity represented dangerous economic regression. The agricultural picture was a tragedy, as production fell 6 per cent below 1961. Shortages grew and inflationary pressures appeared. The Party's interference in economic management caused further dislocations and resentments after it undertook to play favorites among workers when reassigning them to sectors with labor deficits: when coal mines or farms needed extra manpower to make up for production lags, the Party kept its most loyal members in less taxing jobs in industrial plants and services while dispatching politically "expendable" men and women to dig for coal and till land.

To deal with this accumulation of problems, the Novotný regime turned again to the old-fashioned method that combined small concessions with stern political discipline. No attempt was made to come to terms with reality. Stalin's statue, to be sure, had been torn down, but at the Party's Twelfth Congress in December 1962 the only other tangible concession to the political unrest in the country was the appointment of the Kolder Commission to study the purge trials. The KSČ leadership presumably expected that Kolder, one of its "inner circle," would come up with another report confirming that the sentences handed down in the 1950s had been just. The rest of the congress was used to lay down the orthodox law and read the riot act to intellectuals and other troublemakers. Novotný and Hendrych devoted hours of speechmaking to warning writers and others against "bourgeois" and "revisionist" tendencies in their work and to proclaiming the inviolability of the sacred Party line. Simultaneously, the Party quietly continued its accustomed practice of buying off men who might protect the *status quo* with prizes and trips abroad and rewarding even more grandly the tested faithful.

At the end of 1962 Novotný and his colleagues clearly assumed they had the political situation firmly under control—once more that inability to resist self-delusion and to see through the empty verbiage of formal resolutions forced out of servile assemblies—and many foreign observers tended to agree. But within the next year all the cherished illusions and delusions began to break down. From then on, the road for Novotný and his associates was to be downhill all the way. Unquestionably, 1963 was the most important year in Czechoslovakia between 1948 and 1968; it was a year during which all the political, ideological, intellectual, and economic problems suddenly escalated and escaped the control of Novotný's regime.

It is difficult to reconstruct precisely which event, at what point, set the whole process in motion. Events succeeded each other with such speed that they tended to overlap in a flowing stream of onrushing history. The Party's entire structure started to crack despite Novotný's desperate attempts to repair the fissures. Simultaneously, the intellectuals rose in their greatest rebellion since the cultural night fell over Czechoslovakia in 1948. And the economic crisis reached its climax. But it is probable that the single event that set off the chain reaction was the issuance of the Kolder report on the purge trials. For the Kolder Commission found that the trials had been frame-ups, that the "evidence" had often been doctored or fabricated, and that there was a powerful case for reviewing the sentences and rehabilitating the victims.

One is tempted to pause and wonder what made trusted top apparatus Communists—first Barák and then Kolder—resist the powerful political pressures and not only seek the truth but fight for it to emerge. The answer, if there is one, is immensely complex and contradictory. Kolder, despite his history-making stand in 1963, placed himself during the Prague Spring in the camp of pro-Moscow conservatives. Barák, who had fought for justice and the rehabilitations in 1955–1956, made a complete turnabout with his 1957 report and bravely rejoined the battle in 1962. Conversely, men like Dubček and Černík, who were destined to lead the liberal events of 1968, remained silently on the sidelines in 1962 and 1963, notwithstanding their considerable power. (As we shall see, Dubček, in fact, rallied to Novotný's side against the liberal intellectuals.) After all is said, then, the heart, soul, and mind of an apparatus Communist remain enigmas—a strange mystery in terms of human consistency, ethics, and self-respect.

In any event, it was Kolder's report that opened the floodgates of 1963, as the ghosts of Slánský, Clementis, and the other executed and condemned men came back to haunt the Novotný establishment. Although this report was not formally presented until April—and made public in August—there are strong indications that the Party leadership was aware of it early in March and began to act accordingly. Thus, on March 7, Dr. Josef Úrvalek, president of Czechoslovakia's Supreme Court, who had earned this august post as a reward for his role as chief prosecutor in the Slánský trial, resigned "for reasons of health." An official announcement stating that he would subsequently concentrate on research of legal problems of the judiciary, was a telltale sign. Obviously, the regime could not tolerate a Supreme Court president who in short order would be publicly exposed as a criminal manufacturer of false evidence that had led eleven outstanding citizens of the republic to the gallows. But the sacrifice of expendable men was nothing new to Novotný, as he would prove again weeks later.

Having fired Ůrvalek, Novotný went immediately on the offensive lest the Party's supremacy be endangered. Speaking to a Communist militants' meeting in Ostrava late in March, he acknowledged that "we need criticism here as we need salt in our daily food." But he warned that "no one may touch our Communist Party, its program, or our socialist order. . . . This must be and must remain sacred for everyone." Turning on his enemies among the intellectuals, Novotný thundered that the Party had the right "to direct cultural activity, just as it directs and leads the entire life of the country." Artists and intellectuals did "not have a monopoly on criticism" and were not "special people differing from others," not a "godsend to this land so as to judge the people's life from their exalted position like conscience, and on the basis of this human activity, to reach godlike conclusions."

These were brave words. But a week later, when the Party's Central Committee met in a secret session in Prague on April 4, Novotný reshuffled the top leadership in the most drastic manner since the purges of the fifties—except that this time, the political victims were the very men who had engineered the purges.

Karol Bacílek, State Security Minister in 1952 and 1953, who was addicted to wearing a general's uniform, was expelled from the Presidium and the Central Committee and removed as First Secretary of the Slovak Party. His replacement on the Presidium and as head of the Slovak Party was Alexander Dubček. Dubček now held the triple posts of member of the Presidium, member of the Party Secretariat, and chief of the Slovak Party. In practice, this made Dubček second only to Novotný and Hendrych in the Party hierarchy. But if Bacílek's dismissal was dictated by the obvious need to rid the Party of the worst aspects of its Stalinist past, Dubček's emergence at the top of the heap could not by a long shot be regarded as a liberalizing gesture. He had a sound reputation as a loyal Party man, he was schooled in Moscow and, presumably, prepared there for advancement, and he was to remain faithful to Novotný and his repressive policies for a long time to come. One must guard against the belief that so easily spread in Prague in 1968 that Dubček was all along a secret liberal.

The next man purged by Novotný was Bruno Köhler, head of the

Central Committee's Cadres Department, a staunch Stalinist who had played an important role during the trials as the MGB's chief collaborator and the closest confidant of State Security Minister Ladislav Kopřiva. Köhler was now fired from his post as a Party secretary and from the Central Committee and expelled from the Communist Party. Another man expelled from the Party was Alexei Čepička, Gottwald's son-in-law, who had served as Justice and Defense Minister and was one of the principal architects and defenders of the purges.

Novotný and the Central Committee took these steps at the April 1963 Plenum, after receiving the Kolder report. They were sacrificing the very same men whom Barák had accused the year before of being responsible for the purges in his ill-fated letter to Khrushchev. This may have vindicated Barák's judgment, but it did not bring his release from prison. Novotný was not about to set free the man he suspected of being his rival for power.

So drastic were the actions taken by the Central Committee's April Plenum and so shattering was the Kolder report that both were kept secret for a long while—the Party purges and Dubček's ascent for six weeks and Kolder's findings for four and a half months—to give the Party time to explain them to its organizations throughout Czechoslovakia. But the spirit of protest now pervaded the nation, and its intellectuals did not have to await the news of the Central Committee's decisions to swing into action. In any case, Novotný's obvious concessions were no longer enough to stem the rising tide.

The first shot in the intellectuals' open revolt against the Novotný regime was fired at the congress of the Slovak Writers' Union that met in Bratislava on April 22, three weeks after the Central Committee session in Prague. Slovaks had been prime targets during the purges a decade earlier for their "bourgeois nationalism" and, proportional to their numbers, they had suffered even more than the Czechs. In 1963 the reaction against these purges took the form of a revival of Slovak nationalism and protest against the vestiges of Stalinism still alive in Czechoslovakia.

At the Bratislava Congress, it was Laco Novomeský, restored to membership in the Writers' Union, the novelist Ladislav Mňačko, and the poet Karol Rosenbaum, the Union's new secretary, who set the tone for the proceedings. Novomeský spoke of his old friend Vladimir Clementis and told the writers that Stalinism was a "monstrous and horrible" thing which had "wiped out trust, confidence, understanding, yes, even loyalty, in the life and consciousness of thousands and thousands of people." The time had come, he said, for "the whole truth, and nothing but the truth." Mňačko, a burly man who was completing his book *Delayed Reports,* destined to shock Czechoslovakia the following year, turned to the moral problem haunting so many Czechoslovak intellectuals of their once passive acceptance of Stalinist excesses. There was, he said, "an eternal stain on the good name of every one of us, for we all condemned Slánský, Clementis, Novomeský, and others." Rosenbaum, looking to the future, said that "revolutionary changes" were occurring in the Czechoslovak society and that new forces had gathered to block any return to the Stalinist "personality cult" and its "inhuman" methods.

The intellectual ferment quickly infected the universities, as it did in 1956, and on May Day there were antiregime student demonstrations in Prague and Bratislava.

On May 22 the Czechoslovak Writers' Union, which included both Czech and Slovak writers, met in Prague. It took up where it had left off at its 1956 congress and, again, protests and accusations against the situation in the nation were angrily and emotionally voiced. Novomeský spoke of the "collective guilt":

> The tragedy of the whole situation lies not, or not only, in the fact that some believed more and some less a lie and accepted it, some in fear, some in the good faith that they were thus serving a correct cause. It lies in the fact—and this applies to us as writers and journalists in particular—that we tried to persuade our readers of the correctness of the lie, that we misled and confused a whole generation, standing now outside this hall helpless, puzzled, uncertain, and having no ground under its feet. To this generation we must return confidence, trust, and truth; however, we must find them in ourselves first.

Miroslav Valek delivered a prophecy of what 1968 was to be when he urged a struggle for broader freedom within Communism. He said that in "the process of renewal and purification, which our Party has begun to effect, we shall evidently continue . . . it is necessary to continue this in a downward and in an upward direction, in fact in every direction in which it is necessary."

But the real fireworks exploded at the Congress of the Slovak Journalists' Union in Bratislava on May 27 and 28. The star was Miroslav Hysko, a professor at the local school of journalism, who accused the regime of blocking the "process of revival" of the Party and described de-Stalinization in Czechoslovakia as "insincere." He listed a number of top Communist leaders who were responsible, he said, for imposing and preserving Stalinism in the country: notably Premier Široký, a Slovak. Hysko then argued that writers and journalists had the right and the duty to express "correct, that is, Marxist-Leninist, views even if they are in conflict with the subjectivist opinions of certain official persons." Again, a blueprint for 1968 was unfolded as Hysko declared that henceforth journalists should "respect only directives which are not in conflict with the fundamental principles of socialist morality." This, he said, meant that awareness of the Communist Party must be understood "not in a vulgar manner as servile subordination to the directing organ, but in the Leninist spirit, as conscious and devoted service to the cause of the Communist Party and as an objective judgment of all the facts from the standpoint of the unfalsified principles of Marxism-Leninism, which are equally binding on the directed and on those who direct."

This was a call to arms, and it was particularly disturbing to the Novotný regime because it came from Communists seeking to reform the Party rather than from anti-Communists bent on destroying it. What Hysko and the others in Bratislava and Prague were doing was to raise the fundamental issue of *what* Communism should be in Czechoslovakia. In the opening salvo of his battle with the Czechoslovak intellectuals— no longer the sniping of the past years—Novotný struck back at them and the Slovaks a few days later.

Speaking in Košice, the Slovak city where Czechoslovakia's first postwar government had been established in 1945, Novotný attacked Hysko by name, criticized other Communists and non-Communists for recent public speeches, and took to task the editors of *Pravda*, the Slovak Party organ, and *Kulturný Život*, the Slovak cultural publication, for printing articles that represented "an indirect attack on the policy of the Party." This, he said, would henceforth not be permitted. He warned Slovak editors and writers that they were walking down a "dangerous path" and were breaching Party discipline by discussing publicly questions that the Central Committee was preparing to resolve. These questions were, of course, related to the rehabilitation of Slovaks like Husák and Novomeský —a burning issue in Slovakia.

Novotný was not alone in striking back at the Slovaks' protest. Presently, he was joined by Dubček, the new First Secretary of the Slovak Party, who attacked Hysko for publicly discussing internal Party matters. Loyal apparatus man that he was, he hit out at the "undisciplined and impatient comrades who . . . not waiting for the decision of the Supreme Court, try to create the impression that they, and not the Central Committee, were persistently struggling for the rehabilitation of unjustly condemned persons and for the correction of errors."

This, to say the least, was an overstatement. As Dubček spoke, the Central Committee had been sitting for well over a month on the Kolder report and looking for a graceful, safe way out of the quandary of not rehabilitating men it still regarded as enemies without risking new unrest. Dubček may have been counseling patience, but the fact remained that if it had not been for public pressure by the intellectuals and the press, many of the rehabilitations would have been delayed longer.

A case in point was Husák. Husák had been out of prison since the 1960 amnesty, but neither Dubček nor anyone else in authority seemed anxious to rehabilitate him. Finally, in June 1963, following insistent demands in Slovakia, his membership in the Communist Party was restored. His full rehabilitation was still delayed, but Husák now could leave his job at the Bratislava construction firm and, as a Communist in good standing, accept a position at the Institute of State and Law of the Slovak Academy of Sciences. While awaiting his rehabilitation, Husák completed his book on the 1944 Slovak uprising. (This was a period during which Husák's fate was, to some extent at least, in Dubček's hands. We may speculate as to whether this might not have affected his attitude toward Dubček after the Soviet invasion in 1968.)

The intellectuals' campaign seemed to have borne some fruit—and this turned the rebel writers, journalists, and artists into a tangible factor in Czechoslovak politics for the first time. They now began to make their influence felt in the broader sphere of cultural and political freedoms.

In May 1963 the Czechoslovak Writers' Union obtained the formal rehabilitation of the "decadent" Franz Kafka and Karel Čapek, the greatest Czech writers of the century. It may appear ludicrous that this was necessary, but to the writers it was a matter of basic principle. They reasoned that cultural freedom simply could not be restored in Czechoslovakia so long as Kafka and Čapek could not be read and studied. The man behind the rehabilitation of Kafka was Eduard Goldstücker, about to be rehabilitated himself after a prison term connected with the Great Purge. The whole situation had a Kafkaesque touch, but so did everything in Communist Czechoslovakia.

Simultaneously, the first literary works of the new generation of playwrights and writers appeared denouncing Stalinism and stating the case for freedom. Václav Havel, the playwright, was twenty-seven in 1963, when he completed his first full-length play, *The Garden Party*, which was a satire dealing with de-Stalinization and Communist bureaucracy. Rather startlingly, the regime, seeking to be conciliatory, allowed the play to be staged in a Prague theater. It was a smash hit, for the public loved Havel's satirical use of the Communist jargon. Yorick Blumenfeld, an American writer specializing in East European culture, counted that Havel used the word "liquidation," or its variations, some ninety-two times in Act Three alone: the word had been "taboo" for fifteen years and Prague theater-goers could not hear enough of it.

At the same time Ludvík Vaculík, a thirty-seven-year-old novelist, published his *A Busy House*, also an attack on Stalinist practices. This marked Vaculík's entry on the political scene; he was to be one of the principal protagonists in 1967 and 1968. Other works of a similar character were also in progress. Mňačko was getting ready to issue his *Delayed Reports*, and Ladislav Bublik, an older Communist journalist, was completing a devastating novel on life in Czechoslovak prisons during the Stalinist era.

In a country in which the written word commands more attention than tanks, Czechoslovak intellectuals were increasingly capturing command positions. Not only were they writing and publishing again with relative freedom, but the liberals among them were able in 1963 to assume the leadership of both the writers' unions and the journalists' unions and to control the editorial boards of such influential literary magazines as *Literární Noviny* in Prague and *Kulturný Život, Kulturný Tvorba*, and *Plamen* in Bratislava. From these positions, they could influence public opinion and politics to a remarkable extent. Inevitably, the regime struck back at them, and the battle between them and the Party orthodoxy proceeded inconclusively until 1967.

The conclusions of the Kolder report were released on August 22, 1963, after lengthy struggles in the Presidium and Central Committee. They covered 481 cases of rehabilitated Party members; 70 names were listed in the version given to the public. Considering that uncounted thousands of Czechoslovaks had been imprisoned during the purges, this was, numerically speaking, a disappointing document. But its political importance was extraordinary because it included all the principal victims of the purge and because it was generally known that these rehabilitations had been forced by public pressure.

At the same time, the regime quietly released Cardinal Beran, who had completed the full fourteen-year prison term to which he had been sentenced in 1948. But the Party insisted that he be exiled, and Beran went to live in Rome, where he died in 1969, at the age of eighty, never having seen his homeland again.

Slánský, Clementis, and their nine trial companions, executed in 1952, were cleared of all charges of criminal activity, treason, Titoism, and Trotskyism. But, curiously, Slánský, Otto Šling, General Reicin, Otto Fischl, and Karel Švab were not cleared of "political responsibility" or rehabilitated ideologically so far as the Party was concerned. This, evidently, was a face-saving device for Novotný. A bizarre situation was thus created in which Slánský and his four codefendants were "two-thirds" rehabilitated in 1963; their ghosts had to wait five more years for the last "one-third."

For those who survived the purges, rehabilitation had the practical value of freeing them of criminal records and, in applicable cases, of permitting their readmission to the Communist Party, which reopened the doors to decent jobs and sometimes to new political careers. The latter was to be the case with Husák, whose full rehabilitation was granted in December 1963, and with many of the men who were to figure so prominently in the Prague Spring. One intriguing aspect of this process was that most of the Communists deprived of Party membership and imprisoned by their fellow Communists during the Stalinist period were willing and eager to rejoin the Party. Again, the question must be posed as to motivations: was it new faith in the Party, a psychological inability to sever bonds with it despite the sufferings, or rationalized opportunism?

The rehabilitations failed, however, to solve Novotný's political problems. The public recognition that the trials were fabrications without a shred of real evidence required the removal from office of additional persons connected with the purges, since the actions taken against Bacílek, Köhler, Kopřiva, and Čepička were obviously insufficient. There was also pressure from Moscow for speedier de-Stalinization. At the same time, the Czechoslovak economy continued to decline and top-level personnel changes were urgently needed to arrest the deterioration. Industrial production in 1963 dropped by 0.7 per cent and the national income as a whole fell by 3.7 per cent from the preceding year. This was a situation so catastrophic that the initial targets of the current Five-Year Plan had to be reduced three times during the year.

The man chosen as the principal sacrificial lamb was Premier Široký, a power in Czechoslovak politics since 1945. His name had been repeatedly associated with the purges and, as Premier, he theoretically bore the responsibility for the economic debacle. In September, therefore, Široký was dropped as Premier and Presidium member. Deputy Premier Jaromír Dolanský, another old-timer and the man directly in charge of the economy, was likewise fired along with a number of lesser officials. (Dolanský, however, remained on the Party Presidium.)

The new Premier was Josef Lenárt, a forty-year-old Slovak and another new-generation product of the Party apparatus. As it turned out, Lenárt was the man for all seasons, weathering every political tempest and gladly shifting amidst a variety of government and Party posts. The new Deputy Premier in charge of the economy and chairman of the State Planning Commission was Oldřich Černík.

Not yet placed in charge of reforming the crippled Czechoslovak economy but actively groomed for it was Ota Šik, forty-four, Kolder's protégé. Kolder, whose own main interest was in economics, had brought Šik to prominence in 1962, when Šik, then only a minor Party intellectual concentrating on ideology and social and political sciences, was made a member of the Central Committee, Director of the Economic Institute of the Academy of Sciences, and chairman of the Czechoslovak Economic Society. Although Šik's academic background in economics was slim—he lacked a degree in the field—he developed an interest in Liberman's theories of market economy and, later, in Yugoslavia's experiments in collective management. In 1958 he had published *Economics, Interest, Politics*. Kolder, in turn, became interested in Šik's ideas and began to sponsor him. In 1963 Šik was briefly assigned to the Central Committee's Ideological Commission, but early in 1964, as the Czechoslovak economy verged on complete disaster, he was switched to the Economic Commission and started planning the reform. At the same time, he wrote a book about Comecon, *On Problems of Socialist Commodity Relations*.

Having reorganized his government, Novotný undertook once more to put order in the shaky political and economic system.

XII

Novotný: Tyranny of
the Middle Way

Novotný's attempt to consolidate the situation began with a special Ideological Plenum of the Central Committee in December 1963. He was relatively successful, in the sense that the next three years saw a standoff in his battle with the Communist progressives. With some effort he was able temporarily to curb the intellectuals, while the intellectuals themselves needed time to regroup and prepare for future struggles.

But, once again, Novotný mistook a tactical advantage for a political victory and proceeded to act as if de-Stalinization never existed and as if Czechoslovakia's problems could be dismissed out of hand. In so doing, he became entangled in a series of unnecessary clashes and disputes along the entire front—most of them provoked by himself—and in the end he triggered the revolt that overthrew him.

The leadership with which he sought to control the continuously explosive nation was, or appeared to be, ideologically safe, and, in fact, the Czechoslovaks found it less objectionable than the team he had headed before the 1963 purges. Hendrych and Koucký were the pro-Moscow specialists in ideology, propaganda, and culture—which seemed to take care of the most pressing problem of the intellectuals. The security services were in the hands of Strougal, another reliable hard-liner. Kolder and Černík were overseeing the economy from the Presidium and the government, respectively, while Šik planned the economic reform. Premier Lenárt and Dubček, the man in charge of Slovakia, seemed colorless men, as did Foreign Minister Václav David, unconditionally devoted to

191

Moscow. Dubček began to show his individuality only after Novotný started pointlessly tangling with him over Slovakia.

In a striking way, the speeches at the 1963 Ideological Plenum fore-shadowed the vicious and furious attacks delivered five years later, for the same reasons, by pro-Moscow conservatives after the Soviet invasion. What emerged here was the fundamental split between the orthodox Stalinist interpreters of Marxism-Leninism and the new generation to whom socialism meant both justice *and* freedom, the right of dissent, the unhampered flow of ideas, and the capability of each national party to make its own decisions. This was a basic philosophical conflict over the role of Communism in the modern world, and in this sense it went further than the Hungarians had in 1956 in questioning the entire ideology and the place of the Soviet Union in it. The Hungarians had only wanted to get rid of the Russians. The Czechoslovak ideological challenge was attuned to the new ideas sweeping the Communist movement in Europe —notably in Yugoslavia and Romania—in favor of "polycentrism." As the Czechoslovaks set forth this proposition in their still Stalinist country, the same notions were being espoused in a memorandum written before his death by the Italian Communist Party chief Palmiro Togliatti during conferences with the Soviet leadership in Yalta in 1964, and, separately, by the Romanian Communist Party.

The official reaction in Prague was of the usual troglodytic nature. At the Ideological Plenum, the Novotný men spoke of the "untenable licentiousness" of the Czechoslovak press and reproved the literary maga-zines for their "revisionism" and "shameful role" in propagating it. Writers and journalists were accused of attempting "slyly to discredit responsible Party workers" and of applying political "blackmail." Calls went out to strengthen Party control over the press, again a foretaste of 1968–1969, and a warning was issued that if the "revisionist" editors and writers would not conform, they would be replaced by "deeply convinced Communists."

The year 1964 opened with a short-lived effort at a truce between the intellectuals and the regime. But it broke down within a month and Novotný was back at the microphones announcing that "in our country, liberty exists for all who adhere to the principles of socialism and for those who defend its interests, but not for those who would propagate opinions and conceptions foreign to our socialist system and morality." This, of course, barred all dissent.

Because much of the criticism of the regime came from Slovak cultural publications, Novotný presently found himself particularly at odds with the outspoken Slovaks. As seen in retrospect, his tough handling of them was one of the most serious errors that quickened the disintegration of his rule. But Novotný was assuming that all would be well so long as he controlled the formal structure of the Slovak Party. After all, the two top Slovak politicians—Lenárt and Dubček—were his unquestioning supporters and Dubček had publicly recorded his impatience with Slovakia's progressives.

As part of the anti-Slovak campaign managed from Prague, *Rudé Právo* in April began denouncing the Slovak press as "rebellious and ideologically hostile." *Pravda*, the organ of the Slovak Party and a newspaper controlled by Dubček, abandoned its earlier criticisms of the regime and echoed the official line. This only encouraged the rebels to try harder and, in succession, *Kulturný Život, Kulturný Tvorba,* and *Plamen* proclaimed that their interpretation of proper Marxism-Leninism was correct and that they would pursue their line of attack. *Kulturný Život* added fuel to the fire by serializing Ladislav Mňačko's devastatingly anti-Soviet *Delayed Reports.* A Bratislava publishing house followed suit by issuing *Reports* in book form. Three hundred thousand copies had soon been sold, some at high black-market prices. Mňačko, once a Stalinist himself, diagnosed Stalinism not as a conspiracy by a few men but as a basic distortion of the prevailing social system. In Prague, *Literární Noviny* openly proclaimed its admiration for "the unbelievable . . . daring of the author and his publishers."

This was about all Novotný could take. Pavel Stevček, editor of *Kulturný Život,* was fired. Mňačko was removed from the Presidium of the Slovak Writers' Union and barred from running for a seat in the National Assembly in the June 1964 elections. In Prague, Jiří Sotola was dropped as editor of *Literární Noviny.*

Then, on May 2, 1964, about three thousand young people assembled in Prague's Petřín Park for a poetry reading around the monument of Karel Hynek Mácha, a nineteenth-century nationalist Czech poet. Hundreds of policemen, using dogs and blackjacks, rushed in to break up the rally, and the students fought back amidst shouts of "Long live freedom!" and "Down with the Gestapo!" The youths left the park, but in the early evening near the statue of Saint Wenceslas, they staged another demonstration—a forerunner of the great 1968 demonstrations in the central town square.

The Czechoslovak youth's rebellion spread. Popular music and attire were strongly influenced by Western styles; Prague became obsessed with jazz and the big-beat sound as if in retaliation against years of Stalinist monotony and boredom. No longer clandestine, jazz was intently listened to on Voice of America broadcasts, which the regime had ceased to jam. An international jazz festival held during the summer, curiously with official assent, was an overwhelming success. The twist and its successors became the ritual of young Czechoslovaks. Blue jeans and beards appeared in Prague and Bratislava. There were more ways than one, clearly, of combating the regime; the big beat and long hair had turned into political weapons. When John Cogley, then Religion Editor of *The New York Times,* returned from a visit to Prague and other East European capitals, he remarked to me that the common denominator among young people in the Communist countries was "admiration for John Kennedy, strains of 'Strangers in the Night,' long hair, and blue jeans." Unwittingly, America was contributing in its special way to the gathering Czechoslovak revolution. Novotný thus not only had to contend with indigenous styles of protest but also with the legend of Kennedy, American music and dress, the plays of Edward Albee, Arthur Miller, and Tennessee Williams, which Czechoslovak directors were now hungrily staging. In 1964 the Prague rulers could no longer seal off the country from Western influences and ideas. They wanted Western tourists for their hard currency and they wanted trade—and ideas, books, and records followed the visitors.

Again in the fall, on October 11, Prague students rioted for nearly four hours in Wenceslas Square. An American correspondent reported that a youth climbed atop a scaffolding to shout, "Who wants Communists?" The crowd below responded, "Nobody!"

But when Khrushchev was suddenly expelled in October 1964 from all his government and Party posts, Novotný once more misunderstood the situation. Though Khrushchev's policies had caused problems for him, Novotný had had a cordial personal relationship with him, dating back to 1957. Only two weeks before his dismissal, Khrushchev had vacationed with him at a Slovak spa. So, piqued at not being tipped off in advance of Khrushchev's downfall, Novotný fired off a telegram to Moscow expressing Czechoslovakia's regret over this event. Leonid Brezhnev, the new Soviet leader, evidently did not take kindly to this reaction. Though he was the man destined to bring neo-Stalinism back to the Soviet Union and Czechoslovakia, his relations with the old Stalinist, Novotný, never improved.

While the ferment was thus growing in Czechoslovakia, Soviet Communist orthodoxy suffered another blow in Romania. It came in the form of a resolution issued by the enlarged Plenum of the Romanian Party's Central Committee on April 26, 1964. This resolution, now commonly known within the Communist movement as Romania's "Declaration of Independence," had naturally evolved from the more cautious Party declaration of December 1961, which was largely confined to a veiled criticism of the Soviet Union through attacks on Stalinism. If the essentially negative 1961 statement carried nationalistic overtones, the 1964 resolution spelled out in a positive fashion what had now become a firmly established Romanian political and ideological position. Rebel Czechoslovak intellectuals were barely beginning to articulate their new concepts of Marxism, but the Romanian Party with overwhelming unity produced a coherent program of political action.

The crux of this program was contained in the words of the 1964 resolution that "no one can decide what is and what is not correct for other countries and parties. . . . There is not and cannot be a 'parent' party and a 'son' party, a 'superior' and a 'subordinate' party. No party has or can have a privileged position, or impose its line and opinion on other parties."

The resolution listed the principles that the Romanian Communist Party believed must govern relations among Communist parties and countries: "sovereignty . . . equal rights . . . national interest . . . noninterference in internal affairs . . . each party's right to make its own decisions . . . and choose its path to socialism." These principles, the Party said, were a condition *sine qua non* for Communist unity.

The Romanian Party's position, as we have seen, stemmed from, among other things, its consistent opposition to the Soviet Union's plans for Comecon. But chances are that the inclusion of the noninterference-in-internal-affairs clause resulted directly from Khrushchev's abortive attempt in the fall of 1963 to engineer a coup to overthrow Gheorghiu-Dej and his regime. On a higher political level, however, the increasing acrimony of the Soviet-Chinese dispute had simultaneously accomplished two things: first, it gave the Romanians the comfort of knowing that the Chinese Communist Party was likewise rejecting the Soviet concept of a "parent" party; and it convinced them of the absolute need to prevent further excommunications of independent-minded parties from the Communist movement. The Romanian Party, which in 1948 and 1949 had enthusiastically joined in signing the Cominform attack on Yugoslavia, now found common cause with Peking, Tirana, and Belgrade in fighting for Communist "equal rights."

Little is known of the Soviet conspiracy to restore Moscow's sway in Romania in 1963 except that it existed and that Khrushchev must have been rather desperate to sponsor it in the face of the Romanian Party's impressive unity. During July 1963 Khrushchev had assembled in Moscow the top East European Communist leaders, including Gheorghiu-Dej, to press for unanimous acceptance of economic integration in the bloc. Once more, the Romanians opposed it and forced Khrushchev to pigeonhole the project. At this juncture, the Soviets were faced with a peculiar dilemma. Had Romania risen in open defiance of them or of Communism per se—as Hungary had done in 1956—Khrushchev might have had the excuse to mount a punitive expedition. Brezhnev did not hesitate to order an invasion in 1968 when he was convinced that the supremacy of Communism was seriously endangered in Czechoslovakia. But the Romanian Party was in full control of the country. It had no rebel press causing ideological worry and irritation in Moscow. Romania participated in Warsaw Pact and Comecon activities and never considered withdrawing from them. All it did—and, of course, it *was* a lot—was to refuse to follow Soviet guidance blindly. It also refused to take the Soviet side against China. In fact, it had the temerity to try to mediate the dispute. All in all, Bucharest's policies were annoying and even embarrassing but hardly made a plausible case for an invasion, even assuming that the Soviet Union, just emerging from the Cuban confrontation with the United States and beset by the Chinese controversy, wanted to solve the Romanian problem militarily.

Accordingly, Khrushchev sought to find a conspiratorial political solution. He is known to have made a secret trip to Bucharest around September, probably both to serve Gheorghiu-Dej with an ultimatum and to shop around for supporters among the Romanian leadership. But Gheorghiu-Dej and his associates refused to be intimidated. Nobody of any stature in the Party was prepared to join in a coup. Observers of the Romanian scene believe that Khrushchev had hoped to enlist the support of General Bodnaras, but the old Bessarabian declined and, instead, informed Gheorghiu-Dej of it. At that time, Ceauşescu held the post of Deputy Minister of Defense, along with his top Party posts, and his personal influence in the armed forces was great enough to keep the military behind the regime even if Bodnaras had wanted to plunge into plotting.

The Romanians had the self-restraint and the sophistication not to make a scandal of the failed coup. In fact, hardly a word was breathed publicly, and the words that *were* breathed were subtly indirect. Yet indirection, too, can be a weapon and the Romanians used it wisely. Hints were dropped in strategic places and within a week or so most of the nation shared an awareness that *something* sinister on the part of the Russians had been imminent. This was one of Gheorghiu-Dej's ways of marshaling public support, a technique that Ceauşescu was to raise later to the status of a fine art.

At the same time, Romania aggravated her sinfulness toward Moscow by simply ignoring the Soviet Party's proposal early in 1964 for a worldwide meeting of Communist parties to condemn China. Romanian newspapers failed to inform their readers about it for weeks—while the rest of the East European press devoted column after column to it—and the Party made it amply clear it would neither go along with the meeting nor join in any condemnations of China. (As it was, it took the Soviet Union more than five years to organize the conference, and when it was finally held, in June 1969, no condemnation was issued, again largely thanks to Romanian opposition.)

As we have noted earlier, Communist leaders have an obsession with each other's birthdays, using them as occasions on which to express approval or disapproval in what are meant to be "subtle" gestures. The Romanians are also accomplished players at the Communist birthday game. Presumably to emphasize Romanian neutrality in the Soviet-Chinese dispute, Gheorghiu-Dej stayed away from the celebrations in East Berlin in 1963 on the seventieth birthday of Walter Ulbricht. In April 1964 he was the only East European Party boss to boycott the Moscow festivities in honor of Khrushchev's seventieth birthday. In fact, Gheorghiu-Dej called his Central Committee into session for the very same week, a stinging example of deliberate bad manners.

Late in March, *before* his birthday, Khrushchev had suddenly arrived in Bucharest, gone to the Soviet Embassy, and demanded that Gheorghiu-Dej call on him. Since his 1956 visit to Warsaw against the wishes of the Poles, he had evidently developed the habit of dropping in, sometimes uninvited and sometimes unannounced, on his fellow Communist Party chiefs. This second secret trip to Romania within six months was apparently designed to dissuade the Romanians from becoming too intimately allied with China or issuing Party documents at variance with Soviet orthodoxy. In his account of this second visit, Paul Lendvai reports that Gheorghiu-Dej, apprised of Khrushchev's presence in his capital, coldly informed the Soviet Embassy that Romania's head of state "is not accustomed to conducting talks in the buildings of foreign embassies" and that if Khrushchev wished to see him, he could call the Presidential residence in the afternoon. They did eventually meet, and it is certain that the encounter ended in a personal break between them. The next step for the Romanians was to hold the Central Committee session and to issue the "Declaration of Independence."

Throughout 1964, tension between the two governments mounted. Romania decided to proceed on a de-Russification policy which included dropping the Russian language as a compulsory subject in secondary schools and, to the joy of the Romanian intellectuals, replacing much of the heavy Russian literary and theatrical diet with Western imports. In May Deputy Premier Gheorghe Gaston-Marin flew to Washington to negotiate with Averell Harriman a major economic agreement and the elevation of the two countries' legations to the rank of embassies. I remember attending the Romanian reception at Washington's Mayflower Hotel on the last evening of Gaston-Marin's visit and hearing unhappy and poisoned remarks about Romania whispered by other East European diplomatic guests present at the champagne-flowing *fête*. In December the Romanian Party declined the Soviet invitation to participate in the first preparatory meeting for the projected world conference of Communist parties.

The point must be made, however, that much as Romania emphasized her independence in foreign policy, she had made precious few advances in the field of relaxing internal controls. Gheorghiu-Dej believed in each Party's right to find its own way to socialism, but his own concept of it did not include the "humanization" of Marxism that was already preoccupying the Czechoslovaks. Until his death on March 19, 1965, Romania was a Communist police state, quiet but effective. Securitat, the secret police, kept a close check on men and ideas. There were about ten thousand political prisoners in Romania during Gheorghiu-Dej's rule, although most of them were released late in 1964.

Only the advent of Nicolae Ceauşescu as Gheorghiu-Dej's successor in the post of the Party's General Secretary brought a modest relaxation in Romania's internal life. But even Ceauşescu allowed himself no serious experimentation and only in 1968 took the major step of dissociating himself from the memories of Gheorghiu-Dej's dictatorship.

There are many reasons why Romanian Communists showed no desire to preach or practice political reform despite their uncompromising stand on foreign policy. The first appears to be that neither Gheorghiu-Dej nor Ceauşescu believed in political dissent or in the broadening of Communism into a pluralistic political society. The second is that both of them must have been aware that any *overtly* revisionist move would have brought swift Soviet punishment. Moscow may have tolerated—and still tolerates—a degree of heresy and independence in foreign policy, but a challenge to the leading role of the Communist Party was certain to bring instant retaliation. It had happened in Hungary and it was to happen again in Czechoslovakia. Finally, Romania had not had the terrible purges that Czechoslovakia underwent in the fifties. Gheorghiu-Dej and Ceauşescu did not have to contend with the powerful head of steam that was building up for Novotný.

The scope of the crisis had already gone far beyond a relatively simple defiance of the establishment by a small group of restive writers and journalists. The rebels in 1963 were not an isolated minority operating in a vacuum. The entire nation was, in one way or another, to be affected by a cohesive movement pressing for basic changes in Czechoslovakia.

Each day Novotný's options became more limited. Ota Šik was permitted to plan a modest economic reform early in 1967, but the regime realized that it needed the cooperation of scientists, economists, and intellectuals in the Academy of Sciences to make it work. Inasmuch as the Academy was increasingly dominated by progressives, a complete crackdown on them was impossible at the risk of alienating the people Novotný needed most to help lift the Czechoslovakian economy out of the morass.

Almost all the moves Novotný made, negative ones as well as positive, were counterproductive. A product of the Stalinist school of politics in which everything was either black or white, he simply could not cope with the new and highly complex situation. His enforced permissiveness in the cultural field—allowing the publication of books and plays and increased penetration of Western influences—only encouraged the intellectuals, who, having made an impact, became hungry for more successes, while his repressive moves boomeranged.

First, there was the Císař case. During the leadership reshuffle in May 1963 when Dubček had become First Secretary of the Slovak Party, a forty-three-year-old philosopher and journalist named Čestmir Císař was named to the Secretariat of the KSČ. Although Dr. Císař was an apparatus man—unscathed by the purges, he served in 1956 as secretary of the Party's regional committee in Plzeň and came to Prague in 1957 to be deputy editor of *Rudé Právo* and, in 1961, the editor of the KSČ's ideological monthly, *Nova Mysl* (*New Thought*)—he was regarded as a liberal, and his appointment was interpreted as a concession to the rebel intellectuals. But his views were evidently too progressive for the conservative Secretariat, and four months later, in September, when Novotný brought in Lenárt and reorganized the cabinet, he was demoted to the post of Minister of Education and Culture.

Once ensconced in his new post, Císař rapidly embarked on reforming Czechoslovakia's school system, still based on the Soviet-drafted 1953 Education Act. He made the curricula more flexible, cut down on Party ideological indoctrination, and attempted to free professional appointments from Party controls. At the same time, he maintained close ties with the liberal intellectuals and, often, protected them. A plain-speaking, bespectacled man with a crew cut, Císař rapidly won popularity with the students and professors at Charles University in Prague (where he had earned his doctorate in philosophy) and elsewhere. Encouraging dialogue and cultural freedom as he did, he inevitably had to be eliminated by the regime. But he could not be politically liquidated altogether—his standing was too high in the intellectual community—and the solution was to dispatch him as Ambassador to Romania in November 1965. Analysts of Czechoslovak affairs commented at the time that Císař was being sent away not because Novotný disliked or resented him but because he feared him. But in sending Císař to Bucharest, Novotný, once again displaying his talent for making the wrong move, helped to establish a close link between the Czechoslovak progressives and the independent-minded Ceauşescu. This friendship was to pay off richly in the years to come.

Císař's successor in the Ministry of Education and Culture was Professor Jiří Hájek—and this appointment turned out to be one more Novotný error, for Hájek was to emerge in 1968 as one of the leading spokesmen for the Prague Spring. But, in all fairness, Novotný could not be blamed for this choice, because Hájek had behind him a career of Party conformism. Fifty years old when he was appointed Education Minister, Hájek was a man of unusual brilliance and linguistic talents. At first a Social Democrat, Hájek joined the Communist Party after the 1948 takeover. In 1949, at the unusually young age of thirty-four, he was elected to the Central Committee, named Prorector of the Prague School of Political and Economic Studies, and selected as vice-chairman of the Foreign Affairs Committee of the National Assembly.

The turmoil of the 1950s never touched him. While the Foreign Ministry was being massively purged, Dr. Hájek went to New York as a member of the Czechoslovak delegation to the United Nations, remaining there from 1950 to 1953. Returning to Prague, he was appointed Dean of the Faculty of International Relations at Charles University and wrote a book entitled *The Nefarious Activities of Right-wing Socialist Parties*, a pamphlet attacking President Wilson and his role in the creation of the Czechoslovak Republic, and a series of anti-American articles. In 1955 Hájek became Ambassador to London. In 1957 he was appointed Deputy Foreign Minister, and in 1962 he was sent back to New York, this time as the chief of the United Nations delegation. It was from there that Novotný summoned him in November 1965 to give him the Education and Culture Ministry. In view of Hájek's credentials, it was not surprising that Monsignor Rudolph J. Gerber, an American Jesuit university professor and an editor of *America*, wrote after visiting Prague that the new minister had been handed the responsibility of stemming "the cultural tidal wave sweeping the country." But how Dr. Hájek was to carry out this responsibility was something else.

Earlier in 1965 Novotný named Presidium Member Hendrych to the chairmanship of the Ideological Commission of the Central Committee, replacing Vladimir Koucký, the completely pro-Soviet member of the Party's Secretariat. Hendrych was one of Novotný's closest associates and, in the moment of crisis, seemed best suited to assume the direction of the ideological and cultural campaign. He and Hájek, presumably, were to work together, but Hendrych's appointment turned out eventually to be a major fiasco.

One of the regime's first steps in 1965 in attempting to bring the rebel intellectuals under control was to dismiss Dr. Ivan Sviták, a leading young Marxist philosopher, from his post as philosophy professor at Charles University. Sviták, a tall gangling man with a quick and devastating repartee, was one of the first original Marxist thinkers of the new generation and one of the first philosophers in his country to write openly that scientific Marxism-Leninism should not be confused with Party ideology. Not only that, but he had made the statement that philosophers should not be political hacks and "clowns with diplomas" but responsible thinkers. Presently, he was fired from the Philosophical Institute of the Academy of Sciences, expelled from the Communist Party, prevented from teaching and publishing, and deprived of his passport.

The next achievement in the counteroffensive was to force the demise of two highly outspoken literary publications, *Tvař (Face)* and *Knižni Kultura (Book Culture)*. *Tvař*, a publication of the Writers' Union that passionately supported the cause of cultural and political freedoms, was accused of "unashamed liberalism," and the Party demanded that its editorial board be purged. The Writers' Union's Presidium apparently agreed to do so in October 1965, but some three hundred Czechoslovak writers signed a declaration protesting that "administrative measures once again replaced literary discussion." The Presidium insisted on new editors, but *Tvař* refused and, instead, discontinued publication altogether early in 1966. *Knižni Kultura*, published by the Education Ministry, enraged the leadership by frequently printing articles by writers out of favor with the KSČ. The ministry therefore simply ceased to issue it.

In theory, the regime had overwhelming power over these publications because they were published by the government itself or by government or Party-controlled agencies. Moreover, most of Czechoslovakia's intellectuals were Party members and subject to Party discipline. It is strange, therefore, that given their proclivities for a tightly controlled press, Novotný and Hendrych did not lower the boom more often and harder. But the regime was more and more often bogged down in confusion and contradiction, and frequently the right hand did not know what the left hand was doing. The same thing was true in the film industry, which, after 1964, enjoyed a major and brilliant renaissance. Freed from the straitjacket of ideological guidelines, Czechoslovak movie makers were able to produce such gems as Jan Kadar and Elmar Klos's *Shop on Main Street* and Miloš Forman's *Loves of a Blonde* with crackdowns on their freedom occurring only in a random and fitful way.

Liberty was an issue elsewhere in Eastern Europe at the same time. In Bulgaria, the regime of Todor Zhivkov nipped in the bud a military conspiracy apparently designed to bring the country out of its servitude as a wholly obedient Soviet satellite. In Yugoslavia, President Tito in 1966 dramatically fired his security chief in what became a far-reaching internal liberalization.

In the Bulgarian affair, as far as it can be reconstructed, a group of high-ranking Army officers and Foreign Ministry officials had planned a coup for April 14, 1965, either to oust Zhivkov altogether or to neutralize him through forcing the formation of a new government considerably less amenable to Soviet wishes and the Communist orthodoxy. The coup—the only military conspiracy we know to have developed in an East European Communist country since the war—was masterminded by General Ivan Todor-Gorunia, a Deputy Defense Minister and member of the Party's Central Committee; General I. Anev, commander of the Sofia garrison; and Tsolo Krastev, a high-ranking civilian official in the Foreign Ministry. Three other important Army officers were involved. All nine men had been wartime guerrilla fighters and "home Communists." It may be assumed that at least to an extent they were influenced by the Yugoslav example next door.

But the Zhivkov regime, reportedly helped by Soviet intelligence officers, smashed the conspiracy a week before the coup was to have occurred. General Todor-Gorunia committed suicide after his arrest. The others were tried and received prison sentences. The Bulgarian government never told the full story of this abortive conspiracy, but in a speech the following month Zhivkov spoke derisively of a "handful of miserable adventurers." He later told a visiting Western journalist that the plot was "pro-Chinese." (Not quite two years earlier, in December 1963, Bulgaria tried and executed Assen Georgiev, one of its senior United Nations delegates, on charges of "spying" for the United States. This case, too, never received a comprehensive public explanation.) With the failure of the plot, Bulgaria relapsed into her sullen satellitehood.

In Yugoslavia, the cause of domestic freedom gained considerably from Tito's dismissal of Vice-President Alexander Ranković, an Army general who had built a virtually independent power apparatus in the UDBA, the security service, which he headed. The ostensible reason for Ranković's fall and for his subsequent expulsion from the Party following a Central Committee meeting on July 2, 1966, was the discovery that the UDBA had tapped the private telephones of Marshal Tito and most of his top collaborators. The Ranković conspiracy, if that is what it was, could be foiled thanks to the efforts of military intelligence services loyal to Tito; they, in turn, had tapped the telephone lines of the Serb general and his top associates. But the deeper reason was that Ranković—once considered as Tito's potential successor—had found himself at the head of a powerful political group, said by Tito's associates to have been supported by the Russians, opposing the latest economic reforms introduced by Tito. Mixed into this affair was Ranković's position favoring Serb predominance in Yugoslavia, at a time when Tito was desperately attempting to forge real unity among the six federated republics.

The immediate consequence of Ranković's demise was a series of public denunciations of the UDBA which went far to diminish its role in Yugoslav life. A general political relaxation followed. Milovan Djilas was among those released from prison. Ranković himself was not arrested, and seven months later Tito dropped the criminal charges against him and his allies. But to this day Ranković lives under discreet surveillance and under suspicion, regarded by the regime as a "sectarian" guilty of conservative pro-Soviet sympathies. Since the Soviet invasion of Czechoslovakia, he has been watched with special care.

The eighteen-month period encompassing the year 1966 and the first half of 1967 marked the final phase of preparations for the assault on the Novotný regime. But, again, it would be wrong to say that a specific revolutionary conspiracy was afoot in Czechoslovakia. The antiregime movement—actually an antiestablishment movement—was more like a spontaneous internal combustion. Nobody was really in charge of it; there were scores of informal groups engaged in various pursuits with no contact among them and no particular effort to establish any. There were individuals working on specific scientific or cultural projects which simply happened to fit into the over-all trend. Some of them were in the KSČ leadership—such as the economist Šik and Hájek—and others worked in the Academy of Sciences, the film industry, the writers' and journalists' unions, or simply performed the daily tasks of writing for newspapers and magazines, broadcasting on radio and television, and toiling in loneliness over books, poems, and plays.

The striking thing about the mood at this time was that nobody in or out of the Communist Party ever seemed to consider direct political action. No one considered ousting Novotný and capturing power. And, indeed, there was nobody in the top ranks of the KSČ—certainly not Dubček at this juncture—capable of staging a coup to unseat Novotný. After the Prague Spring, I raised this matter with a number of the progressive leaders and, invariably, the answer was that the emphasis had been on changing the situation by rapid internal evolution, definitely not by revolution. This helps to make the point that, first, the Prague Spring was not planned by anyone and, second, when it did come it lacked cohesive leadership.

The intellectual battle for freedom continued in the same fashion as in the preceding years, but at a quickened pace. Because the regime's censors tended to cancel each other out (and some of them were secretly in sympathy with the liberals), Ludvík Vaculík was able to get his novel published: *The Axe*, a bitter study of human transformation in Czechoslovakia under Communism, and a work hailed as an outstanding Czech literary product of the generation. The flavor of *The Axe* comes across well in the comment by the journalist-narrator-hero that he would no longer accept the acts of "self-terrorization" that the Party expected of its members. "That's all the Czech invention is: we terrorize ourselves so democratically that there is no one left to assassinate." The Writers' Union awarded Vaculík its 1966 prize.

But Milan Kundera, another young writer, had the publication of his novel *The Joke* postponed until 1967 because the censor demanded, and Kundera refused to make, a change in a scene describing unarmed soldiers employed in hard labor because of their political "unreliability." Then, rather improbably, the regime named Mňačko, author of *Delayed Reports*, an Artist of Merit, although two years earlier he had been fired from the Presidium of the Writers' Union and was then writing *The Taste of Power*, a novel about a high Communist official who starts out a revolutionary idealist and degenerates into a corrupt tyrant. When finally published, this book did for Czechoslovakia what Milovan Djilas's *The New Class* had done for Yugoslavia thirteen years earlier in denouncing the new "Red bourgeoisie." Prague, of course, provided all the needed examples. Novotný lived in baronial splendor in a heavily guarded villa equipped with a sauna and other facilities in the wooded hills of Kinského Zahrada. Other Party officials also enjoyed considerable luxury and, with few exceptions (Dubček was one of them), spent free holidays at secluded resorts in other Communist countries (they returned the hospitality in Czechoslovakia) and exchanged expensive gifts with their foreign colleagues.

The intellectuals' protest now extended beyond the frontiers of Czechoslovakia. Something akin to international solidarity was beginning to develop among writers and artists in the Communist countries. After the Soviet writers Yuli Daniel and Andrei Sinyavsky had been sentenced to hard labor at a Moscow trial in February 1966, a group of Czechoslovak writers went to the Soviet capital to protest. (In 1968, after the invasion, Soviet intellectuals attempted to reciprocate this gesture, and some of them paid with prison terms for their courage.)

At the Academy of Sciences, a twenty-eight-man team of economists, sociologists, statisticians, historians, physicists, and architects, under Dr. Radovan Richta of the Philosophical Institute, issued in 1966 a comprehensive study of the problems facing Czechoslovakia in the technological revolution. *Civilization at the Crossroads* warned that the Czechoslovak political and economic leadership was unable to understand the meaning of modern technological change and was tending to push the country back to Stalinist methods of extensive industrialization—this at a time when most serious Marxist economists in Eastern Europe had recognized that *intensive* industrialization, coupled with up-to-date automation, was the proper path of development if the Comecon bloc was not to be left light years behind Western Europe, to say nothing of the United States.

While Šik was completing his "New Economic Model" reform and the Richta team was inquiring into the implications of the scientific revolution, the Academy of Sciences launched still another far-reaching project. This one was quite revolutionary, for it touched on the fundamental question of what political changes should accompany economic reform. The head of the commission making this study (appropriately called the New Political Model Commission) was Zdeněk Mlynář, a thirty-six-year-old lawyer and political scientist at the Academy. Mlynář had started out as a very cautious Communist progressive—he had, in fact, antagonized the writers by his criticisms of their acts—but he was to become one of the key leaders of the Prague Spring.

The notion that economic reform cannot function without political reform—both calling for freedom of action and options—was developing strongly not only among the intellectuals, but also, increasingly, among younger members of the government and Party. The Mlynář commission started from the assumption that political change *must* follow economic reform, and its research immediately centered on popular attitudes toward Czechoslovakia's existing political institutions and electoral system. The Czechoslovaks were jumping far ahead of the Romanians and even the Yugoslavs, who still believed that it was possible to liberalize the economy but not the people's lives. A powerful encouragement for those proposing new economics and new politics came during the KSČ's Thirteenth Congress, meeting in Prague from May 31 to June 4, when Šik told a press interviewer that economic changes would necessitate basic political reforms. The ideological profile of the Prague Spring was beginning to emerge. The trend was for reforming some of Communism's basic concepts without attacking Communism itself. In fact, the concept shared by the new ideologues was that the only way Communism could survive was through self-regeneration.

With this new philosophy, new men began to emerge, in and out of the establishment, to give it practical form. In the government and Party, Šik, Hájek, and Císař had become identifiable prophets of the new thinking. Outside the regime, there were Mlynář, Richta, Sviták, Karel Košik, a young Charles University philosopher, and Václav Müller, a brilliant young professor of economics. I remember asking Müller on one occasion what his students thought of Marxist economics. He raised his eyebrows and said, "Even my third-year students know there is no such thing as Marxist economics. . . . There is simply economics."

The great names later associated with the Prague Spring, however, were not yet in evidence on the side of this renaissance. Dubček was mostly holed up in Slovakia running the Slovak Party, though he held a seat on the KSČ Presidium. Ostensibly, he was still loyal to Novotný and on occasions quite abrasive with the rebel intellectuals. But some observers believe that during this period he did more than was realized to protect Slovakia's intellectuals, editors, and writers from Prague retaliation. Černík, who had risen with Dubček in the Party Secretariat and had been a Deputy Premier and chairman of the State Planning Commission since 1963, was elected to the Presidium at the June 1966 Party Congress, replacing the septuagenarian Fierlinger. Presumably, he and Kolder supported the New Economic Model, but if Černík had any positive views about simultaneous political reform, the record does not show it. Josef Smrkovský, who in 1965 had been made Minister-Chairman of the Central Administration of Water Supply, something less than an ideological command post, and who was also a deputy to the National Assembly, was restored to the Central Committee at that same Party Congress, but his voice, too, was conspicuously missing from the progressives' chorus. General Svoboda received the title of Hero of the Soviet Union and the Order of Lenin in 1965, and was named a Czechoslovak Hero of the Republic. He hardly seemed the man to question Communist orthodoxy or defy Soviet wishes.

On May Day 1966 Prague had its by now traditional youth riot. But this year the students were joined by young workers and office clerks. The indifference of the working class, at least of its younger members, toward political change was beginning to crack, although Novotný still believed that the workers would rise to defend his regime. After the usual poetry reading at the Mácha statue in Petřín Park, the young people marched downhill, crossed a bridge over the Vltava, and set off a demonstration at Wenceslas Square. "We want freedom!" "We want democracy!" "A good Communist is a dead Communist!" Policemen were greeted with cries of "Gestapo!" Twelve leaders of the demonstration were tried on May 25 and sentenced to jail terms of from five to seventeen months. Two well-known student leaders, Jiří Müller and Luboš Holeček, escaped sentence but late in 1966 were expelled from Prague University and the Union of Czechoslovak Youth and drafted for military service—an event that served to turn the otherwise nonpolitical Union into a new hotbed of antiregime activism. The Novotný regime had a special talent for awakening opposition.

The regime, blissfully oblivious of change, sought to counteract the growing criticism with the usual turgid rhetoric, the accustomed threats and reprisals. In March, for example, the Party forced the Writers' Union's weekly *Literární Noviny* to form a new editorial board free of progressive "extremists." The Union had by now learned to roll with the punch and avoid pointless showdowns and worked out a compromise, advising the KSČ leadership that the weekly had corrected its ideological deficiencies. It was the same story as in 1956 and 1957: a "good" paper resolution meant more than reality, and the regime was satisfied.

At the Slovak Party's congress in May, Dubček by and large succeeded in staying away from the controversial subject of the intellectuals. The man chosen to read the riot act was Vasil Bilak, a forty-nine-year-old conservative *apparatchik*. Until the age of thirty-two, Bilak was a laborer and a minor Party official in Slovakia. He was wounded in the 1944 Slovak uprising in which both Dubček and Husák had participated. In 1958 Bilak suddenly sprang to prominence when he was named a minister without portfolio in the national government, Vice-Chairman of the Slovak National Council, and its Commissioner for Education and Culture. His academic credentials were a three-year course at the KSČ's Central Committee ideological school. In 1963 Bilak joined the Slovak Party's Central Committee, under Dubček, and was made a member of the Presidium of the National Assembly. Now, discussing the intellectuals' role at the Slovak Party Congress, Bilak declared that there were people and groups of writers who lacked "a firm ideological outline and . . . experience in life." It was an "evil creed," he said, that held that young Communists could avoid political involvement because their elders had backed socialist ideas without reservations. The Party never proposed to dictate to writers and artists, he went on, but it had the duty to stress "what is and what is not in harmony with the aims of our socialist society." He encouraged intellectuals to enter the Party's ranks, but warned that, "it is quite another thing if someone takes a stand running counter to the strategy and the tactics of the Party."

When the KSČ Congress met on May 31, it was Novotný himself who delivered a blast at the intellectuals. In his typical jargon, Novotný deplored the fact that in Czechoslovakia there existed "certain incorrect modes of erroneous political ideas which are also manifested in the one-sided, unobjective, and negative views of our socialist reality and also in the attacks on the Party and its policy." The students, he said, acted with a "destructive attitude toward the values of our society," while the tone of articles in certain cultural publications was "false and foreign to socialism."

Novotný found that some "teachers" of Marxism-Leninism were passively or actively associated with "negativist influences" and, in a veiled threat to his Education and Culture Minister, warned, "We shall make every effort to insure that the trends which harm all youth are radically changed and overcome." He found fault again with the cultural journals, which, hiding behind a "fashionable liberalist gown," were spreading ideologically questionable views. All those distortions, Novotný said, "led to the propagation of abstract humanism conceived in connection with the class standpoint and advocated an uncritical and conciliatory acceptance of diverse currents or forms of bourgeois ideology."

Perhaps unwittingly, Novotný had put his finger on a principal ideological difference between his and the new generation. What he considered dangerous "abstract humanism" the younger Communist thinkers regarded as a vital renaissance of Marxism along human lines. It was a gulf of ideas that never could be bridged.

The year 1967, a crucial year in Czechoslovak history, opened with a two-pronged offensive by the regime. By now, it must have become obvious even to Novotný that his own survival was at stake, and it is small wonder that he devoted himself to an improvement in the Czechoslovak economy and a last attempt to control the dissident intellectuals, whose influence was spreading farther and farther. Using the universities, the theater, the cinema, and the press as their forum, they had become a highly politicized force in Czechoslovakia and commanded a growing audience. The regime's prime concern was that failure to ameliorate the economy would draw the thus far passive workers to join the general unrest.

On January 1, 1967, the New Economic Model reform program designed by Ota Šik and sponsored in the Presidium by Oldřich Černík and Drahomír Kolder officially went into effect. Its theoretical highlights were the creation of a market economy, in which supply and demand would be spontaneously generated and not artificially created; a realistic revaluation of salaries and prices; decentralization in industry; the introduction of incentives for both enterprises and workers; and, in the long run, a form of international convertibility for the arbitrarily pegged Czechoslovak crown. Šik summed it all up in his new book, *Plan and Market Under Socialism*. The objective of the reform was not only to cure the long-accumulated ills of the national economy but also, at the same time, to make it competitive internationally. Czechoslovakia could not modernize industrially unless she could earn hard currency through her exports and thus be able to import Western technology and equipment.

Even the most naïve Czechoslovak economist—or, indeed, every economist in Eastern Europe—knew that the Soviet Union was in no condition to supply this technology to her bloc partners. In fact, the Soviet Union was an increasing drain on the Czechoslovak economy which, between 1960 and 1966, had to provide Moscow with 877 million dollars in credits to cover deliveries of Czechoslovak petroleum-industry equipment for the development of new Soviet oil fields. The Czechs then had to buy Soviet crude oil at twice the world price. Czechoslovakia had accumulated 1850 million dollars in unrecoverable debts from Comecon, including the Soviet Union, for capital investments and trade. These debts could be collected either in nonconvertible bloc currencies, useless in the West, or in unnecessary imports from other Communist countries, such as Bulgarian tomatoes or Polish television sets. Payments for the processing of Soviet raw materials in Czechoslovak plants also were in nonconvertible rubles. Additionally, Czechoslovakia was forced by Moscow to provide assistance to North Vietnam and Cuba in the name of Communist solidarity, a highly expensive proposition, and weapons went to the Arabs.

Starting out with all these strikes against her, Czechoslovakia could rely only on herself to improve and modernize her economy. Actually, some advances had been made following the 1963 crisis, and in 1966 and

1967 per-capita national income was officially reported to have gone up by 7 and 8 per cent respectively. The per-capita Gross National Product stood in 1967 at 1700 dollars, compared with 1532 in the Soviet Union and 1800 in East Germany. Czechoslovak exports were running at the rate of 2.9 billion dollars in 1967, though 33 per cent of them went to the Soviet Union. But farm production, deeply hurt by forced collectivization, still lagged at 1930 levels, and there remained acute shortages in both foodstuffs and consumer goods. Long queues of housewives with string bags waiting in front of food stores at dawn were a typical Prague sight.

To be sure, Šik's reform had limitations. The Czechoslovaks could not, at this juncture, consider a return to private enterprise even at the minimal levels that existed in Poland or East Germany, neither of which were *Socialist* republics. They could not reverse the drain on the Czechoslovak economy caused by Soviet trade and investment policies. And, most especially, they could not openly propose political reforms to go along with these attempts at economic liberalization. At the same time, Party bureaucrats with vested interests opposed decentralization and the regime's problems were further complicated by the fact that the necessary revaluation of wholesale prices resulted in a rise in retail prices that was not compensated for by higher productivity. To make sense, reform could succeed only in a society which politically trusted its leadership, and this was definitely not the case in Czechoslovakia. It was awareness of this factor that had led Šik and many others to argue in Party councils that a political reform was urgently needed. But in the circle of Novotný and his friends these arguments obviously fell on deaf ears.

Rather than look for political flexibility, Novotný again took on the progressive intellectuals in the second phase of his "survival" offensive of 1967. A series of Central Committee meetings was called to find ways of smashing the intellectuals' revolt. Speaking at a February Plenum, Hendrych attacked *Literární Noviny* and *Host do Domu* (the latter published in Brno) for their "liberalism." In a lengthy speech, he hit out at a "secondary, but not insignificant stream of literature, films, and visual arts which in individual works makes poetry out of the hopelessness and absurdity of people estranged from social progress. . . . Creative freedom must not be construed as license for vagueness of views or anarchism, the absolute negation of the life of our society."

Then, at the next Plenum in March, new assaults were made on the writers, movie makers, and philosophers. The regime banned the showing in Czechoslovakia of the films *The Daisies* and *A Report on the Party and the Guests*. But even the regime refused to go along with a proposal made in the National Assembly to ban all progressive film directors as a "fifth column" and "internal enemies of the state."

At the February Plenum, Novotný had announced his decision to split up the Education and Culture Ministry. Professor Hájek remained as Education Minister, but the new Culture Ministry was given to Karel Hoffman, an ultraconservative Party hack with strong ties to Moscow. Hoffman, who was to play an important role in preparing the 1968 Soviet invasion, was elevated to the Culture Ministry from his post as chief of the Central Committee's Ideological Commission. His replacement there was one František Havlíček, another hard-liner.

Since January 1 the regime had had at its disposal a press law which legalized censorship for the first time since the Communist takeover. As Z. A. B. Zeman, a Czechoslovak historian now living in England, points out in his book *Prague Spring*, this law went into effect exactly one century after the adoption of the Habsburg Press Law. The new legislation theoretically confined censorship to the protection of state, economic, and official secrets, but in practice the new Culture Ministry had the authority to determine what constituted these secrets. The law also gave Hoffman the power to license publishing by organizations only, not individuals; this effectively prevented anyone outside of the Party or regime from starting a new newspaper or magazine. Not surprisingly, the new law was greeted with a loud outcry by the writers and journalists who dismissed the official claims that it was a step ahead in "socialist legality."

The regime may have thought it had succeeded in silencing the press critics, but barely a month after the National Assembly's approval of the Press Law, the intellectuals found another outlet through the state-owned radio network. On January 30 Radio Prague began a series of discussion programs on topical internal problems, naming them the Club of Engaged Thinking. Unthinkable thoughts and unspeakable words were thus uttered on the Czechoslovak radio as the panelists joined in demanding political reform to follow the economic reform and telling the nation of the real merits of Tomáš Masaryk and Eduard Beneš, the two presidents whose memories the Communists had relegated to oblivion for nearly twenty years. This was the beginning of Masaryk's rehabilitation—one of the major philosophical and political ingredients of the Prague Spring.

It also marked the entry of Czechoslovak broadcasters into the battle for national freedoms.

As the spring of 1967 drew to its end, the trumpets sounded for the final showdown between Czechoslovakia's progressive Communists and the encrusted orthodox regime of Antonín Novotný.

BOOK FOUR

The Day

In Which the Light of Day

Shines over Czechoslovakia

XIII

Lashing Out—Right and Left

The international context in which the Czechoslovak confrontation—and with it the Communist renaissance—developed in 1967 was one of great concern to the Soviet Union. The immediate cause of this concern was Romania, whose stubborn attitude of independence persisted, sabotaging Soviet plans for Comecon integration, complicating the smooth functioning of the Warsaw Pact military alliance, and undermining Communist unity in Eastern Europe. With Yugoslavia and Albania already long lost by the Soviet Union, the Romanians' "selfish" neutrality in the dispute with China (as an enraged Khrushchev called it when he burst in on Gheorghiu-Dej in 1964) was creating a serious breach in the political, military, and economic front in Eastern Europe, with dangerous strategic implications. Among other problems, Romania's example was being carefully and enviously watched by militant progressive Communists in Czechoslovakia who would have liked, too, to act independently of the Soviet Union in foreign affairs. The progressive Císař, exiled as Ambassador to Romania in 1965, made it his business to keep his Prague friends posted on Bucharest's policies.

Taking up where the "Declaration of Independence" had left off in 1964, Nicolae Ceauşescu delivered the next blow at Soviet geopolitics in a minor speech on May 7, 1966. This speech (oddly unnoticed in the West) urged the scrapping of all military blocs in the world and the removal of troops of all nations from the territories of foreign countries. To be sure, Ceauşescu readily acknowledged that the Warsaw Pact alliance had to be maintained so long as NATO existed, and he offered no hint that Romania was even thinking of leaving the Pact. But his words were disturbingly reminiscent of Tito's "nonalignment," and Moscow knew that for

217

several years Romania had managed to avoid active participation in the operations of the Warsaw Pact. Consequently, Brezhnev rushed to Bucharest to remonstrate with Ceauşescu over the implications of his speech and of his whole policy, notably toward China. He had as little luck impressing the stone-faced Ceauşescu as Khrushchev had had with Gheorghiu-Dej in 1964.

Then, in June, Romania played host to China's Premier Chou En-lai. Ceauşescu handled this visit as artfully as he had handled Brezhnev. To show that the Romanians were truly neutral—and not just deliberately flirting with the Chinese as the Russians were beginning to suspect—Ceauşescu prevailed upon Chou En-lai not to deliver a speech attacking the Soviet Union. In the end, the Chinese Premier had to settle on a noncontroversial and virtually ad-libbed address. Ceauşescu could now claim the unique distinction for a Communist leader of having forced both Brezhnev and Chou En-lai into respecting Romania's position. In Albania after his frustrating Bucharest visit, Chou En-lai sought revenge in barbed remarks against the Romanians, but an open dispute with them evidently did not suit China.

The next episode in Romania's complicated diplomatic game concerned the meeting of the Warsaw Pact's Political Consultative Committee, its governing organ, scheduled to be held in Bucharest in July 1966. Immediately after Ceauşescu's speech and Brezhnev's visit, Romania proceeded to sabotage it. Having discovered that Brezhnev proposed to use the conference to strengthen and streamline the Warsaw Pact, the Romanians started to leak word to Western journalists that they would propose, instead, a "multilateralization" of the alliance. This meant, it was quietly explained in Bucharest, that Romania desired a greater voice in the decision-making process of the Warsaw Supreme Command for each of its members, and that it believed that the post of Supreme Commander should rotate from country to country. The Romanians straightfacedly pointed out that no provision in the Warsaw Pact specified that the command must *always* be held by a Soviet officer. Finally, the carefully managed Bucharest rumor mill produced the information that Romania would also propose the withdrawal of Soviet troops stationed in the bloc countries. As soon as articles in the West on the Romanian position produced the desired result—a sense of alarm in Moscow—the Romanian spokesmen blandly denied that any such plan existed. But the denials were deliberately unconvincing, and the Kremlin did not miss the point.

Accordingly, when the top leaders of the Warsaw Pact met in Bucharest, the Soviet Union shelved its proposals for strengthening the alliance in order to keep Romania from presenting her counterproposals. This was precisely the result Ceauşescu had wanted to achieve. All the conference was able to produce, aside from a resolution attacking American "imperialism," was a declaration calling for the development of bilateral and multilateral relations among European states regardless of their political systems. The declaration also proposed a European security conference, and Ceauşescu piously signed the document.

Just as piously, he used the same declaration six months later to justify the establishment of diplomatic relations with West Germany, Romania's principal trading partner in the West. This obviously was not what the Soviet Union had in mind when the declaration had been drafted in Bucharest and, indeed, the establishment of diplomatic ties with West Germany on January 31, 1967, was a major blow. Seen from Moscow, it was a dangerous penetration by West German "revanchists" into Communist Eastern Europe, a threat to East Germany's political position, and a bad precedent for the other bloc members. To be sure, Moscow had long maintained diplomatic relations with Bonn but, in the Kremlin's reasoning, what was good for the Soviet Union was not necessarily good for her satellites.

Inevitably, this Romanian example was observed in Czechoslovakia. Inasmuch as West Germany was likewise Czechoslovakia's chief Western trade partner and Ota Šik's New Economic Model reform provided for greater commercial links with the West, Novotný agreed to consider diplomatic relations with Bonn. But, in a small-scale repetition of Stalin's ban on Czechoslovakia's participation in the Marshall Plan, Brezhnev promptly talked Novotný out of this idea. Only reluctantly was Czechoslovakia allowed in August 1967 to invite a permanent West German trade mission to Prague, after signing a new twenty-year friendship treaty with East Germany.

New problems with Romania arose early in 1967. The Soviet Union had summoned a conference of the heads of ruling Communist parties and a number of Western parties to meet in April in the Bohemian resort of Karlový Vary to discuss ideological problems, and notably China. Ceauşescu refused to send a delegation on the grounds that Romania disagreed with the conference's "character, procedure, and purpose." This was the first time the Romanians had formally boycotted a top-level Communist meeting (aside from the informal 1965 preparatory session for the planned world conference of the parties). Instead of going to Karlový Vary, Ceauşescu was visited in Bucharest by Tito, who had also declined the Soviet invitation. It was the first time since 1956 that Tito had come to Bucharest, and his visit marked the beginning of an increasingly close relation between the two "revisionist" countries. In March Ceauşescu made a point of rolling out the red carpet for Richard M. Nixon, then titular head of the Republican Party, after Soviet leaders had refused to receive him in Moscow and Poland had turned down his request for a visa. This political prescience was to be rewarded in August 1969 by an official visit to Romania by the man who had in the meantime become President of the United States.

To counteract all these divisive moves in Eastern Europe, Brezhnev devised the strategic-military idea of strengthening the Communist bloc by means of an "Iron Triangle" formed by East Germany, Poland, and Czechoslovakia. This concept was highly welcomed by the Poles and East Germans, who were becoming increasingly nervous over the turn events were taking in Eastern Europe. Soviet troops were stationed in Poland and East Germany, but there were none in Czechoslovakia, and Brezhnev began pressing Novotný to invite Soviet units assigned to the Warsaw Pact to establish bases there. But, given his domestic problems, Novotný concluded that this would be a disastrous gesture on his part and delayed his answer to Moscow. Before long, however, the problem was taken out of his hands.

Throughout Eastern Europe, the Soviet Union had to contend with aging and weakening leaders who no longer commanded meaningful support in their parties and had to have recourse to tough measures to retain power and preserve ideological orthodoxy. Given the available leadership, then, not too much constructive thinking could be expected from the "Iron Triangle" or indeed from the Hungarians or Bulgarians. Only the relatively young and imaginative Ceauşescu was worth watching, but he was a dangerous fellow from Moscow's viewpoint.

At home, too, the Kremlin faced serious problems. Soviet intellectuals, encouraged earlier by Khrushchev, were increasingly vocal and critical, and the conviction of Daniel and Sinyavsky had only aggravated the pressures. New trials were held in 1967 resulting in prison and hard-labor terms for the writers Aleksandr Ginzburg, Aleksei Dobrovolsky, and Vera Lashkova for publicly criticizing earlier arrests and trial procedures.

Meanwhile, the ugly specter of nationalism was again raising its head among the Ukrainians, Crimean Tatars, and Latvians. As early as 1961, the KGB had arrested seven members of an allegedly secret Ukrainian Union of Workers and Peasants who were then tried and sentenced on charges of advocating secession from the Soviet Union (for which, incidentally, the Soviet constitution does provide). In 1965 and 1966 some one hundred Ukrainians, mainly young intellectuals, had been arrested for "agitation" and "dissemination of anti-Soviet propaganda." Among those imprisoned were Vyacheslav Chornovil, a journalist and literary critic, who had compiled a chronicle of the earlier Ukrainian intellectuals' trials; the poet and translator Svyatoslav Karavansky; the historian Valentyn Moroz, who wrote the clandestine *Report from the Beria Reserve*; the well-known literary critic Ivan Dzyuba, who wrote a treatise on *Internationalism or Russification?*; the critic Ivan Svitlychny; the writer Mikhail Horyn; the writer Mikhail Osadchy; and the painter Opanas Zalyvakha.

As in Slovakia, demands for intellectual freedom united with nationalist fervor in the Ukraine, and the fact that Slovakia adjoins the Ukraine, allowing direct communications between the two, was not overlooked by anyone. In a remarkably courageous speech on September 29, 1966, on the twenty-fifth anniversary of the Nazis' wartime massacres of thousands of Jews at Babi Yar, Ivan Dzyuba condemned anti-Semitism in the Soviet Union and pleaded for cultural rights for both the Jews and the Ukrainians: "This is our duty to millions of victims of despotism; this is our duty to the better men and women of the Ukrainian and Jewish nations who have urged us to mutual understanding and friendship; this is our duty to our Ukrainian land in which we live together; this is our duty to humanity." Dzyuba was arrested shortly after delivering his speech. (In one way, then, it took more courage for Soviet intellectuals to protest the denial of their rights than for their Czechoslovak colleagues to do the same, for the latter remained more or less free of the threat of imprisonment. The exception was Jan Beneš, a thirty-one-year-old writer arrested in September 1966 on charges of clandestinely sending literary materials to a Czech-language publication in Paris.)

The Czechoslovak crisis and the eventual decomposition of the Novotný regime revolved, to an important extent, around the issue of anti-Semitism and Israel. On the surface, the Six-Day War of 1967 may appear to be an event totally unrelated to Czechoslovakia. But the Israeli-Arab conflict struck very close to home in Prague. As in so many other areas, it was Novotný's clumsy handling of this question and his obedient imitation of Soviet policies that helped to make it a major Czechoslovak issue.

On May 25 the Foreign Ministry, headed by the pro-Soviet Václav David, had issued a gratuitous statement accusing Israel of creating tensions in the Middle East in concert with "imperialist circles directly connected with oil monopolies." This coincided with the (still unexplained) Soviet warning to the United Arab Republic that Israel was preparing an "attack" on Syria, which had led Cairo to mobilize suddenly and may have been one of the reasons for the eruption of the war.

When war came, the Czechoslovak Foreign Ministry published a "we-told-you-so" declaration charging Israel with "aggression" against the U.A.R. On June 9, as the lightning war neared its end, Eastern Europe's top Communist leaders gathered at an emergency conference in Moscow to agree on a joint policy in the Middle East. Even Marshal Tito came from Belgrade for this conclave. The Soviet recommendation was for a collective breach of diplomatic relations with Israel, and this was instantly accepted. Novotný and Lenárt unhesitatingly voted for the break as did Poland's Gomułka and Premier Cyrankiewicz. Hungary's Kadár and Premier Jenoe Fock, East Germany's Ulbricht and Premier Willi Stoph, and Bulgaria's Zhivkov. Tito cast his vote for it too, but probably more for reasons of his "nonaligned" nations' relationship with Nasser than out of loyalty to the principle of Communist unity. The only dissenters, not unexpectedly, were the Romanians. Ceauşescu and Premier Ion Gheorghe Maurer refused not only to break off relations with Israel but also to sign a joint declaration censuring the Israeli "aggression." To emphasize their protest, they stayed away from the Warsaw Pact summit meeting in Budapest in July.

Czechoslovakia wasted no time in implementing the Moscow decision and, on June 10, became the first Communist state after the Soviet Union to break off relations with Israel. On June 11 Novotný repeated in a speech that Israel was guilty of "aggression."

This anti-Israeli policy had catastrophic repercussions on Czechoslovak public opinion. Czechoslovaks immediately began to equate the present fate of Israel, surrounded by enemies, with Czechoslovakia's in 1938, abandoned by the world after the Munich pact. Those who thought further ahead even saw a parallel between Israel's defiant stand and the current situation of Czechoslovakia in the midst of the orthodox Communist sea. The Israeli war and the accusations of Zionism hurled from Moscow were too reminiscent of the anti-Semitic wave that had accompanied the trial and execution of Rudolf Slánský. A country singularly free of anti-Semitic prejudice, by Eastern European standards, Czechoslovakia tended to associate anti-Semitism with Stalinist oppression. And, finally, many Czechoslovaks were genuinely pleased to see the Soviet-trained and -equipped Egyptian Army swiftly defeated.

Thus, when Ceauşescu explained Romania's policy on the Middle East in a speech at the July session of the Grand National Assembly in Bucharest, he expressed the sentiments of masses of Czechoslovaks: "We wish honestly to tell our Arab friends that we do not understand and do not share the position of those circles that speak in favor of the liquidation of the state of Israel. We do not wish to give advice to anybody, but the lessons of history show that no people can achieve their national and social aspirations against the right to existence of another people."

Naturally, no ranking Czechoslovak official was prepared to take such a stand, but the intellectuals did so at the crucial and emotion-packed Fourth Congress of the Writers' Union meeting in the auditorium of the Transport Ministry in Prague, June 27–29. This meeting, the first congress held since 1963, was the turning point in the campaign against the Novotný regime.

Pavel Kohout, a thirty-nine-year-old playwright who once found fame through his eulogies of Stalin but now had become a fierce liberal and a nationalist, brought the Israeli controversy into the open. (In addition to more than four hundred writers, his audience included the Party's chief ideologue Jiří Hendrych, Karel Hoffman, and the increasingly progressive-minded Hájek.) In what amounted to a public denunciation of the regime's policy, Kohout said that Israel had the right to strike first in the June War because "a country as small as Israel cannot defend itself otherwise than offensively." He took exception to the "one-sided" view of the Middle Eastern crisis presented to the Czechoslovak public by the official press and claimed that Israel was a "model" of socialist development. "In Israel, they have made a garden out of a desert," where nearly the entire Israeli agriculture system has developed along "socialist or Communist" lines. Kohout's position was supported in a subsequent speech by Jan Procházka.

But the most dramatic gesture was made by the novelist Mňačko. In August 1967 he simply left Czechoslovakia for Israel. While en route to Jerusalem, Mňačko issued a statement in Rome explaining his step. It was not published in Czechoslovakia, of course, but within days copies of his statement began to circulate clandestinely in Prague and Bratislava:

I am going to Israel. It is my intention to register my protest against the policy of the Czechoslovak government by this journey. Since in Czechoslovakia one is prevented from speaking out about the Middle East crisis, I am compelled to choose this unusual way.

It is impossible for me to support—even through silence—a policy which leads to the eradication of a whole people and to the liquidation of an entire state. . . .

Generally speaking, I have been unable to understand our policy toward Israel throughout the past. In the West this policy is described as "satellitism." I do not believe this is quite correct. We go beyond the bounds which are required in this respect. We do our job with great eagerness and great alacrity. I believe this is connected with our past which is not yet overcome. In our country the connotations of the political trials of the Stalin era were particularly unpleasant. The Slánský trial served the purpose of producing an anti-Semitic tide. This had, of course, nothing in common with Communist ideology. Its effects have not been reversed up to this moment. The Slánský trial itself and its consequences, the anti-Semitic tide, have not yet been fully discussed and fully explained.

The system in Czechoslovakia must be changed to a very considerable degree if we want to continue as a healthy socialist humanitarian country. This chaos, this system of rubber laws, these opportunities of circumventing the law, and whenever the rulers see fit, these possibilities of applying such laws which do not fit at all in a particular case, this arbitrariness must be eliminated. In this respect, a good deal has already been achieved. However, there are no guarantees that excesses will not occur again.

The regime's response was to deprive Mňačko of his Czechoslovak citizenship, his Communist Party membership, and his title as "Artist of Merit." But this was a feeble reaction, and it really was self-damning.

The Israeli issue, important as it was, was only one aspect of the rebellion now at its peak. The big battle had begun on June 5 with the Fifth Congress of the Union of Czechoslovak Youth. The Union had been part of the official Party apparatus since 1949, and all youths between the ages of fourteen and twenty-six were "eligible" for membership, but over the years membership had dropped alarmingly from its high of 1,112,000 in 1958. No figures were available in 1967, but it was estimated that only 26 per cent of the "eligibles" still belonged to it at the time of the Fifth Congress. One of the Union's principal functions, the formation of "auxiliary policy units," lessened its appeal to the new generation. Nevertheless, the June youth congress was intended to consolidate the Union as a power tool of the regime, and accordingly, Novotný came to address it. (The Soviet Union inexplicably sent Marshal Konev, the aging liberator of Prague, as its chief delegate.) But what the meeting proved was that, despite the usual prefabricated resolutions dutifully approved on the floor, the Union was an empty shell from which the nation's deeply alienated youth was massively staying away. Its real functions were being taken over by informal associations of university students who had no use for Novotný and Konev or for anything they stood for.

The writers' congress three weeks later threw new light on the intellectuals' estrangement from the Prague establishment. The tone for this meeting had been set by the conference of the Slovak Writers' Union in Bratislava on May 11, where the Slovak writers had heard the Party's local ideologue, Vasil Bilak, urge them to "an intensive political activity and confrontation of ideas," while at the same time he sounded renewed warnings that "an artist must not retreat from the socialist world concept and must not yield ground to hostile ideas." So stale were Bilak's pronouncements that the cultural journals in Bratislava and Prague did not even bother to report his speech, although they reported on the speech by the Slovak Writers' Union's First Secretary, Vojtech Mihalik, who propounded the need for "constantly and ceaselessly broadening the scope for a free exchange of views, for a many-sided democratization of the Union's life, for supporting and defending creative work wherever it is engaged in criticizing violations and distortions of man's humanistic ideals." (*Pravda*, the organ of the Slovak Party, likewise printed Mihalik's speech.)

The real fireworks came at the Czechoslovak Writers' Union congress in Prague. Zeman has noted that this congress in effect repeated fifty years later the defiance of the Prague writers in May 1917, whose manifesto "signed the death warrant of the Habsburg Empire."

During preparations for the congress, there were indications that the Novotný regime was still hoping to muzzle the intellectuals. The Ministry of Culture and Information prepared "for official use only" a blueprint of its activities based on the concept that there existed two kinds of art, "an art accessible to only a small number of people" and "an art for the broad masses." The second type of art, the document noted, possessed "chief social significance" and as such must be encouraged. In what was a clear attempt to smuggle "socialist realism" back into Czechoslovak culture, the Ministry offered to "judge important events in cultural life and evaluate their social significance." Simultaneously, the Party ideologues—Hendrych and Hoffman—spent weeks negotiating with the Writers' Union Presidium, notably with Kundera and Vaculík, over the text of the main resolution to be approved by the congress. Here again was that obsession with resolutions which the Party believed could effectively paper over the realities.

Kundera (his *The Joke* had been published a few months before the congress) was the lead-off speaker, and when he finished his speech everyone in the huge hall knew that a real battle had begun. He had stressed that the Czechoslovak civilization had "the greatest flowering in its history" between the two world wars—it was another way of praising the Masaryk period—and gone on to say that "to interrupt that development first by the Nazi occupation, then by Stalinism, almost a quarter of a century altogether, to isolate it from the outside world, to do away with its manifold inner tradition, to reduce it to the level of barren propaganda —that was the tragedy which threatened to remove the Czech nation, once and for all, to the outer suburbs of European civilization."

Addressing himself to the cultural watchdogs of the Novotný regime, Kundera said:

> I know that when freedom is mentioned some people get hay fever and reply that every freedom must have its limits. Of course, every freedom has its limits, given by the state of contemporary knowledge, education, prejudice, and so on. Yet, no progressive period has ever tried to fix its own limitations. . . . Only, in our case, the guarding of frontiers is still regarded as a greater virtue than crossing them.

Pointed in this direction, the writers' congress thundered on. After delivering a critique of the regime's policy on Israel, Pavel Kohout read the text of a letter sent the month before to the Soviet writers' congress by Alexander Solzhenitsyn, the author of *One Day in the Life of Ivan Denisovich*. The letter, which was not read at the Moscow session, struck out at censorship and accused the Soviet Writers' Union of not standing up for the rights of its members:

> The Soviet Constitution does not provide for censorship, which is, therefore, illegal and is never mentioned in public, but under the obscure name of Glavlit [the Central Administration for Literary Affairs and Publishing], it weighs upon our literature, subjecting writers to the arbitrary will of unlettered officials. . . .
>
> The congress should demand and obtain the abolition of all censorship—open or concealed—of artistic works. . . . It should free the publishing houses of their obligation to obtain permission from the authorities before publishing any work. . . .
>
> The Writers' Union . . . has invariably shown itself to be the first among the detractors and in a cowardly fashion abandoned to their misfortune . . . over six hundred innocent writers . . . whose persecution has ended in exile, prison camp, and death.

Reading this letter at the officially sponsored writers' congress was a slap in the face for the Party and, especially, for Jiří Hendrych, its ranking representative, who had already angrily tangled with the writers in an improvised speech full of bitter accusations and contradictions. In the passion of the argument and the heat of the June day, he had taken off his jacket to harangue his enemies. Now, as Kohout read from Solzhenitsyn's letter, Hendrych put his coat back on and furiously stalked from the hall. Later that week, the Soviet government protested to Czechoslovakia that Kohout's presentation of Solzhenitsyn's appeal had constituted an interference in Soviet internal affairs.

Other writers rose to criticize the censorship and demand full cultural freedoms. Among them were Eduard Goldstücker, the literary and cinema critic Antonín Liehm, and the writer Ivan Klima. But the climactic point of the congress was a speech given by Ludvík Vaculík, the prize-winning author of *The Axe*, and his words were the most devastating public indictment of Czechoslovakia's malady in twenty years:

> This congress was not convened after the members of the organization decided to meet . . . but only after the ruling circles . . . graciously gave their consent. In exchange, they expect, as rulers have customarily expected for hundreds of years, to be treated with reverence. I suggest that we not show them reverence. . . . Let us play this game as if we were citizens, as if we had permission to use this playground. And for three whole days, let us act as if we were adult and had come of age. . . .
>
> Here I speak as a citizen of a country which I will never renounce, but in which I cannot live contentedly. . . . I am a Communist Party member, and I would not, and moreover do not, wish to discuss Party affairs. . . . But it so happens that in our country there is almost nothing left that at a certain stage of debate does not become a Party matter.
>
> The regime's confidence was won by the obedient, by those who made no difficulties, by those who asked no questions that the regime itself did not raise. At every stage of the selection, the average man came out on top. And the complicated characters disappeared from the stage—those with personal charm, and particularly those who, because of their qualities and accomplishments, were a measure of the public conscience. So it was a negative selection. What happened to the others? Where are they? What do they think? What are they doing?
>
> You have perhaps noticed that all of us, Czechs and Slovaks, are inclined to feel that in our various jobs we are led by men less capable than ourselves. And all of us, wherever we meet, complain bitterly. This is disgusting. Because the incapable and the lazy, the absolute good-for-nothings and the people with limited intelligence, complain together with those who perhaps have reason to do so. . . . Thus, a false and harmful unity has grown up between men who by no means be-

long together. We are all united by the most miserable impulse imaginable: . . . a common unwillingness. . . . In literature depression, nihilism, and spiritual decay are the fashion. The snobs indulge in orgies. Even the intelligent are becoming stupid. From time to time a clever man feels the need to assert himself—he wants to lash out left and right. But when he looks up and sees what is above him and then looks down and sees that there are people to stamp on him, he must ask himself, "My God, for whom am I doing this?". . .

Just as I do not believe that the citizen and the regime can identify themselves with each other, so I do not believe that art and the regime can like being on good terms with each other. . . . They cannot and never will. They are different. They do not match. What is possible . . . is that they should understand their positions and work out respectable rules for dealing with each other. . . .

Everything our culture achieves, everything good which men have done or created in our country . . . has [come about] despite the fact that our ruling circles have behaved in this way for years on end. These achievements were literally bullied out of them. And indeed much could be done. Something could really be done.

But the government and leadership are spurring us on. . . . Was it not during the writers' congress that Jiří Hendrych, Chairman of the Party Ideological Commission and Secretary of the Central Committee, proclaimed that the Party is striving to develop culture as an active factor in the great struggle between capitalism and socialism, and as an organic part of the socialist revolution and of the Party's policy? Is that not a goal? Is that not leadership? But what sort of leadership? I see only the brakes being applied. . . .

I see and hear that the [regime] retreats only when it sees and hears too strong a resistance. But no arguments convince it. Only failure. Repeated failure, which costs us all money and tries our nerves. I see the return of the bad old days as a long-standing aim and a permanent danger. For what was the meaning of the statement that we have a union, publishing house, and newspapers? A threat that they will take them away from us if we don't behave? . . . But are they really the lords of everything? And what remains of us in the hands of others? Nothing? Then we need not exist. But they should say so. Then it would be perfectly clear that basically a handful of people decide on our existence or nonexistence. What we should do, think, and feel. About everything . . . concerning culture. That is the position of culture in our nation today. . . .

Just as I do not feel very secure in the cultural-political situation, which the regime can apparently bring to a state of conflict, so I have no feeling of security as a citizen outside this room, outside this playground. Nothing is being done to me, and nothing has been done—because such things don't happen any more. Should I be grateful? I don't want to be. I am afraid. . . . I see no firm guarantees whatever. It is true that I see better work in the courts, but the judges themselves do not see any firm guarantees. I see better work by the state prosecutor's office. But do the state prosecutors have guarantees and do they feel secure? If they like, I would be glad to interview them for the newspapers but do you think it would be published? I would not be afraid to discuss with the state prosecutors why unjustly sentenced and rehabilitated people do not automatically regain their original rights. How is it that National Committees do not give them their apartments or houses back? But that would not be published. Why has no one properly apologized to these people? Why don't they have the advantages of those who have been politically persecuted? Why are we miserly about money for them? Why can't we live where we want to? Why can't a tailor go to Vienna for three years or a painter for thirty years to Paris with the opportunity to return . . . as a free citizen, not a criminal?

I see no guarantees. What guarantees? I don't know. And I stop, because at this point I am in great doubt. Do the ruling circles themselves, the government and its individual members, have these guarantees of civil rights without which it is impossible to create—to create even a policy? Before the congress, the Writers' Union weekly, *Literární Noviny,* polled a group of prominent writers and poets asking them what the aim of the Writers' Union should be. The first series of answers was published. The second was banned by the censor. What did the writers want? . . .

Policies devoid of culture evoke struggles for freedom. And yet the regime is annoyed when we constantly talk about it. It does not understand that freedom exists only in places where one does not need to speak about it. The regime is annoyed because people talk about what they see. But instead of changing what people see, the regime wants to change their eyes. And in the meantime we are losing the only valuable ideal: the dream of a citizen who governs almost by himself. Is this dream realizable?

Next year, Czechoslovakia will celebrate the fiftieth anniversary of the First Republic and the twentieth anniversary of the Second Republic. But also the thirtieth anniversary of the Munich Pact, which led to the destruction of Masaryk's First Republic. This First Republic was not socialist. It left a heritage that Czechoslovak historians have so far been silent about. We have had partial successes on the road toward the dream we have aimed at since the beginnings of history.

Our aim was the rise of an independent Czechoslovakia, a gain made by progressive people and progressive politicians, which has not yet been officially recognized and which I propose should be recognized. Because as a result a state was formed which, despite its imperfections . . . brought with it a high level of democracy. And it was a state in which the citizens had no aversion to the ideas of socialism, to the socialism which could be realized . . . only in the second stage of the state's development. After the war . . . the idea of a socially just state was exchanged for a program of socialism. . . .

When we talk about that period, when we seek for explanations as to why we lost so much morally and materially, as to why we are economically backward, the ruling circles say that it was necessary. I believe that from our point of view it was not necessary. Perhaps it was necessary for the spiritual development of the organs of the regime, of the organs which compelled all the supporters of socialism to experience this development with them.

It is necessary to understand that no human problem has been solved in our country for twenty years—starting with the elementary needs, such as housing, schools, and prosperity, and ending with the more refined requirements which cannot be satisfied by the undemocratic systems of the world. For instance, the feeling of full value in society. The subordination of political decisions to ethical criteria. The belief in the value of even small-scale labor, the need for confidence among men, the development of the education of the entire people.

I fear we have not risen on the world's stage and that our republic has lost its good name.

I do not wish to say that we have lived in vain, that nothing of what has happened has any value. It has value. But the question is whether it is only the value of forewarning. But was it necessary for a country which knew precisely the dangers for its culture to be made into an instrument for this kind of lesson? I suggest that in the writers' congress resolution we should state what progressive Czechoslovak culture knew even in the thirties. . . .

We are not trying to restore the First Republic. The writers are socialists and they believe that socialism can create a beautiful new world—but only socialism as they conceive it.

When I criticize the regime, I do not criticize socialism, because I am not convinced that what happened here was necessary, and because I do not identify the regime with socialism, in the way it tries to identify itself. The fate of one need not be the fate of the other. And if the people who exercise power came here and asked us: Can the dream be realized? . . . They would have to take this answer as the expression of our good will and . . . our supreme civic loyalty: "I don't know."

Vaculík's masterful speech—subsequently regarded as one of the basic documents of the Prague Spring—spelled out the disappointments, fears, and hopes not only of Czechoslovakia's intellectuals but of all her citizens. It also described with unprecedented clarity the aims of what soon was to become Czechoslovakia's "democratic socialist revolution."

But as Vaculík had correctly predicted, the regime was "annoyed" that he spoke of freedom, not understanding that "freedom exists only in places where one does not need to speak about it," and struck back. Jiří Hendrych delivered another speech castigating the rebel writers and threatening reprisals. Grabbing Vaculík outside the meeting hall, he accused him of maintaining secret contacts with Czechoslovak émigrés in New York. This was a virtual threat of arrest: Jan Beneš had been in jail since the previous September awaiting trial on charges of having émigré contacts in Paris. But nothing happened to Vaculík, and, despite the official fury, Hendrych agreed to a resolution which urged a revision in the press law to confine censorship to matters affecting national defense and proclaimed that "nothing is a more enduring indictment of a political regime than the absence of a great culture." In one of those classical compromises in which different phrases mean different things to different people, the resolution said:

> Socialism's great opportunity is that its program enables it consciously to defend itself against the dehumanizing aspects of the progress of civilization, against its dehumanizing tendencies. Socialist culture, in its widest sense as a complex of experiences gained in the creation of material and spiritual values, is thus bound up with the freeing of human relations and the winning of greater liberty. To the extent that a socialist society is aware of the humanizing importance of culture and promotes the freedom of science, the arts, and literature, so it tests and strengthens its socialist character.

But the Party forbade the publication of the speeches delivered at the congress—they were to be read by Czechoslovaks only in the spring of 1968—and it readied itself for a final repression of its detractors. Novotný personally took charge of this offensive in a speech delivered on June 30 to the graduating class of the KSČ's Central Committee School in Prague.

"We certainly cannot tolerate accusations that in the past we have been passing through a 'second dark age,' as was indicated by some delegates," Novotný said. "These people attacked the policy of the Party, the country's domestic and foreign policy, asserted coexistence with bourgeois ideology and failed to recognize the class struggle, which today takes very sharp forms when two clearly defined fronts are facing each other in the world." The next day *Rudé Právo* published the text of Novotný's speech, but his rebuttals must have mystified its long-suffering readers because they were not told what "these people" had actually said at the congress.

On July 3 the Prague municipal court, possibly by sheer coincidence, finally tried Beneš for allegedly smuggling literary materials out of Czechoslovakia for the Paris émigré magazine. He was condemned to five years in prison, and Pavel Tigrid, the magazine's editor, to fourteen years in an *in absentia* sentence. Novotný, meanwhile, left for a vacation in the Soviet Union on July 5, the day before the anniversary of Jan Hus's burning at the stake for his reformist heresy.

That Czechoslovakia still lived in a special type of dark age was dramatically demonstrated on August 16, with the mysterious and still unsolved disappearance in Prague of Charles Jordan, the fifty-nine-year-old Executive Vice-Chairman and Director General of the American Joint Distribution Committee, an American Jewish service organization concentrating on Jewish emigration to Israel and elsewhere. Jordan, a Philadelphian, had arrived in Prague from Bucharest on August 14 on a routine visit connected with his activities as operational head of Joint.

On the evening of August 16 Jordan left his suite at the Esplanade Hotel, telling his wife he was going out to buy cigarettes. He never returned. On August 29, almost two weeks later, his body was found floating face down in the Vltava River. Czechoslovak police officials described Jordan's death as the result of drowning, not ruling out the possibility of a suicide. But this explanation was not accepted or believed by the United States government, Joint, or Mrs. Jordan. A strong suspicion of foul play developed, and some of it fell on Soviet agents.

Joint, consequently, retained Dr. Ernst Hardmeier, a famous Swiss legal pathologist and Director of the Institute of Forensic Medicine at the University of Zurich, to conduct a second and independent autopsy. Dr. Hardmeier's findings were that traces of a powerful drug remained in Jordan's pancreas, leading to the now accepted theory that he had been kidnaped and drugged. (Dr. Hardmeier pointed out that the pancreas is the body organ in which a foreign substance would be preserved the longest, and this is why traces of the drug still appeared there despite the fact that the body had been nearly two weeks in the water.)

Dr. Hardmeier's findings were never published—I believe that I am the first to do so—and general interest in the Jordan case quickly died. But, on December 10, 1967, three months after he performed the autopsy, Dr. Hardmeier was found frozen to death in the snow about five hundred meters from his locked car in Forch, a deserted mountainous area on the right shore of the Lake of Zurich. There were no visible signs of a struggle, and, from what is known of the autopsy performed on Dr. Hardmeier's body, he had not suffered a stroke or heart attack. The *Tribune de Genève* and *La Suisse,* two reputable Geneva newspapers, reported on Dr. Hardmeier's mysterious death in their respective December 12 and 13 editions; both hinted at foul play and noted that the famous pathologist had earlier been retained by Joint to examine Jordan's body.

There is no known motive for the apparent kidnaping and murder of Charles Jordan and the subsequent apparent liquidation of Dr. Hardmeier. However, American and Swiss officials familiar with the twin mystery believe that Dr. Hardmeier not only had disclosed that Jordan had been drugged *before* drowning but also held additional evidence corroborating the murder theory. The Swiss authorities have never published the conclusions of the autopsy on Dr. Hardmeier's body, but there are reasons to believe that the Zurich police are convinced he too was murdered.

As for Jordan, a number of theories—none of them conclusive—suggest that he may have been killed because of his activities in promoting Jewish emigration from Eastern Europe. One theory is that the murder may have been carried out by fanatic Arab nationalists. Until the invasion of Czechoslovakia a year later, American diplomats in Prague persistently requested Czechoslovak authorities for further investigations, but they invariably drew a blank. During my stay in Prague in 1968, I raised the question with an acquaintance of mine in the Czech security services. (This was at the time Czechoslovak authorities had launched an investigation into the circumstances of Jan Masaryk's equally mysterious death in 1948.) My acquaintance said, "I suggest strongly you stay away from the Jordan business."

American investigators, however, have evidence to indicate that Jordan was to have been murdered in Romania, before his visit to Prague, but that either the plot was foiled by the Romanian Securitat or the killers simply were unable to carry it out. I was told by a foreign diplomat in Bucharest that he had discovered that Jordan was heavily drugged during a car trip they had made together from the Romanian capital to the town of Braşov on the morning of August 13, 1967, the day before the Jordans flew to Prague. This diplomat said that Jordan was unsteady, almost incoherent, and continuously falling asleep in the car, although he obviously was not intoxicated with alcohol. It appears, therefore, that Jordan's assassins followed him from Bucharest to Prague, where they finally succeeded in kidnaping and killing him.

As far as the American and Swiss governments are concerned, the Jordan and Hardmeier cases remain open. There is no likelihood that Czechoslovak security agents were directly involved in Jordan's death but the incident added to the general tensions already developing in Prague.

After his return from a holiday and a rather disastrous visit to Slovakia in August, Novotný concluded that the time had come to put an end once and for all to the intellectuals' revolt. He and his closest advisers agreed that the time for compromise was over. Speaking to the graduates of Czechoslovak military academies at a reception at Hradčany Castle on September 1, Novotný said that "liberalism" was spreading in the country and that it was imperative to "come out openly against this phenomenon. . . . Democracy and freedom have their limits," he said. "In a socialist state it is not possible to allow the propagation of opinions and ideology harmful to socialism and alien to the Communist Party."

Jan Procházka took up Novotný's challenge. In a long article published by *Literární Noviny* the thirty-eight-year-old Procházka, a candidate member of the Party's Central Committee, paid vibrant tribute to Tomáš Masaryk on September 14, the thirtieth anniversary of his death, as fulfilling the pledge he had made before the writers' congress that Czechoslovak intellectuals would go on fighting for freedom "to the last writer, the last ruler, and the last reader in this world." It was not the first time that Masaryk was being brought back from officially imposed oblivion in recent years, but Procházka's article was a major breakthrough in reviving the legend of the Republic's founder:

> [Masaryk] earned recognition from enemies, and that is something we no longer know, because he honored and tolerated even opinions he himself disagreed with. . . . He gained followers without trying to win them, and without threatening them. . . . A passionate politician who proclaimed honorable principles and, what is more, acted upon them, [he was] all the time a pedagogue and an educator, because he knew that to lead any nation means a continuous struggle with the nation's bad qualities. . . . T. G. Masaryk undoubtedly has a lot to say to contemporary socialist people.

Late in September, Novotný proceeded to carry out his threat that "the propagation of opinions and ideology harmful to socialism" would no longer be tolerated. A special Plenum of the Party's Central Committee met on September 26 and 27 to decree punitive measures. Hendrych, who had come under attack from his conservative colleagues on the Presidium for being too tolerant of dissent, told the Plenum that "the great and concentrated endeavor of our society is being stabbed in the back by the preaching of freedom, democracy, and humanism stripped of their class and socialist meaning."

The Plenum then deprived Procházka of his rank as a Central Committee candidate member. Vaculík, Klima, Liehm, and Mňačko were formally expelled from the Party. Pavel Kohout and Milan Kundera were severely reprimanded. *Literární Noviny* was placed under the direct jurisdiction of Culture and Information Minister Hoffman, who promptly fired nineteen editors and allowed the remaining five to resign. The new staff, Hoffman announced, would know how to infuse the magazine with "Party-minded ideological and political criteria in criticism and journalism." They did, indeed, and when *Literárni Noviny* reappeared early in October under the new management, it was a listless and obedient publication that newsvendors returned each week largely unsold. To prevent the Union from publishing books according to its own lights, the Party removed the Československý Spisovatel publishing house from its control and established two new houses under the Culture Ministry's direction. Editors were fired or reshuffled, paper supply to the Union's publishing concern was cut down, and the Culture Ministry took over administration of the fund for needy writers.

There are no available minutes of KSČ Presidium meetings, but reliable informants claim that both Dubček and Černík opposed this crackdown.

In December the Party restricted foreign travel and, simultaneously, cancelled "for technical reasons" a conference on literature and mass culture with East European writers and critics that the Writers' Union had planned to hold in Prague. The new Presidium of the union was made up of eleven writers who took no sides in the June controversy, four staunch Party-liners, and one liberal—the Moravian poet and editor Jan Skácel.

As far as Novotný was concerned, the rebellion had been smashed. But now he had to cope with the twin problems of the collapsing economy and of mounting Slovak bitterness against his regime. The battered intellectuals may not have believed it, but the end and victory were in sight.

XIV

The Fall of Novotný

Although Novotný had allowed Professor Šik to build his New Economic Model, he did virtually nothing in the course of 1967 to help him put it on the road. The tremendous economic bureaucracy built up during nineteen years of Stalinist management, feeding on a centralized system of decision-making and allocations of everything from credit to labor, was not amenable to Šik's ideas about decentralizing and dismantling this monstrously gigantic machine. Comfortable jobs in the ministries, in economic and labor organizations, industrial plants, and farms were held by loyal Communist Party hacks, and they were not about to be dislodged by the musings of the pint-sized professor in Prague. The industries, grouped in "associations"—Communist cartels really—had no autonomy to deal with each other or the outside world. So utterly was the management of the Czechoslovak economy pervaded by the influence of the Party that virtually no decisions could be made on economic merit. Personal and political considerations almost always prevailed.

Even though the economic reform had been formally unveiled on January 1, 1967, almost nothing meaningful was accomplished during the year because of this sullen and determined opposition on the part of conservative Communist bureaucrats. Šik himself had predicted this phenomenon in *Plan and Market Under Socialism,* when he remarked that the New Economic Model might run into the opposition of "leading economic or social bullies." While he tempered his realism with the optimistic statement that "under socialism . . . every progressive social finding will prevail, sooner or later, as a prerequisite for overcoming growing economic or social contradictions," this was far from happening.

237

In the first quarter of the year, for example, wholesale prices rose by 29 per cent instead of the 19 per cent Šik had planned, chiefly because the powerful heads of the associations were permitted under the reform to calculate their own production costs—which, naturally, they did upward —but did nothing to increase productivity and to render industry more flexible through decentralization. The Communist traditionalists preferred to continue with the closed circuit of arbitrary decision-making by other bureaucrats at the top. This was, in the scathing words of a Prague economist, "pseudo planning." Consequently, shortages not only continued but increased in a more expensive economy. By May, Šik himself was forced to recognize that his earlier optimism had been excessive. He told a foreign interviewer that the New Economic Model was being applied "only in some enterprises and little things. . . . The resistance to it becomes ever sharper and more evil. . . . Naturally, we can continue playing with it. But tomorrow the government will be compelled to introduce the system by force. . . . There will be no other way."

As Novotný was evidently unable to force his immense Party bureaucracy to accept the new reforms, however, the economic situation in Czechoslovakia took a turn for the worse. By the middle of the year, the economy was again in a tailspin. Concentration on "extensive" industrial development still kept up the GNP figures, but in reality the existing state of affairs again bordered on disaster.

The root of the trouble seemed to lie even more in the human sphere than in management or production, though chaos reigned in the latter. Party favoritism had entrenched incompetent men in key positions—as Vaculík had told the writers' congress, "all of us . . . feel that in our various jobs we are led by men less capable than ourselves"—and the workers had utterly lost confidence in their managers. A cartoon published in October in the Prague economic daily *Hospodarské Noviny* showed a doctor telling a potbellied patient, "You are fit for work, Comrade Deputy Manager, but you are certainly not fit for your job." In the huge machine plants, steel mills, and automotive factories apathetic workers resisted the foremen, the foremen turned their backs on the managers, and the managers lied to the ministers in Prague. Czechoslovakia's once-famous quality standards fell so low that foreign buyers were rejecting the products.

Without coherent planning and lacking incentive, workers fell back on absenteeism and job-hopping. Inasmuch as the 1960 constitution guaranteed every citizen a job, no particular effort was required to remain employed and collect the paycheck every month. When overstaffing became too obvious in one sector and another suffered from manpower shortages, workers were shifted from plant to plant and from town to town without much regard for human, social, or economic considerations. To those who complained, the invariable answer was that the law guaranteed employment but did not say where a man was to be assigned. A classic example of prevailing labor policies was the sight in Prague streets of several persons, often women, sharing the simple task of switching tramway tracks at almost every major intersection. Václavské Náměstí, the loudly heralded project for the capital's first pedestrian underpass, was running a year behind schedule and passers-by were forced to walk through twisting passageways between wooden fences to reach one end of the huge square from another. (By that time, Belgrade already had a series of such underpasses, built with less publicity but more efficiency.) The laying of foundations for a projected Intercontinental Hotel Corporation building in Prague was also running at least a year late and then the blueprints for the construction had to be abandoned as unusable.

Housing remained, after nineteen years, a national tragedy. As an embittered economist told me on my first visit to Prague, "We've been so busy building socialism we forgot to build houses." In the big cities—Prague, Bratislava, Brno, Ostrava, Košice—the housing shortage was so drastic that the dramatic human problems it created affected the entire social and psychological make-up of the nation. Young people could not get married because it was virtually impossible to find a flat and the parents' homes were too crowded to accommodate the new couple and, God forbid, their children. Those who married often went on living separately. Estranged husbands and wives seldom sought divorce or separation because it would mean that one of them would become homeless. A divorced woman I knew in Prague would not marry her lover of ten years' standing until her daughter grew up and she could turn the apartment over to her and not lose it altogether. Municipal laws defined how many square meters could be allocated per family.

With only a handful of persons still proprietors of their dwellings, there was no incentive and no real possibility for private construction. The government equipped each city and town with a few showy housing projects, and no statistics existed to indicate the housing deficit. Even these projects, such as those along Prague's Lenin Avenue, were allowed to deteriorate rapidly. Doors did not close, windows were broken, plumbing was shot, and the elevators, when they existed, seldom functioned. A foreign friend of mine waited three years for a state-employed house painter—everybody was state-employed—to finish painting the wood-work in his apartment.

Since sociology as a science had been banned in Czechoslovakia until about 1966, no research was possible into the damage done to the fabric of society by the housing and other economic problems. The Sociological Institute at the Academy of Sciences had only a few trained scientists, and sociology was taught seriously at Charles University only in the last few years. A young woman of my acquaintance who was assigned to spend a year in a Slovak village to study gypsy society pleaded with her American friends for books on basic interviewing techniques. She was agog with admiration and envy when I told her of Oscar Lewis's work among Mexican slum dwellers and Puerto Ricans in San Juan and New York with graduate-student assistants, tape recorders, questionnaires, and classification methods.

Social measurements were possible only on the very certain basis of personal observation and secondhand knowledge. One knew, for example, that suicide and alcoholism rates were extremely high and that abortions were commonplace, but no serious conclusions could be extrapolated from these random data. But, in 1968, a Czechoslovak television director set out to prove in a starkly dramatic way how cynical his fellow countrymen had become about these matters. He placed advertisements in the newspapers seeking to adopt a baby, and received virtually no response. Then he placed a second set of advertisements offering a Fiat 850 in exchange for a baby—and was flooded with responses. The parents, usually mothers, were then willing to appear before the cameras in a sordid version of a "This Is Your Life" program to tell why they would swap children for cars. One woman said frankly she already had too many children, but the family could use a car.

It goes without saying that these economic and social problems and their psychological ramifications were plunging Czechoslovakia into a crisis, and that the resulting discontent was a political peril for the regime. With Šik's reform stalled by bureaucratic opposition, the Party had to strain for real or apparent solutions. Accordingly, the Central Committee devoted most of its attention to economic questions at its February, May, and September Plenums—when it was not engaged in the running battle with the intellectuals. A speech by Jiří Hendrych at the February 8 session showed that the Party leadership believed that the new economic reforms could function alongside traditional cultural and political policies. In effect rejecting Šik's contention that political reform must accompany economic change, Hendrych indicated that the KSČ was still wedded to the Stalinist concept of a rigidly centralized economy, political repression, and strict controls and uniformity in all media of communications.

At the May Plenum, the Central Committee sought to concentrate, and none too soon, on wasteful use of labor, the huge volume of unfinished construction, and production plans inadequately geared to the badly needed foreign trade. The over-all situation was so bad that despite the needs in housing, industrial construction, and plant retooling, the Central Committee decided to cut capital investments by one billion crowns—50 million dollars at the then prevailing artificial exchange rate. Because wholesale and retail shortages added to high production costs and the enterprises' profits were spurring inflation, credit policies were tightened. While the 1967 economic plan called for an 11 per cent increase in exports to the West, by August there was a 2 per cent drop.

In September Alexander Dubček rose at the Central Committee meeting to complain about the malfunctioning of the economic plan. He noted that while the plan had assigned 28 per cent of national investment resources to Slovakia, these investments were actually running at a rate below 22 per cent in the first half of the year. Urging that this imbalance be corrected. Dubček proposed the creation of an investment fund that would better direct the flow of available resources. He was siding, in effect, with Šik in asking for greater decentralization so that Slovaks could share in decision-making at all levels with the more numerous Czechs. Resentment over the economic situation in his region, combined with other complaints about the treatment of Slovakia, was gradually pushing Dubček into open opposition to the regime. In the end, Novotný was to founder on the rock of Slovak dissent.

The Slovak question has existed as long as the Czechoslovak state, and it transcended the Communist power struggles. Prior to World War Two, both Slovaks and Czechs were part of the Austro-Hungarian Empire. But, largely because of geography, their political and cultural orientations went in different directions.

The Czechs, the people of the ancient and historically rich Bohemian and Moravian lands, were Westerners who identified with Vienna and with the West in general. It is, in fact, a *faux pas* to speak in Prague of being in *Eastern* Europe. The Prague people will at once correct the innocent foreigner and remind him that Prague is geographically west of

Vienna and that the Czech lands lie in *Central* Europe. During the Habsburg Empire Bohemia and Moravia, the "Historic Provinces," sent distinguished men to sit in the Vienna parliament, hold high government posts, and in other ways influence the political and cultural life of Vienna, then one of the world's great centers of civilization. Great aristocratic names like Černin and Lobkowitz came from the Czech lands and to this day belong culturally as much to Vienna as to Prague. Count Czernin (which is the way his name was spelled by the Austrians) was the last Foreign Minister of the Empire. The Czech country was also the industrial hub of the region.

The Slovaks, on the other hand, in the easternmost part of the country, hemmed in between the Hungarian plains in the south and the Tatry and Beskidy mountains lining the Polish border to the north, looked to the east. Bratislava, the Slovak capital and a great Danubian harbor, is only one hour by road *east* of Vienna (Prague is six hours from Vienna); culturally and politically it might be days away. During the Empire, Slovak orientation was toward Budapest, the second capital of the Dual Monarchy—which made sense economically, in terms of the Danube basin, and ethnically, as Slovaks and Hungarians were widely interspersed throughout the region. After World War One, when new borders were drawn up, hundreds of thousands of Hungarians found themselves in Czechoslovakia and lots of Slovaks in the new Hungary. (This, incidentally, created another minority problem for Central *and* Eastern Europe between the wars.)

Slovak historical and cultural traditions and identity likewise tended to be weak. Their chief legendary national hero, Jánošík, a nationalist Slovak Robin Hood of the mountains, also belongs to the folklore of the adjacent Polish highlands' Huculs, who called him Janosik (in the Polish tonal version). Oddly enough, or maybe not so oddly, an important passage in Liszt's "Hungarian Rhapsody" is taken from a Slovak-Polish folk song celebrating Jánošík's (Janosik's) exploits. Highland peasants still dance to this tune, and the ancient lyrics speak of brave mountaineers dancing with their axes swinging (the ax was the sidearm of the highland bandits) in old stone cellars. The Slovak language, particularly the dialect spoken in the mountains, is closer to Polish than to Czech.

But the Slovaks, presumably tired of the Austro-Hungarian monarchy and as receptive as everyone else in Europe to the freedom winds of 1848, began developing a cultural and, therefore, national identity in the nineteenth century. When Masaryk on the one hand and the Western Allies on the other were thinking how best to carve up the defeated Empire, the Slovaks opted reluctantly to join the new Czechoslovak Republic. The notion of an independent Slovakia, largely an agricultural country with little industry, was not very viable, but the Slovak nationalists had extracted, or thought they had extracted, a promise of autonomy within a federation from Masaryk and his associates. This was never granted and, as a matter of fact, Czech treatment of the Slovaks was one of the less handsome pages in the history of the First Republic. Inevitably, Slovak nationalism grew between the wars. Its principal spokesman was the Autonomous Party, led by Ondřej Hlínka, a Roman Catholic priest. After the Nazi occupation of Czechoslovakia in 1939, a vassal Slovak autonomous state was set up by Hitler under Monsignor Tiso, the "president" who was executed following the 1945 liberation. At first, the Slovaks took relatively kindly to the idea of their own state even under Nazism, but by 1943 the Slovak National Council was founded as a resistance movement, and the Slovak uprising came in 1944. The resistance was mainly organized by Slovak Communists who led the uprising (as Husák had done) and fought in it (as the Dubček brothers had). The Slovaks, evidently, were tougher people than the Czechs, who had no organized *maquis* of their own.

When the war ended, the Slovak Communists were the most articulate advocates of Slovak nationalism. A curious parallelism developed between the prewar or wartime right-wing Slovaks, who were militant in the Hlínka party, and the Communists, who took up where these old-line nationalists had left off. Husák was the principal spokesman for a federated Czechoslovakia when Beneš and the Moscow Communists met in 1945 to plan the postwar regime. To the Slovak Communists, then as now, there was no conflict between nationalism and loyalties to Communism's "proletarian internationalist concepts." But, by 1950, Slovak nationalism had become "bourgeois nationalism" in the eyes of Moscow and the Gottwald regime in Prague. Clementis paid for it with his life and men like Husák with long prison sentences.

A resurgent cultural and political Slovak nationalism was an obvious reaction to the Great Purge. The opposition of Slovak Communist intellectuals to the Novotný regime, starting in 1963, had as much to do with hunger for cultural freedom and general revulsion against Stalinism as with nationalism. But by 1967, the Slovak Party had split, pretty much as most thoughtful Slovaks had. Intellectuals like Mňačko (he was born in Moravia but wrote in Slovak and thought of himself as a Slovak),

Novomeský, Hysko, and Mihalik favored a Slovak identity within a federal Czechoslovak state. Husák, who had pushed the idea in 1945, strongly supported this position, and his influence again began to grow after his 1963 rehabilitation, though he still chose to remain in the shadows of the Bratislava Law Institute. To an important extent, to be for Slovak rights was to be against Novotný and his centralist ideas, which were a crude version of Masaryk's and Beneš's. From the Slovak viewpoint *everything* was wrong with Novotný because his centralism denied Slovakia both love and money. From there, it could easily be rationalized, and was, that what was wrong for Slovakia was wrong for Czechoslovakia—an argument which led to an alliance of anti-Novotný Slovaks with anti-Novotný Czechs.

In Slovak terms, therefore, even centrists and conservatives had no choice but to join the anti-Novotný line. The difference of opinion within the Party had to do with the important nuance whether Novotný's ouster should lead only to Slovak rights or also to a general liberalization. Some wanted both, on the ground that there could be no rational federalization without political freedom and the give-and-take it implied, just as there could be no successful economic reform without political change. Men like Vasil Bilak, on the other hand, the Slovak Party's orthodox ideologue, fought Novotný on the limited Slovak issue but had no quarrel with the prevailing political system. Husák, who was in the comfortable position of not having to take a public stand in the leadership struggles, supported Slovak interests but, as far as it is known, was silent on the broader issues. A centrist position was taken by Dubček in his dual role as the Slovak Party's First Secretary and as a KSČ Presidium and Secretariat member. As we have seen, Dubček first sought to remain neutral, in fact supporting the Prague establishment, then gradually evolved toward the progressive cause in opposition to the crackdown on both Czech and Slovak intellectuals and to the central government's economic discrimination against Slovakia. When Dubček first openly defied Novotný, he seemed to be doing it more for Slovak than for Czechoslovak reasons. But, by then, the momentum of the anti-Novotný rebellion was erasing dividing lines.

It took Novotný and his special political talent for turning all that he touched into suicidal dynamite to precipitate the final crisis. Returning from his July holidays in the Soviet Union, he and his wife decided to go on one of his rare official trips to Slovakia. It was late August, and Slovakia was celebrating the hundredth anniversary of Matice, the organization that maintained cultural links with Slovaks living overseas, and of the foundation of the first high school where the Slovak language was taught. For reasons known only to himself, Novotný chose this occasion to attack Slovak nationalism. In a speech at Turčanský Svatý Martin, Novotný blandly informed his audience—which included both Dubček and Bilak—that there was no more Slovak problem, that Slovakia's economic growth since 1945 was proof that the region thrived in the centralized system. He spoke of the Košice steel mills (which most independent economists regarded as an example of "pseudo planning" and waste), of the Bratislava petroleum and chemical works, and of the whole new era that Communism had brought to Slovakia. He dismissed talk of a federal state with a misquotation from Lenin that federations should be temporary and not permanent affairs. With public opinion aroused over Prague's policies in the Middle Eastern crisis, Novotný argued that support for the Arabs was part of the "anti-imperialist struggle" and that in backing Israel the West was repeating its policies of backing Hitler at the time of Munich. To most Slovaks this was not only arrant but also offensive nonsense.

After his speech, Novotný met with Slovak Party leaders, among whom were Dubček and Bilak. Someone mentioned that the Matice building, partly a museum, had grown too small and that the Slovaks would welcome a new edifice. No new building was necessary, Novotný replied. In his view, the Matice collection should be moved to Prague and the organization's overseas functions better centralized through the Foreign Institute which the Foreign Ministry operated in Prague. There is no record of Dubček's reaction to this extraordinary proposal, but Bilak, the loyal Party man, lost his temper and shouted at Novotný that he had no right to make proposals so insulting to Slovaks. A bitter argument ensued and Novotný left in a huff, returning immediately to Prague.

The next event in the gathering conflict between Novotný and the Slovaks came at the Party's September Plenum, when Dubček opposed the repressive measures taken by the regime against the intellectuals and accused Novotný of shortchanging Slovakia in the allocation of national investment funds. Though it would be inaccurate to say that he was the standard-bearer of the liberal cause at the time, Dubček's emergence as an active opponent of Novotný and his group can be dated back from this Plenum.

The Plenum was summoned again on Monday, October 30, to debate "The Party's Position and Role in the Current Stage of Socialist Society."

This was intended by the regime as a fundamental review of all the problems facing Czechoslovakia, but the Slovak dispute overshadowed all other issues. When the question of federation arose, Novotný again argued that the Slovak problem had been solved and accused federation proponents of "bourgeois nationalism."

Dubček took it upon himself to answer. Since the September Plenum his relations with Novotný had deteriorated to the point where they were hardly on speaking terms. When Dubček came to Prague on Party business, he had found that on Novotný's order the telephone in his room at the Praha Hotel had been disconnected. (The Praha Hotel was used by the Party for ranking members and foreign guests, and its switchboard was connected to the switchboard of the Central Committee building, a domed edifice on the Vltava's right bank. To call the hotel, one had to call Party headquarters and ask for the Praha.) He was also being followed by the secret police. Dubček outwardly a mild man, knew of these tactics and his anger was aroused.

So, on the second day of the two-day meeting, Dubček rose to charge Novotný with "behaving like a dictator" and with deliberate sabotage of the economic reform. He accused Hendrych, the main speaker at the session, of changing the text of the basic resolution on the Party's role, on which the Presidium had earlier agreed, to damage Slovak interests. In protesting about the resolution, designed to climax a series of meetings held since August throughout the country to convince Party leaders on district and regional levels that the mounting political chaos had to be ended with obedience to the KSČ leadership reasserted, Dubček charged Novotný with incompetent interference in Slovak affairs that was damaging to Slovakia's economy. He repeated his September charges.

Novotný hit back furiously. Addressing himself directly to Dubček, he remarked that if Slovakia wished to rise to the levels of the Czech lands, she had to depend on the assistance of Bohemia and Moravia. If Dubček disapproved of how matters were being handled, the Czech and Slovak economies could be separated and Slovakia could go it alone without Prague's aid.

The argument had entered the realm of threats. Dubček threw a basic challenge to Novotný. It was no longer the question of Slovakia, he said, but of the whole political system in Czechoslovakia. "Before we can talk of economic division, we must discuss political division, starting at the top, with the Party leadership."

Novotný grabbed the microphone to denounce Dubček and his followers as "bourgeois nationalists." The meeting in the great Spanish Hall of Hradčany Castle turned into chaos. It was no longer the customary well-managed session at which the leaders delivered oracular proclamations and then graciously let hand-picked speakers from the membership second the official line. Now the Slovak delegates rallied around Dubček, who was demanding a fundamental change in the KSČ structure, methods, and relationship to the Czechoslovak state. This, he said, was not only a Slovak viewpoint but a basic requirement if the nation was ever to regain trust in the Communist Party. Presently, Czech leaders at the meeting rose in support of the Slovak's offensive. And then Communist back-benchers began urging Novotný's resignation as First Secretary.

By mid-afternoon, the debate had become so bitter that Novotný called for an adjournment. The reason he gave was ill calculated to quiet the aroused tempers: the Party leadership, he said, had to attend a ceremony in another part of the castle celebrating the fiftieth anniversary of the Bolshevik Revolution in Russia and this could not be delayed. The session was adjourned, but before the evening was out a new crisis broke out in Prague.

Shortly after nine p.m., as Novotný and his associates were entertaining Soviet dignitaries at Hradčany Castle and drinking toasts to the Russian Revolution, about fifteen hundred Technical College students from the dilapidated university dormitories in Strahov, on the left bank, began marching downhill in the general direction of the castle. This spontaneous march had no connection whatsoever with the Central Committee row earlier in the day—the students had no way of knowing about it—but was a protest against the trivial but annoying fact that the dormitories suffered from chronic electric-power failures and from lack of heating. Prague autumns tend to be chilly, and now, on the last day of October, it was both dark and downright cold in the student houses. Student leaders had been long complaining about the power breaks and the poor heating but neither the authorities of Charles University nor the Education Ministry paid much attention.

On that particular evening the students had invited several Prague newspapermen to see for themselves what life was like at the Strahov dormitories. Just then, the lights went out once more, and a number of the youths called for a protest march. A crowd was immediately formed and after several passes around the dormitory buildings, the parade moved out into the street and headed toward town. It was a good-natured march as those things go; the boys and girls carried lighted candles, strummed guitars, beat on tambourines, and chanted, "We want light, we want light!"

Presently the students reached an intersection on Loretánské Square. If they continued straight ahead along Loretánská Street, they would have reached the castle in a matter of minutes. Inasmuch as the castle was the Presidential residence, this could have been interpreted as a political demonstration. The students, therefore, turned right and marched down steep and narrow Nerudová Street (named after Jan Neruda) toward Malostranské Náměstí, at the bottom of the hill, and the Vltava bridges.

About halfway down Nerudová Street, the students were intercepted by police. The youths told the police officers why they were marching with their candles. The officer in charge suggested that a delegation be named to deliver the protest to someone in authority. The students refused because they feared that later they might be accused of organizing an illegal demonstration whereas the march had started spontaneously. There was laughter, shouting, and waving of candles. It was all still good-natured and apolitical. Then the crowd turned around and began climbing up Nerudová Street, pursued by police cars. Squads of policemen on foot dispersed the students (who could go nowhere but up) and at least three youths were arrested.

At this point the manifestations ceased to be good-natured. The students, now angry, halted, regrouped, and again started to march down Nerudová. Police reinforcements chased the students back up Nerudová, across Loretánské Square, and all the way to the Strahov dormitories, where they beat the students with nightsticks and fired tear-gas grenades. The riot went on into the small hours of Wednesday, November 1, when it ended with twelve injured students and three policemen taken to the hospital. (One of the students was unconscious and two had concussions.)

There had been student disturbances in Prague many times before in recent years and they had no serious political consequences. But this time the unwarranted police attack on youths engaged in a nonpolitical manifestation produced a significant reaction. The student community became aroused as it never had been before, and word of police brutalities on the night of the riot seeped out from the indignant doctors and nurses at Petřin Hospital to the Prague population. Novotný's police had added one more dimension to the mounting crisis and the people of Prague said later they could feel the tension in the air. But Novotný himself, with his usual imperception, left for Moscow to be present at Soviet celebrations of the October Revolution. He stayed away for over a week.

On November 8, the day of his return to Prague, students at the Philosophy Faculty, the gray-façaded building facing Red Army Square and the Vltava River, held a five-hour meeting to discuss the Strahov riot and its implications. The faculty was also the home of young professors who were apostles of a new Marxist philosophy, and they joined the students in protesting police brutality. The students drafted a letter to Education Minister Hájek demanding public identification and punishment of the policemen responsible for the Strahov beatings, a ban on the use of tear gas, and, of course, measures to solve the electric-power and heating problems in the dormitories. The professors went even further. Their resolution asked for a public apology by Interior Minister Josef Kudrna (who replaced Lubomir Strougal in April 1965 when Strougal was switched to the KSČ Secretariat), an investigation of the role of the police in Czechoslovak life, and the granting of complete academic freedom. They also requested Hájek to transmit their full bill of particulars to the National Assembly. Now Novotný was challenged from all sides.

On November 20 a second rally held at the Philosophy Faculty became a nine-hour sit-in by students and professors, the first time such an event took place in Communist Czechoslovakia. The sit-in was preceded by two meetings of teachers in the Czechoslovak Youth Union to demand explanations of the police brutality. The University Committee of the Communist Party voted for a full investigation (they also went on record as discouraging student manifestations). At the Philosophy Faculty rally, students accused the government and press of attempting to mobilize the workers against them—a reference to published reports, apparently planted by the regime, that the students were arming for a revolution and receiving help from abroad. The newspapers, in offering their version of the October 31 happenings, hinted that the Workers' Militia might be called out, if necessary, to quell the student movements. The entire issue of political freedoms in Czechoslovakia came up for debate. Clearly, the Strahov incident had become a pretext to seek fundamental changes in the nation.

Presumably to the students' and professors' own surprise, Charles University Rector Oldřich Starý and Vice-Rector Eduard Goldstücker attended the sit-in and engaged in a lengthy dialogue with the rebels. (Goldstücker had been named Vice-Rector despite his involvement with the militant intellectuals and his speech at the writers' congress the preceding June—one of the small concessions that the disoriented Novotný leadership occasionally offered its foes in hopes of placating them.) Starý and Goldstücker agreed with the rebels on some points and disagreed on others, but on the whole they were sympathetic. In the end, the meeting issued a virtual ultimatum to the regime to fulfill all the student demands by December 15 or face joint action by the entire Charles University.

On December 4, however, the government took the unprecedented step of admitting officially that the police had engaged in unnecessary violence. It said the leaders of the Strahov march would not be prosecuted and it announced changes in the personnel managing the dormitories. Workers also began to dig trenches for new power cables. But matters had already gone so far that this admission of guilt and these concessions only undermined Novotný's prestige and further weakened his hold on the nation's politics. The truth was that Novotný had his back against the wall and his opponents in the top levels of the KSČ—suddenly there were scores of them—were overtly urging his resignation.

Early in December two events occurred to suggest that Novotný had finally realized the danger facing him.

One was the sudden start of secret maneuvers in central, northern, and western Bohemia—which meant the military encirclement of Prague— by important Czechoslovak Army units on December 4. Inasmuch as winter maneuvers are rarely, if ever, held on such a scale in the snow-covered Bohemian countryside, this pointed strongly to the possibility that Novotný had alerted the Army to stand ready to defend him.

The other event was an urgent request sent to Moscow by Soviet Ambassador Stepan Vasilievich Chervonenko that Brezhnev come as soon as possible to Prague to determine for himself where Soviet interests lay in the now exceedingly divided Czechoslovak situation. The two moves were totally unrelated except that, according to some versions, Novotný had asked Chervonenko for some form of Soviet support. There are, however, strong reasons to believe that Chervonenko had recommended backing Novotný as a sound political proposition, and this appears to be borne out by Jiří Hendrych's subsequent remark that Brezhnev's visit was "in the nature of an intervention in favor of Comrade Novotný." That Chervonenko may have been guilty of such a misjudgment of the Czechoslovak situation is an important point to remember in view of his role in the 1968 invasion. Chervonenko was all along somewhat less than brilliantly successful in his diplomatic career.

A fifty-two-year-old Ukrainian and a protégé of Nikita Khrushchev's, his fellow Ukrainian, Chervonenko was a Party functionary with an academic background in philosophy and education. He emerged from obscurity in 1955 to become the head of the Science and Culture Commission of the Ukrainian Party's Central Committee. Within a year, he was a Secretary of the Central Committee in Kiev and Chairman of the Foreign Affairs Commission of the Ukrainian Supreme Soviet. To improve his knowledge of international problems Khrushchev sent him on Soviet government missions to Poland and East Germany and, in 1959, took him along to Peking for the celebrations of the tenth anniversary of the People's Republic of China. As it developed, the purpose of this visit was to introduce Chervonenko to Mao Tse-tung and other top Chinese officials as the new Soviet Ambassador to Peking.

Though totally lacking in diplomatic experience and in familiarity with Asia, and with his foreign exposure confined to the brief visits in Poland and East Germany, Chervonenko thus started at the top in his new career when he took over the China Embassy in October 1959. As is the case with most Soviet ambassadors, he simultaneously was named to the Central Committee of the Soviet Communist Party. But his five-and-a-half-year stay in Peking appears to have done little to reverse the quickening deterioration in Chinese-Soviet relations. Chervonenko was of course unfortunate in that he arrived on the scene just as the dispute between the two Communist giants began to take shape, and, after all, an ambassador must carry out the instructions of his government rather than grandiosely improvise. This is especially true in the rigid Soviet system. But circumstances seemed to victimize Chervonenko especially badly. His access to direct information steadily diminished. A fellow diplomat in Peking remarked at the time that Chervonenko had to rely on the *People's Daily* to discover what went on at the crucial secret meetings of the congress of the Chinese Communist Party in March and April 1962.

Chervonenko was recalled from Peking five months after Khrushchev's downfall. Perhaps this was due both to his long assignment in China and to the new Soviet leadership's natural desire to be represented in Peking by an envoy not identified with Khrushchev. But his appointment as Ambassador to Czechoslovakia in April 1965 could hardly be regarded as a promotion. Despite everything, Czechoslovakia in 1965 was a dependable satellite and Novotný was firmly in control, so Chervonenko's mission was principally to oversee the placid relationship with Prague and dedicate himself to ceremonial appearances at Hradčany Castle and at meetings of the Czechoslovak-Soviet Friendship Society. He was known in Prague as a superficially pleasant but rather taciturn man; squat and balding, Chervonenko peered at people through his spectacles and said as little as possible. There is no reason to suspect that his personal contacts reached beyond officialdom and the enthusiastically pro-Soviet Czechs and Slovaks who called at the walled Soviet Embassy compound off the wooded Pod Kaštany Square in Prague's diplomatic and residential Bubeneč district.

Chervonenko obviously was not sent to Prague to handle major emergencies, but now, in December 1967, he was facing one. His inclination was to see Novotný survive the crisis—he must have thought that the situation still permitted it—and he presumably expected Brezhnev to reach the same conclusion. The General Secretary of the Soviet Communist Party arrived secretly in Prague on December 8, and it is doubtful that anyone outside of Novotný's immediate entourage had advance notice of his visit. For two days, Brezhnev conferred with Novotný and a large number of Czech and Slovak politicians, asking questions and studying the situation. (The only top leader not in Prague during these two days was Dubček, and a number of Party people noticed that Brezhnev frequently inquired about him.) He gave no indications of whether Moscow would go on supporting Novotný or not. These were two days of awesome tension for Novotný and his allies, as well as for his opponents. If Brezhnev decided to back the besieged regime, his opponents knew they might have to defy Moscow or desist from their efforts to depose Novotný. If, on the other hand, the Russian chose to turn his back on him, Novotný's chances of survival were next to nil. Soviet power was still an enormous factor in the political calculations in Czechoslovakia.

On the evening of December 9 Brezhnev was the guest of honor at a dinner hosted by the KSČ Presidium. All its members were present except for Dubček. Brezhnev sat and ate in silence. Suddenly in the middle of the meal he rose to his feet and announced he was leaving Prague. As for the Party power struggle, he said, "That is, comrades, your Czechoslovak affair. The Soviet Party and the Soviet Union will not interfere in your internal affairs." This remark was to come back to haunt Brezhnev a few months later, when events in Czechoslovakia quickly convinced him that the question of the leadership in Prague *was* very much a Soviet affair.

But, for the moment, he washed his hands of the whole unpleasant problem and, leaving behind a stunned Novotný and his friends, demanded to be driven to the airport.

Brezhnev took one precaution, however, that was to loom subsequently as one of the great ironies of the Czechoslovak drama. En route to Moscow, he stopped off briefly in Bratislava to see Dubček, or, as a Czech Communist said later, to "look him over." Brezhnev's political instincts may have suggested to him that Dubček was the probable winner in the Prague power struggle. Absolutely nothing is known of their conversation that night, but, strangely, Brezhnev appeared to have satisfied himself that Czechoslovakia and the KSČ would fare well in the hands of this quiet Slovak educated in the Soviet Union. Chervonenko was not the only one to be caught in misjudgments.

Josef Smrkovský, who had just been promoted from his chairmanship of the Central Administration of Water Supply to the post of Minister of Forestry and Water Supply, recalled Brezhnev's visit in a speech early in 1968: "When we [the progressive group, actively working for Novotný's fall] got to know that Comrade Brezhnev had been asked, that he was here, we were apprehensive as to why he was here. When we got to know what his point of view was, we were very happy."

The man who was not very happy with the outcome of Brezhnev's visit was Novotný. He may have speculated that his disastrous telegram to the Kremlin in October 1964 deploring Khrushchev's fall may have brought on a long-delayed vengeance on Brezhnev's part. Be that as it may, he was left with only a few important allies, and his last weapon was a counter-conspiracy. It appears almost certain that Novotný decided to stage a military *coup d'état before* his enemies could rally enough forces in the Central Committee to administer the lethal blow. His calculations must have convinced him that most likely he could no longer muster a majority in the Presidium and probably not even in the Central Committee, packed though it was with hand-picked appointees, when it came to a vote.

Novotný's principal partner in this venture was Miroslav Mamula, the shadowy figure who since 1961 had headed the Central Committee's Eighth Department, in charge of security in the Party, the government, and armed forces. (He was the man who had accompanied Novotný during the melodramatic episode on the night of January 24, 1962, when Novotný had personally arrested Rudolf Barák's secretary for allegedly embezzling a thousand dollars.) Virtually nothing is known of his background and Mamula studiously avoided the limelight. But under the Novotný regime he exercised the power that Ladislav Kopřiva, the architect of the great purge, had under Gottwald.

Also involved in the conspiracy was Major General Jan Šejna, a forty-year-old former farmer and *bon vivant,* Mamula's deputy specifically in charge of military security. Šejna, who owed his meteoric Army career to the Party's support, also held the key job of chief of the main Party committee in the Ministry of Defense and was a National Assembly member. When he was a colonel in 1963, at the age of thirty-six, his penchant for glamorous good living propelled him into the company of the establishment writers and movie makers. One of his closest friends was Antonín Novotný, the son of the President and the manager of a Prague publishing house. The third crucial man in the conspiracy was Colonel-General Vladimír Janko, Deputy Minister of Defense. There is no tangible evidence that Defense Minister General Bohumir Lomský had any part in the plot.

Prior to Brezhnev's visit, when the Army maneuvers around Prague began on December 4, Mamula, Šejna, and Janko began proselytizing top military officers and Party leaders for the proposed preventive coup, dropping heavy hints that, if necessary, the Soviet Union would stage an armed intervention to support Novotný and the plot, quoting Chervonenko as the source for it. An effort was made, however, to keep the plan from Slovak officers out of fear that they might betray it. After Brezhnev's visit and his announcement that the leadership struggle was "your Czechoslovak affair," the tactics had to be changed. The plotters were now on their own and could not invoke Soviet backing. The new plan, therefore, was either to launch a full-fledged coup or, at least, to bring troops into Prague when the Central Committee was to meet on December 16, and, presumably, carry out Novotný's dismissal. The idea was to arrest the principal anti-Novotný figures, including Dubček, and thus pressure the Central Committee into abandoning any attempts to change the leadership. The generals advised Novotný, however, that extra time was needed to complete the partial mobilization of the reserves, already under way, and to place the troops in position. Accordingly, Novotný advised the Central Committee that the session would be delayed for several days for "technical reasons."

About December 16—and at this point some of the details become obscure—the conspirators alerted the First Armored Division and the Thirteenth Infantry Division, both stationed at the Mladá military reservation about twenty-five miles north of Prague, to be prepared to move on the capital. At the same time, Mamula drew up warrants for the arrests of the progressives and their friends. Everything seemed ready. But sometime on December 17, a Sunday, Lieutenant General Václav Prchlík, chief of the Army Political Administration, learned of the conspiracy and immediately informed the anti-Novotný leaders, including Dubček.

On December 18, before orders could be given to the troops to enter Prague, a secret emergency session of the Party's Presidium was called, and Novotný was faced with documented charges that he was about to set a *coup d'état* in motion. He denied any knowledge of the conspiracy, but he must have immediately given orders to call off the coup because the Army maneuvers in Bohemia were abruptly halted on the same day. With the Presidium in permanent session, the Central Committee was summoned on December 19, also secretly. As the Presidium members commuted continuously between their own meeting and the Central Committee gathering in the Party headquarters, fighting for support and votes for their respective causes, the first formal attempt was made to unseat Novotný. Although the black Tatra limousines of the Central Committee members were rushing to and fro few people in Prague were aware of the unfolding drama. Almost nobody knew that a military coup and possibly a civil war had been averted by a matter of hours.

But the rebels still could not marshal sufficient power in the Presidium to dethrone Novotný. One of the difficulties was that there was no agreement on his successor. At this stage, Novotný commanded six votes out of the ten in the ruling body: his own vote and those of Jiří Hendrych, National Assembly Chairman Bohuslav Laštovička, Premier Josef Lenárt, Slovak National Council Chairman Michal Chudík (a personal enemy of Dubček's), and Otokar Šimůnek, Czechoslovakia's permanent delegate to Comecon. Pressing for Novotný's ouster were Dubček, Oldřich Černik, Drahomír Kolder, and Jaromír Dolanský. Interestingly, all four were advocates of Šik's economic reform and the last three were the Party's top overseers of the Czechoslovak economy.

After three days of intense struggle, it became clear that the deadlock could not be broken. Novotný had the votes to survive if a vote were taken, but his tormentors had enough power to keep the battle going. A showdown in the Presidium would tear the Party asunder, and both sides preferred to avoid it. In the end, the decision was taken to adjourn for the Christmas and New Year holidays and resume the debates immediately afterward. Late in the evening of December 21, the nation was informed that the Presidium and Central Committee had been meeting since the 19th, but no precise explanation was offered for it. It added up to a temporary standoff, not even a truce, and the citizens of Prague went uneasily about celebrating the holidays.

Both bodies reconvened on Tuesday, January 2, 1968, and the battle resumed. In his New Year's speech, Novotný sought to recoup by suddenly presenting himself as a champion of "socialist democracy" and a defender of Slovak rights. Now, however, word of the power struggle had reached wide political circles and pressure from the informed sector of the public began to influence the politicians in favor of Novotný's removal. The reformers likewise used the holiday break to build up support. Then, according to an unconfirmed but plausible account printed several months later in a London newspaper, Novotný proceeded, true to form, to dig his own grave. For reasons that remain unclear, he accused Hendrych's daughter Zděna during one of the Presidium meetings of being involved in clandestinely sending literary material to the Paris-based Czechoslovak émigré magazine (the charge on which Jan Beneš had been sentenced the previous July). Hendrych angrily shouted at Novotný, "Antonín, you'll never succeed in making another Barák out of me. . . ."

True or not, the fact remains that Hendrych, for years Novotný's closest associate, switched his vote. So did Premier Lenárt, who apparently sensed which way the wind was blowing. When, after three days of infighting, the vote was finally taken late on Thursday, January 4, Novotný was removed from the post of the KSČ's First Secretary. His only backers to the bitter end were Laštovička, Šimůnek, and Chudík; all three immediately and permanently vanished from the Czechoslovak political scene.

At the same time, the Presidium resolved, and the subsequent Central Committee resolution endorsed its decision, "to separate the functions of the President of the Republic and the First Secretary of the Central Committee of the Communist Party." In practice, this meant that Novotný was allowed to remain as President.

(Only two weeks earlier, the National Conference of the Romanian Communist Party had taken precisely the opposite decision in voting for a fusion of Party and government functions. Nicolae Ceauşescu, already the Party's General Secretary, was elected Chief of State, replacing Chivu Stoica. It went to prove that, indeed, the two reform-minded Communist countries of Eastern Europe were choosing their own "paths to socialism.")

In Prague the problem still remained whom to select as the new First

Secretary of the Party. Contrary to the general impression, Dubček was not at the time the recognized leader of the anti-Novotný faction and of the progressives. He was only one of the rebels, and his motivation appeared to be in the first place to protect Slovak interests and in the second place to assure success for the economic reform—two closely related issues, of course, from his viewpoint. The two other Slovaks on the Presidium, Lenárt and Chudík, seemed, however, to have acted out of reasons of personal politics. Lenárt shifted his position when the mood in the Central Committee already pointed to the outcome, but Chudík, a lifetime Party hack, never deserted Novotný. Lenárt thereby saved his political future and Chudík lost it.

How Dubček was finally chosen First Secretary remains unclear, and there are several somewhat conflicting versions. One version is that sometime during the Presidium meeting on the night of January 4–5, Novotný proposed Lenárt even though the Premier's switched vote had helped to bring him down. The victorious faction preferred Černík, who had won respect for his performance as Deputy Premier and head of the State Planning Commission. But neither Lenárt nor Černík had enough support in the Presidium and in the Central Committee. The same version has it that in face of the stalemate, one of the Presidium members, probably Černík, nominated Dubček.

The second version is that Kolder, one of the anti-Novotný leaders, proposed Lubomir Strougal, the onetime Agriculture and Interior Minister and currently Chairman of the Central Committee's Commission on Living Standards and a member of the KSČ Secretariat. Strougal, a hardliner, is said to have declined and to have suggested Černík, who, according to this account, also turned it down. Then, the story goes, Novotný proposed Lenárt, who also refused the job. Finally, Novotný made a motion for Dubček's election, assuming that he, too, would decline. But, says this version, Dubček accepted the nomination and was forthwith unanimously elected.

My own inclination, based on numerous conversations in Prague with Central Committee members and other informed persons, is to accept the version that it was, indeed, Novotný who proposed Dubček—the man who had remained virtually silent during the lengthy debate—to the exhausted members of the Presidium at five o'clock in the morning of Friday, January 5. The total mental and physical fatigue of the ten men in the conference room at that stage may have led them to accept the compromise that Dubček seemed to personify.

It is impossible to tell whether Novotný pointed to Dubček because he expected him to refuse or because he considered the quiet Slovak as the least of all evils. But there may be some validity in the theory I heard in Prague that Novotný, incredibly, still hoped to make a comeback and reasoned that Dubček would be the easiest to push aside. A companion theory is that Novotný regarded Dubček as a loyal apparatus man who, despite his obsession with Slovak problems, would not turn the Party over to "liberals," "revisionists," "bourgeois nationalists," and the like. Finally, it is conceivable that the fact that Dubček seemed to enjoy Brezhnev's sympathies may have swayed Novotný. If this is true, then Dubček had risen to power through not one but two historical ironies.

Czechoslovakia was apprised of Novotný's fall and Dubček's succession by a nation-wide radio announcement at nine p.m. January 5.

XV

Dubček Conducts
the Overture

The extraordinary thing about the downfall of Antonín Novotný and the rise of Alexander Dubček is that it failed to produce an immediate sense of real change, let alone of emerging revolution, in Czechoslovakia. There seemed to be no conscious awareness that not only a political but also a generational break had been made, with the bowing out of the Stalinist old guard and the arrival on the scene of a new breed of Communist. There was no public rejoicing and no demonstrations of triumphant glee in Prague or anywhere else. Even the Slovaks, who for the first time in the republic's history saw one of their sons in the nation's highest political post, appeared to take events in stride. They were evidently pleased over Dubček's ascendancy, as they were over Lenárt's premiership, but no more than that.

For one thing, Czechoslovaks had grown immensely cynical over the continuing game of musical chairs in the last twenty years and were conditioned to the fact that whether Slánský, Gottwald, Zápotocký, or Novotný ran the Party and the government, their lives were defined by the drabness and oppressiveness of their daily existence on the one hand and the empty, bombastic rhetoric of their leaders on the other. Why, many of them asked with a shrug, should anything be different under Dubček? Except for a small elite of political initiates who quickly perceived its significance, the replacement of Novotný by Dubček looked like simply a smoke-filled-room deal with no meaning for the future.

For another thing, the changeover was not accompanied by the usual savage attacks on the deposed leaders and accustomed purges. Instead, there was silence and an outward preservation of the *status quo,* for after a generation of purges and revenge, the new men wished a peaceful and civilized transition, with no blood, no trials, and no prisons. Thus, Novotný remained President, Lenárt Premier, and both the cabinet and the KSČ leadership stayed intact. In fact, the Dubček men, instead of purging the Presidium after January 5, simply moved to add four new members.

These were Jan Piller, a rather conservative Communist who had served as Deputy Premier between 1962 and 1965 and then as Deputy Minister of Heavy Industry; Josef Špaček, the strongly progressive First Secretary of the Brno District Party Committee and, at forty-one, the Presidium's youngest member; Josef Borůvka, the liberal-minded chairman of the agricultural cooperative at Dolany; and Emil Rigo, a conservative Slovak of gypsy origins and chairman of the Party organization in a steel plant. With Špaček and Borůvka tending to favor reforms and Piller and Rigo closer to the conservative persuasion, the power balance was not noticeably altered.

As for Dubček, a virtually unknown figure to the general public, he was keeping almost entirely to himself, making no public speeches and no public appearances, and no fawning sycophants were filling the pages of *Rudé Právo* with the traditional turgid prose through which new personality cults are fashioned in Communist countries.

One usually thinks of the Prague Spring as a great reformation, a repetition almost half a millennium later of the Hussite crusades. But at the outset no drums were beating, no trumpets blaring. Although, later, people in Czechoslovakia began to date events as having occurred "before January" or "after January," the actual month passed without event. The population was mainly preoccupied with its daily problems of earning a living and filling the shopping baskets in the midst of an exceptionally cruel winter.

If, in these opening days and weeks, Alexander Dubček was not acting as a reformer, a crusader, or a revolutionary, it was probably because he never meant in the first place to be any of these things. It could be argued that he was later carried on the crest of the wave of reform, becoming a revolutionary leader *malgré lui.* But Dubček was an extremely difficult man to read, understand, and judge. He had very few, if any, close personal friends. He was a shy, introspective, and complex human being who lacked brilliance but possessed immense intuitive powers and who could be as hard as steel and as tender as the very Czech music of Smetana. In attempting to portray the Dubček of January 1968, one must trust instinct as much as the precious few available facts.

The first objective fact is that he was—and remains a year after his subsequent fall from power—a loyal and dedicated Communist. The son of an old-fashioned socialist turned Communist who brought his family back from the United States to Czechoslovakia after World War One and then took his wife and two sons to the Soviet Union, Dubček grew up in Russia and was tutored in Communism from his youngest years. He gave his entire adult life to the Communist Party and, as his career advanced, went back for three more years in the Soviet Union to study at a high-level ideological school. This background has many meanings for men like Dubček. It implies a bond of allegiance and ideology that is almost impossible to break. It implies an extraordinary self-discipline and the capacity to come to terms with the most taxing and demanding situations when the interest of the Party (of which men like Dubček always think in capital letters) requires it. Meditating about Dubček in the postinvasion days, one is reminded of the defendants in the Slánský trial who accepted their alleged guilt because the Party needed their sacrifice.

Yet, in Dubček, this loyalty and psychological conditioning had to clash sooner or later—and perhaps even before he knew it—with other dimensions of his personality. These dimensions were his Czechoslovak, and Slovak, patriotism and his almost romantic idealism.

It can be taken almost for granted that when he assumed power, Dubček had no specific program to transform Czechoslovakia and her Communism to the point where the Soviet Union would invade. What appears to have happened, therefore, was a process of intellectual, ideological, spiritual, and human evolution that gradually led this otherwise pragmatic but idealistic man along the path of searching for a "human Marxism"—his "Socialism with a Human Face"—and for his country's independence within Communism. It is impossible to define precisely and scientifically what single factor at what single moment touched Dubček the man and began influencing Dubček the Communist politician. A friend of mine who was close to Dubček during the Spring days believes that the change in him came shortly after he took office and, with his newly gained access to the Party archives, discovered in gory and terrible detail what had been the history of the persecutions, brutalities, and injustices in the past twenty years. My friend tells of Dubček's breaking down in tears and vowing that this would never happen again to Communism in his country. This account may be inaccurate and the story may be naïve, but I have no better explanation.

Likewise, the men with whom he came in contact in January and afterward were Communists with a fresh viewpoint. They were the new Marxist philosophers, with a liberal or progressive interpretation of Communism, rejecting the old Stalinist dogma for reasons of personal experience or conviction. Some of them were young, some were middle-aged, and some were simply opportunists. Their influence on Dubček, the leader searching for a "way out" of the wilderness, was immense. But whatever else may be said of him, the fact remains certain that he was not power hungry and that he never sought the trappings of power. When Novotný and his Party leaders wallowed in luxury and corruption, Dubček lived modestly at his Bratislava home with his wife and three children. He drove his own car and his recreation consisted of swimming (and highboard diving) and attending soccer games when his favorite Trečín team was playing. He did not smoke (in contrast with Gottwald's and Novotný's ever-present pipes), and his drinking was confined to an occasional glass of wine. He dressed conservatively and even in warm weather wore a vest. His tastes and way of life, then, were of a Communist petty bourgeois, if such an expression may be used.

Dubček inspired as little worry in Moscow as he inspired promise at home, and he received effusive greetings from the Kremlin the day after his election. Brezhnev, who had inspected him in Bratislava the previous month, wired "hearty congratulations," wished him "successes" in his work, and assured him that the Central Committee of the CPSU was "firmly confident" that the existing "brotherly, sincere friendship" between the peoples of the Soviet Union and Czechoslovakia will "further strengthen and develop."

There is no reason to think that Dubček set out to betray this "brotherly" trust. But in the coming months Dubček developed a different idea of what this "sincere friendship" should be. This evolution began soon after his investiture, as powerful forces of reform began pressing him from every side.

Significantly, these pressures first emanated from older Communists, the victims of the purges of the 1950s. The opening shots came during January from Gustav Husák, fifty-five, and Josef Smrkovský, fifty-seven. Husák the Slovak and Smrkovský the Czech had played major roles in the penetration of Communism into Czechoslovakia in 1945 and in the takeover in 1948. Husák now entered the political picture on January 12 with an article entitled "Older Anniversaries and New Hopes," in the Slovak cultural magazine *Kulturný Život*. This roused a certain interest at the time and was greeted with approval; Husák had considerable intellectual standing and was, after all, a figure of importance in the Slovak Communist world. When it is reread now, however, after Husák ousted Dubček and helped to liquidate the Prague Spring, it sounds positively eerie. It illustrates, among other things, in how short a time an ambitious man can perform a 180-degree political turn:

This struggle for personal and national freedom, for the elimination of national, social, and political suppression is the most typical feature of our history and creates the base of our democratic and revolutionary traditions. It led our peoples to the socialist path in the conviction—as Palmiro Togliatti said toward the end of his life—that "socialism is a system in which the working people have the broadest freedom and in which they actually and in an organized way participate in the management of all social life. . . ."

Democratism is an inherent component part of the great idea of a socialist social system, although in practice this has been frequently forgotten. . . . Social practice in the struggle for freedom and also after the liberation confirmed the principle of revolutionary democratism on which our state was re-established, on which the masses carried through to victory, and on which the new relations between our peoples were arranged.

It would do no harm to recall this. In later development, we had undisputed successes and advances, but also grave shortcomings and deformations. It would be foolish to close the right or the left eye, to see one thing and not another. Our gravest weakness over the years lay in the field of application of the principle of democracy to a broad range of social practice, and this led to the deformed practice by social institutions, to their bureaucratization, to a disturbance in the relations between the leaders and the led, between the authorities and the citizens, with concurrent complications in the fields of politics, the economy, culture, and national relations.

Some people would not have minded rule by kindergarten methods: Take my hand, children, hold onto the cord or you will get lost; do not ask about this, you would not understand yet; wait until you are older; and, if you do not obey, I will punish you. I hope that it logically follows that we are also mature and cultured individuals and citizens, a mature and cultured people. From this it is necessary to draw conclusions for the entire social practice. . . .

The European of today wants to know what is at issue in his state; he wants to understand it, to have a say in it, to take part in deciding on his fate and living conditions, *to elect his leaders* and then—according to their deeds—praise them *or even criticize or depose them.* In short, he wants to have the constitutional principle that "the people are the source of all power" changed into everyday specific practice. The citizen wants to see his civic and national self-realization in the national and state representation; he wants to have guarantees that he can freely apply his right of selection, control, and responsibility. It is a problem of progressing democratization of our social system, a problem of the freeing and development of all creative forces of the population, its physical and mental potential, and its engagement and activity, a problem of the cooperation of millions of hands and minds expressed and guaranteed through the institutions. . . .

In recent years all kinds of things have been and are being remedied in our country. The New Year has stirred the reflections of our people; it has also stirred new hopes that the seeking of ideas and the maturing of thoughts, which we have noticed in our country particularly in recent years, would gradually be expressed in specific results and in the entire social practice, that the efforts we have started to develop for the democratic reform of our society, supported by all the progressive people, would be accelerated and manifested in the solution of questions which have ripened. It is both a process and a struggle. We are convinced that it is inevitable for the modern socialist society. Hopes are being raised by the discussions of the leading Party organs and their echo among the people.

It is also necessary to recall Alexander Dubček's words in *Pravda*'s [of Bratislava] New Year issue: "The past period tested past values and our ability to maintain and multiply them for the present and the future. We are now living through a historical change, a transition to a new quality of socialist society, and this has marked our work and put extreme demands on it." *The election of Alexander Dubček to head our Party imbues his words with programmatic content. And this we can ardently welcome and support.* . . . [Italics added.]

We need today the activity and engagement of all who have at heart the progressive solution of our problems, the modernization of our society, and the completion of the revival process of socialist theory and practice. . . . We can only hope that . . . the new hopes were not mere illusions and that the year 1968 has moved our society on to a new phase of development.

It is curious that it was Husák, then an outsider to the group favoring liberalization, whose voice was the first articulate one after Novotný's fall to summon progressive-minded Czechoslovaks to join in this revival of "socialist theory and practice," that it was Husák who rose to "ardently welcome and support" Dubček's call for a "new quality of socialist society," that it was Husák who was the prophet of the revolution which he later denounced and helped to destroy.

Three weeks after his first article, Husák wrote again in *Kulturný Život* expressing impatience with what he evidently thought was the excessively slow pace of reform. In the magazine's February 2 issue, Husák remarked that the nation was watching the new situation with hope, but at the same time with "old skepticism."

Smrkovský, the man who remained true to his ideas to the bitter end, had set forth his views on the new state of affairs in an article on January 21 in the Prague trade-union daily *Prace*. As a cabinet minister and influential member of the Central Committee, Smrkovský addressed his readers with considerable authority:

> We must determinedly correct, repair, and rectify the deformations of socialism which occurred in the past, and we must not permit new ones to arise. Conflicting opinions about the solutions of problems must be settled in a democratic manner, as is stipulated in the Party statutes. They must not be settled by means of an authoritative pronouncement. High posts of office must not be regarded as held for life. Conditions must be established which permit an honorable discharge from, and a return to, high and even the highest positions. . . .
>
> In the economic sphere, the economic reform must be resolutely continued and developed as a whole and its principles must be "pushed through" to every place of work. In the social sphere, the democratic spirit must be restored and an atmosphere for the exchange, and contest, of opinions must be created, permitting the most valuable and *progressive ideas to prevail over conservative and outdated opinions.* . . . [Italics added.]
>
> The issue is that the whole nation should again rally to bring about an upsurge of all creative forces, to bring about the reconstruction, development, and creation of its socialist people's state, of our Czechoslovak Socialist Republic.

Up to this point, however, all that was really new in Czechoslovakia were these few words from men like Husák and Smrkovský and cautious beginnings of political discussion in the still censored newspapers, radio, and television. To be sure, delegates from Prague went across the country to explain to Party organizations on all levels the essence of the changes resulting from the January 5 decisions of the Central Committee. Špaček, the new progressive KSČ Presidium member from Brno, was the man behind this operation. In some of these briefings, ideas about a new "socialist theory and practice" were mentioned, but the continuing vagueness in Prague inevitably was communicated to the provinces. To the entrenched men of the Party apparatus, who had thrived in the Novotný days, all this verbiage was somewhat disturbing but far from alarming. They, too, were cynics and had heard brave new words spoken before and then forgotten. And to the most of the fourteen million people of Czechoslovakia—the nine million Czechs, the three million Slovaks, and the two million of the ethnic minorities—the remote echoes of the drama played out within the labyrinths of the Communist Party were academic and unrelated to their lives and their world.

Perhaps more than anyone else in Czechoslovakia, writers and journalists were conscious of the immense potential in the new situation. They were the men who had so greatly contributed to set the whole process of change in motion, and now they rushed to exploit the first victory.

The Central Committee of the Writers' Union assembled on January 24 in Prague for the first time since the Novotný regime had penalized the organization and its members the previous September for their defiance in June. This time, there was no overt interference by the Party and no pressure by the authorities to influence the election of new officials or to force the writers to produce ideologically acceptable resolutions. Hendrych, Hoffman, and all their acolytes seemed suddenly to have lost interest in what the writers said or did.

Meeting in this new freedom, the Union elected as its chairman Eduard Goldstücker, a middle-aged man who probably tended to be more moderate than his fiery younger colleagues. Jan Procházka was defeated in his bid for chairmanship but was chosen vice-chairman, along with Miroslav Valek, a Slovak writer. Milan Kundera joined them on the Union's Presidium. Then the Union announced that starting in March it would resume publishing the weekly magazine which the Culture Ministry had taken away from it last September. Since the writers felt that the regime had polluted the magazine's old name (*Literární Noviny,* which means *Literary News*), they decided to rename it *Literární Listy* (*Literary Letters*).

The reorganized Writers' Union became the first solid outpost of the new reform movement, and its plans to publish *Literární Listy* promised to equip the progressives with their own channel of communications with the public. The Union and *Literární Listy* were to remain throughout the Prague Spring and for a while afterward a mainspring of the liberal movement.

Even if already in January the Party's old-line ideological watchdogs and censors had moved into the wings on their own, the chances are that the Writers' Union could not have elected its liberal leadership and prepared to publish *Literární Listy* without Dubček's assent. Similarly, when Goldstücker announced that the Union would seek the release from prison of Jan Beneš, action was taken fairly promptly. Beneš was freed on March 22, less than two months later; this was an unprecedented move in Communist Czechoslovakia, where intellectuals normally did not obtain commutations of prison sentences.

But liberalization was not proceeding smoothly and uniformly. On January 23 the Central Committee of the Slovak Party in Bratislava elected Vasil Bilak as First Secretary to fill the vacancy left by Dubček. Although he had once tangled with Novotný over Slovak matters, Bilak by no stretch of imagination could be considered a progressive. Instead, his election indicated that conservative forces still controlled the Slovak Party and that with Dubček in Prague they would tighten their hold over it. Bilak's rise to power was the first tangible demonstration that the KSČ would split widely, rather than unite, in the wake of Novotný's removal and the advent of reformers. As future events would show, Dubček in the end was caught between his two fellow Slovaks, Husák and Bilak. But Bilak at least had the distinction of consistent and, in his own way, honest behavior through the approaching crisis.

Not quite four weeks after he took office, Alexander Dubček flew to Moscow for a two-day visit intended, in effect, to be his formal introduction to the Soviet leadership. He arrived in the Soviet capital on January 29, and met with Brezhnev and President Nicolai Podgorny to discuss topics ranging from the "deepening cooperation" between Czechoslovakia and the Soviet Union to various international problems, the most important being the forthcoming session in Budapest in preparation for the world Communist parties' conference scheduled for November.

The Kremlin had been trying to arrange this conference since 1964, as a follow-up to the 1960 meeting which condemned Tito's Yugoslavia, but it had been consistently blocked by the Romanians and certain West European parties. During 1967 Romania again defied Moscow as Ceauşescu flatly refused to go along with an anti-Israeli policy and, instead, built up Romania's economic and cultural relations with Israel. In December 1967 this Romanian independence was rewarded in Foreign Minister Corneliu Manescu's election as President of the United Nations General Assembly, the first Communist diplomat to earn this distinction. Now the Kremlin wished to assure itself that Czechoslovakia under Dubček would not embark on any line disruptive of its world policies, the Warsaw Pact, or Comecon activities.

There is no reason to believe that the Soviet leaders met Dubček with coolness or suspicion, or to infer that because the visit was arranged for late January and not immediately after Dubček's assumption of power a deliberate slight was intended. It is a standard procedure for new Party chiefs in Eastern Europe to visit Moscow to be inspected at the Kremlin and then to make "protocol calls" on their opposite numbers in the bloc. But these visits are arranged as a matter of mutual convenience, unless a crisis is in the making, and a lapse of four weeks is not unduly long. In any event, Dubček had received Brezhnev's warm congratulations on

January 6, and nothing particularly alarming had occurred in Czechoslovakia in the interim to change the Soviet attitude toward him.

In Moscow, Dubček assured his hosts that Czechoslovakia's relations with the Warsaw Pact and Comecon would not be affected by the leadership change and that, naturally, he would send a delegation to Budapest the following month.

That Dubček passed the Moscow test with flying colors was demonstrated in the official communiqué, in which his visit was characterized by "warm friendship, sincerity, and complete identity of views on all matters discussed." The conversations, it said, had resulted in a "friendly understanding which corresponds to the character of fraternal relations between the two Parties." On the rigidly measured scale of Moscow communiqués, this certainly indicated the highest form of Soviet approval. Only when a communiqué curtly refers to a discussion's having been held in a "frank and comradely spirit" may one conclude that it broke down in total disagreement. Such communiqués were to be issued later in the year.

Immediately after the August invasion, the Soviet press offered a completely different account of the Brezhnev-Dubček conferences in Moscow in January, claiming that serious warnings were issued to the Czechoslovak leader of the dangers to socialism developing in his country. But this latter-day version is singularly unconvincing. Aside from the elections in the Writers' Union five days before Dubček's Moscow trip, there were no tangible developments in Czechoslovakia of a nature likely to fill the Kremlin with such dire premonitions. The Soviet press, however, excels at hindsight and finds it easier to rewrite history than to predict it. As one Prague editor remarked to me after the invasion, the greatest problem facing Soviet historians is "how to predict the past."

On February 4 Dubček met with János Kadár at the border town of Komárno. They had known each other for a long time, and Dubček, who speaks fluent Hungarian, favorably impressed Kadár with his plans for Czechoslovakia's future, especially in the economic field. Hungary, too, was moving ahead with a cautious economic reform. On February 7 Dubček conferred with Władysław Gomułka in the Moravian industrial town of Ostrava near the Polish border. On February 19 Vladimir Koucký, the strongly pro-Soviet member of the KSČ Secretariat in charge of international relations, flew to Bucharest to acquaint the Romanian leadership with the Czechoslovak situation. The only notable omission in this protocolary fence-mending in Eastern Europe was Dubček's failure to meet with Walter Ulbricht, who was to be one of his chief tormentors in the ensuing months.

In February the reform movement picked up momentum and acquired shape and direction. Getting the economic reform going seriously, emphasizing freedom of expression and public debate of national issues, insistence on justice and legality—these were the chief ingredients of what the young Communists in the editorial offices, the rapidly multiplying discussion groups, the classrooms of Charles University, and even the trade-unions were calling "Socialism with a Human Face." It was a felicitous expression, well fitting the Czech temperament, which inclines toward humanism and lyricism.

The Prague Spring has been described as a revolution. The Russians, of course, prefer to call it a "counterrevolution." I believe that in seeking to analyze the Czechoslovak experiment it is important to define precisely the terms and meanings and shy away from clichés and slogans. My own view is that what was attempted in Prague in 1968, first instinctively and then consciously and programmatically, was a revolution in the deepest philosophical sense, undertaken in the context of a Western-oriented European society with a long civilizing tradition. The Czechs were building from a philosophical, humanistic, and cultural background that had its roots in the times of Saint Wenceslas at the turn of the millennium and had developed with amazing consistency and unity of purpose through the Hussite experience and the Tábor Mountain crusades, the seventeenth-century risings against the Habsburgs, the intellectual impact of Comenius, participation in the modernization of the Austro-Hungarian Empire, and, finally, in the flowering of mature thought and nationhood in Tomáš Masaryk's First Republic.

The advent of Communism in Czechoslovakia, a country with left-of-center but democratic proclivities, was a deformation in this historical process, not because of the Marxist ideology per se but because of its overwhelming Stalinist content, with the added distortion of representing the alien Soviet interest at the expense of Czechoslovakia's national interest.

The Czechoslovaks' reaction—starting in 1956 and culminating in 1967 and 1968—was, therefore, the response of a freethinking civilized *Western* society to a colossal political aberration transported from the East in the baggage train of the Soviet armies. I think it is significant that this reaction found interpreters among the older Communists with extensive Moscow

connections—the Smrkovskýs, the Husáks (the latter being opportunisti-
cally but intellectually attuned to the times), the Kriegels, and the Gold-
stückers—as well as among the new Communists like Dubček, Špaček,
Šik, Císař, and Mlynář, and among theoreticians like Košik, Václav Müller, Milan Hübl, and Sviták. The battle that developed in 1968 was, then,
essentially between believers and philistines, between the men of thought
and the primitives. Among the leading figures of this period, only Gustav
Husák succeeded in finding himself on both sides within the short period
of eight months.

The emerging Czechoslovak philosophers of Marxism were the first
Westerners living in a Communist society to apply modern critical analysis to socialism. After Marx and Engels, practical Marxist thought was
the province of Easterners with Byzantine encumbrances—Lenin and
Trotsky. Furthermore, both of them were already operating in a practical-
power context of directing a revolution and then a country. The torrent
of thoughts and words spewed out by Stalin, Khrushchev, Brezhnev, and
their ideological minions can by no stretch of charity be classified as
philosophy.

To be sure, the West has produced in the interim serious Marxist
ethical and aesthetic thought and philosophy with Jean Jaurès, the Webbs,
Harold Laski, Antonio Gramsci, with Ernst Bloch, Jean-Paul Sartre,
Albert Camus, and Roger Garaudy. Herbert Marcuse had jazzed up old
Marxist concepts in a cocktail of neoanarchist and Chinese revolutionary
ideas, but he offered little that was fresh, original, or, for that matter,
constructive in terms of the world's real problems. In all cases, however,
the Western thinkers were free of practical problems of political administration coping with change and conflict, except for Palmiro Togliatti,
whose influence grew rather than diminished after his death, not only in
the Italian Party but throughout the Communist world. The young Czechoslovak philosophers were engaged in translating modern Marxist concepts into political action.

The rest of Eastern Europe has produced no more than tentative rethinking of Marxism after the installation of Communist regimes following World War Two and this, too, always stopped at the water's edge.
Georgy Lukacs was neutralized by the Hungarian regime and was, in any
case, by the time the Czechoslovak phenomenon arose, an octogenarian.
Poland's Leszek Kołakowski, who made important contributions to the
new philosophy in Eastern Europe, had already left for North America
when the Czechoslovaks moved along with their Marxist revolution.

Czesław Miłosz has been away too long to represent new Polish thought. Adam Schaff, once a member of the Central Committee of the Polish Communist Party, did express the new trends in *Marx and the Individual*, published in 1965, in which he argued that "he who fails to see that man holds the central position in the socialist idea disregards what is most important in it, and does not understand it at all." But Schaff, too, has been silenced. Aside from the Czechoslovaks, only Milovan Djilas remains the prophet of the new Marxism, and his *The Unperfect Society* may well be a milestone in contemporary socialist history.

In Czechoslovakia, the incipient revolution early in 1968 was the product of an intellectual and emotional marriage of politicians and philosophers. In terms of Communist practicalities, it bore the imprint of the "Yalta Testament" of Italy's Palmiro Togliatti and his concept of "unity within diversity" (something the very un-Communist John F. Kennedy had also propounded for modern society in the second half of the twentieth century). It was not surprising, then, that one of the most violent reactions against the Soviet invasion of Czechoslovakia came from Togliatti's heirs in the Italian Communist Party.

Stripping away the slogans of the Prague Spring—even the famous "Socialism with a Human Face"—what made the Czechoslovak experiment a true twentieth-century revolution was that it undertook to wed socialist concepts of social economic justice with the West's traditions of political, cultural, and scientific freedom. It had never been attempted in a Communist society, and its critics were quick to say that its humanistic Marxism was a contradiction in terms. But the Czechs, a bridge in themselves between East and West, believed themselves capable of this synthesis.

Human socialism, then, was the philosophy of the Czechoslovak revolution, and it was a tragedy for Marxism and socialism that Brezhnev's tanks temporarily interrupted this East European renaissance before it could be fully and freely tested.

The practical dimensions of the revolution—consistent economic reform and a reassessment of the role and function of the Communist Party in a modern socialist state—could not be rationally considered until freedom of expression and public debate and dialogue were established. For twenty years all Czechoslovakia had heard was a monotonous soporific monologue which had prevented dissent and birth of new ideas. Now the time had come to release the stream of opinions.

Late in January a group of journalists and writers called on Jiří Hendrych, still the official Party ideologue, to ask for the abolition of press censorship. In 1967 and before, Czechoslovak journalists, with a few notable exceptions, had not distinguished themselves as fearless fighters for freedom of expression, and the brunt of the battle in Prague, Bratislava, and Brno had been borne chiefly by writers, playwrights, and poets. Scores of newspaper writers and editors, who later redeemed themselves with extraordinary courage and imagination, were content to toe the Party line in their reporting and editorials. Foreign correspondents stationed in the West for Czech and Slovak dailies and the news agency ČTK contributed the same kind of insipid, uniform, one-sided, and venomous reporting as their colleagues of *Pravda*, *Izvestia*, Tass, *Trybuna Ludu*, and *Neues Deutschland*. But now the journalists, too, joined the fray.

Surprisingly, Hendrych agreed that the time had come for censorship to be jettisoned. He did not have the power the change the 1967 press law, and the Party and the government, still feeling their way, were not yet prepared to do so. Therefore, freedom of the press simply happened. The censors remained in the editorial offices, but they put away their blue pencils and scissors. They were not tarred and feathered, they simply and naturally switched to more constructive tasks like brewing coffee or fetching beer. The journalists were not vindictive—this was not in the spirit of the quiet revolution—and they welcomed the help with the beverages. Some of the more objectionable censors, who no longer felt at ease in the newspaper offices, began staying home or just turning up to punch the time clock.

Between February 1 and 3, the Seventh Congress of Unified Agricultural Cooperatives met in Prague. Normally, a farmers' gathering is not a major political event, but this was the occasion on which Alexander Dubček chose to make his public debut. On February 1, the day after his return from Moscow, he addressed the eighteen hundred delegates.

In his shy and quiet manner, peering down at his text through his spectacles, Dubček began by saying that the achievements of "socialist construction" confirmed the "correctness" of the Party's line on the socialist reconstruction of agriculture. The decisions of the KSČ's Central Committee Plenum on January 5 opened "a wide sphere for manifold activities of the people and set into motion all forces of society." Unlike Novotný, who never missed a chance to deliver a forceful pep talk,

Dubček simply said that the new leadership trusted the farmers, along with the workers, and looked forward to their genuine support and co-operation in the tasks ahead. Democracy was just as important as discipline, he told his audience, albeit that in the past official emphasis had been on the latter.

"Democracy," Dubček said, "is not only the right and chance to pronounce one's own views, but also the way in which people's views are handled: whether they have a real feeling of coresponsibility, codecision, whether they really feel they are participating in making decisions and solving important problems. . . . Government organs must strive to create the optimum conditions in which farmers can apply their skills and initiative, not to give orders on when and how to reap and sow."

Then Dubček announced that the Party was preparing an "Action Program" designed to spell out and codify the aims of the "new socialist society," to clarify "the present political tasks of the Party in the sphere of society, state, and economy." This program was the Magna Carta of the Czechoslovak revolution and, on February 6, the Presidium held a formal session to discuss it. The Presidium also took the consistent step of announcing that "meetings of the Central Committee should be held in an atmosphere which would enable *free criticism and creative exchange of views* as well as evaluation of different proposals and standpoints."

In a radical departure from past practice, the Presidium also promised that "information about the discussions of the Central Committee of the Communist Party of Czechoslovakia and its Secretariat will be published." This was tantamount to the proclamation of functioning democracy within Communism. And the Presidium, though still weighted with Novotný and his conservatives, went one more step in announcing that elected bodies, presumably meaning the National Assembly, would be Czechoslovakia's policy-making organs instead of the Party apparatus. The new regime was engaging in a genuine separation of powers, destroying the pernicious and all-pervading role of the Communist Party in all the fields of national life.

The new democracy had already begun to function spontaneously at the farmers' congress. After Dubček's speech, the congress ceased to behave like all the stage-managed gatherings of the past. Unscheduled speakers rose to ask questions and voice criticisms. The usual predrafted resolution was scrapped and a new one produced amidst excited debates on the floor. It called for the creation of a national farmers' organization free to advocate farm interests and influence national policy makers, a full democratization of the collective farms, and the granting to them of the same rights enjoyed by other organizations in Czechoslovakia.

On February 25 Smrkovský went before the microphones of Radio Prague to discuss the "Czechoslovak socialist road," and to argue, among other things, for the separation of Party and government administrative organs. In subsequent newspaper articles, one of them in *Rudé Právo,* he took up the related themes of the autonomous socialist development and of Czechoslovakia's place on the world scene. "It is incumbent on us," Smrkovský wrote in the Party newspaper, "on Czechs and on Slovaks, to enter courageously into unexplored terrain and in it to look for our Czechoslovak socialist road. This is, in the last analysis, our duty . . . to ourselves . . . and to the whole international socialist movement." In another article, he set forth the daring thesis that there must exist a measure of equality among Communist countries. Industrialized and developed Czechoslovakia needed to create a "type of socialism which would have something to say even to the industrial countries of Europe with their mature revolutionary workers' movements." Smrkovský's point was that henceforth the Czechoslovak Communist Party should orient itself to Western Europe.

It was implicit that Czechoslovakia must in some way and some day free itself of excessive Soviet tutelage. The corollary was that Czechoslovaks must concern themselves with their country's lopsided relationship with the Soviet Union—the Comecon edicts, the credits and the deliveries to Russia, the vast but artificial trade—before the national economy could live again after its long stagnation. At this point, therefore, Yugoslav and Romanian concepts of economic independence entered the Czechoslovak picture. It was logical, then, that the awareness followed that political independence, too, was crucial.

In a radio commentary on February 20, Evžen Löbl, onetime Deputy Minister of Foreign Trade who had returned to his economic studies in Slovakia after eleven years in prison, raised this complex and explosive problem. How long would it take Czechoslovakia to adjust its "unequal relations with the Soviet Union" in the economic realm? The same week the Defense Ministry's weekly publication *Obrana Lidu* took it upon itself to defend Yugoslavia from earlier criticisms by the Cominform and other Communist organs. It praised the Yugoslavs for standing up to Moscow's pressures to follow its example.

That the population was likewise equating domestic liberalization with anti-Soviet sentiment became evident on February 15 when the Czecho-slovak ice-hockey team beat the theretofore undefeated Soviet Union 5-to-4 at the Olympic Games in Grenoble, France. Ice hockey is Czecho-slovakia's most popular sport—Czech and Slovak kids play it on frozen ponds and even in the streets the way American kids play sandlot base-ball—and on the day of the Grenoble game hundreds of thousands of people were before their television sets and glued to their radio receivers. Victory over the Soviet Union with its obvious symbolism electrified the nation and thousands of Czechoslovaks poured out into the streets in joyful celebrations. The importance of ice hockey in Czechoslovak-Soviet relations was emphasized again dramatically in 1969 when the Czechoslo-vaks once more beat the Soviets. Smrkovský, another distinguished victim of the 1969 hockey match, spoke rather prophetically on the perils of ice-hockey politics in a speech to students on March 13, 1968:

> Many of you, of course, may think that the relationship between us and the Soviet Union is not one of equals. It's because you have taken no interest in politics; you have been interested in politics for only two months. You thought that here, in our Republic, the Soviet Union was in the driver's seat. If anyone is still thinking that, my young friends, he is terribly wrong. Those times are behind us. Comrades, our relations are now built on the principle of equality, on the principle of sover-eignty. That's the truth. . . . Very often we see young people giving way—especially at hockey matches—to their dislike of the Soviet Union. Well, look here, to love or not to love, that's everybody's private affair. Nobody can force that on you. But you must think over this one fact: look at the map, when you go back to school, or at home, look at the frontier, who our neighbor is, because we must live politically. . . . Don't take lightly what I'm saying now and don't play around, don't underestimate your responsibility for the safety of our state.

By mid-February, it was evident that the debate in Czechoslovakia could not be contained within the limits of an intellectual exchange of views on what might be best for the country. Entrenched apparatus men as well as the Soviet officials around Ambassador Chervonenko at his tightly guarded Bubeneč compound did not need much imagination to perceive that the *status quo* was changing before their very eyes. More and more, whispers were heard that a "counterrevolution" might be in the making.

But just as the progressives' leadership remained amorphous, the con-servatives, too, had no impressive figure around whom to build a counter-movement. And between the two camps, there lay a vast mass of people (in *and* out of the Communist Party) who were confused, disoriented, and uncertain in their hearts and minds over the quickening pace of events. All the positions, however, were relative. Men like Smrkovský, Šik, and Slovakia's Husák wanted to move faster and faster. Dubček, who appeared as a dangerous radical to the conservatives and presumably to the Soviet Embassy, was in reality a centrist who hoped that a reformist's happy medium could be achieved. But soon none of the protagonists could any longer control their own attitudes or those of their partisans. Czechoslovakia was rapidly caught between opposing dynamics.

The conservatives' foremost weapon was the argument, mouthed surreptitiously at certain Party meetings, that the liberals' reform would strike at the core of the workers' most vital interests. The workers were told that if Šik and his collaborators were allowed to carry out the reform, thousands and thousands of jobs would be lost, salaries would drop, and prices would rise, and Czechoslovakia's economy would be distorted beyond remedy. It was rather strange for men who had run the Czechoslovak economy into the ground to present themselves now as the champions of working-class interests. And, curiously, the progressives were actually disturbed over this attack, for they underestimated the growing appeal of their own cause and overestimated the conservatives' persuasive powers. The nation's eventual reaction was to surprise both sides.

One of the arts of politics is to know when to quit when you are behind. This art had still not been mastered by Novotný even after his expulsion as the Party chief. He took seriously the fact that he had been permitted to remain as President of the Republic and—probably to the dismay of his fellow conservatives, who must have known he was through—took it upon himself to act as a spokesman for the antireform faction. On February 17, for example, he addressed thousands of workers at the huge ČKD works in Prague on the wisdom of his past policies and warned against the awesome perils of the Dubček-inspired course. (It was characteristic of "Socialism with a Human Face" that Novotný not only still sat at Hradčany Castle but was free to deliver political speeches. It would have been inconceivable for the Soviet Party to let Khrushchev run about after his political demise and beat the drums publicly against the new Brezhnev establishment. This was the difference.) Novotný considered the ČKD complex as the apple of his eye—it was one of the enterprises especially pampered by his regime—but he aroused only polite, slightly bored applause. The speech was duly published in the uncensored newspapers, but, not surprisingly, his words had the opposite effect of what he had hoped. As Z. A. B. Zeman has pointed out, "Novotný in fact helped the cause of reform by forcing the debate into the factories, into the open air of public life."

The Dubček regime was not interested in purges, but there were men in powerful and influential positions who could no longer be tolerated, for there was the risk that reforms would be blocked from within. The two key areas where the progressives urgently needed control were the ideological and cultural sector and the security apparatus. Dubček was not yet ready to reshuffle the Presidium or the cabinet, which meant that Hendrych, Hoffman, and Kudrna could not yet be fired. Their personal influence had been drastically diminished by the march of events, but both in the KSČ and in the government these "operational" men still held levers of power. Then, for psychological reasons, it would have suited Dubček to see Novotný removed. There was an obvious incongruity in his continued presence as head of state and commander-in-chief when everything he stood for was being swept away. But the proper opportunity had to be awaited.

On February 16 the Ideological Commission of the Central Committee held its first post-Novotný meeting to map out its new course. The session had the peculiar character of blindman's buff. The Party ideologists were to a man Novotný appointees and straight dogmatists and it was a bit much to ask them to come up suddenly with a liberal interpretation of Marxism. But the Commission solved its problem with jargon and some personnel changes. The Party's cultural policy, it proclaimed, had been "critically evaluated" and it was now believed necessary to "consistently overcome a simplified approach to culture and intellectuals." Party officials should concentrate on their ideological and political tasks and not take over the functions of the state bodies. This meant, among other things, that Hendrych and Hoffman were being told to stop dictating to the intellectuals and interfering with them.

Two days earlier, for example, the Czech Section of the Writers' Union had formally asked the Party to intercede on its behalf with the Culture Ministry to obtain a permit for the publication of its new magazine, *Literární Listy*. The Ministry had been dragging its feet on it for a number of weeks and resisting the Union's request for an allocation of enough newsprint for a press run of 150,000 copies of a sixteen-page magazine. (Instead, Hoffman's Ministry offered the Union newsprint for 50,000 copies of a ten-page publication.) The Party and the Ideological Commission must have acted favorably on the writers' request because *Literární Listy*'s first issue, rich in political and cultural comment, came out on February 29 and its 150,000 copies were immediately snapped up. It could not have been done without Dubček's approval.

The Ideological Commission also fired as its head František Havliček, a hard-line Party hack who had held the job since March 1967, when he replaced Pavel Auersperg, a historian and former private secretary and speechwriter of Novotný's. Auersperg was one of those interesting Czechoslovak Communist intellectuals who switched allegiances and viewpoints according to the influences under which he found himself at a given time. Unlike Husák, however, Auersperg was not possessed with a power hunger. He lost his post in 1967 because of his progressive instincts, and in 1968 he helped to shape the revolution's program, but in 1969 he was to return to the conservative fold. It would probably be unfair to describe Auersperg as an opportunist: he just seemed to run ahead of the political trends of the day, regardless of the direction. He seemed to confirm Victor Hugo's famous dictum that the chief difference between a man and a cow is that a man may change his mind as often as he wants while the cow always chews the same grass. In any event, Havliček, who had replaced Auersperg, was succeeded by Jaroslav Kozel, a conservative nonentity, which may well have suited the Party at this juncture. Kozel held the post too short a time to have any kind of effect.

The cleanup in the security apparatus began on February 8. On that day, the KSČ's Control and Audit Commission—the Party's powerful disciplinary organ—met to take up plans for "a more profound evaluation of the control activity in the Party. . . ." It announced that "the evaluation of the work of the . . . Commission and the entire control system in the Party will make it possible to formulate in a more responsible and exact way the position, tasks, and structure of the Central Control and Audit Commission," as well as the "main lines of its activities" pending the Fourteenth Party Congress. In plain language, this meant the Party would no longer seek to impose blind discipline on its members and punish transgressors.

On February 19 the Presidium met under Dubček's chairmanship to review the draft of the Action Program, whose preparation the new First Secretary had announced on February 1, and to take the unprecedented decision that both members and alternate members of the Central Committee, along with lower-ranking Party organizations throughout the country, "should actively join in its elaboration." The draft should be submitted for consultation with regional Party committees, it said, and then openly discussed in the Central Committee's commissions. This was another departure from the precedent under which both the Central Committee and the Party organizations were simply informed of programs drafted and approved in the Presidium. The three men who drafted most of the Action Program were Ota Šik, emphasizing its economic aspects; Radovan Richta, head of the team of the Philosophical Institute, which had produced the earlier study on *Civilization at the Crossroads*; and the historian Auersperg. Zdeněk Mlynář, soon to become the official Party ideologue, helped to write the political sections. It goes without saying that the confused Ideological Commission of the KSČ had little, if anything, to do with the Action Program's elaboration.

The same Presidium meeting removed Miroslav Mamula from the directorship of the Central Committee's ill-famed Eighth Department, which looked after security matters. Mamula had been, in effect, Czechoslovakia's top security agent and a close associate of the Soviet KGB. Although the security service was in theory subordinated to the Interior Ministry, Mamula ran it directly with the aid of Deputy Interior Minister Viliam Šalgovič, a Slovak and a truly sinister personage on the Czechoslovak scene. A tough, swarthy, bespectacled man in his late forties, Šalgovič was also a KGB liaison officer and played a most important role in the preparations for the Soviet invasion. The security apparatus was like a state-within-a-state governed by Mamula and Šalgovič with virtually no reference to the Interior Ministry or even the Party Presidium. Firing Mamula, whom Dubček assigned to work as a clerk at the aircraft plant at Letňany, represented the first major act in dismantling the secret police and placing it under the government's orders. But, of course, the STB men did not simply vanish. They wormed their way into the woodwork and waited until they could re-emerge, as they did after the invasion. No official reason was given for firing Mamula, but initiates knew that he had been removed because of his involvement in the December plot to stage a preventive military coup on Novotný's behalf. It would have been rather difficult for Dubček to tolerate in a high position the man who had signed the warrant for his arrest.

Replacing Mamula was Lieutenant General Prchlík, the man who had warned Dubček of the coup and then prevailed upon the regional commands to remain neutral in the power struggle. Named in charge of the Army Political Administration to replace him was Major General Egyd Pepich, a Slovak who later was to cast his lot with Husák. The only key Novotný man still retaining a top-sensitive security job was Major General Šejna, Mamula's young deputy in the armed forces and a coconspirator in December. But before the new regime could formally remove him, he took matters in his own hands and precipitated a major political crisis that, in fact, ended Novotný's regime once and for all.

On February 22–23 Czechoslovakia went through the motions of cele-brating the twentieth anniversary of the Communist takeover in 1948, although the actual date was February 26. It was an anniversary that few people cared to remember, let alone pretend to cherish, but one that could not be ignored. Brezhnev, Gomułka, Kadár, and Ulbricht came to help in the festivities—it was their first *in loco* inspection of the new re-gime—and the anniversary turned into a test of sorts of whether Commu-nism was Communism in Czechoslovakia. Ceaușescu also came to Prague, but his inspection was of a different nature. Dutifully, red banners and streamers were draped over the façades of Prague's buildings, and flags were hoisted upon the roofs and entryways of houses. The huge red flag of the KSČ was raised on its mast in the courtyard of Hradčany Castle opposite the Czechoslovak tricolor. Other accustomed features were apparent, too—but it all seemed even more hollow than in previous years. The newspapers published photographs of Brezhnev being greeted by a half-smiling Dubček at the airport and other news and television clips showed Ceaușescu's poker face, the officious smiles on Gomułka's and Kadár's faces, and Ulbricht's goateed scowl.

For Dubček, the celebrations posed a delicate problem which he faced squarely and openly. If Brezhnev and his acolytes had come to inspect Czechoslovak Communism, he would explain and interpret for them what this Communism meant in 1968. In his speech at the main ceremonies, Dubček skipped rapidly over the usual Communist platitudes and assur-ances of fraternal unity and came straight to the point:

> In the early 1950s our people lived through one of the great dramas in all their history. Never before had it been possible to effect, within such a short historical period, such profound transformations in the socioeconomic, political, and ideo-logical life of the country. Unfortunately, the magnitude of the errors and short-comings which the then leadership of the Party, regrettably, failed to avoid corresponded to the scale of those truly gigantic processes. There were many setbacks also in inner Party life, the consequences of some of which are still felt by us. . . .
>
> In the atmosphere of false suspicion these problems and equally serious socio-political problems were compounded by such negative phenomena as violations of socialist legality from which not only Communism suffered. I think that the task of true rehabilitation of the dignity of all those who during the first and, espe-cially, the second world wars honestly served the Republic, the cause of its pro-

gressive developments, and the victory of socialism in our country is an integral part of our present-day efforts for the all-around democratization of the entire society and the Party. We must remove, along both state and Party lines, all the injustices done to people, and we must do so consistently and without reservation.

Science and culture are probably the most complex and delicate branch of Party activity. For here we are dealing with educated people whose work requires deep understanding and appreciation and does not tolerate stagnation, set formulas, impatience, or haste. Neither cultural nor scientific creation is free of difficulties, setbacks, and errors. It is influenced not only by shortcomings and defects in our work which lead to disenchantment and disillusionment. We do not always correctly appraise the significance, impact, and, more important, the causes. As a result, in this field we have had more frequent undesirable conflicts that tend to aggravate relations between Party bodies and scientists and artists. However, these shortcomings, which occur in every field, cannot and should not prompt us to base our policy toward scientists, writers, cinema workers, artists, and other cultural workers on distrust of their public activity, its content and direction. On the contrary, our policy must be based on trust and fruitful constructive cooperation. We must eliminate everything that tends to hamstring scientific and artistic creation, everything likely to breed tensions. . . . However, the Party cannot relinquish its right and duty to see to it that artistic creation helps to form socialist man.

I do not think we can win over the younger generation by reproaching it or by telling it that everything it enjoys had to be won by hard effort. For young people all this is workaday reality, something they take for granted. They do not regard it as something that had to be fought for. However, that is not the central point. . . .

The enthusiasm of the youth cannot be restricted to constantly praising our achievements. Our young people want to have achievements of their own, bring to reality their dreams and ideas, just as older people did in their young days, when the revolution gave them the opportunities. The youth must not be given gifts, things won for it by others. It must be afforded the conditions necessary to develop its own initiative, work for its own goals, that will enable our young citizens to perform their duty as a generation. . . .

Latterly, the old view of the Party as a force which, instead of giving political leadership, decides minor issues in an authoritarian way has again gained dominance. . . . No one is likely to deny that this understanding of leadership was largely responsible for the fact that the work of many of our administrative, economic, and public institutions was largely deprived of meaningful content and responsibility, that public initiative was not encouraged, and that many of our undertakings bore the stamp of formality. . . .

For the Party, to carry through its leading role in the present situation means first and foremost to create the necessary preconditions for the growth of creative initiative, to provide greater scope for confrontation and exchanges of opinion, to make it possible for every Communist to be informed thoroughly, objectively, and in good time about events in his own country and abroad, so that he may possess a point of view with regard to the Party's policy and, particularly, in framing the Party's political policy and in its actions, especially in the sphere in which he is employed. In brief, it means that at present, while retaining the essential centralism, we should lay the greatest accent on developing more, and above all deeper, democratic forms, and this not only in the upper Party echelons, but especially "lower down" in the organizations and among the membership.

Harry Schwartz, an editorial writer for *The New York Times* with an eye for Kremlinological detail, has pointed out that in reporting Dubček's speech, Moscow *Pravda* omitted all these passages. The rest of the address dealt with the Czech and Slovak problem, and there was the hint that a new arrangement would be worked out to solve the nationality question.

It is a fair assumption that Brezhnev and his Soviet colleagues—Ukrainian Party boss and Politburo member Pyotr Shelest, the Soviet Party's Central Committee Secretary in charge of relations with ruling Communist parties Konstantin F. Katushchev, and Regional Party Secretary L. S. Kulichenko—took a dim view of Dubček's words. The Soviets' suspicion that they were witnessing "revisionism," if not an incipient "counterrevolution," was strengthened, and this was the last time that even an effort was made to present Soviet-Czechoslovak relations as cordial. In his speech, Brezhnev ran through the standard phrases of Communist rhetoric for such occasions, but he made the significant point of praising Czechoslovakia's *past* achievements and her struggle against nationalism. Brezhnev's reaction was, of course, not unexpected, but what were Władysław Gomułka's thoughts as he listened to Dubček's views on the role of the Communist Party? Twelve years earlier, he, too, had attempted a similar liberalization of Communism but was beaten back and eroded by the threat of Soviet power. Now sixty-three and a "realist," Gomułka sat in Prague hearing of a brave new program for Czechoslovak young people, as back in Warsaw new ferment was rising among Poland's youth.

The following day Novotný spoke at an anniversary rally at Prague's Old Town Hall. It was, to say the least, an anticlimactic occasion used by the President of the Republic to praise himself and to repeat roughly the same ideas expressed the preceding afternoon by Brezhnev. The Czechs were spared, however, the customary military parade, which was both apt and ironical.

That morning, the Defense Ministry's weekly *Obrana Lidu* published an article by Major General Pepich, for the first time disclosing publicly that the President and his associates had attempted to stage a military coup the December before. He did not name General Šejna directly, but the hint was strong enough for Šejna to take it and flee Czechoslovakia two days later. It was the beginning of a major scandal.

Accompanied by his eighteen-year-old son and a young woman said to be the boy's girl friend, Šejna crossed the border into Hungary on February 25, then drove to Yugoslavia and finally to Italy. In Rome, he presented himself to the American Embassy to ask for political asylum in the United States. It was, indeed, a most curious situation—a pro-Soviet Czechoslovak general, a trusted associate of the Soviet armed forces, was seeking American protection against a liberalizing Communist revolution essentially oriented toward the West. Šejna received asylum chiefly because he was too valuable a source of military intelligence to be turned down. CIA agents took charge of him in Rome and secretly transported him to the United States, where he was taken to an unknown location in the Washington area near CIA headquarters at Langley, Virginia. Now why did Šejna choose the United States for a haven rather than the Soviet Union, with which he had professional and ideological ties? A possible answer is that Šejna, who appreciates the finer things of life, calculated that he would be safer and better off in Washington than in Moscow: the Kremlin is notorious for its dislike of losers and, besides, he had a great deal to offer the Americans and absolutely nothing to the Soviets.

For many months, both before and after the Soviet invasion of Czechoslovakia, Šejna remained a tap for the CIA, feeding it military information on his own country and the Soviet Union—it is said that he had visited secret Soviet rocket-testing installations—and providing a cascade of security data and personal identifications. Several months after Šejna's defection, I was told by Czechoslovak military-intelligence sources in Prague that his diplomatic passport for travel to "Socialist countries"—Hungary and Yugoslavia—had been validated a few months earlier by Soviet officers at the Warsaw Pact headquarters, a routine step necessary because of his familiarity with Soviet and Warsaw Pact military secrets. This apparently, is what made it possible for him to cross the Hungarian border on February 25 in one more ironic touch in this whole extraordinary situation. I reported the story of the passport validation in a report filed from Prague to *The New York Times,* but Šejna, questioned about it by the CIA, insistently denied it. I am still satisfied that the story was accurate and that Šejna denied it to remove any suspicion that his defection was stage-managed in Moscow.

The Czechoslovak public was not apprised of Šejna's flight until March 1—although the Western press and radios carried the news earlier—but by that time the National Assembly, meeting in secret session under the chairmanship of Novotný's friend Laštovička, had deprived the general of parliamentary immunity so that he could be sued for a criminal offense. This offense, reported by Prague newspapers in late February, was that Šejna, once a farmer, had "embezzled" twenty thousand dollars' worth of sweet clover and alfalfa from the government.

This somewhat absurd development had wide-ranging consequences. On February 28 Marshal Ivan I. Yakubovsky, Supreme Commander of Warsaw Pact forces, flew to Prague for urgent and confidential meetings with Dubček, Novotný, Premier Lenárt, and Defense Minister Lomský. Šejna's defection and its intelligence and security implications were obviously discussed, but it also appears possible that Yakubovsky came to study the possibility of a Warsaw Pact invasion of Czechoslovakia. After the intervention in August, Czechoslovak Army intelligence officers estimated that staff contingency planning for the attack must have begun late in February, for, they believed, six months were required to prepare the movement of over half a million men with armor, artillery, and full logistic support from five countries.

The disclosure of Novotný's plans for a military coup and the involvement of Mamula, Šejna, and Deputy Defense Minister Janko made Novotný's continuance as President untenable. Loud demands for his resignation echoed throughout Czechoslovakia, and, on March 8, the Army General Staff published an open letter on Šejna's defection which directly attacked Novotný and Mamula and demanded that the President resign. Novotný's reaction the following day was to strip Šejna of his military rank and all his distinctions and medals—a somewhat unethical step if one considers that it was Novotný who had enlisted Šejna's aid in the abortive conspiracy in the first place—but it was already much too late to save the Presidential skin. On March 13 Czechoslovakia's ambassador in Washington, Karel Duda, delivered a note to the State Department requesting that Šejna be extradited on criminal charges under the provisions of the 1925 extradition treaty. A criminal warrant covering the "embezzlement" was attached. Then, on March 14, General Janko shot himself.

On March 5 the KSČ Presidium, meeting under Dubček's chairmanship, deprived Hendrych of his responsibilities for over-all ideological policies and placed him instead in charge of politico-organizational matters. The new chief ideologue was Josef Špaček, the young and liberal member from Brno. Hendrych was to remain for a while longer in the Presidium but now chiefly as a figurehead. The same meeting set up a system for the flow of information from the Party's top bodies to the basic organizations and vice versa. This was designed to implement the earlier decision calling for full consultations throughout the Party and an open debate of the Action Program and other new policies. The Presidium also began debating a new press law to replace the 1967 legislation and formally do away with censorship.

The new democratic system began to function when, during the weekends of March 9–10 and March 17–18, Presidium members held sixty-seven meetings with Party regional and district organizations to review the draft Action Program and other new policy ideas. Party delegates presented to the Presidium proposals and suggestions for bringing the KSČ rank and file out of its long stagnation, democratizing the Party and public life in general, applying "Marxist-Leninist" solutions to the nagging nationalities question, clarifying the relationship between the workers and the intellectuals, solving the accumulated economic problems, and facing the demands of the youth. Grass-roots pressure was also brought to bear on the Presidium to proceed speedily with the rehabilitation of purge victims.

Now that the Presidium encouraged Party members to speak out, it was flooded with criticisms and complaints about "mistakes" and "aberrations" over the past years. The Party organizations insisted on the firing of officials—including President Novotný—who had discredited themselves through their earlier activities before the eyes of the Czechoslovak nation. And, finally, the Presidium discovered a powerful groundswell in favor of secret-ballot elections. Nothing like this had happened before in the history of the KSČ as, for the first time since 1945, Party members became active protagonists in the political process and not just observers or victims. Dubček's notion, of course, was that the Party must regain—or acquire—a flexibility that would make it acceptable to the nation. The new Marxist dream was that the Communist Party should hold power through popular consent and not through force.

It was characteristic of the new mood that the Prague newspaper *Večerní Praha*, taking to heart the Presidium's injunction for free speech, on March 12 attacked its own publisher, the city committee of the KSČ, for forcing it earlier that month to print a statement designed to "disorient the public" with which the editors had disagreed. The head of the Prague committee was Martin Vaculík, an old-guard Communist (no relation to the fiery novelist Ludvík Vaculík). The same day a Radio Prague commentator protested the jamming of Radio Free Europe programs in Czech and Slovak; citizens should be allowed to hear the broadcasts they chose without government interference, he remarked. The following day Radio Prague, now increasingly a bastion of liberalization, criticized the Soviet press for its silence on Czechoslovak developments. (Pending some decision on how to handle the Czechoslovak rebellion, the Soviet media had adopted the method of simply ignoring it. The Kremlin was obviously not prepared to keep its domestic opponents informed of how Czechs and Slovaks were going about *their* democratization.) By now, protests and denunciations of old practices were streaming from all sides in the Party, the government, and the many organizations that had for so long served as obedient transmission belts of KSČ power.

On March 13 two Party organizations in the Interior Ministry passed resolutions protesting the "dilatory" stance of its leadership and of departmental heads toward the functioning of the security apparatus. The resolutions stressed that this failure to clean up the secret police—for this was what they were talking about—"considerably influenced the attitude of the public toward members of the national security force." In other words, the secret police had decided that it craved popular approval. Already the day before, Interior Minister Kudrna had publicly apologized to Charles University students and condemned the "unnecessary brutality" of individual policemen in the Strahov riots, announcing that seven policemen had been punished, that all the injured students would be paid damages. Henceforth all uniformed police would wear numbered badges so that they could be easily identified.

But, inevitably, these measures were coming too late. On March 14 the Presidium of the National Assembly, until January a pliant tool of the regime, passed a vote of nonconfidence in Kudrna and Prosecutor General Jan Bartuška. It also instructed the president of the Supreme Court to take energetic steps to accelerate the rehabilitations. At the same time, ninety-two law instructors at Charles University sent an open letter to Bartuška charging him with responsibility for delaying the review of the purge trials. On March 15 Novotný had no choice but to dismiss his Interior Minister and Prosecutor General, and the KSČ Presidium immediately approved this step. It also confirmed the dismissal of Michal Chudík from the chairmanship of the Slovak National Council and of Miroslav Pastyřík from the leadership of the Central Council of the Trade-Unions by their respective organizations. (Such was the national temper that both bodies had rejected their voluntary resignations in order to dismiss these men with votes of no confidence.) František Barbírek, a rather conservative apparatus man, became the Slovak National Council's acting chairman. The Council immediately proceeded to call for a new relationship between Czechs and Slovaks and for full legislative powers for itself. In the labor council, Pastyřík's dismissal was accompanied by wide criticism of the organization's past slavish practices and by demands that it now acquire an independent role. Karel Poláček, chairman of the powerful Metal Workers' Union and a progressive, was elected as the new head.

Simultaneously, the Party organization at the Foreign Ministry—the principal graveyard of the 1950s purges—met to criticize the pro-Soviet Foreign Minister, David, and, indeed, Czechoslovakia's entire foreign policy. The group urged the punishment of those responsible for the "deformations" of the past years and proclaimed that Czechoslovak foreign policy must acquire its own identity while remaining in alliance with the Soviet Union.

Elsewhere, too, the prevailing mood was one of self-criticism and of pressure for changes in leaders and programs. These stirrings came from such unrelated organizations as the Association of Ukrainian Working People in Czechoslovakia, the National Conference of the Peace Movement of the Catholic Clergy, the Young Pioneers, the Presidium of the Central Council of the Union of Czechoslovak Youth, and the Prague University Council. The youth division of Svázarm, the national paramilitary organization, broke away and announced it would reconstitute itself as the Czechoslovak Boy Scout Movement. The Boy Scouts had been proscribed in 1948 as an "imperialist" tool. The Writers' Union, never lacking in new ideas, proposed a Club of Critical Thought. The People's Party and the Socialist Party, all along obedient members of the Communist-led National Front, busied themselves with revitalization schemes, suddenly realizing that something of an independent future might loom ahead. The National Front itself proposed secret elections for May 19 for the National Committees throughout the country. The Central Publication Board, the censorship organ, proposed the end of censorship.

Czechoslovakia's orthodox Communist society was thus suddenly coming apart after twenty years and, like a healing wound, new tissues were growing in the body politic. But it was still only a beginning and it was clear that even more dramatic changes must come. When Dubček convened the KSČ Presidium on March 13–15, the leadership group announced that it had prepared personnel changes to be submitted to the forthcoming Plenum of the Central Committee. This meant, of course, that most of the members of the old Presidium had signed their own political death warrants. In the meantime, Čestmir Císař was brought back from exile at the embassy in Romania and named Central Committee Secretary in charge of Education, Science, and Culture. In a preview of things to come, the Presidium also announced that an end would be put to all the "deformations" in Czechoslovak life, that rehabilitations would proceed apace, and that the electoral process would be restored. But, significantly, it warned against all "extremisms."

With everything being questioned and the idols and taboos laboriously constructed during two decades falling by the wayside one after another, it was understandable that things which the regime had wanted to obliterate in the Czechoslovaks' consciousness were now remembered with new clarity. The most important of these remembrances concerned Masaryk. On March 7 Czechoslovaks spontaneously celebrated the 117th anniversary of Tomáš Masaryk's birth and, on March 10, the twentieth anniversary of the mysterious death of his son Jan. Delegations from official organizations and uncounted thousands of students, workers, and just plain Czechs made the pilgrimage to the little walled cemetery at Laný, twenty-five miles southeast of Prague, where Tomáš and Jan Masaryk lie buried side by side. Newspapers, magazine articles, and radio and television programs brought the story of Tomáš Masaryk's life into every Czechoslovak home. His portrait, often showing him proudly astride his horse, appeared in store windows and homes; Masaryk buttons and postcards materialized at the little outdoor stands on Václavské Náměstí. The buttons were sold by the thousands, along with Dubček buttons, and they were intensely traded in the busy curbstone exchange of buttons and insignia in front of the Europa Hotel.

The restoration of the Masaryk myth had a twin effect on Czechoslovakia. On a plane that was both sentimental and political, Tomáš Masaryk was the great example to be imitated in what people were hoping would now turn into the Third Republic. But if the memory of the old President brought yearnings for the liberties associated with his epoch, the observance of his son's death pushed to the fore the long-harbored suspicion that he had been murdered by Soviet MGB agents or on their orders. Inevitably, the surfacing of this suspicion became an added ingredient in the mounting anti-Soviet sentiment.

But the future of Czechoslovakia was still the central theme of national interest. On March 17 Dubček addressed Party functionaries in Brno as a part of the Presidium's consultations throughout the country in preparation for the final unveiling of the Action Program. There, he took another step in explaining the KSČ's new program—including the independence of the judiciary—as well as in sounding a note of caution. He repeated again that Czechoslovakia's loyalty to the Soviet Union and other Socialist states remained intact under his regime and appealed to editors and broadcasters not to make the presentation of the great problems of the nation too "precipitate." This was necessary, he said, so that "our entire society may really be able to master the problems set forth." The Party expected the press to "aid the enforcement of the basic trend" in the new policy and to influence "the active attitude of the wide strata of citizens toward the Party policy." He praised the media for involving public opinion in Czechoslovakia's new political process: they had accomplished, he said, "much meritorious work," and "it has been a long time since the citizens' interest in our domestic political events was so great." But, he also remarked, press activities had occasionally displayed an "imprudent character." As the progressive leaders were to do with increasing emphasis in the weeks and months to come, Dubček was seeking to communicate to the journalists his concern that they might get out of hand and provide an excuse for a Soviet crackdown.

On March 13 and 20 it was Smrkovský's turn to address himself to the youth, setting forth the objectives of the Party's renaissance and cautioning them against excesses. Speaking before several hundred persons at the Lucerna banquet and dance hall in downtown Prague, Smrkovský impressed his young audience so much that on March 20, when he again spoke to the Young Communists and others, six thousand people crowded the Prague Congress Hall, built to accommodate half this number. A gray-haired man with a crew cut and a pleasant smile, Smrkovský quickly became a favorite of the crowds and, in a sense, the day-in-day-out spokesman for the revolution.

"You have the right and the duty to be more radical and more revolutionary," he said. "We older people have to see to it that during this great transformation of our country, of our state, nothing happens that would mean a catastrophe."

Following Smrkovský on the speakers' stand was Mrs. Marie Švermová, the Politburo member arrested at the outset of the 1950s purges, who was just about to be rehabilitated. Taking her listeners back to the black days of the previous decade, she remarked, "I had been better off in prison than living at a time when people, in a tremendously strained atmosphere, under psychological pressure, demanded a sentence, a sentence of death, for all those who had been described as criminals."

The six-hour session at the Congress Hall finally sent a resolution to the National Assembly demanding Novotný's resignation, a formal end to censorship, free travel abroad, a more effective economic reform, and, above all, "the truth" about everything. The resolution, however, emphasized that Czechoslovakia must remain a socialist state and never revert to capitalism and urged that "equal relations" be established "with the socialist countries, especially the Soviet Union."

The Czechoslovak press at the same time was purging and rejuvenating itself. On March 21, the Central Committee of the Union of Czechoslovak Journalists voted to convene an extraordinary congress to elect a new General Secretary, following the resignation of Adolf Hradecký. The same week, *Rudé Právo* took the extraordinary step of announcing that henceforth it would contribute "independently" to the formulation of KSČ policy. New editors were named for *Večerní Praha*, the youth daily *Mladá Fronta*, and the Bohemian provincial organ *Jihočeská Pravda*.

On March 20 the Presidium of the National Assembly met to discuss "the political situation in the country" in connection with the Presidential problem. Several Assembly committees urged a special plenary session to consider a motion of no confidence in Novotný. The Assembly's Deputy Chairman, Chudík, the pro-Novotný Presidium member from Slovakia, turned in his resignation.

The sense of crisis deepened. Dubček and the Party Presidium called the Central Committee into session for March 28. Simultaneously, the new leadership took security precautions. Intelligence reports had it that Soviet troops were moving on Czechoslovakia's eastern border, in areas adjacent to Slovakia, so the Army High Command canceled all major military exercises until after the Central Committee Plenum. Remembering how Novotný, Šejna, and Mamula had used the December maneuvers to try to stage a preventive military *coup d'état*, the Dubček group was taking no chances that they might awake the next day surrounded by tanks.

On March 21 pressures on the Party came from the Catholic church. Bishop František Tomášek, Apostolic Administrator of Prague, handed Dubček a petition signed by Czechoslovak bishops, priests, monks, nuns, and 22,317 Catholic laymen asking for the normalization of relations between the church and the state. Dubček promised to study it. A few hours earlier, the Presidium of the Peace Movement of the Catholic Clergy, a pro-Communist organization, dismissed its chairman, Josef Plojhar. Dr. Plojhar, a member of the Catholic People's Party, was also Minister of Health. He was replaced in the Peace Movement, which was to vanish altogether within a few months, by Bishop Tomášek.

On March 22 Novotný finally capitulated and submitted to the National Assembly his resignation as President of Czechoslovakia.

ESTEEMED COMRADES, DEPUTIES:

This is to notify you that I have decided to resign the office of President of the Czechoslovak Socialist Republic. I have made my decision after careful consideration, with regard to the internal situation at the present time, and motivated by the wish to help by this step the further development of the socialist society, the strengthening of our socialist country.

Please believe me that as President I have always endeavored to base my work on the interests of our working people, the interests of our country, in accord with our socialist aims.

I have striven as President to contribute to the strengthening of the international status of our Republic and to ensuring its security.

I was proposed by the Central Committee of the Communist Party of Czechoslovakia for the office of President, and confirmed by you, comrade-deputies.

I have already notified the Presidium of the Central Committee of the Communist Party of Czechoslovakia of my decision to resign the Presidency.

Please accept my thanks for your cooperation with me.

I wish our socialist country, the Czechoslovak Socialist Republic, many new achievements on her road ahead, in the interest of our people, in the interest of progress and peace.

Comradely yours,
A. Novotný

Later in the day, the Presidium of the National Assembly voted to accept Novotný's resignation. Under the provisions of the Constitution, the Presidential powers were transferred forthwith to the cabinet until the election of a new President. Premier Lenárt became Czechoslovakia's Acting President.

An era had come to an end. After nearly twelve years Antonín Novotný vacated Hradčany Castle, where he had resided as the third "worker President" since the 1948 Communist takeover. Except during a few feeble political convulsions in the months to come, Novotný became, by unspoken agreement between his foes and former friends, Czechoslovakia's leading nonperson.

On March 23 Dubček and four of his colleagues were summoned to a meeting with Warsaw Pact leaders in Dresden. The official communiqué on this surprise session issued by Tass emphasized that the main topic was a report by the Prague delegates on "the course of the realization of the decisions of the January Plenum of the Czechoslovak Communist Party which was directed at effectuating the line of the Czechoslovak Party's Thirteenth Congress."

This, of course, was double talk designed to create the totally misleading impression that the January Plenum, which had ousted Novotný from the Party's leadership and installed Dubček, had carried out the "line" of the Thirteenth Congress.

The reality was that Brezhnev, Gomułka, Kadár, Ulbricht, and Zhivkov had become greatly alarmed over the developments in Czechoslovakia since their joint visit to Prague the month before. Now they pressed Dubček for explanations as to just where he proposed to lead Czechoslovakia under his Action Program. He was in a rather difficult position before this self-constituted Communist inquisitional court, because only Černík among his fellow delegates could at that point be counted upon to support his progressive line. The three others were clearly in the conservative camp: Acting President and Premier Lenárt, Presidium member Kolder, and Slovak Party chief Bilak. Lenárt and Kolder had voted against Novotný in January, but now they were squarely in opposition to Dubček's policies.

Dresden was the first major confrontation between Czechoslovak liberals and Warsaw Pact hard-liners, but the split between them was papered over in the words of the Tass communiqué, which blandly announced that "confidence was expressed that the working class and all workers of the Czechoslovak Socialist Republic . . . will guarantee the further development of socialist construction in the country." Returning to Prague and anxiously pressed for an explanation of what had happened at the meeting, Dubček acknowledged that, indeed, fears had been voiced over possible dangers to socialism in Czechoslovakia. He said, however, that he had been able to assure his fellow Communist leaders that all was well in his country as far as the fortunes of Communism were concerned. To minimize the impression that Dubček had been called on the carpet, official announcements also spoke of discussions covering economic cooperation within Comecon.

Czechoslovakia was not the only problem on the minds of Brezhnev and his Warsaw Pact associates. From the beginning of 1968, much of

Eastern Europe had been in a state of dangerous ferment. Within weeks of Novotný's ouster, surging anti-Soviet sentiment had exploded in Warsaw and, a week before Gomułka arrived in Dresden, the Polish capital had witnessed its worst riots since 1956. The Romanians had added to the tension by walking out of a Communist parties conference in Budapest in February and refusing to attend the Dresden meeting. It must have seemed to the men in the Kremlin that the spirit of 1956 was being reborn.

The Polish unrest began, not surprisingly, with intellectual and artistic problems. They revolved around Adam Mickiewicz, one of Poland's great poets of the nineteenth century who had also been a fierce spokesman for Polish independence following the Russian occupation of the country's eastern and central regions in the wake of the partition of 1795. A native of Wilno, in the Lithuanian province of eastern Poland, Mickiewicz had belonged to secret anti-Russian societies, notably the Philomathians, who attracted chiefly poets and writers. In 1836 Mickiewicz was among the signers of the manifesto demanding freedom for Poland. Exiled to Paris, he became editor of the *Tribune des Peuples,* a publication advocating independence and egalitarianism for the Poles. But above all, Mickiewicz was a poet and a playwright. A romantic contemporary of Chopin, another exiled Polish patriot of genius, his accent on Poland and things Polish was recurrent in all his works from the epic poem *Pan Tadeusz (Sir Thaddeus)* to his outspokenly anti-Russian play *Dziady (Ancestors).* The Czarist rulers of Poland applied the same censorship methods to Mickiewicz as their Soviet successors were to apply a century later to their own and other East European artists, but in 1897 a more benign Russian governor permitted the erection of a statue of Mickiewicz in the center of Warsaw. No speeches were permitted when the monument was unveiled, but the thousands of Poles standing around the statue of the slim young man lost in thought wept unabashedly.

Even after the installation of the Communist regime in 1946, Mickiewicz remained a classical author to be read and studied. Then, in January 1968, Warsaw's National Theater conceived the idea of staging *Dziady.* In the context of 1968, this decision obviously had powerful political connotations. The producers must have remembered Mickiewicz's old dictum to "measure your powers by your purposes, not your purposes by your powers."

Night after night, then, Warsaw audiences cheered lines like "Full well I know the kind of grace the Muscovite will show ripping the fetters from my feet and hands to rivet on my spirit yet heavier bands!" and the remark in the play that "the only things that Moscow sends us are jack-asses, idiots, and spies." Within a week, *Dziady* acquired the proportions of a major anti-Soviet demonstration and presently Gomułka personally ordered a ban on further performances.

This ban fitted into a larger campaign of repression in Poland against intellectuals and Jews. Already in 1966 the Marxist philosopher Kołakow-ski had been expelled from the Communist Party for telling a rally of Warsaw students that it would be pointless to celebrate the tenth anni-versary of the Polish October because the nation still lacked liberty. Following the Middle East war in 1967, the Gomułka regime not only broke diplomatic relations with Israel, but embarked on a domestic campaign against "Zionist elements" at home. In the best tradition of anti-Semitism, Jews were expelled from jobs and deprived of apartments. Though the Jewish population had dropped from three million in 1939 to some thirty thousand in 1968—the Nazi exterminations had so dramat-ically reduced it—official anti-Semitism was now practiced with the verve of prewar days. This gave rise to bitter jokes, like the story of the com-manding general of the Polish Air Force banning further celebrations in the officers' mess of victories of Israeli Mystères and Mirages over Soviet-built MiGs: the officers, the story went, were delighted to see the MiGs destroyed for Polish anti-Soviet reasons—"because we have just dis-covered that Israelis are Jews." Another rather macabre story had a Warsaw Jew tell a friend that all was well with him although he had lost his ministry job, his daughter had been expelled from the university, and the family was deprived of its apartment; "You should see the fun I have," he added, "denouncing the Poles who hid me during the Nazi occupa-tion."

By March the situation had become a crisis. The Polish Writers' Union protested the ban on *Dziady,* and Kołakowski emerged from self-imposed silence to say that Polish culture was being destroyed by the regime. Thousands of Polish students occupied Warsaw University buildings, and the regime sent the militia and armed workers to oust them. In the fighting that went on for several days, scores were injured, and it devel-oped that the student leaders included the sons and daughters of some of the top figures in the Party and government.

Immediately afterward, the Party blamed the student riots on "Zionist" agents. Gomułka, who twelve years earlier had fired the imaginations of Poles as a great patriotic Communist leader, went on radio and television on March 19 to say that "a significant part of the student youth of Warsaw and of other academic centers has been deceived and misled by forces contrary to socialism." To him, the moderate reformers were just as dangerous as the "radicals" demanding a break with the Soviet Union. Clearly, Gomułka was not about to tolerate experiments with "Socialism With a Human Face" in Poland. Four days later he went to Dresden to the Warsaw Pact's inquisitional questioning of Dubček. Communist informants say that Gomułka and East Germany's Walter Ulbricht began then to urge Brezhnev to start thinking of a possible invasion of Czechoslovakia. There are reasons to believe, however, that the idea had already occurred to Brezhnev and his marshals.

At the Dresden meeting, the Warsaw Pact leadership did not have the company of President Ceauşescu of Romania. Only four weeks earlier, a delegation of the Romanian Party, led by Paul Niculescu-Mizil, a member of the Presidium's Standing Committee, had walked out of the preparatory meeting in Budapest for the world Communist conference, after a Syrian Communist leader had attacked them for maintaining diplomatic relations with Israel. However, Ceauşescu attended a summit meeting of the Warsaw Pact in Sofia, March 5–8. There, his contribution to Communist unity was his continuing refusal to sign the nuclear nonproliferation treaty, on the presumed grounds that Romania did not want to tie her hands in any future contingency. This made Romania the only Warsaw Pact nation to stand against the treaty. The same attitude was taken, of course, by both France and China, which have nuclear weapons.

Although the communiqué of the Dresden meeting refrained from direct attacks on Prague, the East German propaganda machine launched an assault on the Czechoslovak reformers four days later, on March 27, and on the eve of the crucial session of the KSČ's Central Committee. In contrast with the belabored Dresden communiqué, which said the meeting had "strengthened relations among socialist countries on a basis of cordial friendship, equality, mutual trust, mutual support and non-interference in the affairs of other states," Professor Kurt Hager, the chief ideologist, said in a speech before an East Berlin Philosophers' Congress, "In their campaign against our socialist constitution, West German propaganda centers refer . . . to the events in Czechoslovakia. They diligently quote statements by Forestry Minister Smrkovský; they produce in great detail the attacks of journalists and writers against the Central Committee and the leading role of the Party. They openly express their sympathy with these statements and phenomena in the Czechoslovak Socialist Republic. . . . The behavior of Smrkovský and others fills them [the West Germans] with hope that the ČSSR might be engulfed in the turmoil of evolution."

As soon as Hager's speech was read in Prague, Foreign Minister David, himself an orthodox hard-liner, called in East German Ambassador Peter Florin to deliver a formal protest. Simultaneously, the Czechoslovak Ambassador in East Berlin protested in person to East German Foreign Minister Otto Winzer and Secretary of the East German Party Erich Honecker. In March the East Germans banned the circulation of the Prague German-language daily—published for the German minorities in Czechoslovakia but normally available in East Berlin—presumably to prevent the spread of the contagion. Radio Prague programs had begun to be jammed both in East Germany and Poland.

In Moscow, *Pravda* unveiled the new line of indirectly but unmistakably attacking Czechoslovakia through criticism of the Western press. On March 28 an article denounced "slanders" in Western newspapers "presenting the relations between the Communist parties of the Soviet Union and Czechoslovakia in a false light, using the old formula about 'Soviet interference.'" But *Pravda* claimed this was in vain because "in actuality, the relations among socialist countries have been and are being built on the basis of Party friendship, equality and confidence, mutual support and noninterference in each other's affairs." For whoever's benefit this line was being expounded, it was not to last much longer. In fact, events in the next few days were to change the situation in Czechoslovakia and throughout the Communist world.

The crucial and long-awaited Plenum of the KSČ Central Committee opened in the Spanish Hall of Hradčany Castle on March 28, with Alexander Dubček in the chair. Nearly three months had elapsed since he took power, and truly revolutionary changes had occurred in Czechoslovak society. Now Dubček and his associates, obviously undaunted by the Dresden inquisition, were ready to spell out the revolutionary program and to bring in their own men to carry it out.

But the committee's first order of business was to name a new President of Czechoslovakia. The committee voted to accept Novotný's resignation, then adjourned briefly to let the Presidium and National Assembly agree on a new chief executive. Considerable support had developed, especially among the young people, for the candidacy of Čestmir Císař, the onetime Education Minister and Ambassador to Romania and currently in charge of education and science in the Central Committee. Dubček and his advisers, however, appeared to feel that Císař lacked sufficient stature on the one hand and was too identified with the extreme progressive wing of the Party on the other. The point was made during one of the Presidium meetings that to elect Císař would constitute too much of a provocation to the Soviet Union.

The alternate choice was General Ludvík Svoboda, seventy-two, who had been Defense Minister in 1945, then a Deputy Premier, and finally, through a series of errors, a prisoner during the purges of the 1950s. The white-haired, blue-eyed, and grandfatherly Svoboda was among the first to be rehabilitated and, in 1965, was named a Hero of the Soviet Union. Since his rehabilitation, he had spent his time writing military history. He appeared to be the perfect candidate for a figurehead President, certain to please the Czechoslovaks as well as Moscow, and Dubček proposed his name to the Presidium. The idea was immediately accepted. Even Novotný, still a Presidium member, voted for the old general. On March 30 the National Assembly voted on the Party's recommendation: Svoboda, the only candidate, received 282 votes out of 288 ballots cast. Much was made of the fact that in Czech the word "*Svoboda*" means "freedom." The new President was meant to be a figurehead, but his elevation was considered a happy omen for Czechoslovakia. Prague citizens noticed another significant omen: neither soldiers nor policemen any longer wore red-star insignia on their caps. Nobody seemed to know who had given this order, but it was another sign of the changing times.

The Central Committee reconvened on Monday, April 1. The main speaker was Dubček, and he proceeded to outline the ideas of the Action Program, the new role of the Communist Party, and all the policies of "Socialism with a Human Face" that had been accumulating in Czechoslovakia since January.

Addressing the Central Committee in his slow, grave voice, Dubček recognized that after January, when the new leadership "opened the door to the new developments and took the lead, it could have no detailed plan as to how these events would unfold." This spontaneous process, he argued, had advantages over the former Party methods in which everything had been manipulated in advance. Yet Dubček was eminently aware of the fears and suspicions both among the old-line Communists at home and among his Warsaw Pact allies that the events in Czechoslovakia were endangering the supremacy of the Communist Party. With this in mind, Dubček told the Central Committee, "Many people have been taken by surprise to such an extent that they are expressing fears whether the Party is not giving way to pressures, whether it will not give up its positions, if it is not being pushed by these developments, and whether it will be able to deal with incorrect attitudes and harmful demands which always occur in that kind of process."

And, to be sure, political stirrings that few, if any, Communist states would tolerate were beginning. Only the day before, on March 31, three thousand former political prisoners met in Prague to form an association they called K-231, which stood for the number of the law "for the protection of the Republic" under which they had been imprisoned. The K-231 Clubs organized branches throughout the Republic with the avowed aim of obtaining rehabilitation, justice, and indemnification for the victims of the terror. But, inevitably, there were founder members of the K-231 who were already thinking of turning the clubs into a political group. Under Communist law, whatever parties existed in Czechoslovakia (the KSČ and the captive Socialist and People's parties) and professional and youth organizations had to be fitted into the all-embracing National Front or be organs of the Communist Party itself. But the K-231 at this stage had no thought of joining the National Front. It asked the Interior Ministry for a registration permit and, pending a decision, simply proceeded to function. I remember discussing the future of the club with one of its leaders, an elderly retired general who had spent twelve years in prison for attempting to flee Czechoslovakia in 1949. He told me that at the moment the K-231 did not regard itself as a political group, but, he added significantly, "It is hard to predict where the political momentum may carry us."

Among Communist and non-Communist intellectuals, a number of philosophers and writers were making plans to launch as soon as possible an organization they were to call the Club of Committed Non-Party Members. Among their leaders was the philosopher Ivan Sviták. As the ideas of this club crystallized, it became increasingly clear that what they had in mind was a political party that perhaps could someday challenge the KSČ in an open election.

Dubček was aware of all these movements. There was, he told the Central Committee, an "enormous amount of differentiated and opposing interests and attitudes, representing certain short- and long-term interests of the most varied social groups." He warned that the rebirth of "certain nonsocialist modes" and the cries for "revenge" must not be legalized "under the cover of democracy and rehabilitation." The fundamental concept held by Dubček and his friends—and this is a key point that has to be borne in mind about the inebriating days of the Prague Spring—was that the Communist Party—changed and rejuvenated—could carry the day democratically in the face of all the other surging ideas. "Let us not be afraid of this wave but let us learn from it," he said. "Confidence in the Party and self-confidence within the Party are growing."

In expounding these new notions, Dubček had already consciously embarked on a collision course with Brezhnev. Four days after Dresden and the day before Svoboda's election to the Presidency, the Soviet leader had delivered an ideological speech before an audience of Moscow Communists that was unmistakably addressed to Czechoslovakia. In this speech, Brezhnev emphasized the need for the monopoly of the Communist Party's "guidance and directing influence," ignoring the importance of the ideas "from below" that now loomed so crucial in the renaissance of the Czechoslovak Party. As Prague was granting its intellectuals unprecedented freedoms of thought and action, Brezhnev was advocating still tighter controls. "The ideological struggle in our times," Brezhnev said, "is the sharpest front of the class struggle." "Capitalism" was feeding on "nationalist and revisionist elements" in the Communist countries.

But Dubček's view of history and of the future was devastatingly different. To Dubček, the year 1968—unlike the Stalinist days of the Cold War—called for the realization "of the new phase of socialist revolution in the epoch of nonantagonistic relations." This, he said, led to "the need to develop, shape, and create a political system that would correspond to the new situation." What was necessary was a new program of Marxist revolution attuned to the world of the late 1960s: "Because of the scientific theory with which the Party is equipped, because of the Party's historical achievements, because the process of reform and the entry into the next stage of development of our country is being accomplished under the auspices of the Party, we think that we have the right to declare—with a better justification than ever—the Communist Party goes on being the decisive, organized, progressive force in our society."

Dubček went on to explain that while the Communist Party must make a decisive impact on the society, it must defend its positions through persuasion and not through force. "Authority must be renewed. . . . It is never given to anyone once and for all."

Having matured in three months from an apparatus man to an ideologue with a program, Dubček now proceeded to insist that within the new framework, Czechoslovakia must develop a "socialist democracy" in which the KSČ, the government, and the National Assembly would each play its separate role against the background of the independence of all "social and interest organizations." This was, indeed, a new Communist compromise: Dubček emphasized that he was not proposing a return to the pre-1948 formal parliamentary system, but, at the same time, was recommending that every Czechoslovak organization—be it the Army or the Sokol sports clubs—cease operating as obedient transmission belts for the Communist Party.

This, of course, was the intellectual crux of the Action Program. Its chief features were free ideological play under Communist guidance, a real economic reform, and the rehabilitation of the terror victims. Dubček requested the Central Committee to rescind the September decision expelling the writers Ivan Klima, Ludvík Vaculík, and Antonín Liehm from the KSČ and to suspend the disciplinary action against Milan Kundera and Pavel Kohout. The committee did so. (By coincidence, the regional court at Ústí-nad-Labem, a north Bohemian city, acted on the same day to revoke the convictions of 1954, approved by the Supreme Court, condemning eleven Social Democrats for alleged "antistate activities" to prison terms of from eight to twenty-four years.)

Between April 2 and 4, the Central Committee dealt the final blow to the old Party leadership and produced a new KSČ Presidium, Party Secretariat, cabinet, and National Assembly directorship. But it was a reflection of a deepening split within the Party that Dubček could not, despite his wide popular support, hammer together a fully progressive leadership but had to compromise with the old guard. This inability to impose himself over the KSČ was to plague him to the very end.

In the Party, Novotný, Hendrych, Laštovička, Dolanský, Šimůnek, Chudík and Lenárt resigned their Presidium seats. Pastyřík lost his seat as an alternate Presidium member. Hendrych was dropped from the Secretariat and his post as chairman of the Central Committee's Ideological Commission. In a farewell speech on April 2, Hendrych said, "For the fear for the unity of the Party I tried to reconcile extremes that were irreconcilable. . . . That was my worst mistake." Koucký, the pro-Moscow Secretary, chairman of the Central Committee's Legal Commission, and member of the Ideological Commission, went the same day. Martin Vaculík, the Prague boss, was removed as a member of the Secretariat. Pavel Hron, head of the Central Committee's Control and Auditing Commission, was likewise fired.

Novotný, who while speaking for over an hour in his defense was often interrupted with derisive laughter, was deprived of his last remaining post as chairman of the National Front. But he managed to slip in a warning against the new trends, saying that "negative forces in the country are being activated." Referring to the mounting attacks on his conservatives, he said that, "in connection with rehabilitation, when everything is supposed to be rehabilitated, a campaign has arisen that can do nothing but harm to the Party." Novotný's parting shot was his remark that "we must not be confused because everyone says nowadays that he is for socialism."

In the decapitation of the old leadership, Laštovička resigned as National Assembly Chairman and Chudík as its Vice-Chairman and head of the Slovak National Council.

But the new Presidium proved to be far from satisfactory to the progressives, and strategic posts in the KSČ Secretariat were uncomfortably occupied by conservatives who had no use for Dubček's policies and wasted no time in sabotaging them. In the eleven-man Presidium, Dubček could count only on Smrkovský (who was also named Chairman of the National Assembly); young Josef Špaček from Brno; František Kriegel, the heart specialist and Spanish War veteran who simultaneously was chosen chairman of the National Front; and Oldřich Černík. The identifiable conservatives were Vasil Bilak, First Secretary of the Slovak Party and long an enemy of the liberals; Drahomír Kolder; Oldřich Švestka, the strongly pro-Soviet editor of *Rudé Právo*; Jan Piller; and Emil Rigo. František Barbírek, the new head of the Slovak National Council, tended to stay neutral. So the Presidium was split right down the middle. The three alternate members of the Presidium were Martin Vaculík and Antonín Kapek, head of the ČKD engineering works, both staunch conservatives, and Lenárt, who increasingly veered toward the orthodox wing.

Kolder, Lenárt, and Alois Indra, former Minister of Transportation under Novotný, were the conservatives. Císař was the only out-and-out liberal. Slovakia's Stefan Sadovský was a centrist with progressive sympathies. The Central Committee's Secretariat had Dubček, Císař, Zdeněk Mlynář, and Václav Slavik as progressives; Indra, Kolder, and Lenárt as conservatives; and Sadovský and Oldřich Voleník as "neutrals." Miloš Jakeš, an outspoken conservative, was named to run the key Central Committee Control and Auditing Commission. But Špaček headed the Ideological Commission.

It was with this mixed bag of progressive and conservative Communists that Dubček launched the Action Program, approved on April 5, 1968, by the Central Committee after its members had discussed it in floor speeches.

The Action Program, a sixty-three-page document, proclaimed as its basic tenet that there existed a special "Czechoslovak way to socialism," and it dismissed Brezhnev's insistence on continued class struggle with the statement that "the Party decisively condemns the attempts to set individual classes and groups of socialist society against each other . . . and it will remove every cause creating tensions among them."

Addressing itself to the economic situation as it had existed in the pre-January days, the Action Program lashed out at the favoritism dispensed by the Party in the name of Communist "egalitarianism." This "false egalitarianism" had been one of the main brakes on intensive economic development and the improvement of the standard of living. "[It] is harmful because it protects lazy good-for-nothings and irresponsible workers against self-sacrificing and industrious people, unqualified against qualified workers, technically and professionally backward men against gifted people with initiative."

In a major departure from precedent, the Action Program specifically removed the ban on non-Communists in top industrial, educational, and other jobs. The emphasis was on a coherent and creative society led but not stifled by the Communist Party. The Action Program called for full rehabilitation of the victims of the past, for the creation of a federalized Czecho-Slovak Republic, and for a new constitution to replace the Soviet-model charter of 1960. The problem of freedom of opinion and culture was thus expressed: "The social influence of the arts is not without political significance. We shall take care that freedom of opinion, guaranteed by the Constitution, is fully respected. The Communist Party cannot, however, renounce its task to inspire and to give up the attempt to make works of art help effectively to shape the socialist man in his struggle for the transformation of the world."

In the foreign-policy section, the Action Program duly took note of the struggle against "the forces of imperialist reaction" and pledged friendly relations with Communist countries and parties. But it refused to isolate Czechoslovakia from the West: "In regard to developed capitalist countries, we shall actively pursue the policy of peaceful coexistence. Our geographic situation as well as the needs and opportunities of an industrial country demand a more active European policy aimed at the development of mutually advantageous relations and the safeguarding of the collective security of the European continent."

Summing up the hopes and expectations of the Czechoslovak Communist Party at this watershed, the Action Program concluded with these words:

> We now have to go through unusual situations. We shall experiment, give socialist development new forms, use creative Marxist thinking and the experience of the international workers' movement, rely on the correct understanding of social development in Czechoslovakia. It is a country which bears the responsibility, before the international Communist movement, for the evaluation and utilization of its relatively advanced material base, uncommonly high level of education, and undeniable democratic traditions. If we did not use such an opportunity, nobody could ever forgive us.

On April 6, the day after the Action Program was approved and the Central Committee concluded its historic session, Premier Lenárt submitted the resignation of his government to President Svoboda. Immediately, the President asked Oldřich Černík, the new Presidium member and the champion of economic reform, to form a new cabinet.

Two days later, on April 8, Černík produced the new government that, with the new Party leadership, was to lead Czechoslovakia along the brave new path of "human socialism." But just like the Party leadership, the Černík cabinet offered an odd mixture of men who both supported and opposed the Action Program and all it represented.

Among the five Deputy Premiers, Slovakia was represented by Gustav Husák and Professor Petr Colotka, an intellectual. Both were regarded as solid progressives. Husák's direct responsibility was the preparation of a new electoral law, a new constitution, and the federalization of the Czech lands and Slovakia. Another liberal Deputy Premier was Ota Šik. The fourth Deputy Premier, František Hamouz, was a colorless man whose task was to represent Czechoslovakia on Comecon. Surprisingly, the fifth was Lubomir Strougal, who had been Novotný's Interior Minister. With him, the pro-Moscow conservatives had a foothold in the cabinet. Curiously, then, the Prague Spring's government was born with the elements of its own destruction built in. Barely six months were to elapse before Černík, Husák (who in April was not even a member of the Central Committee), and Strougal were to emerge as the trinity bent on destroying the Prague Spring on Moscow's behest. Eighteen months later, Husák and Strougal were to share the power alone as Černík, too, fell by the wayside.

The twenty-three-man cabinet offered other curious combinations. The liberal wing was represented by Interior Minister Josef Pavel, veteran of

Spain and one of the first purge victims; Foreign Minister Jiří Hájek, protector of the intellectuals in the last Novotný phase; Culture Minister Miroslav Galuška, who had served as ambassador in London; Education Minister Vladimir Kadlec; Justice Minister Bohuslav Kučera; and Consumer Goods Industry Minister Mrs. Božena Machačová. But the cabinet also included Oldřich Pavlovský as Minister of Internal Trade, a man who was so pro-Soviet that his own staff refused to work with him; Minister of Foreign Trade Václav Valeš, with strong conservative sympathies; Minister of Chemical Industry Stanislav Razl, who was to join in time the pro-Soviet forces; Mines Minister František Penc, a colorless conservative; and Defense Minister Lieutenant General Martin Dzúr, whose role before and after the invasion remains wrapped in mystery. Dzúr, a Slovak, had fought in the German Army, deserted in the Soviet Union to join the Czechoslovak brigade fighting alongside Soviet troops, became a Communist Party member, and enjoyed a rapid rise in the Czechoslovak Army culminating in a course at the Soviet General Staff School and the post of Deputy Defense Minister in 1962.

As seen from the outside, the new Czechoslovak regime was something of an iceberg. The visible heroes and advocates of the new "socialist democracy" were Dubček, Svoboda, Smrkovský, and Černík, and, on a lower level, Ota Šik, Špaček, Pavel, Hájek, and Galuška. And there were the liberal intellectuals ranging from Ludvík Vaculík to Goldstücker and Liehm. But hidden beneath the waters were the foes of reform: Bilak, Indra, Kolder, Strougal, and Lenárt—and the mystery men Husák and Dzúr.

XVI

The Prague Spring

From the outset, the new leadership was a house divided. More and more, Dubček had to act as arbiter and moderator, to keep alive the progressive spirit without unduly antagonizing the conservatives and Moscow.

It was a perilous balancing act, and it was proper to ask whether Dubček at this juncture of events was truly leading the revolution, as his speech to the KSČ Central Committee suggested, or was simply being carried on the crest of its wave. Actually, both evaluations may have been accurate: there were areas of policy, such as economic reform and the renaissance of the Party, in which he wished to proceed with deliberate speed, while in other areas—the mounting questioning of *all* Marxist-Leninist dogmas and the increasing freedom of speech—he would have preferred caution. But the situation was too fluid and fast moving to permit him to stabilize his own thinking.

Even in the field of economic reform Dubček was under pressure from both sides. When the Economic Council was established on April 12 to plan major economic decisions, it was the conservative Strougal, a man not notably versed in economics, who became its head. Ota Šik, the architect of the reform, was not even vice-chairman but simply an ordinary member. In the Presidium, the member in charge of the economy was Kolder, a strong conservative with close Moscow connections despite his earlier championing of the economic reform and his anti-Novotný stand. From the very beginning, then, the reform was again being stymied. Šik wanted to move rapidly with industrial decentralization, the creation of a competitive market economy, and encouragement to limited private enterprise in the hands of families, but Strougal and Kolder succeeded in blocking his efforts.

Dubček and his progressive friends soon realized that the March-April Plenum had not even begun to solve the political problems. Out of the Central Committee's 110 members, at least 40 were solid conservatives and at least 30 others tended to the *status quo* rather than to reform. The roster of the conservatives on the Central Committee included men like Novotný, who had been allowed to keep his seat, Bilak, Barbírek, former Foreign Minister David, Dolanský, the eternal Zdeněk Fierlinger, Hendrych, Hoffman, Chudík, Indra, Kapek, Kolder, Koucký, Kudrna, Laštovička, Lenárt, Lomský, Vilém Nový (back in the conservative camp after his years in prison), Pastyřík, Internal Trade Minister Pavlovský, Jan Pelnař, Presidium members Piller and Rigo, Šimůnek, Švestka, Deputy Premier Strougal, and Martin Vaculík. Most of these men, the progressive leaders realized, would have to be expelled from the Central Committee if the Action Program were ever to be properly implemented. Novotný no longer counted in the calculations, so thoroughly had he been discredited, but the new orthodox command was crystallizing around Bilak, Kolder, Indra, Hoffman, Koucký, Strougal, Kapek, Piller, and Rigo. These were the men who already in mid-April were preparing a counter-offensive, marshaling domestic allies, and plotting with the Soviet Embassy and Chervonenko. The progressives' plan to defeat them was twofold: to eliminate at least twelve of the most objectionable members at the Plenum late in May and then to hold the Fourteenth Party Congress sometime late in the summer to bring in a whole new Central Committee with the support of what it was hoped would be progressive delegates to be elected throughout the country in preparation for the congress.

All these strategic and counterstrategic plans were laid during April. From the progressives' side, one of the most powerful thrusts came as early as April 2 in the form of an article in *Student* by Ivan Sviták, who claimed that new evidence had been unearthed to indicate that Jan Masaryk had been murdered and demanded an immediate investigation to ascertain the truth. So sensitive was this issue that the following day, April 3, the Prosecutor General's office assigned Dr. Jiří Kotlar, head of the investigation department, to reopen the case. The implication was obvious from the outset that if Jan Masaryk had indeed been murdered, then the Soviet Union had something to do with it. On April 16 *Rudé*

Právo added further credence to the murder theory by asking in print what role "Beria's gorillas" had played in this affair. Clearly with tongue in cheek, *Rudé Právo* then appealed to "our Soviet friends" to provide help in clarifying the circumstances of Masaryk's mysterious death.

Once the implications of Soviet criminal involvement in the Masaryk case were brought into the open, the Czechoslovak press plunged headlong into the whole issue of Stalinist terror and the function of Soviet and Czechoslovak security services in it. In mid-April, the Defense Ministry's *Obrana Lidu* published an article by Lieutenant Colonel Milan Richter, the new chief military prosecutor, declaring that "it must be said frankly that the most flagrant illegalities did not originate in our country but were a direct result of Beria's 'long arm.'" Colonel Richter wrote that "after the Twentieth Congress of the Soviet Communist Party, the chief [Soviet] advisers of the former Czechoslovak Minister of Defense, Generals Makarov and Likhachev, were sentenced to death in Moscow." Actually, Makarov and Likhachev had been the top MGB liaison officers in Czechoslovakia preparing the Slánský trial, after completing the Rajk trial in Budapest. The Czechoslovak Defense Minister at the time was Čepička, Gottwald's son-in-law. Now that the fashionable thing in Prague was to blame the Soviet Union for the purges, Karol Bacílek, Security Minister in 1952, came forth with a statement that they had been imposed on an unwilling Gottwald by Stalin and told the story of Anastas Mikoyan coming to Prague to set the stage for the trials. Bacílek, obviously, was preparing his own defense, but it was too late.

The flood of revelations about the purges was now accompanied by a wave of suicides. Dr. Josef Breštanský, Vice-President of the Czechoslovak Supreme Court, was found on April 2 hanging from a tree in the woods of Babice south of Prague. He had been missing since March 28, and his death was officially described as suicide. Breštanský, who had had the task of reviewing the purge trials, was said to have been personally involved in their preparations. On April 26 Dr. Josef Sommer, who had served as the Ruzyň prison doctor in 1951 and 1952, killed himself at his Prague home. Among Sommer's victims had been General Pavel, the new Interior Minister. On April 27, Lieutenant Colonel Jiří Počepický, chief of investigations in the Prague public security department, shot himself in a forest near the health resort of Maríanské Lázně. At the same time, the Military Prosecutor's Office announced that the suicide in March of former Deputy Defense Minister Janko—the general involved in the abortive Novotný coup conspiracy—had been politically motivated.

Janko, the investigators said charitably, had feared that the new trends in Czechoslovakia were "going too far to the right" to suit him.

Meanwhile, the Czechoslovak Communist Party's Action Program and quickening developments in Czechoslovakia led to deepening concern in Moscow. The Soviet press ignored the Central Committee session and the Action Program for a full week, but the Soviet Party's Central Committee met on April 9–10 to hear Brezhnev's report on ideological problems in general and Czechoslovakia in particular. Addressing himself to the theme of "Pressing Problems of the International Situation and the Struggle of the Communist Party of the Soviet Union for Unity of the World Communist Movement," Brezhnev, it was reported, dealt at length with the Prague events, although the text of his speech was never published. But the official communiqué made a point of stressing "the significance of the Dresden meeting."

The Moscow Central Committee session was a major milestone in contemporary Communist history inasmuch as the communiqué said that the body had "confirmed anew the readiness of our Party to do all that is necessary for the steady political, economic, and defensive strengthening of the Socialist Commonwealth." This was a preview of what was to become known later as the Brezhnev Doctrine, or the right the Soviet Union had arrogated to itself to intervene militarily in any Communist country where it felt socialism was in danger. Ostensibly speaking of Soviet problems, the communiqué added that the Central Committee had "ordered an irreconcilable struggle against hostile ideology" and that it had declared that "the strengthening of all the ideological activities of our Party assumes special significance."

When *Pravda* finally got around on April 12 to reporting the April 5 proceedings of the KSČ Central Committee Plenum, it constructed its account around the speeches of the fiercest conservatives expressing their fears over "excesses" and dangers to Communism. As the alleged star speaker of the Prague Plenum, *Pravda* selected a totally obscure Central Committee candidate member named Bohus Chnoupek who denounced "rightist excesses" and threatened that the workers would take to the streets to defend the correct brand of Communism. In other words, Soviet readers gained the impression that the Prague meeting was a victorious defense of orthodoxy. The news story on the Action Program emphasized passages that made the KSČ and the Soviet Party appear as two peas in a pod. But the same issue of *Pravda* came up with a two-page article on ideological purity and warnings against "revisionism." The context was clear to even the densest *Pravda* readers.

The rising attacks on the Prague reformers were not confined to *Pravda* and Comrade Chnoupek. Shortly after the approval of the Action Program, Vasil Bilak had this to say about Czechoslovakia's newly emancipated press, radio, and television:

> The Communists employed in radio and television must realize that radio and television are instruments of state policies, that they have not ceased to be instruments of the ideology and policies of the socialist state, and that for this reason they cannot serve anything else than the interests of the socialist state.
>
> I think that it is a shortcoming in the work of the mass-communications media not to have properly reflected all the wealth of ideas and suggestions contained in the many documents of the Central Committee, in Comrade Dubček's speeches. . . . Every thesis deserves to be thoroughly explained and commented upon in order that the views and the minds of the people be united toward positive work.
>
> Naturally, it is more comfortable to collect sensational reports, to reprint articles from the bourgeois press, to publish all sorts of unilateral statements, but it is of little social value. Those who work in this fashion probably do not realize that they are ignoring the progressive role of their own Party and that they do injustice to many honest people.

But neither the Soviet nor the Czechoslovak imprecations seemed to have any effect on the rising momentum of the Prague revolution. The original anti-Novotný coalition had been dispersed during the debates over the Action Program and the leadership changes, and now the battle was on between the two camps. Dubček and his allies had somehow succeeded in pushing the Action Program through the Central Committee, but the reaction against it was coming strong. On the other hand, the progressives were consolidating their positions. On April 9 President Svoboda named Miloš Čeřovský as the new Prosecutor General. On April 18 the National Assembly confirmed Smrkovský as its chairman. Dr. Otmar Boček was elected Supreme Court President. And on the same day, the KSČ Presidium instructed Premier Černík to present recommendations for "bilaterally advantageous economic cooperation between Czechoslovakia and the Soviet Union." This was clearly intended as an effort to end the *unilateral* situation in which Czechoslovakia supplied the Soviet Union with machinery and raw materials, receiving in exchange unusable ruble credits. The instructions to Černík coincided with reports that the Prague government urgently needed four hundred million dollars in hard-currency credits to retool its obsolescent industry with Western equipment. Prague, the story went, had first asked Moscow to pay back some of its debts in hard currency. When rebuffed, it was said, Prague had turned to the International Monetary Fund, though Czechoslovakia was not a member, and to a West European consortium. The report, published in Western newspapers, had so annoyed the Soviet Union that on April 17 the Finance Ministry issued a specific denial. But in general, no opportunity was lost to show where Czechoslovak sympathies lay. When a group of North Vietnamese students at Prague University burned an American flag during an antiwar demonstration on April 27, a delegation of *Czechoslovak* students appeared the next day at the chancery of the United States Embassy to offer their apologies and present a new flag. But the only flag the students could produce was the old forty-eight-star banner. Seldom had the American diplomats in Prague been so moved as on that day.

The latter part of April was largely devoted to rehabilitation procedures, among other pressing concerns. To do justice to the victims of the purges and subsequent punishments was one of the key points of the Action Program and one of the most burning issues in Czechoslovakia. To an important extent, the reputation of the new regime rested on its fulfillment of its rehabilitation pledges. On April 25 the Party recommended "complete Party and political rehabilitation" of Zdeněk Hejzlar, former chairman of the Czechoslovak Youth Union, who had been expelled from the KSČ in 1952 on "the basis of a tendentious, false, and framed charge." Hejzlar was presently named director of the Czechoslovak State Radio. Simultaneously, Dr. Boček, the new President of the Supreme Court, ordered a review of the 1962 trial of former Interior Minister Barák, the only important Czechoslovak figure still in prison. General Pavel, the new Interior Minister, canceled the ministry's decision of August 1967 that deprived Ladislav Mňačko of his Czechoslovak citizenship for having gone to Israel. Nine philosophy professors at Charles University were rehabilitated by a special commission of their faculty. In a ground-floor office at the Czernin Palace, a hand-written notice on the door announced that the Rehabilitation Commission of the Foreign Ministry was meeting there from April 26 on. And the Prague Municipal Court reopened the 1949 "subversive activities" cases of the late General J. Kutlvašr, two other officers, and two civilians.

On April 29 President Svoboda performed the symbolic act of returning the Order of Socialism and the Order of February 25, First Class, to the family of Rudolf Slánský and the Order of February 25, First Class, to the family of Otto Šling. The two men were now fully rehabilitated and vindicated almost sixteen years after their deaths.

The last week of April also witnessed the presentation by Černík's cabinet of its program to the National Assembly. Implementing the philosophy contained in the Party's Action Program, it set forth the principle that henceforth the government would be primarily responsible to the National Assembly rather than the Party. This was a democratic step in the right direction, but the fact remained that all the top cabinet and National Assembly officials were at the same time leaders of the KSČ (both Premier Černík and National Assembly Chairman Smrkovský were members of the Party Presidium), so the gesture tended to be more symbolic than real. But, as events were to show, the National Assembly took itself very seriously. The government also pledged to redefine the responsibilities of the Interior and Justice ministries to assure complete legality in all their proceedings. It was not in vain that Interior Minister Pavel had been one of the most brutally tortured prisoners of the 1950s purges; now he was in the vanguard in assuring the protection of citizens' rights.

At the same time, Prague received two visitors who were somewhat less than welcome. One of them was Soviet Marshal Yakubovsky, Supreme Commander of the Warsaw Pact forces, and he came ostensibly to meet the new Party and government heads. But it was his second visit in a month, and it left many Czechs quite uncomfortable, even though it would seem normal for the Pact's Supreme Commander to pay a visit to a member state. The second visitor was Bulgaria's Todor Zhivkov. He came to sign a new treaty of friendship, cooperation, and mutual assistance—an undertaking that was to seem rather peculiar four months later. Zhivkov had just weathered a conspiracy in the Bulgarian region of Vratsa, and he was confident and self-assured as he surveyed the Czechoslovak scene.

The month of May brought both hope and fear to the Czechoslovaks. The hope was that their revolution for "Socialism With a Human Face" would succeed, and the fear was that Soviet power would kill it before it reached fruition. Yet, as the sun bathed Prague in its golden rays on May Day, the overwhelming sentiments were faith and joy.

In Communist countries, May Day is usually celebrated with military parades and heavy Party rhetoric. In Prague, May Day had become associated since 1961 with student freedom riots against the police and a sense of ugly and desperate frustration. But in 1968 it was a day of fulfillment. The hero of the day was, of course, Alexander Dubček. His long Pinocchio nose pointing up and his blue eyes twinkling, he smiled and laughed as the crowds cheered him wherever he went. He was his usual shy self, but he accepted gifts of flowers, signed autographs, and allowed himself to be mobbed by admirers until the police reluctantly and apologetically surrounded him with a protective cordon.

Unlike past May Days, this one did not have Communist crowds brought to downtown Prague in trucks and busses by the Party to hail the leader. This time, the people came spontaneously and in enormous numbers. Boy Scouts, Sokol athletes, and bearded students paraded before Dubček, and other Czechs waved American and Israeli banners and good-natured posters. On the Václavské Námešti and in the Old Town Square the mood was of a country fair. The girls were pretty and the men smiled and cheered.

On a more solemn note, President Svoboda used the occasion of May Day to confer the title of Hero of the Czechoslovak Socialist Republic posthumously on Vladimir Clementis and Josef Frank, the former Deputy General Secretary of the Communist Party, who were executed with Slánský in 1952. He awarded, in memoriam, the Order of the Republic to Ludvík Frejka, former head of the Economic Division of the Presidency; Rudolf Margolius, former Deputy Minister of Foreign Trade; André Simone, former editor of *Rudé Právo*; and Osvald Zavodský, former chief of state security. Among the survivors of the purges, the coveted Order of the Republic went to former Deputy Foreign Ministers Vavro Hajdu and Artur London; former chief of Presidential security Leopold Hoffmann; and Mrs. Marie Švermová. Bedřich Geminder, the executed head of the Party's international relations' section, was posthumously awarded the Order of Labor.

But almost overnight the joy of May Day turned into the fears of survival. Reality had abruptly returned. On May 2 President Svoboda found it necessary to appoint Vladimir Koucký, the ousted member of the KSČ Secretariat and a leading Moscow-line follower, to be Czechoslovakia's ambassador to the Soviet Union. On May 4 Defense Minister Dzúr publicly confirmed reports that during his visit the previous week Marshal Yakubovsky had proposed that joint maneuvers of Warsaw Pact armies, including Soviet forces, be held as soon as possible on Czech-oslovak territory. General Dzúr explained somewhat lamely that the full extent of the maneuvers had not yet been decided on, but that, most likely, they would be in the nature of "staff exercises" rather than full-fledged war games comparable to the 1966 Vltava maneuvers. This piece of news sent chills up the spines of Czechoslovak readers. It did not require much imagination to realize that Warsaw Pact maneuvers in Czechoslovakia at this juncture would represent a powerful pressure on the Prague reform leadership. As a Czech friend remarked to me, "How do we know they will leave once we let them in?" It was the beginning of a long nightmare of Soviet military maneuvers that haunted Czechoslo-vakia up to the very day of invasion.

In the evening of May 3, hours after Dzúr's announcement, thousands of Czechs, young and old, converged on the Old Town Square for what had been a previously authorized rally. But now the mood was ugly and bitter. The demonstration immediately developed into an anti-Com-munist and anti-Soviet affair. Speaker after speaker told of imprisonments and injustices of the past; others protested anti-Semitism in Poland and urged restoration of diplomatic relations with Israel. There were calls for democracy and freedom for political parties. The police did not interfere and, presently, the demonstrators thinned out and, little by little, straggled home.

But at midnight, unknown to the citizens of Prague, Dubček, Černík, Smrkovský, and Bilak flew to Moscow "on the invitation of the Central Committee of the Soviet Communist Party." It was obvious that the sum-mons had come suddenly and that the Kremlin leaders intended to have a showdown with the Prague team over a long list of problems including the planned Warsaw Pact maneuvers; a secret meeting on April 25 of the Soviet Party's Central Committee had discussed Czechoslovakia. The Czechoslovak delegation had three reform leaders—Dubček, Černík, and Smrkovský—and one pro-Moscow conservative, Bilak. Less than thirty-six hours later, after conferences with Brezhnev, Kosygin, Podgorny, and several other officials, the delegation flew home. The real results of the mission were wrapped in mystery, for the official communiqué spoke simply and rather ominously of the meetings' taking place in a "com-radely atmosphere," which is Communist shorthand for cold disagree-ment.

Deep concern and a kind of malaise spread over Czechoslovakia. Dubček felt it necessary to tell something to his people and *Rudé Právo* carried an "interview" reporting that there had been economic discussions in Moscow and that, in the political sphere, "our Soviet friends received with understanding our explanation of our endeavors aimed at the further development of socialist democracy and at the strengthening of the Communist Party as its leading force." This was, in effect, an admission that the Soviets had called Dubček on the carpet and that he had had to defend his policies to the hilt. What Bilak's role had been was not revealed, but Dubček went on to say that the Soviets

expressed the conviction that the Czechoslovak Communist Party, which enjoys the support of the overwhelming majority of Czechoslovak people, will be able to successfully implement its aims. . . . It is customary among good friends not to hide behind diplomatic politeness but to speak openly as equals. It was in this spirit that our Soviet comrades expressed their anxiety lest the process of democratization in our country be abused against socialism. It must be said that our Party has frequently, since the January Plenum, emphasized its fundamental disagreement with antisocialist excesses and considers it an inseparable part of its policy to oppose these excesses with determination.

Dubček's rather frank statement served only to deepen the concern in Prague. It had now been publicly admitted that the Soviets felt "anxiety" about the Czechoslovaks, and the feeling in Prague was that such anxiety might well be transformed into hostile actions. For the first time since January, serious and responsible people in Prague spoke of the possibility of a Soviet invasion. That their premonitions were correct was confirmed in an article published in *Pravda* on August 22, 1968, the day after the invasion. In it, the Kremlin belatedly offered *its* version of what happened at the May 4 talks in Moscow with Dubček and his colleagues:

At the May 4 Moscow meeting, the Czechoslovak Communist Party leaders themselves spoke about the seriousness of the situation in the country. More than that, they said that the negative features of the internal political development in the country "go beyond the limits of our purely internal affairs and affect the brotherly countries, for example, the Soviet Union, Poland." And it was impossible to disagree with this.

The Czechoslovak leaders said also that they were prepared to take the necessary measures in order to master the situation. They said, then, literally the following: "The enemy acts. He wants to turn events in the interests of counterrevolution."

They recognized that the enemy was trying first of all to discredit the Communist Party, weaken its influence on the masses, that there was a growing demand to create a legal political opposition to the Communist Party of Czechoslovakia, which could by its nature become only an antisocialist opposition, and that "if firm steps are not employed, this may degenerate into a counterrevolution." They said that they know the persons specifically guilty of this and affirmed they possessed evidence of these persons' connection with the imperialist circles and that an end will be put to this.

Not only in retrospect but also on the basis of facts known at the time in Prague, this *Pravda* version appears to be a work of fiction—unless the "they" mentioned in the account referred only to Bilak. It is completely improbable that Dubček and Smrkovský—and even Černík—would have acknowledged in May that a "counterrevolution" was threatening Czechoslovakia. They did not do so after the invasion, and they refused to accept the Soviet insistence on "counterrevolution" even as late as mid-1969. It is possible, of course, that in separate meetings Bilak may have said all these things, for he had always believed them. But it is striking that Moscow waited until *after* the invasion to publish this account when it only represented a post-factum justification.

There remains the uncertainty as to whether the Soviet leaders used the occasion to extract from Dubček the agreement to Warsaw Pact maneuvers in Czechoslovakia and to the permanent stationing of Soviet troops to help "defend" the Western frontiers of the "Socialist camp." Some foreign commentators, who were not in Prague at the time, have suggested that Dubček made a commitment of this nature and failed to inform his colleagues or the public at home. But desperate foot-dragging by the Czechoslovak government over the maneuvers for many more weeks renders this speculation highly unlikely. As events were to show, the maneuvers were in the end forced on Defense Minister Dzúr, bypassing to a large extent the Party and government leadership.

Dubček could enjoy a brief respite from the mounting Soviet pressures when, on his return to Prague, he found Luigi Longo, General Secretary of the Italian Communist Party and a kindred spirit. Longo, a man in the tradition of Palmiro Togliatti, publicly expressed the Italian Party's solidarity with Czechoslovak efforts to develop a "socialist democracy." It was welcome support from the world's largest nonruling Communist Party.

Dubček had been home from Moscow only two days when Soviet pressure resumed. On May 7 Tass denied as "mendacious and provocative" the reports printed in the Czechoslovak and Soviet press that Jan Masaryk's death might have been a murder connected with the activities of "advisers from Soviet security agencies." The next day Polish Ambassador Władysław Janiurek delivered a protest note to the Prague

Foreign Ministry against the reporting of events in Poland by Czech press, radio, and television. This related to a spate of comments by the independent-minded Czechoslovak journalists on anti-Semitism in Poland and the persecutions of students involved in the March disorders. But the Czech official who received the note replied with immense dignity that the Czechoslovak press was free and could not be told by the government what it should or should not publish.

Late on May 8, still unknown to the Czechoslovaks, leaders of the Warsaw Pact countries began gathering in Moscow for a meeting with Brezhnev and Premier Kosygin. Dubček had not been invited—making it obvious that Czechoslovakia was the subject of the conference—and Ceauşescu stayed away, faithful to his principle of boycotting meetings designed to condemn other Communist parties (or worse). (He had presided during April over a session of the Romanian Party's Central Committee that rehabilitated the executed Justice Minister Pătrăşcanu and placed the blame on former Interior Minister Alexandru Draghici. Ceauşescu, acting like the Czechs, deprived Draghici of all Party and government functions and promised more rehabilitations and more "socialist legality.")

May 9 was a day of extreme tension in Prague—the greatest since January. It was a holiday commemorating the twenty-third anniversary of Prague's liberation from Germany by Soviet tanks. The ancient capital was draped in red flags; long red streamers covered the façades of public buildings—from Communist Party headquarters to the downtown police station on Bartolomějska Street—to help create a solemn mood of gratitude to the Soviet Union for the 1945 liberation. But the Czechs' hearts were not in it. Thousands of them had gathered four days earlier on the site of a monument to American soldiers in Plzeň to wave the Stars and Stripes and deposit flowers—the monument had been torn down after the 1948 Communist takeover, but people came all the same to pay tribute, and for the first time the Czechoslovak Communist government officially recognized the United States' role in the liberation of Czechoslovakia. So in Prague on May 9 the commemorations were stilted and officious. Marshal Konev and a group of tight-lipped Soviet generals were on hand for the day's events, but pessimistic Czechs were saying that they had come to discipline the Czechoslovak armed forces and prepare the way for the Warsaw Pact maneuvers—if not for an invasion.

Eager to see the official activities, I drove past the 1945 Soviet tank monument in Smíchov on my way to the Julius Fučik Park of Culture.

On the sprawling lawn, children were crawling over several vintage Soviet tanks—the Czechs, even the young ones, were not to forget who had liberated them—while at a near-by outdoor auditorium Marshal Konev and his companions unsmilingly watched a performance by a Red Army dance ensemble.

The Czechs were still worried over Dubček's sudden visit to Moscow, despite his assurances in *Rudé Právo* that the Soviets "have understood our efforts to strengthen our socialist democracy." They were too cynical and skeptical to accept this explanation at face value after Dzúr's announcement of the maneuvers and Marshal Konev's presence in Prague. At the same time, well-informed Party progressives began quietly telling a few foreign journalists that the Kremlin leaders had warned Dubček that a dangerous similarity was emerging between the Hungarian revolt of 1956 and the Czechoslovak experiments of 1968. Dubček, according to this account, had disagreed. But few among the informed Czechs believed that the Russians could be so easily put off. Late in the afternoon I had a drink with a Czech journalist friend. "You will see," he said, "the damned Russians will invade us sooner or later."

In the course of the day, good news came down from Hradčany Castle that President Svoboda had decreed a fairly far-reaching political amnesty benefiting several thousand persons. It covered persons who left Czechoslovakia illegally and remained abroad; in the case of other political offenses, prison sentences up to three years were wiped off and others shortened. Those who had served eight years in prison were to be released at once.

But no sooner had the announcement of the amnesty been broadcast than gloom again descended. Word had come from Moscow of the Warsaw Pact leaders' meeting and the worried talk was that action against Czechoslovakia was imminent. Reports from Warsaw, East Berlin, and other points swept Prague that tank-led Soviet army columns were advancing across Poland toward the Czechoslovak border. The conjunction of the Moscow conference and the reported Soviet troop movements seemed too much of a coincidence. Newspaper editors throughout the world began thinking of a war, and one American correspondent in Prague was urgently requested to write a dispatch discussing the possibilities of a "Vietnam in Czechoslovakia."

Soviet military movements on the Polish side of the Czechoslovak frontier have been verified beyond doubt, but it remains a matter of conjecture whether an armed intervention in Czechoslovakia was contemplated at this point. It was known in Western intelligence circles that the Soviet Union normally kept only one understrength mixed armor and motorized division of some twelve thousand men in Poland. This division was permanently stationed near Legnica, in southwestern Poland, about sixty miles north of the border-crossing point of Nachód and along one of the main communication routes to East Germany. But excited reports from Western military attachés in Poland on the evening of May 9 spoke of military movements vastly exceeding one division. Other sources quickly reported that the Soviet command had sent into Poland the First Carpathian Army, normally based in the Ukraine between Lvov and Užgorod, and that this force was now advancing toward Czechoslovakia's northeastern frontiers.

It was, indeed, ironical that this was how the twenty-third anniversary of Prague's liberation was being commemorated. Some of my Czechoslovak military friends theorized during that night that the Russians were simply engaging in a show-the-flag demonstration to warn Dubček of peril ahead if he persisted in his program. They stressed that the Western military attachés in Warsaw had been deliberately tipped off about the sudden Soviet troop movements. To compound this purposeful deception, several of them—notably the French attaché—were then prevented from approaching the Czechoslovak border for several days. Be that as it may, governments throughout the world stayed awake all that night. So did the newspaper correspondents in Prague—and I remember finally going to bed only when morning rose over the tense city.

Another school of thought held that the Kremlin leadership had, indeed, favored a quick military operation on May 9–10 to remove the "Dubček cancer" before it could spread further. This idea developed after Dubček's visit to Moscow the previous week, the argument went, and this was why the Warsaw Pact leaders had been so urgently convoked to the Soviet capital on May 8 to give their approval to the operation. Militarily, an invasion on a much smaller scale than was to occur in August was already feasible in May as, according to Czechoslovak military intelligence, troop movements and logistic support operations, including the air force, had been initiated sometime late in February as contingency planning. On the correct assumption that the Czechoslovak armed forces would not fight, the country could have been occupied as expeditiously with two hundred thousand men in May as with the five hundred thousand men who were activated in August.

The problem, however, appeared to be lack of unanimity among the planners. Among the Warsaw Pact allies, János Kadár was squarely opposed to the "police action" pushed by Gomułka and Ulbricht. As I was to learn later from Hungarian Communist sources, Kadár argued to the very end that a "political solution" must be found for the Czechoslovak crisis. Older and mellowed, he surely remembered the tragedy of Budapest that had put him in power twelve years earlier. Zhivkov presumably would have gone along with whatever decision the Kremlin made; only token Bulgarian contingents were eventually to participate in the Czechoslovak invasion after being ferried over the Black Sea to the Soviet Union.

And we still do not know, of course, the division of opinion in the Soviet Politburo. It is by no means certain that all or even most of its members were "hawkish" in May, and there remain doubts that the Red Army command was entirely sold on the operation. It appears that Brezhnev and the Ukrainian Party boss Shelest were the earliest and most articulate spokesmen in favor of the invasion. Premier Kosygin and Mikhail Suslov were said at first to oppose it for the time being. Among the officers, Warsaw Pact Commander Marshal Yakubovsky and General of the Army Aleksei A. Yepishev, Chief of the Political Administration of the Soviet Army and Navy, seemed to prefer quick and decisive action. But Defense Minister Marshal Andrei A. Grechko was still, contrary to widespread reports, on the cautious side in May.

A possible explanation why no invasion was attempted in May—assuming that one had been actually planned—is that it would have lacked sufficient political plausibility. The Soviet propaganda machine had barely begun to crank out material portraying Prague as the site of a sinister antisocialist "counterrevolution" or "imperialist plot"—and thus a convincing political context for a military intervention was still missing. But there are sound reasons to believe that economic and political sanctions against Czechoslovakia were discussed at the May 8 Moscow summit. While Kadár, it is said, again discouraged a joint Comecon action, there are indications that already late in April the Soviet Union had begun to cut down on grain deliveries to Czechoslovakia. Zdeněk Mlynář said so in an interview with an American correspondent in Prague early in May, but when the story was published he announced that he had been misquoted.

Whatever may have happened during these ten days in May, the episode served to underscore how easily the Soviet Union—acting out of a sense of underlying insecurity—may be led to the brink of a military attack against a Communist nation dabbling in what she regards as heresies. It also illustrates how quickly a "tank psychology" developed during the flowering of the Prague Spring. This "tank psychology" was never absent from Czechoslovakia until it climaxed in the August invasion, and it returned anew early in 1969 when the Russians once more felt threatened by the Czechoslovaks. The most extraordinary thing about the Soviet Union's involvement in Czechoslovakia, indeed, was that it never stopped feeling threatened there from the day its tanks first entered Prague on May 9, 1945.

May, then, was a curious month in Prague, a month of elation and depression, of optimism and pessimism. On the high political and military levels, it was a time for public and secret consultations between the Czechoslovaks and the Soviets, and for mysterious or half-explained visits. Press attacks on Czechoslovakia mounted in the Warsaw Pact capitals and Prague replied in kind. The Czechoslovaks seemed determined to protect their political gains, and the elderly President Svoboda took it upon himself to tell the world, "Our goal is democratic regeneration." In the best Czech way, he spoke these words on the one-hundredth anniversary of the first rally at which the Czechs asserted their national identity within the Austro-Hungarian Empire. Accompanied by Dubček, he drove on May 10 to the mountain village of Říp, some thirty miles from Prague, to voice Czechoslovakia's dedication to democracy.

Below the political level, life was excitedly bubbling in Prague and elsewhere in the country. Czechs and Slovaks have a capacity for living on two separate planes at once: they can worry themselves to distraction over the dangers facing them and, at the same time, derive tremendous enjoyment from the pleasures of the moment. This gift, no doubt, helped them to survive everything from the burning of Jan Hus to the Soviet invasion half a millennium later.

May was the month of the Prague Spring Festival, and it fitted well with the nation's spirit. When the festival opened, President Svoboda was the guest of honor at Smetana Hall. No other Communist President had ever attended the opening of the festival, and the audience wept with emotion as the old general stood erect to hear a rendition of Smetana's "Our Country"—within short months the theme music of Czech resistance. Czechs and the year's first tourists soon fought over tickets to the

National Theater, Smetana Hall, and the House of Artists for the festival performances. The young American pianist Julius Katchen, the Greek pianist Gina Bachauer, and the violinist Henryk Szeryng gave recitals. The Concertgebouw Orchestra from the Netherlands and the Budapest Symphony Orchestra played series of concerts. All twenty-two of Prague's theaters played every night to capacity audiences. The Burian Theater presented František Langer's play *The Horseback Patrol*, a long-forbidden story of Czechoslovak legionnaires fighting the Communists in Russia in 1918. The National Theater offered a new production of *Who's Afraid of Franz Kafka?*, which was the Czech translation of *Who's Afraid of Virginia Woolf?* (Kafka, rehabilitated posthumously in 1963, was one of the symbols of the new revolution.) The celebrated Czech mime Ladislav Fialka was showing his white-powdered face at another theater. Movie houses were sold out for showings of *Closely Watched Trains* (the American Academy Award winner in 1968 for the best foreign film) by the young Czech director Jiří Menzel, and a whole series of new Czechoslovak films shortly to become world famous. Prague's nightlife also soared skyhigh. At a dark downtown establishment called the Reduta Jazz-Klub, a combo went through Dave Brubeck's "Set Five" with perfect precision and an eerie touch of the Bossa Nova. Muscles and bribes to doormen were needed to get into the night clubs, where dance bands still sounded nineteen-thirtyish and one danced the fox trot in the prewar way.

It did seem somewhat incongruous that life could go on so richly and gaily as Soviet troops maneuvered menacingly along Czechoslovakia's frontiers. But there was a melancholy counterpoint to all this in a smash-hit play called *The Last Stop*, which Jiří Šlitr and Jiří Suchy, famous playwright-actors and composers, presented in the Semafor basement theater. The musical play, set in a hospital whose chief doctor was named Antonín (after Novotný), was about a patient who was clearly Czechoslovakia. At the end, the patient dies and the hospital is suddenly transformed into a demented tavern.

At lunch one day, Šlitr was despondent and pessimistic. His musical really predicted the end of the Prague Spring, he thought. "What you see here is a spring between two winters." A middle-aged lady bearing an illustrious Czech name wanted desperately to believe that the liberalization would work, but, she told me, "Let's be realistic: how long can the Russians stand for Dubček?"

The Dubček regime had no choice but to go along with the brinkmanship. On May 10 it took official cognizance of the Soviet movements in Poland; ČTK, the government news agency, issued a statement that "the diplomatic correspondent of the Czechoslovak radio was told in informed circles that the Czechoslovak government had been informed in advance of the regular maneuvers of the Warsaw Treaty countries in the region of southern Poland. The correspondent added that the reports of some news agencies that this was a move against Czechoslovakia was considered in Czechoslovak political circles to be a political provocation."

This, of course, was totally inaccurate. Czechoslovak military intelligence ignored the troop movements in Poland until late in the evening of May 9. Only the following morning did Warsaw Pact liaison officers in Prague tell the Defense Ministry that "maneuvers" were under way. Not willing to excite the population but forced to acknowledge the situation, the regime thus chose the indirect form of quoting a radio "diplomatic correspondent." But nobody in Prague was fooled.

The ČTK statement may have spoken of "political provocation" from the West, but the real provocation was now coming from the East. Speaking for the Communist Party on May 11, *Rudé Právo* took to task both the Warsaw Pact summit meeting and an East German newspaper which had claimed that American troops had been introduced into Czechoslovakia under the guise of participating in a joint movie production. Of the Moscow meeting, *Rudé Právo* remarked that "contrary to similar meetings in the past, the official communiqué does not mention unanimity and unity, from which foreign correspondents deduce that full harmony among all the participants was not achieved." With Czechoslovakia's and Romania's absence, the combination of Soviets, Poles, East Germans, Hungarians, and Bulgarians had "appeared for the first time" in a Warsaw Pact conference. The article concluded with the sarcastic hope that "at this time, there was no 'excommunication' of Czechoslovakia or her Communist Party on the part of the participants" in the Moscow meeting—an obvious allusion to Yugoslavia's "excommunication" by the Cominform.

Rudé Právo's special indignation, however, was reserved for East Berlin's *Berliner Zeitung*'s charge that American soldiers were disguised as extras in the filming of *The Bridge of Remagen*, a movie about a World War Two incident on the Rhine River being produced in Czechoslovakia by David Wolper, an American who bought eight unarmed American-built tanks from the Austrian Army to use in the shooting. Wolper paid the Austrians with Volkswagen cars for the obsolete tanks, and the only United States military in Prague at the time was a retired colonel acting as a technical adviser. The *Berliner Zeitung* allegation was "simple nonsense" and "scandalous mystification," *Rudé Právo* said, yet, unbelievably, East German propaganda went on for months with the ploy, for the "tank" story was immediately reproduced in three other East German publications. The Warsaw Pact propaganda machine had swung into action.

In Moscow, *Literaturnaya Gazeta*, the organ of Soviet intellectuals and all along one of the principal Soviet siege guns aimed at the Czechoslovaks, launched on May 8 an attack on Jan Procházka, deliberately misspelling his name and accusing him of anti-Marxist and anti-Soviet attitudes. The next day, this article was reprinted in *Neues Deutschland*. On May 12 *Neues Deutschland* ran an editorial charging Professor Antonín Snejdarek, head of the Prague Institute of International Politics and Economics, with "supporting attacks on the Czechoslovak Communist Party and turning against the foreign-policy line laid down by the government." Subsequent articles accused Czechoslovak reformers of working hand in hand with "West German revanchists." On May 14 *Sovetskaya Rossyia* viciously attacked Tomáš Masaryk as an "absolute scoundrel" and said that in 1918 he had "paid" two hundred thousand rubles to have Lenin assassinated. Warsaw's *Trybuna Ludu* pitched in with its own charges against Prague, partly piqued by Charles University's offer to employ four Polish Jewish professors expelled from Warsaw University. By late May the propaganda pattern had become clear: it was directed by the Soviet Union and faithfully followed by East Germany and Poland; Hungary and Bulgaria remained as silent as possible.

The Czechoslovaks wasted no time in responding to the attacks, and angry polemics developed. A commentary carried by Radio Prague on its international service on May 13 said that the Soviet, East German, and Polish attacks were "demagogy of such a caliber that it takes the breath away, even from people who are quite accustomed to things along this line. . . . We know from our own experience with what methods and application of tricks and formulations a group of individuals can present itself as an entire Communist Party or the entire working class. After the last twenty years we are of the opinion that socialism cannot be built without democracy."

This concept was taken a step further on May 13 when *Rudé Právo* published a questionnaire asking its readers whether they thought that Communism could be compatible with democracy. Among the twenty-two questions were:

> Does the internal democratization of a Communist Party provide a sufficient guarantee of democracy?
> Can you speak of democracy as being socialist when the leading role is held only by the Communist Party?
> Should the Communist Party carry out its leadership role by devotedly promoting free progressive socialist development or by ruling over society?
> Does the new political system have to provide free and democratic platforms for the wide-ranging requirements of the various groups and strata of people in a socialist society in forming its political decisions?
> Is the Czechoslovak way of constructing and developing socialism our own internal matter that must be decided by the sovereign will of our people?

The questionnaire was published as Dubček was meeting in Prague with the Party's regional chiefs to map out the continuing course of his liberalizing policies. He told them that the Central Committee would meet late in May and that the regional organizations must start preparing for the Party congress in the summer. But a typical Soviet reaction to the democratization policies and the public criticism that went with it came that week from two Moscow newspaper correspondents in Prague. Chatting with American colleagues, one of them pointed to the *Rudé Právo* questionnaire and remarked indignantly: "Can you call *this* honest socialist criticism? . . . We consider honest criticism when a paper like *Izvestia*, for example, publishes an article criticizing pollution in the Volga River. Now, that's constructive criticism."

The Prague government moved on May 14 to be even more explicit about its plans for reform. For the first time since the Communist takeover, a news conference with no holds barred was held by the Premier and Deputy Premiers Šik and Husák. Western reporters not only outnumbered Warsaw Pact correspondents but virtually monopolized the meeting, in which the three officials good-humoredly and fully answered all the questions.

The eighty-minute session was opened by Premier Černík, who declared that the new regime's "guiding principle" was "to stress the democratic rights and freedom of citizens." He announced that new legislation was being prepared to guarantee freedom of the press and the right of assembly, that a new constitution would be drafted for a federal Czecho-

Slovak state, and that a new electoral law would be written. Then Deputy Premier Husák addressed himself to the electoral law and the federal state, and Šik unveiled his further plans for decentralizing the economy to make it competitive at home and abroad. Answering a question, Černík said Czechoslovakia had invited Soviet Premier Kosygin for a visit but that he was "not expected soon."

Kosygin materialized in Prague three days later, however, evidently taking the Czechoslovak regime by surprise. He arrived in the late afternoon of May 17, five hours after an eight-man mission of high-ranking Soviet military chiefs led by Defense Minister Grechko had landed at the Prague airport.

What had prompted these two sudden visits? Veterans were reminded of Khrushchev's sudden arrival in Warsaw with a high-level military team at the height of the October 1956 crisis. Others compared Kosygin's appearance with Brezhnev's visit in Prague the previous December in the futile attempt to save Novotný's political life.

In any event, a sense of crisis spread through Prague on that warm day. On May 15 Yugoslavia's Foreign Minister Marko Nikezić had told a news conference in Prague that Czechoslovakia's democratization would affect other Communist countries—and this had set off speculations that Yugoslavia was advocating the renewal of the Little Entente she had formed with Czechoslovakia and Romania in 1920 and 1921. The implications for Soviet interests of a Communist Little Entente reaching from the heart of Central Europe to the Balkans were so tremendous that this alone may have precipitated Kosygin's trip. On May 16 Gomułka and Premier Cyrankiewicz had suddenly flown to Budapest for consultations with Kadár. Clearly, a process of reviewing the whole Czechoslovak affair was again under way.

The Grechko mission arrived in Prague at twelve-thirty-five p.m. aboard an Ilyushin-18 jet airliner, and there had been just enough advance notice for several Czechoslovak journalists to gather at the airport. Among the Soviet generals was Yepishev, head of the armed forces' political administration. A recent report in a Paris newspaper had said that he had told the Soviet Party's Central Committee on April 25 that the Soviet Army stood ready to move in response to an appeal for help from *a* Czechoslovak government. As General Yepishev, a short, plump, bemedaled man, walked into the terminal, Duna Havlíčkova, a pretty and elegant reporter for Prague television, thrust the microphone into his face to ask whether he had really advocated intervention in Czechoslovakia. No such question has ever been asked publicly of a Soviet general, and Miss Havličkova's inquiry was followed by a moment of stunned silence that the television audience savored fully. Then Yepishev produced a weak smile and said in Russian, "This is a stupid thing." The only official explanation for the Grechko mission's presence in Prague was that it had come to become acquainted with Czechoslovakia's new military leaders.

On the seven p.m. television news program, the Prague station presented again the Yepishev-Havličkova exchange; then the announcer broke in to say that Kosygin had just landed in Prague. As was learned later, the regime had been informed of Kosygin's trip when he was already flying to Prague. Dubček, Černík, Smrkovský, Foreign Minister Hájek, and Soviet Ambassador Chervonenko barely had time to reach the airport to greet him. Such was the official confusion surrounding his arrival that the first television announcement said implausibly that the Soviet Premier had come "for a short holiday and treatment." Only an hour later ČTK issued a communiqué that Kosygin had been invited by the Central Committee and that "it was expected that Mr. Kosygin's stay in Czechoslovakia will be used for a continuation of the exchange of views with leading Czechoslovak officials on questions interesting both sides."

Were the Soviets attempting a last-minute reconciliation or setting the stage for a final showdown? The presence in Prague of the two top Soviet officials coincided both with bitter polemics in the press and with a new attempt by the antireform conservatives to challenge Dubček at the approaching session of the KSČ Central Committee. After spending the night at the Kramař Villa, the official guest house, Kosygin drove up on the morning of May 18 to Hradčany Castle for conferences with the Czechoslovak leadership and then departed with his granddaughter for the Karlový Varý spa as if to confirm that he had indeed come for a health cure. An announcement said that he would spend ten days in Karlový Varý.

Kosygin had apparently arrived in an outwardly dovish mood and in the evening of May 18 the regime felt sufficiently encouraged to let ČTK issue a story that according to "authorized Czechoslovak sources" the conversations with the Soviet Premier had shown that "the path of the further development of socialism upon which Czechoslovakia has embarked is meeting with understanding among Soviet leaders." This was, of course, a restatement of what Dubček had said on May 6 on his return from Moscow. But Party officials authorized to talk to selected foreign newsmen insisted that this time the evaluation was accurate. After the talks in Moscow and the subsequent Warsaw Pact summit meeting, a military intervention in Czechoslovakia had been a "real possibility," but, these officials said, Moscow had concluded that no government that would "request" Soviet help could be formed in Prague in time and the plan had been dropped. It may have been wishful thinking, but the Party officials who talked to us on the evening of May 18 insisted that the Kremlin was disenchanted with Czechoslovakia's pro-Soviet conservatives. This, they said, resulted in the more conciliatory approach.

As these Party officials reconstructed the events of early May, Dubček had received the text of the minutes of the Soviet Party's Central Committee meeting of April 25 before going to Moscow, the text in which he was accused of being a "revisionist" and a "prisoner of antisocialist forces," and General Yepishev had, indeed, proposed intervention in response to a "call" from Prague. Dubček apparently was partly successful in demolishing these charges, and no decision was taken in Moscow. But when the Warsaw Pact leaders convened three days later, Ulbricht and Gomułka resumed their pressure for immediate action. For a day the fate of Czechoslovakia hung in the balance. Then the Kremlin leaders again decided against an immediate move. They agreed to push Ulbricht's second proposal that eleven thousand Soviet troops be stationed in Czechoslovakia on the West German border, and they ordered the May 9 troop movements as a psychological concession to the East Germans and as a warning to Dubček.

Now, with Kosygin in Karlový Vary, the Czechoslovak leaders felt that the worst danger was over, and ČTK was authorized to say that Kosygin would discuss economic-assistance questions with Dubček and Černík. As the Soviet Premier rested, some ten thousand Czech students paraded through Prague with anti-Soviet slogans and posters—one of them said LET US GIVE YOU THE CURE, KOSYGIN—and cheers for Masaryk and Beneš. The gay and good-natured students were supervised by student "policemen" wielding huge sausages instead of clubs, and one medical student carried a mock camera with the inscription SECRET POLICE. The real police ignored the demonstration, as it did a meeting later in the evening of five thousand members of the new KAN Clubs of Committed Non-Party Members.

The curious thing about Prague in these May days was that the sense of inevitable doom as in a Greek tragedy—people knew that something *had* to happen sooner or later—blended with total incongruity in the day-to-day events. In Prague, students were parading with sausages as Marshal Grechko and his advisers took a measure of possibilities of invading the country. In Karlový Varý, Premier Kosygin spent Sunday, May 19, taking the waters, unrecognized among the thousands of East and West German tourists. In a dark overcoat and a pearl-gray Homburg hat with a silk band, he strolled with his granddaughter Irina and five discreet Soviet security agents from watering station to watering station. In the afternoon, he took a nap at the Victorian-style yellow-stucco Villa Javorina.

But reality reasserted itself on Wednesday, May 22. Marshal Grechko and his team suddenly returned to Moscow amidst reports that they were disturbed over Kosygin's excessively conciliatory and relaxed attitudes. Communist sources in Prague reported worriedly that Grechko felt it urgent to be the first to acquaint the Kremlin with the "real" Czechoslovak situation. Two days later the Czechoslovak regime announced that Warsaw Pact military maneuvers to "test cooperation and commands under conditions of modern warfare and to improve the combat readiness of troops and staff" would be held in June on Czechoslovak and Polish territories. This was a radical change in plans: on May 4 Defense Minister Dzúr had publicly announced that "staff exercises" would take place only late in the year, since summertime maneuvers would interfere with harvesting. And whereas Dzúr had spoken only of "staff exercises," the new announcement mentioned improvement of "combat readiness" of Pact troops. There could be no question that Grechko had scored a victory while Kosygin held his conferences in Karlový Varý, and that the maneuvers were a major political move.

A few hours before the announcement was made Kosygin had rushed back to Prague, breaking off his "cure" four days ahead of time. He immediately called on President Svoboda at Hradčany Castle, and visibly disoriented Czechoslovak officials spoke of sudden "new difficulties" in the negotiations. The previous evening Kosygin had a "hard" session with Dubček and Černík. The next day Kosygin left for Moscow without any explanation why his holiday had been shortened, departing two hours ahead of the announced time in order to avoid newsmen.

As events were to show, this was the last attempt by the Soviet Union to obtain a peaceful settlement of the Czechoslovak crisis. Now that Dubček and his colleagues demonstrated they would not be talked or bribed out of the "socialist democratic" revolution, other means would have to be used. The military maneuvers had already been forced on Prague—though the civilian leaders around Dubček may not have perceived their full significance—and now an ominous new relationship developed between the Soviet Union and Czechoslovakia.

XVII

Socialism with a Human Face

Despite the rising external threat, attention turned again to the domestic struggle for "Socialism with a Human Face." Now the interest centered on the Central Committee Plenum Dubček had called for May 29.

At this stage, the division in the KSČ was clear between the liberals and the conservatives who openly enjoyed Soviet support. For the liberals, the approaching Plenum was an opportunity to get rid of as many as possible of the forty hard-liners on the 110-member Committee and to push even further with democratization. For the conservative band, captained by Bilak, Kolder, and Indra, the Plenum was the chance to demonstrate that the "revisionists" lacked popular support and that brakes should be placed on the Action Program. The conservatives also hoped to maintain the *status quo* in the Central Committee to gain time for a counteroffensive later in the year or even for an intervention by the Warsaw Pact powers. Increasingly, the old-guard Communists were heard complaining that the Soviet Union was not acting with sufficient determination and firmness to curb the "traitors."

Dubček himself was locked in something of a centrist position. His sympathies were obviously with the Action Program, but he was also disturbed by the growing polarization. He realized that if the liberals were allowed to go unchecked, the Soviets might decide to strike. And he knew he did not have enough votes to clear out the conservatives altogether; naturally, he could not risk a defeat on the floor. Late in May, therefore, he began urging caution. On his behalf, Císař and Mlynář, the two liberal Party secretaries, met with editors and broadcasters to ask them to tone down their attacks on the Soviet Union and to avoid polemics even under provocation. They recommended that public debate on Czechoslovakia's political life be conducted in calmer tones and that nothing be said or done to indicate to Moscow that the Communist Party's sacred "leading role" was being questioned.

But, as Dubček must have realized, it was difficult if not downright impossible to slow down a process that had acquired its own momentum and dynamics. The editors agreed with Císař and Mlynář that caution was advisable, but if a Soviet or Polish newspaper delivered another broadside against Czechoslovakia there was no way of preventing a response.

At the same time, the leadership was committed to its own program and this, too, added momentum to the revolution. In mid-May, for example, the government took a major step in restoring freedom of religion in the country. As a result of negotiations between Bishop Tomášek and Mrs. Erika Kadlecová, Undersecretary for Religious Affairs in the Culture Ministry, three Roman Catholic bishops were allowed to resume the direction of their dioceses after eighteen years. Simultaneously, the government agreed to let the Vatican propose candidates to fill the five diocesan vacancies resulting from the deaths of their bishops. This meant, in effect, the end of the direct control of the state over Czechoslovak churches that had been imposed in 1948. It foreshadowed, among other things, the disappearance of the Peace Movement of the Catholic Clergy, the pro-Communist front organization, and the complete withdrawal of the regime from interference in church affairs. When I called on the sixty-eight-year-old Bishop Tomášek at the Archbishop's Palace across the square from Hradčany Castle, he told me with satisfaction that while problems still remained, the "first big steps" had been taken in normalizing church-state relations.

Meanwhile, rehabilitation procedures moved apace. On May 22 the Prague Municipal Court canceled the 1949 prison sentences against a group of Foreign Ministry officials and professors. Among them was Dr. Antonín Sum, who had been Jan Masaryk's private secretary and who had been condemned to twenty-two years. On May 23 the National Assembly's Committee on Constitutional Law approved a draft law on court rehabilitations covering illegal trials between 1948 and 1956. On May 25 President Svoboda awarded General Karel Klapálek, a victim of the purges, the title of Hero of the Czechoslovak Socialist Republic. On May 27 Interior Minister Pavel created a commission to "evaluate cases of unlawful procedures" committed by the security services and the prison service that had infringed upon citizens' rights. This drastic step opened the way to prosecutions of secret-police agents. Earlier in the month Mňačko triumphantly returned from Israel after Pavel restored his citizenship.

Liberalization in its most meaningful sense was thus in full swing when the Central Committee met at Hradčany Castle on the morning of May 29. In the days preceding the session, the leadership had been flooded with letters and telegrams demanding the ouster of the conservatives, and now a small crowd gathered in front of the iron gates to applaud the arrival of Dubček, Černík, Smrkovský, and the other progressive leaders. Novotný, making his first public appearance since his resignation, was booed good-naturedly.

But it quickly became apparent that the progressive forces did not control the necessary two-thirds of the votes in the Committee to expel *any* of the conservatives. Novotný's old Central Committee was not about to purge itself, even if it had put Dubček in power in January and begrudgingly approved his Action Program in April. The best the progressives could do was to expel Novotný—the conservatives were willing to throw him to the wolves at this point—and to suspend his and six other former officials' Party membership pending investigation of their role in the purges of the 1950s. (Suspended in addition to Novotný were former Security Minister Bacílek, former Justice Minister Stefan Rais, former Premier Široký, former Prosecutor General in the Slánský trial Josef Úrvalek, former head of the KSČ Cadres Commission Köhler, and former Presidium member Pavel David.) This was only a modest victory for the Dubček faction.

The expulsion of Novotný and the suspensions of the other six Party members were ordered on the first day of the Plenum, but the next day the nation's attention was drawn away from the continuing session by news that Soviet troops had begun to enter Czechoslovakia for the Warsaw Pact maneuvers. On its evening news program on May 31, Prague television showed films of Soviet truck convoys entering Slovakian towns from the Užgorod area.

The suddenness of the troop movements took Czechoslovakia by surprise, and Czechoslovak military-intelligence officers reported that these arrivals had not been cleared with the Defense Ministry. Defense Minister Dzúr had announced on May 24 that maneuvers would be held in Czechoslovakia and Poland in June, but when a mission from Warsaw

Pact headquarters had reached Prague on May 29, headed by Soviet General Ivan Kazakov, chief of staff of the Warsaw Pact Command, a brief announcement had simply said that Soviet, Polish, Hungarian, and Czechoslovak troops would participate in the war games. Now total confusion reigned over the timing and the scope of the maneuvers, and it was clear that even Defense Minister Dzúr did not know exactly what was happening, or else he was not telling the whole truth. On the evening of May 30, for example, Dzúr told a radio audience that "small units" from each of the four countries would participate in "command staff exercises." But then he said that each participating division would be represented by "two or three hundred men" and Defense Ministry sources were able to report that "at least" ten divisions would thus be represented. At this point, therefore, the "staff exercises" had already grown to at least three thousand.

There were more contradictions. Dzúr had said on May 24 that the maneuvers were designed to test "combat readiness" of Warsaw Pact troops, but on May 30 he spoke only of "communications units," and Foreign Minister Hájek insisted at a simultaneous news conference that no combat forces would be involved. As Western military attachés and foreign newsmen in Prague pondered just what kind of exercises the Warsaw Pact Command had in mind, General Dzúr increased the confusion by saying that the Soviet units "are bringing in special signal equipment, which we ourselves will use for our own maneuvers later in the year." One perceptive Western diplomat remarked that it looked as if the Soviets were installing sophisticated communications devices to be used, if needed, in the case of invasion. The speed with which microwave and other communications installations materialized throughout Czechoslovakia on August 21 seemed to confirm fully this prediction.

The concern caused in Czechoslovakia by all this military activity was reflected on May 31 by the Prague Socialist newspaper *Svobodne Slovo*, which linked the maneuvers with reports that the Soviet Union wished to station troops permanently in the country. Existing "special circumstances" in Czechoslovakia, the newspaper added, raised questions about the validity of earlier denials about the stationing of Soviet troops.

All this excitement over the maneuvers succeeded completely in overshadowing the Central Committee meeting, which adjourned on June 1. The progressives succeeded in obtaining the additional resignation from the Committee of former Defense Minister Lomský, while Dubček scored his only real victory when the Committee agreed to call the "Extraordinary" Fourteenth Congress of the KSČ for September 9. This, of course, involved a matter of opposing strategies. Dubček was banking on the delegates elected to the congress during the summer giving him a progressive Central Committee in September. The conservatives were betting on the opposite result and, as likely as not, on other events that would aid their cause.

In an article filed from Prague to *The New York Times* on June 2, I quoted a high Czechoslovak official who, I thought, summed up well the situation in his country:

> It is politically so untactful, not to say crude, to organize military exercises in Czechoslovakia the very day the progressives in the Central Committee are trying to evict the "Stalinists" that even the Russians must have known better if some overwhelming consideration had not arisen.
>
> To ask us to accept that there is no relationship between the fight in the Central Committee and this sudden Soviet yearning for immediate exercises with Warsaw Pact staffs and Signal Corps specialists—thousands of them—is to demand that we stretch our imagination beyond reason. . . .
>
> We've been escalated out of the "sandbox" exercises by a bunch of generals into something we cannot quite measure ourselves. . . . The question is how to handle this sandbox plot.

That a plot was afoot against the liberalizing revolution was now crystal clear to one and all. In the Central Committee session, Dubček had come under powerful fire from the conservatives and, in a sense, the whole scenario had been reversed. Whereas Dubček had hoped to rally the progressives against the conservatives, he ended up defending himself from their attacks. The "Stalinist" group, encouraged by the entry of the Soviet units for the "maneuvers" in Czechoslovakia, had shown greater cohesion and self-assurance than at any time since January. The final result was the publication of a five-point resolution that was distinguished by its lack of real meaning. It proposed:

> 1. To ensure the leading political role of the Communist Party in society;
>
> 2. To safeguard the development of socialism and the freedom of workers and all working people;
>
> 3. To strive to ensure that the new political system corresponds to the developments of socialism;
>
> 4. To oppose all attempts at violating the legal order and disrupting the state apparatus;
>
> 5. To further develop the relations of Czechoslovakia with the Soviet Union, the other socialist countries, and the international Communist movement based on the principles of internationalism.

If anything, this was a regressive resolution, in terms of what had been thus far accomplished in Czechoslovakia. Knowing this, Dubček finally decided to take off his gloves: he ceased to be a peace-making centrist and plunged headlong into the battle. Two days after the conclusion of the Central Committee session, he flew to Brno, a liberal stronghold, and in a rare public speech before six thousand Party officials delivered a frank account of the political situation.

The refusal of the "rightists" to resign voluntarily from the Central Committee had led him to call an Extraordinary Party Congress on such unusually short notice, Dubček said; "rightists" and "conservatives" posed the "greatest danger" to Czechoslovakia's democratizing process. For the first time publicly he called them "reactionaries" and, in effect, linked their activities to the Soviet Union. As the Party officials continuously interrupted him with thundering applause, Dubček noted that "in meetings, rallies, and public appearances we have always formulated our attitude toward the Soviet Union and we have rejected all attacks against our alliance as well as against our own Party. How, then, is it possible that we have now been witnessing so many negative reactions, particularly in the past month and a half?"

> It must be clearly said that we do not pretend our policy to be an example for others. We will not measure, according to our needs and conditions, the policies of other socialist countries. . . .
> We have reserved the right to arrange our internal affairs according to our conditions and traditions. Let us not take this right away from others, and let us not interfere, through publicizing various of our views, in the internal affairs of other socialist countries.
> Let us not do unto others what we would not wish others to do unto us.

While he spoke in Brno, Dubček's associates were preaching the gospel of Communist democracy to Party units across the country from Bohemia to Slovakia. Both the progressives and the conservatives knew they were engaged in a race against time and that the coming weeks would tell who was to be the winner when the Party membership began electing Congress delegates.

Early in June I accompanied Eduard Goldstücker and Antonín Liehm, chairman and vice-chairman of the Writers' Union, on a political barnstorming tour of Ostrava, a coal-and-steel town in northern Moravia. The intellectuals were fully involved in the effort to proselytize the rank and file for the liberal cause, and Ostrava was chosen because of a belief that the workers there were proconservative out of fear of the economic reform. But the overflow meeting in the City Hall auditorium proved the opposite. There was talk of political freedom, rehabilitations, and economic improvement. The audience asked questions and applauded the answers as Goldstücker and Liehm took turns explaining the new revolution.

But the conservatives, too, were active. Vasil Bilak, the boss of the Slovak Party, took East Germany's Ambassador Peter Florin around Slovakia to address local Party meetings and presented Florin with a fifty-volume set of Karl Marx's works in Slovak. But the right-wingers generally preferred to work quietly in closed meetings with limited leadership groups known to be sympathetic to them. A key strategist in the conservatives' operation was Alois Indra, the forty-seven-year-old KSČ Secretary and former Transportation Minister and State Planning Board chairman under Novotný. As early as May, conservative Communists talked of Indra as the Soviet choice to replace Dubček "when all this nonsense is over." Poland's dogmatists also approved of Indra, who had met confidentially with Edward Gierek, up-and-coming Polish Party boss in Silesia.

The conservatives' tactics included the distribution of tens of thousands of unsigned leaflets accusing the progressives of betraying socialism. A typical leaflet, read at a Prague factory, said: "The inventors of the new model of socialism—Goldstücker, Šik, Kriegel, and Císař—try to deceive us for their mercenary interests. Under the slogan of 'liberalization,' they fight their way into the leadership and try to take over the power. Actually, they want to restore the first bourgeois Republic by revisionist means."

In Prague, Dubček showed no open concern over the situation, though he was known to be working eighteen or twenty hours a day at his Central Committee office. As the weather turned hot, he developed the habit of taking predawn walks in the city's streets from the Hotel Praha, where he still maintained his residence. When the occasional passer-by recognized him, Dubček would stop to chat. One dawn I ran into him and we exchanged pleasantries. For a man under so extraordinary a strain, he seemed almost eerily relaxed and serene. In the coming months he was to need all his reserves of serenity.

On June 13 Dubček and Černík flew to Budapest to sign a new Treaty of Friendship, Cooperation, and Mutual Assistance with Hungary in what seemed like a momentary relaxation in the tensions building up between Czechoslovakia and her nominal allies. This visit gave Dubček the opportunity of a long private talk with his friend—and defender—János Kadár. What advice, if any, Kadár gave Dubček is not known, but he consistently worked to prevent a final break between Russia and Czechoslovakia. And, surprisingly, National Assembly Chairman Smrkovský led a delegation of deputies to Moscow for a leisurely ten-day visit from June 4 to 14. He met with Brezhnev, who, according to a press report, denied with "tears in his eyes" that the Soviet Union ever considered halting Czechoslovakia's democratization. But, on the whole, the visit was rather cool, and Smrkovský found himself criticizing in public speeches some "excesses" of Czechoslovak journalists. On June 17 Foreign Minister Hájek went for two days to East Berlin. It appeared that the Czechoslovaks and their tormentors were again on speaking terms. But, as usual, Communist diplomacy had its touch of unreality.

At home, events moved with their accustomed daily contradictions. On June 6 Interior Minister Pavel was forced to name Viliam Šalgovič as his deputy in charge of the secret police. Šalgovič was head of the secret police during Mamula's reign and was a particularly sinister figure. For whatever reason Pavel made Šalgovič a deputy minister, he soon had ample reason to regret it bitterly. But on the same day the National Assembly elected Leopold Hoffmann, a Spanish War veteran and a prisoner during the 1950s purges, as chairman of its Defense and Security Committee. During the same week, Rudolf Barák was released from prison after serving six years. He was the last well-known political prisoner to be put at liberty.

All this did not lessen Soviet military pressures on the Czechoslovaks. Early in June, Defense Minister Dzúr was secretly requested to authorize the participation of Soviet tanks and aircraft in the planned Warsaw Pact "staff exercises." Whether he did so or not, strong elements of a Soviet tank division quietly moved into Czechoslovakia from Poland on the night of June 3–4 and set up camp in the restricted Czechoslovak Army reservation of Libáva, northeast of Frýdek-Místek and about thirty miles from the Polish border. I was told about it on June 4, by a Defense Ministry friend, who also advised me that large-scale Soviet troop movements across Czechoslovakia would start the following day in preparation for the "sandbox exercises."

There had been so much confusion about these exercises that I decided to go and see for myself. Early in the morning of June 5 I set out from Prague in my rented Simca with my Czech driver in the general direction of Libáva. Along the highway from Prague to Hradec Králové, we ran into a number of Czechoslovak Army Military Police traffic controllers and several portable radio transmitters set up in the fields. My driver then noticed that at the approach to each bridge along the way new signs had been posted doubling the permissible maximum weight of vehicles. From this we concluded that heavy military traffic was imminent. Leaving Hradec, we saw three MiG-21 jet fighters making low passes over the city. Between Hradec and Olomouc, the big Moravian town, there were more M.P. traffic controllers. In Olomouc we spotted several canvas-covered vehicles resembling rocket carriers with Hungarian license plates. Past Frýdek-Místek we found the road leading to the Libáva reservation closed off. We turned back and between Hranice and Olomouc caught up with the tail of a long Soviet Army convoy.

The convoy moved slowly, and we were able to pass it, along with a number of other Czechoslovak passenger cars and busses. The long Soviet column (it included more than a hundred vehicles) was made up chiefly of closed communications vans of the Signal Corps, canvas-covered trucks with soldiers in brown overseas caps, field kitchens, and Gasik-type staff cars carrying officers. There was no attempt at secrecy, and the column was led by a blue Czechoslovak police cruiser. The Russian soldiers waved at the people along the highway, most of whom waved back. It seemed like a friendly visit. We tracked the convoy all the way to the outskirts of Prague, where it veered north to the Mlada Army reservation. This was, as it turned out, the concentration point for the Soviet troops which, on June 18, began the long-awaited "staff maneuvers" in western Bohemia under the command of Marshal Yakubovsky. From this single sighting on one day two weeks before the official start of the exercises, it was easy to conclude that the total forces had to run into many thousands, representing all the key branches of the Soviet Army. When *The New York Times* published my story of the Soviet troop movements the next day, I was widely denounced by my colleagues in the lobby of Prague's Alcron Hotel for "wild exaggeration." As it turned out later, I had erred on the conservative side. Subsequently, it became known that the Soviets had introduced sixteen thousand troops in Czechoslovakia for the "maneuvers."

This, incidentally, was the day Robert Francis Kennedy died of wounds following the shooting by Sirhan Sirhan in Los Angeles. News of his death had a tremendous impact in Prague. It was a rainy evening, but thousands of Czechs stood patiently in line to sign the condolence book at the American Embassy. They made a strange contrast with the Soviet Army columns.

The start of the Warsaw Pact maneuvers on June 18 was another electrifying shock, and it brought Czechoslovakia to a full realization of the danger it was in. The next day, June 19, Dubček addressed a national rally of the People's Militia at the Prague airport. As First Secretary of the KSČ, he was commander of this force of armed workers, and he had gathered them to still demands for the militia's disbanding and, at the same time, attract them to the progressives' cause. But conservatives were in control of the militia, and the meeting turned into a demonstration in favor of the Soviet Union and Communist orthodoxy. As Dubček listened incredulously, the militiamen approved a resolution declaring that "we shall not permit anyone to blacken or threaten the principles of the construction of Socialism and Communism which were formulated by V. I. Lenin and for whose realization we laid the foundation in February 1948. . . . We do not agree with and divorce ourselves from," the resolution went on, "the irresponsible actions of some journalists who try to break our friendship by spreading various distortions from the bourgeois press."

This was a great coup for the conservatives, and the resolution was promptly sent to the Soviet Embassy and, two days later, published in *Pravda*. Immediately, "resolutions" of support from Soviet workers streamed to the Czechoslovak militiamen. Moscow's satisfaction over this stand was, however, to be short-lived. Two months later, the members of the armed workers' force had ceased to be admirers of the Soviet Union.

Meanwhile, the Soviet press resumed its attacks on the Prague progressives. Among other attacks, *Pravda* published a vicious assault on Císař, the liberal KSČ Secretary, accusing him of ideological heresy and ties with other "deviationists" who had betrayed Marxism. *Svobodne Slovo* rose to Císař's defense, but attacks on the reformers continued to come from the ranks of Czechoslovak conservatives who, presently, turned to anti-Semitism. Indignantly, *Rudé Právo* printed the text of an anti-Semitic letter sent to the Writers' Union and addressed to Goldstücker, charging that the reformist policies were the work of Jews and that they harmed the workers. "Don't worry, your time will come, your days are numbered, you disgusting Jew." Goldstücker wrote an open letter in reply, reminding his readers that anti-Semitism had figured in the Slánský trials of the 1950s. Pro-Soviet groups had been trying to play the anti-Semitic card in Czechoslovakia on many occasions, but this had never found receptivity among the Czechs as it had among the Poles.

But the progressives did not give up the battle. On the contrary, the regime and its supporters now went on the offensive in anticipation of the elections of delegates for the Party congress. The workers still had to be convinced of the need for the economic reform and it fell to Deputy Premier Šik to disclose in a series of television talks to the nation the brutal truth about Czechoslovakia's economic situation. The national economy, he said, was an "empty cupboard" from which no more "hand-outs" could be given. Depressing statistics were cited to show in what shape Czechoslovakia had been left by past regimes. Half of the steel production was of low quality, only one-third of Czechoslovakia's manufactured products met world quality standards, the Czech worker had to work 117 hours to buy a transistor radio while a West German required only 12 hours, Czechoslovakia ranked extremely low in housing construction, and the nation was suffering enormous losses by exporting heavy industrial products below production costs (the last a reference to trade arrangements with the Soviet Union).

The National Assembly, meanwhile, began to translate promises into deeds. On June 26 it struck out the censorship provision from the Press Law. Then it approved a law on rehabilitations of victims of past purges and persecutions. Yet there was a sense of impending tragedy. The time had come, the more thoughtful Czechoslovaks concluded, to state their hopes and fears before the nation and before the world.

On June 27 a manifesto, drafted at the suggestion of a group of Czechoslovak scientists and written by the novelist Ludvík Vaculík, was addressed to "workers, farmers, civil servants, artists, scientists, technicians, and everybody." This became known—simply as Two Thousand Words—throughout Czechoslovakia; immediately it was the great document of the Prague Spring. I reproduce it here in full:

The life of our nation was first threatened by the war. Then followed another bad time with events which threatened the nation's spiritual health and character. The majority of the nation hopefully accepted the program of socialism. Its direction got into the hands of the wrong people, however. It would not have mattered so much that they did not have sufficient statesmanlike experience, practical knowledge, or philosophical education if they had at least possessed more common sense and decency, if they had been able to listen to the opinion of others, and if they had allowed themselves to be gradually replaced by more capable people.

The Communist Party, which after the war possessed the great trust of the people, gradually exchanged this trust for offices, until it had all offices and nothing else. We must put it this way, and those Communists among us know it to be so and their disappointment over the results is as great as the disappointment of the others. The incorrect line of the leadership changed the Party from a political party and an ideological alliance into a power organization which became very attractive also to egotists avid for rule, calculating cowards, and unprincipled people. Their influx into the Party affected its nature and conduct. Its internal organization was such that honest people could not gain influence in it without shameful incidents, and could not change it to bring it consistently in line with the modern world. Many Communists fought this decline, but they did not succeed in preventing what happened.

The situation in the Communist Party was the pattern and cause of a similar situation in the state. The Party's linking with the state led to the Party's becoming accustomed to remaining aloof from the executive power.

There was no criticism of the activity of the state and economic organizations. Parliament forgot how to proceed, the government forgot how to rule, and the directors how to direct. Elections had no significance and the laws lost their weight. We could not confide in our representatives in any committee, and if we could trust them we could not ask them to do anything because they could change nothing. It was still worse that we could not trust even one another. Personal and collective honor declined. Honesty led nowhere and it was futile to speak of appreciation of ability. Therefore, most people lost interest in public affairs; they were concerned only with themselves and with money. These bad conditions also brought the result that now one cannot even rely on the money. Personal relations were spoiled, joy in work was lost; in sum, the country reached a point where its spiritual health and character were threatened.

We are all responsible for the present state of affairs. The greater responsibility rests with the Communists among us. The main responsibility, however, rests with those who were component parts or instruments of uncontrolled power. It was the power of an opinionated group placed, with the help of the Party apparatus, everywhere—from Prague to each district and community.

The apparatus decided what one might or might not do; the apparatus directed the cooperatives for the cooperative members, the factories for the workers, and the national committees for the citizens. No organization actually belonged to its members, not even the Communist organization.

The main guilt of and the greatest deception perpetrated by these rulers was that they presented their arbitrariness as the will of the workers. If we wanted to believe this deception, we would now have to blame the workers for the decline of our economy, for the crimes against innocent people, for the introduction of censorship which made it impossible for all this to be written about; [we would have to say that] the workers were to blame for the mistaken investments, for the losses in trade, for the shortage of apartments. Naturally, no sensible person believes in such guilt on the part of the workers. We all know and, in particular, each worker knows that in practice the workers did not decide anything. Someone else controlled the workers' representatives' vote. While many workers thought they ruled, rule was exercised in their name by a specially educated group of officials of the Party and state apparatus. In effect, they took the place of the over-thrown class and themselves became the new authority.

For the sake of justice, we will say that some of them long ago realized this bad game of history. We know them now by the fact that they are redressing wrongs, correcting mistakes, returning decision-making power to the [Party] membership and the citizens, and limiting the authority and the numbers of the apparatus of officials. They are with us against the obsolete views in the Party membership. But many officials are still opposing changes and they still carry weight! They still hold instruments of power, especially in the districts and in the communities, where they may use these instruments secretly and with impunity.

From the beginning of the current year we have been in the midst of the reno-vating process of democratization. It began in the Communist Party. We must say this, and the people among us outside the party who, until recently, expected no good to come from us, also know it. We must add, indeed, that this process could not begin elsewhere. After a full twenty years only the Communists could give something like a political life; only Communist criticism was in a position to make a basic assessment of things; only the opposition within the Communist Party had the privilege of being in contact with the enemy. The initiative and efforts of democratic Communists, therefore, is only one installment in the repayment of the debt the entire Party incurred with the people outside the Party, whom it kept in a position in which they did not have equal rights. Therefore, no gratitude is due the Communist Party, although it should probably be acknowledged that it is honestly striving to use the last opportunity to save its own and the nation's honor.

The revival process is not bringing [about] any very novel things. It is producing ideas and suggestions many of which are older than the errors of [Czechoslovak] socialism and others of which emerged from beneath the surface of visible events. They should have been expressed long ago; however, they were suppressed. Let us not cherish the illusion that these ideas are now victorious through the force of truth. Their victory was decided rather by the weakness of the old leadership which, obviously, was first weakened by an untrammeled rule of twenty years. Obviously, all the wrong elements hidden in the foundations and the ideology of this system had to mature until they gained their full form.

Therefore, let us not overestimate the significance of the criticism from the ranks of writers and students. The source of social change is the economy. The right word carries significance only if it is spoken under conditions which have already been duly prepared. Duly prepared conditions: in our country, unfortu-nately, we must understand this term to mean our general poverty and the com-plete disintegration of the old system of rule in which politicians of a certain type calmly and peacefully compromised themselves at our expense.

Thus, truth is not victorious; truth simply remains when everything else goes to waste. There is no cause for a national celebration of victory; there is merely cause for new hope.

We turn to you in this moment of hope, which, however, is still threatened. It took several months for many of us to believe that we could speak out, and many still do not believe it. Nevertheless, we have spoken up, and so many things have been revealed that somehow we must complete our aim of humanizing the regime. Otherwise, the revenge of the old forces would be cruel. We turn mainly to those who have so far only waited. The time which is coming will be decisive for many years.

The approaching season is summer—with its vacations and holidays, when, according to old habit, we will want to leave everything. We can be certain, however, that our dear adversaries will not indulge in summer recreation, that they will mobilize those who are indebted to them, and that even now they are trying to arrange for calm Christmas holidays! Let us try to understand it and respond to it. Let us renounce the impossible demand that someone higher up must always give us the only possible interpretation of things and one simple conclusion. Each of us will have to be responsible for drawing his own conclusions. Commonly agreed-upon conclusions can be reached only by discussion, and this requires the freedom of expression which at present is the only democratic achievement of the current year.

In the coming days we shall have to display our initiative and determination.

Primarily, we shall oppose the view, should it arise, that it is possible to conduct some sort of democratic revival without the Communists or possibly against them. This would be both unjust and unreasonable. The Communists have the developed organizations, and we should support the progressive wing within them. They have experienced officials, and, last but not least, they also have in their hands the decisive levers and buttons. Their Action Program has been submitted to the public; it is a program for the initial adjustment of the greatest inequality, and no one else has any similarly specific program. We must demand that local action programs be submitted in each district and each community. Here, we shall have suddenly taken very ordinary and long-expected correct steps. The Czechoslovak Communist Party is preparing for the congress which will elect a new Central Committee. Let us demand that it be better than the current one. If the Communist Party now says that in the future it wants to base its leading position on the citizens' confidence and not on force, let us believe this as long as we can believe in the people whom it is now sending as delegates to the district and regional conferences.

Fears have recently been expressed that the process of democratization has stopped. This feeling is partly a manifestation of fatigue caused by troubled times, and it is partly due to the fact that the season of surprising revelations, resignations from high places, and intoxicating speeches of unprecedented verbal boldness is past. However, the struggle of forces has merely become somewhat less evident. The fight is now being waged over the content and implementation of laws, over the scope of practical steps to be taken. In addition, we must give the new people—the ministers, prosecutors, chairmen, and secretaries—time to work. They have the right to this time, so that they can either make good or prove impossible. Apart from this, one cannot presently expect more of the central political organs.

The practical quality of the future democracy depends on what becomes of the enterprises and what will happen in them. In all our discussions it is the economists who control things. One must seek out good managers and see to it that they get good positions. It is true that, compared to the mature countries, we are badly paid, and some are even worse off.

We can demand more money—it can be printed, but at the same time its value diminishes. Let us rather demand that directors and chairmen explain to us the nature and extent of expenditures they want in order to produce, to whom they want to sell their products and at what price, the profit from this, what part of it is invested in modernization of production and what can be distributed.

Under apparently boring headlines, a very hard struggle is going on in the press relating to democracy and the manager. As producers, the workers can intervene in this struggle through their choice of the people whom they elect to the enterprise management and enterprise councils. As employees, they will do what is best for themselves when they elect as their representatives in the trade-union organs their natural leaders, capable and honest people regardless of their party affiliation.

If at this time we cannot expect more from the present central political organs, we must achieve more in the districts and with regard to the Communists. Let us demand the resignation of people who have misused their power, who have harmed public property, or who have acted dishonestly or brutally. We must find ways and means to induce them to resign—for instance, through public criticism, resolutions, demonstrations, demonstrative work brigades, collection drives for gifts to them when they withdraw, strikes, and boycotts. But we must reject methods that are illegitimate, indecent, or gross, since they might use them to influence Alexander Dubček.

We must so generally decry the writing of insulting letters that any letter of this kind which they may yet receive could be considered a letter they had sent to themselves. Let us revive the activity of the National Front. Let us demand public meetings of the national committees. On issues which no one [official] wants to know anything about, let us set up special citizens' committees and commissions. It is simple: a few people convene; they elect a chairman, keep regular minutes, publish their finding, demand a solution, and do not let themselves be intimidated.

Let us change the district and local press, which has degenerated to a mouthpiece of official views, into a platform for all positive political forces. Let us demand the establishment of editorial councils composed of representatives of the National Front, or let us found new papers. Let us establish committees for the defense of the freedom of expression. Let us organize a special order-maintenance service in our meetings. If we hear strange news let us check on it, let us send delegations to the people concerned, and let us publish their replies, possibly nailed to trees. Let us support the security organs when they prosecute genuine criminal activity. We do not mean to cause anarchy and a state of general insecurity. Let us avoid disputes among neighbors. Let us renounce spitefulness in political affairs. Let us reveal informers.

The heavy vacation traffic throughout the Republic will arouse interest in the constitutional arrangement of the Czechs and Slovaks. We consider the federation a method of solving the nationality question; aside from this, it is one of the important measures aimed at democratizing conditions. This measure cannot by itself ensure better living conditions for the Slovaks. The problem of the regime—in the Czech regions and in Slovakia individually—is not solved by this. The rule of the Party-state bureaucracy may still survive—in Slovakia especially, because it has "ensured greater freedom."

The recent great apprehension results from the possibility that foreign forces may interfere with our internal development.

Being faced with all these superior forces, the only thing we can do is decently to hold our own. We can assure the government that we will back it, if necessary, even with weapons, as long as the government does what we gave it the mandate to do, and we can assure our allies that we will observe our alliance, friendship, and trade agreements. Excited reproaches and underground suspicions necessarily make the position of our government more difficult without being of any help. At any rate, we can insure equal relations only by improving our internal conditions and by carrying the process of revival so far that one day at elections we will elect statesmen who will have sufficient courage, honor, and political wisdom to establish and maintain such relations. This, by the way, is the problem of absolutely all governments of all small countries in the world.

This spring, as after the war, a great chance has again been given us. Again we have the possibility of taking into our hands our common cause, which for all practical purposes we call socialism, and giving it a shape which will better correspond with our once good reputation and with the relatively good opinion which we once had of ourselves. This spring has just ended and will never return. In the winter we will know everything.

With this we conclude our statement to the workers, farmers, civil servants, artists, scientists, technicians, and everybody. It was written at the suggestion of the scientists.

As published in *Literární Listy*, the trade-union newspaper *Prace*, the youth newspaper *Mladá Fronta*, and the agricultural organ *Zemedelske Noviný*, the manifesto carried seventy signatures. They were not, the document said, "a complete collection of all of the people who agree with us, but merely a selection from the various groups of citizens whom we reached at home." It is useful to record some of the names of the original signers, a true cross section of the Czechoslovak society. The roster is also the roster of the men and women who later rose in resistance against the Soviet invasion. Thus:

Beno Blachut, member of the National Theater Opera in Prague and "National Artist";

Vera Časlavská, Olympic prizewinner;

Rudolf Hrusinsky, actor and stage manager;

Jaromil Jires, film producer;

Vera Kavečová, director of the ophthalmic clinic of Charles University;

Karel Košik, professor of philosophy and member of the Central Committee;

Jiří Kral, director of the Prague Institute for Sports Medicine;

Karel Krautgartner, conductor of the Czechoslovak Radio Dance Orchestra;

Jiří Menzel, cinema director;

Alfred Radok, stage manager and "National Artist";

Jiří Raska, Olympic prizewinner;

Jaroslav Seifert, poet and "National Artist";

B. Sekla, director of the Biological Institute of Charles University;

Zdeněk Servit, director of the Physiological Institute of the Academy of Sciences;

Jiří Šlitr, composer;

Oldřich Starý, Rector of Charles University and member of the Central Committee;

Jiří Suchy, poet;

Jiří Trnka, stage manager, film maker, and "National Artist";

Ludvík Vaculík, writer and author of the manifesto;

Jaroslav Vojta, member of the National Theater and "National Artist";

Jan Werich, actor and "National Artist";

Colonel Emil Zátopek, Olympic prizewinner;

Dana Zátopková, Olympic prizewinner.

Then there were the names of factory workers, private farmers, a sow breeder, engineers, physicians, lawyers, teachers, singers, and economists. The day Two Thousand Words was published, tables were set up in the streets of Prague and other cities for others to sign it. There must have been tens of thousands of signatures on it in the end.

The text of Two Thousand Words was read in Moscow on June 27 within hours of its appearance in the four Prague newspapers, transmitted in full by the Soviet Embassy in Prague. The reaction of the top men at the Kremlin bordered on hysteria. Brezhnev telephoned Dubček

to protest against this official proclamation of a "counterrevolution"—
Pravda is the source for the information about this telephone call—and
the entire political power of the Soviet Union was mobilized to force the
Czechoslovak regime to denounce and disown the document.

That the Soviet leaders should have reacted with such an extraordinary
degree of alarm to Two Thousand Words offers an important insight into
the Kremlin psychology and its leaders' incurable insecurity. I remember
discussing the Prague manifesto with a high-ranking East European
Communist diplomat who explained the Soviet reaction in this manner:

> You must bear in mind that for fifty years the Russians have learned to consider
> as "official" everything that is printed in a newspaper published in a Communist
> country. The Soviet Union has never had a free or even independent-minded
> press. When something is published in *Pravda* or *Izvestia* or a provincial news-
> paper or even a scientific weekly, everybody assumes that it is the official pro-
> nouncement of the Party or government. It must be the official line, because other-
> wise it could not be published. Therefore, when the Russians in Moscow read
> Two Thousand Words in *Literární Listy* and the other Prague newspapers they
> automatically took it for granted—it was a Pavlovian reflex—that the manifesto
> spoke for Dubček and all the others in the leadership. It just did not occur to them,
> because it could not occur to them after fifty years of conditioning, that Vaculík
> and all the people who signed the document were private citizens expressing
> private opinions. The Russians have become prisoners of their own thinking and
> reading habits. Being highly suspicious of the Czechs in the first place, their
> natural conclusion was that the manifesto had to be the work of the regime. What
> you are dealing with is the mentality that "if it is written black on white, then it
> is official."

In addition, Two Thousand Words could be interpreted as one wished to
interpret it. It had called for a better and more honest Communist Party,
but Moscow chose to read this as a challenge to the Party's "leading role."
It had urged peace and order and avoiding disputes "among neighbors,"
but the Kremlin ignored this appeal. Its pledge to the government that
"we will back it, if necessary, even with weapons" was read at the Kremlin
as a call for an armed "counterrevolution." Its expression of (obviously
justified) fear that "foreign forces may interfere with our internal development" was taken to mean an indictment of the Soviet Union. And,
finally, the ultimate challenge was read into the concluding statement:
"This spring, as after the war, a great chance has again been given us.
Again we have the possibility of taking into our hands our common cause,
which for all practical purposes we call socialism, and giving it a shape
which will better correspond with our once good reputation and with the

relatively good opinion which we once had of ourselves. This spring has just ended and will never return. In the winter we will know everything." As *Pravda* was to interpret it in its August justification of the invasion, this was an "open call to struggle against the Communist Party of Czechoslovakia and against the constitutional power." Telling its version of June 27, *Pravda* was to report that "the leadership of our Party called A. Dubček's attention to the danger of this document as a platform for further activization of counterrevolutionary actions," and Dubček "replied that the Central Committee Presidium is considering the problem, that the [Soviet] appeal will be given the sharpest evaluation, and that the most decisive measures will be taken."

What Dubček, Černík, and Smrkovský actually thought of Two Thousand Words is, of course, academic. The reality on this afternoon of June 27 was that Moscow was angrily demanding action and that Czechoslovakia was filled with thousands of Soviet troops. For all practical purposes, Czechoslovakia was already an occupied country, for at a moment's notice Marshal Yakubovsky's troops could swing into action and gain control of all the strategic spots in the nation and additional divisions, poised on the borders, could be called in to provide swift assistance. If the Czechoslovak Army were to fight back, which was improbable, the Soviet Union could within hours move further divisions and back them up with unlimited air power. I was reminded of a casual remark an Eastern European journalist had made to me when the maneuvers began. "You know," he said, "if the Czechs ever get one inch out of line, Yakubovsky could drive up to the castle and say to Svoboda, 'Look here, I have news for you: you are an occupied country.'" And as I was to learn later, the Soviet Union had in addition concentrated three hundred thousand troops along the Czechoslovak borders.

Before the end of the afternoon of June 27, therefore, Dubček had called the KSČ Presidium into session. Bilak and Kolder bitterly reproached him for having allowed the situation to reach the point where "such a document" could have been issued. The so-called neutral Presidium members nodded their agreement. Consulting with his liberal colleagues—Smrkovský, Černík, Špaček, and Kriegel—Dubček sadly agreed that Two Thousand Words had to be denounced. Within hours, a special announcement from the Presidium described the manifesto as a "clear threat to the entire democratization process." In Bratislava, the Presidium of the Slovak Party, loyal to Bilak, issued an even harsher condemnation. General Samuel Kodaj, a Slovak, rose in the National

Assembly to denounce the manifesto. Speaking next, Premier Černík obtained from the Assembly the unanimous approval of a condemnation of all those who created "a climate of nervousness, apprehension, and legal uncertainty." Dubček expressed his "grave concern" over the situation. And Alois Indra proceeded to cable all regional Party organizations warning them against "counterrevolutionary incitement."

The next day Dubček again denounced the manifesto but also invited the citizens to join in the process of national renewal. Simultaneously, Party conferences opened in one hundred districts, and delegates began to be elected to the KSČ Congress.

Prague's official denunciation of the Vaculík manifesto seemed to calm the storm, but nobody could tell whether the Soviets had really been assuaged and the danger was over. Optimists were inclined to think that the crisis had passed and a relatively quiet summer loomed ahead. Thousands of Czechs and Slovaks began to leave their city homes for the countryside; others motored to Austria, Yugoslavia, Italy, and elsewhere in Europe for their holidays. Conversely, thousands of foreign tourists filled Czechoslovakia and, incongruously, their cars mixed on the roads with the Soviet, Polish, and Czechoslovak tanks and troop trucks still involved in the maneuvers. Outwardly, Czechoslovakia was tranquil, and the foreign tourists watching the clock on the tower of the Old Town Hall in Prague or camping around Karlový Varý and the Slovak spas had little inkling of the drama seething about them.

The pessimists, on the other hand, thought that the worst still *had* to come. Some of the liberal intellectuals reasoned that the situation could not remain suspended and unresolved. Either Czechoslovakia completely and irrevocably halted the entire democratization process, restored press censorship, and found new leaders; or the liberalizing revolution would keep gathering momentum and inevitably force a Soviet intervention. Dining with me late in June, a prominent Prague journalist said, "Let's be logical. The movement has too much momentum and has aroused too many hopes to be stopped. Dubček will not stop it and, short of an upheaval, he cannot be removed from power. Therefore, the Russians will have no choice but to invade us. It is logically and historically inevitable that an invasion will come." Yet, this man was in a minority. Even those who foresaw new crises and new tensions could not bring themselves to admit the possibility that the Soviet Union would invade Czechoslovakia, a fellow socialist country. "This is 1968, not 1956," they said. "We live in a changed world, Khrushchev could smash Hungary in 1956, but Brezhnev can no longer smash Czechoslovakia in 1968."

On July 1 Radio Prague announced that the Warsaw Pact maneuvers had ended, and on July 3 Marshal Yakubovsky said the exercises had accomplished all their objectives and that some Soviet units had already begun to depart. But, as usual, the truth about the Soviet troop movements was wrapped in mystery and contradictions. Independent observers saw no signs of troop departures and, instead, numerous communications installations were spotted. They did not look temporary to trained eyes.

Whether the Kremlin had reached a final decision on Czechoslovakia is, of course, unknown. Evidently, the Soviet Union would have preferred to see Dubček collapse of his own accord and obviate a military attack. But the contingency planning for an invasion was already so advanced that Moscow could keep both options open for a while longer. The position of the United States and NATO was a factor in Soviet calculations, but all indications were that Moscow was convinced that Washington would not react militarily. Nearly 550,000 American troops were committed in Vietnam, and the American forces in Europe had no capability of striking in defense of Czechoslovakia short of unleashing a nuclear war. This, the Russians knew, was highly improbable. The Kremlin could assume—and the assumption proved to be correct—that the United States would tolerate an intervention in Czechoslovakia. To Brezhnev and Kosygin, the Yalta concept still remained valid, and it was bolstered by the realities of Vietnam.

On July 3 Kadár went to Moscow on an official visit and, apparently, the Soviets finally convinced him that an intervention in Czechoslovakia might well be necessary to "preserve socialism" and that Hungarian troops must participate in the joint operation. In Kremlin speeches that evening, both Brezhnev and Kadár derided the United States as a "rotten and disintegrating" society, as if to persuade themselves and the world at large that the Americans simply could not and would not interfere in Eastern Europe. Brezhnev then went on to say that "apologists for the bourgeois order are prepared to pose in any pseudo-socialist clothes" and "under the mask of national forms" to destroy the socialist system and "weaken the brotherly ties among socialist countries." In another preview of his "doctrine," Brezhnev announced that the Soviet Union "can and will never be indifferent to the fate of socialist construction in other countries." Kadár, in turn, declared that Hungarian Communists expressed "full solidarity with the Communists, with those who defend the power of the working class, the cause of socialism against the encroachments of dogmatists, revisionists, the class enemies. . . . We understand the sense of the struggle, and we are prepared to extend international aid by all means." There could be no clearer way to announce an invasion, but few international statesmen took it seriously. Brezhnev was sounding as Khrushchev had in 1956, and Kadár's words in Moscow in 1968 echoed his own words in Budapest twelve years before as he rode to power in the wake of Soviet tanks.

On July 8 Dubček received almost identical letters from Brezhnev, Ulbricht, Kadár, Gomułka, and Zhivkov demanding that he attend a Warsaw Pact summit meeting to discuss the threat to Communism in Czechoslovakia raised by Two Thousand Words. The manifesto, then, had not been forgotten in Moscow and was again being used to force Prague into submission. The Presidium met on July 9 to consider this virtual order and, by a majority vote, decided to refuse to attend the proposed summit. This time, even the "neutrals" sided with the progressives, and only Bilak, Kolder, and Alternate Member Kapek voted to accept the summons. The reply the government sent suggested that any general conference be preceded by bilateral discussions. This was playing for time.

On July 10, as the Soviet press reopened fire against the "counter-revolutionary forces" in Czechoslovakia, the National Assembly in Prague elected Císař, the liberal detested by Moscow, to head the new Czech National Council. Whether or not this was calculated to irritate the Russians or simply constituted the developing Czech political process, the Kremlin took it as another provocation. On July 11 *Pravda* published a long article headlined "Attack Against the Socialist Foundations of Czechoslovakia" in which the situation was compared to Hungary in 1956. The signers of Two Thousand Words were "counterrevolutionaries linked to foreign imperialism," *Pravda* said, even more ingenious in their subversive work than the Hungarian "counterrevolutionaries" the last time around. *Literaturnaya Gazeta* attacked Presidium member Kriegel for voicing sympathies for the Vaculík manifesto, and *Pravda* came back to the attack with dire warnings that "individual leaders" in Czechoslovakia were attempting to "minimize the danger of this counterrevolutionary statement."

This, again, was a promise of intervention, but, in the usual incongruous way, *Pravda* also announced on July 12 that the Warsaw Pact maneuvers in Czechoslovakia had "just" ended. There was no explanation of what had happened since Yakubovsky had first announced their completion nine days earlier, except for a later statement from the Czechoslovak Defense Ministry that the troops' departure had been delayed because of "misgivings about internal Czechoslovak developments."

But the begrudged evacuation of the Soviet forces was, at best, a feint. Immediately, Soviet and other Warsaw Pact troops began an allegedly defensive antiaircraft exercise along Czechoslovakia's frontiers under the code name of Operation Sky Shield. This was to be announced on July 25. Meanwhile, the invitations were issued for the Communist summit meeting in Warsaw. The Czechoslovak Presidium replied on July 12 that it still preferred preliminary bilateral talks as it had proposed on July 9. On July 14 the conference opened. The Soviet delegation was made up of Podgorny, Brezhnev, Kosygin, Ukrainian Party boss Pyotr Shelest, and Konstantin F. Katushev, the Party Secretary in charge of relations with ruling Communist parties—a most impressive team. Gomułka was the host, and Ulbricht, Kadár, and Zhivkov attended with their top associates.

On July 15 they drafted a highly belligerent letter to Czechoslovakia, published only on July 17 after a session of the Central Committee of the Soviet Party in Moscow. It was Shelest who explained the Warsaw Letter to the Plenum, while Suslov, the Party ideologist who had not gone to the conference and was known to oppose the military intervention, sat in silence.

On the day the Warsaw Letter was being drafted, the Kremlin received another slap in the face from Prague. It took the form of a statement by Lieutenant General Prchlík proposing basic changes in the Warsaw Pact. He suggested that all the Pact partners have an equal voice in its decisions (which was also Ceaușescu's view) and that the Pact never be used for political objectives. This was presumably an attempt to warn against the Warsaw Pact's preparations to invade Czechoslovakia.

But the Warsaw Letter, delivered in Prague on July 16, made it amply clear that the Communist alliance had every intention of acting politically:

> It is our deep conviction that the offensive of the reactionary forces, backed by imperialism, against your Party and the foundations of the socialist system in the Czechoslovak Socialist Republic threatens to push your country off the road of socialism and thus jeopardizes the interests of the entire socialist system. . . .

We cannot agree to have hostile forces push your country from the road of socialism and create a threat of severing Czechoslovakia from the socialist community. This is something more than your cause. It is the common cause of our countries, which have joined in the Warsaw Treaty. . . .

You are aware of the understanding with which the fraternal parties treated the decisions of the January plenary meeting of the Central Committee of the Communist Party of Czechoslovakia, as they believed that your Party, firmly controlling the levers of power, would direct the entire process in the interest of socialism and not let anti-Communist reaction exploit it to grind its own ax. We shared the conviction that you would protect and cherish the Leninist principle of democratic centralism. . . .

Unfortunately, events have taken another course.

Capitalizing on the weakening of party leadership in the country and demagogically abusing the slogan of "democratization," the forces of reaction triggered off a campaign against the Communist Party of Czechoslovakia and its honest and devoted cadres, clearly seeking to abolish the Party's leading role, subvert the socialist system, and place Czechoslovakia in opposition to the other Socialist countries. . . .

Antisocialist and revisionist forces have laid hands on the press, radio, and television, making them a rostrum for attacking the Communist Party, disorienting the working class and all working folk, spewing forth uncurbed antisocialist demagogy, and undermining friendly relations between the Czechoslovak Socialist Republic and the other Socialist countries. . . .

This is precisely why the reaction has been able publicly to address the entire country and to print its political platform under the title "Two Thousand Words," which contains an outright call for struggle against the Communist Party and constitutional authority, for strikes and disorders. This call represents a serious danger to the Party, the National Front, and the socialist state, and is an attempt to introduce anarchy. . . . Far from being repudiated, this platform, being so extensively circulated at a responsible moment on the eve of the Extraordinary Congress of the Communist Party of Czechoslovakia, has, on the contrary, found obvious advocates in the Party rank and file and its leadership, who second the antisocialist calls. . . . A situation has thus arisen which is absolutely unacceptable for a Socialist country. . . .

Matters have gone so far that the joint staff exercises of our troops, with the participation of several units of the Soviet Army . . . , are being used for groundless accusations of violations of the sovereignty of the CSSR. . . .

Czechoslovakia can retain her independence and sovereignty only as a Socialist country, as a member of the Socialist community. . . . It is our conviction that a situation has arisen in which the threat to the foundations of socialism in Czechoslovakia jeopardizes the common vital interests of other Socialist countries. . . .

Each of our parties is responsible not only to its working class and its people but also to the international working class and the world Communist movement, and it cannot evade the obligations following from this. . . .

That is why we believe that a decisive rebuff to the forces of anti-Communism and decisive efforts to preserve the socialist system in Czechoslovakia are not only your task but ours, too.

The cause of defending the power of the working class and of all working people, as well as Czechoslovakia's socialist gains, demands that a bold and decisive offensive should be launched against right-wing and antisocialist forces; that all the defensive means set up by the socialist state should be mobilized; that a stop should be put to the activity of all political organizations that come out against socialism; that the Party should take control of the mass-information media—press, radio, and television—and use them in the interests of the working class, of all working people, and of socialism; that the ranks of the Party itself should be closed on the principled basis of Marxism-Leninism; that the principle of democratic centralism should be undeviatingly observed; and that a struggle should be undertaken against those whose activity helps the enemy. . . .

We express the conviction that the Communist Party of Czechoslovakia, conscious of its responsibility, will take the necessary steps to block the path of reaction. In this struggle, you can count on the solidarity and all-around assistance of the fraternal Socialist countries.

In stating that "Czechoslovakia can retain her independence and sovereignty only as a Socialist country, as a member of the Socialist community" and in warning that "a situation has arisen in which the threat to the foundations of socialism in Czechoslovakia jeopardizes the common vital interests of other Socialist countries," the Warsaw Letter was an ultimatum to Prague to desist or be invaded.

Dubček convened the Presidium to prepare a reply, rejecting the accusations and calling the Central Committee into session for July 19. This Czechoslovak reply was much more moderate in tone than the Warsaw Letter, but it was firm in declaring that the Party would pursue its course and that it did not see the "counterrevolutionary" dangers claimed by its partners.

On the same day President Ceauşescu and Yugoslavia's Foreign Minister Nikezić issued statements in Bucharest and Belgrade in support of Czechoslovakia. The two governments foresaw that danger to Czechoslovakia was a danger to them, and both Ceauşescu and Tito privately advised Dubček and President Svoboda that they were ready to fly to Prague on a moment's notice to offer their moral support. But the Czechoslovaks declined these offers on the grounds that the visits would be premature. They felt that it might be more useful to keep Ceauşescu and Tito in reserve for the final crisis.

In its reply to the Warsaw Pact chiefs, the KSČ Presidium said:

The several fears expressed in your letter were also expressed in the resolution of our May plenary session of the Central Committee of the Communist Party of Czechoslovakia.

However, we see the causes of the conflicting situation mainly in the fact that these conflicts accumulated over the years preceding the January plenary session of the Central Committee of the Communist Party of Czechoslovakia. . . .

Not even the Party itself can remain untouched by internal disputes which accompany the process of unification along the lines of the Action Program. One of the negative aspects of this process is the violation of the principles of democratic centralism in the dealings of some Communists, mainly arising from the fact that for many long years the old Party leadership applied bureaucratic centralism and suppressed internal Party democracy. . . .

We do not, however, see any realistic reasons for statements calling our present situation counterrevolutionary, for statements about an immediate danger to the basis of the socialist system, for statements that Czechoslovakia is preparing a change in the orientation of its socialist foreign policy, or for statements that there is a concrete danger of separating our country from the Socialist society. . . .

The basic orientation of Czechoslovakia's foreign policy was conceived and confirmed at the time of the fight for national liberation and in the process of the socialist reconstruction of our country: it is alliance and cooperation with the Soviet Union and the other Socialist countries. We shall strive for a deepening of friendly relations between our allies—the countries of the world socialist system—on the basis of mutual respect, sovereignty and equality, mutual esteem, and international solidarity. . . .

We do not hide the fact—and we stated this plainly at the May Plenum of the Central Committee—that there exist today tendencies aimed at discrediting the Party, attempts to deny it its moral and political right to lead society. But if we ask the question whether such phenomena can be correctly judged as a threat to the socialist system, as a decline of the political role of the Communist Party of Czechoslovakia under the pressure of reactionary, counterrevolutionary forces—then we come to the conclusion that this is not so. . . .

In accordance with the resolution of the May Plenum of the Central Committee of the Communist Party of Czechoslovakia, a binding political socialist platform of the National Front is being created on the initiative of Communists. All the political components of the National Front adopted the program statement made on June 15, 1968, which clearly accepts the historically won leading role of the Communist Party of Czechoslovakia and which expresses the principles of a socialist system and socialist domestic and foreign policy. . . .

There is, in our opinion, a decisive aspect to the present situation: the rise in authority of the new, democratic policy of the Party in the eyes of the broadest masses of the workers and the growing participation of the overwhelming majority of the people. The overwhelming majority of the people of all classes and sectors of our society favors the abolition of censorship and is for freedom of expression.

The Communist Party of Czechoslovakia is trying to show that it is capable of a different political leadership and management than the discredited bureaucratic police methods [of the past]. . . .

At the present time the interests of socialism in our country can be served best by a measure of confidence in the leadership of the Communist Party of Czechoslovakia and of full support for its policy by our fraternal parties. For this reason we have proposed, as a prerequisite of successful joint discussion, bilateral meetings of the representatives of our parties. . . .

We discussed the proposals of the five parties to hold a meeting in Warsaw at two sessions of the Presidium of the Central Committee of the Communist Party of Czechoslovakia—on July 8 and 12. . . . Unfortunately, our meeting of July 12 was superfluous because, regardless of its outcome, the meeting in Warsaw had already been convened for July 14—a fact we learned only through ČTK on the afternoon of July 13, at a time when the representatives of the five parties were already on their way to Warsaw. . . . We think that the common cause of socialism is not advanced by the holding of conferences at which the policy and activity of one of the fraternal parties is judged in the absence of its representatives. . . .

We see it as an important task to hold the bilateral talks which we have proposed in the nearest future. It would then be possible to assess the possibility of a common meeting of the Socialist countries and to agree on its program and composition, and the time and place of its convening.

On July 18 Dubček spoke on television to reaffirm the Party's rejection of the Warsaw Letter's claims of "counterrevolution." He sounded calm and self-confident as he told the nation the contents of the official reply, and the following day the Central Committee unanimously endorsed the action. Ironically, Soviet pressures were creating a sense of unity in the Czechoslovak Party that Dubček and his colleagues had not been able to achieve a month earlier. Even the pro-Moscow activists—Bilak, Kolder, Indra, and the others—found it wiser to join the show of national unity. If the Kremlin had any understanding of the Czechoslovak mentality, this alone might have caused it to pause and consider the implications of the actions it was now actively preparing. But the Soviet leadership was already committed to the proposition that the Czechoslovak revolution must be destroyed, and it could not entertain thoughts of caution. It gave short shrift to a proposal from the French Communist Party to convene all the European Communist parties to discuss the Czechoslovak problem.

On July 19, the day of the KSČ Central Committee Plenum in Prague, Moscow resumed the offensive on two fronts. *Pravda* reported that a cache of American weapons had been found in Czechoslovakia near the West German border, a new suggestion that "imperialists" were behind the Czechoslovak events. For weeks, the Soviet Union had been criticizing the Prague regime for alleged secret ties with West Germany, even though the Czechoslovak Foreign Ministry had said publicly that the

Munich Pact of 1938 must be declared void if diplomatic relations were to be established between the two countries. (As has been noted, the Soviet Union and Romania already had diplomatic relations with Bonn.) And in the same issue, *Pravda* claimed that "secret" Pentagon and CIA documents had been discovered disclosing plans to overthrow the Prague regime.

The second Soviet move was to take Prague up on its proposal for bilateral talks; the Russians invited the *entire* KSČ Presidium to meet with the Politburo somewhere in the Soviet Union—Moscow, Kiev, or Lvov —on July 22 or 23. The Czechoslovaks' reaction was predictable and, in the light of subsequent events, extremely wise. It refused to travel to the Soviet Union and insisted, instead, that the meeting be held on Czechoslovak territory *after* the departure of the last Soviet detachment from the maneuver force. Dubček and his colleagues did not need to spell out their reasons: every Czech and Slovak realized that once the Presidium was in the Soviet Union, its members might never be heard from again. There was a long history of mysterious disappearances in the Soviet Union, Imre Nagy's being only the most recent. So anxious was the Soviet leadership for the confrontation with the Czechoslovak Presidium—it had become a question of almost obsessive face-saving—that to Prague's own great surprise it agreed. *Pravda*, in disclosing this on July 22, told its readers that while the Czechoslovak leaders still failed to understand the "counterrevolutionary" dangers, they had shown their desire to improve relations with their socialist allies and that a direct discussion would be highly constructive. But at the same time, *Pravda* hurled another set of accusations against "right-wing antisocialist forces" in Czechoslovakia "encouraged and supported by imperialist reaction." Also on July 22 Ambassador Chervonenko handed the Foreign Ministry in Prague a secret note demanding that Warsaw Pact troops be permanently stationed in Czechoslovakia and protesting General Prchlík's remarks on the Warsaw Pact structure.

If the Dubček regime felt that it had scored at least a partial victory in obtaining the Politburo's agreement to come to Czechoslovakia and the final withdrawal of Soviet troops, this feeling was extremely short-lived. On July 23 a series of events occurred which demonstrated that the Soviet Union was not only keeping all its options open, but also applying new psychological pressure. An official announcement from Moscow said that "large-scale" maneuvers of Soviet support and supply troops had begun along Czechoslovak borders in the Ukraine as well as in the western part of the Russian Republic, in Byelorussia and Latvia. The announcement said the new maneuvers, slated to end on August 10, were being held under the command of Marshal Ivan K. Bagramyan in order to work out procedures for the organization of rear-area facilities, delivery of supplies to front-line troops, and repairs of military equipment. Reservists were called up and civilian transport requisitioned. Though an observer might have concluded that the Russians had simply gone maneuver-happy in this summer of 1968, professionals realized at once that the Red Army was putting the final touches on its logistic arrangements for the support of invasion forces. The antiaircraft Operation Sky Shield was simultaneously unfolding along Czechoslovakia's borders, for the benefit of the air units already earmarked for a possible intervention.

While the final withdrawal of Soviet troops from Czechoslovakia had been announced on July 22, the very next day an inquiring British reporter found a Soviet force of two thousand men with tanks, armored cars, and mortars bivouacked east of the central Slovak town of Zilna. The tanks had not been placed on their transporters, he discovered, and the brigade was showing no signs of leaving. Since it was unlikely that this particular unit was the only one being left behind in Czechoslovakia, it seemed obvious that the Russians were not keeping their word and not evacuating the country prior to the planned conference.

Simultaneously, the Soviet press launched a new salvo of attacks on Czechoslovak leaders. *Izvestia* printed a letter by an unidentified Czech historian charging Interior Minister Pavel with complicity in organizing rigged trials and "condemning innocent men" to death during the Stalin era. This was patent nonsense, because Pavel had ceased to be Deputy Interior Minister and was himself arrested in 1951 before the purges went into high gear. But the *Izvestia* letter claimed that Pavel, now "cynically backing the rehabilitation of surviving prisoners," should be punished for his earlier "crimes." It seemed like a return to the fantasy world of the 1950s, as the Soviets prepared their public opinion for what was to come. The same morning, *Red Star*, the Soviet military newspaper, took to task General Prchlík for his comments on the Warsaw Pact and called them "an undisputed slander."

On July 25 the KSČ Presidium decided that some concessions were in order, and it abolished the Armed Forces and Security Department of the Central Committee and transferred General Prchlík, its head, to regular Army duty, preferring to abolish his department altogether than to fire him. The Soviet press chose not to publish this news. A statement by the

Defense and Security Committee of the Czechoslovak National Assembly that the defense of the country was fully assured—especially on its borders with the capitalist states—likewise failed to mollify Moscow. The Committee had also pledged that internal security and Czechoslovakia's relations with its socialist allies were protected.

Late on July 25, a Thursday, Czechoslovaks were apprised that the fateful meeting of the KSČ Presidium with the Soviet Politburo would be held on Monday, July 29, at an undisclosed spot in Czechoslovakia, presumably near the Soviet border. The sense of crisis deepened. On July 26 *Literární Listy* issued a special edition with an appeal by Czechoslovak intellectuals to their leaders. Written by Pavel Kohout, it said:

> Comrades, we are writing to you on the eve of your meeting with the Politburo. ... As many times before in the history of mankind, a few men will decide the fate of millions. It is difficult, and we want to help you by expressing our support.
>
> The history of our countries over the past centuries is a history of bondage. Except for two short intervals we have been condemned to create our national existence illegally. We have several times stood on the brink of disaster.
>
> The moment has come when, after many centuries, we have found the beginnings of hope not only for ourselves but for others. The moment has come when we can prove to the world that socialism is not an emergency solution for underdeveloped countries but the only true alternative for civilization.
>
> We expected the whole Socialist camp to be the first to welcome this development sympathetically. Instead we are being accused of treason. We receive ultimatums from comrades who by their declarations prove their lack of knowledge of our development and situation. We are accused of crimes we have not committed. Intentions are attributed to us which we did not and do not have.
>
> Comrades, it is your historic task to prevent such a danger. It is your mission to convince the leading representatives of the Soviet Communist Party that the process of regeneration in our country must be carried out in accordance with the interests of our country and of progressive forces on all continents.
>
> All we are striving for can be expressed in four words: socialism, alliance, sovereignty, and freedom.
>
> In socialism and alliance lie our guarantee to fraternal countries and parties that we will not allow any development threatening the true interests of nations with whom we have been fighting side by side for twenty years in a common cause. Our sovereignty guarantees that we will not repeat the serious mistakes which have brought us to the brink of crisis in the past.
>
> Explain to your partners that the extreme voices which are heard here and there in our internal discussions are precisely the products of the bureaucratic police system which has stifled creative thought for so long and pushed a number of people into internal opposition.
>
> Convince them by quoting innumerable examples to show that the authority of the Party and the position of socialism here are incomparably stronger now

than ever before. Tell them that we need freedom, peace, and time to become better and more reliable allies than before.

Simply speak on behalf of the people who in these days have ceased to be an abstract term and have become a force creating history.

Act, explain, but unanimously defend the way we have embarked upon and which we do not intend to leave alive. During the next few days we will follow your dealings hour by hour. We await your reports with impatience. We think of you. Keep us in mind. You are writing a fateful page of the history of Czechoslovakia. Write with deliberation but above all with courage. We trust you. At the same time we appeal to all citizens who agree with us to support this message.

This document, a *cri de coeur* of the Marxist liberals, logically followed Two Thousand Words, but it also was an almost unprecedented nationalist pronouncement. Within hours of its publication, hundreds of copies had been posted on walls all over Czechoslovakia and tables had been set up in the streets where citizens could sign this appeal to the country's leaders. Nobody knows how many signed; it may have been millions.

In the evening Dubček met with a workers' delegation in Prague. He promised them that he would win more freedom of action from the Soviet Union. Czechoslovakia did not wish to push its differences with Moscow to an open break, he said, but, "We know what we want. . . . We must not get nervous, because nervousness leads to insecurity. These difficult times demand the utmost circumspection and deliberation, and the least passion. . . . Be assured that we shall succeed. We shall succeed not only in defending our ideas but in getting more freedom of action. . . . Such an attitude of our Party and people will be the greatest support in the talks."

Czechoslovakia now stood on the brink of her greatest crisis in thirty years. But the mood was not the defeatist mood of 1938, when in Munich "they decided about us, without us." Now, the leadership was firm, and the nation trusted it. A Prague journalist said, "This is more like England in 1940."

On Sunday, July 28, Moscow and Prague officials announced that the meeting of the Soviet Politburo and the Czechoslovak Presidium would open the next day at Čierna-nad-Tisou. This obscure village is a railroad stop in the southeastern corner of Slovakia where the Czechoslovak, Soviet, and Hungarian borders meet. It is about ten miles north of the river Tis (the Hungarians call it Tisza), which enters Slovakia briefly from Hungary and then meanders along the Soviet-Hungarian border before returning to Hungarian territory. The rail line through Čierna is a secondary one running from Chop, in the Soviet Ukraine, to Slovenské Nové Mesto, in southern Slovakia. Čierna itself is less than five miles from the Soviet border.

Čierna suddenly became a center of world attention as a train from the Soviet Union brought nine members of the Soviet Politburo and a train from Bratislava brought President Svoboda and all eleven members of the Czechoslovak Presidium for their historic confrontation. There was no precedent in Communist history for such a conference. During the Polish crisis in October 1956 Khrushchev brought only three Politburo members to Warsaw. When the Budapest uprising erupted a month later, two Politburo members went to Hungary. The only explanation for it was the deep distrust among the Soviet leaders, obviously still divided among themselves over the Czechoslovak affair, and their reluctance to let a small group make a decision on behalf of the entire Politburo.

This, then, was the line-up at Čierna: The Soviet team was made up of the General Secretary of the Soviet Party, Brezhnev, sixty-two; Premier Kosygin, sixty-four; Chief of State Podgorny, sixty-five, who tended to be a mediator; the ideologist Mikhail Suslov, sixty-six, who had been in Budapest in 1956 but now favored caution in Czechoslovakia; Ukrainian Party boss Pyotr Shelest, sixty, an advocate of radical action against Prague; Aleksandr Shelepin, fifty, former head of the KGB and a "hawk"; Arvid Pelshe, sixty-nine, the Latvian Party boss with a past in the secret police and an enemy of nationalists; Kyril Mazurov, fifty-four, head of the Byelorussian Party and also a hard-liner; and Gennady Voronov, fifty-eight, a technocrat who probably opposed tough measures. (The Politburo members left in Moscow to mind the store were Dmitri Polyansky and Andrei Kirilenko.)

The Czechoslovak delegation was led by Dubček and also included the seventy-two-year-old President Svoboda, who was not at the time a Presidium member. The others were National Assembly Chairman Smrkovský and Josef Špaček, both liberal progressives; Premier Černík, who was still then a progressive; František Kriegel, a liberal; Drahomír Kolder, a hard-line conservative; Vasil Bilak, the Slovak Party boss and probably the most pro-Moscow Presidium member; Oldřich Švestka, a Stalinist; František Barbírek, a Slovak "neutral"; Emil Rigo, a conservative gypsy Communist; and Jan Piller, a conservative.

Aside from the individual political views of the Soviet and Czechoslovak delegates, one striking fact was that Čierna was a confrontation of old and young men. The average age of the Soviet team was just under sixty-one, while the average among the Czechoslovaks, excluding President Svoboda who attended ex officio, was just over forty-seven.

The meeting was planned for one day but lasted four—such were the divergences between the two delegations as well as within the Prague contingent. The first session began in the morning of Monday, July 29, at the heavily guarded Čierna movie theater. But even before the discussions started, the Russians had set a propaganda campaign in motion. *Pravda*'s issue of that morning, rushed to Čierna, emphasized Czechoslovakia's economic dependence on the Soviet Union. As the conference got under way, Brezhnev read a long prepared statement accusing Czechoslovakia of betraying international socialism and serving the "imperialist" cause. He quoted at enormous length from Czechoslovak publications to prove his point and argued that freedom of the press was threatening the Communist Party's "leading role" in Czechoslovakia and, in turn, driving the country away from the Warsaw Pact and Comecon.

On the day the Čierna meeting opened, Western military intelligence services observed the movement of seventy-five thousand Soviet troops in East Germany in the direction of the Czechoslovak border, and other divisions were spotted in Poland deploying south. Two East German divisions were seen on the move, supplementing the Soviet main force. All these units were intended as reinforcements for the divisions already massing around Czechoslovakia. Whether this was part of mounting psychological pressure on Dubček and his associates or was simply the continuation of invasion preparations, neither the Prague leaders nor the NATO commanders could determine at that moment. It could, in fact, have been both—as Moscow clearly was playing to the hilt its stratagem of deception and potential surprise. In any case, the military moves and the political operations were perfectly synchronized at that juncture, and the Russians could, to the last minute, keep all their options open at Čierna.

At Čierna, Dubček rejected all these charges and insisted that the only aim of the revolution was the implantation of "Socialism with a Human Face." President Svoboda, siding with Dubček, angrily reddened when Brezhnev spoke of socialist "treason." The rest of the day was taken up with back-and-forth remarks by various of the participants. The meeting was adjourned at ten-thirty p.m., and the Soviet train took the Kremlin delegation back to Chop for the night. But Dubček was restless and spent much of the night strolling around Čierna and chatting with the

railway workers, who expressed their support for him. Czechoslovak police kept the hundreds of newsmen at bay, not even letting them enter the
village.

The next day, newspapers in Hungary and Bulgaria expressed new criticisms of Czechoslovakia. *Nepszava* in Budapest wrote that "our historic
experiences show that hostile forces will inevitably become involved in
the process of correcting mistakes and will use every opening to their own
advantage." Sofia's *Rabotnichkeskoe Delo* said that the "threat to socialism in Czechoslovakia is growing every day," that "internal reaction and
imperialist centers" were pushing Czechoslovakia toward "revisionism
and restoration." *Pravda* printed a letter from ninety-nine workers in a
Prague automotive plant protesting against the calls for the withdrawal of
Soviet troops from Czechoslovakia.

On Wednesday, July 31, a crisis developed in the talks. The positions
of the two sides were completely irreconcilable, and the conservatives on
the Czechoslovak delegation drew back from the discussions. At one
point, Brezhnev became furious over a remark Kriegel had made and
called him a "dirty Galician Jew." Then he was taken ill, or pretended to
become ill, and the discussions ceased as he returned to his railroad car.
However, Dubček visited him and the talks were resumed. Feelings were
running high, though; a banquet and news conference were canceled.

Although no details of the final session held on Thursday, August 1,
were ever published, I have sound reasons to believe that during it Dubček either made important concessions or created the impression that he
had done so. Shortly after the invasion, a high Czechoslovak official told
me—and I so reported in *The New York Times*—that Dubček and Brezhnev had worked out a six-point agreement. According to this version,
Dubček promised to "establish control over the Czechoslovak press"; to
prevent the organization of any political groups outside the National
Front; to take measures to strengthen the People's Militia and other security forces; to assure the protection of conservative Communists opposed to the liberalization program; to end the press polemics with the
Soviet Union; and to remove from the Prague leadership at least two of
the liberals most objectionable to Moscow. These were Kriegel and
Císař.

With the possible exception of the last point, this sounds quite credible.
While these commitments met, in principle, most of the Soviet objections,
they were couched in sufficiently general language to give Dubček very
considerable leeway in implementation. And it is possible that all of them

meant different things to Brezhnev on the one hand and Dubček on the other. Proof that Brezhnev was willing at this stage to settle for general rather than specific assurances was seen in the fact that the brief communiqué issued after the meeting announced that a full-fledged Warsaw Pact meeting would be held in Bratislava two days later. This would not have been possible unless the two sides felt they had reached some form of an agreement. But since no record is available of the Čierna talks, it may never be proved whether it was the Soviet Union or Czechoslovakia that broke the alleged accord.

Returning to Prague that evening, Dubček told newsmen that he had good news and that the people of Czechoslovakia could sleep peacefully. But citizens of Prague were suspicious and not so easily satisfied. The four days of silence during Čierna had raised tensions intolerably and now the people wanted explanations. Late at night, more than five thousand Czechs gathered at the Old Town Square to insist on some form of reassurance or report. There were calls for Dubček to appear. Presently, Smrkovský arrived and was led to a balcony from which to address the crowd. Sounding and looking exhausted, he kept repeating that the leaders had not "betrayed" the cause of the revolution, but questions were hurled at him relentlessly. Again there were cries for Dubček. Smrkovský took a deep breath and said, "I ask you, comrades, be so kind as to leave Dubček alone a bit! . . . That comrade sleeps only three hours a day. What he has got to carry in his head and on his shoulders . . . nobody can even imagine. I can assure you that Comrade Dubček would tell you in his Slovak the same things I have said in my Prague Czech, for we both speak the same language."

On Saturday, August 3, the Warsaw Pact leaders met at the Hall of Mirrors of Bratislava Castle to elaborate a document as long as it was meaningless. This Bratislava Declaration was signed by Dubček, Brezhnev, Gomułka, Ulbricht, Kádár, and Zhivkov, and the signing ceremony was followed by the usual embraces and kisses on the cheek by all present. The question remained who had misled whom.

From the Czechoslovak viewpoint, the Bratislava Declaration was a victory, even if an ephemeral one. The document refrained from mentioning "counterrevolutionary" dangers in Czechoslovakia and said nothing of the Socialist states' obligation to help socialism in sister states. Czechoslovakia was not even mentioned by name. In this sense, it appeared that the Communist leaders had junked the Warsaw Letter and its ultimatum and had produced instead a general and ambiguous statement of socialist principles. (The signers committed themselves to cooperation on the basis of "equality, sovereignty, national independence, and territorial integrity," and spoke piously of socialist construction: the "many-sided tasks of creating a socialist society in each of our countries are easier to solve with mutual help and support." The document contained the standard charges against the United States over the war in Vietnam and against Israel for its "aggressive" policies in the Middle East.) From the Russians' viewpoint, since it was improbable that the Kremlin had suddenly been convinced that no dangers existed in Czechoslovakia, it probably was useful to paper over the disagreements and place a brief moratorium on the dispute—so as to have time either to better prepare the conservative leadership in Czechoslovakia for the next showdown or to organize the invasion militarily.

In any event, the Czechoslovaks and the Western press cried victory. (That in itself may have been the error. The Russians do not like to be shown up for fools.) The consensus was that the crisis was over. More Czechs and Slovaks left for vacations, among them Deputy Premier Šik and Foreign Minister Hájek, who went to Yugoslavia. On television, August 4, Dubček spoke in optimistic tones.

But even in the midst of this jubilation there were pessimists who wanted to look beyond the piece of paper that was the Bratislava Declaration. It was too pat to be true. Their suspicions seemed confirmed by the fact that Soviet troops had not moved away an inch from the Czechoslovak borders after the fraternal feast in Bratislava. During a week I spent in Washington in early August, I was apprised by high American officials that four hundred thousand Warsaw Pact troops stood on Czechoslovakia's frontiers and that at least three hundred Soviet combat aircraft were concentrated on Polish and East German airfields, minutes away from Czechoslovak targets. The final build-up, detected by Western intelligence on July 29, had now been completed. But the troops had not yet received the order to strike. Once more, Moscow was keeping the options open. And, above all, it was closely watching events in Czechoslovakia.

One of the things it watched with immense interest was Tito's visit to Prague, August 9 and 10. When Tito called on President Svoboda at Hradčany Castle, thousands of Czechs smashed through the heavy iron gates to invade the wide courtyard to surround and try to embrace the

Yugoslav leader. The implications of this visit were so obvious (Romania's President Ceauşescu was due in Prague the following week and talk of a new Little Entente was revived) that *Rudé Právo*'s conservative editor Švestka decided to cut coverage of it down to a minimum. This led to a dispute within the newspaper and Švestka peremptorily fired three of his top editors, including Foreign Editor Jiří Hochman.

Domestic political developments, picking up momentum, also worried the Soviets. The elections of delegates for the KSČ congress on September 9 had been completed, and it was obvious that the progressives had carried the day. Within a month Dubček would have a liberal Central Committee. The Slovak Party scheduled its own congress for August 26, and there were reasons to think that Bilak—the man who had sided with Brezhnev in Čierna—might be ousted from his post of First Secretary. On August 10 *Rudé Právo* published the text of drafts for new Party statutes that were to be submitted to the forthcoming congress. Prepared by a commission headed by Špaček, the drafts virtually eliminated the sacred principle of "democratic centralism" in proposing that whenever a decision was taken by a majority, the minority had the right to go on expressing its views. This struck at the very heart of the orthodox principle of Communist discipline. The new texts also provided for open discussions and secret balloting.

The newspapers in Prague, meanwhile, were writing openly about the quickening reforms and the possible outcome of the Party congress. If Dubček had indeed committed himself at Čierna to "control" the press, he evidently had not gotten around to it. A small park off Příkopi Street, which is Prague's financial center, was turned into a forum for discussions —it promptly became known as Hyde Park—and citizens, young and old, gathered every evening to listen to impromptu speeches and to debate the issues of the moment. A new campaign was started to disband the People's Militia, though the regime moved quickly to discourage it.

On August 11 new Soviet maneuvers began along the east, southeast, and northern borders of Czechoslovakia. Troops were probably being placed in positions for the attack. It is also believed that a few days earlier new pressures had converged on the Kremlin to set the military intervention in motion. Gomułka and Ulbricht had both let it be known that they thought Brezhnev had erred in bogging himself down at Bratislava instead of attacking at once, while the Indra-Bilak group in Prague were insisting to Soviet Ambassador Chervonenko that no more time be wasted. They apparently succeeded in convincing him that they were in a position to form a rival regime rapidly and appeal for Soviet help. Chervonenko relayed this view to Moscow with his own recommendation.

On August 12 Ulbricht met with Dubček in Karlový Varý to seek a commitment for a struggle against "antisocialist forces" and the stationing of Warsaw Pact troops in Czechoslovakia. He also wanted a pledge that Dubček would consult him before entering into any talks with West Germany. The meeting, which lasted only a few hours, was chillingly cold and Ulbricht went home empty-handed. He instantly telephoned Brezhnev in Moscow; the time for action, he believed, had come.

It is impossible to pinpoint with any precision just when the Kremlin decided to proceed with the invasion of Czechoslovakia. But the available evidence suggests that at least a preliminary decision was reached on August 10—a week after Bratislava—and that the start of the new maneuvers the following day formed part of the preinvasion pattern. Soviet units in East Germany reportedly were placed on emergency alert on August 14. On August 16 Marshal Grechko, the Defense Minister; Marshal Yakubovsky, the Commander-in-Chief of the Warsaw Pact armies; and General Yepishev, the head of the Soviet Army's Political Administration, flew to East Berlin for the final inspection. The following day they visited Warsaw, presumably for the same reason.

On August 14 the Soviet press had resumed its attacks on "counter-revolutionaries" in Czechoslovakia with an article in *Literaturnaya Gazeta*. On August 16 *Pravda* published a long article charging Dubček's regime with failure to live up to the Bratislava Declaration, whatever this meant. On the same day Dubček warned the Czechs against "too much freedom" and repeated that alliance with the Soviet Union was the "alpha and omega" of Czechoslovak foreign policy.

Between August 15 and 17 much of Dubček's time was taken up with President Ceauşescu's visit. On the evening of the 15th I attended a reception for Ceauşescu given at Hradčany Castle by President Svoboda. It was the last relaxed evening in Prague. Thousands of guests milled through the vast halls of the castle as Svoboda, Dubček, Černík, and Smrkovský sat in a corner with Ceauşescu and his associates eating and chatting with animation. Ambassador Chervonenko stood by himself in a corner of the room and watched the Czechoslovak leaders. He must have known already that the invasion was imminent. I happened to stay late, and after the Romanian guest departed, I encountered Dubček, who was standing alone in the middle of a room with a glass of wine in his hand. I introduced myself and suggested that given the world interest in his person he might wish to grant *The New York Times* an interview. Dubček smiled and agreed it seemed like a good idea, but, he said, he was too busy and would I wait until after the Party congress? We shook hands and he soon left the castle.

After Ceauşescu's departure on August 17, events began moving with inordinate speed. Dubček secretly flew to Komarno, on the Hungarian border, in response to an urgent invitation by Kadár. The Hungarian leader, speaking with Moscow's knowledge, blamed Dubček for his "failure" to carry out the Čierna and Bratislava promises and repeated Brezhnev's earlier demand that Kriegel and Císař be eliminated from the top KSČ leadership. As Ulbricht had done five days earlier, he insisted that Czechoslovakia agree to the stationing of Warsaw Pact forces. Dubček called a Presidium meeting on his return to Prague, and a new appeal for restraint was issued.

It was already too late. The die had been cast.

Late on August 17, as Dubček was meeting with the Presidium, a special Soviet Aeroflot plane landed at Ruzyň airport bringing a team of ranking KGB specialists. They contacted the Soviet Embassy and immediately began meeting with trusted officials of state security at the Interior Ministry to prepare the measures to be taken when the occupation came. Their principal ally was Deputy Interior Minister Šalgovič in over-all charge of the secret police. Interior Minister Pavel naturally was ignorant of the plot, as were his young aides. This was the first step in Czechoslovakia to set the intervention in motion.

On August 18 *Pravda* again attacked the Prague leadership and expressed indignation over the Czechoslovak situation. Specifically, *Pravda* complained that the ninety-nine workers at the Auto-Praha plant who had earlier signed a letter demanding the presence of Soviet troops in Czechoslovakia had been punished and demoted. It seemed like an implausible pretext to justify an invasion, but this was all *Pravda* had available that day. In checking out the story at Auto-Praha, it appeared that the letter had been signed by only forty-four workers—the others were members of their families—and that they had done it in the name of the plant's Party organization without consulting their fellow employees. The Auto-Praha Party secretary promptly confirmed that the man who had gathered the signatures had been suspended from his position for infringing discipline.

A Radio Prague commentator said, "Nothing is settled. . . . We must again say no, so as to gain more concessions. . . . The future will not be easy."

In Moscow, foreign diplomats felt no sense of imminent crisis, and there is nothing to suggest that, despite the latest broadsides fired by the Soviet press, they were advising their governments that an invasion was about to be set in motion. The tension had now lasted so long that a false sense of security had descended on the diplomatic community. It had been common knowledge that for nearly a month powerful Soviet forces were concentrated along Czechoslovakia's frontiers; few, if any, of the ambassadors in Moscow felt impelled to warn their capitals. No alarm was detectable in Washington, in the West European capitals, or at NATO headquarters. President Johnson was watching from the White House the preliminary proceedings at the Democratic Convention in Chicago, and Secretary of State Dean Rusk was preparing to fly there to expound on the foreign-policy plank in the party's platform. The Soviet stratagem of deception was working perfectly.

But, unknown to the diplomats, Brezhnev, Kosygin, and Podgorny had returned to Moscow on August 16 from their summer vacations at the Black Sea. Just as secretly, other members of the Politburo and numerous members of the Central Committee began slipping into Moscow during the weekend. Brezhnev spent much of Sunday, August 18, telephoning Ulbricht, Gomułka, Kadár, and Zhivkov to inform them that the Soviet leadership had decided to order the invasion. They had to be advised inasmuch as their troops were to participate in the intervention.

The following day an emergency meeting of the "enlarged Politburo" —the full membership plus alternates and key members of the Central Committee—was secretly held in the Kremlin to confirm the decision to invade. Afterward, Brezhnev dispatched a letter to Dubček chastising him in the strongest terms for betraying the "spirit" of Čierna and Bratislava, but with no hint that the invasion was now imminent. It could have been read in Prague as just another Soviet expression of displeasure. Premier Kosygin's assignment on that day was to send a message to President Johnson advising him that he was agreeable to the summit meeting Johnson had pressed to discuss Vietnam and disarmament. Kosygin suggested that a joint announcement be made on Wednesday, August 21, though he surely knew that by then Czechoslovakia would have already been occupied. These were the extremes to which the Soviet leadership had gone to assure the most perfect deception. Politically and militarily, everything was now ready.

In Prague, Monday, August 19, was a quiet summer day. In the morning six Czech and Slovak Roman Catholic bishops were received by President Svoboda to discuss cooperation between the state and the church. It was the first time since 1948 that a Czechoslovak President had received a delegation of bishops.

The Prague newspapers, responding to Dubček's appeal of the previous Saturday, refrained from polemics with the Soviet press and confined themselves to reprinting without comment Moscow's most recent attacks. But there must have been a touch of premonition among the editors. *Svobodne Slovo* wrote of the Tito and Ceauşescu visits that "the talks with our Yugoslav and Romanian friends gave us moral support for the next days, support that we shall probably still need to a great extent because all has not been won on either the home front or the foreign front." The Catholic newspaper *Lidova Demokracie* said the two visits had deep meaning for Czechoslovakia because "we subconsciously suffered from a complex of 'being alone' or 'going it alone' at decisive moments . . . and no wonder, because in 1938 we saw for ourselves the value of 'friendship' that is only on paper and is mere promises."

A small item distributed by ČTK announced that Czechoslovak Army divisions would exercise on Wednesday and Thursday in Bohemia with the presence of Warsaw Pact observers. With all the maneuvers that had been held on and off since May, few readers paid attention to this item. Yet it was significant, because it showed that the Soviet military had prevailed upon the Czechoslovak Defense Ministry to let in Warsaw Pact "observers" and to send tank units away toward the West German border.

Over Radio Prague a worried commentator warned that "while we are engaged in academic discussions, disguised conservatives behind our backs are eliminating political activists and journalists from key posts, quietly and behind closed doors, as under Novotný." He was referring to the purge at *Rudé Právo* and other attempts by Moscow-line Communists to recapture some of their lost positions.

Otherwise it was a routine day. Premier Černík officially denied a report that Czechoslovakia was considering credits from the World Bank and Western firms, but conceded that individual firms would like to receive credit lines from firms in "capitalist countries" to increase their production. A deputy minister of heavy industry announced that Japanese manufacturers might wish to produce small passenger cars in Czechoslovakia. Two Soviet journalists improbably arrived to attend a summer seminar on European security at Kokorin, in central Bohemia. The Interior Ministry said it had received eighty new applications for registrations from a variety of organizations. A public-opinion poll—polls had become the rage in Czechoslovakia, as everybody wanted to know what everybody else thought—showed that bad management was responsible for the country's catastrophic economy. Another poll disclosed that fifty-five per cent of those asked thought that confidence in journalists had risen recently and eight per cent believed it had fallen.

Sometime in the evening Dubček received the long letter from the Central Committee of the Soviet Party signed by Brezhnev reproaching the KSČ for disregarding the Čierna and Bratislava decisions. There was no suggestion that the Soviet Union was contemplating an invasion—certainly not the following day. Dubček did not show the letter to any of his associates that evening. The regular Presidium session was scheduled for the following morning, and he proposed to read it at that time.

On Tuesday, August 20, Dubček started his day reading a long article by *Rudé Právo*'s editor. Švestka, under the rhetorical title, "Why the Communist Party?" Švestka's patronizing conclusion was that "the Communist Party of Czechoslovakia has a big chance today. . . . In the closest cooperation with the fraternal parties of the working class of the other Socialist countries, it is implementing its aims: to build a free society according to the *original* ideas of Marx, Engels, and Lenin." The rest of the article was a tedious defense against his staff's charges that he was turning *Rudé Právo* into a stronghold of conservatism on the eve of the KSČ congress.

The Presidium session began at two p.m., four hours late. Discussions of preparations for the September Party congress took all afternoon and early evening; then Kolder and Indra—who usually attended Presidium meetings in his capacity of Party Secretary—insisted that the body take up a long report by Jan Kaspar, a right-wing official of the Secretariat, analyzing the political situation since the Čierna and Bratislava conferences. Dubček must have noted the coincidence between this proposal and Brezhnev's letter of July 19 that he had in his pocket, but he had no reason for further suspicions. What he did not know was that under the plan painstakingly prepared in Moscow, the Presidium was supposed to vote on a resolution to be introduced by Bilak and Indra—based on Kaspar's report—just as Soviet troops entered the country. Bilak, Kolder, Švestka, Indra, and Alternate Member Kapek, all of whom knew precisely when the invasion was to start, had assured the Kremlin a few days earlier that a resolution condemning the "counterrevolution" would be approved and Dubček would simultaneously be ousted from his post. The next step was for the new KSČ leadership and Indra, who would be Acting Premier, to issue a proclamation inviting Warsaw Pact forces to save socialism in Czechoslovakia.

In the advance planning of this coup, nothing was left to chance. At four p.m., two hours after the Presidium session began, Deputy Interior Minister Šalgovič called to order an extraordinary meeting at the Interior Ministry, across the river from the Central Committee building. All the trusted chiefs of security departments and sections were present, as were several Soviet KGB agents who had arrived in Prague the Saturday before. Their leader was an officer named Vinokurov. This meeting proved conclusively that Interior Minister Pavel had not succeeded in the preceding four months in eliminating pro-Soviet elements from the secret police. Despite the opposition of General Kotov, the chief KGB "adviser" to the ministry (whom the government could not eliminate either), Pavel had fired Deputy Minister and state security chief of staff Klima and at least three heads of departments, but this had made no difference. When, inexplicably, he brought Šalgovič back as Deputy Minister, the whole Soviet-controlled apparatus had been reorganized.

Now Šalgovič was informing his colleagues that the invasion would take place that evening and handing out assignments for the night. Klima and other fired officials were advised to be ready to report for duty when the alert was sounded at eleven p.m. As to the security officers attached to the ministry, Lieutenant Colonel Bohumil Molnar, who commanded the Prague region state security, was ordered to have his men ready to arrest the Party's progressive leaders. A KGB agent named Mukhin was to supervise this operation. The Second Department of the ministry, headed by Lieutenant Colonel Josef Rypl, was charged with preventing unauthorized radio broadcasts after the invasion, particularly if Dubček's Presidium succeeded in preparing a proclamation against the intervention. The Department's Seventh and Thirteenth sections were to cooperate in this endeavor with Karel Hoffman, former Culture Minister and currently director of the Central Communications Administration. Lieutenant Colonel Vanek—who with Rypl, assisted Šalgovič in planning the over-all operation—ordered the Second Section to have its agents guard all the "capitalist foreign missions" in Prague as well as the Yugoslav and Romanian embassies during the night. (This was to prevent Czechoslovak citizens from taking asylum when the invasion came.)

In case any of the Interior Ministry's officials had any doubts about the propriety of the operation Šalgovič was setting in motion, he quickly informed all concerned that he was acting in conjunction with the Party's Central Committee. He even claimed he had a direct telephone line to Dubček, though it seemed to make little sense that the First Secretary would be issuing instructions for his own liquidation.

At six p.m. Miroslav Sulek, Director-General of ČTK, arrived at his office off Václavské Náměstí with copies of the "proclamation" inviting Warsaw Pact intervention and a statement by the councils of ministers of the five invading countries.

Aside from people in the Soviet Embassy and KGB officials, the chances are that no more than forty or fifty men in Prague were privy that Tuesday to knowledge that an invasion was only hours away. But Czechs are people with a strong sense of premonition. In making my rounds on August 20, I was aware of malaise and uneasiness. At lunch at the Hotel Esplanade, a leading progressive editor expressed concern that "something bad" would happen to prevent the holding of the September Party congress. There would be "provocations," he said, and perhaps even riots in which Dubček would have to use the police against the people. We parted on a nervous note.

When I returned to my hotel that afternoon to write a dispatch on this new pessimistic mood of Prague, an American news agency was carrying a report that the Soviet Party's Central Committee was meeting in Moscow. A little later I heard on the radio that the KSČ Presidium was in session. With the three or four of my foreign colleagues lingering in Prague during that hot August I shared premonitions that something was about to occur. And, indeed, the invasion machinery had been set in motion, and the deed would soon be done.

BOOK FIVE

The Night Again

XVIII

The Invasion

Precisely at eleven p.m., Tuesday, August 20, Soviet, Polish, East German, Hungarian, and Bulgarian troops crossed Czechoslovakia's borders at eighteen points, coming from the north, northeast, east, and south. Airborne troops equipped with light tanks, armored cars, and antitank artillery were landed in the early hours of Wednesday, August 21, in Prague and Bratislava. An airlift operation working with clocklike precision brought the huge Soviet AN-12 transport planes to Prague's Ruzyń airport at one-minute intervals. They were guided from a taxiway by an Aeroflot aircraft that had arrived from Lvov at ten-thirty p.m. Tuesday and awaited the start of the airlift; it was a mobile control tower. Another unscheduled Aeroflot plane late Tuesday had brought a group of Soviet officers in civilian clothes—the advance command contingent—who rushed to the Soviet Embassy to coordinate movements with Ambassador Chervonenko and the KGB and Czechoslovak security officials.

At the moment the invasion began, the Soviet Union made two simultaneous diplomatic moves. In Washington, Soviet Ambassador Anatoly Dobrynin had requested a six p.m. appointment with President Johnson —there was a five-hour time difference between Central Europe and Washington—but he could not be received at that time. His mission was to inform the United States that the intervention in Czechoslovakia was, in effect, a local affair within the socialist camp and should not be regarded as a threat to America or its NATO allies. But since Johnson could not receive Dobrynin, the United States learned of the invasion from an Associated Press dispatch filed from Prague. For many hours, American military commanders in Western Europe were of no help in

377

diagnosing the situation because the Russians' jamming of Czechoslovak radar defenses had spilled so far over West Germany that they were totally in the dark as to what was happening.

Actually, the Russians had jammed NATO radar on several occasions in the past, and the first reaction was that just another Soviet military exercise was under way. Later, Western intelligence people speculated whether the Soviet Union had developed a new and highly sophisticated radar system to have been able to cover so effectively its operations on the night of August 20. In any case, nearly two hours elapsed before NATO commanders—and Western governments—realized that Czechoslovakia had been invaded, and the chances are that the first word to reach them came from Radio Prague broadcasts and news reports.

That NATO should have been caught unaware is surprising when one considers the amount of intelligence data that was available to it. For months, Warsaw Pact ground and air deployments were monitored by American "spy-in-the-sky" orbiting satellites, U-2 photo-reconnaissance aircraft, NATO's own radar installations, secret electronic devices eavesdropping on Soviet military teletype, microwave, and voice traffic and decoding it, Western military attachés in Eastern Europe, and CIA and West Germany's BND agents. NATO chiefs thus had the full picture of the military developments around Czechoslovakia, and there was no shortage of intelligence analysis suggesting the plausibility, if not probability, of an invasion. Yet, mysteriously, the recipients of all this intelligence input seemed unable or unwilling to interpret it adequately. Perhaps the most valuable element in the Soviet stratagem was the West's psychological inability to believe that the Kremlin would actually stage an invasion.

The result was that NATO failed to order a full military alert even in late July and early August. By normal standards, the Warsaw Pact build-up at that time would have justified a state of alert, inasmuch as nobody could safely predict just what the Soviet intentions might be. Instead, a rather ineffectual state of "vigilance" was ordered early in August. When the invasion finally came, NATO's communications network failed to function efficiently, and much vital information on the actual Soviet movements reached the responsible commanders only after considerable delay. As British Defense Secretary Denis Healey was to explain it later, "as the crisis developed in August, it revealed weaknesses in NATO—a failure in communications, not only between governments themselves, but also between governments and the military."

In Prague, meanwhile, Ambassador Chervonenko's first diplomatic move was to drive to Hradčany Castle shortly after eleven p.m. to inform President Svoboda that his country had been invaded in the name of socialist solidarity by the forces of a nation which the old general had revered as a friend. There is no record of Svoboda's reaction; he immediately went to the Central Committee headquarters, where Dubček, conducting the Presidium meeting, had himself just learned of the invasion.

Up to that moment—just before midnight—everything had gone as planned. Troops of five Warsaw Pact nations were streaming into Czechoslovakia without meeting the slightest resistance. Marshal Yakubovsky, the Warsaw Pact Supreme Commander, had drafted a textbook operation, immensely aided by the long weeks that Soviet troops and signal corps specialists had spent in Czechoslovakia during the June and July maneuvers. The actual execution of the invasion was equally brilliant, under the direction of General Ivan G. Pavlovsky, Soviet Deputy Defense Minister and commander of Soviet ground forces. There was no reason, actually, why it should not have been. There was nobody to oppose or stop the overwhelmingly powerful thrust which engaged close to half a million troops by the time General Pavlovsky had everything—from tactical nuclear weapons to Bulgarian soup kitchens— in place a week later.

In the first forty-eight hours, General Pavlovsky committed elements of twenty-four Warsaw Pact divisions in the invasion, close to two hundred thousand men, not counting the air support and airlift units. Involved in the initial operation were forces from sixteen Soviet, three Polish, two East German, two Hungarian, and one Bulgarian divisions. The small Bulgarian contingent had to be flown first from Varna, in Bulgaria, to Odessa, in the Soviet Union, and thence to the staging areas on the Czechoslovak–East German border. This complicated maneuver was made necessary by Romania's absolute refusal to let Bulgarian troops cross or even overfly her territory (a policy Ceauşescu was to maintain when Bulgarians were being repatriated months later), but the Soviet Union was determined that Bulgaria be represented in the "fraternal" action.

But while the Soviet military might function perfectly *in vacuo*, its political power failed as soon as it met the first resistance. And this resistance came the instant that word of the invasion reached the KSČ Presidium at eleven-forty p.m. Tuesday. This was when the scenario so lovingly elaborated by Ambassador Chervonenko collapsed in its entirety.

As he had worked it out with Bilak, Indra, Kolder, and Švestka, the Presidium had indeed bogged down in discussing the resolution urging an end to "anti-Communist propaganda" in Czechoslovakia. But, more important, there was not enough support to force it through. The "neutrals"—Lenárt and Barbírek—were sitting on their hands. They evidently were not ready to see Dubček ousted. Barbírek, in fact, spent an extravagant amount of time away from the council room, washing his hands and making casual telephone calls. The Dubček-led progressives could thus hold their own.

News of the invasion then, quite contrary to the Soviet script, changed the picture in the progressives' favor and not against them. Premier Černík brought the word (Defense Minister Dzúr had telephoned him). Dubček looked as if he had been struck in the face. He produced the Brezhnev letter, which gave no sign that an invasion would come, and read it to the Presidium. Dubček said, "I declare on my honor as a Communist I had no suspicion, no indication, that anyone would want to undertake such measures against us." There were tears in his eyes as he added, "That they should have done this to me, after I dedicated my whole life to cooperation with the Soviet Union, is the greatest tragedy of my life."

But he recovered quickly. As President Svoboda arrived, Dubček ordered that a proclamation to the nation be drafted. Indra disappeared instantly and drove to the Soviet Embassy. Bilak, Kolder, Rigo, and Švestka stayed behind long enough to vote against this new proclamation. But its approval was the first blow to the Soviet Union's political plan. The proclamation said:

TO ALL PEOPLE OF THE CZECHOSLOVAK SOCIALIST REPUBLIC:

Yesterday, August 20, 1968, at about eleven p.m., the armies of the Soviet Union, the Polish People's Republic, the German Democratic Republic, the Hungarian People's Republic, and the Bulgarian People's Republic crossed the state borders of the Czechoslovak Socialist Republic. This took place without the knowledge of the President of the Republic, the Presidium of the National Assembly, the Presidium of the Government, and the First Secretary of the Communist Party Central Committee. The Presidium of the Central Committee was then in session, preoccupied with preparations for the Extraordinary Fourteenth Party Congress. The Presidium calls upon all citizens of the Republic to keep the peace and not resist the advancing armies, because the defense of our state borders is now impossible.

For this reason, our Army, the security forces, and the People's Militia were not given the order to defend the country. The Presidium considers this action [the invasion] to be contrary to the fundamental principles of relations between Socialist states and a denial of basic norms of international law.

All leading officials of the Party and the National Front remain at their posts, to which they were elected as representatives of the people and members of their organizations according to the laws and regulations of the Czechoslovak Socialist Republic. The appropriate constitutional organs have called into session the National Assembly and the Government of the Republic, and the Presidium of the Central Committee is convening the Party Central Committee in order to deal with the situation that has arisen.

> Presidium of the Central Committee of the Communist Party.

Radio Prague began to broadcast the proclamation shortly before one-thirty a.m. Wednesday, but Hoffman's and Šalgovič's agents managed to cut off the medium-wave transmitter in mid-sentence. Radio technicians succeeded in sending it through another Prague channel, and within minutes the nation was informed of the true situation. I heard the first part of the proclamation over my radio in the hotel room and the balance through a wire transmission in the garage of the Alcron Hotel. The Soviet plan had run into its first obstacle. A leadership had survived the first hours of the invasion and could communicate with the people.

The second Soviet problem was that the teletype operators at ČTK simply refused to transmit the text which Sulek had left behind of the alleged invitation to the Warsaw Pact armies. They placed test tapes on their machines and vanished in the night. Radio Prague was held by announcers and technicians loyal to Dubček and they, too, would not handle the spurious announcement. Therefore, the Soviets found themselves in the extraordinary position of controlling the country militarily and being unable to give the Czechoslovaks their version of what they were doing there. This undermined from the very outset the "credibility" of the whole operation as an intervention "requested" by Czechoslovakia, and it remained bereft of credibility forever after.

If the Czechoslovak Party and government, in the words of the dawn proclamation, instructed their military and security forces not to resist the invasion because it was "impossible," this raised fundamental questions not only of policy but about the Czech and Slovak temperaments. In the first place, the intervention had been ordered because Moscow took the calculated risk of assuming that Czechoslovakia would not defend itself even though it had the largest and strongest army in the Warsaw Pact after the Soviet Union's—two hundred thousand men under arms, equipped with tanks and jet aircraft. General Pavlovsky, to be sure, threw half a million men into the invasion in case of resistance, but this was a normal military precaution. If Brezhnev had thought that Czechoslovakia would fight—as Stalin apparently assumed Yugoslavia would do in 1948–1949—then, it could be argued, the Kremlin might have concluded that a bloodbath in a fellow Socialist country was too high a price to pay for destroying the Prague Spring, and other means would have been sought.

The Czechoslovak argument was subsequently that in the certainty of defeat no government has the right to sacrifice its people. This was the decision President Beneš had made after Munich in 1938 and again when the Nazis marched into Prague in 1939. Svoboda and Dubček acted similarly in 1968. Does the foreigner have the right to make moral judgments about this? Nations such as the Poles, the Yugoslavs, and the Greeks fought to the bitter end against all odds in World War Two and built up formidable resistance movements. The Czechoslovaks did not and, at least in the eyes of other Europeans, their behavior raises the delicate question of honor. It also raises the question of long-range practicality.

After the Nazi invasion of Czechoslovakia and Beneš's choice not to fight, George F. Kennan commented that this resolve "perhaps most important of all has preserved for the exacting tasks of the future a magnificent younger generation—disciplined, industrious, and physically fit—which would undoubtedly have been sacrificed if the solution had been the romantic one of hopeless resistance rather than the humiliating but truly heroic one of realism." In 1968 Czechoslovakia chose this "realism" again and with it an extraordinary, imaginative kind of passive resistance that for the next nine months kept national pride aloft and immensely embarrassed the Soviet Union. But in the end "realism" became a contagion, a way of life, and little by little even the pride was eroded as the nation finally accepted the true reality: it had lost the Prague Spring. History has shown that the Czechs know better than anyone how to wait for the next chance. But an engaged observer cannot help wondering what would have been the course of events in Czechoslovakia and Eastern Europe if Czechoslovakia had resolved to fight on August 20, 1968.

But as this is written two years after the invasion—and a certain sense of perspective on all these events has already emerged—I am increasingly tempted to think that the issue of whether the Czechoslovak armed forces and nation should have fought the invaders is already overshadowed by the *political* consequences of the nation's resistance. The facts are that, on the one hand, no organized military attempt was made to block the invasion, even for a few days, and, on the other hand, that Czechoslovak defiance of Soviet *diktats* has never really ended. To be sure, the Prague Spring ceased to exist as a political and ideological enterprise. But the spirit of the Prague Spring is far from dead, and the Soviet Union has been unable to solve the fundamental problem it faces not only in Czechoslovakia but in all of Eastern Europe. One must conclude that the invasion has been a resounding political fiasco for the Kremlin, even if Dubček and his followers have been effectively removed from power and the fiction has been created that Czechoslovakia is now a loyal member of the Moscow camp. If this were not so, it would not have been necessary for Soviet troops to stand poised to intervene in Prague again on the first anniversary of the invasion. The profound meaning of all this is that, no matter what their power, the Russians can never feel secure in Czechoslovakia.

The invasion on the night of August 20–21, 1968, did not, therefore, mark the end of the Czechoslovak story but, instead, the beginning of a new phase. This phase opened the instant the so-called allied troops entered Czechoslovakia expecting a quick military and political triumph, but discovered, literally within minutes, how atrociously the Kremlin planners had misunderstood and misinterpreted the situation in the country. In fact, things went wrong from the very first moment, when the conspiracy in the KSČ Presidium collapsed and the Party and government leadership was able to get to the nation first with its proclamation.

This simple fact dashed the Russians' carefully prepared plans for the immediate creation of a puppet Party leadership and government. Instead of awakening on the morning of the 21st to be told that foreign "fraternal" troops had arrived at the request of a new regime, Czechoslovaks learned that the nation had been invaded. Even before advance elements of the invasion forces could reach the key strategic targets in Prague, the resistance had therefore already begun. And it began spontaneously.

As the huge Soviet AN-12 transports disgorged the paratroop units and the light armored vehicles in the darkness at Ruzyň airport and the tank columns converged on Prague from the East German and Polish crossing points, thousands of Czechs poured out into the streets of the darkened capital. Some were jolted out of their sleep by the roar of the landing aircraft. Others had heard the Presidium's proclamation over the radio and now were telephoning each other and battering on each other's doors with the awesome news. Cars filled with young people raced through the streets, their horns blaring, calling for manifestations at the Old Town Square and Wenceslas Square. They were the vanguard of the force that was to give brief, bloody battle to the invaders in the heart of the city.

Dubček and his supporters in the Presidium remained at the Central Committee building—it was another misconception on the part of the planners to think that they would rush to seek asylum at foreign embassies—to face what might come. At two in the morning Bohumil Šimon, the tough leader of the powerful Prague Party organization, burst in with a proposal that the Extraordinary Fourteenth Party Congress, scheduled for September 9, be called immediately into session, that a general strike be organized, and that an appeal to the Communist parties of the world be drafted. Dubček agreed, and the moves that Šimon and his colleagues initiated were to turn the tables on the Russians in less than forty-eight hours.

Černík left KSČ headquarters as soon as the proclamation was written and drove to his office at the yellow building in Klarov, across the river, where the government Presidium functioned in the former Straca military academy. His idea was to convene the cabinet to assure that Czechoslovakia had an operating government. But just before three a.m., as he was summoning the ministers, Soviet troops broke into the building and a squad of paratroopers arrested him at bayonet point. While other officials were lined up against the wall, Černík was taken away by the crimson-bereted paratroopers, placed in an armored car, and driven to an unknown destination.

For reasons still unclear, the Central Committee building remained unoccupied for another ninety minutes. Dubček, Smrkovský, Kriegel, Špaček, Václav Slavik, and a number of lesser Party officials had made no move to leave. But at about four-thirty a.m., three Soviet armored cars led by a black Volga with Soviet Embassy license plates arrived at the green-domed structure. The troops evidently had to be guided by Soviet diplomats, KGB, and pro-Soviet Czechoslovak security agents. Within minutes, more armored cars, truckloads of paratroopers, and a column of tanks surrounded the Central Committee building. The soldiers, submachineguns at the ready, were posted twenty yards apart. Nobody could leave or enter. A group of officers and civilians presently made their way upstairs and Dubček, Smrkovský, Kriegel, and Špaček were placed under detention. Slavik somehow escaped arrest. The four detained leaders were kept in the building under Soviet military guard as General Pavlovsky and Ambassador Chervonenko either awaited further instructions or pondered the next moves. In the small hours of the morning two Czechoslovak civilians, presumably security agents, led away Čestmir Císař, the Party Secretary and chairman of the Czech National Council, to the security police downtown headquarters on Bartolomějska Street.

By then, Prague was cut in two by Soviet tanks blocking all the bridges over the Vltava. Other units surrounded Hradčany Castle on the hill on the left bank of the river and the Foreign Ministry a quarter of a mile away, and set up an armed camp at the Soviet Embassy in Bubeneč. On the right bank, Soviet tanks and troops gradually surrounded not only the Central Committee building but the National Assembly, the Prague television station on Maxim Gorky Square, newspaper and magazine offices, ČTK, the headquarters of the Writers' and Journalists' unions, and, late in the morning, the Academy of Sciences. This pattern of occupation made it clear that the first targets in Prague were to be the centers of political and ideological thought and action—whatever had been said, and would be said, about the need to defend Czechoslovakia from "Western imperialists."

All the invading tanks and vehicles were painted with a wide white stripe to distinguish them from the identical Soviet-manufactured Czechoslovak equipment.

As day broke over Prague, the Soviets had captured the entire city with one vital exception—Radio Prague, which at four-thirty a.m. resumed broadcasting from its main studios at Vinohradska Street, a block away from Wenceslas Square. In total disregard of the physical occupation of the capital and now the whole country, Radio Prague was calmly functioning as a service of the legal government of Czechoslovakia. It repeated the Presidium proclamation and went on transmitting a stream of up-to-the-minute reports. In this incredible state of affairs, Czechoslovaks saw themselves surrounded by invading tanks but could listen to a radio and, subsequently, television network denouncing the occupation and methodically organizing a resistance. Radio and TV technicians had rapidly restored the transmission facilities and, oddly, neither the Soviets nor the Czech traitors were able to silence these voices of freedom. As the Czechs proved within a few hours, not even Soviet tanks were a deterrent. As much as anything else, the story of the Czechoslovak radio was a measure of the colossal political fiasco of the invasion.

Because Prague was divided into two, we journalists, too, split up operations. Around four a.m., just before the bridges were closed to traffic, I drove from the *Times* office at the Alcron Hotel, just off Wenceslas Square, to the American Embassy on the left bank, taking with me our Czech secretary and interpreter Kitty Voleniková. I had been able to send several hundred words about the invasion over the Alcron Hotel Telex to the *Times* bureau in London, but I became worried about the Telex lines being shut down by the Russians. International telephone connections had been interrupted at midnight. The embassy, however, had a Telex of its own and I hoped I could use it if all else failed. Peter Rehak of the Associated Press, who had told the world of the invasion with his flash from the Alcron Telex, came along too. Clyde Farnsworth, a *Times* correspondent who had arrived in Prague the previous afternoon on a routine visit to gather economic information, remained at the Alcron to cover the right bank. As it turned out, the fact that we had a correspondent on each side of the river gave the *Times* a tremendous advantage in covering the developing story. At the embassy, Ambassador Jacob D. Beam had already arrived from his Bubeneč residence, and his staff was functioning with extraordinary smoothness and efficiency that was to characterize it for weeks and months to come. Beam (since appointed Ambassador to Moscow) was cool, unruffled, and under the circumstances immensely friendly and understanding of our problems. It was his kindness in allowing us to use the embassy Telex at will—the embassy communicated with Washington through separate classified facilities—that made it possible for the *Times,* the Associated Press, and later other American news organizations to keep up an uninterrupted flow of news from Prague. I shudder when I think what some other American ambassadors of my acquaintance—less courageous and independent-minded than Jake Beam—might have done under the circumstances. As it was, Kitty Voleniková and I were installed in the ambassador's waiting room with our radio and typewriter and this became the *Times* office for days to come. Peter Rehak, who speaks Czech and Slovak, took turns with Kitty monitoring the radio, and then Peter and I alternated at the Telex. I must say the Telex worked like a charm.

By early morning vast confusion reigned in Prague. Soviet troops and token Bulgarian units were in control of the city, but they could not communicate with the people they came to occupy. About four a.m., before Radio Prague resumed broadcasting, by sheer chance we caught the weak transmission on the 210-meter band of a station identifying itself as Radio Vltava. Even my limited knowledge of Czech made it obvious that the announcer was a German speaking Czech with an atrocious accent. Vltava, we soon realized, was the station of the "allied command," broadcasting from East Germany, and it transmitted the text of the proclamation of the invading governments in a pathetic attempt to explain the intervention. To make sure that the Czechoslovaks were aware of it, copies of the proclamation were being dropped from aircraft and helicopters and distributed from the Soviet tanks to a furious population:

OUR BROTHERS, CZECHS AND SLOVAKS!

The governments of the Bulgarian People's Republic, the Hungarian People's Republic, the German Democratic Republic, the Polish People's Republic, and the Union of Soviet Socialist Republics appeal to you.

Responding to the request for help from leading Party and state leaders of Czechoslovakia who have remained faithful to socialism, we instructed our armed forces to go to the support of the working class and all the people of Czechoslovakia to defend their Socialist gains, which are increasingly threatened by plots of domestic and foreign reactionary forces.

This action is based on the collective commitment that the Communist and workers' parties of the fraternal countries adopted at Bratislava and on the commitment to support, strengthen, and defend the socialist gains of every nation and to stand up to imperialist plots.

Counterrevolutionaries incited and supported by imperialists are grasping for power. Antisocialist forces that seized positions in the press, radio, and television have attacked and smeared everything created by the hands of industrious Czechs and Slovaks in the twenty-year-long struggle for socialism.

Enemies have incited people against the cadres dedicated to socialism; they have undermined the foundations of legality and the legal order, wantonly removed class-conscious workers and peasants from the political life of the country, and persecuted honest members of the intelligentsia who refused to take part in their actions. Trampling Socialist laws under foot, counterrevolutionary forces preparing to seize power have created their own organizations. And all this was being masked by demagogic phrases about democratization! We believe that the Czechoslovak people, dedicated to the ideals of socialist democracy, will not be deceived. True freedom and democracy can be guaranteed only through strengthening the leading role of the working class and of its vanguard—the glorious Communist Party of Czechoslovakia.

The January session of the Central Committee of the Czechoslovak Communist

Party, which marked the beginning of the effort to rectify the mistakes of the past, had called for attainment of this very goal. Our parties and nations supported the justified aims to strengthen and further perfect socialist democracy.

In recent months, the antisocialist forces, working in clever disguise, have concentrated their efforts on undermining the foundations of socialism. A number of people who had penetrated the state and Party leadership of Czechoslovakia offered cover for these subversive actions and thus helped the counterrevolution to rally its forces for the final struggle to seize power.

Czechoslovak leaders kept declaring, at the Soviet-Czechoslovak meeting at Čierna-nad-Tisou and at Bratislava that they intended to guard the interests of the workers and defeat the reactionary forces that were attempting to undermine socialism. They promised that they would strengthen the unity of Czechoslovakia and the fraternal Socialist countries.

These assurances and commitments were not fulfilled, however, which further encouraged the antisocialist forces and their foreign protectors to strengthen their hostile activities. The enemy was preparing to throw the country into chaos.

The counterrevolutionaries expected that, in the complicated and strained international situation brought about by the aggressive actions of American imperialism and especially by the revanchist forces in West Germany, they could succeed in detaching Czechoslovakia from the community of Socialist states. But these are vain hopes. The Socialist states have sufficient strength to support a fraternal country and defend the cause of socialism.

Dear friends!

Your class brothers have come to your aid today.

They did not come to meddle in your internal affairs but to help you fight the counterrevolution, defend the cause of socialism, and remove the danger threatening the sovereignty, the independence, and the security of your homeland.

The armies of the fraternal allied countries came so that no one could take away your freedom gained in our common struggle against fascism, so that no one could bar you from advancing on the shining road to socialism. These troops will leave your territory after the danger to the freedom and independence of Czechoslovakia has been removed.

We believe that the close unity of the fraternal nations of the Socialist commonwealth will prevail over the plots of the enemy.

Long live Socialist Czechoslovakia!

Long live the friendship and brotherhood of the nations of the Socialist countries!

Council of Ministers of the Bulgarian People's Republic
Council of Ministers of the Hungarian People's Republic
Council of Ministers of the German Democratic Republic
Council of Ministers of the Polish People's Republic
Council of Ministers of the Union of Soviet Socialist Republics.

It is difficult to say whether this extraordinary document sinned more by naïveté than by cynicism and deception. To invade an allied and friendly nation and tell it that "your class brothers have come to your aid today" must be, by all tests, an insult to the good faith and the intelligence of the population. To have assumed that the Czechs and Slovaks would believe that the intervention had really been requested by "leading Party and state leaders" was a mistake that only someone as divorced from Czechoslovak reality as Ambassador Chervonenko could have promoted. Finally, the appeal served to create the record for the Soviet lack of credibility in the ensuing months: not only no Czechoslovak Communist, no matter how pro-Soviet, ever admitted to requesting the invasion, but such notorious conservatives as *Rudé Právo*'s editor Švestka and ex-Presidium members Kolder and Piller specifically and publicly denied that they had thus "betrayed" their country.

An interesting sidelight was that the "proclamation" was signed only by the five *governments* and not by the leaderships of their Communist parties. In most cases, to be sure, the same men are leaders of both government and Party, but Communist protocol often finds it necessary to make the distinction. And, gratuitously, the "proclamation" made two statements that no sane Czechoslovak could possibly believe: that the occupiers "did not come to meddle in your internal affairs" (if not, Czechs asked, why did they come at all?), and that their troops would leave Czechoslovakia "after the danger to the freedom and independence of Czechoslovakia has been removed."

Having so breathlessly told the Czechoslovaks why it had invaded their country, Moscow proceeded to offer a justification for world consumption. It was based on the same elements, but it is worth recording it to recapture the extraordinary flavor of the whole undertaking. In the form of a statement by Tass, it was broadcast at five-twenty-five a.m. over Radio Vltava so that the Czechoslovaks would know what the world beyond was being told:

Tass is authorized to state that Party and government leaders of the Czechoslovak Socialist Republic have asked the Soviet Union and other allied states to render the fraternal Czechoslovak people urgent assistance, including assistance with armed forces. This request was brought about by the threat that has arisen to the Socialist system existing in Czechoslovakia, emanating from the counterrevolutionary forces that have entered into collusion with foreign forces hostile to socialism. Further aggravation of the situation in Czechoslovakia affects the vital interests of the Soviet Union and other Socialist states.

The decision is fully in accord with the right of states to individual and collective self-defense provided for in treaties of alliance concluded between the fraternal Socialist countries. The decision is also in line with vital interests of our countries in safeguarding European peace against forces of militarism, aggression, and revanchism, which have more than once plunged the peoples of Europe into wars.

Soviet Army units together with units of other allied countries entered the territory of Czechoslovakia on August 21. They will be promptly withdrawn from the Czechoslovak Socialist Republic as soon as the threat to the security of the countries of the Socialist community is eliminated and the legal authorities find that the further presence of these armed units is no longer necessary.

The actions that are being taken are not directed against any state. They serve the purpose of peace and have been prompted by concern for its preservation.

The fraternal countries firmly and resolutely counterpose their unbreakable solidarity to any threat from outside. No one will ever be allowed to wrest a single link from the community of Socialist states.

This was, in a sense, more honest than the five-power "proclamation," and it added two new dimensions. First, Tass acknowledged, as the "proclamation" did not, that "Further aggravation of the situation in Czechoslovakia affects the *vital interests* of the Soviet Union and other Socialist states [italics added]." Moscow was thus placing less emphasis on the seemingly selfless desire to help Czechoslovak "socialism." Second, it hinted at what was to become a few weeks later the so-called Brezhnev Doctrine of limited sovereignty when it said that the decision to invade was in accord with "the right of states to individual and collective self-defense" in the interests of the "socialist commonwealth."

Now that the invasion was explained as best it could be under the circumstances, the Soviet political-military command turned its attention to the much more complicated problem of what to do in Prague, which now lay under its physical control. The day had barely started when the Moscow chiefs could already chalk up two major defeats.

The first defeat was that "the working class and all the people of Czechoslovakia" made it unmistakably and rapidly clear that they had no interest whatsoever in having the Warsaw Pact armies "defend their socialist gains." In the streets—it happened in Prague as well as in Bratislava, Brno, Liberec, Košice, and a score of other cities—citizens spat at the tanks and troopers, hurled garbage and insults, and, in many instances that first morning, tried and succeeded in setting the armored vehicles afire. The Soviet soldiers, told by their commanders that they were coming to save Czechoslovakia from a "counterrevolution," were startled and uncomprehending of the violent reaction. Youths ran up to the tanks to stuff petrol-soaked flaming rags into their exhaust pipes and dozens of the T-55s and brand-new T-66s exploded and burned in the squares and streets of Czech and Slovak towns. When the tanks could not be directly attacked, young people painted swastika signs on them. The Russians, frightened of what they thought might develop into urban guerrilla warfare, fired back, sometimes in self-defense, sometimes without provocation. In the first hours of the morning there were scores of dead and hundreds of wounded. The Czechoslovak Army, obeying the Svoboda-Dubček orders, was not resisting, but the people—blinded by tears of rage and hatred—tried to fight.

If the street reaction stunned the Russians, the politicians' reaction did so even more. As precious hours ticked away, they continued to be unable to reveal the leaders who they said had called for the intervention or to form a pro-Moscow Party leadership or government. A contingency plan called for maintaining a semblance of constitutional continuity under General Svoboda, but the old man would not budge. At Hradčany Castle, President Svoboda—virtually a prisoner—stubbornly refused to take any part in forming a new leadership. Instead, he met with the cabinet ministers who made their way to the castle. When Alois Polednak, a Communist liberal deputy, succeeded in reaching him on the telephone at nine-thirty a.m. Svoboda told him he had requested Soviet permission to inspect Prague's streets and visit the Central Committee. At ten-seven a.m. scores of deputies convened an emergency session of the National Assembly (it was to remain in permanent session for six days) despite the Soviet troops outside, and drafted an appeal to the five Warsaw Pact governments demanding the withdrawal of the invasion forces. A delegation led by the octogenarian Zdeněk Fierlinger went to the Soviet Embassy to deliver this protest.

Rather than collapsing, then, as predicted by Chervonenko, Czechoslovak society was arming itself for a political struggle, and even the men who were counted upon to show solidarity with the intervention were angrily joining the liberal camp. And the explosion of nationalist sentiment prevented Russia's most trusted friends from coming forward to try and take over the government on her behalf. It was virtually a matter of physical safety for them to remain hidden or silent. The night attack had unified Czechoslovakia—and the Communist Party—as nothing else could have done: a fact which Moscow did not understand then or later.

Early on the morning of August 21 at the Soviet Embassy Ambassador Chervonenko and General Pavlovsky conferred with the handful of Czechoslovak conservatives who had taken refuge there—Indra, Bilak,

Piller, Kolder, Barbírek, Lenárt, Švestka, and a few others—on how next to proceed. No decision was made over the fate of Dubček and his associates held prisoner at the Central Committee building or of Černík, who was under guard at the airport. But the group agreed that maximum effort must be made during the day to convene the Party's Central Committee somewhere in Prague to create a political leadership. The Russians and their friends were nonplused, and improvisation took the place of the painstakingly drafted blueprints.

The second major Soviet defeat—occurring at the same time—was that Radio Prague was still on the air. At six a.m., it broadcast a personal appeal from Dubček—he was under Soviet guard but his personal movements were not yet controlled and, presumably, he could telephone out— urging the population to go to work as usual. At six-thirty-five, the even voice of a Prague announcer asked the people to "remain calm" and respond to the occupation with passive resistance. A few minutes before seven, Prague television began transmitting, using the suburban Cukrek antennas. (Soviet troops had occupied the main Strahov transmitter.) At eight-twelve, it broadcast a statement from the Academy of Sciences protesting the occupation.

But shortly before seven a.m., the Soviet command had decided that Radio Prague must be taken by force. Tanks began moving up Wenceslas Square toward the radio building on Vinohradska Street, and other units moved down from the eastern suburbs. But thousands of people were filling the huge square and other crowds were forming in the Old Town Square. At seven-fifteen, Radio Prague urged the people in the Old Town Square to disperse and take down the barricades they had built from streetcars and buses. "Self-control is our best weapon," the woman announcer said quietly. The man's voice that followed her—a woman and a man alternated at the microphones—added that the first clashes were taking place downstairs.

A moment later, the woman said; "We appeal for calm and self-control. Do not allow yourselves to be provoked! . . . Armed defense is out of the question. . . . Reports arrive that the first shots are being fired in front of the Prague building of the Czechoslovak radio, where six tanks are in position. . . . The troops fire tracer bullets—perhaps even live ammunition. . . . We do not know how much longer the radio will be able to continue broadcasting. . . . We are in a hurry. . . . People on Wenceslas Square are trying to stop vehicles of the occupation troops with their bodies. . . ."

There was a moment of silence. At seven-eighteen Radio Prague read another message from Dubček: "I beg you to maintain calm and to bear with dignity the present situation. I appeal to you for calm." The radio announcer added, "So do we."

At seven-twenty-five, a Soviet tank column was deployed in front of the Radio Prague building. But enraged youths erected a barricade a few hundred yards away at Wenceslas Square. The announcer repeated that "several hundred people are trying to stop the advancing tanks with their bodies."

As Kitty Voleniková and I heard the broadcast at the American Embassy, there were shots in the background. Soviet aircraft were buzzing the radio station. Then Smetana's slow, sad "Moldau Suite" was played. The woman announcer came back at seven-thirty-five to say, "When you hear the Czechoslovak anthem, the broadcasting of Radio Czechoslovakia will come to an end. It will mean the radio has been occupied. When you hear voices on the radio you are unfamiliar with, do not believe them!"

Tears were streaming down Kitty's face as she took notes. I, too, felt on the brink of tears, which is not a reporter's usual professional reaction. There was another moment of silence. Then came the strains of the Czechoslovak anthem. It is all over, I thought, and I went upstairs to the Telex to file a dispatch that the Czechoslovak radio had finally been silenced.

When I returned ten minutes later, Radio Prague, as if by magic, was broadcasting again. Somehow, the announcers succeeded in remaining at their posts and their communications network remained intact. This time, the male announcer was saying that the Ministry of Foreign Affairs, surrounded by Soviet troops, was requesting that the radio transmit its statement that the occupation was "unjustified." As I was to learn later, the man coordinating the flow of information at the Foreign Ministry was Karel Dufek, the foreign press chief, onetime Spanish War volunteer and a purge victim in the 1950s. Dufek had reached the ministry at dawn and was putting together news-agency dispatches—the ministry had incoming teletypes—and domestic and foreign broadcasts to keep his chiefs informed of the situation. Foreign Minister Hájek was on vacation in Yugoslavia, but Acting Minister Václav Pleskot, a man who had never overly sympathized with the reform program, was at his desk and he and his aides drafted the protest notes to the invading governments. Dufek was to remain at his post for days.

At eight-fifteen a.m., Radio Prague broadcast this address from President Svoboda:

DEAR FELLOW CITIZENS:

During the last few hours a complicated situation has arisen in our country. At the present moment I cannot tell you any more. As President of the Czechoslovak Socialist Republic, I address you with the full responsibility I accepted when I assumed office, and I urgently ask you to maintain reason and complete calm.

Aware of your civic responsibility and in the interest of the Republic, do not allow any unpremeditated actions to occur. With the dignity and discipline you have shown during the past few days, await further measures by the constitutional authorities of the Republic.

Then Radio Prague went off the air once more. This time Soviet troopers had burst into the studios and interrupted the broadcasting. This was the crucial moment of the battle for the building. Soviet tanks were firing wildly along Vinohradska Street, their cannon shells and machine-gun bullets hitting the buildings and the parked cars. Other tanks fired at the National Museum, the majestic building that sits at the top of Wenceslas Square, and smashed through the barricades. But the young people, many of them long-haired boys and girls in slacks, fought the tanks with their bare hands, setting them on fire with flaming torches and hitting at them with branches fallen from the trees.

Clyde Farnsworth was in the square, and later he filed this dispatch to our newspaper: "This reporter saw four slain young Czechoslovaks, one with his head blown off, minutes after a machine gun from a Soviet tank had opened up on their truck. . . . People wept in the streets. They screamed defiance at the tanks. One tank was left a flaming wreck and two retreated in flames near the Prague radio building. . . . A young student looked up at the Museum, which had just been sprayed with machine gun fire, and said: 'Not even the Germans did that during the war.' "

Radio Prague was occupied, but the broadcasting did not cease for long. Radio Ostrava, in Moravia, took over, and then Plzeň, Bratislava, and scores of other broadcasting centers carried on the fight. This gave the Prague radio technicians time to set in motion an amazing clandestine network that for two weeks kept the resistance alive.

The underground network had evidently been planned for months ahead—though none of the Prague radio and television people ever admitted it—and it was run with professional smoothness by Zdeněk Hejzlar, director of Radio Czechoslovakia, and Jiří Pelikan, the forty-two-year-old director of state television and a popular National Assembly deputy. Hejzlar and Pelikan went underground with their staffs of technicians and announcers. By noon "Legal and Free Radio Czechoslovakia" was functioning—to the wrathful dismay of the Soviet command. This broadcasting was done from a dozen secret locations in Prague—cellars, private apartments, empty lofts, and some sites so obvious that the Soviet security agents would have been embarrassed had they known how close they were—and, subsequently, other Czech and Slovak towns. When the broadcasters had reason to suspect they were about to be located by Soviet triangulation teams, they moved to other prepared spots. Sometimes the listeners were told there would be brief silence "while we move." The moves were made on foot, in taxis, private cars, and, often, in ambulances which carried broadcasting equipment and announcers disguised as doctors and nurses. The Russians never found a single secret station or intercepted a move from one site to another. This was simply because there was no Czech who would tell the Soviets anything, Initially, Czechoslovak Army and Interior Ministry radio stations aided the clandestine network with advice and equipment. The afternoon of August 21 heard an Interior Ministry station warning the Plzeň broadcasters to leave because "the Russians are approaching." But after two days, no assistance was required, and even television was back on the air from secret studios in Prague, Brno, Ostrava, and Bratislava with news and discussion programs and even humorous skits against the occupation.

In Prague's streets the fighting went on all day. Youths paraded with Czechoslovak banners, some dipped in the blood of the victims, shouting, "Dubček, Dubček, Dubček!" and "Russians go home!" In a way, the Soviet troops showed remarkable restraint in the face of the massed hatred against them. They had orders to fire only in self-defense and, relative as this concept may be, they followed the discipline imposed by their commanders. This probably explains why there were *only* thirty killed—and not, say, three thousand—in Prague on August 21. There were casualties in the afternoon when two Soviet ammunition trucks exploded in front of the radio station and hundreds were wounded by ricocheting bullets as the Soviet troopers fired submachinegun bursts into the air or over the demonstrators' heads. But what the Soviet Union wanted was political submission and not a bloodbath.

This submission, however, seemed further and further away. At noon a two-minute protest strike brought all movement in Prague to a standstill. People halted in their tracks. For two minutes there was terrifying silence in the golden capital. Then, as the radio resumed broadcasting, an avalanche of protest telegrams came from the unions, factories, military commands, artistic groups, and, it seemed, every organized group in Czechoslovakia.

Eleven cabinet members met at Hradčany Castle under the chairmanship of Minister of Consumer Goods Industry Mrs. Božena Machačová to signify the continuity of government even in the absence of Premier Černík. At twelve-fifty-five p.m., the Free Radio, now a channel for all official communications, issued their statement:

> 1. We stand firmly behind all the legally elected constitutional and political authorities, and we firmly support today's proclamation of the Presidium addressed to all people.
>
> 2. We consider the occupation of the Czechoslovak Socialist Republic, which took place without the agreement and knowledge of the Czechoslovak government, an illegal act, contrary to international law and the principles of socialist internationalism.

It is interesting to note that among the signers were Minister of Chemical Industry Stanislav Razl and Minister of Foreign Trade Václav Valeš, both of whom later joined the Soviet-imposed government—Razl as Premier of the Czech Regions under the 1969 federalization act and among the most enthusiastic supporters of the new order. It took the crucible of the postinvasion months to separate the men consistent in their beliefs from those who were willing to be swayed and thereby rewarded. At the moment, however, the tremendous outburst of nationalist revulsion against the invasion had almost everyone on the side of the angels.

Meanwhile, a decision had to be made on what to do about Dubček and his companions. At nine a.m., Lieutenant Colonel Molnař, one of the pro-Soviet security commanders with prior knowledge of the invasion, gathered ten of his officials and three KGB agents in his office to order them to take Dubček, Smrkovský, and Kriegel into custody. Molnař assumed that Interior Minister Pavel was also at the Central Committee building, and he issued orders for his arrest also. Both the KGB and the Czechoslovak security men were eager to capture Pavel; earlier, they had arrested five of his aides. But there seemed to be surprisingly little enthusiasm among Molnař's men about arresting Dubček.

After some discussion, the group drove to the Soviet Embassy in five cars. There, a uniformed Soviet major with an automatic rifle and another Soviet officer took command of the contingent. Presently, the Soviet and Czechoslovak agents drove to the Central Committee. A KGB man said,

"Who among you is a hero? Who will go to Dubček and say, 'In the name of the Revolutionary government, led by Comrade Indra, you are hereby taken into custody'?" There was silence until an agent named Hoffman volunteered for the job. Six men were chosen to carry out the arrest and they brought Dubček, Smrkovský, and Kriegel to the office of Party Secretary Císař, where the KGB people had set up their command post. Pavel could not be found. It was about eleven a.m. The three leaders were ordered to raise their arms, and they were searched. But the arresting party seemed to have no instructions what to do next. Soon nineteen Soviet tanks led by KGB officers Nalivaiko and Mukhin arrived at the Central Committee—also to make the arrests—but they found the liberal leaders already detained. There were hurried consultations in the next three hours, and other Party members, including Presidium Member Špaček, were arrested.

Finally, at about two p.m., Dubček, Smrkovský, and Kriegel were taken in a Soviet armored car to Ruzyń airport, under heavy escort. Premier Černík had already been there since dawn. But even at this stage the Soviets seemed uncertain what to do about their prisoners. They were manacled and placed aboard a Soviet plane that flew them to the Try Duby military airport in Slovakia. From there, the four men were driven to a barn near the spa of Sliac and kept there all night under Soviet guard. It appears that they were prompted with rifle butts to keep moving. What happened at Sliac remains unknown—none of the four leaders ever revealed the details of their imprisonment—but as Premier Černík was to tell the cabinet after his release, "I feared for my life and that of my comrades." All that is known is that from Sliac they were removed, on August 22, to the Trans-Carpathian town of Mukachevo and then to the Soviet city of Lvov and apparently put in the local prison. They were not allowed to change clothes, were barely fed, and were mistreated and insulted. What the Soviet government had in mind for them at this point will never be known. They may have been used as temporary hostages or perhaps were being kept for a show trial Moscow may have been planning at that juncture. There is the possibility that the Soviets may have been considering a summary execution. But there also is the possibility that the Kremlin had no idea what to do with its prisoners.

Back in Prague, the resistance and the defiance were mounting. Radio Prague began issuing calls to the delegates to the Fourteenth Congress to rush to the capital and meet at once. It said the congress would open the following day, August 22, at the ČKD industrial plant. The National

Assembly, presided over by First Deputy Chairman Josef Valo, issued a proclamation demanding freedom for the imprisoned leaders, protesting the invasion and the placing of Soviet troops at the parliament, urging the immediate withdrawal of the occupation forces, and advising the nation that "if necessary, you will surely be able to defend yourselves by a general strike."

The cabinet met again under Mrs. Machačová, and in the name of the "Government of the Socialist Republic of Czechoslovakia" issued a lengthy proclamation broadcast by the clandestine radio at seven p.m. It asserted its determination to "discharge its constitutional functions and insure normal life in the country" despite the arrest of the top leaders, again demanded the withdrawal of the Warsaw Pact armies, and warned the nation not to allow "the establishment of any government other than one elected under free and democratic conditions."

As night fell over Prague and the first day of the occupation drew to an end, the Soviet Union found itself in the extraordinary position of having invaded Czechoslovakia and imprisoned and abducted its leaders, but of being unable to impose its will on the defiant nation. All the Soviet occupiers could do was to fill the night with the sound of gunfire. Lieutenant General of the Guards Ivan Velichko, Commander of the Allied Troops in Prague and the Central Bohemian Region, issued from his headquarters in the northern suburb of Troja an order for a ten-p.m.-to-five-a.m. curfew to defend the capital's population from "the dangers connected with actions of extreme and hooligan elements." "Hooligan" is a favorite word in the Soviets' lexicon to describe any person actively opposing them. General Velichko, as divorced from reality as his supreme commanders, also announced that "I consider it indispensable that radio and television broadcasting and the publishing of dailies, weeklies, and other printed matter be made subject to the approval of the relevant authorities."

The reply to this order came from the Prague editors, as they secretly printed illegal issues of the next day's newspapers and from the Free Radio which, at ten-thirty p.m., broadcast this new proclamation from President Svoboda:

DEAR FELLOW CITIZENS:

I am addressing you for the second time on this fateful day. We are going through exceptionally grave moments in the history of our nation. Military units of the Soviet Union, together with units of the Polish People's Republic, the Bulgarian People's Republic, the German Democratic Republic, and the Hungarian People's

Republic, entered the territory of our Republic. This took place without the agreement of the constitutional authorities of the state, which, however, because of their responsibility to the nations of our homeland, must urgently deal with the situation that has arisen in order to bring about an early departure of the foreign troops.

As far as current conditions allow, I have sought during this day to work toward that end. Today I convoked a plenary session of the National Assembly. This evening I spoke with members of the government about some of the urgent problems related to the task of restoring normal conditions to the country. Tomorrow I shall continue these discussions—hopefully, also with Premier Oldřich Černík. I am aware of all the problems and difficulties called forth by the present situation. I turn to you again, dear fellow citizens, with the urgent request that you maintain the greatest prudence and avoid everything that could provoke regrettable actions with irreparable consequences. I sincerely address this appeal especially to our youth.

I appeal to all of you—workers, peasants, members of the intelligentsia—to demonstrate again by your attitude your relationship to socialism, freedom, and democracy.

For us there is no way back. The Action Program of the Communist Party expresses the vital interests and needs of all the people of our homeland. We must, therefore, continue the task we have begun. We shall not lose faith. We will all join together, and together with the Communist Party and the National Front we will remain united for the sake of a better life for our nation.

The unbelievable had happened. A peaceful European nation had been invaded under a tenuous and false pretext by the Soviet Union and four of its allies in the first such act on the European continent since the Nazis occupied Czechoslovakia in 1939. How did the world react to it?

I submit that a shock greater only than the invasion itself was, precisely, the lack of a reaction. The Soviet Union may have utterly misinterpreted the internal situation in Czechoslovakia—except for the assessment that Czechoslovak armed forces would not be ordered into combat—but it was absolutely correct in its assumption that the so-called Free World would accept the invasion with no more than pious expressions of regret and condemnation. This, for example, was all that President Lyndon B. Johnson, then fighting a disastrous war allegedly against Communism in Vietnam, was capable of when word of the invasion reached him in Washington. Johnson did summon a midnight meeting of the National Security Council at the White House—less than five hours after the news of the attack had reached him—to examine the global implications of the invasion and to plan for the contingency that the Soviets might not halt at Czechoslovakia's western and southern borders. Concern arose over the fate of Romania and Yugoslavia—to whom the same "socialist solidarity" treatment might have been applied —and even Austria.

It must be made clear at once that at no time did the Czechoslovak progressive leaders hope or expect that the United States and the West would rally to their defense militarily. Choosing not to fight themselves, men like Dubček and Svoboda certainly did not encourage the start of World War Three on Czechoslovakia's behalf. They knew from the outset that, as usual, Czechoslovakia was alone in her battle. The strategic considerations were equally obvious to the Soviets: they knew that with an army of six hundred thousand men bogged down in Vietnam, the United States —to say nothing of NATO—was incapable of handling the five hundred thousand Warsaw Pact expeditionary force armed with the most modern weapons. The United States Seventh Army in West Germany, at the far end of a trans-Atlantic supply line, would not have had a chance against General Pavlovsky's force fighting from its home base.

Within forty-eight hours of the invasion, close to two hundred thousand Warsaw Pact troops had entered Czechoslovakia, nearly fifty thousand of which were concentrated in and around Prague, and they were supported by an estimated three hundred aircraft, not counting airlift transport. It stands to reason that the Soviet Union threw such an overwhelming force into Czechoslovakia not only to discourage internal resistance, but to make it plain to the West that any military reaction was doomed to dismal failure. A political-military by-product was, of course, to demonstrate to the West that Soviet power could not be challenged in Europe in a conventional war. That the NATO commanders were taken by utter surprise on the night of August 20 served to prove this point quite convincingly.

But where, the Czechoslovaks wondered, was any kind of meaningful political and moral support? They saw President Johnson so deeply engaged in the Vietnam war and so obsessed with his hope for a disarmament "summit meeting" with Premier Kosygin as to rule out any energetic political response to the invasion. It became obvious that the first concern in Washington and the NATO capitals was whether the *détente* with the Soviet Union might be spoiled by the invasion of Czechoslovakia—and how quickly Czechoslovakia might be forgotten as an inconvenient element in the big-power games. This, obviously, embittered (though it did not demoralize) the Czechs, and it was no surprise that among the thousands of signs and graffiti appearing in Prague on invasion day was the slogan MUNICH = YALTA. It expressed the Czechs' conclusion that, just as the 1938 Munich Pact had led to their country's occupation by the Nazis, the 1945 Yalta agreement among Churchill, Roosevelt, and Stalin had resulted in the 1968 invasion. The Czechs were and are convinced that at Yalta the world was divided into two spheres of influence—Soviet and American—and that it so remains. As they were in the Soviet sphere, they reasoned, they could barely expect sympathy from the West, except for a few tears shed in newspaper editorials and in formal statements issued by some Western leaders.

Among other Czech arguments, which are worth being recorded, was that Western policy was polluted with such an immense dose of cynicism and immorality that in the end it was bound to infect its practitioners. Individual Czechs in Prague and elsewhere showed great friendship for Americans, especially the newsmen, but the accusation of a moral "sell-out" was always close to the surface. In the end, the Czechs shrugged their shoulders and said, "What else could we have expected?"

My own personal reaction, as I watched the Soviet tanks rumbling down Prague's streets, was a profound disenchantment over the failure of Americans to protest the invasion. It seemed to me to be not only inconsistent but a betrayal of the American liberal sense of decency to battle the Administration over the Vietnam war—rightly, I thought—but to dismiss out of hand the Soviet attack on Czechoslovakia. It was with a sense of shame that most American newsmen in Prague read the remarks of Senator Eugene J. McCarthy, a liberal standard-bearer, appearing to shrug off the invasion and suggesting that President Johnson had overreacted in calling the National Security Council in the middle of the night. We were aware, of course, that the intervention in Czechoslovakia coincided with the Democratic Convention in Chicago, but we found it hard to accept such a one-sided approach to world problems by otherwise intelligent and presumably well-meaning people. And if a segment of the American New Left was able to take Czechoslovakia in its stride, it had found itself totally out of step with all the world leftist movements, with the obvious exception of the Soviet Communist Party's Politburo.

The curious fact was that the most powerful and emotional reaction against the invasion came from Communists of all persuasions. The Czechoslovak affair was, and remains, the greatest watershed in Communist history since the Russian Revolution. In Moscow, a small brave band of Soviet intellectuals staged a protest parade in Red Square, and paid for it with heavy prison sentences. That was more than American liberals could bring themselves to deliver in Washington, New York, or Chicago. Even in East Germany, whose troops participated in the invasion, courageous people protested publicly.

The Czechoslovak cause won support from the powerful Italian Communist Party—the largest in Western Europe—and its Secretary-General, Luigi Longo, led the violent protests. The British, Swiss, Belgian, and Scandinavian parties joined in denunciations of the invasion. The big French Party was rocked by its greatest internal crisis since the war, as a progressive wing led by Roger Garaudy forced through the Central Committee a resolution condemning the attack. Interestingly, the tiny American Communist Party was among the few foreign parties to offer unqualified support for the Soviet intervention.

That China and Albania denounced the invasion was, of course, in line with their anti-Soviet policies. But the angriest and the most sincere revulsion came from those whose reaction might have put them in line as the next Soviet targets: Romania and Yugoslavia.

In Bucharest, President Ceauşescu convoked his Party's Central Committee on August 21 and delivered the most emotional public speech of his life. Vast crowds gathered in front of the Party headquarters to cheer Ceauşescu and Czechoslovakia and berate the Russians. On August 22 Ceauşescu called the Grand National Assembly into session to approve a resolution declaring that "the only path for ending the created conflict is the immediate withdrawal of all the foreign troops from the territory of the Czechoslovak Socialist Republic, the creation of conditions so that the fraternal Czechoslovak people, the Party, and the lawful Czechoslovak government may be able to settle their internal affairs without any outside interference." Ceauşescu, who had visited Prague only four days before the attack, gravely assured his nation that he had found nothing in Czechoslovakia to justify the invasion in the name of socialism or anything else. (It must be remembered that Romania is a Warsaw Pact member, even if a foot-dragging one, and Ceauşescu was fully aware of the danger of a Soviet thrust into his country to solve once and for all the Kremlin's problems in Communist Eastern Europe.)

In Belgrade, Marshal Tito likewise spoke in condemnation of the Czechoslovak invasion. He, too, had been in Prague that same month. A few days later, Ceauşescu and Tito met to consider joint defense measures if the Soviet Union was indeed determined to restore Communist orthodoxy with force from the Tatra Mountains to the Adriatic.

It took fellow Communists, then, to defend a democratic revolution in Czechoslovakia. The democrats of the world sat on their hands.

In Prague, the Communist idea of democracy, meanwhile, was faring much better than one had the right to expect. Through the night of August 21–22, hundreds of delegates streamed from all over the country to the capital for the Fourteenth Party Congress. They were reaching Prague in disguise and with false papers (prepared with amazing speed) despite Soviet roadblocks and the vigilance of KGB-controlled Czechoslovak security agents. Only the Slovaks—except for five delegates—were unable to get to Prague. Among those turned back was Gustav Husák, a Deputy Premier in the government, but not a member of the Party hierarchy. In the light of what we have learned later about Husák, one may wonder just how hard he had tried to reach the congress.

As the pro-Dubček delegates streamed into Prague, the men whom Moscow had chosen to bring the new regime to life were meeting at the Praha Hotel in an attempt to give credibility to the invasion and provide a native political framework for the Soviet intervention. Under the prodding of the pro-Moscow leaders at the Soviet Embassy, twenty-two members of the Central Committee—all of them obscure conservatives—gathered at the Praha in midafternoon, August 21. They, it was believed, would provide the political solution that had been lacking since the Warsaw Pact troops entered Czechoslovakia.

But it was a desultory meeting held under the protective cannon of Soviet tanks. By early evening the total number reached fifty persons, about one-third of the Central Committee's membership. Among the later arrivals were Presidium members Drahomír Kolder, Vasil Bilak, and František Barbírek, and Party Secretary Alois Indra. They were accompanied by Soviet officers who remained for the rest of the session. Jan Piller came alone, as did such top conservatives as Karel Mestek, Vilém Nový (the first Party official arrested in the Stalinist purge in 1950), and Miloš Jakeš. Also on hand was Martin Vaculík, once the boss of the Prague Party and alternate member of the Presidium; he was generally regarded as a conservative, yet it was he who appeared a few hours later at the Fourteenth Congress to give an account of what had happened at the hotel, and the liberal congress elected him to the new Central Committee.

At the hotel meeting, Vaculík reported, Piller rose to offer a resolution opposing the Fourteenth Congress on the grounds that it would "aggravate" the situation. But the meeting was not making the kind of progress the Soviets needed. In Vaculík's words, "Despite the presence of the occupation officers, none of the Central Committee members present could confirm that any person or Czechoslovak authority had requested the occupation of the country by the armed forces of the signatories of the Warsaw Letter." Not even Indra, Bilak, or Kolder was willing to stand up and accept the responsibility.

The Soviet strategy was coming apart. The best the conference could achieve was a communiqué supporting the section of the Dubček Presidium's proclamation that urged calm, prudence, and order. The invasion was designed to halt the reform movement in Czechoslovakia, but the Praha meeting cautiously insisted that there must be no return to the "pre-January conditions" and confirmed the Action Program as the basis for further KSČ activity. In deference to Soviet wishes, the communiqué proposed that contacts be established with the commanders of the foreign troops, and the meeting sent teletype messages to regional Party committees that, as Vaculík put it, "called for collaboration with the occupiers." Vaculík's own conclusion was that "the communiqué accepted the occupation of Czechoslovakia as a reality, but it failed to take into consideration the second reality—that is, the outrage and open opposition of the Czechoslovak population to the action of the signatories of the Warsaw Letter."

When the Praha meeting broke up at one-thirty a.m. Thursday, August 22, the Soviet political plan had not advanced an inch. It had not been possible to form a new Party leadership or identify for the skeptical nation the "leaders" who had called for the invasion. The political fiasco of the operation must have been obvious even to Ambassador Chervonenko. During the night, a more direct course of action was decided at the Soviet Embassy, as Chervonenko and General Pavlovsky hung at the end of the telephone line to Moscow. With about a dozen Czechoslovakians present, it was simply decided to form a "collective Party leadership" to replace Dubček. Because agreement could not be reached even within such a limited group, the Russians decided that pending the subsequent selection of a KSČ First Secretary, the Party would be run by a troika made up of Bilak, Indra, and Kolder. The problem was not so much that any of them insisted on the top spot but that none of them wanted to be singled out as the chief "quisling." At the same time, a cabinet list for a "Government of Workers and Peasants" was drawn up, and

Indra was designated Premier to replace the imprisoned Černík. Among the proposed ministers were such nonentities as Oldřich Pavlovský, Minister of Internal Trade before the invasion, who for long weeks dared not come to his own office.

All this looked fine on paper, or relatively so, but the Russians insisted that the cabinet must have President Svoboda's approval, anxious that constitutional continuity be maintained and reluctant to do away with the old man who held the title of Hero of the Soviet Union. In the morning of August 22, Piller and Chervonenko drove up to Hradčany Castle to inform Svoboda that the KSČ would be run by a troika and to ask him to approve the new government.

But the old general, in full Army uniform, refused even to discuss the situation. He is said to have told them that Černík remained in his view the legal Premier of Czechoslovakia and that only with him would he discuss matters pertaining to the government. There is, of course, no record of this conversation—Piller later denied that he had even been there—but reliable reports said it was an angry one, with the President insisting that the release of the imprisoned Czechoslovak leaders was the first condition for any steps toward what Chervonenko kept calling "normalization" of the situation. As the two emissaries left the castle, the deadlock was stronger than at any time since the invasion. I saw a member of the Central Committee that morning—he was hurrying to the Party congress—and he said that the Soviets might have no choice in the end but to impose a military government. "There are no Kadárs among us," he said. Whether Moscow was contemplating this obviously unpalatable step—it would have been a public admission of utter political failure—is unknown. But tension mounted in Prague, and the frustrated Russians concentrated on repressive measures.

Troops occupied the offices of the newspapers that had not been closed the previous day, and, at about eight a.m., a unit of Soviet soldiers began searching through the files of the Academy of Sciences. Later, someone found there copies of the unit commander's recommendations for medals to be given to several of his officers who distinguished themselves in diligent search. He failed to mention, however, that some of his soldiers had defecated on the Academy's library books, and when his attention was called to this practice, he told his men that "uncultured acts" were not permitted. The Central Telegraph Office was occupied in midmorning—it had evidently been forgotten on the previous day—and foreign newsmen worried that their Telex would now be cut. Even the American Embassy

Telex operated through the Central Telegraph Office. But, miraculously and inexplicably, the Russians never disrupted the Telex connections. Early in the morning Soviet armored cars sprayed the Children's Hospital with machine-gun fire. At eleven o'clock, General Velichko issued an order forbidding the putting up of posters on the walls, banning public meetings, and maintaining the nightly curfew. By that time, Prague was one immense collage of anti-Soviet posters and signs, some humorous and some plain insulting. Street signs told the Russians that Moscow was eighteen hundred miles away, and a poster informed "Ivan" that his "Natasha" slept with someone else while he was on duty in Prague. Signs for and portraits of "Dubček-Svoboda" covered walls and the windows of stores and homes. On the baroque façade of the National Museum, where Soviet machine-gun fire the day before had left a patchwork of scars, scribbled signs said RUSSIAN CULTURE and SOUVENIRS OF RUSSIA.

While the Soviet-sponsored political activity remained paralyzed, the Czechoslovak Communist liberals, now enjoying almost total national support, moved to the counteroffensive. On Wednesday they had been stunned and disoriented; now they had a new sense of assurance, armed with the superbly functioning Free Radio network, imaginative television, and the clandestine press (all the newspapers were appearing under their own names: *Rudé Právo, Svobodne Slovo,* and so on) distributed by volunteer soldiers, policemen, and students. Throughout Prague, tens of thousands of citizens proudly wore the Czechoslovak tricolor and the first Dubček buttons.

At nine a.m., 162 deputies of the National Assembly, most of whom had slept in the Assembly building, resumed the plenary session. The total membership is 300, so a quorum was available. With Soviet tanks and paratroopers at the doors, the Assembly calmly drafted and approved this resolution:

> The National Assembly of the Czechoslovak Socialist Republic, duly elected by the Czechoslovak people as the supreme organ of state power and duly convened by the President of the Republic, categorically protests to the governments and parliaments of the five states of the Warsaw Pact and declares that no constitutional organ of the Czechoslovak Socialist Republic was empowered to discuss the arrival of foreign troops . . . nor has approved any such discussions, nor has invited the occupation troops of the five states of the Warsaw Pact.
>
> The National Assembly categorically demands the urgent arrival of a competent and responsible political leader, or leaders, of the five states of the Warsaw Pact, who could authoritatively explain to the supreme organ of state power in Czechoslovakia the illegal acts that have taken place.

It took courage to demand these explanations from the occupying forces, who by now had over five hundred tanks in and around Prague (foreign newsmen and diplomats worked out a remarkably effective system for detailed assessment of the growing Soviet forces in the area), and the Czechs and the Slovaks had quickly acquired it. A call went out for a one-hour protest strike at noon, and Czechoslovak flags went up at the statue of Saint Wenceslas. Fresh-cut flowers were placed on the pavement where youths had been killed by Soviet guns the day before. Crowds carrying banners paraded in front of the muzzles of the Soviet tanks.

At eleven-eighteen a.m., Vladímir Kabrna, a thirty-seven-year-old member of the Central Committee, opened the secret Extraordinary Fourteenth Congress of the Communist Party in an auditorium of the ČKD industrial plant in the Prague district of Vysočany. That the congress, within twenty-four hours of its convocation, could be held in secret in the heart of Prague, under the noses of the Soviet troops, was an astounding feat of political organization, legerdemain, and deception. And it was to have a profound effect on subsequent developments.

The organizers of the congress succeeded simply because they did the *obvious* thing. The clandestine radio had been summoning delegates to be at the ČKD plant in Prague at eleven o'clock in the morning, Thursday, August 22. The Russians immediately assumed that the congress would therefore be held at another hour, probably on another day, and most certainly in another place. It was a fine example of how devious and Byzantine minds can be self-defeating. Convinced that the congress could not possibly sit when and where the Party said it would sit, the Soviet command made no effort to surround the Vysočany plant. And no special attention was paid to the six a.m. shift of workers arriving that Thursday morning. The Russians and the security agents did not know that the men and women dressed as workers and seeming to be workers were not workers but Party delegates. The plant security officers normally check the workers' papers as they enter the gates, and they did so on this morning as well. But, also unknown to the Soviets, these ČKD security men were part of the vast conspiracy. The only somewhat unusual element was the number of ambulances that kept entering and leaving the grounds. Their function was to bring to the meeting the Party leaders who were so well known that they might have been recognized if they had walked in with the morning shift and came, instead, disguised as patients, doctors, nurses, drivers, and attendants.

Somewhat over nine hundred delegates were on hand when the congress was called to order. Others arrived with the noon shift, using the same procedures, and in the afternoon. When the meeting adjourned at nine-fifteen p.m., the total attendance was 1192 delegates out of the 1543 elected during the summer.

Security measures for the congress included the mobilization of the ČKD People's Militia. With submachine guns and rifles at the ready— and with their lone antitank gun—they covered the entrances to the plant. If Soviet troops had discovered that the congress was in session, the militiamen were ready to protect the delegates. This was even more extraordinary because, as a rule, the People's Militia, which was made up of older Communists, had opposed the Dubček reformers. But here, too, the Soviet invasion had accomplished the miracle of fusing total unity. Czechoslovak television cameras and scores of Communist reporters were likewise smuggled into the plant. A special contingent of real workers was assigned the task of creating the impression that the ČKD was busily at work.

It is impossible to tell who were the brains behind this complex operation mounted with such speed and attention to detail. But the top organizers probably included Bohumil Šimon, the forty-eight-year-old Prague Party boss who first proposed the calling of the congress within three hours of the invasion, and the Party Secretary Čestmir Císař, who was released from arrest by friendly security agents late on Wednesday.

The congress did several basic things. It elected a 27-member enlarged Presidium and a new 144-member Central Committee, reaffirmed its trust in Dubček, and issued a resolution threatening "measures" if its demands for the release of Party leaders imprisoned by the Russians and for immediate negotiations on the withdrawal of the invading troops were not met. In its selection of Presidium and Central Committee members, the congress also demonstrated that the Party was now entirely committed to the progressive line. Not a single known conservative was elected, but the congress did pick Gustav Husák *in absentia* for the Presidium, presumably on the theory that he was a Deputy Premier identified with Dubček and a power in Slovak politics even though until then he held no Party post. I was aware even then that a number of progressives had doubts about Husák, and in my story for *The New York Times* that evening I included the observation that he "has taken generally liberal positions, but some liberals distrust him."

The congress chose Venek Silhan, a relatively unknown economist and industrial plant manager, to act as the KSČ First Secretary until Dubček could resume office. Dubček, Smrkovský, Kriegel, Černík, and Špaček were re-elected to the Presidium, and new members included Císař; Deputy Premier Ota Šik, who was already on the Soviet blacklist; the Writers' Union's chairman Eduard Goldstücker; Bohumil Šimon; Deputy Premier Petr Colotka; Milan Hübl, the head of the Party's Ideological School and an ardent liberal; Zdeněk Hejzlar, the man in charge of the clandestine radio; and Stefan Sadovský, a Slovak who later turned out to be a leading pro-Soviet figure.

Then the congress delegates addressed this letter to Dubček:

DEAR COMRADE DUBČEK:

The Extraordinary Fourteenth Party Congress that met today sends you warm comradely greetings. We thank you for all the work you have done for the Party and the Republic. The repeated calls of "Dubček, Dubček" coming from our young people carrying the bloodied state flag through Prague bear ample testimony that your name has become the symbol of our sovereignty. We protest against your unlawful imprisonment and the imprisonment of the other comrades.

The congress re-elected you to the new Central Committee, and we continue to consider you our leading representative. We firmly believe that the conduct of their destinies will be restored to the Czech and Slovak nations and that you will return to us.

To the people of Czechoslovakia, the congress had this to say:

COMRADES, CITIZENS OF THE CZECHOSLOVAK SOCIALIST REPUBLIC:

Czechoslovakia is a sovereign and free Socialist state founded on the free will and support of its people. Its sovereignty, however, was violated on August 21, 1968, when it was occupied by troops of the Soviet Union, Poland, the German Democratic Republic, Bulgaria, and Hungary.

This action is being justified on the grounds that socialism was endangered and that the intervention was requested by some leading Czechoslovak officials. However, yesterday's Central Committee proclamation, the second radio broadcast of the President of the Republic, the proclamation of the National Assembly and the Government of the Republic, and the statement of the Presidium of the Central Committee of the National Front make it clear that no competent Party or constitutional authority has requested such an intervention.

There was no counterrevolution in Czechoslovakia, and Socialist development was not endangered. As was demonstrated by the tremendous confidence shown in the new leadership of the Party of Comrade Dubček, the people and the Party were fully capable of solving by themselves the problems that have arisen. Indeed, action was being taken that was leading toward the realization of the fundamental ideas of Marx and Lenin on the development of Socialist democracy. At the same time, Czechoslovakia has not breached its treaty commitments and obligations; it has not the slightest interest in living in future enmity with the other socialist states and their peoples. These obligations, however, were violated by the troops of the occupying countries.

Czechoslovakia's sovereignty, the bonds of alliance, the Warsaw Pact, and the agreements of Čierna and Bratislava were trampled underfoot. Several leaders of the state and Party were unlawfully arrested, isolated from the people, and deprived of the opportunity to carry out their functions. A number of establishments of the central authorities have been occupied. Grave injustices have thus been committed.

The congress resolutely demands that normal conditions for the functioning of all constitutional and political authority be immediately created and that all detained officials be released forthwith so that they can assume their posts.

The situation that was created in our country on August 21 cannot be permanent. Socialist Czechoslovakia will never accept either a military occupation administration or a domestic collaborationist regime dependent on the forces of the occupiers.

Our basic demand is, of course, the departure of foreign troops. If the stated demands are not complied with, particularly if, within twenty-four hours, negotiations are not begun with our free constitutional and Party leaders for the departure of foreign troops and if Comrade Dubček does not make a timely statement to the nation on this matter, the congress requests all working people to stage a one-hour protest strike on Friday, August 23, at twelve noon. The congress has also decided that if its demands are not accepted it will undertake further necessary measures.

In Wenceslas Square, meanwhile, about twenty thousand persons had congregated for a manifestation that was to climax at noon in a one-hour work stoppage. The people of Prague were not waiting for the KSČ congress. Mimeographed leaflets were circulating telling Czechs to have nothing to do with the invaders. The crowd was a heaving and swelling sea of red, blue, and white from the flags and small tricolor pennants that every person seemed to be carrying or wearing. A man with a loudspeaker announced that the Party congress was being held somewhere in Prague. The crowd cheered and sang the national anthem. The Soviet tankers shifted uncomfortably atop their armored vehicles. Some of them climbed inside the tanks and the turrets began turning.

At noon Prague was filled with one great sound. Sirens on rooftops, locomotive whistles in the railway yards and stations, factory whistles, horns of cars and buses, and streetcar bells merged in a rising and rolling wave of sheer sound. It marked the beginning of the protest strike. Then, the sound died as suddenly as it began. In the square, now lit by the noon sun, thousands of persons simply sat down on the pavement and remained motionless for an hour. Everywhere traffic stopped. People neither walked nor talked. Silence engulfed Prague. The Soviet soldiers, caught in the midst of this immense mass of humanity, were alone and isolated. If silence could kill, it would have killed that noon in Wenceslas Square in Prague.

On the second day of the occupation the political control of Czechoslovakia was entirely in the hands of the progressive Communist leaders, overwhelmingly supported by virtually the entire nation. The Soviet government clearly could not tolerate this. Accordingly, Soviet representatives in Prague took new steps, and still another phase of the crisis was inaugurated.

As it developed later, this latest phase of the crisis was the most dangerous, and it was to last for four excruciating days. Pitted against the Soviet Union's need for some form of conclusive action to end a ridiculous state of affairs—and the Kremlin was painfully aware that the invasion was becoming a laughingstock—was the Czechoslovaks' stubborn determination to resist with all the means at their command. The last forty-eight hours had proved that these means were numberless.

At eleven-thirty a.m. August 22—just as the Fourteenth Party Congress was convening—General Pavlovsky and Ambassador Chervonenko called on President Svoboda at Hradčany Castle to demand in no uncertain terms that the President accept a government headed by Indra and a Party leadership made up of the Indra-Bilak-Kolder troika. They told Svoboda that the counterrevolution was spreading and that the "allied forces" would tolerate it no longer. Only the patience, the good will, and the understanding of the "allied command," they said, had prevented the occupation troops from taking sterner measures. But time was running out. The resistance must cease. Czechoslovakia's leaders had until six o'clock in the evening to accept the proposals; otherwise, they suggested, the Soviet command might have no choice but to form an "occupation regime," force General Svoboda to resign, and establish martial law.

President Svoboda stood his ground. To do so was brinkmanship of the first order, but the old man had evidently decided that Pavlovsky and Chervonenko were bluffing. He knew the Soviet Union and the Russians well enough to realize that a military government was not what Moscow desired. He was also aware that sentiment against the Russians was running so high that a bloody revolt could erupt at any moment. He staked his position on the assumption that the Soviet Union could not really afford a repetition of the 1956 Budapest slaughter. And, furthermore, the extraordinary unity of his nation had given him a negotiating position that was stronger than perhaps he realized. He told the general and the ambassador, therefore, that no discussions could be pursued so long as Dubček and the other leaders remained imprisoned. He could not control his people much longer unless they were released, Svoboda said. Besides, he added, the situation had reached the point where he could no longer negotiate only with Pavlovsky and Chervonenko, who, after all, had no power of decision; it was urgent, he said, that a meeting be arranged with the top Warsaw Pact leaders. After three hours of inconclusive talks, the Soviet emissaries left, telling Svoboda they would communicate his views to Moscow.

Just then, calls went out for a major anti-Soviet demonstration at five p.m. There were rapid consultations, mainly by telephone, among Svoboda and his ministers and the Party leaders at the ČKD congress. The consensus was that this might be a Soviet provocation and that a demonstration must be avoided at all costs. The Czechs could not risk a bloody confrontation that would give the Soviets the excuse to claim that the regime could not maintain public order. Immediately, the clandestine radio chain began broadcasting appeals against the planned demonstration. "It is an act of provocation!" the radio announcers kept repeating. But, as five o'clock approached, crowds were forming again in Wenceslas Square. Young people were arriving in trucks draped with Czechoslovak flags. The Russians moved in additional tanks; the armor was now drawn up in a solid wall along the National Museum with cannon pointing down at the expanse of the square and the growing crowd. A police car pulled up at the foot of the square and a captain spoke over the loudspeaker. "Come on, boys," he said. "Don't be foolish. Disperse. Why hand the occupiers a pretext? Don't you understand what they want?"

Reluctantly the crowd obeyed. Student volunteers appeared to assist the handful of uniformed policemen directing cars away from the square. Presently the area became empty. The Soviet tankers relaxed. The immediate danger of a clash had passed. The Czechs, almost childishly, were congratulating themselves on their discipline.

But the political battle went on. At nine p.m. Bilak, Kolder, and several other conservative leaders went to see Svoboda at the castle, apparently to press him to accept the Soviet-sponsored regime. This time, Svoboda had with him his daughter and his son-in-law Milan Klusak, who had recently returned from a diplomatic assignment at the United Nations. My liberal friends told me that Klusak was a Soviet sympathizer and they expressed concern that he might influence the elderly President in the wrong direction. Their evaluation of Klusak was not incorrect in principle, but at this stage Svoboda was not being influenced by anyone. The President once more rejected the idea of the Indra government.

Shortly before eleven p.m.—as Soviet tanks fired their cannon along the Vltava River—Svoboda received a call from Chervonenko telling him that the Soviet leaders were ready to receive him in Moscow the following day to open high-level negotiations. Svoboda said he would leave in the morning. The cabinet was in permanent session at the castle under the chairmanship of Deputy Premier Lubomir Strougal, the highest-ranking member of the government then in Prague. It was one of those Czecho-slovak ironies that it was Strougal who was informed by the President of the Moscow mission and was asked to appoint two members of the government to accompany him to the Soviet capital. Strougal immediately proposed Husák and Defense Minister Dzúr. The first outlines of what was to be the Husák-Strougal alliance in the months to come thus emerged as early as the evening of August 22. The National Front named Justice Minister Bohuslav Kučera, a Socialist, to represent it on the delegation. An interesting sidelight to the cabinet discussion that night was an order to Deputy Interior Minister Šalgovič—the man who directed the security services in preparing the invasion—to report at once to the Presidential Military Office "because of the abnormal situation that reportedly has developed in state security." The communiqué said this was ordered on the advice of Interior Minister Pavel, "who regularly takes part in the government deliberations." Actually, Pavel was working from a secret hideout to avoid arrest by the KGB.

Svoboda went to sleep after two a.m., Friday, August 23, planning to fly to Moscow in the morning. But at six a.m., he telephoned his wife at their villa at Jeleni Prikop (this was the Presidential residence) to say that he had just been informed that a government had been formed without his knowledge and he was canceling his trip. In reconstructing the confused hours of that night, it appears that Indra, presumably acting on his own, proclaimed himself Premier. He must have concluded that negotiations in Moscow might end his chances for the premiership. In any event, Svoboda telephoned Chervonenko to tell him the Moscow visit was off. The ambassador rushed up to the castle to assure him that no government had been created behind his back and that the Soviet leadership was awaiting him for the negotiations. At seven-fifty a.m. Svoboda called his wife again to say he was leaving. At eight-forty-five the clandestine radio—still acting as the official channel—broadcast Svoboda's departure statement:

> Yesterday—that is, on August 22, 1968—I had discussions with representatives of the Soviet Union on how to solve the situation created by the entry of Soviet and other troops on Czechoslovak territory, especially on how to restore the functions of the constitutional organs of the Czechoslovak Socialist Republic. When these discussions did not produce a satisfactory result, in the [early] morning hours I asked members of the government, who at this time are still at Hradčany Castle, to give their consent to direct talks with the highest representatives of the Soviet Union. This morning, the Ambassador of the Soviet Union expressed a positive attitude of the Soviet leadership to such talks.
>
> The following people will accompany me for the talks: Husák, Dzúr, Piller, Bilak, Indra, and Kučera. We shall inform the National Assembly of our trip.
>
> Dear citizens, I want to thank you for your support and trust, and I ask you to give further support to my next approach. I urge you to maintain calm and restraint and to help, through your attitude of awareness, create favorable conditions for the coming discussions with Soviet representatives. We hope that we shall emerge from this situation, which threatens tragic consequences for our people and our country, with honor and assure you that we are continuing on the path of democratic development of our socialist homeland in the spirit of the January plenary meeting of the Central Committee. We expect to return home this evening and immediately to inform the constitutional organs, as well as you, dear citizens, about the talks.

Although Svoboda had said that Piller, Bilak, and Indra were flying with him to Moscow, spokesmen hurried to tell newsmen that the three conservatives were *not* going as members of the official delegation but simply at their—and the Soviet Embassy's—request. Still, Svoboda's mention of their names immediately aroused fears that a "deal" had been made, and at nine-twenty a.m. the Free Radio reported that the President had asked it to broadcast the clarification that his trip was being made on his own initiative and that "he assures everyone that he has not signed proposals to establish a collaborationist government." Svoboda also took along his secretary, Novak, his son-in-law, Klusak, and his personal doctor. At nine-thirty a.m. the Presidential aircraft left Ruzyň airport for Moscow. It was the start of one of the bravest and most heartbreaking missions in modern history.

There is no detailed account available—and no written record is known to exist—of the tortured Moscow negotiations between the Soviet leadership and the Czechoslovak delegation of which President Svoboda was the official head. What there is for the chronicler to assemble are brief references to the dramatic character of the negotiations that the returning leaders offered in their public speeches, a few obviously incomplete private accounts obtained at second hand, some minor personal indiscretions, and a mass of unverified rumor. Just as Dubček, Smrkovský, Černík, and Kriegel always shied away from describing publicly or even privately their personal experiences in the hands of the Russians, so all the other Czechoslovak participants have remained singularly tight-lipped about the day-by-day story of the negotiations. It goes without saying that no Soviet version can be obtained. The reconstruction one can make of the four days of the Moscow negotiations remains, therefore, unsatisfactory and full of gaps. Certain insight can be gained from the over-all knowledge of the situation as it then prevailed, and this allows some assumptions as to what might have gone on in the Kremlin. And, of course, there is the backdrop of the simultaneous events in Prague that adds to the understanding of the broader story.

Svoboda and his companions arrived at Moscow's Vnukovo airport shortly before one p.m., local time, Friday, August 23. The Soviets chose to make a festive occasion of it and Party General Secretary Brezhnev, Premier Kosygin, and President Podgorny were on hand to greet them. A Soviet military band played both national anthems and both the airport and the route into the city were decorated with Czechoslovak flags. Photographs and films later released in Moscow showed Svoboda standing in an open car with the Soviet leaders and waving to the crowds. There were pictures of warm embraces between Svoboda and his hosts. No Western news correspondent in Moscow actually saw any of these scenes and some suspicion remains that the photographs were largely a laboratory product. Whatever the case, in the light of what had happened in Czechoslovakia earlier that week and of what was to happen in the Kremlin in the ensuing days and nights, there was a touch of the macabre and the cynical in this reception.

The moment the Czechoslovaks reached the Kremlin a complete curtain of secrecy descended over the proceedings. There are excellent reasons, however, to believe that Friday afternoon and evening were spent almost entirely in a showdown between Svoboda and Brezhnev and Kosygin over the fate of the four Czechoslovak leaders imprisoned by the Soviets. The most reliable accounts agree that Svoboda told the Russians he would not negotiate anything until the four men were freed. This was the position he had taken in Prague on invasion day and he maintained it stubbornly in Moscow. He is believed to have told the Soviet leaders that, if nothing else, the clandestine Party congress in Prague the day before had demonstrated overwhelming Communist support in Czechoslovakia for the leaders. He reportedly added that unless they were released and brought to participate in the negotiations, no agreement reached in Moscow could possibly be binding upon the nation. He predicted a bloody revolt in Prague.

The Russians countered by insisting that a counterrevolution had arisen in Czechoslovakia and that Dubček, Smrkovský, Černík, and Kriegel were largely responsible for it and must be punished. According to one account, Brezhnev volunteered to turn them over to Svoboda for a show trial. The old President, who suffers from high blood pressure, is said to have turned red in the face and exploded. Dubček and Černík were his legally elected fellow leaders in the government and Party, he shouted, and he would not tolerate accusations against them.

The Russians demanded that a "way out" must be found, that the Fourteenth Party Congress was "illegal," and that an agreement must be worked out on that basis. Svoboda answered that nothing could be discussed so long as his companions were in prison. One report, published so insistently as to have acquired the appearance of a confirmed fact, is that Svoboda threatened to commit suicide in the Kremlin if the four men were not freed at once. A participant in the discussion said that at one point Svoboda drew his service revolver to show his determination. I am inclined personally to believe in this suicide threat. Despite his benign appearance, Svoboda is a stubborn and an emotional man—it is sometimes forgotten that the pragmatic Czechs are also, down deep, sentimental Slavs—and he has a high sense of honor. And at this stage the issue for him had become one of honor.

The deadlock remained unbroken throughout the day. Unbeknownst to Svoboda, however, the Soviet authorities had brought Dubček, Černík, Smrkovský, and Kriegel from Lvov to Moscow late Thursday night and kept them in a secret detention place. Their fate had now turned into a bargaining element for both sides. Somewhere in the discussion, Brezhnev is said to have remarked to Svoboda that Soviet forces were in a position to destroy Prague if they wished, and that the President should bear it in mind; having gone this far in Czechoslovakia, the Soviet Union would go further if necessary. Again, it was for Svoboda to decide whether Brezhnev was bluffing. He must have thought so, because he stood firm.

From the moment he arrived in Moscow, Svoboda was cut off from all information from Prague. Attempts in the Czechoslovak Foreign Ministry to phone him and in the Defense Ministry to reach General Dzúr failed. The Svoboda team was thus ignorant of what was occurring in Prague during the day. But the Russians, of course, knew everything, and they were thus aware that at noon another general strike—even more drastic than on the day before—had paralyzed all of Czechoslovakia for one hour. Responding to the call by the Fourteenth Congress, millions of Czechs and Slovaks had simply vanished from the streets of their cities and towns, leaving the Soviet troops completely alone.

Simultaneously, a new dimension of resistance had erupted. Responding to the Free Radio's appeals, the people began turning the nation, and especially Prague, into a geographical no man's land. Immediately following the invasion people everywhere had removed road signs or turned them around to confuse the movements of the occupying troops. On numerous occasions Soviet, Polish, or East German units reached wrong destinations, throwing much of the logistical planning into a cocked hat. (In one instance, a Polish tank column wound up back on Polish territory after wandering over the countryside for hours.) And in towns and villages, the authorities and the population refused to sell the tired and thirsty troops food or beverage. Everywhere, even water was refused. Later in the week the mayor of a town near Prague told a Soviet commander who was complaining about the hostility of the people, "You may have water, but you cannot have friendship."

Now, in Prague, the radio launched the campaign of "Streets Without Names." The citizens were instructed to remove or paint over street signs and even house numbers. "The mailman will find you, but the Russians won't," a Prague announcer said. (Many citizens feared arrest by the KGB.) Newsvendors were warned not to provide subscribers' lists to anyone. By Friday evening, not a single street sign remained in place. They were torn off, splashed with paint, or replaced with signs reading DUBČEK AVENUE or SVOBODA SQUARE. Even longtime Prague residents had trouble finding addresses. During the night curfew, Soviet soldiers fired at young men and girls removing the street signs. But this was no solution, and, by midafternoon, Soviet sentries and tank crews were desperately searching for maps of Prague. Foreign tourists' cars were stopped by Soviet patrols demanding maps. Czech security agents loyal to the Soviets were assigned to the commanders of tank and armored car patrols to help them find their way. A Soviet tank captain said plaintively, "I was ordered to move my unit to a midtown street, but nobody will tell me where it is."

President Svoboda's stubbornness in Moscow and mounting resistance in Czechoslovakia finally produced results. Early Friday evening a Moscow announcement said that the talks, which Svoboda had hoped to complete that same day, were not concluded and would go on for another day. This was the only word Czechoslovaks had of what was happening in the Kremlin. At midnight, the two delegations met again. Svoboda, Husák, and Dzúr were the only spokesmen for the Czechoslovak side as the conservative trio was ignored by both Svoboda and the Russians. There was another explosive discussion. Suddenly Brezhnev announced that in the interest of Soviet-Czechoslovak friendship the Soviet government had decided to release Dubček, Smrkovský, Černík, and Kriegel and bring them, as free men, to the conference table. Svoboda asked whether this also meant that on their return to Prague they could resume their official posts. Brezhnev, annoyed, said yes, he supposed so. Between four and five a.m. Saturday, August 24, the four leaders were brought to the Kremlin. Reports say that they were fatigued beyond description, dirty, and wearing torn clothes. Svoboda, in tears, embraced them with warm emotion. There were no greetings exchanged with the three conservatives—Bilak, Indra, and Piller—hovering in the background.

In an unprecedented way, Svoboda had won a great victory for his cause, and, very possibly, he had saved the lives of his four companions. There is no record of leaders arrested by Soviet authorities being released under the pressure of their colleagues and promoted to the status of negotiators on an equal footing with those who detained them. It was an obvious defeat, no matter what Brezhnev had said about the interests of friendship, and both sides knew it. But it had become imperative to get off dead center and thus Svoboda had his way. At six-twenty a.m. Radio Prague reported that Husák had telephoned from Moscow that "Comrades Dubček, Smrkovský, and Černík . . . are also taking part in the negotiations."

A tremendous feeling of relief—and victory—spread throughout Czechoslovakia. Everyone agreed that it was the nation's unity, as expressed in the Fourteenth Party Congress resolutions, that had forced the Russians to liberate the leaders. Svoboda became even more of a hero in the eyes of his fellow citizens. The only thing that worried them was that

Husák had not mentioned Dr. Kriegel. But presently it was learned that he, too, was free but that Brezhnev had absolutely refused to let him take part in the negotiations. It was a matter of personal hatred: Kriegel was the man whom Brezhnev had called at Čierna a "dirty Galician Jew . . ."

The freeing of the four men was, however, only the beginning of the real negotiations. Having won his initial point, Svoboda now had to face the Russians' long list of demands. The basic one—of sixteen points—was, in effect, a legalization of the invasion, providing for the permanent stationing of Soviet troops in Czechoslovakia (the Russians kept calling it "temporary") and for a long series of political measures designed to curb the reform movement, strengthen Czechoslovakia's conservative Communists, and eliminate from the leadership a number of individuals especially objectionable to Moscow. Brezhnev also insisted that the Fourteenth Party Congress be declared illegal and null and void. This was a political touchstone; the Russians obviously could not live with a Party leadership that had so roundly denounced them.

In Prague, where Lubomir Strougal, as the only Deputy Premier on hand, was in charge of the government, an extraordinary thing happened. The cabinet met in special session to dismiss Deputy Interior Minister Šalgovič, Russia's chief security agent in Czechoslovakia. The cabinet ordered that his activities—meaning, presumably, the preparations he made for the invasion on August 20—be investigated and declared all his decisions invalid. Interior Minister Pavel, whom Šalgovič and the KGB had tried so hard to arrest on the day of the invasion, took personal charge of the secret police and proceeded to dismiss Lieutenant Colonel Molnař, chief of security in the Prague region and the man who had personally ordered Dubček's arrest. He also dismissed all the STB officials connected with the invasion preparations. "I am also ordering the commander of state security headquarters and his deputies to maintain an orderly performance of duties in accordance with the laws of the Czechoslovak Socialist Republic and with the Action Program of the Party and thus assure the restoration of a good reputation to all sectors of the Interior Ministry in harmony with post-January developments." The officers loyal to Pavel, arrested on invasion night, were freed.

Saturday remained a day of tensions in Prague. A woman was killed by tank fire as she stepped down from a streetcar in Klarov, opposite the Council of Ministers building, and there was scattered firing all day long. A fifteen-minute stoppage in midmorning developed into a minor anti-Soviet demonstration. General Velichko issued a new curfew order claiming that "members of the Soviet Army have been murdered and tanks set on fire. . . . In order to stop the provocative actions, I order the commanders of army groups and their detachments to take the most decisive measures against persons who attempt to attack members of the allied armies." No sooner did night fall than Soviet patrols began firing at pedestrians and vehicles in the streets. Several persons were killed and two ministers had their cars fired on.

All day there was no news from Moscow—except for a second telephone report from Husák that the talks were continuing—and concern grew again. But at ten-forty-five p.m. Radio Prague broadcast this message from Svoboda:

DEAR FELLOW CITIZENS:

First of all, I want to ask you to accept heartfelt greetings from all the comrades accompanying me. I told you before my departure that I expected to return that same evening and to report to you on the results of the negotiations. I want you to know that I would not stay one minute longer in these difficult moments if it was not urgently required in the interest of our Socialist Republic. Immediately after our arrival in the Kremlin, we started our discussions with the leading representatives of the Soviet Union. We considered it essential that Comrades Dubček, Černík, and Smrkovský should also take part in our negotiations. I can announce to you that these comrades are already, along with us, taking part in the preparations for further negotiations. And that is also the reason we have extended our stay in Moscow. I am turning to you again, dear fellow citizens, in my own name, in the name of Comrades Dubček, Černík, Smrkovský, and the other comrades present here, with a request to remain calm, sensible, and confident. Go responsibly about your work in the factories, in the fields, in all places of work. Such a loyal attitude on your part will be the best support you can give us in our further negotiations.

On Sunday, August 25, the tense negotiations continued in Moscow, and in Prague the Soviet command made moves to increase the pressure on the Czechoslovak negotiators. During the night, Soviet troops had entered several ministries and disarmed units of the People's Militia. The cabinet met Sunday morning and noted in a communiqué that "so far the commander of the occupation forces has not kept the promise he gave to President Svoboda concerning the relinquishment of government buildings and the securing of the activities of government organs." It said, acting for all the world as if Czechoslovakia were truly sovereign, that "with respect to the conduct of the occupiers, the government instructed our Ministry of Foreign Affairs to lodge a protest with the occupation governments against their armies' behavior toward the civilian population."

A noteworthy fact about this brave announcement was that it was signed by Deputy Premier Strougal, a man whose attitude toward the Soviet Union and the occupation was to undergo such a drastic metamorphosis that by early 1970 he was leading a government totally subservient to Moscow. Later Sunday morning Strougal added his signature to a joint letter sent to President Svoboda from the government, the Party Presidium, and the National Assembly. (Silhan signed for the Presidium and Valo for the Assembly.) The lengthy letter made the point that Svoboda might not possess information on the situation in Czechoslovakia since his departure and told him that "our people resolutely reject the occupation as illegal, unconstitutional, and groundless and demand the departure of the occupation armies."

Reflecting upon the circumstances under which Svoboda's team was forced to negotiate in Moscow, the letter advised the President that "already two attempts have been made to occupy the transmitting station at the Ministry of Foreign Affairs, which is our only link with our embassies and other offices abroad and also our only link with you."

> The occupation organs have so far failed in gaining the support and the cooperation of the population. This failure heightens their nervousness. The National Assembly and other organs of the country possess evidence of acts of force. We emphasize that we do not consider it normal that there should be a lack of communication between ourselves and your delegation in Moscow about the contents of your negotiations in Moscow. . . .
>
> A dangerous factor is the growing fatigue and nervous tension of the occupation armies and of our population. The tension on both sides has now increased as a result of the unforeseen extension of your stay and the stay of other officials out of the country. . . . We consider that a necessary precondition of your further negotiations is for you to be more fully and precisely informed about the real state of affairs.
>
> We therefore recommend that information be given you by a special consultative group composed of representatives of the Central Committee, the National Assembly, and the government, whose presence in Moscow you could urgently request. We are also submitting for your consideration the suggestion that your negotiations be interrupted temporarily and for a brief period and you return to Prague along with Comrades Dubček, Smrkovský, and Černík.

Svoboda did not reply directly to the suggestions that a delegation fly from Prague to brief him or that he return with Dubček. Perhaps he could not answer. But starting Sunday afternoon a number of Communist politicians, representing both the progressive and the conservative wings of the Party, made their way to Moscow. The pro-Moscow faction was reinforced by the arrival of František Barbírek, Emil Rigo, and Oldřich Švestka—all former Presidium members—and Miloš Jakeš, the tough former chief of the disciplinary Control Commission, and the onetime Premier Lenárt. The Dubček group was strengthened by the appearance of Zdeněk Mlynář and Prague's Bohumil Šimon. Czechoslovakia's ambassador to Moscow, Vladimir Koucký, an old Stalinist, joined the delegation on the spot. Not counting Kriegel, there were now eighteen Czechoslovaks negotiating with the Soviet leaders in the Kremlin. Obviously it was not a homogeneous or even a coordinated delegation. The conservatives, who had become a majority, huddled among themselves and occasionally consulted with the Russians. They had virtually no contact with the progressives except through Svoboda and Husák. The brunt of the talks was carried by Svoboda, Husák, Černík, Dubček, and Smrkovský, and for them it was a harsh and exhausting task. The Soviet delegates refused to authorize that a record be kept of the negotiations, so the Czechoslovaks had to take notes almost surreptitiously.

Now that they had the Prague team across the table in the Kremlin, Brezhnev and his associates talked tough and demanded a complete capitulation. Soviet troops were to remain in Czechoslovakia until a "normalization" occurred, but nobody cared to define what "normalization" meant. (This word was to plague Czechoslovakia for an indefinite time.) Censorship was to be reimposed. Reforms were to be abandoned. Men ideologically unpalatable to Moscow were to be removed: Brezhnev mentioned Foreign Minister Hájek—then in New York trying to make a case for Czechoslovakia before the United Nations Security Council—Deputy Premier Šik, Interior Minister Pavel, Císař, and several other liberals.

These were the demands that the Russians presented on Sunday to President Svoboda. The sixteen points were never made public, but a few days after the delegates returned from Moscow I was able to obtain the list from a high-ranking member of the Party. We published it in *The New York Times* on September 8. The points were:

    1. The characteristics of [Czechoslovak] political development . . . will be changed in accordance with the Soviet type of socialism.

    2. The declarations of the Fourteenth Party Congress are not valid.

    3. The strengthening of socialism [will come] through press censorship.

4. The Czechoslovak side will declare that there was a counterrevolution.

5. The mass communications media may not speak or write against the allies.

6. Together with the withdrawal of troops, the other groups [Soviet security organs] will also be removed.

7. Interior Minister General Josef Pavel is asked to be relieved from his functions because he was not ready to cooperate with the Soviet security organs.

8. A commission will probably be formed consisting of the representatives of the five [Warsaw Pact] states and Czechoslovakia to decide what can be approved as reparations [for damages caused by the invasion] and what cannot.

9. The international situation must be adjusted in accordance with the agreement in Bratislava.

10. Czechoslovakia will issue a document that the government did not request the United Nations and will not request the United Nations to discuss the [Czechoslovak] subject.

11. The question of ministers: The release from their functions of Ota Šik and of Prof. Jiří Hájek.

12. A declaration that the [Czechoslovak] border with West Germany is not prepared for defense and must, therefore, be secured by the allies.

13. The results of the Moscow negotiations are strictly secret and will not be published.

14. The further strengthening of friendship and alliance with the Soviet Union and with the states of the Socialist camp.

15. A declaration that the persons who worked for the Soviet Union . . . will not be persecuted.

16. The statement that the Fourteenth Congress is not valid will be made when the foreign troops have left the country.

The Russians insisted that the Moscow Agreement be based on these points. Svoboda and his associates realized that Czechoslovakia must make far-reaching concessions, but they were determined to make a stand on several basic points. This took up all Sunday and Monday. Thus, Svoboda won his point that the word "counterrevolution" would not be mentioned in the joint declaration that was being prepared. Several times the negotiations threatened to break down over this issue, but, in the end, the Russians gave in. Then Svoboda wrested from Brezhnev an agreement —it was Point 16—that a formal declaration on the nonvalidity of the Fourteenth Congress would be made only when the occupation troops left. Point 6, on the withdrawal of Soviet security organs along with the troops, was also the result of Svoboda's insistence. The Czechoslovak group pressed for compensations for damages caused by the invasion, but all Moscow would accept was the formation of a commission.

On all the other points the Czechoslovaks capitulated. They agreed to the stationing of Soviet troops in the country pending "normalization" and in recognition of the allegation that the border with West Germany was not adequately defended. They accepted censorship and the enforcement of the "Soviet type of socialism." They agreed to the cabinet purge.

This is not to say, however, that these conditions were easily accepted. Svoboda, Dubček, and Smrkovský fought inch by inch to resist what would appear as a compromise. But, as the hours passed, it developed that within Svoboda's own group a tendency toward "realism" was developing. It was represented by Husák, who increasingly urged Svoboda and the others to be "reasonable," and—more surprisingly—by Premier Černík. He, too, had been imprisoned and mistreated by the Soviets, but he must have decided that there might be a future for him and for Czechoslovakia if they were "realistic" and accommodating. Svoboda, pressed by his son-in-law Klusak, also began gradually veering in this direction. Dubček seemed to see some merit in listening to Husák's and Černík's arguments. This left Smrkovský alone. Finally he was presented with the ultimate argument: Soviet power. The Czechoslovaks were coldly informed that if no agreement could be reached along the general lines proposed, Prague could—or would—be attacked. They were told in chilling detail what was the disposition of Soviet troops around the capital.

In Prague, estimates by Western military attachés and the few American newsmen who tried to keep track of the occupation troops' movements were that the capital was ringed on Sunday, August 25, by at least three Soviet divisions equipped with tanks, self-propelled artillery, and rocket launchers. The latter were surface-to-surface Scuds, the Soviet equivalent of the United States Army's Honest John tactical battlefield missiles. The Scuds, which have a range of about a hundred miles, may carry nuclear or conventional high-explosive warheads. We had no idea whether the Scuds around Prague carried nuclear warheads—those of us who made forays around the city to check on the Soviet deployment could not get close enough to the rocket batteries to determine whether fueling equipment required for nuclear launchings had been emplaced alongside the mobile launchers—but we theorized that in an operation of this type the Russian commanders would have probably wished to have atomic weapons available.

Our count further showed that between Friday morning, when President Svoboda had flown to Moscow, and noon Sunday, Soviet forces in and around Prague had been increased from about forty thousand to seventy thousand troops. We calculated that two armored divisions and one mechanized infantry division plus support battalions of artillery and housekeeping troops were deployed around Prague in a radius of twenty miles. The artillery consisted of net-camouflaged 155-mm. howitzers and 160-mm. mortar launchers. Additional mortar companies posted in the suburbs were armed with 81-mm. tubes. The azimuth and elevation of the artillery pieces and the positioning of the mortars suggested that shells could be lobbed directly into the center of Prague. Inside Prague— including Ruzyń airport and the Troja reservation in the northern sub- urbs—troops totaling at least another division were deployed. At least five hundred tanks were in position inside and around the capital, in addition to battalions of armored cars and armored personnel carriers. There were several battalions of paratroopers and regular infantry.

Inside Prague, eighty tanks were stationed at the Julius Fučik Culture and Sports Park, on the left bank of the Vltava. There were upward of fifty tanks in the Letná Park, adjoining the Interior Ministry. Smaller tank units on the left bank were deployed at Hradčany Castle, the Foreign Ministry, the Štefánik Infantry Barracks, and the Soviet Embassy in Bubeneč. Fifty or more tanks sat in the large plaza near the Defense Ministry and in the avenues leading to it. On the right bank, a column of thirty to forty tanks lined Dlouhá Street behind the Old Town Square. Forty tanks were at the park facing the railroad station the Czechs still call Woodrow Wilson. Twenty to thirty tanks occupied Wenceslas Square. A total of probably one hundred and fifty more tanks were scat- tered throughout the right bank area, guarding ministries, newspaper offices, the KSČ Central Committee, and various downtown squares and intersections and the Vltava bridges.

This formidable force was supported in depth by what was estimated on Sunday as two hundred thousand additional Warsaw Pact troops throughout Czechoslovakia. By the middle of the second week, the total was believed to be close to six hundred thousand troops. Curiously, NATO headquarters at Brussels insisted subsequently that the invading armies never exceeded two hundred and fifty thousand troops. This led to bitter arguments because the military attachés of the NATO countries in Prague were in agreement that the occupation armies were certainly upward of a half-million and they were so informing their defense minis- tries. In the end, the professional consensus in Prague was that NATO was deliberately minimizing the scope of the invading forces to cover up the embarrassment caused to its intelligence chiefs who had been taken completely by surprise by the invasion. This was a dangerous game of self-delusion. When I visited NATO headquarters late in October, I was taken to task by high-ranking United States Army and intelligence officers for my insistence that at least five hundred thousand Warsaw Pact troops had entered Czechoslovakia. They said their information indicated that I had exaggerated it by a hundred per cent. I could find no satisfactory explanation why their estimates were so much at variance with the figures projected by the NATO military attachés in Prague.

Another example of how NATO and American military experts had misinterpreted the magnitude of the Warsaw Pact move in Czechoslovakia was provided early in November by Alain C. Enthoven, then Assistant Secretary of Defense for Systems Analysis, when he formally retracted a memorandum he had written immediately after the invasion saying that "neither the short- nor the long-term threat to NATO's Center Region has undergone a major change" in the wake of the intervention. In November Enthoven wrote that "the net threat—including the availability of forces and the possible [Warsaw] Pact willingness to risk their use against NATO territory—has significantly increased." In a letter to a United States Senator, Enthoven requested that his earlier estimate be deleted so that "the error will not be perpetuated."

But on Sunday, August 25, these were highly academic considerations as far as the population of Prague and the Czechoslovak team in Moscow were concerned. There are sound reasons to believe that this was the most dangerous moment of the entire crisis, for the Soviet leaders were not ruling out the use of their military power if the Svoboda group proved too obdurate. If power were to be used, the Soviet commanders had two basic options. One was to use their armor in Prague in a series of psychological and terror operations, such as the destruction of certain buildings by point-blank shelling. The second alternative would have been to remove the forces from the city and submit it to bombardment from the positions ringing Prague on the pretext, for example, that armed "counter-revolutionaries" were threatening an uprising. The fact that the Soviets had rushed reinforcements into the Prague area while the negotiations were going on in Moscow seems to support the belief that punitive military action was being contemplated as an element of pressure on the Svoboda negotiators to break down their resistance.

That an attack on Prague was indeed threatened was clearly indicated in Svoboda's and Smrkovský's speeches when they returned to Prague after the signing of the Moscow Agreement. Speaking to the nation in the afternoon of August 27, General Svoboda said, "Developments in our country in recent days threatened hourly to produce the most tragic consequences. As a soldier, I know what bloodshed can result in a conflict between civilians and an army with modern equipment. Consequently, as your President, I considered it my duty to do all I could to insure that this does not happen, that the blood of peoples that have always been friends is not spilled senselessly."

Speaking on August 29, Smrkovský put it this way:

> Our negotiations in Moscow were of an unusual nature. . . . As everyone can figure out for himself, to make decisions in this situation was extremely problematic. The occupation of our country by Warsaw Pact troops was a stern reality. Our communication with home was limited; we received very little or no information, and sometimes we had to depend more on our faith in the firm attitude of our people than on any factual knowledge of the situation. However, the attitude of our partners was made known to us rather accurately, and we also guessed that there might be certain difficulties in which the external military intervention found itself politically. . . .
>
> We could have rejected any type of compromise and prodded the development of things to the point where the foreign troops would stay on our territory permanently, with all the consequences this would have for the sovereignty of the state, the political rights, the economy, and for possible new human sacrifices such a contentious development would likely have caused. I emphasize that we did bear in mind that there is a certain point at which nothing is left but to reject any submissive settlement, at which it is better to expose one's breast to the bayonets in the interest of the honor and the character of the nation. . . .
>
> But our deliberations were not easy. . . . They went on virtually for a day and a night, and we realized that the outcome could be regarded by the people of our country and by history either as acceptable or as a betrayal. . . . I ask you to believe that we did not keep silent, that we did clash sharply and repeatedly—both with our partners and among ourselves—and that we used every argument available to us.
>
> We, too, had to act and decide in the shadow of tanks and aircraft on our territory.

But Prague was singularly peaceful on Sunday, a sunny day, and there seemed to be no awareness among the citizenry of the immense dangers facing the city. The people chose simply to ignore the tanks and the armed soldiers, and acted as if there were no occupation troops there at all. Parents strolling with their children in the sun stared straight through the Russians. Young boys and girls developed the habit of walking up and down past a line of soldiers, almost brushing against them, the way you walk along a row of trees or bushes. Young people in love walked about hand in hand and looking into each other's eyes. The churches were open and many people went quietly to mass. On Charles Bridge the ancient stone statues of saints did not seem to notice the self-conscious jack-booted Soviet officers photographing each other in front of them. In the Vltava the ducks and mallards swam as usual, and a few fishermen ventured out with their boats.

In the evening, after the curfew, there was the usual burst of firing. Heavy machine guns rattled just before midnight somewhere near the empty Presidential castle. A two o'clock in the morning on Monday the American Embassy caught fire. There was a skeleton staff of diplomats on duty as well as the five-man Marine detail and a half-dozen newsmen using the Telex to file late copy. At first we thought the great old building—a lovely palace once belonging to a noble family of the Dual Monarchy—had been hit by incendiary bullets as the smoke rolled out of the roof. Then we realized that the old wooden beams and rafters in the attic had caught fire from the heat of the embassy's incinerator, in which classified papers had been burned steadily for two days. At one point flames were shooting up so high from the roof that we thought the building was lost. The fire department could not come because of the curfew, and, for the same reason, Ambassador Beam could not reach the embassy from his residence. But the combined efforts of the Marines, diplomats, and newsmen—and an American movie actor who once worked as a forest ranger in the West and happened to be spending the night at the embassy —saved the old structure.

On Monday, August 26, several Soviet soldiers invaded the embassy garden to eat apples in the orchard. Two Marines, unarmed, went up to the pavilion atop the gardens to hoist the Stars and Stripes. Then Mark Garrison, the embassy's Political Officer, a young and talented diplomat who also happens to speak Russian, marched up the hill to expel the trespassers. "These are American apples," he said. "You cannot eat them." The Russians, perplexed, dropped the fruit and departed.

At nine-fifteen a.m., a fifteen-minute anti-Soviet demonstration was staged. All the sirens sounded and car horns were tooted. This seemed to frighten the Russians. Volleys from submachine guns were fired in the air. At the Strašnice crematorium, near a field where Soviet mortars were emplaced, a burial service was held for Zdeněk Přihoda, the first Czech youth to be killed in the invasion. At noon the cabinet met under Strougal's chairmanship to write a protest to the Soviet government, demanding "immediate and effective measures against the inexplicable and nonpermissible acts committed by members of the Warsaw Pact armies who have occupied the Czechoslovak Socialist Republic." It demanded that General Pavlovsky keep his promise to free the government buildings. The National Assembly was still in permanent session. Someone set up a special place for the men to shave and the women deputies to wash and dry their hair. Later the deputies, who had been sitting in for five days, were shown the film *Capricious Summer*, produced and directed by Jiří Menzel. The Presidium of the Writers' Union met secretly and issued a proclamation asserting that "the long uncertainty as to whether the Soviet Union is to play the role of an apostle or of a gendarme in the Socialist camp has finally been overcome. . . . The great socialist power is returning to the tried and tested traditions of Cossack diplomacy." Late in the afternoon, the radio announced that at six p.m. all the main roads leading to Prague would be sealed by Soviet forces and that "shooting cannot be excluded" in case of violations. Tension was mounting again as there was no word from Moscow on the progress of the negotiations.

But, shortly after eight p.m., the Soviet contingents suddenly left the building of the Council of Ministers in Klarov. To some acute observers this was a sign that an agreement must be in the offing in the Moscow talks. They were right. That same evening President Svoboda and seventeen Czechoslovak politicians, including Dubček and Smrkovský, were placing their signatures on the text of a joint Soviet-Czechoslovak secret agreement and a public communiqué telling the world what had been decided at the Kremlin. Only František Kriegel, who had been kept out of the talks, did not sign. Zdeněk Mlynář, one of the early Party progressives, who signed the documents, said later he understood how President Beneš must have felt in 1938. The Czechoslovaks accepted the agreement in a state of total mental and physical exhaustion, and most of them believed sincerely they were saving their country from bloodshed and destruction.

Here is the text of the communiqué:

During the talks, in a free comradely discussion, the two sides considered questions relating to the present development of the international situation, the activization of imperialism's machinations against the Socialist countries, the situation in Czechoslovakia in the recent period, and the temporary entry of troops of the five Socialist countries into the territory of the Czechoslovak Socialist Republic.

The participants expressed their mutual firm belief that the main thing in the present situation is to carry out the joint decisions adopted in Čierna-nad-Tisou and the provisions and principles formulated by the Bratislava conference, as well as to implement gradually the practical steps following from the agreement reached during the talks. The Soviet side stated its understanding of and support for the position of the leadership of the Czechoslovak Communist Party and the Czechoslovak Socialist Republic, which is determined to proceed from the decisions adopted at the January and May plenary meetings of the Central Committee of the Czechoslovak Communist Party, in the interest of improving the methods of management of the society, developing socialist democracy, and strengthening the socialist system on the basis of Marxism-Leninism.

Agreement was reached on measures aimed at the speediest normalization of the situation in the Czechoslovak Socialist Republic. The Czechoslovak representatives gave information on the planned immediate measures aimed at meeting these goals. The Czechoslovak representatives stated that all the work of the Party and state organs in all the sectors of their activity will be directed at ensuring effective measures in the interest of the Socialist system, the leading role of the working class, and the Communist Party and developing and strengthening friendly relations with the peoples of the Soviet Union and the entire Socialist community. Expressing the unanimous striving of the peoples of the Soviet Union for friendship and brotherhood with the peoples of Socialist Czechoslovakia, the Soviet representatives confirmed their readiness for the broadest sincere cooperation on the basis of mutual respect, equality, territorial integrity, independence, and Socialist solidarity.

The troops of the allied countries that temporarily entered the territory of Czechoslovakia will not interfere in the internal affairs of the Czechoslovak Socialist Republic. Agreement was reached on the terms of the withdrawal of these troops from the territory of Czechoslovakia, depending on the normalization of the situation in the Republic. The Czechoslovak side gave information that the supreme commander of the Czechoslovak armed forces had issued appropriate orders aimed at preventing incidents and conflicts capable of disturbing peace and public order. He also instructed the military command of the Czechoslovak Socialist Republic to be in contact with the command of the allied troops.

In connection with the discussion in the United Nations Security Council of the so-called question of the situation in the Czechoslovak Socialist Republic, the representatives of the Republic stated that the Czechoslovak side had not requested the submission of this question for consideration by the Security Council and has demanded its removal from the agenda. The leading representatives of the Czechoslovak Communist Party and the Soviet Communist Party confirmed their determination to carry out resolutely in the international arena a policy meeting the interests of strengthening the solidarity of the Socialist community and the cause of peace and international security.

As heretofore, Czechoslovakia and the Soviet Union will resist with determination the militaristic, revanchist, and neo-Nazi forces that strive to reverse the results of World War Two and to encroach on the inviolability of the existing borders in Europe. Both sides also confirmed again their determination to fulfill unswervingly all commitments under multilateral and bilateral agreements concluded between Socialist states, to strengthen the defensive power of the Socialist community, and to increase the effectiveness of the defensive Warsaw Pact. The talks were held in an atmosphere of frankness, comradeship, and friendship.

The turgid prose of this declaration—which ranks among the most incredible documents of our generation, I think—deliberately concealed the far-reaching concessions and commitments exacted from the Czechoslovaks. The actual agreement, it will be recalled, provided in its thirteenth point that "the results of the Moscow negotiations are strictly secret and will not be published." The idea was that the conditions imposed on Czechoslovakia would be gradually spelled out for the nation. Even the Soviet Union realized that to disclose the truth—or even part of it—in the immensely explosive atmosphere prevailing in Czechoslovakia could lead to a dramatic reaction, and at this point both governments wanted to avoid it. As a sop, presumably, the declaration vaguely described the Soviet Union as supporting the principles of the January and May Plenums of the KSČ Central Committee which had moderately defined the objectives of the Prague reformers: the January Plenum was acceptable to Moscow because it had been so inarticulate in its formulations; the May Plenum had been Dubček's last effort at caution and compromise. But the April Plenum—when the Action Program was voted on—was conspicuously not mentioned in the Moscow communiqué.

The key phrase in the communiqué was, of course, that "agreement was reached on the terms of the withdrawal of [the allied] troops from the territory of Czechoslovakia, *depending on the normalization of the situation in the Republic.*" Having introduced the arbitrary concept of "normalization," the Soviets gave themselves a free hand to proceed as they wished. The passage pledging that the armies that "temporarily" entered Czechoslovakia would "not interfere in the internal affairs" of the country was a semantic decoy. It was not the Soviet Army but the Soviet Union itself that had given itself the right of interference—hence the invasion. Nevertheless, there were to be occasions when the Soviet forces stood on the verge of new intervention, or "interference." The giveaway sentence making it immediately clear that the troops on the "temporary" mission would remain indefinitely in Czechoslovakia was the reference to the decision "to increase the effectiveness of the defensive Warsaw Pact." The Soviet argument even before the Moscow negotiations had been that Warsaw Pact troops must be stationed in Czechoslovakia to protect the West German frontier.

In all fairness, however, it must be noted that Svoboda emerged with several concessions in Czechoslovakia's favor, at least in a relative sense. In the first place, he had successfully resisted Soviet pressure to acknowledge that a "counterrevolution" had taken place in his country. This not only afforded Prague considerable flexibility in its future dealings with Moscow but also permitted the release from prison of Dubček and his companions and their return to office, and it was a propaganda and political defeat for the Kremlin because it removed from the public record the justification for the invasion that it had been trumpeting to the world all week long. Likewise, no reference was made to the allegation—loudly used in the first hours of the occupation, when Moscow thought it had a collaborationist regime ready and waiting to assume power—that the "fraternal" troops had arrived in response to a call from Czechoslovak leaders. This unhappy myth was laid to rest once and for all. On balance, therefore, Svoboda did better than could have been expected under the terrible circumstances in which he was negotiating. This fact is clearer now than it was on August 26, 1968.

Svoboda scored a final point in the last-minute drama played out at Vnukovo airport at dawn on Tuesday, August 27. When the Czechoslovak leaders gathered at the terminal for departure for Prague at two a.m., someone noticed that Kriegel was not present. Svoboda made inquiries and was told by Soviet officials that Kriegel was ill and would not be flying home with the rest of the group. Svoboda refused to accept this explanation and, along with most members of the delegation, said he would not leave without Kriegel. There was another showdown, more consultations among the Soviet leaders, and, presently, Kriegel was brought to the airport, about three a.m. (That he was ill was true. He is a diabetic, and the Russians had apparently refused to supply him with sufficient insulin.)

As the Czechoslovaks boarded the plane for the flight home, Soviet armor in Prague began withdrawing from many strategic points in the capital. Clyde Farnsworth and I had stayed up all night awaiting Svoboda's return—we had been tipped off by friends in Czechoslovak military intelligence that an agreement had been signed and the delegation was about to come back—and periodically throughout the long dawn we checked Hradčany Castle to see whether the Presidential standard, signifying Svoboda's presence in the capital, had been hoisted. Shortly before five a.m. we were told that the Soviet troops were moving away. Clyde drove downtown and returned with the report that the Vltava bridges were clear of tanks and that the armor had also been withdrawn from the Štefánik Infantry Barracks and a number of government buildings. Heavy Soviet units remained elsewhere in Prague. A few minutes after six the delegation aircraft landed at Ruzyň. Only Indra had remained behind in Moscow with his Soviet friends, and I was told that he was ailing.

But I had the distinct feeling that this man who had hoped to become Premier in a Soviet-sponsored regime was simply in no hurry to come home and face his fellow citizens.

At eight-five a.m. Radio Prague—still broadcasting from its clandestine studios but now considered the official Czechoslovak station—announced that Svoboda and his companions had returned to Prague, and, presently, the Presidential standard went up on Hradčany's roof. At eight-fifteen a brief taped interview with Smrkovský, sounding on the verge of collapse, was broadcast. "It's hard for me to speak. By means of the radio, I wish to pay my profound respect to this nation, which has accomplished so much. We have all come back, including Kriegel."

Now the nation awaited word from its leaders on what had been decided in Moscow about its fate. A writer I knew whom I met in Wenceslas Square that morning said mournfully, "I wonder if, again, they've decided about us without us."

XIX

The End and the Beginning

It was not quite ten o'clock in the morning Tuesday, August 27, when Smrkovský arrived at the National Assembly to report, in his capacity as chairman, on the Moscow Agreement. A big crowd awaited him and Smrkovský's black car could advance only very slowly. Anxious and questioning faces peered into the automobile and people waved to him and smiled gently. Smrkovský, suddenly looking years older, barely acknowledged the greetings. The Soviet tanks had left the National Assembly during the night, and there was only the churned-up soil turned by their tracks in front of the building. Smrkovský received a thunderous ovation as he entered the Assembly, but inside the deputies who had been in permanent session since the previous Wednesday simply stood quietly in tribute. Speaking in tired, somber tones, Smrkovský told them of the negotiations and the agreements, the reimposition of censorship, the liquidation of political associations, and so on. The session was a closed one, but word quickly reached the people outside and spread throughout the city.

Later in the morning, Premier Černík presided over a cabinet meeting at Hradčany Castle. Svoboda was present and the government took its first decisions to implement the Moscow pact. Dubček had gone to the Central Committee to brief his Party associates. At two-forty p.m. Radio Prague broadcast the text of the Moscow communiqué, and gloom fell over the capital. The Czechs were sufficiently adept at reading—or listening—between the lines to have understood at once the meaning of the declaration. Anger and frustration rose in the country, and spontaneous meetings of Party organizations and other groups began sending protest telegrams to Radio Prague. The announcers read some of them, then

435

appealed for calm, and said Svoboda and the other leaders would soon be addressing the nation.

Awaiting the speeches, Radio Prague played the entire Beethoven Fifth Symphony—the "Victory Symphony"—a fine touch of pride and defiance. Then Svoboda began speaking. He started by explaining the danger of bloodshed that had menaced Czechoslovakia as he negotiated in Moscow. He went on:

> I do not want to deny the fact that painful wounds caused by the events of these days will long remain. . . . The place of our country in today's world is and cannot be anywhere but in the Socialist community. . . . I have returned with all these comrades, who are forthwith resuming the offices to which they have been democratically appointed. . . . This is the first and for us important step toward normalization of life in our country. Naturally, the departure of the armies of the Soviet Union and the other Socialist countries from our territory bears on this. We have, above all, achieved agreement in principle on a gradual implementation of the complete departure of the armies. Pending this, their presence is a political reality.

But Svoboda wanted to reassure the nation that the government was not abandoning the reform programs of 1968:

> In the spirit of the January, *April* [my italics], and May plenary meetings of the Central Committee of the Communist Party of Czechoslovakia, we want to continue to develop the Socialist social system and strengthen its humanist, democratic character, as expressed in the Action Program and the government's policy declaration. . . . We want to carry on building our country as the real homeland of the working people. We shall not retreat a single step from these aims. We shall naturally not allow them to be misused by those to whom the interests of socialism are alien. To that end, all of us must now purposefully and with determination direct our efforts.

The President's words did not allay the Czechs' bitterness and frustration. More and more protest resolutions and telegrams streamed to Radio Prague and they were immediately broadcast. In Wenceslas Square and in the Old Town Square crowds of young people gathered. There were cries of, "A second Munich!" At five-thirty Dubček went on the air, so obviously in a state of complete exhaustion that some of his sentences sounded incoherent and others were slurred beyond understanding. Often his voice trailed off into silence. But in the light of the rapidly mounting tension in Prague and throughout Czechoslovakia, he evidently felt he must speak at once to seek and find comprehension among his fellow citizens.

The life of our people will take place in a situation whose reality does not depend on our will alone. We were fully aware of this fact during the entire time, just as you feel it. . . . It is necessary to prevent further suffering and further losses at all costs, because they would not alter the real conditions, and the abnormal situation in our homeland would be prolonged. The fact that we are determined to prevent bloodshed does not mean that we want passively to submit to the situation that has been created. . . . The Soviet representatives, too, want to contribute to the normalization of our relations.

In today's reality, we are faced with the task of finding a way out of the present situation in Czechoslovakia. First, we have an agreement on the phased departure of troops of the five states from the territory of our Republic. Consequently, any distrust aroused about this matter is groundless and harmful. That agreement, that standpoint, is the fundamental prerequisite for our future activities. We have agreed that troops will be moved immediately from villages and towns to areas reserved for them. This is naturally connected with the ability of our own Czechoslovak organs to ensure order and normal life in individual areas. In this respect, the government of the Republic has already proceeded today to take appropriate measures in order that our organs may implement steps to regulate our civil life. It would, therefore, be very imprudent and dangerous to take any actions that would hold up the movements and eventually the departure of the troops of the five states from our country. The final aim of our entire endeavor is to effect the complete withdrawal of these troops as soon as possible. On the basis of the Moscow negotiations, the government is already taking specific steps in this direction. . . .

I want to point out most seriously that the normalization of conditions includes the requirement that each individual should not act on the basis of passions and mass psychosis without knowledge of the facts. In this complicated period, we must not succumb to passions and psychoses. . . . This support will strengthen us all the more and will be an obligation for us not to abandon, in this complicated time, our striving for the expression of humanist and socialist principles.

It might seem a paradox that I speak about this just now. But we must have faith in our strength and faith in our people. . . . We are returning to work with the determination to create conditions for continuing this policy with as few mistakes as possible. . . . To ignore the real situation could lead in some places only to adventure and to anarchy. . . . The first thing we need is the quickest possible consolidation and normalization of the situation in the country. . . . For this very reason, we trust that you will assist us today . . . with your continued confidence and active participation. We trust you will do this if we must carry out some temporary, exceptional measures restricting the degree of democracy and freedom of expression we have achieved. . . . This reality must not be ignored.

It was remarkable, really, that despite all the concessions they had been forced to make, Dubček and Svoboda still could talk of keeping alive the spirit of the Prague Spring. And even more remarkable—as events were to show—was that they meant it. From the first moment, then,

Dubček had made up his mind that even in an occupied country it was still possible to keep one's dignity, one's defiance, and one's allegiance to ideas that had become basic in Czechoslovakia in the short eight first months of 1968. Listening to him that afternoon, I believed that Dubček was being either naïve or simply determined at all costs to pacify public opinion. But I misjudged both Dubček and his people and their extraordinary gifts of imagination and improvisation.

For the time being, though, Dubček wanted to avoid an explosion before his people fully understood what had happened and what possibilities loomed ahead. He, therefore, warned his fellow citizens: "Broadcasts of some radio transmitters, after the speech of the President of the Republic, Comrade Svoboda, have been spreading mistrust and doubts about the Moscow negotiations and about the measures being prepared for the withdrawal of troops. We warn very emphatically against such a course. Inflammatory words are easily broadcast into the atmosphere. It is necessary to see the link between such speech and responsibility for additional loss of life, and material damage, which even now is far from small."

It was a measure of the extraordinary trust Czechoslovaks had in Dubček that within minutes of his radio speech their mood changed. The same organizations that all day long had been approving and sending protest resolutions now began forwarding communications of support for Dubček. The slogan—"We are with you; be with us!"—that was to swamp Czechoslovakia within a few days had not yet been coined. But an invisible bond of confidence was suddenly restored between this quiet and self-controlled man and millions of Czechs and Slovaks. A curious political alchemy was operating in Czechoslovakia, drawn from the nation's whole experience, and it seemed to explain the astounding unity during that first week, as well as during all the subsequent events.

Meanwhile, Dubček went on sharing with his people his emotions on his return from the Moscow negotiations. "I want to state quite frankly," he said in his radio broadcast, "that we paid dearly for the experience we now have, that we must conduct our policy with determination and consistency. We must also take care to see to it that the present complicated situation is not taken advantage of by elements and tendencies to which socialism is alien. We shall guard decisively and consistently our socialist policy in Czechoslovakia for the future. . . ." Then he lapsed into a silence lasting one, two, three minutes. I thought he had simply passed out from emotion and exhaustion. Then he regained his voice: "Dear listeners, I ask you to forgive me if every now and then there is a pause in this largely improvised speech and impromptu appearance. I think you know why it is. . . ." People listening at their radio sets at home and to their transistors in the streets wept unashamedly. It was a moment of perfect communion between a leader and his people.

Later in the afternoon, new appeals went out to the nation. The Central Committee issued a statement thanking everybody for having behaved so well, with special words of appreciation for the broadcasters and newspapermen who worked from their clandestine posts to keep the nation together: "We also thank all those who work in the mass media of communications, who, being unable to go to their usual places of work, have succeeded in establishing, with the assistance of specialized enterprises and of many citizens, new posts where they were able to work and who have communicated the will as well as the feelings of the people in the fateful hours of trial." The Central Committee then told Czechoslovakia: "We are with you; be with us!"

In the evening, Svoboda, Smrkovský, Černík, and Dubček signed a proclamation to "All the People of Czechoslovakia" that "your confidence is an obligation to us. . . . However, it is our duty, with which you have entrusted and charged us, to govern. Make that possible for us if you ask us to serve you."

The nation's sense of pride was expressed on August 28 in a proclamation by the National Assembly declaring that it was convinced that "our Army is capable of securing our western frontiers" and calling on the government "systematically and resolutely to insist on the establishment and consistent fulfillment of specific time limits for the speediest possible withdrawal of foreign troops from our country." It also demanded that "the undisturbed, free activity of all constitutional, government, and state organs, and of all legal mass media of communications, should be made possible and secured without delay. . . . At the same time, we insist that all our citizens who have been illegally detained and imprisoned by Czechoslovak or foreign organs since August 21 be released."

But it was incumbent on Premier Černík, the "realist" among the four leaders, to inform the country that the Moscow Agreement had ruled out what the National Assembly called "the undisturbed, free activity . . . of all legal mass media of communications." The secret Moscow Agreement had specified that socialism would be "strengthened" through "censorship," and, accordingly, Černík announced in a radio address that "the government approved . . . some extraordinary measures concerning the press, radio, and television required by the abnormal situation in which it is necessary to assert the government's influence on the radio, television, and Czechoslovak News Agency."

A new state of affairs came into being in Czechoslovakia with the signing of the Moscow Agreement and the return of the Republic's leaders to Prague. The period that lasted from August 28, the day after the nation's leaders re-established their rapport with their people, until November 16, when the increasingly grim realities of life under Soviet occupation marked another milestone, was to be an eerie, often unbelievable interlude. Political forces ominously clashed within Czechoslovakia, and the nonconformity and imaginative daring of the Czechs and Slovaks exposed the Soviet Union to trials and challenges that Brezhnev and his companions could never have predicted.

I think the first thing to be said of this period is that the world had never before witnessed a military occupation quite like the one the Soviets, rather than the Czechoslovaks, had to endure in Czechoslovakia. They had to deal with a government and a Party leadership so obviously opposed to it as to make the entire occupation a mockery for long months. Its leaders were men whom the Kremlin had first imprisoned and threatened to destroy, but whom it had been forced to bring back to positions of relative power because of the vacuum that would otherwise have developed. The Russians, as they have proved on so many occasions, like to think in terms of black and white, but the situation they created in Czechoslovakia was at best viscous gray. Not only the leaders but Czechoslovak society as a whole operated elusively, eel-like, disconcertingly. The Russians, to be sure, had an abundance of bayonets in Czechoslovakia. But soon they discovered the truism of the dictum ascribed, I believe, to Winston Churchill that you can do everything with bayonets except to sit on them. As the situation developed in Czechoslovakia after the signing of the Moscow Agreement, it became painfully clear that "normalization" meant one thing to the Kremlin and another thing to the Czechoslovaks.

The psychological and military momentum that the Soviets still enjoyed when they had Svoboda and his colleagues in Moscow had now vanished. After a few days it became obvious that the Russians had two choices: to set in motion instant and brutal repression or to roll with the punch and hope that a slow, inexorable process of internal erosion within the Czechoslovak leadership and society might someday produce the results that the invasion had been designed to bring. It appears that the first possibility—what the Writers' Union had called in August the "tried and tested traditions of Cossack diplomacy"—had crossed the minds of some Soviet leaders.

But the Soviet Union was in fact in an improbably weak political and ideological position. We now know in general outlines that deep dissensions had arisen within the Soviet establishment over the manner in which the Czechoslovak problem had been handled. The Soviet marshals, who were initially believed to have favored the intervention, were reported to be remonstrating with the political leaders—Brezhnev, *et al.*—for having forced the Red Army into action when the political situation was obviously unprepared for the intervention. Many diplomats in Moscow believed that the marshals were reluctant to order their troops to kill in cold blood as a means of forcing the Czechoslovaks into submission. Likewise, it was believed, some Politburo members, like Mikhail Suslov, feared that repression would damage the unity of the international Communist movement even more than the invasion did. (Suslov was still intent on convening in Moscow in November the long-delayed world Communist conference and he knew that war in Prague would ruin any chance of it.) In the end, then, the Kremlin chose the patient way and Prague subtly capitalized on it with its maddening minuet of a concession here and a defiance there.

The contradictions began, in fact, with the Russians themselves. About a week after the invasion, it dawned on someone in the Kremlin—aides to Foreign Minister Gromyko, reportedly—that the presence of East German troops in the occupation forces in Czechoslovakia posed a serious international problem for the Soviet Union. There was no peace treaty with East Germany and the use of Ulbricht's East German units in a foreign military operation could have been construed as a violation of the Potsdam Treaty, though this notion evidently never occurred to the State Department. Both East and West Germany had been rearmed by their respective sponsors, but the West German Army was kept at home. Moscow was at that time engaged in an obscure diplomatic maneuver to prove that the arming of West Germany was in contravention of two articles of the United Nations Charter. Although the purpose of this short-lived maneuver was never made clear, the stationing of East German troops in Czechoslovakia was clearly a mistake, and within a week of the invasion they were quietly withdrawn.

To assuage Ulbricht's feelings, an East German commandant and liaison officers remained attached to General Pavlovsky's command. Radio Vltava went on broadcasting from East Germany—it later turned out to be a transmitter of the East Berlin Radio International—and the occupation newspaper *Zpravý*, a scurrilous sheet written in bad Czech, continued to be printed in Dresden until it moved its operations to an abandoned Czechoslovak Army printshop in Mlada. (Soviet psychological warfare teams had the peculiar notion that the Czechoslovaks would accept the occupation if they were forced to read *Zpravý* and Moscow's *Pravda*. Thousands of copies of *Pravda* were flown daily from Moscow and foisted on the population by Soviet tank crews and patrols. They made excellent little bonfires in the streets of Prague.)

In terms of Czechoslovak politics, one contradiction followed another. On August 28 Premier Černík set up a voluntary censorship system—principally banning the use of the word "occupation" in reference to the presence of the Warsaw Pact troops in Czechoslovakia and forbidding attacks on the "foreign troops"—but simultaneously he fired Miroslav Sulek from the directorship of the news agency ČTK and replaced him with Jíndrich Suk. Now Sulek was a member of the original invasion conspiracy, and he was the man charged with sending out over the ČTK wires the "request" of Czechoslovak leaders for the invasion, a task in which he failed because of his subordinates' sabotage. A few days earlier the KSČ Presidium had dismissed Švestka, a signer of the Moscow Agreement, from his post as editor of *Rudé Právo* and replaced him with the moderately progressive Jiří Sekera, who, in turn, rehired the two liberal deputy editors Švestka had thrown out. Interior Minister Pavel, with Deputy Premier Strougal's blessings, had removed Colonel Šalgovič, another conspiracy member, from his job as boss of the secret police when Svoboda was negotiating in Moscow. Šalgovič went to his native Slovakia to re-emerge later, somewhat improbably, as Czechoslovak consul in Budapest and, finally, as the Party boss in Plzeň. Jan Zaruba, another Deputy Interior Minister, committed suicide. Drahomír Kolder was exiled to Sofia as economic counselor to the Czechoslovak Embassy there. His constituents in Moravia voted to deprive him of his seat in the National Assembly. Thus, rather incredibly, the people being purged before and after the Moscow Agreement were the top pro-Soviet officials and they were being replaced with Dubček liberals.

Also on August 28 an intriguing political situation that was to have immense consequences began developing in Bratislava. There, the Slovak

Communist Party held its congress, and it dropped Vasil Bilak, the notorious pro-Soviet leader, as its First Secretary. Elected in his place was Gustav Husák, Deputy Premier under Černík and one of the two official government delegates assigned to accompany President Svoboda to Moscow. This choice marked the formal beginning of Husák's ascent in national politics.

Except among a few unusually perspicacious Prague liberals, Husák was generally regarded as a progressive. He had spent eight years in prison under the Novotný regime, and, it was recalled, he was among the first to urge, in January, a more rapid reform policy by the then still hesitant Dubček leadership. He was a Slovak nationalist of old standing, which, it was assumed, made him unpalatable to Moscow and the orthodox Communists. His apparent patriotic ardor and liberalism had been rewarded by the clandestine Fourteenth Party Congress that elected him both to the KSČ Central Committee and Presidium.

But as soon as he was elected head of the Slovak Party, Husák did a most peculiar thing. He announced that he was resigning from both his KSČ posts on the grounds that the Fourteenth Congress was not valid because most of the Slovak delegates had been unable to attend it. Even more curiously, he publicly appealed to Dubček to resign as well from the bodies established by the clandestine conclave. The first reaction in Prague was that Husák was simply trying to make matters easier for Dubček, who, at that point, was facing the problem of how to reconcile the preinvasion and postinvasion Central Committees and Presidiums, both of which he headed. But the Husák game was vastly subtler and more complex. For one thing, it was noted in Prague that one of the principal Soviet demands in Moscow was to have the Fourteenth Congress declared illegal, something that Dubček was loath to do because this meeting may have well helped to save his life.

This internal political operation was taking place as the Soviet press resumed charges of "counterrevolution." *Izvestia* wrote on August 28, "We cannot close our eyes . . . to the difficulties created by the activation of antisocialist forces and their reluctance to accept a loss of their position. . . . Counterrevolution in Czechoslovakia is not a myth and it still makes its presence known, striving to exacerbate the situation, confuse the people, incite provocations and turn unstable people against fraternal countries, and, in a word, to push the country from the path to socialism." Tass for its part declared that "counterrevolutionaries" were seeking to "stir up nationalistic hysteria and sow anarchy and disorder. . . . Party members have joined the counterrevolutionaries and are striving to split the Communist Party and to undermine its ability to act."

On August 29, the day Prague newspapers began to reappear legally under the self-censorship rule and the nocturnal curfew was lifted for the first time since the invasion, Josef Smrkovský announced in a radio speech there were plans afoot to impose formal censorship and to disband non-Communist political organizations such as the KAN Clubs of Committed Non-Party Members and the K-231 Clubs of former political prisoners. Indicating that the National Assembly would be asked to draft a new censorship law, Smrkovský said that "we shall have to take special measures in the field of radio, television, and the press to prevent writings against the foreign-policy requirements and the interests of the Republic." Speaking sadly of this and other concessions Czechoslovakia would now have to make, he remarked, "We never thought we would have to pay the price we paid on the night of August 20–21." In what was the most honest appraisal of the situation thus far made in Prague, Smrkovský commented that, in truth, Czechoslovakia had "no real guarantees, other than our own wisdom," that the occupation troops would be withdrawn even if she fulfilled her end of the bargain. He told the Czechoslovaks that "after the first reaction of pain and indignation, I ask you to reflect with calm and coolness."

This was a day of worry and concern in Prague as the force of Dubček's assurances two days earlier began to wear off. Jiří Pelikan and Zdeněk Hejzlar, who headed the television and radio systems and had been the inspirers of the clandestine broadcasting, were replaced on "temporary vacation," evidently under Soviet pressure.

On August 30 General Velichko, the Soviet commander in Prague, promised his troops would be withdrawn from the capital altogether if all the anti-Soviet posters and signs were promptly removed. The Czechs engaged in a frenzy of wall-cleaning. A friend of mine in the Central Committee told me in the afternoon—we met furtively in a crowded downtown coffeehouse—that the Russians had obtained Svoboda's agreement to fire General Pavel from the Interior Ministry and to replace him with Jan Pelnař, an unknown Communist politician from Plzeň whom Moscow seemed to trust. The following day, as the Central Committee met at Hradčany Castle in the first open session since June, the government indeed dismissed General Pavel in Pelnař's favor. In the evening I had a drink with a Prague editor I knew well. He was unusually pessimistic and told me that "Dubček is being gradually forced to become his own

Kádár." This, however, turned out to be a misjudgment. It was Gustav Husák who was more and more acquiring Kádár's characteristics.

On September 1, however, Dubček and his associates astounded all the observers as the Central Committee, concluding a two-day session, seemed to end the Party crisis by producing a stunningly liberal twenty-one-man Presidium. The Committee enlarged itself to 187 members by absorbing most of the progressives elected by the underground Fourteenth Congress. The Presidium retained Dubček, Černík, Smrkovský, and Josef Špaček from the former liberal contingents and added President Svoboda as an honorary member. New progressive members were Zdeněk Mlynář; Vladímir Kabrna, the man who opened the Fourteenth Congress; Moravia's Václav Neubert; Václav Slavik, a friend of Dubček's; Libuse Hrdinová, the woman member of the invasion Presidium; Prague's ardently liberal Bohumil Šimon; and the Slovak liberals Václav Simeček, Anton Tazky, and Josef Zrak. The only hard-line conservatives—in a gesture toward Moscow—were Bilak and Piller. The centrist contingent were Evžen Erban, an economist; Jarolim Hettes, a man who later returned to his once conservative leanings; Josef Pinkava; and Slovakia's Stefan Sadovský. The Presidium alternates were Karel Polaček, the Trade-Union Council's progressive chairman; and the conservatives Josef Lenárt and František Barbírek.

Perhaps the most important of all, Husák was elected to the Presidium after having refused a similar post in the body selected by the Fourteenth Congress. His new and great prominence was reflected in a subsequent article in *Rudé Právo* which for the first time listed him after Dubček, Svoboda, Smrkovský, and Černík as one of the leaders "who proved in the moments of the hardest test that they fully deserve our trust." This was a true accolade, and Husák now formally joined the inner circle. His new self-appointed task, as it soon became clear, was to capture this circle from within.

Aside from the special case of Husák, however, the great mystery was how the Dubček forces succeeded in forming the most liberal Party leadership in Czechoslovak Communist history ten days after the Soviet-led invasion. If Moscow had feared that the Fourteenth Congress would have elected a progressive Central Committee on its original September 9 date, the group now in ostensible control of the Party exceeded the liberals' most daring dreams. Diplomats and foreign newsmen speculated that Dubček blithely ignored the Russians and took literally the commitment that Soviet troops would not interfere in Czechoslovakia's internal affairs. We were struck by the notion that Dubček, after all, really proposed to move ahead with his reform program in disregard of the ideological motivations of the Soviet invasion.

I must confess, however, that at this point we paid insufficient attention to Husák and the men in the Presidium who would soon become his quiet but effective allies: Sadovský, Erban, Hettes, and Pinkava. We underestimated the potential importance of Bilak and Piller in a future test, and we attached too much significance to the presence of such liberals as Mlynář, Kabrna, Neubert, Slavik, Hrdinová, and the three Slovaks. We did not correctly foresee the role Černík was to play, and we forgot that the Moscow faction held the vital Control Commission through Miloš Jakeš, a man with a long memory and excellent files. There perhaps was too much faith in the political acumen of President Svoboda —he knew how to be tough under fire but seemed increasingly lost in the complicated political byplay—and, in the end, the real progressive hard core was reduced to Dubček, Smrkovský, and Šimon. Conceivably, all these facts were clearer to the Russians. For the time being, however, the progressives had a lease on life and they used every moment of it to act as thorns in the Russian bear's side.

But, quietly, the Soviets were exacting their price, too. Pavel's dismissal was followed by the "resignation" on September 3 of Deputy Premier Ota Šik. Kriegel had been left out of the Presidium. Čestmir Císař ceased to be a Party Secretary to become chairman of the mainly decorative Czech National Council. Pelikan and Hejzlar were removed. The removal of the men truly objectionable to Moscow had been virtually completed. Only Foreign Minister Hájek still held his post, but he was still abroad and the ministry was run by Václav Pleskot, a man who did not mind obliging the Soviet Union on important matters. As Western correspondents, we could feel the new chill at the Foreign Ministry, and now even men like Dufek, the foreign-press chief, were sarcastically critical of our work.

September was a seesaw month. The defiance was still very much in the air. Hundreds of youths kept vigil at the statue of Saint Wenceslas, still decorated with flags and flowers. Resolutions demanding the withdrawal of Soviet troops kept coming out of industrial plants and civic organizations throughout Czechoslovakia. The newspapers were appearing regularly and legally under the loose voluntary censorship administered by a liberal-minded Culture Ministry official named Josef Vohnout. Soviet tanks and troops still held the key points in Prague and armored cars and jeeps patrolled the city at night. But, politically, the pressure seemed to be principally on the pro-Moscow conservatives. On September 5, for example, both Oldřich Švestka, *Rudé Právo*'s former editor, and Jan Piller found it advisable to publish statements disclaiming that they were among those who called for the invasion. "I did not betray my country, or our Communist Party, or my Communist convictions," Švestka wrote. "Rumors claiming that I was among those who had called for the troops of the Warsaw Pact are not true. . . . The future will certainly tell the truth about those who were called collaborators and traitors. Today I have no other alternative than to declare before our Party and our people that I did not betray my country." Piller said in his statement he had never dealt "with anybody" about "entering or forming some new government." He insisted that the Praha Hotel meeting on August 21–22 dealt with efforts to release Dubček from Soviet captivity and that his visit to President Svoboda concerned the negotiating trip to Moscow.

The men in evidence were the liberals. Dubček visited Prague factories and urged the workers to support the process of "humanizing" socialism. On the evening of September 5 Prague television, resuming broadcasting from its own studios, presented Smetana's opera *Dalibor* (*Faraway Forest*), on the theme of peasants rising against their oppressors. The Czechs were perfecting their handling of symbolism.

Moscow may have had faith in the patient approach, but the situation was becoming frankly embarrassing and something had to be done about it. Soviet First Deputy Foreign Minister Vasily V. Kuznetsov, former chief Soviet delegate to the United Nations and a veteran negotiator, arrived in Prague on September 6 to take matters in hand. (He came with Chervonenko, who had been urgently summoned to Moscow two days earlier.) Kuznetsov met immediately with Svoboda, and it appeared that he had been sent to Czechoslovakia on a protracted assignment to oversee "normalization" as the discredited Chervonenko evidently was unable to do. The behavior of Soviet troops also became somewhat more menacing. Seven miles east of Prague, over a hundred medium tanks were parked in a circle, as if ready to move at a moment's notice. The howitzers and mortars remained pointed at the city, and there was an accelerated movement of armored cars in the capital's streets. Again, there was a sense of crisis.

As Kuznetsov made his rounds—he saw Dubček in Prague after the Presidium had authorized him to negotiate the gradual withdrawal of

Soviet troops—Gustav Husák made his first major speech, and this spread a chill among the liberals. Husák told the Slovak Party's Central Committee in Bratislava that action might be taken shortly to prevent Czechoslovaks from leaving the country indiscriminately. He remarked that the country's borders could not be turned into a "promenade boulevard" and that "panic" had to be stopped because it interfered with normal work.

Husák's speech was particularly significant because in recent days he had become the object of lavish praise on the part of the Soviet and Polish press. Czechoslovaks have sensitive political antennas and they sensed that the unsmiling Slovak was grooming himself, or was being groomed, for the top job. The smart money in Prague was on Husák as the man who would, sooner or later, replace Dubček. In his Bratislava speech, Husák said that the internal-security apparatus would have to be strengthened—this was a Soviet demand dating back to Čierna—but he hurried to assure his audience that no liberals need fear arrest or persecution. The day after his speech Husák received Kuznetsov in Bratislava.

It was becoming increasingly clear who were the men with whom the Russians were prepared to work, and their choice not surprisingly fell on the new "realists." Husák was visibly in Soviet favor, and on September 10 Premier Černík flew to Moscow with Deputy Premier František Hamouz and Foreign Trade Minister Václav Valeš for a one-day visit, ostensibly to discuss economic matters. This was Černík's first trip to the Soviet Union since August 21. But this time he was received with warmth and cordiality; it was said in Prague that Černík was the official whom the Kremlin had selected for all the important negotiations, Husák being designated to oversee political matters at home as part of the process of isolating Dubček.

Černík's return from Moscow coincided with a proclamation signed by him, Svoboda, Dubček, Smrkovský, and Husák guaranteeing freedom of artists, scientists, and intellectuals to maintain their contacts with the outside world. The proclamation also appealed to Czechoslovaks not to flee abroad—a milder version of what Husák had said in Bratislava.

On September 11, exactly three weeks after the invasion, Soviet tanks left Prague for encampments in the countryside. Husák's and Černík's activities had presumably satisfied Kuznetsov that "normalization" was finally progressing and that the first phase in the withdrawal of Soviet troops could be set in motion. Infantry units and the armored cars remained in the city, but for the first time since the dawn of August 21 the menacing tanks were no longer there. In Plzeň—where banners spelled out the slogan of "We are with you; be with us!"—President Svoboda told workers, "We must fulfill the Moscow Agreement so that we can demand the fulfillment of the Agreement by the other side," and he observed that "unpopular measures" were looming ahead—a reference to formal action by the National Assembly preparing to legalize press censorship as part of the price for the departure of the Soviet tanks from Prague.

Another payment was the reinforcement of the secret-police apparatus. This, too, had been demanded by Moscow and mentioned by Husák earlier in the month. I was naturally interested how this would work, and on September 12 I went over to the Interior Ministry to interview its chief of public relations, Captain František Dubský. He was a gregarious young man in a sports jacket, and over bottles of beer served during our morning talk he assured me that there were no Soviet "advisers" attached to his ministry—so far. Only later did I discover that Dubský belonged to Šalgovič's group in charge of preparing the ground for the invasion on the night of August 20. But already then I had the uncomfortable feeling of being followed as I drove around Prague and in the country-side, and of the STB taking an excessive interest in my activities. That week I also discovered that Miroslav Mamula, who had been in charge of security in the KSČ Central Committee, was back on the job with an office in Party headquarters. The Stalinists purged in the early days of the Prague Spring were creeping out of the woodwork.

The day after my visit to the Interior Ministry, Premier Černík an-nounced in a speech that the National Assembly had approved un-specified new legislation on increased security powers "to strengthen the public order." He explained, however, that both the police and the Army would be used to assure order. Černík spoke after 257 deputies had voted to restore the censorship provision to the Press Law. Three months earlier, in the same Hradčany Castle hall, the deputies had voted to re-move censorship as part of the "democratic socialist" revolution. This time only two of them voted against censorship. It was a sign of the times. Deputy Premier Petr Colotka, a Slovak who once served on the Inter-national Court of Justice, was named to head a new Committee for Press and Information charged with the enforcement of preventive censorship. Czechoslovakia, at least legally, was back where she had been nine months earlier. And Černík added to the general gloom by remarking that "under the present situation there is no room for great promises."

As September drew to a close, Prague was a city of changing moods, of hopes and fears. Despite censorship, the dailies and the weeklies succeeded in keeping alive the spirit of resistance. Each article made the people smile and say to each other, "See, we're still alive and kicking." But in the leadership there was new concern over Soviet intentions, and, on September 14, Dubček addressed the nation on this subject. "I beg you again and again not to let anyone misuse you," he said; but, still the optimist, he remarked of his fading liberalization policies, "we are not ready to abandon them."

At best, this was a relative hope. Dubček avoided speaking of the censorship and of the purges of his close associates. He left it to Mlynář, the increasingly disenchanted liberal, to confirm publicly that the clandestine Fourteenth Congress had been declared void. All that was left in reality of the Prague Spring was the continuing rehabilitation of the victims of the 1950s purges, the freedom to travel abroad, and preparations for the establishment of a federalized Czecho-Slovak state. Other than that, there was sadness. A poem inked on a rain-drenched sheet of paper was placed at the foot of Saint Wenceslas's statue on a gray Sunday:

TO OUR FALLEN
Who will heal the pain; who will cure the wounds
That burn in our hearts—who will answer?
WHY?
Death came from afar in iron, in steel,
Young lives were smashed by machine guns.
Over the graves of the fallen, life goes on.
Who would not cry over the beloved dead?
Now our people stand firmly, stand proudly.
Your grief and defiance you must nurture in your hearts,
But the cruel morning you must remember well.

The nation felt the grief and showed its defiance when it could. In *Rudé Právo,* thirteen leading economists published an open letter challenging the Soviet charges that the economic reform proposed by Šik was based on "bourgeois theories" that would lead to unemployment, lower living standards, and the entry of "foreign monopolies" in Czechoslovakia. Jaroslav Seifert, the aging poet who had led the 1956 writers' revolt, said on television, "Our aim is freedom of the individual, sovereignty of the nation, and democratic socialism." The youth weekly *Mlady Svet* published a cartoon touching on the refusal of Czech women to have any dealings with the Russians. "As far as I am concerned, the girls here are frigid," a Soviet soldier said to his companion in the cartoon's caption.

In the unending pattern of action and reaction, Soviet troops reoccupied outspoken Party newspapers in Ostrava and in Zvolen, Slovakia, and ordered the editor of a newspaper in Banská Bystrica, Slovakia, to be fired. On September 19 Foreign Minister Hájek was finally forced to resign ten days after he returned to Czechoslovakia. This seemed to complete the Soviet list of undesirable persons to be removed from the regime. Moscow had the further satisfaction of hearing Mlynář, still head of the Party's Legal Commission, admit that the radio and television crews had acted "illegally" when they went underground on invasion day, but it was saddening for Czech liberals to see one of their own turning against the progressive cause. Their ranks were thinning out in the leadership, but elsewhere they held firm.

At a trade fair in Brno, Svoboda and Dubček received a heroes' welcome from huge crowds. Prague's liberal *Reportér* magazine, in its first legal postinvasion issue on September 20, published a public-opinion poll showing that ninety-nine per cent of those questioned regarded Dubček "as the leading personality of our lives." *Reportér* also ran a poem by the nineteenth-century Czech poet Jan Neruda entitled "Moving Ahead": ". . . Only before our people do we bow our heads." In northern Slovakia, a meeting was held to honor the memory of Vladimir Clementis.

In relations between the Soviet Union and Czechoslovakia, the seesaw pattern prevailed continuously. First, the KSČ Presidium had authorized Dubček to open new negotiations with Moscow on troop withdrawal, but a trip late in September was canceled because of disagreements with Kuznetsov, still operating as the proconsul in Prague. Then, Černík announced that the Warsaw Pact troops would begin leaving within a few days. He emphasized, however, that "certain contingents . . . will remain among us," confirming the belief that at least two Soviet divisions would be based permanently in Czechoslovakia. (Earlier, newsmen had seen permanent quarters going up for the Russians.) At the same time, however, he reopened the whole invasion controversy by claiming that the Prague leaders had made no commitments to the Russians at Čierna. This point—and the question of the "counterrevolution"—would plague Czechoslovakia for years.

To justify its claim of "counterrevolution," the Soviet Union issued late in September a book entitled *On the Events in Czechoslovakia*. Allegedly assembled by "Soviet journalists," this volume promptly became known as the "Soviet White Book," and was printed in a variety of languages. The book liberally quoted in and out of context from articles in the Czechoslovak and Western press and offered its own conclusions in every instance. In its capacity to annoy the Czechoslovaks, it became a companion to *Zpravý*, the occupation newspaper, which the Soviet troops still insisted on spreading throughout the country. (One evening an American radio reporter was detained by Soviet Marines and kept for twenty minutes inside a truck before being sent home with an armful of copies of *Pravda* and *Zpravý*.) But presently Moscow concluded that the time had come for a serious ideological explanation of the Czechoslovak invasion.

This took the form of a major front-page article in the September 26 issue of *Pravda* under the title "Sovereignty and the International Duties of Socialist Countries." Written by the commentator Sergei Kovalev, the article became widely known for its presentation of the Brezhnev Doctrine of Limited Sovereignty and is still considered a basic Soviet policy document despite subsequent disclaimers that it was intended as such. Its main thrust was that military intervention by one or more socialist countries in another socialist country is justified if socialism appears to be in danger. So seriously was this article taken in the Communist world that President Ceauşescu, among others, made a point of publicly denouncing the "so-called doctrine of limited sovereignty" as a pernicious influence in Socialist relations. The *Pravda* article said in part:

> The measures taken by the Soviet Union, jointly with other Socialist countries, in defending the Socialist gains of the Czechoslovak people are of great significance for strengthening the Socialist community. . . .
>
> We cannot ignore the assertions, made in some places, that the actions of the five Socialist countries run counter to the Marxist-Leninist principle of sovereignty and the right of nations to self-determination.
>
> The groundlessness of such reasoning consists primarily in that it is based on an abstract, nonclass approach to the question of sovereignty and the rights of nations to self-determination.
>
> The peoples of the Socialist countries and Communist parties certainly do have and should have freedom for determining the ways of advance of their respective countries.
>
> However, none of their decisions should damage either socialism in their country or the fundamental interests of other Socialist countries, and the whole working-class movement. . . .
>
> This means that each Communist Party is responsible not only to its own people, but also to all the Socialist countries, to the entire Communist movement.

Whoever forgets this, in stressing only the independence of the Communist Party, becomes one-sided. He deviates from his international duty. . . .

Just as, in Lenin's words, a man living in a society cannot be free from the society, a particular Socialist state, staying in a system of other states composing the Socialist community, cannot be free from the common interests of that community.

The sovereignty of each Socialist country cannot be opposed to the interests of the world of socialism, of the world revolutionary movement. . . .

From a Marxist point of view, the norms of law, including the norms of mutual relations of the Socialist countries, cannot be interpreted narrowly, formally, and in isolation from the general context of class struggle in the modern world. The Socialist countries resolutely come out against the exporting and importing of counterrevolution.

Each Communist Party is free to apply the basic principles of Marxism-Leninism and of socialism in its country, but it cannot depart from these principles. . . .

Concretely, this means, first of all, that, in its activity, each Communist Party cannot but take into account such a decisive fact of our time as the struggle between two opposing social systems—capitalism and socialism. . . .

It must be emphasized that when a Socialist country seems to adopt a "nonaffiliated" stand, it retains its national independence, in effect, precisely because of the might of the Socialist community, and above all the Soviet Union as a central force, which also includes the might of its armed forces. The weakening of any of the links in the world system of socialism directly affects all the Socialist countries, which cannot look indifferently upon this.

The antisocialist elements in Czechoslovakia actually covered up the demand for so-called neutrality and Czechoslovakia's withdrawal from the Socialist community with talk about the right of nations to self-determination.

However, the implementation of such "self-determination"—in other words, Czechoslovakia's detachment from the Socialist community—would have come into conflict with its own vital interests and would have been detrimental to the other Socialist states.

Such "self-determination," as a result of which NATO troops would have been able to come up to the Soviet border, while the community of European Socialist countries would have been split, in effect encroaches upon the vital interests of the peoples of these countries and conflicts, at the very root of it, with the right of these people to Socialist self-determination.

Discharging their internationalist duty toward the fraternal people of Czechoslovakia and defending their own Socialist gains, the U.S.S.R. and the other Socialist states had to act decisively and they did act against the antisocialist forces in Czechoslovakia. . . .

People who "disapprove" of the actions of the allied Socialist states are ignoring the decisive fact that these countries are defending the interests of all of world socialism, of the entire world revolutionary movement.

The system of socialism exists in concrete form in some countries, which have their own definite state boundaries; this system is developing according to the specific conditions of each country. Furthermore, nobody interferes in the concrete measures taken to improve the Socialist system in the different Socialist countries.

However, the picture changes fundamentally when a danger arises to socialism itself in a particular country. As a social system, world socialism is the common gain of the working people of all lands; it is indivisible and its defense is the common cause of all Communists and all progressives in the world, in the first place, the working folk of the Socialist countries.

The Bratislava statement of the Communist and Workers' parties says of Socialist gains that "support, consolidation, and defense of these gains, won at the price of heroic effort and the self-sacrifice of each people, represents a common international duty and obligation for all the Socialist countries."

What the right-wing antisocialist forces set out to achieve in recent months in Czechoslavakia did not refer to the specific features of Socialist development or the application of the principle of Marxism-Leninism to the concrete conditions obtaining in that country, but constituted encroachment on the foundations of socialism, on the basic principles of Marxism-Leninism.

This is the nuance that people who have fallen for the hypocritical nonsense of the antisocialist and revisionist elements still cannot understand. Under the guise of "democratization" these elements were little by little shaking the Socialist state, seeking to demoralize the Communist Party and befog the minds of the masses, stealthily hatching a counterrevolutionary coup, and they were not duly rebuffed inside the country.

Naturally the Communists of the fraternal countries could not allow the Socialist states to be inactive in the name of an abstractly understood sovereignty, when they saw that the country stood in peril of antisocialist degeneration.

The actions in Czechoslovakia of the five allied countries accord also with the vital interests of the people of the country themselves. . . .

Formal observance of the freedom of self-determination of a nation in the concrete situation that arose in Czechoslovakia would mean freedom of "self-determination" not of the popular masses, the working people, but of their enemies.

The antisocialist path, "neutrality," to which the Czechoslovak people were pushed would bring it to the loss of its national independence.

World imperialism, on its part, supported the antisocialist forces in Czechoslovakia, tried to export counterrevolution to that country in this way.

The help to the working people of Czechoslovakia by other Socialist countries, which prevented the export of counterrevolution from abroad, constitutes the real sovereignty of the Czechoslovak Socialist Republic against those who would like to deprive it of its sovereignty and give up the country to imperialism.

The fraternal Communist parties of the Socialist countries were for a long time taking measures, with maximum self-restraint and patience, to help the Czechoslovak people to stop the onslaught of antisocialist forces in Czechoslovakia. And only when all such measures were exhausted did they bring armed forces into the country.

The soldiers of the allied Socialist countries now in Czechoslovakia proved by their actions indeed that they have no other tasks than the tasks of defending Socialist gains in that country.

They do not interfere in the internal affairs of the country, are fighting for the principle of self-determination of the peoples of Czechoslovakia not in words but in deeds, are fighting for their inalienable right to think out profoundly and decide their fate themselves, without intimidation on the part of the counter-revolutionaries, without revisionist and nationalist demagogy.

Those who speak about the "illegal actions" of the allied Socialist countries in Czechoslovakia forget that in a class society there are not and cannot be nonclass laws. . . .

Formal juridical reasoning must not overshadow a class approach to the matter. One who does it, thus losing the only correct class criterion in assessing legal norms, begins to measure events with a yardstick of bourgeois law. . . .

There is no doubt that the actions of the five allied Socialist countries in Czechoslovakia directed to the defense of the vital interests of the Socialist community, and the sovereignty of Socialist Czechoslovakia first and foremost, will be increasingly supported by all those who have the interest of the present revolutionary movement, of peace and security of peoples, of democracy and socialism at heart.

Brezhnev was to associate his name with this extraordinary doctrine when, addressing the congress of the Polish Party on November 12, he said, "When external and internal forces hostile to socialism try to turn the development of a given Socialist country in the direction of a restoration of the capitalist system, when a threat arises to the cause of socialism in that country—a threat to the security of the Socialist commonwealth as a whole—this is no longer merely a problem for that country's people, but a common problem—the concern of all Socialist countries."

Neither the *Pravda* commentator nor Brezhnev offered a definition of what constitutes such a "threat" and who is to be called upon to summon the Socialist states to the aid of the presumed victim. The Brezhnev Doctrine is a purely arbitrary instrument in the hands of the Soviet Union.

It was under this arbitrary doctrine and the equally arbitrary concept of "normalization" that Czechoslovakia went on facing up to Soviet pressures. In the closing days of September one way to do this for the young people was to join the Communist Party in the hopes of asserting their influence from within. In the month after the invasion there were 7200 new applications, sixty-four per cent of them from people under the age of thirty. Another way was to pay tribute to ancient Czechoslovak heroes. On September 28, the day of Saint Wenceslas, hundreds of Czech youths attempted to march with their flags to Saint Vitus Cathedral, which stands behind Hradčany Castle and where a High Mass was being said at dusk. But the march was dispersed by police under the stern eye of a huge Soviet major with Mongol features who rolled up in a patrol jeep with armed paratroopers. Still another way for the Czechs to show their sentiments was to fill the basement Semafor theater for the opening of the season with a musical revue by Jiří Suchy and Jiří Šlitr. A sign on the door said THEATER STOPS WHEN BURSTS OF LAUGHTER ARE MUFFLED BY THE BURSTS OF GUNFIRE.

Classically, Soviet interventions or pressures result in the exodus of intellectuals and other politically committed people. The Czechoslovaks, however, fought their battle by staying home. Many of the intellectuals active in the Prague Spring who were caught abroad by the invasion or left immediately afterward began returning in the autumn. Suchy was among those who came back and so were the writers Pavel Kohout and Jiří Mucha, the film director Jiří Menzel, and the famous actor Jan Werich. Ludvík Vaculík was seen calmly taking the air in Wenceslas Square. Jaroslav Seifert, Václav Havel, and Jan Procházka concentrated on keeping the Writers' Union going. When the Soviet press attacked Eduard Goldstücker, the Union's absent chairman, the Union replied in kind and the newspapers published its retort. A group of liberal editors and writers signed a manifesto urging intellectuals to stay in Czechoslovakia and others to return. "You are needed," they were told. As in the past, then, the intellectuals and the artists provided the backbone of the resistance.

The Russians, meanwhile, were digging in for the winter. The Thirteenth Czechoslovak Division evacuated the vast Mlada reservation twenty-five miles north of Prague to make room for one of the Soviet divisions earmarked for permanent duty in Czechoslovakia. This was to be the main Soviet base in the vicinity of the capital. Other wintering forces were installed near Rozvadov, on the West German border, in the Olomouc area in Moravia, and southeast in Slovakia. Marshal Yakubovsky, the Warsaw Pact commander, came to inspect his troops and the Prague leaders were again told that "normalization" must proceed better and faster before excess forces could be withdrawn.

On October 3 Dubček, Černik, and Husák flew to Moscow. (The trip had been delayed by an argument over the inclusion in the delegation of National Assembly Chairman Smrkovský, whom the Soviets refused to receive. Smrkovský had become a chief target for Kremlin antipathy, for the Russians decided he was the culprit behind the delays in "normalization." He agreed to stay home.) After two days of tough negotiations in which Dubček argued for at least a residual preservation of liberalization and Černik and Husák again took the "realist" stand, a new agreement was signed committing Prague to a further tightening of Czechoslovak freedoms.

The communiqué summed it up this way: "The Czechoslovak delegation stated that the Central Committee of the Communist Party of Czechoslovakia and the Government of the Czechoslovak Socialist Republic would take every measure to insure the fulfillment of the Moscow Agreement. . . . They will step up efforts to raise the leading role of the Communist Party, intensify the struggle against antisocialist forces, take the necessary measures to place all mass-information media at the service of socialism, and reinforce the Party and state organs with men firmly adhering to positions of Marxism-Leninism and proletarian internationalism." Put in plain language, this meant a commitment to total censorship and a purge of the progressives remaining in influential posts. The payment for this apparent capitulation after six weeks of resistance was Moscow's willingness to sign a treaty on withdrawal of the occupation forces and the permanent stationing of Soviet units in Czechoslovakia.

But "capitulation," like "normalization," has different meanings in Moscow and in Prague. The day after the delegation returned from Moscow, the Czech press exploded in accusations against the Warsaw Pact news media for spreading "lies" and "insults" about the country's leaders and, as the trade-union newspaper *Prace* put it, for "twisting facts" and "spreading untruths and gossip." A Prague editor, asked how he explained these charges in the light of the latest commitment that the press be placed "at the service of socialism," smiled and said, "We are dealing here with very vague concepts." The Party Presidium issued a communiqué promising that the latest Moscow agreement would not infringe the "legal rights of citizens"—fears of political arrests had again arisen in the country—and, as if to show disdain for Moscow, young Czechs began organizing Dubček Fan Clubs. The clubs distributed Dubček's pictures and buttons, but also promoted serious discussions of his political ideas. Thus the minuet went on.

Still, reality could not be ignored altogether, and on October 11 Dubček went on television to advise his followers that "democracy needs a certain discipline." His listeners noticed that Dubček's tone, too, was changing. It was poignant to hear him admit that there had been "deficiencies" in the liberalization program and that "everything is harmful that disrupts our alliance with the Socialist community, everything which undermines the leading role of the Party, everything which is aimed against the political or economic substance of the socialist system." Coming closer than he had ever done before to the Soviet ideological line, Dubček said that Czechoslovakia had learned that it could not overlook the effects of its internal activities on "our Socialist allies" and that it was impossible to ignore their "opinions and fears."

These admissions, which must have cost Dubček an emotional effort, were rewarded in the way in which the Kremlin rewards obedience. On October 14 Černík returned to Moscow to discuss the troop treaty with Premier Kosygin. Two days later the Soviet Premier came to Prague to sign the pact that in effect legalized the invasion and Moscow's right to keep an undisclosed and presumably unlimited number of forces in Czechoslovakia. The ceremony at the Foreign Ministry was conducted with classical Communist heartiness, and—as Dubček remained in the background—Černík, the realist, said the treaty was "a step toward strengthening the defense" of Czechoslovakia and all the Socialist countries "in the face of growing revanchist efforts of West German militarist forces."

In the military sense, the August invasion had accomplished its aims. The treaty did not specify for how long Soviet troops would remain in Czechoslovakia—it said that the arrangement was "temporary"—and their mission was simply explained as the defense of socialism from "imperialism." This, of course, vested the entire flexibility in the hands of the Soviets. Invoking threats to peace, the necessity of maneuvers, or just about anything that sounded plausible, Moscow was free to maintain in the country as many divisions as it wished and to reinforce them without further consultation.

Soviet troops were now officially garrisoned in Poland, Hungary, East Germany, and Czechoslovakia, and the Soviet forward defense line ran north-south from the mouth of the River Elbe on the North Sea to Bratislava on the Danube, bringing it within sight of Vienna, and then curving southeast along the borders of Hungary with Austria and Yugoslavia. Strategically, the new arrangement filled out the salient on West Germany's and NATO's southern flank in Bavaria as well as giving the Russians control of both sides of the Danube east of the vital Vienna juncture. As far as the mobility of Warsaw Pact armies went, freedom of operations in Czechoslovakia added an important area of maneuver for both offense and defense. Under a theory shared both by NATO and by Warsaw Pact experts, control of Czechoslovakia gave Moscow an approximate defensive advantage of forty-eight hours in the unlikely event of a Western attack in the south. In other words, the Soviets could maintain sufficient troops in central and western Czechoslovakia to hold back a conventional Western thrust for two days, the time needed to rush in massive reinforcements.

But, of course, this was pure theory. The concept of a Western conventional attack in the nuclear age from West Germany, in either the north or the south, against the Soviet Union's immense land military apparatus was so absurd as to obviate further analysis. The likelihood of American or NATO troops' penetrating Czechoslovakia in peacetime—with the tolerance of a Dubček type of Communist liberal regime—to mount a direct strike at Poland or the Soviet Union likewise belonged to the realm of fantasy. As a strategic move, therefore, the Soviet invasion accomplished little of real defensive military importance from the Soviet viewpoint. It unquestionably improved the Soviet offensive position in Central Europe if Moscow ever planned to use her vast conventional forces to break out into the West. The ease and speed with which the Soviet command hurled over half a million men into Czechoslovakia in little over a week served to demonstrate that an operation of similar or even greater scope would just as easily be set in motion against West Germany, and the American force of less than two hundred thousand men along with the West German Army could do little to deter it. But, again, this was strategic nonsense. A Soviet land attack on the West would so obviously bring nuclear retaliation that the advantage of garrisoning Czechoslovakia remained limited.

In winning the legal right to station troops in Czechoslovakia, therefore, the Soviet Union achieved only psychological and political gains. It presumably satisfied its nearly psychotic need for a *cordon sanitaire*—a need that included, of course, the full political control of Czechoslovakia. In this sense, the Soviet leadership took its own Brezhnev Doctrine with more seriousness than the ideological cynicism of the document suggested at first sight. The Soviet Union was ideologically so uncertain of Eastern Europe in the late 1960s that a Czechoslovak "detachment" appeared as a threat to the viability of the whole system. As seen through

Soviet eyes, a successful Czechoslovak experiment in "Communist democracy" could—and probably would—spread to East Germany, Poland, and, in time, Hungary. That Ulbricht and Gomułka were the chief advocates of the Soviet invasion seemed to make this point conclusively. The Hungarians, who had not altogether forgotten 1956, could probably have lived with it and so could Kadár. It was, then, with utmost seriousness that the Soviet Union invoked in the Brezhnev Doctrine her vital interests and those of the other "Socialist states"—or, at least, regimes. Only stubborn Romania refused to welcome a "temporary" stationing of Soviet troops. But she was flanked on three sides.

One is again brought to the conclusion that the August invasion was essentially a political and not a military undertaking. The vigor of Czechoslovakia's resistance in the weeks and months after August 21 presumably reinforced the Kremlin's view that a permanent armed force was essential in Czechoslovakia if that country was to remain faithful to Soviet dictates on everything ranging from Comecon to the nature of poetry.

The treaty signed by Kosygin and Černík provided that the chief responsibility for the defense of the western border remained in Czechoslovak hands—which, in itself, contradicted the military defensive argument for the invasion—and the dispositions of Soviet forces after the Warsaw Pact troop departures (beginning on October 21 with the withdrawal of Hungarian units) underlined what the Soviets really had in mind. By early November, when all the Hungarian, Polish, and Bulgarian troops and most of the Soviet forces were pulled out, it developed that Czechoslovakia was garrisoned by the Soviets in a way which had no strategic value but a very considerable political one. The Soviet bases ran in a diagonal line from the west to the southeast, slicing the country in two. The line was anchored in the west on the West German border, then jumped to the Mlada base north of Prague, continued southeast into Moravia, and ended in Slovakia in the southeast. "It's a hell of a way to defend Czechoslovakia from Western attack," a Western military attaché remarked after studying the Soviet troop dispositions. But, just as clearly, this deployment provided a perfect security screen for internal control purposes. From the Mlada base and the headquarters town of Mlada Boleslav, Soviet armor could reoccupy Prague in less than one hour, barreling down the broad E-14 highway. The troops in the west could reach Plzeň just as fast. The Moravian center of Czechoslovakia could be controlled from Olomouc, and reinforcements could rapidly move south from Poland. Slovakia could be held by the forces in its eastern region, which could advance easily on Bratislava.

A curious security situation surrounded this redeployment situation. Whereas the Soviet authorities made not the slightest effort to prevent Western newsmen from observing the movements of their troops into Czechoslovakia in August and their subsequent positioning in September and early October—nobody, for example, said a word to me after I described in *The New York Times* the emplacements of the nuclear-capability Scud missiles—a curtain of secrecy descended when the forces began to depart and relocate. Several newsmen were arrested and expelled when they observed the loading of Soviet armor onto trains at Benešov, south of Prague. Others were reprimanded for poaching around the Mlada area. I have reasons to believe that my article in *The New York Times* describing the permanent positioning of Soviet troops along the west-southeast axis, and making the point it was politically motivated, was among the causes of my subsequent expulsion from the country.

The Soviet-Czechoslovak treaty on the stationing of troops—it was approved on October 18 by 228 votes to 4 with 10 abstentions in the suddenly supine National Assembly—provided that Soviet troops would not interfere in internal Czechoslovak affairs. But enormous naïveté was required to take this seriously. The very presence of Soviet troops in Czechoslovakia constituted overwhelming political interference, and this was aggravated by the free admission on both sides that the withdrawal of the troops was conditioned on "normalization." When the occasion arose, the Kremlin had no hesitations about threatening to use troops to help maintain "public order." Finally, the signing of the treaty made it illegal for the Czechoslovaks, individually or collectively, to go on demanding the departure of the occupation forces. The legal farce that the Soviet troops were in Czechoslovakia under a freely signed contractual arrangement took care of this point.

But all this still did not mean that the Czechoslovaks gladly accepted what was being done to them and that they were beaten into submission. There was still the defiant press, and the intellectuals and the artists; there were the workers and the students; basically, there were still just plain people who would not conform.

Late in October, as the occupation troops were withdrawing, I toured the Polish border area around the town of Nachód. The people of this town were not acting defeated. Their main square was still named after Tomáš Masaryk and the main street was called Dubček Avenue. Store windows were decorated with portraits of Dubček, Svoboda, and Masaryk in preparation for the celebrations of the fiftieth anniversary of the Czechoslovak Republic.

The Academy of Sciences, congregating ten thousand of the best brains in Czechoslovakia, issued toward the end of October a twelve-thousand-word document rebutting point by point the allegations in the "Soviet White Book." Prepared in separate sections by the Academy's philosophers, historians, economists, and sociologists, the document called the Soviet explanations "lies," "inventions," "distortions of Marxist-Leninist thought," and "flights of schoolboy logic":

> The metaphysical conception of socialism as a perfect system leads logically to the conclusion that any criticism of deficiencies and contradictions is considered indiscriminately as revisionist and antisocialist and is identified with counter-revolution and reaction.
>
> Counterrevolution usually presumes the intervention of reactionary governments with the aid of armies, blockades, organizations of armed uprisings, sabotage, banditry, etc. . . .
>
> If we shift this concept into the sphere of opinions, any opinion not entirely in conformity with a certain up-to-date conception may be interpreted simply as being counterrevolutionary. This is a dangerous logic, paralyzing the Party and Marxist theory.

It had to be noted, of course, that the Academy's comments were not drafted by raging right-wingers, but by serious Marxist thinkers, Communists all, reflecting modern Marxist thought in opposition to the old Moscow dogmas. It was ideologically the most damaging study issued since the invasion and the formulation of the Brezhnev Doctrine, but *Reportér,* had no qualms about publishing it in its entirety for all the Czechs to read and reflect on.

As the anniversary of the Republic approached, the Prague leaders, sensing the rising unrest, issued warnings to the population to avoid all "extreme attitudes." A communication signed by Svoboda, Dubček, Smrkovský, and Černík suggested that dire consequences might follow irresponsible actions. This was a curious way of dealing with a treaty that specified that Soviet troops would not interfere in domestic affairs. But what the Prague regime was doing was obviously contradictory. Prior to the Prague Spring, there had been no formal celebrations since 1948 of the anniversary of the Republic Masaryk established in 1918. But this year, a national holiday was declared, plans were made for solemn ceremonies involving the Central Committee, the National Assembly, and the National Front. Prague was a sea of Czechoslovak flags and banners—in contrast with previous years, when October 28 was celebrated as the Day of Nationalization and only red flags were brought out for the occasion. It did not take much perspicacity to foresee that there would be anti-Soviet demonstrations, and the popular mood was even more bitter against Moscow because the government had chosen that week to announce the suspension of the experiments with workers' councils in industrial plants, one of the main features of the economic-reform plan. What the Soviet officials said to the Czechoslovaks about the dangers of organizing a nationalist celebration at this particular point is not known, but the government went ahead with the plans.

On the eve of the celebrations photographs and busts of Masaryk blossomed forth everywhere. In Wenceslas Square, vendors had a bonanza selling Masaryk medals. On October 27 the government made a point of paying special tribute to all former presidents of Czechoslovakia. On a cold windy morning, a ceremony was first held at the midtown mausoleum where Gottwald and Zápotocký were buried. Floral wreaths were placed by a high-level delegation, but there was not one plain citizen on hand to watch it. In the afternoon the group flew by helicopter to the tiny cemetery in Laný, where Tomáš and Jan Masaryk are buried. A thousand persons made the pilgrimage. Then the Communist regime's representatives flew on to Sezimovo Ústí, south of Prague, where Beneš is buried and his widow lives alone.

In Prague, the National Assembly met solemnly at Hradčany Castle to approve the federalization of the Czech lands and Slovakia, one of the pledges in the April Action Program. On the same day the government opened the nation's treasure vaults in the back of the castle to let the population inspect the Bohemian crown jewels for the first time since 1958. This, too, was an unusual step for a Communist government living under the threat of Soviet tanks, but the Czechs immediately turned it into a silent demonstration of nationalism: an estimated hundred thousand people saw the jewels after standing in a kilometer-long queue in the biting cold wind. The silence was broken only on the morning of October 27, when the crowds loudly cheered Dubček, Černík, and Smrkovský arriving for the National Assembly session.

On October 28—the anniversary day—major anti-Soviet demonstrations broke out throughout Prague—to nobody's particular surprise. From morning until late at night, students and workers with Czechoslovak flags marched in the capital chanting, "Russians go home!" "Down with Brezhnev!" "Long live Masaryk!" "We want freedom!" In Wenceslas Square, irate crowds shouted "Russian murderers out of Prague!" and spat on passing Soviet military vehicles.

There were moments of high tension. After a solemn session in honor of the Republic—attended by the cabinet, the entire KSČ Central Committee, National Assembly deputies, and diplomats—ended at noon at Hradčany Castle, a vast crowd had massed in front of the gates. They waved their flags, shouted imprecations at the Russians, and demanded that Svoboda and Dubček come out to speak to them. The crowd was so dense that the police gave up attempts to control it. The Palace Guard was brought out to prevent the demonstrators from smashing through the wrought-iron gates and into the courtyard. The guardsmen strained against the gates from inside as the crowd—including women, old men, and children—pushed from the outside. Ambassador Chervonenko and his military attaché had to drive out through a back gate under police guard. But when Jiří Hájek, the ousted Foreign Minister but still deputy, entered the square, the people caught him and carried him on their shoulders amidst deafening cheers.

In the afternoon ten thousand persons paraded through the Old Town Square and a column of marchers made its way to the Soviet district headquarters on Hastalska Street to burn copies of *Pravda* and shout, "Russians go home!" Armored cars and sentries with bayonets on their rifles guarded the headquarters, and they would not be provoked. But a potentially serious incident was avoided when Education Minister Vladímir Kadlec, a popular figure, persuaded the young demonstrators to march away. A police roadblock and the presence of water-cannon trucks dissuaded another youth group from marching on the Soviet Embassy in Bubeneč, across the Vltava River. In the evening crowds blocked the approaches to the National Theater, where Svoboda and Dubček were the principal guests at a performance of *Libuse*, a patriotic opera by Smetana. The Czechoslovak leaders were cheered, but the crowd prevented Chervonenko's limousine from drawing up at the theater. The demonstrations, the biggest since the invasion, went on long past midnight. The next day, as if to keep the spirit alive, the Czechoslovak Composers' Union sent a letter to the government asking for a guarantee of freedom in the arts, science, and education. For good measure, the composers also charged that Moscow was violating the August and October agreements by interfering in the nation's domestic affairs.

Now the resistance was visibly on the upswing. The Czechs and the

Slovaks were regaining self-assurance, as their special political alchemy
went to work once more. On October 30 Svoboda and Dubček were
cheered in Bratislava as the federal status was signed into law. Dubček,
as if drawing new strength from his Slovak home surroundings, spoke
emotionally to promise that liberalization policies would go on and that
only the "excesses" would be curbed. Husák, too, spoke but he was largely
ignored. In Prague, the Union of Czechoslovak Journalists approved a
resolution demanding full access to political information and a ban on
Zpravy, the occupation newspaper. *Reportér* published the speech Mrs.
Gertruda Sekaninová-Cartková had delivered in the National Assembly
on October 18, when she was one of the four deputies voting against the
troops stationing treaty. She had said that the occupation was illegal
and that the treaty should have specified when *all* Soviet troops would
leave Czechoslovakia. On November 1 Prague television transmitted an
hour-long program in which "witnesses for the defense"—a colonel in
Army uniform, a newspaper editor, an economist, and a worker—answered starkly, "Not true," when passages from the "Soviet White Book"
offering examples of "counterrevolutionary" activities before the invasion
were read to them. The program was, of course, a complete violation of
the censorship rules against discussions of the invasion. But the Czechs
were again in a cocky mood. National sentiment was expressed in an
editorial in *Politika*, the weekly ideological journal of the KSČ Central
Committee: "It would be tragic if the Party and state leadership were
restoring confidence in our allies in such a way that they would lose the
confidence of their own people." This, of course, was precisely the
dilemma facing Dubček.

And anti-Soviet sentiment was running higher and higher. On November 6, the eve of the fifty-first anniversary of the Russian Revolution,
Czech youths ripped down Soviet flags from a number of Prague buildings. Police had to cordon off the National Theater to prevent demonstrations against Kuznetsov and Chervonenko as they attended a gala performance of *Swan Lake*. On November 7 Soviet flags were ripped from
government buildings and at least ten of them were burned. All afternoon,
crowds of students and workers battled the police around Wenceslas
Square, and late in the evening water-cannon trucks were brought to
disperse a menacing crowd. (Earlier in the day, the Czech police for the
first time used tear gas to quell the demonstrations.) The entire Western
diplomatic corps, except for a Greek and a French diplomat, boycotted
the evening anniversary reception at the Soviet Embassy.

The Russians and Czechoslovak Communist conservatives then had their turn to react. During the November 7 riots there was a strong possibility that Soviet troops would be summoned back to Prague. But Kuznetsov, who was in permanent contact with the Czechoslovak leaders, decided against it. In the political realm, the new policy was to use the approaching KSČ Central Committee session to undercut the position of Dubček and his progressive companions, and the Russians concluded they could live with one more demonstration and avoid the unnecessary perpetuation of the crisis. With an aroused population, the Russians reasoned, the political operation might become more complicated.

Once more, the liberals were feeling the gathering pressures. When Dubček went to the Olšany cemetery on November 7 for a tribute to Soviet World War Two dead, he had a foretaste of the trend. As he departed, a large group of old-guard Communists attending the ceremony shook fists in his face and shouted, "Long live the Soviet Union!" "Long live the Soviet Army!" Dubček did not react, except for a wince. Earlier, looking ill, he had to join Soviet generals and diplomats in singing the "Internationale" at the monument to the Soviet soldiers. I noticed that his blond hair was turning gray. Now the conservatives were emerging from their hideouts to campaign against the Dubček progressives. Their visible organization was the so-called Liben group, named after the Prague district where they met, and it was a conglomeration of six hundred pro-Soviet Communists led by Josef Jodas, a former brewery worker in his sixties. The Liben group, however, enjoyed high favor among the Soviet officialdom and conservative politicians such as Bilak and Piller. Their activities increasingly worried the liberals.

The government, too, was taking steps against the progressives. On November 8 it ordered the suspension for one month of *Reportér* magazine and prepared to shut down the KSČ ideological organ, *Politika*, as well. On November 10 the police were called out to protect members of the Czechoslovak-Soviet Friendship Society holding an early-morning meeting in downtown Prague. The members were entertained by a Soviet Army dance group and heard speeches by top conservatives promising a return to the "good, old days," but angry crowds jeered outside. The next day Černík announced on television that the government would not tolerate any further anti-Soviet outbursts because "they could lead to chaos and even tragedy." *Politika* was closed down the same day. But, paradoxically, this was also the day the Soviet command pulled all its remaining troops out of Prague. After nearly three months, the last armored cars disappeared from the capital.

All attention, however, was centered on the KSČ Central Committee Plenum opening on November 14. The assumption was that that was when the Soviets would deliver the final lethal blow. So rife was the speculation that a Prague newspaper found it necessary to write that rumors of an impending *putsch* were nonsense. But both sides were working feverishly. The progressives felt their cause might not fare too badly, as thousands of pro-Dubček resolutions were streaming in from all over the nation. But the conservatives' plans were well prepared. So were the plans of Gustav Husák.

When the Plenum began, Dubček promised in his keynote speech that the new Party program would reconcile "humanistic socialism" with the "harsh realities" of the Soviet military presence. It sounded like an impossibly tall order and when the Committee finally issued its main resolution it was so contradictory as to appear virtually meaningless. Each side could, in effect, interpret the resolution according to its biases.

But the crucial event was the recasting of the leadership in a way that effectively isolated and neutralized Dubček. The subtly contrived coup consisted in forming an eight-man Executive Committee of the Presidium. Its chairman was still Dubček, but the only true ally he had on the new body was Josef Smrkovský, whose own political powers were quickly eroding. The real power in the Executive Committee was in the hands of a troika made up of Husák, Černík, and Lubomir Strougal. Strougal was simultaneously made head of the Czech Affairs Bureau of the Party. Although there was no separate Czech Communist Party, Strougal had, in effect, become Husák's opposite number. With Husák as chief of the Slovak Party, Strougal head of the Czech Bureau, and Černik Premier, all the levers of power were held by them.

The other members of the Executive Committee mattered little. President Svoboda, increasingly tired and often absent from Prague, had apparently accepted the Husák-Černík-Strougal "realistic" line and was unlikely to join Dubček in any showdown. Rather unkindly, given his courage in August, he was being frequently compared to Marshal Pétain. Stefan Sadovský, groomed by Husák to take over the Slovak Party, was entirely on his side. Evžen Erban, the National Front Chairman, was a nonentity and certain to go with the majority.

Under this new arrangement, the Soviets did not need to load the

Executive Committee with such conservative stalwarts as Bilak or Piller. It was smoother and easier to run the country through Husák, Černik, and Strougal—all of whom had been associated with the Prague Spring. The average citizen was not yet quite aware of the new roles these three men were playing. It was useful, therefore, to maintain illusions. But, the November Plenum effectively marked the end of the Prague Spring.

XX

Into the Future

The November Plenum was a turning point in the Czechoslovak situation, though ten more months were to elapse before the Soviet Union and its collaborators were able and ready to apply the final death blow to what had been the hopes of 1968. Basically, Moscow still faced in November the same problem it had faced in August, namely the nation's deep revulsion against the invasion and its consequences. Ironically, the Soviet Union and men like Husák, Černík, and Strougal still had to take public opinion into account, even though the progressive leadership had been smashed for all practical purposes and the country was now legally filled with Soviet troops.

In itself, the power of public opinion continued to be an amazingly important factor. Nothing like it had been experienced before in a Communist country—certainly not in one occupied by Soviet troops—but the reality that the new leaders had to face was that a premature step could set off a new and major crisis. ("We don't really need leaders," a prominent Prague journalist said to me late in November as new acts of defiance kept occurring with astounding regularity.) Literally and figuratively, therefore, the Soviets and their partners had to bide their time. For three days immediately after the Plenum they had to tolerate a sit-in strike by tens of thousands of university and high-school students demanding the return of the lost freedoms. There was the danger that industrial workers would join the strike, and the leadership issued frenzied calls for calm and reason. *Reportér* magazine won the lifting of its suspension after its editors threatened, incredibly, to sue the government. Again, rather than provoke a well-publicized scandal, the regime gave in. Once more, assurances were given that there would be no "return to the 1950s," no political arrests, and no persecutions. The vital thing was to quiet down the situation and get the people back to work. For Czechoslovakia also faced what was rapidly becoming a catastrophic economic situation. Productivity had fallen off alarmingly, and the disruptions caused by the invasion were now being reflected in shortages of fuel and food. Prague shivered in the late-autumn cold weather.

At this point the question arises why men like Dubček and Smrkovský chose to stay on and not resign and eliminate the fiction of Party unity that Husák and his companions wanted to maintain. One obvious answer is that both Dubček and Smrkovský were and are disciplined Communists, conditioned during a lifetime not to do anything that might harm the Party. Both of them had emerged from their imprisonment in August without a word of personal complaint or self-pity. They accepted humiliations in the Soviet Union and again in Prague, as their authority dwindled from day to day. A second answer, which does not necessarily contradict the first one, is that both men feel powerful obligations to their supporters and to Czechoslovakia in general. It may be argued that they were convinced that so long as they remained in public life—in positions that were at least theoretically important—a residue of hope could survive in the country. They had become identified so strongly with the Prague Spring that their voluntary departure might be interpreted as a betrayal of the ideals they had sponsored and as a sign that further resistance, even in the people's hearts, was useless. If this is true, and I am tempted to think that it is, then the services Dubček and Smrkovský continued to render in the short time that was left to them after the November Plenum were far greater than may have been realized. It is an arguable point, I believe, that nothing would have pleased the Russians and Husák more than to see Dubček and Smrkovský quit and leave the field to them. If Dubček has a sense of history, as he must, then he may regard his services late in 1968 and through most of 1969 as a bridge to a better future he hopes still awaits Czechoslovakia.

Late in 1968 his presence, for example, was a counter to the tone that Husák sought to give Czechoslovak politics. It was becoming increasingly difficult to separate Husák's statements from articles in *Pravda*, and irreverent Czechs began referring to him as "Husák-Rusak" ("Husák-the-Russian"). On November 20, for instance, Husák charged in a speech that the current danger was "from the right" and "from growing anti-socialist forces outside the Party," and attacked the press in which, he said, "right-wing opportunist forces . . . had acquired great power."

On November 29 I cited in an article in *The New York Times* a Prague professor who remarked to me that "the reports of our death are vastly exaggerated." A student, who used to visit our Prague office, was shocked by our gloom and said, in English, "We shall overcome—sooner or later." On the same day František Kriegel in the National Assembly protested the attacks on him printed in *Zpravý*, and the Assembly's Presidium, chaired by Smrkovský, demanded that the government protest to the Soviet Union against the distribution of *Zpravý*. The fight went on.

But, as usual, the Soviets responded with pressures. On December 8 Svoboda, Dubček, Černík, Husák, and Strougal flew to Kiev to meet with the top Soviet leadership. The one-day conference apparently dealt both with the difficulties of the "normalization" and with the composition of the Czech and Slovak governments to be formed when federalization became effective on January 1.

I, too, felt the pressures. On Thanksgiving Day, I was summoned to the Foreign Ministry to receive a "serious warning" from Dufek, the foreign-press chief, about what he described mysteriously as my activities that were "incompatible" with my functions as an accredited newspaper correspondent. Naturally enough, I inquired what activities he was referring to. Dufek, speaking in the presence of an underling, avoided my eyes and said, "You are too intelligent not to know what I mean." I persisted in my questions, but to no avail. Dufek was evidently under instructions to tell me nothing. Simultaneously, I learned later, Ambassador Beam was being informed by a high Foreign Ministry official that the "serious warning" had been delivered to me. His questions, too, went unanswered. At this point I knew that my expulsion from Czechoslovakia was only a matter of time.

For weeks, my Czech employees had been summoned to secret-police headquarters and questioned about my activities, and I was now followed continuously when I drove in Prague and the surveillance was ostentatious. One day a young lady, the daughter of a prominent conservative Communist politician, appeared in my office to offer me Dubček's personal papers. She was a friend of Dubček's, she said, and his concern with his historic role had made him desirous of having his version of the events published in the West. Whether this was a "provocation," as such things often are, I do not know. But I did know that my hotel office was wired for sound, and I politely declined the offer. A case was being built against me—for reasons I ignored—and I awaited further developments.

In the first week of December I was apprised that the Academy of Sciences had prepared a "Black Book," describing in detail the events of the invasion week, including the activities of the secret police on invasion night and other gems of this type. I was able to procure a copy, but it seemed unwise to translate it from Czech into English and process it into story form in Prague. The "Black Book" was a fairly clandestine publication, and I was reluctant to bring in outside translators for the job; by the same token, I did not want to involve my permanent Czech assistant in it. Consequently, I decided to take the book to Vienna, where numerous translators were available and where my wife and my son could enjoy a brief respite from the difficult life in Prague.

Returning to Prague on December 13, I was told that the Foreign Ministry wished to see me on Monday, December 16. I was absolutely certain that my expulsion was now imminent. I was right. Dufek again received me in the presence of his underling to advise me coldly that since I had not heeded the "serious warning" of the month before, I was to leave Czechoslovakia as soon as possible. I suggested that it would be a waste of time to ask for explanations. Dufek agreed and gave me forty-eight hours to go. He was polite and uncomfortable. But as soon as I returned to the hotel, the radio and the ČTK news agency carried a Foreign Ministry announcement that I was being expelled because I had taken "an interest in secret military questions," bribed Czechoslovak citizens for military data, and obtained confidential information from the government and the Communist Party. I wish it had been true that I was able to obtain confidential information from the government and the Party; but I am still at loss as to why the Prague government, or the Soviet government, had me expelled. As to Dufek, he was rewarded in mid-1969 with an appointment as Ambassador to Brazil, presumably for his diligent handling of the foreign press.

With deep sadness, I turned the office over to a *Times* colleague and left Prague for the last time on December 18. A secret-police car accompanied me to the airport, and I flew away to Paris, profoundly moved by the courage of a great many Czech friends and acquaintances who had risked wishing us Godspeed. Someday, I trust, I shall return to a different Czechoslovakia.

On January 1, 1969, Czechoslovakia became a federated state. Černík retained his post as Federal Premier, and Stanislav Razl, the Minister of Chemical Industry, became Premier of the Czech region. He was among the ministers who so violently denounced the Soviet invasion on August

21. Stefan Sadovský was named Premier of Slokavia. Husák continued to run the Slovak Party and Strougal its Czech counterpart.

Czechoslovakia was living through a hard, cold winter. The press was still putting up a brave resistance, and the trade-unions were threatening to strike if Smrkovský were ousted from the Party Presidium or the Assembly chairmanship. He was under violent attack from conservative Communists, with anonymous pamphlets describing him as "two-faced" (an expression that was to become current in 1969 in the denunciations of all progressive politicians).

But, on January 8, all this political pressure and counterpressure was overshadowed by a tragic event. An eighteen-year-old Prague student named Jan Palach set himself on fire in the middle of Wenceslas Square in protest, as his suicide letter explained, against the erosion of freedoms in Czechoslovakia. He was "Torch Number One," his letter said, in a suicide squad of young students determined to shock the world into realization of what was happening in Czechoslovakia. Palach died of burns the following day. Hundreds of thousands of Czechs attended his funeral in a vast but silent outpouring of grief that was also a heartfelt protest against the occupation. Not a single incident occurred during Palach's funeral, for this was a day of national mourning and dignity. Prague students renamed Red Army Square facing the Philosophy Faculty Jan Palach Square. In ensuing weeks a rash of immolations in Czechoslovakia numbed the country.

Meanwhile, Husák—now the dominant personality on the Czechoslovak scene—was making no headway in uniting the profoundly split Communist Party around the so-called principles of the November Plenum, which meant subordination to the Soviet viewpoint on all matters. Palach's suicide gave new courage to the Communist progressives, and the struggle went on unabated. There was no end to the defiance. The press simply could not be controlled, and when the playwright Václav Havel found a secret microphone in his house he turned it into a major scandal by publishing a bitingly sarcastic account of his dealings with the police over it. What the Soviet Union and Husák needed was a pretext to crack down hard.

The pretext came—but from a totally unexpected side. On March 28, a Friday, the Czechoslovak team defeated the Soviet Union 4-to-3 in the world ice-hockey championship match in Stockholm. To the millions of Czechoslovaks watching the game on television and following it on the radio, the hockey victory was a metaphoric victory over the Soviet Union and a retribution for the August invasion. In Prague and other Czechoslovak cities, thousands poured out into the streets to celebrate the triumph. But the celebration quickly turned into violent anti-Soviet riots. In Prague, the first target was the office of the Soviet Aeroflot airline on Wenceslas Square. Demonstrators smashed the neon sign, broke the plate-glass window, invaded the office, and carried the furniture and the files into the square to start a merry bonfire. People climbed the Saint Wenceslas statue to place Czechoslovak flags on it. It was like the invasion week. Elsewhere in the country, Soviet military headquarters were attacked and Soviet vehicles burned. Sixty-five Czechoslovak policemen were injured in the clashes.

The Soviet Union reacted with undisguised anger. *Pravda* wrote on March 31 that "events of recent days have shown that the right-wing antisocialist forces once again seek to aggravate the situation in Czechoslovakia." It charged that Smrkovský was "among the participants in the anti-Soviet manifestations," though the Prague government denied it at once.

On April 1 Defense Minister Marshal Grechko and Deputy Foreign Minister Vladimir Semyonov arrived in Prague. Semyonov handed President Svoboda a strongly worded protest note and warned him verbally that if the government was unable to maintain peace and would not request Soviet help, the Red Army would intervene directly and demonstrators would be run over by the tanks. After a nightlong session, the KSČ Presidium issued a communiqué criticizing the press for its handling of the hockey riots and announcing tough new measures to establish peace. On April 3 Dubček addressed the nation on television: "We are experiencing the most serious days since August. . . . I am turning to you with an urgent request for peace and discipline and also for support for the measures which we have to take." He spoke after the Presidium had voted down demands for his immediate resignation. The Czechoslovaks' new bitterness was only increased when the Soviets beat the Czechoslovak team 1–0 in the final game to retain the championship.

Preventive censorship, resisted by the Czechoslovak press since late August, went into operation on April 4. Police measures were tightened and joint police-Army patrols appeared in the streets. Smrkovský was reprimanded by the KSČ Presidium for his speeches. When the Journalists' Union protested, the eight-man Executive Committee of the Presidium hit back with a declaration that the newspapermen were insincere, "protected antisocialist forces," and were defying Party policy. It would tolerate no opposition to the censorship. Marshal Grechko and Semyonov conferred in Bratislava with Husák in what appeared to be the launching of the final political operation against Dubček. Then, on April 13, Grechko went home, evidently satisfied that matters were again firmly in hand. The day before Radio Prague first announced and then two hours later denied that additional Soviet troops were coming to Czechoslovakia.

Husák's open bid for power began on April 11, when he went to the Slovak town of Nitra to deliver a speech violently attacking the KSČ leadership—his own companions—for opening the way to "antisocialist and hostile" forces. The Party, he said, had given too much "free scope" to antisocialist forces after Dubček had assumed power. "It is necessary," he said, "politically to defeat and remove from public life hostile anti-socialist forces."

The meeting of the Central Committee was scheduled to open in Prague on April 17, but Husák chose to remain at his Slovak base in Bratislava until the last moment to plan his campaign away from the pressures in the capital. He did not appear in Prague until the evening of April 15, the day Smrkovský, fighting for his political life, said in a statement published in *Rudé Právo* that he had erred in claiming in a January speech that the main danger in Czechoslovakia was from the conservatives rather than from the "right-wing" progressives. But Smrkovský's fate was already sealed, as Husák let it be known that the Slovak members would vote to oust him from the Presidium and its Executive Committee.

On April 16 Husák delivered his master stroke. He met privately with progressive members of the Committee to convince them that Dubček had become a liability to both the Party and Czechoslovakia because his prestige had been eroded to the point where he could no longer effectively deal with Moscow. What was needed, he argued, was a leader who enjoyed the confidence of both wings of the Party and had Moscow's ear. The problem ahead, he patiently explained, was to win as soon as possible the final withdrawal of Soviet troops. In his talk, Husák showed himself to be sympathetic to the basic ideas of the progressives though he gently deplored the mistakes of the past. Presently, Husák appeared to be winning the support of the progressives. It was a brilliant move because it obviated a tough fight in the Central Committee the next day. When Husák left the caucus, Dubček's fate was sealed.

The Central Committee met at two-thirty p.m. Thursday, April 17, at Hradčany Castle with Premier Černík, an ally of Husák's, in the chair. But now the change of guard was only a formality. In the words of the official communiqué, Dubček was the first one to speak and "he briefly analyzed the present political crisis, its causes, and indicated ways out—to strengthen the leading role of the Party in all spheres of social life, to pass everywhere from words to deeds, to rapidly normalize friendly relations with the Socialist countries." Then, the communiqué said, he proposed changes in the leadership:

> Comrade Dubček recommended changes in the structure of the executive bodies of the Central Committee of the Czechoslovak Communist Party that should lead to an increase in the action potential of those bodies and of the whole Party. In conclusion, he asked to be released from the function of First Secretary. He recommended that the Central Committee elect Dr. Gustav Husák, member of the Presidium of the Central Committee of the Czechoslovak Communist Party, to this function.

Svoboda, Černík, Strougal, and Sadovský spoke in support of Dubček's "recommendations" and the Committee voted "to comply with the requests of Comrade Dubček" and re-elected him to the new Presidium. Then the Plenum, by "a large majority in secret ballot," elected Husák First Secretary.

Smrkovský was the other major casualty of the day, as he was dropped from the Presidium (reduced from twenty-one to eleven members). In addition to Husák and Dubček, the new Presidium included President Svoboda, Premier Černík, Strougal, Sadovský, Evžen Erban, Karel Polaček of the trade unions, Bilak, Piller, and Petr Colotka.

For Husák, now fifty-six years old, this was the culmination of the campaign for power he launched the day after he returned from Moscow and the signing of the first postinvasion agreement with the Soviet Union. It was an odd vindication for a man who spent eight years in prison under a Stalinist regime—to win power on the basis of a policy that proposed, in effect, a return to the closest thing to modern Stalinism. And it was also odd that his victory was based on the denunciation of the very ideas he had urged fifteen months earlier, when Dubček had assumed power.

But the new leaders realized that Dubček's removal had been a risky step, so great was his continued popularity. Consequently, both Svoboda and Husák immediately went on television to urge calm in tribute to Dubček, the man they had just ousted. Svoboda found it necessary to say that "the name of Comrade Dubček will be permanently linked in all our minds with the post-January policy of the Communist Party of Czechoslovakia." Husák said, "Keep calm. Preserve peace. Support this course. . . . We expect the wide participation of the masses, of every citizen in creating our policy, in its realization and its control. We are not giving up on any fundamental principles of our post-January policy. But we have to know what to do and when."

Husák's elevation to power ushered in an era of toughness in Czechoslovakia not seen since the fall of Novotný in January 1968. The new First Secretary was determined to eradicate every vestige of the Prague Spring's liberalism, and he dedicated the balance of 1969 to this pursuit. The Party, he believed, must be unified along traditional lines acceptable to the Soviet Union, and his country must be fitted back into the Warsaw Pact, Comecon, and all the Communist enterprises sponsored by Moscow. But if he succeeded in the latter effort, the KSČ remained split as ever; events during the year made it clear that the Czechoslovaks had still not come to terms with the reality of the August invasion and its consequences. In the latter part of the year, therefore, Husák turned to political purges (as if oblivious that he had once been purged himself).

In fairness to Husák, however, it must be recorded that from the outset he bluntly warned Czechoslovakia that he would tolerate no opposition. In his maiden speech to the Central Committee on April 17 he said, "One does not get ahead with a popular policy, being nice to everybody. We shall not make popular policy. We have to struggle without mercy for questions which we have agreed to solve and for the tasks which the Central Committee will impose." He told the Party that "counterrevolutionary" tendencies existed in Czechoslovakia during the anti-Soviet riots in March and added, "I am not afraid of that expression."

As for Dubček, he was named chairman of the new Federal Assembly, though the Central Committee criticized his earlier "shortcomings," in the place of Smrkovský. Not yet quite ready to jettison Smrkovský altogether, Husák arranged for him to be named chairman of the Assembly's new House of Nations.

Though some Prague liberals tried to console themselves with the thought that Husák was so complex a personality that he would not necessarily become a tool of Moscow, the Soviet Union did not hide its support for him. On April 22, five days after his election, he traveled to Moscow for the celebrations of the ninety-ninth anniversary of Lenin's birth. There, Ivan V. Kapitonov, a Soviet Party Secretary, delivered a capsule summation of what the Prague Spring had been in Soviet eyes and what had become of it, as Husák and Premier Černík applauded: "History and life have shown that the cause of socialism is invincible, that any attempts of reaction to turn Czechoslovakia from the Socialist road are doomed to failure."

The balance of 1969 and the opening months of 1970 brought the final liquidation of what had been the Prague Spring. As the Soviet grip over Czechoslovakia tightened, neither Moscow nor the new Prague leadership needed to preserve appearances any longer. A far-reaching purge removed from positions of influence—and even from Party membership— all those associated with the experiment in "human Marxism." Men identified with the Novotný regime surfaced again. Mamula, for example, was made the Party boss in Ostrava, and Šalgovič in Plzeň.

At the September 1969 Plenum of the Central Committee, Dubček was removed from the Party Presidium and Smrkovský lost his parliamentary post. Early in 1970 Dubček was expelled from the Central Committee and, in effect, became a political nonperson in Czechoslovakia. Smrkovský, Pavel, Hájek, and scores of other leaders were expelled from the Party altogether. Colonel Zátopek, the Olympic champion, was cashiered from the Army and assigned to a city sanitation crew. Editors and writers who formed the backbone of the 1968 experiment were relegated to jobs in factories and farms. A handful of the most outspoken progressives— among them the chess Grand Master Ludek Pachman and television commentator Vladimir Škutina—were imprisoned late in 1969 on unspecified charges and remained under detention.

An ironic twist in this liquidation process was that Gustav Husák fought hard to protect Dubček's personal safety, perhaps even his life. As reports circulated in Prague late in 1969 that the Soviet Union and the triumphant Czechoslovak hard-liners again demanded that Dubček be placed on trial on charges of fostering the "counterrevolution," Husák succeeded in winning for him the post of Czechoslovakia's Ambassador to Turkey.

In Ankara, where Dubček assumed his new duties in December, his safety seemed assured, at least insofar as he was escaping a trial. It could be that Husák had privately hoped that Dubček would use this opportunity to seek asylum in Turkey and stay in the West. Perhaps Dubček had thought about it. What we do know is that Dubček—still a disciplined and loyal Party member despite all his reverses—never uttered a word in public during his stay in Turkey. As far as we know, he never attempted to flee.

But Dubček's diplomatic exile was not enough to satisfy his foes. In January 1970 the Party announced in Prague that his membership was being suspended pending new investigations possibly presaging formal charges against him. Shortly thereafter, Oldřich Černík—along with Husák the original postinvasion "realist"—was ousted as Federal Premier to be replaced by Lubomir Strougal, once Novotný's creature. Then events moved rapidly and inexorably.

In March, Mrs. Dubček returned to Prague alone—for reasons never made clear. The orders to return might have been a form of pressure on her husband. On May 25, the KSČ Presidium voted 7-to-4 in a secret meeting to expel Dubček from the Party, the minority votes being cast by Husák, President Svoboda, Slovak Premier Petr Colotka, and National Front Chairman Evžen Erban. Two days later Dubček was brought back from Ankara. His reprieve had ended. On May 29 Premier Strougal said that no political trials were being prepared, but, he remarked ominously, "legal means" would be applied against those who harmed "Socialist society."

The beginning of the end for Dubček came on June 24, when the Central Committee convened at Hradčany Castle. Its first move was to demand that Dubček be formally relieved of his ambassadorship. President Svoboda, too old and too tired to fight any longer, complied at once. In the evening, a brief communiqué announced that "President Ludvík Svoboda today recalled Alexander Dubček from his post as Ambassador to Turkey, in connection with his assignment to other duties." The "other duties," as it turned out, were to be an office job in a factory in Slovakia. On June 26, the Central Committee confirmed Dubček's expulsion from the Party, fired Černík from his new post as chairman of the Federal Committee on Technology and Investments, and suspended his Party membership. Colotka and Erban were removed from the Presidium.

Ironically, Dubček's expulsion from the Party he had faithfully served for thirty of his forty-eight years was formalized one day before the second anniversary of the Two Thousand Words manifesto. Now, the Prague Spring was officially buried. The glorious days of "We are with you; be with us!" were gone, and gloom and despair deepened in Czechoslovakia.

Yet history has its own way and its own logic. To Czechoslovakia, 1968 meant something altogether different than it did to the dogmatists of the Kremlin. The hopes it had raised could not be obliterated by the invasion and its long, dramatic aftermath. They seem to be alive still, as darkness has once more descended on the land of the Czechs and the Slovaks. In the nineteenth century the great Czech poet Jan Neruda looked at the past and the future when he wrote:

> Even if thunder rolls and our bones freeze
> It is no different from what we suffered through the ages.
> We will move ahead. . . .

A Short Bibliography

Adamic, Louis. *The Eagle and the Roots*. Garden City, New York: Doubleday, 1952.

Blumenfeld, Yorick. *Seesaw: Cultural Life in Eastern Europe*. New York: Harcourt, Brace & World, 1968.

Chapman, Colin. *August 21st. The Rape of Czechoslovakia*. London: Cassell, 1968.

Churchill, Winston S. *The Second World War. Triumph and Tragedy*. Boston: Houghton Mifflin, 1953.

Chysky, J., Skalnik, M., and Adamec, V. *A Guide to Czechoslovakia*. Prague: Artia, 1965.

Dallin, David J. *Soviet Espionage*. New Haven: Yale University Press, 1955.

Desgraupes, Pierre, and Dumayet, Pierre, eds. *Praga. Quando os Tanques Avançaram*. Rio de Janeiro: Editôra Expressão e Cultura, 1968.

Djilas, Milovan. *The Unperfect Society. Beyond the New Class*. New York: Harcourt, Brace & World, 1969.

Glaser, Kurt. *Czechoslovakia. A Critical History*. Caldwell, Idaho: The Caxton Printers, 1961.

Gluckstein, Ygael. *Stalin's Satellites in Europe*. London: George Allen and Unwin, 1952.

Kennan, George F. *From Prague after Munich. Diplomatic Papers 1938–1940*. Princeton: Princeton University Press, 1968.

Korbel, Josef. *The Communist Subversion of Czechoslovakia 1938–1948. The Failure of Coexistence*. Princeton: Princeton University Press, 1959.

Lasky, Melvin J., ed. *The Hungarian Revolution*. New York: Frederick A. Praeger, for the Congress for Cultural Freedom, 1957.

Lendvai, Paul. *Eagles in Cobwebs. Nationalism and Communism in the Balkans*. Garden City, New York: Doubleday, 1969.

Lewis, Flora. *A Case History of Hope*. Garden City, New York: Doubleday, 1958.

Littell, Robert, ed. *The Czech Black Book*. New York: Frederick A. Praeger, 1969.

London, Artur. *L'Aveu dans l'engrenage du procès de Prague.* Paris: Gallimard, 1968.

Miłosz, Czesław. *The Captive Mind.* New York: Alfred A. Knopf, 1953.

Mňačko, Ladislav. *The Seventh Night.* New York: E. P. Dutton, 1969.

Rauch, Georg von. *A History of Soviet Russia.* New York: Frederick A. Praeger, 1957.

Reisky de Dubnic, Vladimir. *Communist Propaganda Methods. A Case Study on Czechoslovakia.* New York: Frederick A. Praeger, 1960.

Rose, William John. *The Rise of Polish Democracy.* London: G. Bell & Sons, 1944.

Schwartz, Harry. *Prague's 200 Days.* New York: Frederick A. Praeger, 1969.

Taborsky, Edward. *Communism in Czechoslovakia 1948–1960.* Princeton: Princeton University Press, 1961.

Thomas, Hugh. *The Spanish Civil War.* New York: Harper & Row, 1961.

Truman, Harry S. *Memoirs. Vol. I. Year of Decision.* Garden City, New York: Doubleday, 1955.

Wechsberg, Joseph. *The Voices. Prague 1968.* Garden City, New York: Doubleday, 1969.

Weisskopf, Kurt. *The Agony of Czechoslovakia '38/'68.* London: Elek Books, 1968.

Wolfe, Bertram D. *Khrushchev and Stalin's Ghost.* New York: Frederick A. Praeger, 1957.

Zeman, Z. A. B. *Prague Spring: A Report on Czechoslovakia 1968.* New York: Hill & Wang, 1969.

Periodicals, Transcripts, and Special Materials

Croan, Melvin. "Czechoslovakia, Ulbricht, and the German Problem." *Problems of Communism*, January–February 1969. Washington, D.C.: United States Information Agency, 1969, Vol. XVIII.

"Czechoslovakia: The Brief Spring of 1968." *Problems of Communism*, November–December 1968. Washington, D.C.: United States Information Agency, 1968, Vol. XVII.

Gabor, Robert. "The Organization and Strategy of the Hungarian Workers' (Communist) Party." New York: National Committee for a Free Europe, Research and Publication Service, 1952.

"Hungary's Fight for Freedom," a special 96-page picture report. *Life*, 1956.

"In Quest of Justice: Protest and Dissent in the USSR." *Problems of Communism*, July–August 1968, September–October 1968. Washington, D.C.: United States Information Agency, 1968, Vol. XVII.

Mayer, Milton. *A Study of the Czech Resistance. The Art of the Impossible.* Santa Barbara, California: Center for the Study of Democratic Institutions, 1969.

The Revolt in Hungary: A Documentary Chronology of Events. New York: Free Europe Committee. [ca. 1956–1957?]

Smith, Canfield F. "The Rocky Road to Communist Unity." *East Europe*, February 1969. New York: 1969, Vol. XVIII, No. 2.

"United Nations Report of the Special Committee on the Problem of Hungary."
General Assembly Official Records: Eleventh Session. New York: United Nations
General Assembly, 1957, Supplement No. 18 (A/3592).

Whalen, Dr. Joseph G. "Aspects of Intellectual Ferment and Dissent in Czechoslovakia." U.S. Committee Print, 91st Congress, 1st Session. Washington, D.C.:
U.S. Government Printing Office, 1969.

Index